'O' LEVEL *made simple* **MODULE - I**

INTRODUCTION TO INFORMATION TECHNOLOGY

(Based on NIELIT MAT-O1.R0 Syllabus for 'Multimedia & Animation Technology')

MAT-O1.R0

by

Prof. Satish Jain
B.Sc., B.E.(IISc), M.E.(IISc), M.Tech.(IIT Kanpur),
Wing Commander (Retd.)
Ex Professor of Information Technology,
Institute of Information Technology & Management
GGS Indraprastha University, Delhi.

Ambrish K.Rai
B.E (E & T) System Administrator,
National Micro

and

M. Geetha
B. Com., Dipl Computer Science

REPRINTED 2023

FIRST EDITION 2015

ISBN: 978-81-8333-523-2

Distributors:

BPB PUBLICATIONS
20, Ansari Road, Darya Ganj
New Delhi-110002
Ph: 23254990/23254991

DECCAN AGENCIES
4-3-329, Bank Street,
Hyderabad-500195
Ph: 24756967/24756400

MICRO MEDIA
Shop No. 5, Mahendra Chambers,
150 DN Rd. Next to Capital Cinema,
V.T. (C.S.T.) Station, MUMBAI-400 001
Ph: 22078296/22078297

BPB BOOK CENTRE
376 Old Lajpat Rai Market,
Delhi-110006
Ph: 23861747

Published by Manish Jain for BPB Publications, 20 Ansari Road, Darya Ganj, New Delhi-110002 and Printed by Manipal Technologies Limited, Manipal

www.bpbonline.com

Dedicated to

Lord Ganesha, Lorg Murgan, Sri Raj Rajeshwari and *Sri Sai Baba*

whose blessings overcome all hurdles in life

PREFACE

This book is based on the MAT.O1.R0 syllabus for *Introduction to Information Technology* examination. The objective in bringing out this book in this form is to explain to the students, technical concepts in an easy-to-understand language and in a simple manner. It is felt that most of the books available in the market do not cover the entire syllabus to meet the needs of the students. The syllabus set for this paper requires very thorough study of Information Technology used in Multimedia and Animation Technology. Towards achieving this goal, we have pressed into service all our practical experience in Computer Science as well as in teaching field. This book should meet the requirement of students from any stream namely, commerce, science or arts.

The book covers hardware, software, and operating systems as well as binary, and other number systems used in digital computer. The book also covers software packages namely, Word, Excel, PowerPoint. Each software package is discussed with ample number of examples and screens. The book also covers different types of intellectual property rights including copyrights, trademarks, patents, industrial design and trade secrets. The book also discusses computer networks, Internet and Handheld Devices such as Mobile and Tablets. It also covers HTML and Publishing Tools to create Web pages. In addition, the book also explains impact of Information Technology on Society.

We have made this book user friendly by adding updated glossary of technical terms at the end of this book. These would be very handy as ready reference for key concepts of major topics discussed in this book. The glossary of technical terms will be specially helpful to students in answering objective questions asked in the examination. A set of past NIELIT Questions papers is included at the end of this book to help the students to prepare for the future examinations.

A special feature throughout this book is that the important and crucial information has been shown with parallel and horizontal lines with a (☞) mark to draw attention of the reader, thus, providing a digest of concept(s) presented on those pages.

We shall feel obliged to the readers if they send us their critical opinion regarding the presentation, readability and coverage in this book and give us suggestions, if any, to improve the subject matter.

19th September, 2014

Authors

MAT.O1.R0 : Introduction to Information Technology

Outline of Course

S. No.	TOPIC	Minimum hours
1.	Computer Appreciation	04
2.	Computer Organization	11
3.	Operating Systems	13
4.	Office Automation	12
4.	Intellecutal Property Right and Copyright Issue	04
5.	Handheld devices	04
6.	Basic Networking and Internet	08
7.	Information Technology and Society	04

Theory	**=**	**60**
Practicals/tutorials	**=**	**60**
Total	**=**	**120**

Detailed Syllabus

1. Computer Appreciation: 04 hrs

What is a computer, basic structure of computer, data representation in computer [Binary number system, Hexadecimal number system, Binary to Decimal Conversion, Decimal to Binary Conversion, Binary Coded Decimal (BCD) Code, ASCII Code, UNICODE], representation of visual data.

2. Computer Organization: 11 hrs

2.1 Central Processing Unit (02 Hrs)

Fundamentals of Control Unit, Arithmetic Unit, Instruction Set, Register. Concept of Processor Speed, illustration with popular processors. Basic introduction to CPU

2.2 Memory and Storage (02 Hrs)

Memory Organization, RAM, Read Only Memories, Flash memory. Basics of other storage devices - HDD, CD/DVD, Blue-Ray, magnetic tape etc.

2.3 Input Devices (02 Hrs)

Keyboard, Mouse, microphone, trackball, joystick, Scanner. OMR, Bar/QR-code reader, MICR Digitizer, Card Reader, cameras, fingerprint scanner and other biometric devices, tablets etc.

2.4 Output Devices (02 Hrs)

Display (CRT, LCD, LED), Printers - Dot matrix, Inkjet, laser, Plotters, Projector and visualiser.

2.5 Ports and Interfaces (01 Hrs)

Serial and Parallel ports, Connectors: DIN, RCA, AV; USB, Fire wire (IEEE1394), HDMI

2.6 Computer Software (02 Hrs)

Relationship between Hardware and Software; System Software, Application Software, compiler, assemblers, linkers, loaders

3. Operating Systems: 13 hrs

3.1 Basic concepts of OS (04 Hrs)

Function of OS; Basic concept of resource management, CPU, memory, I/O; Power-up process: BIOS, Bootstrap Loader; File systems and user management.

3.2 Case Study

3.2.1 Microsoft Windows (03 Hrs)

An overview of different versions of Windows, Basic Windows elements, files management through Windows, Using essential accessories: Systems tools- Disk Cleanup, Disk defragmenter

3.2.2 Linux (03 Hrs)

An overview of Linux, Basic Linux elements: System Features, Software features. File Structure, File handling in Linux.

3.2.3 Mac Environment (03 Hrs)

Overview of Mac OS, features of the Mac OS. File and User management, GUI and Mac devices and tools

4. Office Automation: 12 Hrs

Word Processing, Spreadsheet, Presentation tools, HTML Tools, Publishing tools.

5. Intellectual Property Right and Copyright Issue: 04 Hrs

Introduction to Intellectual Property Right and Copyright Issue, Exceptions to Copyright Protection, Guidelines for Clearance, Copyright Elements, Payments, Collaboration.

6. Handheld Devices (Mobiles and Tabs) 04 Hrs

Features of different handheld devices like - mobile phone, smart phone, Tablets, introduction to Android as OS for hand-held devices, Concepts of Apps, some popular applications.

7. Basic Networking & Internet: 08 Hrs

Overview of the Internet, protocols, Basic definition: networks and topologies; Access networks and physical media, Concept of OSI protocol Layers. TCP/IP (features of IPV4, IPV6), WWW, FTP, E-mail, DNS ISP. Concept of multimedia streaming. Basics of Wireless communications, Introduction to Wi-Fi, Bluetooth, GSM, CDMA, GPRS, 3G, 4G.

8. Information Technology and Society: 04 Hrs

Social Networks, e-Governance, e-Commerce, e-Learning, IT-ethics

USEFUL TIPS FOR THE EXAMINEE

Dear Reader,

Every examination has its peculiarity and the best results are often obtained by identifying that particular feature and working with the help of right strategies, which in turn can be adopted by correctly analyzing the question paper.

The 'MAT.O1.R0' Examination being no exception to this rule, the authors present an effective aid to guide you to analyze the question paper and thus help to chalk out your own effective plan of action.

The instructions given on the first page of the question paper should always be read *very* carefully. As the answer sheets of Part ONE will be evaluated with the help of a computer, you have to be extra cautious.

The answer sheet contains separate boxes for writing answers to each question in this part. You should read the following paragraphs to avoid mistakes and clear the first part without any difficulty. (A specimen copy of the answer sheet for filling Part ONE answers of sample papers for objective questions is included at the end of this book.)

How to avoid mistakes?

If you are not sure about a particular answer - *do not fill* the box in the first try itself, but make an attempt later. After having given an initial reading to all the questions, first attempt only those questions about which you are very ***sure*** regarding the correct answer. It is while taking a second go at the questions, that you answer the remaining ones, always making sure that you spend only a *limited* amount of time on each one of them. Finally, go through all the answers once decided and fill the boxes with black ink as per the instructions given in the question paper.

How to answer the questions of Part TWO?

Once you have done well in Part ONE, rest assured, passing Part TWO will not pose much of a problem, if you have effectively followed the instructions given below. While answering Part TWO, the time limit should be strictly kept in mind and every effort must be made to complete all the questions, by keeping the answers brief and to the point. Remember you can also resort to making a sketch/diagram in your answer wherever possible, instead of describing it in words, because "a thousand words of description can be effectively expressed by a small diagram." As the number of questions are normally more for an average student, this precious time saved, enables you to have a wider coverage of the paper.

While attempting the descriptive type of questions, keep a check on the length of your answers and keep in mind the time frame available for answering the remaining questions.

The last stage, being the revision stage, you should save at least 5 to 10 minutes to revise all your answers. Try to find the gross errors, like units of measurement, or wrong question number you might have put for a specific answer, etc. This does happen because of the inherent tension of the examination.

How to prepare for the "Introduction to Information Technology" Examination?

Having familiarized with the format of the examination paper, let us turn our attention on the strategy for preparing for it.

This book has covered the complete syllabus in an easy to understand manner. It is advised, however, that in addition to this book, you should also refer to a few books on Information Technology. This will enable you to broaden the horizon of your knowledge.

Make your own notes, by reading each topic from this book and other standard books. Once you are quite sure about the comprehension of the topic, try to answer the Descriptive Type Questions given at the end of each chapter of this book.

In the second reading, go through the sample papers given at the end of the book. Solve these papers without consulting any book. After you have answered them, compare your response with the relevant matter available in the text of this book. Where you find your answers differ, re-study that part again.

Last, but not the least, you should simulate examination conditions by conducting a demo examination, taking any of the sample papers given at the end of the book and attempting to complete the answers within the stipulated time. After a day or two, evaluate your answers and if any doubts still persist, clarify them from a good text book or a computer specialist immediately. This way, you will be sure about the subject and will have confidence while answering the actual question paper.

WISH YOU A GRAND SUCCESS in the MAT.O1.R0 Examination, and a very bright future in the field of computer science.

Authors

Contents

Introduction to Information Technology

CHAPTER 1

Computer Appreciation

1.1 WHAT IS A COMPUTER?

A computer is a very versatile electronic machine created by man. Computers have made a great impact on our everyday life. Their presence is felt in almost every aspect of life be it at home, school, college, office, industry, hospital, bank, retail stores, railways, research and design organizations, etc.

A computer is basically a programmable computing machine. Earlier computers were used for complex computations. They were costly and hence only large organizations could afford them. Then technological advancements in design and fabrication of semiconductor devices, namely, the microprocessor has made it possible for smaller organizations and even individual's to afford. These computers cannot be asked for faster calculations but also for storing and retrieving information. They can be used to control chemical processes and machines. They can even measure and display physical and electrical quantities and send photographs electronically.

The word 'computer' comes from the word *compute*, which means to calculate. So, a computer is normally considered to be a calculating device that can perform arithmetic operations at an enormous speed. But more accurately, it may be defined as a device that operates upon data for calculation.

☞ *A computer can, not only store and process data, but also retrieve data, i.e., gather data from its memory or storage as and when required. Thus, a computer is a general term that refers to an electronic data processing machine used for a wide range of activities.*

A Personal Computer (PC in short) refers to small electronic data processing machine meant for individual use (See Figure 1.1).

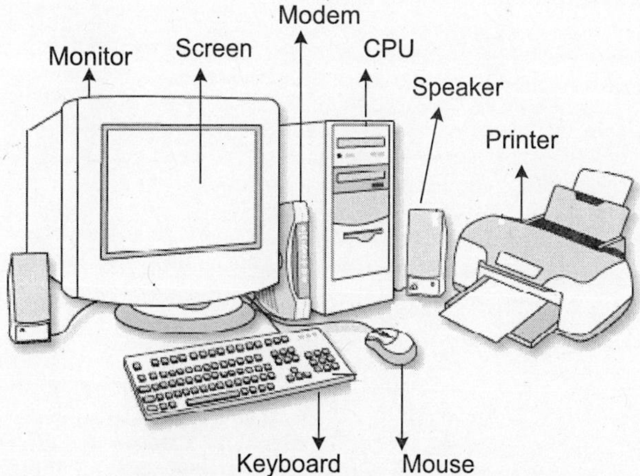

Figure 1.1 A Personal Computer (PC)

There are two basic types of computers, which include:

(a) Analog
(b) Digital

1.1.1 Analog Computers

Analog computers handle or process information of a physical nature. For instance, temperature, pressure, etc. These are based on the measuring of analog or equivalent physical value.

1.1.2 Digital Computers

Digital computers process information which is essentially in a binary or two-state form, namely, zero and one. In computing, we mostly refer to the *digital* type of computers.

Digital computers fall into different ranges called microcomputers, minicomputers, mainframes and supercomputers, which can be further classified in ascending order of size–small, medium, large and very large.

1.2 BASIC STRUCTURE OF A COMPUTER

The five major functional units of a digital computer are:

(a) Central Processing Unit (CPU)
(b) Input units
(c) Output units
(d) Storage devices
(e) Communication interface

CPU is the brain of a computer. The other parts are used to transfer data and to communicate with the CPU. The CPU constitutes the main memory, control unit and arithmetic logic unit.

A block diagram of the basic computer organization is shown in Figure 1.2.

In this Figure, the solid lines are used to indicate the flow of instructions and data. The dotted lines represent the control exercised by the control unit. The Figure shows the basic arrangement of different units of a computer. It depicts the five major building blocks, or functional units of a digital computer system. These five units correspond to the five basic operations, namely, inputting, storing, processing, outputting and controlling data, carried out by all computer systems. The five units are explained in brief as given below.

Inputting: Refers to the process of entering data into the computer with the help of, an input device, such as a keyboard.

Storing: Refers to the storage of data and instructions in the computer's main memory, for manipulations.

Processing: Refers to performing operations (both arithmetic and logical) or manipulation of data entered into the computer so that useful information may be gathered from the entered data.

Outputting: Refers to the process of showing the information or result to the user either on screen (monitor) or on paper (through printer).

Controlling: Refers to directing all the above processes, in coordination. This controlling is done by the Control Unit (CU) in a CPU.

☞ *A CPU is the brain of a computer. Its primary function is to execute programs.*

In addition, a CPU also controls the operation of all other components, such as memory, input and output devices. Under the CPU's control, programs and data are stored in the memory and results are displayed on the monitor or printed on paper.

1.2.1 Hardware

The physical components of a computer are known as hardware. Such physical components may be electronic, electrical, magnetic, mechanical or optical. These include microprocessors, Integrated Circuits (ICs), hard disks, floppy disks, optical disks, colour monitor, keyboard, printer and plotter, etc.

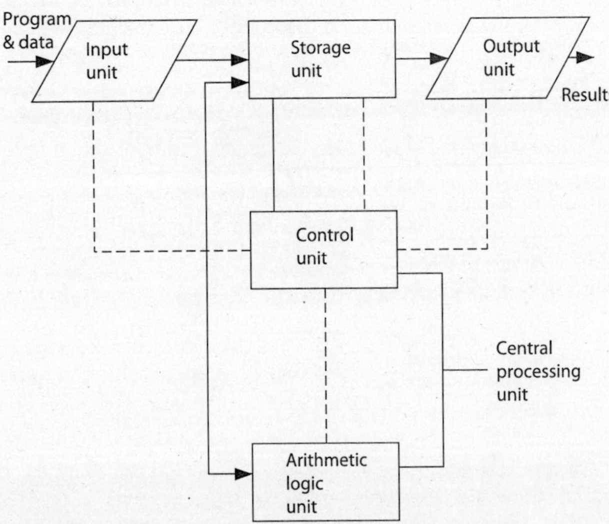

Figure 1.2 Block diagram representing a computer system

The set of computer programs, procedures and associated documentation related to the effective operation of a computer system are termed as *software*. A sequence of instructions given to a computer to perform a particular task is called a *software* or *a program*.

1.2.2 Input Devices

Data and instructions are entered into a computer through input devices. An input device first converts desired input data and instructions into a suitable binary form (i.e., 0 and 1) and then feeds it into the CPU. The commonly used input device is the keyboard. A number of other input devices have been developed that do not require typing. These are:

(a) Mouse
(b) Joystick
(c) Trackball
(d) Light pen
(e) Graphic tablet
(f) Touch screen

The above listed devices permit the user to select an image on the computer screen by pointing to it. Therefore, these devices are also called *pointing devices*.

Voice input systems have also been developed. A microphone is used as an input in such devices. In applications, where computers with vision are required, namely robots and computer-based security system, computers use optical and semiconductor devices that are sensitive to light. Such input devices produce digital signals corresponding to images, pictures etc.

1.2.3 Output Devices

Output devices are used to transfer information stored in the computer or the result of any processing done to the outside world. There are several types of output devices available today, but the most commonly used ones include video monitors and printers. Printers provide a printed record of data and information on paper. A detailed discussion of output devices is given in Chapter 2.

1.2.4 Central Processing Unit (CPU)

The primary function of a CPU is to execute instruction or programs. Besides, it also controls the operation of all other components, such as memory, input and output devices. Under the processing unit's control, programs and data are accepted from the input devices and stored in the memory. Outputs are displayed on the video screen or printed on paper once the processing of a program is complete.

The processing unit of a small computer normally has a single processor, whereas the one for a bigger computer may contain a number of processors. Each processor, in a large processing unit, performs a specific task assigned to it.

The major parts of a CPU are:

(a) Primary or Main memory
(b) Arithmetic and Logic Unit (ALU)
(c) Control unit

1.2.5 Memory

The *Memory* is an essential component of a computer system. It is required by the computer system to store instructions and data. Memory can be divided into the following two types:

(a) *Primary* or *Main Memory*: It is one which is directly connected to the CPU or part of the CPU in some PCs (Personal Computers).
(b) *Secondary Memory*: It is external to CPU.

Primary Memory or Main Memory

Primary memory is a small but relatively fast storage unit that stores data and instructions which are used by the CPU. This type of memory is also known as Main Memory. Primary memory is a temporary memory. It retains its contents only for the time that the computer is switched on. As soon as it is switched off, the main memory loses its contents.

Secondary Memory or Auxiliary Memory

Secondary memory or secondary storage devices are permanent storage units used for storing programs and data. They use the principle of magnetization for storing 1 and 0. Therefore, they are also known as *magnetic memory*. They are non-volatile, i.e, the memory retains its contents even when power is switched off.

Examples of secondary storage devices include magnetic tapes, magnetic disks, compact disks, magnetic bubble memory, magnetic drums, zip disks, etc. The relatively slow magnetic tapes are used for storing very old files. Magnetic disks are used for storing data for backup purposes.

A disk that is permanently attached to the computer unit and cannot be easily removed by user is called the *Hard Disk*. A *Floppy Disk* is a removable disk. A new breed of disks called zip disks (of the size of floppy disks) and pen drives are now available which enable you to store about 2 GB or more of data on them.

1.3 DATA REPRESENTATION IN COMPUTER

Data representation refers to the methods used internally to represent information stored in a computer. Computers store lots of different types of information, such as numbers, text, sound and graphics.

Data Types: Registers contain either data or control information. Control information is a bit or group of bits used to specify the sequence of command signals needed for data manipulation.

Data are numbers and other binary-coded information that are operated on possible data types in registers:

- Numbers used in computations
- Letters of the alphabet used in data processing
- Other discrete symbols used for specific purposes

All types of data are represented in binary-coded form except binary numbers.

Number System: A number system of base, or radix, r is a system that uses distinct symbols for r digits. Numbers are represented by a string of digit symbols. For example, Binary 0, 1 and base is 2. Decimal 0, 1,2-9 and base is 10. Octal 0, 1,2-7 and base is 8. Hexadecimal 0,1,2-9,A,B,C,D,E,F and base is 16.

Conversion: From decimal to its equivalent representation in the radix r system. Most Significant Digit (MSD) Least Significant Digit (LSD) terms are used for this.

1.4 BINARY NUMBER SYSTEM

Binary number system consists of 2 digits namely, 0 and 1. It has a base (or *radix*) 2. For example, 1011_2 is a binary number. The subscript 2 at the end of this number indicates the base of the number. Table 1.1 gives the list of binary representations of decimal digits.

Table 1.1 Binary Equivalent Numbers for Decimal Digits

Decimal Numbers	Equivalent Binary Numbers
0	0000
1	0001
2	0010
3	0011
4	0100
5	0101
6	0110
7	0111
8	1000
9	1001

1.4.1 Decimal to Binary Conversion

Although there are multiple ways of converting decimal numbers to binary numbers, the most commonly used is the *dibble-dabble* method. In this method, the decimal number to be converted is repeatedly divided by 2. The remainders 0s and 1s so obtained are then read in the reverse order to obtain the binary equivalent of the decimal number.

Example 1

Convert decimal number 1975_{10} to binary equivalent number.

Answer

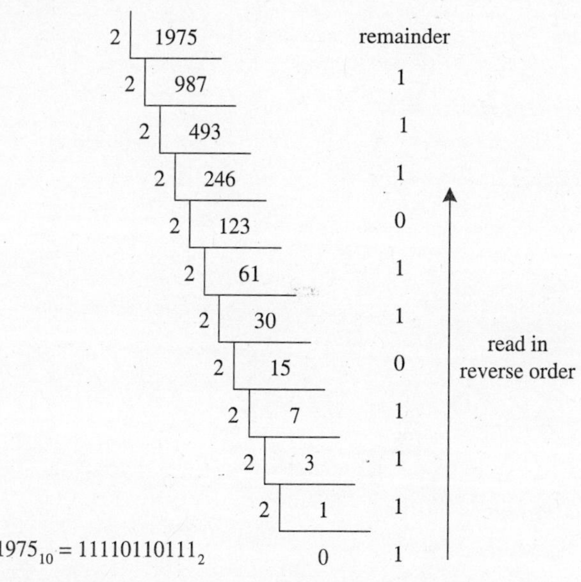

Example 2

Convert decimal number 43 to binary equivalent number.

Answer

Quotient	Remainder	
		(LSB)
43 ÷ 2 = 21	1	↑
21 ÷ 2 = 10	1	
10 ÷ 2 = 5	0	
5 ÷ 2 = 2	1	
2 ÷ 2 = 1	0	
1 ÷ 2 = 0	1	(MSB)

Therefore, 43 (Decimal Number) = 101011 (Binary Number). Note that the first remainder is the Least Significant Bit (LSB) and the final remainder is the Most Significant Bit (MSB).

1.4.2 Binary to Decimal Conversion

The decimal equivalent is obtained by multiplying each binary digit with its positional value. The right most bit has positional value 2^0, the second right most bit has value 2^1 and so on.

Example 3

Convert the binary number 11001 into its decimal equivalent.

Answer

11001 (Binary Number) $= 1 \times 2^4 + 1 \times 2^3 + 0 \times 2^2 + 0 \times 2^1 + 1 \times 2^0$
$= 16 + 8 + 0 + 0 + 1$
$= 25$ (Decimal Number)

$\therefore (11001)_2 = (25)_{10}$

Example 4

Convert 11110110111_2 to decimal equivalent number.

Answer

$11110110111_2 =$
$1 \times 2^{10} + 1 \times 2^9 + 1 \times 2^8 + 1 \times 2^7 + 0 \times 2^6 + 1 \times 2^5 + 1 \times 2^4 + 0 \times 2^3 + 1 \times 2^2 + 1 \times 2^1 + 1 \times 2^0 = 1975_{10}$

Example 5

Convert 11010 (binary number) to its decimal equivalent.

Answer

Bit position from the right hand side:

	1	1	0	1	0
	5th	4th	3rd	2nd	1st

11010 (Binary Number) $= 1 \times 2^4 + 1 \times 2^3 + 0 \times 2^2 + 1 \times 2^1 + 0 \times 2^0$
$= 16 + 8 + 0 + 2 + 0$
$= 26$ (Decimal Number)

Example 6

Convert 1011 (binary number) to its decimal equivalent.

Answer

Bit position from the right hand side:	1	0	1	1
	4th	3rd	2nd	1st

1011 (Binary Number) $= 1 \times 2^3 + 0 \times 2^2 + 1 \times 2^1 + 1 \times 2^0$
$= 8 + 0 + 2 + 1$
$= 11$ (Decimal Number)

We use the following technique. To indicate the *base* of a number, we use suffix, i.e.,
$(11)_{10} = (1011)_2$
We use suffix 10 to indicate that it is a decimal number. We use suffix 2 to indicate a binary number.

1.5 HEXADECIMAL NUMBER SYSTEM

The hexadecimal number system has the radix (base) as 16. Its digits range from 0 to 9 and A to F. Thus in a hexadecimal number system, decimal number 10 is represented by A, 11 by B, 12 by C, 13 by D, 14 by E and 15 by F. The decimal number 16 is represented as 10 and 17 by 11 in hexadecimal number system.

A hexadecimal digit is represented by four binary bits. For instance, the number 5 is represented by 0101 hexadecimal equivalent. The digit A of hexadecimal is 1010 in 4-bit binary representation.

1.5.1 Conversion of Hexadecimal Numbers to Decimal Numbers

For conversion of a hexadecimal number to its equivalent decimal number we use the weights of digits of the number. It means:
The weight of *n*th digit of the number from the right hand side = ***nth digit* × (*Base*)$^{n-1}$**

The following examples will illustrate the conversion procedure:

Example 7

Convert the hexadecimal number 4B7 to its equivalent decimal number.

Answer

7 is the 1st digit of the number from the right hand side. Therefore, its weight is 7×16^0, or $7 \times 1 = 7$.
B is the 2nd digit of the number from the right hand side. Therefore, its weight is $B \times 16^1$, or 11×16^1 where 11 is decimal equal of B.
4 is the 3rd digit of the number from the right hand side. Therefore, its weight is 4×16^2.
Therefore, 4B7 (hex.) $= 4 \times 16^2 + B \times 16^1 + 7 \times 16^0$
$= 4 \times 256 + 11 \times 16 + 7 \times 1$
$= 1024 + 176 + 7$
$= 1207$ (decimal)

Example 8

Convert the hexadecimal number 2B61 to its equivalent decimal number.

Answer

2B61 (hex.) $= 2 \times 16^3 + B \times 16^2 + 6 \times 16^1 + 1 \times 16^0$
$= 2 \times 4096 + 11 \times 256 + 6 \times 16 + 1 \times 16^0$
$= 8192 + 2816 + 96 + 1$
$= 11105$ (decimal)

1.5.2 Conversion of Binary Numbers to Hexadecimal Numbers

The base of the hexadecimal number system is 16. But $16 = 2^4$. Therefore, in order to convert a binary number to hexadecimal, make 4-bit binary groups (each group contains 4 binary bits) of the binary number. After forming the groups, each group of 4 binary bits is converted to its hexadecimal equivalent. Let us see the following examples. The groups are formed starting from the right most bit or the least signification bit.

Example 9

Convert the binary number 01101111 to its equivalent hexadecimal number.

Answer

$(01101111)_2$	= (0110) (1111)	{groups of 4 bits}
	= 6 F	
	= 6 F	{in hexadecimal number}

Example 10

Convert the binary number 101001101 to its equivalent hexadecimal number.

Answer

The formation of groups of 4 bits each in an integer binary number is made from right hand side to left.

101001101 = (1) (0100) (1101)

In the above expression, we see that the group of the most significant binary bits contains only 1 binary bit. This can be extended to 4 binary bits by adding three zeros in Most Significant Bit (MSB) positions. If MSBs are extended by adding zeros, the number remains unaffected. Therefore, the given number may be grouped as follows :

$(101001101)_2$ = (0001) (0100) (1101)
= ↑ ↑ ↑
1 4 D {hexadecimal equivalent}

i.e., $(101001101)_2$ is = 14D in hexadecimal number system.

1.5.3 Conversion of Hexadecimal Numbers to Binary Numbers

To convert a hexadecimal number to its equivalent binary number, each digit of the given hexadecimal number is converted to its 4-bit binary equivalent. Let us see the following example:

Example 11

Convert the hexadecimal number 6B8 to its equivalent binary number.

Answer

$(6B8)_{16}$ 6 B 8
↓ ↓ ↓
= (0110) (1011) (1000) {Binary equivalent of each digit}
= $(011010111000)_2$

1.6 BINARY CODED DECIMAL (BCD) CODES

In BCD code, a decimal number is represented by four binary bits. If a decimal number has two or more than two digits, each decimal digit is represented by its 4-bit binary equivalent. For example, 40 is represented by 0100 0000 in BCD code. Binary equivalent of a decimal number is different from the binary code of a decimal number. The binary equivalent of the decimal number 22 is 10110, But its BCD code is 0010 0010.

Table 1.2 shows standard BCD codes for typical decimal numbers.

Table 1.2 Standard BCD Codes

Decimal Number	Standard BCD code
0	0000
1	0001
2	0100
3	0011
4	0100
5	0101
6	0110
7	0111
8	1000
9	1001
10	0001 0000
11	0001 0001
12	0001 0010
13	0001 0011
14	0001 0100
15	0001 0101
55	0101 0101
85	1000 0101

The most common BCD code is the 8421 BCD code. The BCD equivalent of a decimal number is written by replacing each decimal digit in integer and fractional parts with its 4-bit binary equivalent. Here 8, 4, 2 and 1 represent the weights of different bits in the 4-bit groups, starting from the (MSB) Most Significant Bit (to extreme left) and proceeding towards the Least Significant Bit (LSB).

This feature makes it a weighted code, whose main characteristic is that each binary digit in the 4-bit group representing a given decimal digit is assigned a weight, and for each group of four bits, the sum of the weights of those binary digits whose value is 1 is equal to the decimal digit which they represent.

For example, if we look at Table, we find that the decimal digit 9 when represented in 8421 BCD is 1001. Now the decimal digit assigned to first 1 is 8 and to the second 1 is 1. If we add 8 and 1 we get the required decimal number which is 9.

To perform addition in BCD by first adding in binary, and then converting to BCD afterwards. Conversion of the simple sum of two digits can be done by adding 6 (i.e., 16 – 10) when the 5-bit result of adding a pair of digits has a value greater than 9.

Example 11

Add 9 + 8

Answer

1001 + 1000 = 10001
9 + 8 = 17

Note that 10001 is the binary, not decimal, representation of the desired result. In BCD as in decimal, there cannot exist a value greater than 9 (1001) per digit. To correct this, 6 (0110) is added to that sum and then the result is treated as two nibbles:

10001 + 0110 = 00010111 => 0001 0111
17 + 6 = 23 1 7

The two nibbles of the result, 0001 and 0111, correspond to the digits 1 and 7. The 17 in BCD, which is the correct result.

1.7 ASCII Code

ASCII (American Standard Code for Information Interchange) (pronounced "askee") is the most common alphanumeric code used to represent characters like A, B, C, numbers and other symbols. The current standard alphanumeric code is the ASCII code. This code allows manufacturers to standardize computer hardware, such as keyboards, printers, and video displays.

ASCII code uses either 7 or 8 bits for data representation. The 7 bits in ASCII code format can be represented as:

$$x_6x_5x_4x_3x_2x_1x_0$$

where each x is either a 0 or 1. For instance, uppercase letter A can be coded as:

1000001

and lowercase letter a can be coded as:

1100001

Similarly there are ASCII codes for special characters. Some examples include:

010 0100 ($)
010 1011 (+)
011 1101 (=)

Hitting a key on the keyboard sends the corresponding ASCII code to the computer. For example, when you hit the spacebar of your computer, 010 0000 is sent to the computer.

With 7 bits, only 128 characters can be coded. Characters include letters, digits, special symbols, punctuation marks and control characters. Table 1.3 (a) lists the ASCII codes.

Table 1.3 (a) ASCII codes

Characters or Abbreviations	Hex Codes for 7-bit ASCII	Characters or Abbreviations	Hex Codes for 7-bit ASCII
NUL	00	DLE	10
SOH	01	DC1	11
STX	02	DC2	12
ETX	03	DC3	13
EOT	04	DC4	14
ENQ	05	NAK	15
ACK	06	SYN	16
BEL	07	ETB	17
BS	08	CAN	18
HT	09	EM	19
LF	0A	SUB	1A
VT	0B	ESC	1B
FF	0C	FS	1C
CR	0D	GS	1D
S0	0E	RS	1E
S1	0F	US	1F
SP	20	P	50
!	21	Q	51
"	22	R	52
#	23	S	53
$	24	T	54
%	25	U	55
&	26	V	56
'	27	W	57
(	28	X	58
)	29	Y	59
*	2A	Z	5A
+	2B	[	5B
,	2C	\	5C
–	2D	]	5D
.	2E	^	5E
/	2F	—	5F
0	30	'	60
1	31	a	61
2	32	b	62
3	33	c	63
4	34	d	64
5	35	e	65

(Contd...)

Characters or Abbreviations	Hex Codes for 7-bit ASCII	Characters or Abbreviations	Hex Codes for 7-bit ASCII
6	36	f	66
7	37	g	67
8	38	h	68
9	39	i	69
:	3A	j	6A
;	3B	k	6B
<	3C	l	6C
=	3D	m	6D
>	3E	n	6E
?	3F	o	6F
@	40	p	70
A	41	q	71
B	42	r	72
C	43	s	73
D	44	t	74
E	45	u	75
F	46	v	76
G	47	w	77
H	48	x	78
I	49	y	79
J	4A	z	7A
K	4B	{	7B
L	4C	|	7C
M	4D	}	7D
N	4E	~	7E
O	4F	DEL	7F

Table 1.3(b) Control Characters and their Definition

Control Character	Definition	Control Character	Definition
NUL	NULL	DC2	DIRECT CONTROL 2
SOH	START OF HEADING	DC3	DIRECT CONTROL 3
STX	START TEXT	DC4	DIRECT CONTROL 4
ETX	END TEXT	NAK	NEGATIVE ACKNOWLEDGE
EOT	END OF TRANSMISSION	SYN	SYNCHRONOUS IDLE
ENQ	ENQUIRY	ETB	END TRANSMISSION BLOCK
ACK	ACKNOWLEDGE	CAN	CANCEL
BEL	BELL	EM	END OF MEDIUM
BS	BACKSPACE	SUB	SUBSTITUTE
HT	HORIZONTAL TAB	ESC	ESCAPE
LF	LINE FEED	FS	FORM SEPARATOR
VT	VERTICAL TAB	GS	GROUP SEPARATOR
FF	FORM FEED	RS	RECORD SEPARATOR
CR	CARRIAGE RETURN	US	UNIT SEPARATOR
SO	SHIFT OUT		
SI	SHIFT IN		
DLE	DATA LINK ESCAPE		
DC1	DIRECT CONTROL 1		

Some control characters used in serial communications are: ENQ, ACK, NAK, etc. ENQ is used for enquiry, ACK is used for acknowledge which is and NAK for negative acknowledgment used to indicate errors in reception. Table 1.3(b) lists the control character codes.

☞ *In the 8-bit ASCII code, the eighth bit is often used as a parity or check bit to determine the correctness of data.*

A parity bit is added to the 7-bit ASCII code to form the 8-bit ASCII as:

$$x_7x_6x_5x_4x_3x_2x_1x_0$$

where x_7 is the parity bit. The parity bit is used only to confirm if the data is received correctly or not.

1.8 EBCDIC

EBCDIC (Extended Binary Coded Decimal Interchange Code) is 8-bit character encoding system which is mostly used on International Business Machines (IBM) Mainframe computer system. It has also been working with non-IBM platforms, such as Fujitsu-Siemens' BS2000/OSD, OS-IV, MSP, MSP-EX, HP MPE/iX, and Unisys VS/9 and MCP. EBCDIC codepages are language-dependent with no taxonomy and hence beneficial for non-standard usage. These codepages work on the original EBCDIC character coding. Newline convention has been added to EBCDIC codepages for inserting (NEL), i.e., NEXT LINE code between lines.

1.9 UNICODE

Unicode is an industry standard allowing computers to consistently represent and manipulate text expressed in most of the world's writing systems. Unicode's success at unifying character sets has led to its widespread and predominant use in the internationalization and localization of computer software. Each character or symbol is defined by a 32-bit number. The code can define 2^{32} characters or symbols.

1.10 REPRESENTATION OF VISUAL DATA

Using the computer to convert data into picture form. The most basic visualization is that of turning transaction data and summary information into charts and graphs. Visualization is used in Computer-Aided Design (CAD) to render screen images into 3D (Three Dimension) models that can be viewed from all angles and which can also be animated.

When dealing with data that take on only a few distinct values, it is quite easy to form a bar chart or a pie chart that visually represents the frequency of occurrence of each value of the data. An example shows how to use the Frequency function:
The frequency function has two arguments - the first is the range of cells containing values to be analysed; the second is the range of cells containing the upper values of each group banding.

The second argument (the group upper limits) will exclude any values which exceed the highest category or banding. The function allows you to take account of this and extend the range of analysis to an additional category which contains all values that exceed the specified upper limit.

1. Identify a range of data on which you want to perform your frequency analysis (B2:B13) (See Figure 1.3).

	A	B
1		Trained Staff
2	Ward A	12
3	Ward B	14
4	Ward C	8
5	Ward D	6
6	Ward E	4
7	ward F	14
8	Ward G	19
9	Ward H	22
10	Ward I	14
11	Ward K	15
12	Ward L	20
13	Ward M	27
14		

Figure 1.3 Displaying a range of data

2. Create a vertical range of cells containing the upper bandings with which you wish to group your data (i.e., 0-12, 13-16, 17-20, 21-24).
3. Highlight a vertical range of cells in which you wish the analysis to be reported (E2:E6). Note that by extending this output range by one extra cell, you can capture all values above the maximum banding (i.e. over 24) (See Figure 1.4).

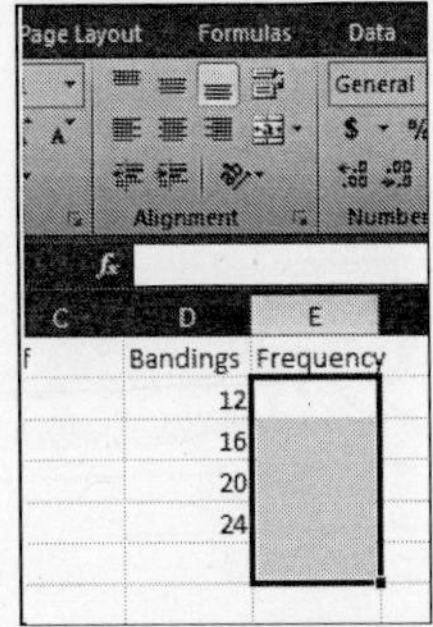

Figure 1.4 Selecting a range of cells (E2:E6)

4. With the whole output range highlighted, type the formula. = FREQUENCY(B2:B13, D2:D5) in the formula bar.
5. Do not press Enter key. This is an array function and therefore requires you to use the alternative key strokes of Ctrl + Shift + Enter.

D	E
Bandings	Frequency
12	4
16	4
20	2
24	1
	1

Figure 1.5 Displaying result of FREQUENCY() function

6. The results will then be automatically entered in all 5 cells (E2:E6). You will notice (in the formula bar) that the formula appears with curly brackets '{}' around it. This indicates that it is an array function. If you type the formula in a single cell and do not enter it using the correct key combination, the function will only return the first value (i.e., 4) (See Figure 1.5).

It is not necessary to have the output range adjacent to the range of bandings. It can be placed anywhere so long as the number of cells is sufficient. You may wish to place the results directly into a table. The function can be of assistance in grouping data to be displayed on a graph as shown in Figure 1.6.

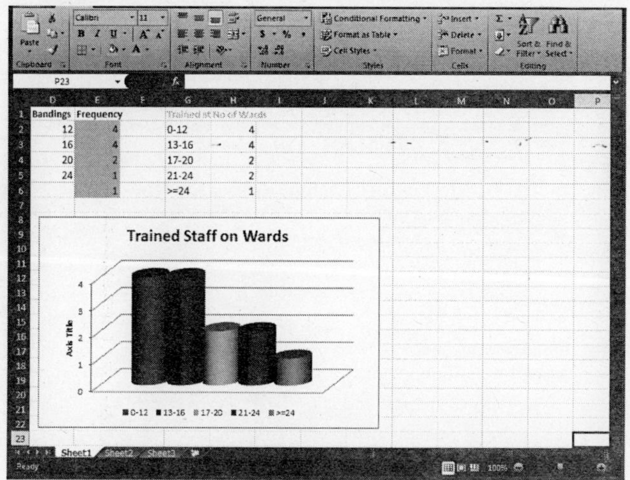

Figure 1.6 Visual representation of given data

REVIEW QUESTIONS WITH ANSWERS

1. Multiple Choice

1.1 The difference between main memory and storage is that main or primary memory is _______ and secondary memory or storage is _____________.
a. Temporary, permanent b. Permanent, temporary
c. Slow, fast d. None of the above

1.2 Which of the following holds the ROM, CPU, RAM and expansion cards?
a. Hard disk b. Floppy disk
c. Motherboard d. None of the above

1.3 The language that a computer can understand and execute is called:
a. Machine language b. Application software
c. System program d. None of the above

1.4 Computers use the ___________ number system to store data and perform calculations.
a. Decimal b. Hexadecimal
c. Binary d. Octal

1.5 There are __________ bits in one byte.
a. 4 b. 8
c. 16 d. 32

1.6 The text code originally used in personal computers:
a. EBCDIC b. Extended ASCII
c. Unicode d. ASCII

1.7 The binary number system has a base:
a. 2 b. 4
c. 8 d. 16

1.8 If even parity mechanism is being used system using ASCII code for data transfer, incorrect receipt data byte is:
a. B5 b. 1
c. 2 d. None of the above

1.9 The widely used code in data communication is:
a. 8-bit ASCII b. EBCDIC
c. 7-bit ASCII d. None of the above

1.10 RAM means:
a. Random access memory b. Read also memory
c. Read access memory d. Random also memory

1.11 In analog computer:
a. Input is first converted to digital form
b. Input is never converted to digital form
c. Output is displayed in digital form
d. All of the above

1.12 Which one of the following is a secondary storage device?
a. CD-ROM b. RAM
c. ROM d. OMR

1.13 1 Kilo bits is:
a. 1000 bits b. 1024 bits
c. 512 bits d. 1048 bits

1.14 During data processing, the actual execution of the instructions takes place in the:
a. Output unit b. Control unit
c. Hard disk d. Arithmetic logic unit

1.15 Which devices can understand difference between data and programs?
a. Input device b. Output device
c. Memory d. Microprocessor

1.16 CD-ROM drive uses:
a. Magnetic storage technique
b. Optical storage technique
c. Solid state storage technique
d. Electronic storage technique

1.17 Number system using strings of 0's and 1's is termed as:
a. Decimal number system
b. Binary number system
c. Hexadecimal number system
d. Octal number system

1.18 Indicate which of the following best describes the term 'software':
a. Operating system programs
b. Application programs
c. Both (a) and (b)
d. None of the above

1.19 Which of the following is the largest memory size?
a. Terabyte b. Gigabyte
c. Kilobyte d. Megabyte

1.20 Which one of the following is not an input device?
a. Microphone b. Mouse
c. Scanner d. None of the above

2. State whether the following statements are True or False

2.1 Computers cannot help in decision-making processes.
2.2 ALU is a part of CPU.
2.3 A floppy disk containing program in it, is not a magnetic storage device.
2.4 The main advantage of computer graphics is that it substantially increases productivity.
2.5 Hybrid computer is a mixture of both digital and analog computers.
2.6 VDUs can be used both as input and output devices.
2.7 OCR is a device that scans written or typed text and transforms it into computer readable form.
2.8 The processing of one program after the other without user intervention is an example of batch processing.
2.9 Access to data stored on magnetic tape is random.
2.10 A microcomputer is called so because it consists of the microprocessor.
2.11 When we move from the outer most track to the innermost track in a magnetic disk, the density increases.
2.12 Computer software is normally classified as system software and application software.
2.13 The group of 8 bits is used to represent a byte.
2.14 Firmware program resides in the ROM portion of a computer.
2.15 A linker can combine object modules from multiple files.
2.16 Editor is a software program which is used to interactively review and modify text material.
2.17 Logical errors in a program can be identified by the computer.

3. Match the following:

3.1	Unicode	a.	Binary Number System
3.2	Radix or base 2	b.	Industry Standard using 32 bits
3.3	QWERTY	c.	Address
3.4	Megahertz	d.	Storage unit
3.5	Analog computers	e.	Computer keyboard keys
3.6	Parallel port	f.	Measure of microprocessor speed
3.7	Serial port	g.	Pressure, temperature measures analogus
3.8	Number used to identify a storage location	h.	Printer
3.9	Holds data to be processed and instructions to be executed	i.	Mouse
3.10	CPU	j.	Brain of computer

4. Fill in the blanks

a. Security	b. Prime	c. Input devices
d. Computer	e. 1101	f. Direct
g. Binary	h. CPU	i. Brain
j. Main	k. Secondary	l. Memory
m. Positional number system	n. Basic input output system	o. Laser printer
p. Animation	q. Byte	

4.1 Floppy disk is an example of ________ access of data retrieval.
4.2 Mouse is a ________ input device.
4.3 ________ is a general purpose machine that manipulates facts according to a set of instructions.
4.4 The CPU is the ____________ of a computer system.
4.5 Hard disk is an example of __________ memory.
4.6 Symbols 0 and 1 represent __________ states.
4.7 Data and instructions are entered into a computer through ________.
4.8 Both data integrity and system __________ are required to protect a person's right to privacy.
4.9 Primary function of _________ is to execute programs.
4.10 Binary equivalent of 13 is __________.
4.11 BIOS stands for _________ .
4.12 Registers are high speed _________.
4.13 _________ is an important component of multimedia.
4.14 __________ is most commonly used to output graphics in hard copy form.
4.15 ________ is used to measure computer memory which is equal to eight bits.

Answers

1.	1.1	a	1.2	c	1.3	a	1.4	c	1.5	b	1.6	d
	1.7	a	1.8	b	1.9	a	1.10	a	1.11	b	1.12	a
	1.13	b	1.14	d	1.15	a	1.16	b	1.17	b	1.18	c
	1.19	a	1.20	d								
2.	2.1	F	2.2	T	2.3	F	2.4	T	2.5	T	2.6	F
	2.7	T	2.8	T	2.9	F	2.10	T	2.11	T	2.12	T
	2.13	T	2.14	T	2.15	T	2.16	T	2.17	F		
3.	3.1	b	3.2	a	3.3	e	3.4	f	3.5	g	3.6	h
	3.7	i	3.8	c	3.9	d	3.10	j				
4.	4.1	f	4.2	b	4.3	d	4.4	i	4.5	k	4.6	g
	4.7	c	4.8	a	4.9	h	4.10	e	4.11	n	4.12	l
	4.13	p	4.14	o	4.15	q						

Short Questions with Answers

*1. Perform the following:
 a. Convert $(1100110110001)_2$ to decimal.
 b. Convert $(2057)_{10}$ to binary.

*2. a. What is hexadecimal number system?
 b. Convert $(1023)_{10}$ to hexadecimal.

*3. What is a computer? What are the different characteristics of a computer?

*4. Write short notes on: (a) ASCII code and (b) EBCDIC code.

*5. Write short notes on:
 a. Motherboard b. Microprocessor

Answers to Short Questions

1. a. $1100110110001 = 1 \times 2^{12} + 1 \times 2^{11} + 0 \times 2^{10} + 0 \times 2_9 + 1 \times 2^8 + 1 \times 2^7 + 0 \times 2^6 + 1 \times 2^5 + 1 \times 2^4 + 0 \times 2^3 + 0 \times 2^2 + 0 \times 2^1 + 1 \times 2^0$

$= 4096 + 2048 + 0 + 0 + 256 + 128 + 0 + 32 + 16 + 0 + 0 + 0 + 1$

$= (6577)_{10}$

b. $(2057)_{10}$

2	2057	remainder
2	1028	1
2	514	0
2	257	0
2	128	1
2	64	0
2	32	0
2	16	0
2	8	0
2	4	0
2	2	0
2	1	0
	0	1

read remainders in reverse order

$(2057)_{10} = (100000001001)_2$

2. a. *Refer Section 1.5 and 1.5.1*

b.

16	1023	remainder
16	63	15 = F
16	3	15 = F
	0	3 = 3

so, $(1023)_{10} = 3FF$

3. A computer is an electronic machine which processes raw data to give meaningful information. Characteristics of a computer are:
   1. Speed: Computer is a very fast device. It can execute basic operations like addition or subtraction at a few microseconds for small machines and nano seconds for large onces.
   2. Accuracy: Computer gives consistently accurate results. Its accuracy does not go down even when the machines used for days together.
   3. Storage capacity: A large volume of information can be stored in the memory of a computer. The information can be retrieved correctly when desired.
   4. Diligence: A computer is free from problems of boredom or lack of concentration. It can work for long hours with the same accuracy and speed.
   5. Versatile: Computers can perform different types of jobs efficiently. They can work with different types of data and information, such as graphics, visuals, audio, video, etc.
4. *Refer Section 1.8*
5. a. Motherboard is the Printed Circuit Board (PCB) which is assembled in computers to hold CPU and memory. Other components, such as sound and video card, hard drives, network drives, Universal Serial Bus (USB) or FireWire slots, etc., are applied to it for better and fast data processing.

   b. Microprocessor is a multipurpose and programmable device which accepts data and information as input, processes them according to given instructions, and displays results as output. It operates on numbers and symbols which are arranged in the binary form. Arithmetic Logic Unit (ALU) and control logic are the two prime components of a microprocessor. The function of ALU is to perform arithmetic operations, such as addition, subtraction, and logical (AND, OR, NOT) operations. The function of control unit is to generate control signals which controls the flow of data between the processor, and memory and peripherals

DESCRIPTIVE TYPE QUESTIONS

1. What is a computer? What are the advantages and disadvantages of a computer?
2. What are the main components of a PC system? Explain each component.
3. Explain the block diagram representing a computer system with the help of illustration.
4. What is the role of input and output devices in a computer system? Name some of the input and output devices used with computers.
5. What are the five basic operations performed by any computer system? Explain each one of them.
6. How many types of memory does a computer have? Justify the need for each type.
7. (a) Convert the binary number 11001 into its decimal equivalent.

   (b) Convert hexadecimal number 759 to its binary equivalent.
8. What is ASCII? Why is it used?
9. Convert$(6806)_{10}$ to Binary and $(7305)_8$ to Hexadecimal.
10. Convert Decimal to Binary (a) 13 (b) 106 (c) 84.
11. Convert Binary to Decimal (a) 10010 (b) 101010.
12. Convert Hexadecimal number 9FAB to its Binary equivalent.

CHAPTER 2

Computer Organization

2.1 INTRODUCTION

The internal arrangement of different parts of a computer is known as computer organization. This arrangement differs from one computer system to another. However, the basic organization remains the same for all types of computer systems.

All computer systems perform five basic operations:

(a) Inputting
(b) Storing
(c) Processing
(d) Outputting
(e) Controlling

Computers receive most data from either the keyboard, scanner, mouse or disk. Information is saved on a pen drive or hard disk. Data is manipulated or processed by the processor(s) and the resulting output is either displayed on a monitor or printed on paper.

In Figure 2.1 shows the basic computer organization. It depicts the five major building blocks, or functional units of a digital computer system which correspond to the basic operations performed by all computers.

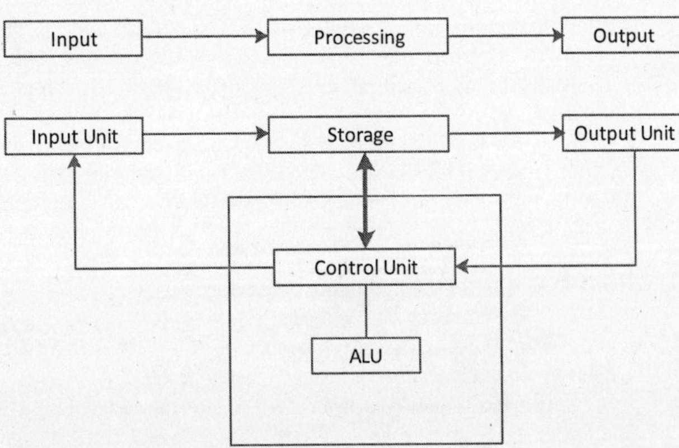

Figure 2.1 Block diagram representation of a computer system

2.2 CENTRAL PROCESSING UNIT

The Central Processing Unit (CPU) is the *brain* of any computer system. In a human body, all major decisions are taken by the brain and all other parts of the body function as directed by the brain. Similar to the human brain, in a computer system, all major calculations, manipulations and comparisons are made by the CPU. The CPU is also responsible for activating and controlling the operations performed by all other units of the computer system.

The major parts of a CPU are:

(a) Arithmetic and Logic Unit (ALU)
(b) Control Unit (CU)
(c) Registers
(c) Main Memory or Primary Memory

2.2.1 Arithmetic Logic Unit (ALU)

The ALU contains the electronic circuitry that executes all arithmetic and logical operations on the data made available to it. The data required to perform the arithmetic and logical functions are inputs from the designated registers. All calculations, including comparisons, are made by the ALU. The data and instructions, stored in the primary memory, are transferred to the ALU for processing.

Results generated in the ALU are transferred to the primary memory. After completion of processing, the final results are sent to an output device, such as printer.

ALUs are designed to perform the four basic arithmetic operations–add, subtract, multiply, divide–and logic operations or comparisons, such as less than, equal to, or greater than. Figure 2.2 shows the different parts of a computer system from the layman's point of view.

In this Figure, the calculator represents the central processing unit and the clock carries out the control function for different operations of the computer. The input and output devices are shown for the keyboard input and the monitor output, respectively. This Figure gives more of a conceptual working of the digital computer. The actual block diagram representation, containing the jobs done by each part is shown in Figure 2.2.

2.2.2 Control Unit

It controls all other units in the computer. The control unit instructs, the input unit, where to store the data after receiving it from the user. It controls the flow of data and instructions from the storage unit to ALU. It also controls the flow of results from the ALU to the storage unit. The control unit is generally referred as the central nervous system of the computer that controls and synchronizes its working.

The CU controls the input and output devices transfer of data to the primary storage. The individual instructions in programs located in the primary storage. One at a time instructions are retrieved from the primary storage. The IR (Instruction Register) holding the current instruction and an instruction pointer to hold the address of the next instruction. Each instruction is interpreted (decoded) so that it can be executed.

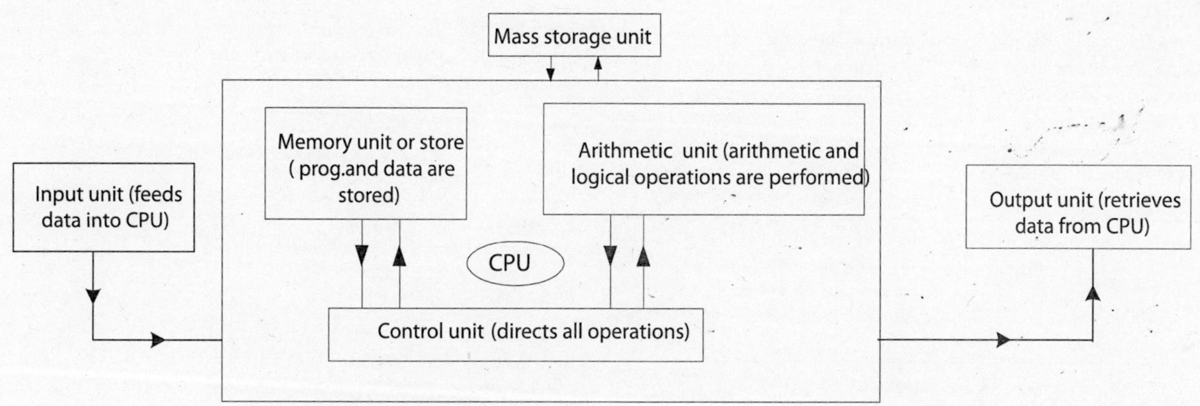

Figure 2.2 Organization of different components of a digital computer

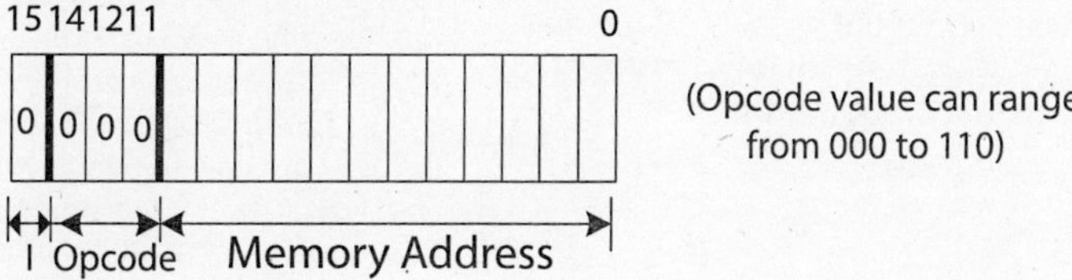

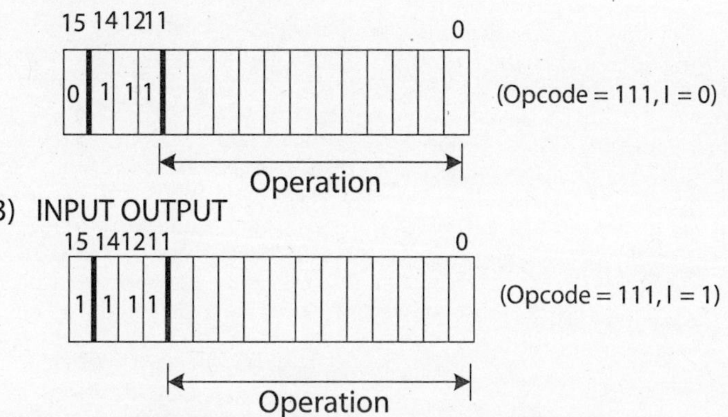

Figure 2.3 Basic Computer Instruction Formats

☞ *Control unit obtains instructions from the program stored in the main memory, interprets the instructions, and issues electrical signals that cause other units of the system to perform their functions.*

2.3 INSTRUCTION SET

An instruction set, or Instruction Set Architecture (ISA), is the part of the computer architecture related to programming, including the native data types, instructions, registers, addressing modes, memory architecture, interrupt and exception handling, and external (Input/Output) I/O. An ISA includes a specification of the set of opcodes (machine language), and the native commands implemented by a particular processor.

It is a command given to a computer to perform an operation on some data. There are three types of instructions shown in Figure 2.3 and each of these instructions consist of three parts.

These three parts of an instruction are called fields. Suppose we have a 16-bit instruction word. Then, the three parts of this instruction would have the following fields:

(a) A 3-bit operation code (opcode field). The value of opcode specifies the operation, such as addition, subtraction, etc., to be performed.

(b) An *I* bit, which is a single bit specifying the addressing mode.

(c) The remaining 12 bits long address field specifies the address of the main memory or the register reference operation or the I/O operation.

If opcode is 111, then depending on *I* bit value, it is either a register reference or an input/output instruction.

If the value of opcode field is a value other than 111, then the instruction is a memory reference instruction. The memory reference instruction means that the operand is stored in memory. The address part in the instruction specifies the address of the operand.

☞ *Note that in this case I bit is not acting as a addressing mode bit. If I bit is 1, it is an Input/Output instruction and the address field specifies the operation to be performed. If I bit is 0, it is a register reference instruction and the address field indicates the operation to be performed on the register.*

2.3.1 Addressing Mode

The techniques for specifying the address of the operands are known as addressing modes. If we want to add two numbers, then we need to bring one of them from the memory to the temporary register and the other in the Accumulator. We can get the address of the number stored in the memory in two ways:

(a) Direct address mode
(b) Indirect address mode

Direct Address Mode

In direct addressing mode, the instruction itself contains the address of the data (operand) in the memory. The operand will be present at some location in the memory and that address of the main memory is provided in the instruction. That is, the address field of the instruction contains the effective address. For example:

BUN A Branch to the instruction in location A

LDA A Load the operand stored at location A into accumulator (AC)

In case of memory reference instructions, the value of *I* bit determines the addressing mode. That is, if *I* bit in the instruction is 0, then the address contained in address field of the instruction is the address of the operand in the memory. That is, bits 0-11 contain the effective address.

Indirect Address Mode

If value of *I* bit is 1, then the address field contains the address of the memory where the effective address is stored in the memory. This is known as Indirect addressing. In other words, the 12-bit address field of the instruction holds the address of the memory word that points to the address of the operand in the memory. For example, if an instruction contains address 40 and the value of *I* is set to 1, then the address 40 is the address of memory where the address of the operand is stored. So, if 1024 is stored in memory location 40 then the effective address of the operand is 1024. This method is indirect addressing.

2.3.2 Memory Reference Instructions

Memory reference instructions are those instructions where the operand to be operated upon is fetched from the memory.

2.3.3 Register Reference Instructions

Register reference instructions are those instructions in which the operand to be operated upon is already present in a register. In such cases, the opcode = 111, I = 0 and the rest of 12 bits represent the operation to be performed.

2.3.4 Input and Output Instructions

Input output instructions are those instructions that are used for interacting with user, i.e., getting data from the user or showing data to the user on a monitor or printer.

2.4 REGISTER

Registers are used to quickly accept, store, and transfer data and instructions that are being used immediately by the CPU. There are various types of registers those are used for various purpose. Among of the some mostly used registers named as AC or Accumulator, Data Register or DR, the AR or Address Register, Program Counter (PC), Memory Data Register (MDR), Index Register, Memory Buffer Register.

These registers are used for performing the various operations. While we are working on the system then these registers are used by the CPU for performing the operations. When we gives some input to the system then the input will be stored into the registers and when the system will gives us the results after processing then the result will also be from the registers. So that they are used by the CPU for processing the data which is given by the user.

The number of registers that a CPU has and the size of each (number of bits) help determine the power and speed of a CPU. For example, a 32-bit CPU is one in which each register is 32 bits wide. Therefore, each CPU instruction can manipulate 32 bits of data. The number of registers varies from computer-to-computer, there are some registers common to all computers. Functions of these registers are described below.

1. **Memory Address Register (MAR):** This register holds the memory addresses of data and instructions. This register is used to access data and instructions from memory during the execution phase of an instruction. Suppose CPU wants to store some data in the memory or to read the data from the memory. It places the address of the required memory location in the MAR.
2. **Program Counter (PC) Register:** The Program Counter (PC), commonly called the Instruction Pointer (IP) in Intel x86 microprocessors, and sometimes called the instruction address register. The PC keeps track of the address of the instructions which is to be executed next. So it holds the address of the memory location, which contains the next instruction to be fetched from the memory.
3. **Memory Buffer Register (MBR):** This register holds the contents of data or instruction read from, or written in memory. It means that this register is used to store data/instruction coming from the memory or going to the memory. A word to be stored in a memory location must be transferred first to MBR from where it is written in memory.
4. **Instruction Register (IR):** It holds an instruction until it decoded. Some computers have two instruction registers, and so they can fetch and save the next instruction while the execution of the previous instruction is going on.

5. **Index Register(IR):** A hardware element which holds a number that can be added to (or, in some cases, subtracted from) the address portion of a computer instruction to form an effective address. Also known as base register. An index register in a computer's CPU is a processor register used for modifying operand addresses during the run of a program.
6. **Accumulator Register (A):** This register is used for storing the results those are produced by the system. When the CPU will generate some results after the processing then all the results will be stored into the AC register.
6. **Input/Output Register:** It is used to communicate with input/output devices. All input information such as instructions and data are transferred an input device is found in this register. Similarly, all output information to be transferred to an output device is found in this register.

2.5 CONCEPT OF PROCESSOR SPEED

A processor, or "microprocessor," is a small chip that resides in computers and other electronic devices. Its basic job is to receive input and provide the appropriate output.

The processor is a unit of computer system that interprets instructions and executes them. The microprocessor is the heart of the computer. A PC's (Personal Computers) performance depends on the capability and speed of the microprocessor. The processing speed of a microprocessor is usually measure in Millions Instructions Per Second (MIPS). The MIPS rating is used to specify the integer computation performance of a processor. The processing speed of a microprocessor for floating point computation is measured in Millions of Floating Point Instructions Per Second (MFLOPS). It speed is the rate at which a processor can complete a processing cycle. It is typically measured in Megahertz (MHz) or Gigahertz (GHz). One megahertz is equal to one million cycles per second, while one gigahertz equals one billion cycles per second. This means a 1.8 GHz processor has twice the clock speed of a 900 MHz processor.

A microprocessor is a combination of arithmetical, logical unit and control unit on a single integrated chip. It requires power supply, clock system and the main memory to function as a complete PC. Microprocessor is also used in many other digital devices besides PCs and workstations. It works on the binary digits 0 and 1. The CPU of a less powerful computer may contain a single microprocessor. The CPU of a bigger workstation may contain a number of microprocessors on one or more motherboards. The major parts of a microprocessor includes:

(a) Arithmetic Logical Unit (ALU)
(b) Control Unit (CU)

☞ *The combination of ALU and CU is known as a microprocessor.*

Processors are, distinguished from each other by the following criteria:

- The architecture, the presence and size of cache memory, the inclusion of a floating point math co-processor, etc.
- The size of data that can be manipulated at one time: 16 bits, 32 bits, or 64 bits. The word bit means binary digit.
- The size of the external bus, that is, the width of the path data. For instance, with 64 bits bus, 8 characters can be sent simultaneously, while a 16-bit bus requires four separate operations to perform the same data transfer.
- Maximum addressable memory, which limits the amount of memory that can be installed in the computer.
- The internal and external clock frequency, that is, the speed at which the processor itself works and the speed at which it can communicate with other components.

8-bit Microprocessor

An *8-bit microprocessor* can handle a combination of 8 bits at a time. These bits are formed by 0s and 1s, such as 10011000, 01110001, etc. The most popular 8-bit microprocessor was Intel 8085. But they are now superceded by more powerful ones.

16-bit Microprocessor

A *16-bit microprocessor* manipulates 16 bits at a time. Thus, a 16-bit computer means that the word length of this computer is 16-bits and the processor manipulates 16-bits of data at a time. An example of 16-bit microprocessor is Intel 80286.

32-bit Microprocessor

A 32-bit microprocessor, means that its word length is 32 bits. Some examples are Intel 80386, 80486, etc. These types of microprocessors were used in expensive PCs earlier.

64-bit Microprocessor

64-bit microprocessors are used in very powerful workstations server and mini computers. An important 64-bit microprocessor based computer is DEC's (Digital Equipment Corporation) Alpha Server.

2.6 TYPES OF PROCESSOR

2.6.1 Pentium MMX Processor

Intel released its newest processor, Intel Pentium with MMX (Multimedia eXtension)Technology in January 1997 (See Figure 2.4). It is an evolutionary design, adding some enhancements and new capabilities to the "classic" Pentium. The main difference between the Pentium with MMX and the Pentium Classic is the inclusion of the MMX instruction set extensions. Running software on a Pentium MMX will result in a significant increase in performance over the regular Pentium at the same clock speed.

The Pentium with MMX is pin-compatible with the regular Pentium and goes in a Socket 7 just like the old chip. However, there is one important difference between the two: the Pentium with MMX uses split-rail voltage, i.e., 3.3 volts for the external voltage and 2.8 volts for the core.

Features of Pentium MMX Processor

MMX processor has the following enhancements over the previous generation of x86 processors (80486):

- **Doubled Primary Cache:** The Pentium with MMX has 16 KB for each of the level 1 data and instruction caches (Regular Pentium processor had 8 KB code and 8 KB data cache).
- **Improved Cache Mapping:** The primary cache is now 4-way set associative instead of 2-way.
- **Deepening of Internal Pipelines:** Both of the internal integer executions units are increased from 5 to 6 stages.
- **Better Use of Internal Pipelines:** More types of instructions can be run in parallel down the two execution pipes than on the older Pentium, so more use is made of the second pipe.
- **Improved Branch Prediction Unit:** Branch prediction was enhanced in comparison with Pentium processors.
- **Improved Instruction Decoder:** The instruction decoder is more efficient than the Pentium's decoder.

Figure 2.4 Pentium MMX processor

2.6.2 Dual Core Processor

Dual core refers to a CPU that includes two complete execution cores per physical processor. It has combined two processors and their caches and cache controllers onto a single integrated circuit (Silicon Chip). Dual core processors are well suited for multitasking environments because there are two complete execution cores instead of one, each with an independent interface to the front side bus. Since each core has its own cache, the operating system has sufficient resources to handle most compute intensive tasks in parallel.

Multicore is similar to dual core in that it is an expansion to the dual core technology which allows for more than two separate processors. In a single core or traditional processor the CPU is fed strings of instructions executes it and then selectively store in its cache for quick retrieval. When data outside the cache is required, it is retrieved through the system bus from Random Access Memory (RAM) or from storage devices. Accessing these slows down performance to the maximum speed the bus, RAM or storage device will allow, which is far slower than the speed of the CPU. In a dual core processor, each core handles incoming data strings simultaneously to improve efficiency. Now when one is executing the other can be accessing the system bus or executing its own code. To utilize a dual core processor, the operating system must be able to recognize multithreading and the software must have Simultaneous Multithreading Technology (SMT) written into its code. SMT enables parallel multi threading wherein the cores are served multi-threaded instructions in parallel. Without SMT the software will only recognize one core. Adobe Photoshop is an example of SMT-aware software. SMT is also used with multiprocessor systems common to servers. A dual core processor is different from a multiprocessor system. In the multiprocessor there are two separate CPUs with their own resources. In the dual core processor, resources are shared and the core resides on the same chip. A multi processor system is faster than a system with a dual core processor, while a dual core system is faster than a single core system. Dual core processors do not require a new motherboard, but can be used in existing boards that feature the correct socket. For the average user the difference in performance will be most noticeable in multitasking until more software is SMT aware. Servers running multiple dual core processors will be seen an appreciable increase in performance.

Features and Benefits

Outstanding Dual Core Performance With its two execution cores, the Intel Core Duo processor is optimized for multithreaded applications and multitasking. We can simultaneously run multiple demanding applications, such as graphics intensive games or serious number-crunching programs while downloading music or running virus scanning security programs in the background.

Power Efficiency Demand for greater power efficiency in computing is on the rise from desktop to laptop PCs. With an Intel Core Duo processor, we get a balance of great dual core computing capabilities and power savings. Its enhanced voltage efficiency supports cooler and quieter system designs as compared to traditional desktop and laptop PCs. And thanks to the innovative energy efficient technologies built-in, the Intel Core Duo processor is able to transfer power only to those areas of the processor that need it, thereby enabling laptops to save power and desktops to have thinner, sleeker designs.

A Vibrant Media Experience The Intel Core Duo processor enables Intel Viiv technology and Intel Centrino Duo mobile technology multimedia experience to be all the more vibrant. Featuring Intel Digital Media Boost, the Intel Core Duo processor enables accelerating technologies for applications, such as CAD (Computer-Aided Design) tools, 3D (Three Dimesion) and 2D (Two Dimension) modeling, video editing, digital music, digital photography and gaming. This is one of the key ingredients that help Intel Viiv technology and Intel Centrino Duo mobile technology to give you a truly rich multimedia experience.

Smarter, More Efficient Designs The Intel Core Duo processor features Intel smart Cache which helps deliver a smarter and more efficient cache and bus design to enable enhanced dual-core performance, and power savings.

☞ *The Intel Core Duo processor is Intel's first mobile dual-core processor and a key component of the new Intel Centrino Duo mobile technology platform.*

2.6.3 Intel Core 2 Duo Processor

The latest generation of Intel x86-compatible processor, Core 2 Duo microprocessor family. It was introduced on July 27, 2006. The Core 2 Duo processors include two cores, each core having 32 KB L1 data and 32 KB L1 code caches, and both cores having shared 2 or 4 MB L2 cache. The Core 2 Duo CPUs run at lower frequency than Pentium 4 processors, but they offer excellent performance due to more efficient architecture:

- Each processor's core can execute up to 4 instructions per cycle.
- Shared L2 cache allows the same copy of data to be used by both cores. Another advantage of shared L2 cache is that more heavily loaded core can use bigger portion of L2 cache - up to the full size of the cache.
- 128-bit SSE instructions can be executed at sustained rate of one 128-bit instruction per cycle.

Core 2 Duo architecture includes other performance enhancing features. One of these features is a "macrofusion". This feature allows the processor to load and execute common instruction pairs as one instruction.

The performance of Core 2 Duo family is much higher than the performance of Pentium 4. Lower processor speed of Core 2 Duo and Extreme processors are also translated into lower power consumption. Core 2 Duo E6600 and E6700 processors have thermal design power 65 Watt (75 Watt for Core 2 Extreme x6800), while less efficient Pentium 4 Extreme Edition 3.73 GHz has thermal design power of 115 Watt.

The Intel Core 2 Duo divided into desktop processors and mobile processors. The desktop processors are split into three code names. Conroe, which uses the 65-nanometer and made in August 2006. Allendale 65-nm, in January 2007 and Walfdale, in January 2008 (See Figure 2.5).

Figure 2.5 Intel Core 2 Duo processor

Types of Core 2 Families

Core 2 Duo: Core 2 Duo was the first family of desktop-class microprocessors based on Core microarchitecture. The first Core 2 Duo processors had much lower core frequency and approximately the same FSB (Front Side Bus) frequency and level 2 cache size as Pentium D microprocessors. They had better performance than the fastest Pentium D 960 due to much more efficient microarchitecture.

Core 2 Quad: Core 2 Quad microprocessors are essentially two Core 2 Duo CPUs in one package - two cores are located on one die, two other cores are on another die, and both dies are packaged together. The level 2 cache on these processors is shared between two cores. These CPUs have higher (about 50% higher) Thermal Design Power than dual-core microprocessors running at the same frequency. The quad core CPUs have the same performance as the Core 2 Duo processors in single-threaded applications, and are faster or considerably faster in multi-threaded applications. Performance difference in games between quad and dual core microprocessors is highly dependent on the game, and varies from no difference at all to 20% performance advantage for quad core CPUs.

Core 2 Extreme is a brand name for the best performing desktop Core 2 microprocessors. These processors were always faster than other Core 2 Duo and Core 2 Quad. Only Extreme processors had higher core frequency, they also had unlocked clocked multiplier which allowed to increase their frequency above nominal. Extreme processors had other features that increased their performance even further. Higher bus frequency, twice as many cores, and / or large level 2 cache. Being faster than any other Core 2 Duo and Core 2 Quad on the market, these CPUs were almost twice more expansive than the most expensive Core 2 Duo / Quad microprocessor.

Core 2 Solo is a family of low power microprocessors based on Core microarchitecture. These processors have only one core. Like other mobile Core 2 families, the Core 2 Solo CPUs have additional low-power modes along with Dynamic Acceleration technology. Solo processors have much lower Thermal Design Power than Core 2 Duo mobile microprocessors - 5.5 Watt versus 25 or 35 Watt.

Main Features and Benefits

Each Intel Core 2 Duo CPU has its two cores placed on a single die, which is a wafer of semiconductor material. The 65-nm chips are bigger than the 45-nm ones. The Core 2 Duo division has a 1.06 to 3.33 GHz processing speed range, 533 to 1,333 MHz data bus speed range; a 2MB, 3MB, 4MB or 6MB Level 2 cache, or secondary memory bank; and a maximum power consumption range of 10 to 65 watts. The mobile processors tend to be the less powerful but more energy efficient Core 2 Duo chips.

2.6.4 Intel Core i3 Processor

Core i3 Core-branded microprocessors was introduced on January 7, 2010. It is originally based on Westmere (enhanced Nehalem) micro architecture, Core i3 CPUs were eventually transitioned to Sandy Bridge, and later to Ivy Bridge architecture. Common features of all Core i3 generations are dual-channel DDR3 memory controller, HD-capable graphics controller, and separate DMI interface to peripheral devices (See Figure 2.6).

All processors have per-core 256 KB level 2 cache, large level 3 cache shared between two cores, as well as support for basic and some advanced microarchitecture features, such as SSE4 instructions, and Virtualization and HyperThreading technologies. Sandy Bridge and Ivy Bridge CPUs also added support for Advanced Vector Extensions.

Intel Core i3 currently consists of desktop and mobile Core i3 families. Desktop Core i3 microprocessors are packaged in 1155- and 1156-land Land Grid Array (LGA) packages, and require socket 1155 or socket 1156 motherboards. Mobile Core i3 CPUs are manufactured in 1023-ball BGA (Ball Grid Array), 1288-ball BGA or 988 micro-PGA packages. BGA processors are soldered directly on motherboards, and PGA processors utilize socket G1 or G2.

Figure 2.6 Inter Core i3 processor

Basic Features of i3

The basic feature of the i3 features are highly improved as compared to previous version of the processor by Intel. i3 processors have 3.06 GHz and 2.93 GHz core speed which is very high as compared to the previous configurations of Intel processors. They have four processing threads that enables multithreading and multitasking. 4 MB additional Cache memory is also provided inside the processor. Double channeled DDR (Digitalized-Image Data Record) with 1333 MHZ memory sequence. Some of the popular and leading features of i3 processors are listed below.

- i3 processors is featured with accuracy and high performance. The users with the high throughput rates, and also reduced time in executing the programs by the processor.
- It is fully equipped by the latest HD graphics with powerful and advanced video engine that provides smooth high quality display along with the 3D graphics capabilities.
- It also provides hyper threading technology to its users which enable the multitasking capability of both user and the system. The systems with i3 processors can perform execution and compilation of two tasks simultaneously without causing the executing delays and debuggers errors. They are so responsive that output of the programs can be generated at the same time too. More than seven applications can run simultaneously on the system with i3 processor built on the motherboards.
- i3 processors are smarter, faster and more adaptive in all kinds of networking scheme. They can be used with any of the hard disk configurations.
- They are also famous in the markets by the name of desktop processor because of the great quality resolution. Integrated components on the motherboards also makes i3 processors unique in their architecture and circuit installations.

Advantages of i3

The advantages that are of great use in the field of computers and technology. Some of them are listed below.

- Dual core processing has the ability to run two independent programs with one hardware.
- i3 processors have improved Pentium base, they have totally new architecture with more integrations and high speed performance structure.
- Hyper threading technology also enables user to enjoy the high speed and better performance with more reliable outputs. It has 4 tasking threads that allows user to easily execute 3 to 4 programmes at a time.
- Smart memory and cache sequence allow user to enjoy the optimized and efficient data access both direct and sequentially. Effective shortcuts have reduced the access time of the file and system.
- HD graphical features also make these processors distinguished from the others because they are considered as best in their resolution.

2.6.5 Intel Core i5 Processor

Intel Core i5 microprocessor family, released in September 2009, is a family of processors with medium-level performance as compared to Core i7. The i5 processors include many features found in Core i7 CPUs. It is single-die(IC) quad-core design, on-die(IC) DDR3 memory controller, point-to-point protocol used to communicate with I/O devices, 256 KB level 2 cache (per core), large shared level 3 cache, SSE4 instructions, and support for such features as Virtualization technology and Turbo Boost technology (See Figure 2.7).

Basic Features of Intel i5 Processors

As i5 processors are more advanced as compared to the i3 or all the previous versions of the processors. It has lot of features that deals the advanced technologies in a very respectable way. Some of the basic key Intel i5 features are as follows:

- Basically i5 processors are introduces to do the intelligent networking and enhance the performance of different purposes, such as for gaming, faster procession, reliable data transmission, etc.
- One of the important feature of the i5 processors is that it automatically manages the power supply where needed and does not break the speed and the performance of the system.
- It also allows the user to enjoy the heavy applications with the higher rate such as HD video composing, composing a music.
- It also provides the opportunity to the users to use the system with multitasking.
- It also able to increase the memory of the system and help users to work with the high bandwidth and great performance.
- A big feature of the i5 processors is that they have ability to run two multitasking processors together that are generally called as dual processors and can increase the working performance of the system efficiently.

- Turbo Boost technology of i5 processors is the key beneficial feature of the i5 processors that allow the users to do their regular and important working with the help of heavy applications.
- It also consists of Hyper Threading technology that enables the users for multitasking and improves their business or working by working on the two different tasks at the same time.

Advantages of i5 Processors

There are many more benefits of the i5 processors because they are advanced form of the processing units. Some more important benefits of the i5 processors are given below.

- Providing high quality visualization for advanced applications.
- High performance with the help of dual processor technology.
- HD graphics enhance the video graphics and applications related to the same architecture.

Figure 2.7 Intel Core i5 processor

2.6.6 Intel Core i7 Processor

Intel developed different types processors for the users for the sake of faster working as compared to the previous versions. After the development of i3 and i5 processor, Intel introduces a new version, i.e., i7 processor that is comparatively a lot more faster than the old ones. Basically i7 processors were designed to meet the challenges of the intelligent and the fastest working performance of the computer system. They were designed in 2008 and were announced in 2009 just after the i5 processors. i7 processors have ability to handle all the problems and working of the latest computer systems and provide the quality systematic to technological world (See Figure 2.8).

Features of i7 Processors

There are many features of i7 processors that are more advanced as compared to the previous or the old versions of the processors invented by the Intel Company. Some of the latest technological features of the i7 features are as follows:

Figure 2.8 Core i7 processor

- With the help of i7 processors, users can enjoy the high speed working with the additional feature of the multitasking, i.e., using two different documents or the files at the same time.
- Dual core technology is also a part of i7 processors that provide reliable and high data rate working performance to the customers.
- It is the Turbo Boost technology. This technology provides the high performance to the system to the users to overcome the work load of different applications on the system and maintain the speed of the system.
- Like i5 and i3 processors, i7 also have a feature of Hyper threading technology enhances the activity and the speed of the system by managing the multitasking, work load and different types of heavier applications of the users.
- i7 processors are so advanced to deal with the integrated memory of system and have ability to increase the memory up to 1066 MB and provide the working speed of 25.6 GB/sec.

Technical Specifications of i7 Processors

Some technicalities specifications of i7 processors that encourages the customers to buy the processing units are as follows:

- i7 processors have integrated memory up to 1066 MB and can provide the faster working for applications.
- i7 processors are also able to supports cache that is very important for the high rate performance and can support up to 8 to 12 MB.
- Highest clock speed of the newt poking of the i7 processors is 3.2 GHz. That is why these are very famous among the users to meet the requirements of the latest technological/professional world.
- There are many other technologies that really make the processors and the system powerful, such as high visualization, and can support up to 64 bits, with the help of these specifications system maintains the working of the BIOS (Basic Input/Output System) and other chipset devices.

- There are different types of cores involved on the manufacturing of the Intel i7 processors but the common cores that are involved are Bloomfield or Lynnfield etc.

Advantages of i7 Processors

i7 is latest processors for the systems that are able to support dual processors technology and provide the fastest and the convenient working performance to the users. Due to its advancement, i7 processors has many advantages, some of them are listed below:

- They are faster from the old versions of the processors given by the Intel and can support dual processor technology.
- Provide high data visualization technology to the users to view the high quality images and video graphics. Better then i3 and i5 family processors.

On top of all advantages, the only major disadvantage of the i7 processors is that they are very expensive to install in systems. And people who have specific requirements in profession they use it, i7 are not used that commonly.

2.7 MEMORY AND STORAGE

All computers require storage space and memory to run programs and store files. There are different types of memory and storage, and each has its own purpose.

2.7.1 Memory Organization

The *memory* is an essential part of a computer system. It is required by the computer system to store instructions and data. In the most general sense, secondary memory refers to external systems, such as disk drives or tape drives. But actually, main memory refers only to the fast semiconductor storage (RAM) directly connected to the CPU. Memory can be divided into the following two types:

(a) *Primary Memory:* These are the memory chips which are directly connected to CPU or they are parts of CPU in PCs.

(b) *Secondary Memory:* These are the memory units which are external to CPU.

☞ *Memory is an electronic circuitary that allows data to be stored and retrieved in 0 and 1 form. The secondary memory stores data and keep it even when the electricity to the PC goes off whereas the primary memory looses its contents on switching off power supply.*

2.7.2 Memory Hierarchy

The total memory of a computer system is organised as the hierarchy of memories. Table 2.1 gives the summary of the different levels of memories.

Table 2.1 Memory hierarchy

Memory	Size	Access Time [Nano (10^{-9}) sec]	Managed by	Backed by
Cache Memory	Less than or equal to 4MB	3-10	Hardware	Main Memory
Main Memory	Greater than or equal to 1GB	80-400	Operating System	Disk
Disk Storage	Greater than 1GB	5,000,000	Operating System /User	Magnetic Tape

(*Contd...*)

Figure 2.9 show a block diagram of hierarchy of memory organization in a computer. In this Figure, observe that there is *Main Memory* that communicates directly with the CPU. There is *Auxiliary Memory* or *Secondary Memory* which indirectly communicates with the main memory through Input/Output processor. Also note that *Cache Memory* is present in between the CPU and main memory.

Now you may ask, what is the need of such a hierarchy of memories, when the same purpose can be met with a single large sized memory system. Economics and performance are the basis for such an hierarchy for memory organization. Secondary memory devices namely, zip disks, floppy disks, hard disks, as well as CD-ROMs (Compact Disk Read Only Memory) are the cheapest and have large storage capacity, but they are slow in accessing or storing data.

☞ *Access time is the average time required to locate and fetch an instruction or data from the memory.*

Comparison of Different Types of Memories

Main memory has less storage capacity and are made up of *electronic integrated circuits*. These are more expensive as compared to auxilliary memory but are much faster. That is, the access time required to fetch data or instruction is in the range of nano (10^{-9}) second.

The cache memory is the most expensive, smallest and fastest memory with least access time. It holds only those program parts and data which is currently and frequently used by the processor. This enhances CPU's performance. The cache memory is expensive because it has complicated circuits associated with it for faster access. You would have observed in Figure 2.9 that access time is directly proportional to the storage capacity of a memory. Therefore, you cannot expect to get a faster performance by installing a large sized main memory. The access time of large sized memories is very large. Hence, such a step would decrease the speed instead of increasing it.

Why Hierarchical Memory System?

Had we used a single large sized memory system, the CPU would have taken considerable amount of time to locate an instruction or data. That is, the access time would have been too large. However, using an heirarchical memory system, the currently used program and data can be loaded into the main memory and thus processed very fast. The programs which are not manipulated currently, can be kept in the slow auxiliary memory. As and when these are needed, they can be loaded into the main memory. The cache memory holds even more frequently used programs, such as subroutines and data. Thus, it will further enhance processing speed of the CPU.

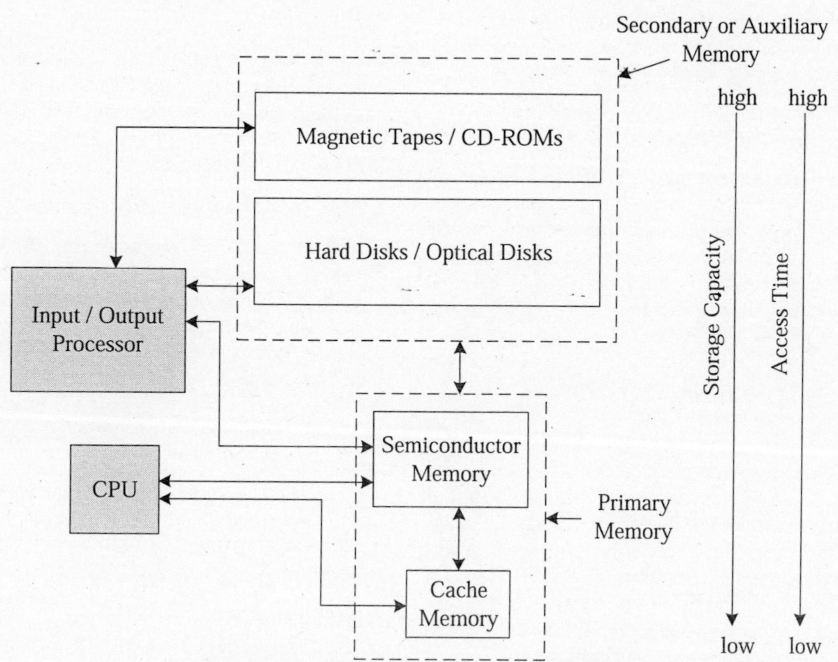

Figure 2.9 Hierarchy of memory organisation

2.8 MAIN MEMORY OR PRIMARY MEMORY

Primary Memory, also known as *Main Memory*, is one of the important parts of the computer, because memory's size determines the length and number of programs that can be stored at a time. Its size also indicates the amount of data that can be processed quickly.

Primary memory is a fast RAM made up of ICs (Integrated Circuits) called *cells*. The main memory is directly addressed by the CPU.

☞ *Main Memory is a small and relatively fast storage unit that stores data and instructions which are being currently used by the CPU.*

Main memory is divided into the following two types.

(a) RAM (Random Access Memory)
(b) ROM (Read Only Memory)

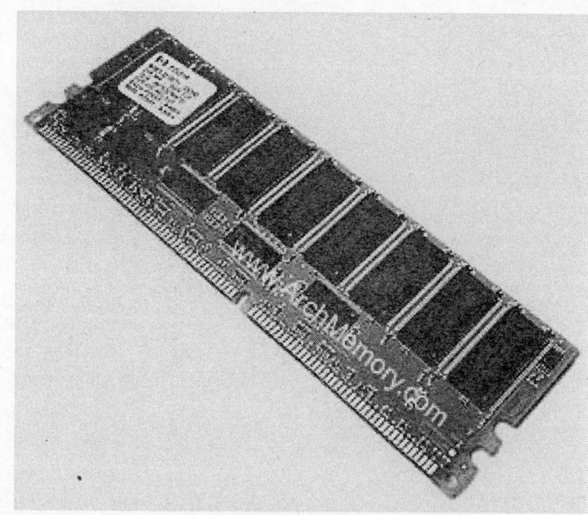

Figure 2.10 RAM chip

2.8.1 RAM (Read/Write)

RAM stands for Random Access Memory and it is a read/write memory. Information can be written to as well read from RAM (See Figure 2.10). The storage locations can be accessed in any order, i.e., Random Access is possible. Term *Random Access Memory* is not appropriate since ROM is also a random access device. Hence we can better call it a *read/write* memory.

RAM is a volatile memory. It retains the data as long as it is supplied with power. When power supply is switched off or interrupted, the stored data in the RAM is lost. RAMs of various capacities are available, for example, 256 MB, 512 MB, 4 GB, 8 GB and so on.

Static and Dynamic RAM

There are two important types of RAMs: static RAM and dynamic RAM. Static RAMs can retain stored information as long as the power supply is on. But a dynamic RAM loses its stored information in a very short time (a few milliseconds) even though the power supply is on. Therefore, dynamic RAMs have to be refreshed periodically, generally every 2 milliseconds. Dynamic RAMs are cheaper and have high packing densities but moderate speed. They consume less power. They are used where a large capacity of memory is needed. Static RAMs are costlier and consume more power. They do not need refreshing circuitry. They have higher speed or shorter access time as compared to dynamic RAMs. Static RAM and dynamic RAM are also written as SRAM and DRAM, respectively.

SDRAM (Synchronous Dynamic RAM)

SDRAM (synchronous DRAM) is a generic name for various types of Dynamic Random Access Memory (DRAM) that are synchronized with the clock speed that the microprocessor is operating. This tends to increase the number of instructions that the processor can perform in a given time. The speed of SDRAM is rated in MHz rather than in nanoseconds (ns). This makes it easier to compare the bus speed and the RAM chip speed.

RDRAM (Rambus Dynamic Random Access Memory)

RDRAM (Rambus Dynamic Random Access Memory) is a memory subsystem that can transfer up to 1.6 billion bytes per second. The subsystem consists of the RAM, the RAM controller, and the bus (path) connecting RAM to the microprocessor and devices in the computer that use it. Direct Rambus (DRDRAM), a technology developed and licensed by the Rambus Corporation, is the latest version and is expected to help accelerate the growth of visually intensive interfaces, such as 3-D, interactive games, and streaming multimedia.

Rambus is intended to replace the current main memory technology of Dynamic Random Access Memory (DRAM). Much faster data transfer rates from attached devices, such as video games using FireWire and the Accelerated Graphics Port (AGP) make it important to reduce the bottleneck in getting data into the computer. Direct Rambus (DRDRAM) provides a two-byte (16 bits) bus rather than DRAM's 8-bit bus. At a RAM speed of 800 MHz (800 million cycles per second), the peak data transfer rate is 1.6 billion bytes per second. Direct Rambus uses pipelining to move data from RAM to cache memory levels that are closer to the microprocessor or display unit. Up to eight operations may be underway at the same time. Rambus is expected to fit into existing motherboard standards. The components that are inserted into motherboard connections are called Rambus In-line Memory Modules (RIMMs). Such components can replace conventional dual in-line memory module.

DDR RAM

Double-Data-Rate Synchronous Dynamic Random Access Memory, also known as DDR SDRAM or DDR RAM for short, is a type of very fast computer memory. DDR RAM is based on the same architecture as SDRAM, but utilizes the clock signal differently to transfer twice the data in the same amount of time. In a computer system, the clock signal is an oscillating frequency used to coordinate interaction between digital circuits. Digital circuits designed to operate on the clock signal may respond at the rising or falling edge of the signal. SDRAM memory chips utilize only the rising edge of the signal to transfer data, while DDR RAM transfers data on both the rising and falling edges of the clock signal. Therefore, it attains the higher speed.

☞ *A DDR RAM is essentially twice as fast as SDRAM.*

EDO RAM

EDO (Extended Data Output) RAM is a type of RAM chip that improves the time to read from memory on faster microprocessors, such as the Intel Pentium. EDO RAM was initially optimized for the 66 MHz Pentium. For faster computers, different types of SDRAM are recommended.

SIMM (Single In-Line Memory Module)

SIMM is a type of memory module used for random access memory in personal computers. It differs from a DIMM (the most predominant form of memory module today) in that the contacts on a SIMM are redundant on both sides of the module. In SIMMs, a slender circuit board is dedicated to store memory chips. Each chip is capable of holding 8 to 9 chips per board, the ninth chip usually an error checking chip. The typical bus from the chip to the motherboard is 32-bits wide.

☞ *One should be very careful about the orientation of the SIMM when inserting them into the socket. Many sockets have key tab to prevent the module from inserting in reverse.*

DIMM (Double In-Line Memory Module)

DIMM includes a series of random access memory integrated circuits. These modules are mounted on a printed circuit board and designed for use in personal computers. DIMMs began to replace SIMMs as the predominant type of memory module as Intel's Pentium processors began to control the market.

2.8.2 ROM (Read Only Memory)

ROM is a permanent type memory. Its contents are not lost when power supply is switched off (See Figure 2.11). The user cannot write into a ROM. Its contents are written into at manufacturing time. ROMs store permanent programs and other types of data which are needed by the computer to execute user programs. ROMs store functions, such as sine, cosine, logarithm, square root, exponential and code conversion tables, etc. An example of a ROM is Toshiba Mask ROM, TCS 534000, 512 K × 8 bits.

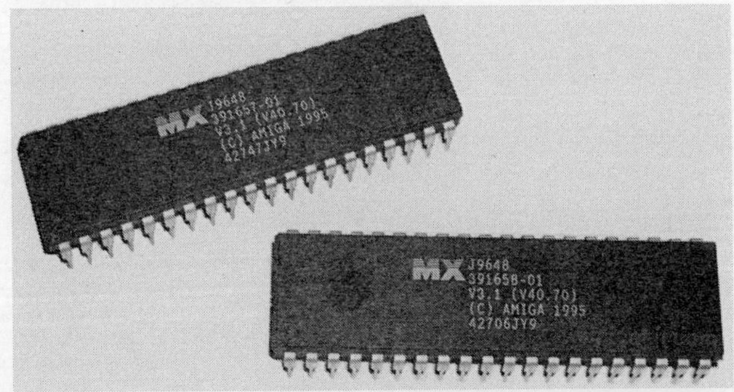

Figure 2.11 ROM chip

☞ *ROM is a semiconductor-based memory that contains instructions or data which can be read but not modified. To create a ROM chip, the designer supplies a semiconductor manufacturer with the instructions or data to be stored.*

ROMs are further classified as:

(a) PROMs (Programmable ROMs)

(b) EPROM (Erasable PROM)
(c) EEPROM (Electrically Erasable PROM)

PROMs (Programmable Read Only Memories)

The contents of PROMs are decided by the user. User can store permanent programs, data or other information in a PROM. The instrument known as *PROM programmer* is an electronic equipment used for programming the ROM. The PROMs are programmable once only, i.e., user cannot write information again and again in them. IC745287 is a type of PROM available commercially.

EPROM (Erasable PROM)

An EPROM is an erasable PROM. The stored data in EPROMs can be erased by exposing them to high intensity short wave ultraviolet light for about 12 minutes. When an EPROM is exposed to ultraviolet light the entire data is erased. EPROMs are cheap, reliable, and hence they are widely used. EPROMs are used to store programs which are permanent but need updating. The permanent programs which are at the research and development stage also need to be stored in EPROMs because they are modified several times. Where updating or changes in programs at the development stages are required, EPROMs are far more economical than PROMs because they can be reused. An example of EPROMs is Intel's 87C257.

EEPROM (E^2PROM)

This is an electrically erasable PROM. The chip can be erased and reprogrammed on the PC's motherboard on a byte-to-byte basis. It requires much shorter time, a few seconds as compared to 10-20 minutes for EPROM. Intel 2816A is a 16K (2K x 8) EEPROM available commercially.

☞ *E^2PROM requires 21 Volts pulses for writing or erasing and 5V for read operation.*

Volatility of Memory

Volatile memory is the memory whose contents are lost when power is switched off. A computer's main memory, made up of dynamic RAM or static RAM chips, loses its contents immediately upon interruption of power. A random access memory is volatile but secondary memory containing magnetic elements is not volatile, because they retain stored data when even power supply is switched off.

2.9 CACHE MEMORY

Cache memory (pronounced as the "cash memory") is placed in between the CPU and the main memory. It is faster than the main memory. Hence access time is much less than that of the main memory. The access time of a cache memory is 15–25 nanoseconds (ns) whereas that of the main memory is 80 ns. One nanosecond = $\mathbf{10^{-9}}$ second. The cache memory stores instructions and data which are to be immediately executed. It is used to reduce the average access time for address, instructions or data which are normally stored in the main memory. Thus, it increases the operating speed of the system. Cache memory is much costlier than the main memory. From economical considerations, the size of cache memory is usually smaller than that of the main memory. Sometimes cache is used to store only instructions. One such type of cache is used in 68020 processor. It has 256-byte instruction cache, which allows it to pre-fetch instructions from the main memory and store them in the cache during the period when the system bus would otherwise be idle. The microprocessor 68030 has both 256-byte instruction cache and 256-bit data cache.

The high-speed memory used for the Cache purpose is very costly, the reason why is not used as the main memory. The information frequently required by the processor is kept in the cache memory by the Cache controller. This Cache controller ensures that the data required by the processor in the next memory access is available in the cache memory. This improves the speed of the computer very much because if the required data is in the cache memory it is made available to the CPU without any wait state. When the required data is available in the cache it is called a hit. In case of a cache hit the processor immediately reads or writes the data in the data cache line. The proportion of accesses that result in a cache hit is known as the hit rate, and is a measure of the effectiveness of the cache.

When the required data is not available in the cache memory it is called a miss. In case of a miss, most caches allocate new entry, which comprises the tag just missed and a copy of the data from memory. The reference can then be applied to the new entry just as in case of a hit. Misses are comparatively slow because they require the data to be transferred from the main memory. This transfer incurs a delay, since the main memory is slower than cache memory.

☞ *Cache memory is a high-speed memory built-in the processor and used between the main memory and the processor.*

The performance of the cache depends on the following:

- Speed and size of the cache memory.
- The logic used to read data around the memory area read by the CPU.
- The logic used to guess next required data by the processor.

Most of the new microprocessors have cache memory added in the CPU chip itself to speed up the process even further. Even on these CPUs with built-in cache, you can add external cache memory.

2.9.1 Levels of Cache

In standard PCs, we find processors with Level 1 (L1) and Level 2 (L2) cache. Some processors like the Intel Itanium have three levels of built-in cache, but these are used only for very special server applications.

Level 1 (L1) Cache

Level 1 cache is built into the actual processor core. It is a piece of RAM, typically 64 or 128 KB size, which operates at the same clock frequency as the rest of the CPU. Thus, we could say the L1 cache is part of the processor.

☞ *The L1 cache is also known as internal cache or primary cache, because it is a part of same chip as the microprocessor.*

L1 cache is normally divided into two sections, one for data and another for instructions. For example, an Athlon processor may have a 32 KB data cache and a 32 KB instruction cache. If the cache is common for both data and instructions, it is called a unified cache.

☞ *The main limitation of the L1 cache is its size, as this cache is designed as the internal part of the processor.*

Level 2 (L2) Cache

The Level 2 cache is normally much larger (and unified), such as 256, 512 or 1024 KB. The purpose of an L2 cache is to constantly read in slightly larger quantities of data from the RAM, so that these are available to the L1 cache.

Traditionally, the L2 cache is connected to the front side bus (See Figure 2.12).

CPU Type	L2 cache
Pentium, K5, K6	External, on the motherboard
Pentium Pro	Internal, in the CPU
Pentium II, Athlon	External, in a module close to the CPU
Celeron (Ist generation)	None
Celeron (later gen.), Pentium III, Athlon XP, Duron, Pentium 4	Internal, in the CPU

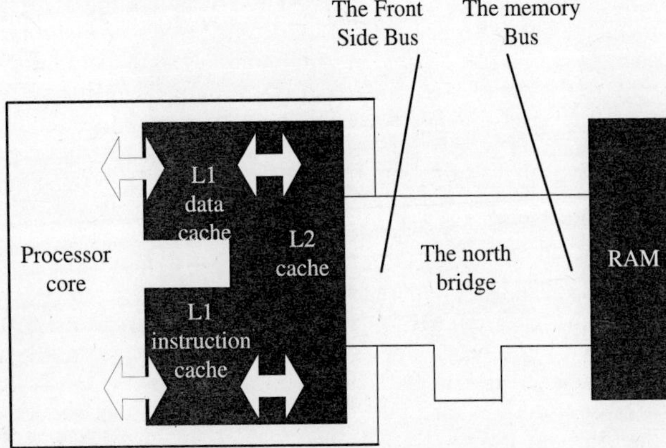

Figure 2.12 Levels of Cache and the North Bridge

2.10 SECONDARY MEMORY

You cannot store data in the main memory of a PC permanently. Firstly because it is very expensive and secondly its contents are erased when the computer is turned off. In order to preserve or save the work which you have done on your computer (permanently for future use) before you shut it off, you need storage media, such as compact disks (CDs) and hard disks, DVD (Digital Versatile/Video Disk), ZIP disk, Pen drive, Blue-Ray Disk, etc.

2.10.1 Floppy Disk

Also called a disk or diskette, a floppy disk is a removable storage disk used for storing data. It is called a floppy disk because the round film inside the disk's plastic shell is flexible (floppy). You can take a backup of any important information from the hard disk in a floppy. This will prevent loss of information in case the hard disk fails or is infected with virus. You can use a floppy disk to store and move data easily from one PC to another.

Floppies are available in $3\frac{1}{2}$" size with a capacity of 1.44 MB or 2.88 MB.

Protecting a floppy disk

A floppy disk has a write-protection notch or tab that is used to prevent accidental erasure of data. Floppy disks should never be exposed to heat, dust, moisture, water and strong magnetic fields. The exposed area (the film) of the disk should never be touched with the hand. Every floppy disk is enclosed in its own protective cover. The front of this cover is smooth, while the rear side has visible roughness. A label is pasted on the top front side of the disk to keep track of the disk. You should use a marker to write on the label so that each floppy can be identified.

How to write-protect a floppy disk?

Write-protection of a disk means that you should not be able to erase or write over the disk. This helps in preventing the loss of important data due to carelessness. You can still read a disk which is write-protected. To write-protect a $3\frac{1}{2}$ floppy, you need to locate the top corner hole with a sliding notch. Move the notch so that you can see through this hole. In this position of the notch, the floppy is write-protected and no one can erase the contents of the disk.

Care of Diskettes

The diskettes that you will be using to store text require special care in handling. So follow these rules carefully.

(a) Keep floppies in their protective covers when not is use.

(b) Avoid bending them.

(c) Insert them into disk drives carefully, with the pasted label side up.

(d) Do not touch the area of the diskette that is exposed through the window of the envelope.

(e) Do not expose floppies to sunlight, high temperature extremes or strong magnetic fields.

2.10.2 Hard Disk

A hard disk is a device used for mass storage of data. The data stored on a hard disk can be retrieved at a very fast speed, it being a direct address device. Unlike floppies, CDs, zip disks, etc., you cannot easily remove a hard disk from a PC.

Structure of a Hard Disk Drive

A hard disk drive is made up of a group of disks or disk platters, piled on top of one another in an airtight, dustproof case.

Each platter is a thin, circular metal plate coated on both sides with a magnetic material. Most of today's disk platters have a 3.5" diameter (See Figure 2.13). Bigger hard disks are used in Mainframe computers, and the smaller ones in PCs and microcomputers. A PC uses 80 GB or more capacity of hard disk. Seven or more of these disks are mounted on a central shaft which rotates at speeds of 2,400 or more revolutions per minute (rpm). These platters are placed half-an-inch apart from each other and each has an upper and lower surface. Further, each surface has a corresponding read/write head attached to a moveable arm. The arms between the two platters carry two read/write heads. Therefore, a 6-platter disk is referred to as a twelve-head disk.

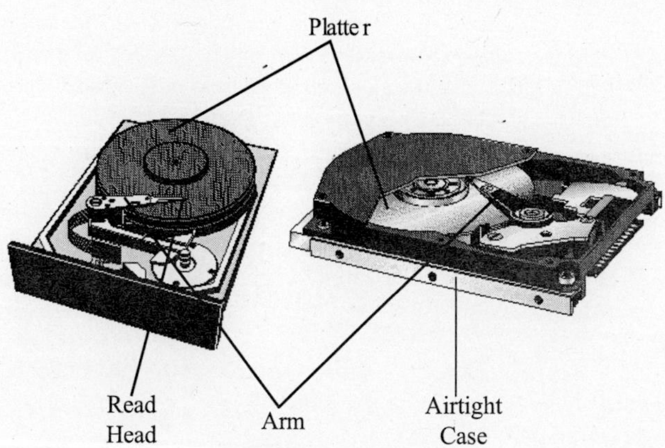

Figure 2.13 Hard disk

All the disks of a hard disk drive, therefore move simultaneously, as the central shaft rotates, in the same direction and at equal speed. In a disk pack, information is stored on both the surfaces of each disk plate, except the upper surface of the top plate and the lower surface of the bottom plate which are not used. Each disk also consists of a number of invisible concentric circles called *tracks*. Tracks are numbered from outside, starting with 0.

The group of tracks having the same track number on different platters form a *cylinder*. Thus a disk pack having 10 disk plates will have 18 recording surfaces and 18 tracks per cylinder.

Each track is further subdivided into sectors. Note that sectors vary in size. Sectors near the centre of the platter are smaller than the ones near the outer edge.

☞ *Although sectors vary in size, the amount of data stored in each of them is the same. This is because sectors towards the centre of the platter are denser than the sectors at the edge.*

The time taken to reach the particular track of a disk is known as the *latency time*. The time taken to read a record on the track is called the *seek time*. The total time, i.e., the sum of latency time and seek time is called the *access time* of a disk pack.

Storage Capacity

The more disk surfaces a particular disk pack has, the greater will be its storage capacity. But the storage capacity of a disk drive also depends on the tracks per inch of surface and the bits per inch of track. The total number of bytes that can be stored on a disk pack is:

Number of cylinders × Tracks per cylinder × Sectors per track × Bytes per sector.

The total number of bytes that can be stored is calculated as:

Bytes per sector × Sectors per cylinder × Number of cylinders × Number of heads.

For example, a hard disk drive having 14 heads, 723 cylinders and 51 sectors each sector can store 0.5 KB has a storage capacity of 258 MB.

$$14 \times 723 \times 51 \times 0.5 = 258{,}111.00 \text{ KB} = 258 \text{ MB}.$$

Example 1

A disk pack has a movable head for each of the 12 recording surfaces. Each surface has 400 tracks. Each track has 16 blocks and each block has 128 words of 32 bits. Calculate the total storage capacity of the disk pack.

Answer

No. of recording surfaces = 12
No. of tracks on each surface = 400
No. of blocks on each track = 16
No. of words in each block = 128
No. of bits in each word = 32

∴ Storage capacity in bits
= (No. of recording surfaces) × (No. of tracks on each surface) × (No. of blocks on each track) × (No. of words in each block) × (No. of bits in each word)

$$= 12 \times 400 \times 16 \times 128 \times 32 \text{ bits}$$
$$= \frac{12 \times 400 \times 16 \times 128 \times 32}{8} \text{ bytes}$$
$$= \mathbf{37.5 \times 2^{20}} \text{ bytes}$$

Accessing Data

Data is recorded on the tracks of a spinning disk surface and read from the surface by one or more read/write heads.

The moving-head-system has one read/write head for each disk surface, each mounted on an access arm which can be moved in and out. So, in this system, each read/write head moves horizontally across the surface of the disk and is able to access each track individually. Each usable surface of the disk pack has its own head and all the heads move together.

The disk pack on some disk storage devices is permanently fixed in position, while on others, it can be removed and replaced one in a matter of seconds. So the storage capacity of a removable disk pack system is virtually unlimited because the storage space can be increased without the heavy expense of buying another complete device.

As a hard disk is more stable, being rigid and contained in a dust-free environment, and its track and bit densities are much higher than those of floppy disks, it can store more information which can be accessed at rates faster than those for floppy disks. The access time is less than 20 ms.

2.10.3 Magnetic Tape

Magnetic tape is one of the most popular storage media for large volumes of data that are needed to be sequentially accessed and processed. The tape is a plastic ribbon usually 1/2 inch wide that is coated on one side with an iron-oxide material which can be magnetized. The tape ribbon itself is stored in reels of 50 to 2400 feet, in small cartridges or cassettes. It is similar to the tape used on a tape-recorder except that it is of higher quality and more durable. Like the recorder tape, the computer tape can also be erased and reused again and again.

Bits are recorded as magnetic spots on the tape. Seven or nine bits are recorded to form a character along with a parity bit. The tape consists of concentric circles called *Tracks*. Read/Write heads are mounted one in each track to write and read data (See Figure 2.14).

These tapes can be started, stopped, moved forward or backward or can be re-wound. But it cannot directly read any data, located in between other data.

Figure 2.14 shows how a data is recorded on a magnetic tape. A label is a small block of information used in tape processing that makes the beginning or end of a file or the beginning or end of the tape. It can contain other information, such as the number of records in the file or files on the tape. A label that is at the beginning of a tape is known as the *header label* and the one at the end of a tape is called the *trailer label*. The *leader* is a portion of the tape that is left blank for winding the tape on the other spool with the help of hand.

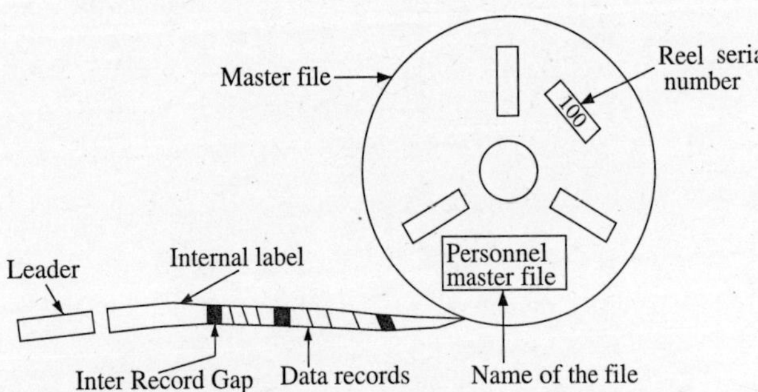

Figure 2.14 Data Recorded on a magnetic tape

Advantages of Magnetic Tapes

The advantages of magnetic tape are given below.

Economical A 0.5 inch wide reel of tape costs much less than other data storage devices. A typical 0.5 inch wide reel of magnetic tape is 2,400 feet long and is able to hold 800, 1600, or 6250 characters per inch of this length. Thus, if 6250 characters are held per inch and if the tape is 28,800 inches long (2400 feet times 12 inches), then the maximum capacity of the tape is 180 million characters.

Fast Input/Output As already discussed, data transfer rate for a magnetic tape can be in excess of 1 million bytes per second.

Long Term Storage Since the reel is compact and weighs less than one kilogram, it obviously occupies much less storage space and is much easier to handle. Large computer centres make use of extensive tape libraries, which contain thousands and thousands of reels of stored information and may occupy an entire room in an organization. The data stored on magnetic reels kept in cool environment and away from dust can be retained for years and retrieved as and when desired.

Reusable An additional cost benefit is that tapes can be erased and reused many times.

Disadvantages of Magnetic Tapes

Only Sequential Recording and Access Magnetic tape is a sequential access device and hence data recorded on tape cannot be addressed directly. Data can only be retrieved serially. So if a required data item is at the end of a tape, all the earlier parts have to be read before accessing this item. If random access is frequently required, then magnetic tape is not a suitable storage medium for such a requirement. Too much operator time would be required to load and unload tapes and too much machine time would be wasted in fetching the exact data that is needed.

Inconvenient for Storing Large Number of Small Records To isolate one record from another stored on a tape, an inter-record gap is provided between two adjacent records. Also, some portion of the tape at one end is left unrecorded for threading purposes. A tape is used for such a requirement.

Non-standarization of Drives makes Compatibility Difficult Variability of tape densities can be a problem since some drives cannot read tapes recorded at very high or very low densities.

2.10.4 Magnetic Disk

Magnetic disks are direct or random access storage devices, and are the primary storage medium used with computers for fast access to programs and data.

A magnetic disk storage is one in which data are stored as a series of magnetized spots on the flat surfaces of disks. A common spindle rotates the disk spinning at speeds of 60 or more revolutions per second. Disks are analogous to turntables. The flat sides of the disk platter are the recording surfaces, the tone arm is the access arm, and the stylus (needle) is the read/write head.

Tracks and Sectors

The disk surface comprises several tracks arranged in concentric circles. The greater the number of tracks, the more is the storage capacity of the disk. The smaller the spots, the more the bits per inch and hence greater the storage capacity. Most disks hold the same number of bits on each track, even though the outer tracks are physically longer than the inner ones. The circular tracks are further divided into segments, called sectors, which determine the least amount of data that can be read or written back to the disk. A sector can contain several records, or one record can span several sectors (See Figures 2.15 and 2.16).

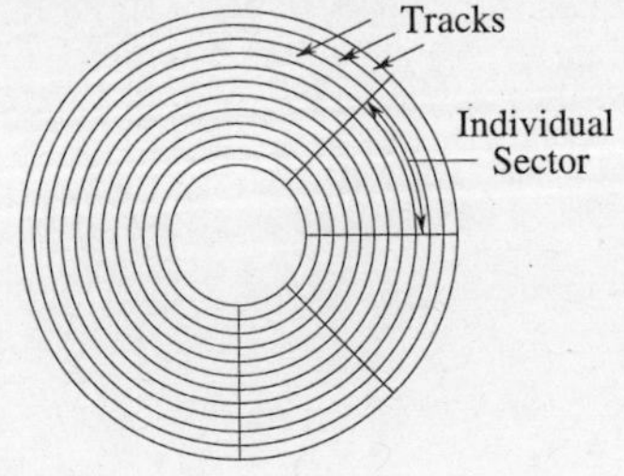

Figure 2.15 Sectors on a disk

☞ *Seek Time is the time taken to position the read/write head over the required track.*

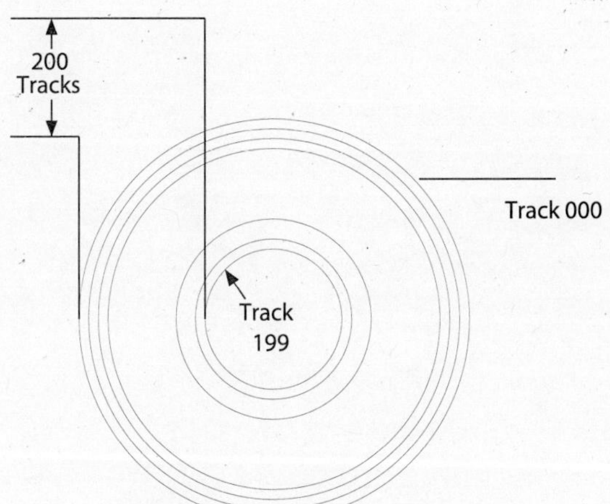

Figure 2.16 Tracks on a disk

Advantages of Magnetic Disks

- Magnetic disks follow direct access mode for reading and writing the data files, thereby making an ideal device for accessing frequently accessed data.
- Magnetic disks are used for both online and offline storage of data.
- Magnetic disks are easily moveable from one place to another because of their small size.
- The data transfer rate of disks is much higher than magnetic tapes.

Disadvantages of Magnetic Disks

- Magnetic disks must be stored in a dust-free environment in order to protect them from crashing.
- Magnetic disks are not ideal devices to use in scenarios where the file access required is of sequential nature rather than direct or random nature.
- Magnetic disks are more expensive than the magnetic tapes.

2.10.5 Compact Disks (CD)

A CD (Compact Disk) is a round disk with a hole in the center that stores data.

A CD is a very high capacity disk which can store about 600 million characters or roughly 300,000 pages of text (See Figure 2.17).

Figure 2.17 CD

The original CDs were read only media, i.e., they can be used only for reading purpose, no changes can be made on the stored data, but now many different technologies have come up to make CD-R (Compact Disk-Recordable) and CD-RW (CD-Rewritable) media and device, using which one can write the data as well as read data from these optical storage devices.

☞ *A CD is mainly used to store permanent information that does not require any change, such as encyclopedia, dictionary, etc.*

The CD is made out of a clear piece of polycarbonate plastic. The CD has different layers that enable the CD drive to read data from the CD. The layers that make up the CD depend on the type, and the number of times that you can write data on the CD.

The basic layers of the CD are:

- Polycarbonate plastic–layer of the disk.
- Aluminium–Reflects the laser beam from the CD-drive like a mirror that reflects light.
- A crylic–Protects the CD layers.
- Label–Enables you to name the CD for identification.

Compact Disk-Recordable (CD-R)

In CD-R (Compact Disk Recordable) text once written cannot be erased. The CD-R is useful to backup data. The CD-R is also used to create music CDs that can played on music systems.

Most common CD-Rs now-a-days store 700 MB information and 800 MB CD-Rs are also widely available. Maximum capacity of a CD-R nowadays is 860 MB. Actually, maximum capacity of a CD is not strictly defined, depending of production technology and the quality of the disk the maximum capacity could be pushed up to about 875 MB.

☞ *CD-R disks are useful for backing up data that must not be modified.*

CD-Rewritable (CD-RW)

The CD-RW disk enables you to rewrite data, to the disk. The data when not required can be erased from the disk.

☞ *The CD-RW disk are useful for transferring data from one system to another, or for storing files that are to be updated regularly.*

CD-ROM Drive

The CD-ROM drive can read data from the CD-ROM disk or the Audio CD. If one has a CD drive in his/her computer system, then that drive can be used to play music by putting normal Audio CDs in them and also one can watch movies by putting video CDs in the same CD drive.

The CD-ROM drives have a variety of controls on their front panel. The most common are listed as follows:

- Head phone jack – used to connect a set of head phones to the CD-ROM and listen to audio output.
- Value control button – used to control head set volume.
- Start/Stop button – used to start or stop CD playing.
- Eject button– used to manually eject a CD or CD tray.

CD-ROMs drive comes in a variety of types classified by the X factor for example 1 x (Single speed) 2 x (double speed), 3x (triple speed), 4x (quad speed), 6x, 8x, 10x, 12x, 16x, 32 x and higher. There are driver being advertised as 100 x. These drives use hard drive space to cache the CD contents and provide faster speeds (1.5 Mbps).

The mechanism of a CD-ROM drive has ben discussed. It has one motor for rotating the disk and another for moving the laser head, which is guided by slides. A third motor drives the disk insertion and ejection mechanism. The disk can be placed in a protective case called caddy. A button on the front of the disk drive activates the motorized ejection of the disk.

A head phone jack and a volume control knob can also be found on the front of most units. Special software enables almost all CD-ROM drives to play audio disks.

CD-R Drive

The CD-R drive can read data from the CD-ROM, Audio CD, and the CD-R disk. The CD-R drive can also write data to the CD-R disk. This drive is useful for backing up data that must not be modified on a CD-R disk.

The CD-R drive can write to the CD-R disk in a single session or using multiple sessions. In the single session, the data is written to the CD-R disk and the connection is closed such that the CD-R is finalized and no data can be further added to the CD-R disk. Using multiple sessions you can continue adding data to the CD-R disk until the disk is full.

CD-RW Drive

The CD-RW drive enables you to read, write and also rewrite data to the CD-RW disk. This is useful for transferring data from one system to another, especially data files that are large in size such as video movies files.

Characteristics of CD-ROMs

Large Capacity Compared to magnetic tape, CD-ROM provides random access data retrieval and data indexing and the disks have a shelf life of more than 40 years. But it is more expensive than tape. CD-ROM is limited to 680 MB of data, making it impractical for large volume applications and, to-date, recordable disks are not erasable and reusable.

Not Reusable They are written once and can be read again and again. Thus they cannot be reused for storing new data.

High Cost Since the technology is still new, therefore the cost of these storage devices is still high compared to magnetic tapes.

2.10.6 Combo Drive/DVD Drive

A Combo drive is a type of optical drive that combines CD-R/CD-RW recording capability with the ability to read DVD media. The device was created as a mid-range option between a CD burner and a DVD burner. Combo drives are becoming less and less common on new systems, though they do occasionally appear in lieu of CD-only drives on low-end computers to lower production and sale costs (See Figure 2.18).

Figure 2.18 DVD Drive

2.10.7 WORM disks

WORM stands for Write Once Read Many. WORM disks allow users to create their own CDs by using a CD-R (CD-Recordable) drive. WORM disks are CDs that are purchased blank and written onto using the CD-R drive. The information recorded on a WORM disk can be read by any ordinary CD-ROM drive. But data can be written only once. Data once written cannot be overwritten. Because of their large capacity and non-alterable property, WORM disks are the preferred choice for archival storage.

2.10.8 DVD

DVD stands for Digital Versatile/Video Disk, is the next generation of optical disk storage technology. It is a faster CD that can hold cinema like video, better than CD audio.

There are various variations of DVD. DVD-ROM or DVD-R are physical formats and DVD-video or DVD-audio are application formats. DVD-ROM is the base format that holds data.

DVDs are of same diameter and thickness as CDs, and they are made using some of the same materials and manufacturing methods. Like a CD, the data on a DVD is encoded in the form of small bits and bumps in the track of the disk.

There are five recordable versions of DVD-ROM. DVD-R for general, DVD-R for authoring, DVD-RAM, DVD-RW and DVD+RW. All recordable drives can read DVD Rom disks, but each uses a different type of disk for recording. DVD-R can record data once (sequentially only), while DVD-RAM, DVD-RW and DVD+RW can be rewritten thousands of times. Various capacities of DVD are given below:

(a) The most common type of DVD is DVD-5 (1 side, 1 layer) having 4.7GB of storage. Double-sided DVDs are rarely used.
(b) DVD-9 8.54GB Single sided, Dual layer.
(c) DVD-10 9.40GB Double sided, Single layer.
(d) DVD-14 13.24GB Double sided, One side single layer, one side dual layer.
(e) DVD-18 17.08GB Double sided, Dual layer.

2.10.9 USB Drive

USB flash drives, or pen drives, are NAND-type flash memory data storage devices integrated with a USB (Universal Serial Bus) interface. They are typically small, light-weight, removable and rewritable. It is a flash memory card that plugs into the computer's USB port. It emulates a small disk drive and allows data to be easily transferred from one machine to another. A USB drive is also known as a flash drive, pen drive, keychain drive, key drive, USB key and memory key (See Figure 2.19).

Figure 2.19 Pen drive

Advantages of USB Drive

Pen drives offer potential advantages over other portable storage devices, such as floppy disks. The advantages are as follows:

(a) It is more compact, faster, holds more data, and is more reliable

(b) It uses the USB mass storage standard, supported natively by modern operating systems, such as Windows, Linux and UNIX.

To access the data stored in a pen drive, the drive must be connected to a computer through a USB host controller. Pen drives are active only when plugged into a USB connection and draw all necessary power from the supply provided by that connection.

2.10.10 Blu-Ray Disk

A Blu-ray disk is a high density optical disk storage medium, which is used for the storage of all high-definition digital formats like audio, video, and play-station games and so on. They have the same physical appearance as a DVD. The name Blu-ray is actually a combination of the colour blue and ray. Here blue refers to the blue colour of the laser that is used for its reading and ray refers to the optical ray (See Figure 2.20).

Figure 2.20 Blu-ray disk

Blu-ray was developed by the Blu-ray disk Association with more than 180 members. The data capacity of blu-ray disk is very large because Blu-ray uses a blue laser (405 nanometers) instead of a red laser (650 nanometers). This allows the data tracks on the disk to be very compact. This allows for more than twice as small pits as on a DVD (See Figure 2.21). Because of the greatly compact data Blu-ray can hold almost 5 times more data than a single layer DVD i.e. 25 GB. Just like a DVD Blu-ray can also be recorded in Dual-Layer format. This allows the disk to hold up to 50 GB.

Types of Blu-Ray Disk

Similar to a DVD, BD also has different versions according to its application. The common types are:

(a) **Blu-Ray Disk Read Only Memory (BD-ROM):** This type of BD can only be read but cannot be written over. The content will be pre-recorded.

(b) **Blu-Ray Disk Recordable (BD-R):** This BD is mainly used for storage of PC data.

(c) **Blu-Ray Disk Re-writable (BD-RW):** This BD is mainly used for storage of PC data. The contents in this disk can be written over and over.

(d) **Blu-Ray Disk Re-writable (BD-RE):** This BD is mainly used for recording of data to be used in HDTV. This disk can also be written over again and again.

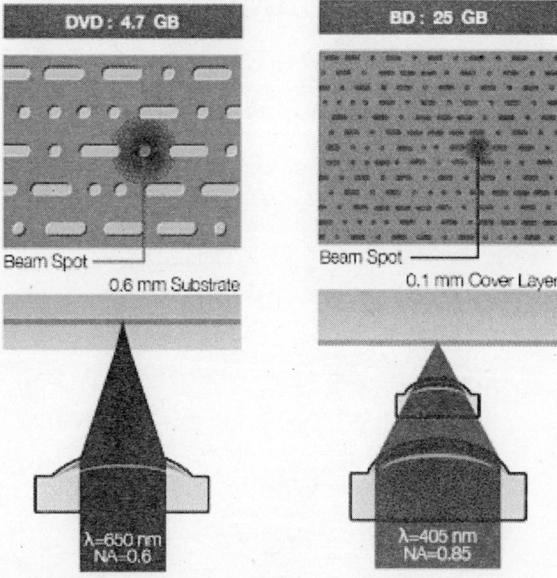

Figure 2.21 Comparison of DVD and Blu-ray Disk (BD)

Advantages of Blu-Ray Disk

Advantages of Blu-Ray disk are as under:

(a) The *sleek design* of blu-ray helps in skipping from any part of the disk to the other.

(b) *Multiple programs* like using the same disk for watching a video as well as recording can be done at the same time.

(c) Watch *HD in its maximum quality* with very little loss.

(d) You can *make your own playlists.*

(e) The programs present on the disk can be *re-ordered in any way* you like.

2.11 INPUT DEVICES

Data and instructions are entered into a computer through input devices. An input device converts input data and instructions into a suitable binary form which is stored in the memory of a computer.

The most commonly used input device is the keyboard. A number of other input devices, also known as pointing devices, have also been developed which do not require data entry by typing. Examples include mouse, light pen, graphic tablet, joy stick, track ball, touch screen, etc. Each of these devices permit the user to select something on the monitor screen by pointing to it. Therefore, these devices are also called pointing devices. Voice input systems have also been developed. A microphone similar to the one used with a public address system is used for voice input.

2.11.1 Keyboard

Programs and data are entered into a computer through a keyboard which is attached to a computer. A keyboard is similar to the keyboard of a typewriter. It contains letters, digits, special characters, function keys and some control keys. When a key is pressed, an electronic signal is produced, which is detected by an electronic circuit called *keyboard encoder* (See Figure 2.22).

A computer includes all the keys found on a typewriter plus some additional keys. These additional keys are cursor control (i.e., moving the cursor around on the screen), insert, delete, and scroll control keys. There are a total of 101 keys (some have more). At the right side of the keyboard is the numeric keypad with numbers and basic mathematical symbols.

The numeric keypad can also be used for cursor control. This double function of numeric keypad is controlled by the Num Lock key.

☞ *At the top of the keyboard are function keys (F1 to F12). Their functions depend upon the program being run.*

The keyboard contains a small built-in processor. When you press a key, this processor detects it and sends a number (binary number) corresponding to that key (*scan code*) to the *keyboard controller*, located on the motherboard. This code is transmitted to the processor (CPU). The CPU then processes it using a program called *keyboard driver*. The *keyboard driver* translates the codes into their corresponding characters.

Different Types of Keyboards

The different types of keyboards are available in market, depending on the layout of the keyboard are, QWERTY and AZERTY. The QWERTY keyboards are most commonly used now-a-days The types of keyboards vary according to their connection with the CPU, the application, the layout of the keys and some special function keyboards.

Wireless Keyboards

The wireless keyboards use three basic types of connections. These are:

(a) Bluetooth Keyboards

(b) Infrared (IR) Keyboards

(c) Radio Frequency Keyboards

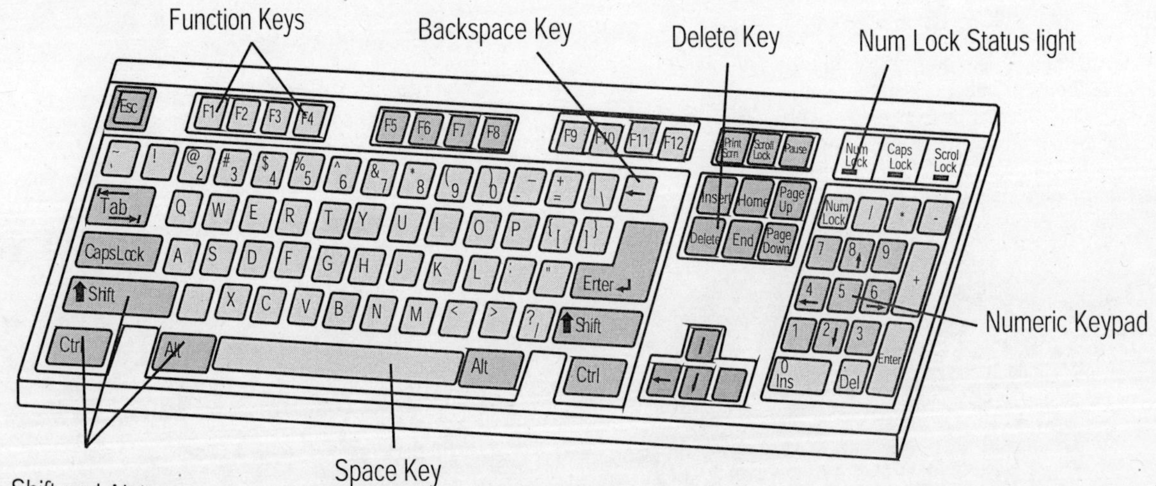

Figure 2.22 Keyboard depicting different keys' functions

The bluetooth keyboards use a bluetooth technology, which provides a greater range than the radio frequency keyboard and infrared keyboards.

The radio frequency keyboards get the required power from batteries or has a USB cable to charge the keyboard. The infrared keyboard are to be kept in the line of sight of the receiver. On the other hand, the radio frequency keyboards provide a greater range than the infrared keyboards. The radio frequency keyboards offer a greater mobility than the bluetooth and the infrared keyboards (See Figure 2.23).

Figure 2.23 Wireless keyboard

Wired Keyboards

There are two wired connections that connect the keyboards to your desktop computers. These are:

(a) PS/2
(b) USB

The *PS/2 keyboards* are very commonly used and they are called so because they use the PS/2 connection. They are one of the cheapest keyboards that are available in the market. The *USB keyboards* use a USB (Universal Serial Bus) to connect to the CPU.

☞ *The PS/2 and USB keyboards are usually plug and play. Other types of keyboards are a bit expensive and require expensive software applications to be installed.*

2.11.2 Mouse

A mouse is a pointing device, which is held in one hand and moved across a flat surface. Figure 2.24 shows a type of mouse or puck.

The mouse can also be used to draw sketches, diagrams, etc., on the monitor screen. It is also moved on the graphic tablet for drawing work. The mouse is also used to edit text. For editing a text on the screen, the cursor can be quickly placed close to the desired point of the screen by moving the mouse.

One type of mouse uses a rolling ball; others use optical sensing techniques. They are linked to the PC with a cable or by using infrared light. A typical mouse has two or three buttons.

What the mouse buttons do depend on the application program running in your PC. In some systems, it is also possible to specify independent functions to the buttons.

☞ *Signals from the mouse are processed by a program called mouse driver.*

Figure 2.24 Mouse

A mouse can be connected to computer system in one of the following ways:

(a) Using a serial port
(b) A bus connection
(c) PS/2 mouse port
(d) USB port
(e) Wireless

Let us read these different types of mouse connections in detail.

Serial Mouse

A serial port is the most common method of connecting a mouse. A serial mouse is connected to either (Communications) COM1 or COM2 port, i.e., to any one of the available serial port on the computer. Connecting a serial mouse is very easy as one needs to just plug in the connector attached to the mouse wire to the vacant serial port on the PC.

Sometimes, one needs to configure the mouse driver to specify the COM port used for the mouse, but most of the new mouse driver software can automatically sense the port to which the mouse is connected and auto-configure themselves.

Bus Mouse

Difference between a bus mouse and a serial mouse is this. A serial mouse is connected to a serial port, whereas the bus mouse is connected to a special board made just for the mouse.

This special mouse adapter board is installed into the PC's expansion slot and then the mouse is connected to the connector provided at the back.

PS/2 Port Mouse

Now-a-days, many computers come equipped with special mouse port for connecting the mouse. This method is similar to the bus mouse approach except that the mouse control circuitry is directly built into the motherboard of the PC and not connected to a separate card.

☞ *This type of mouse is called PS/2 mouse because these connectors are common with IBM's (International Business Machines) PS/2 range of computers.*

USB Mouse

The USB port can be used to connect a mouse. As the mouse is not required during power on/bootup process, no special BIOS (Basic Input/Output System) is required for handling USB mouse.

Hardware installation of the USB mouse requires just plugging in the mouse to the USB port. Operating system, such as Windows XP will automatically install it in the PC.

Wireless Mouse

In this type of mouse, everything is similar to the conventional mouse except that no cable is used to connect the mouse to the computer system. (See Figure 2.25)

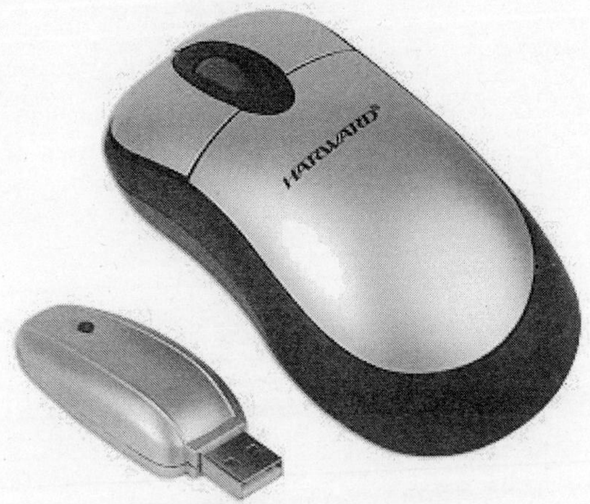

Figure 2.25 Wireless mouse

Basically there are two types of wireless mouse:

(a) Infrared Wireless Mouse

(b) Radio-controlled Wireless Mouse

Infrared Wireless Mouse Infrared mouse communicates with the receiving unit connected to the main system unit using infrared light. As the infrared light can not pass through objects, this requires that an infrared mouse to be in direct line of sight with the receiving unit connected to the main system.

Radio-controlled Wireless Mouse When the radio-controlled wireless mouse is moved, radio signals are transmitted by it to a special receiver unit connected to the main system. The radio signal received by the receiver is sent to the computer as any normal mouse signal received through the cable is sent.

Most of the Infrared wireless mouse and radio-controlled Wireless mouse require the mouse to be within six feet of the receiving unit.

As the radio signal can pass through objects, the radio-controlled mouse need not be in the line of sight with the receiving unit.

In case, more than one wireless mouse is being used at one place, they cause different radio frequencies, so one need not worry about signal from one mouse getting disturbed by the signal from another mouse.

☞ *Before connecting the mouse, it is safe to turn the computer off and unplug it. If your mouse is a USB device, your computer may be kept on.*

2.11.3 Joystick

A joystick is also a pointing device. It is used to move the cursor position on a monitor screen. Its function is similar to that of a mouse and is used for playing games.

A joystick contains a spherical ball at its lower end as well as at its upper end (See Figure 2.26). The lower spherical ball moves in a socket. The joystick can be moved right or left, forward or backward. The electronic circuitry inside the joystick detects and measures the displacement of the joystick from its central position. This information is sent to the processor.

Figure 2.26 Joystick

2.11.4 Graphics Tablet

A *graphics tablet* is a graphic input device that functions like a drawing tablet. It can be used for sketching new images or tracing old ones, selecting from menus or simply for moving the cursor on the screen, all of which can be provided within a single program. The user makes contact with the graphic tablet with a device called a cursor, which is a pen-like instrument that is connected to the tablet by a wire or without wires (See Figure 2.27). For sketching, the user draws with the tablet cursor and the screen cursor "draws" a corresponding image. For tracing an existing image, the screen cursor is often not required. The tablet picks up the drawing as a series of X-Y coordinates, either as a continuous stream of coordinates, or as end points.

Figure 2.27 Graphics Tablets

Menu selection is accomplished by a tablet overlay or by a screen display. The tablet cursor selects an item by making contact with it on the overlay, or by controlling the screen cursor.

2.11.5 Microphones

A microphone, which was originally invented by Emile Berliner in 1877, is a device which allows you to record voices or sounds and place them onto computers, generally as a wav file. Microphones can also be used with other applications, such as a voice dictation program or a voice conference program (See Figure 2.28).

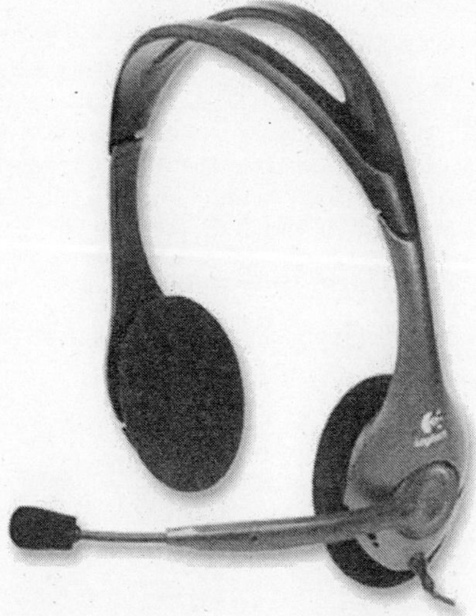

Figure 2.28 Microphone with earphone

When connecting the microphone to the back of the computer, the microphone will be placed in the hole which generally has Mic or Microphone written next to it.

Generally, microphones are a separate computer component. Some manufacturers are integrating microphones into computers. Integrated microphones can also be found on laptops and some desktop monitors. Integrated microphones are usually a small hole in front of the computer which when spoken into will record your voice.

2.11.6 Touch Screen

A *touch screen* is a computer display screen that is sensitive to human touch, allowing a user to interact with the computer by touching pictures or words on the screen. Touch screens are used with information kiosks, computer-based training devices and systems designed to help individuals who have difficulty n manipulating a mouse or keyboard. Touch screen technology can be used as an alternative user interface with applications that normally require a mouse, such as a Web browser. Some applications are designed specifically for touch screen technology, often having larger icons and links than the typical PC application. Monitors are available with built-in touch screen technology or individuals can purchase a touch screen kit.

Advantages and Disadvantages of Touch Screens

Some of the advantages and disadvantages are:

- **Proximity to the Screen:** If you are using a touch screen monitor you have to be close to the screen in order to touch it. This can be frustrating if you have a big desk and you keep your monitor in a place where you have to reach for it. If you are not using a touch screen monitor, you can be as far away from the screen as your keyboard or mouse will allow you.
- **Accuracy:** Unless you are using a stylus pen, a touch screen monitor may not be all that accurate, depending on the size of the icon as it relates to your finger. Small objects on the screen may be hard to touch if you are using your finger, whereas it is easy to click with a mouse or keyboard.
- **Speed:** It is much faster to click something using your finger or a stylus pen than it is to move a mouse or keyboard arrows. Speed can make a huge difference while playing a fast-paced game.
- **Desk Space:** You will have more desk space when you own a touch screen monitor since you are not required to hook up a standard keyboard and mouse. Also, you can put food on the desk without worrying about it spilling something on the keyboard or mouse. If the computer is for your business, you do not have to worry about needing to replace the keyboard or mouse due to careless customers or employees.
- **Cleanliness:** Another disadvantage of touch screen monitors is that the displays get dirty frequently because of constant touching with oily or sweaty fingers. Fortunately, touch screen monitors are made out of glass or something similar, so it is easier to clean than a regular monitor.
- **Simplicity:** Another disadvantage of touch screen monitors is that the displays get dirty frequently because of constant touching with oily or sweaty fingers. Fortunately, touch screen monitors are made out of glass or something similar, so it is easier to clean than a regular monitor.

2.11.7 Scanner

A scanner is a hardware device which is used to scan text or images into the computer. Sometimes the information, picture or text that is available on paper is needed on the computer. The basic function of a scanner is to convert a document into digital format. Scanners are basically desktop analog-to-digital converter. They take analog visual things, documents, magazine papers, photos, business cards, etc., and turn them into digitized bitmaps that a specialized software package can understand and translate into PC readable file.

Types of Scanners

Different types of scanners are used for different applications. The capability and cost of scanners differ from type to type. Scanners required for industrial purpose are different from the ones meant for home use or in small offices. Scanners are of three types. They are:

(a) Flatbed scanner
(b) Sheetfed scanner
(c) Handheld scanner

Let us discuss each of them in brief.

Flatbed Scanner

A Flatbed scanner is also known as desktop scanner and it works just like a photocopier. It allows the user to place a full piece of paper, book, magazine, photo or any other object onto the glass surface of the scanner. It then scans that object and convert it into digital form (See Figure 2.29).

Figure 2.29 Flatbed Scanner

Sheetfed Scanner

A Sheetfed scanner, also known as rollerfed scanner, works like a fax machine. The image is passed over a roller where it is captured. These scanners are very versatile in scanning loose sheets of paper (See Figure 2.30).

☞ *Sheetfed scanner is less expensive when compared to the flatbed scanner. The latter can scan and store images from books without having to remove the page, which is not possible in the case of the rollerfed scanner.*

Figure 2.30 Sheetfed Scanner

Handheld Scanner

A handheld, or portable, scanner is an optical scanner which is designed to be moved by hand across the object or document being scanned. Today, a hand scanner is extensively used with a PC or a word processor as an image input device. It is used for optically reading image or data from a document. This kind of scanner is operated by hand (See Figure 2.31).

Figure 2.31 Handheld scanner

☞ *Handheld scanners are used for a number of applications, such as for barcode readers at points-of-sale of products or services, for recording data from documents for later reproduction or processing, and for translating documents.*

Handheld scanners can be classified into:
(a) General purpose
(b) Special purpose

Most handheld scanners are directed to general purpose uses, so that they can read and store information designed for various applications. The other category of handheld scanners is directed to the scanning of very specific types of images to provide a particular form of information. The best known type of scanner in this category is a bar code scanner, which is used to obtain the identification of a product with a bar code.

Advantages of Handheld Scanner

They are inexpensive and are portable.

Disadvantages of Handheld Scanner

It can be tedious to drag the handheld scanners correctly. While scanning, it will be difficult to have a straight scan. If it is moved too slow/fast, it can cause distortion in the image being scanned.

2.11.8 Trackball

A trackball is also a pointing device and contains a ball which can rotate in any direction. The user spins the ball in different directions to move the cursor on the monitor (See Figure 2.32). The associated electronic circuitry detects the direction and speed of the spin and sends this information to the processor. This type of pointing device is normally used in a laptop computer.

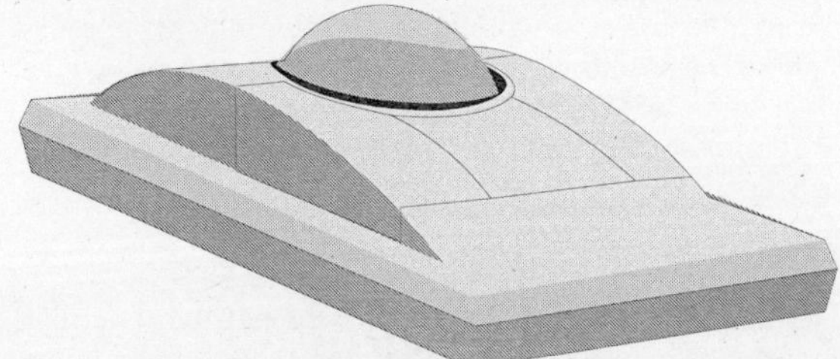

Figure 2.32 Trackball

2.11.9 Light Pen

A light pen is a pointing device, which is used to select a displayed menu option on the monitor. It is a photosensitive pen-like device capable of sensing a position on the monitor screen when its tip touches the screen. When its tip is moved over the screen surface, its photocell sensing element detects the light coming from the screen and the corresponding signals are sent to the processor. The menu is a set of programmed choices offered to the user. The user indicates his/her choice by touching the light pen against a desired description of the menu (See Figure 2.33).

The signals sent by the light pen to the processor identify the menu option. A light pen is also used in handheld pad type small devices for writing small messages and sending them over e-mail.

Figure 2.33 Light pen

2.11.10 Optical Mark Reader (OMR)

Optical Mark Readers (OMRs) are special scanners used for recognizing a pre-specified type of mark made by pencil or pen. For example, in the objective test paper of DOEACC (Department of Electronics Accreditation for Computer Courses), you mark your answers on a special sheet by darkening a small square, using a pen or pencil. These answer sheets are fed into the computer using the optical mark reader. The computer can then evaluate the answer sheets. The use of OMR is not limited to the grading of objective type tests. In fact, any input data that is in the nature of a choice or selection can be recorded for OMR input.

OMR focuses light on the page being examined and the light pattern reflected from the dark marks is then detected. Figure 2.34 shows the OMR characters.

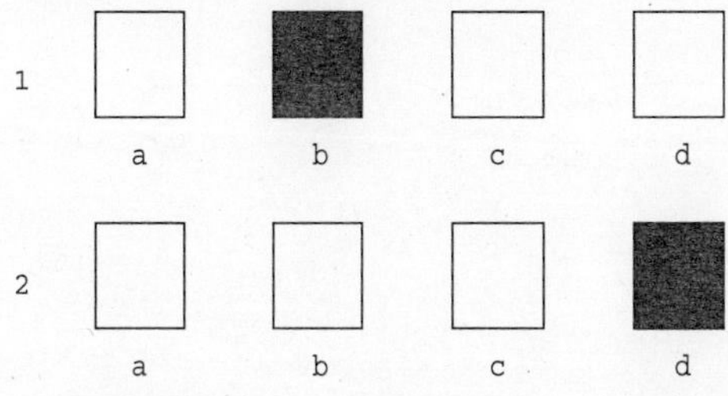

Figure 2.34 Optical marks in an answer sheet

2.11.11 Bar code Reader

Bar code readers are special devices used to read bar coded data. Bar code is a specialized code used for fast identification of items. It consists of a series of small lines, known as bars. The actual coding of the bars is the width of the bar, not the height. These are primarily used for identification of goods, such as books, postal packages, badges, etc. (See Figure 2.35).

2.11.12 Magnetic Ink Character Recognition (MICR)

MICR (Magnetic Ink Character Recognition) detects the special encoded characters on bank cheques and deposit slips. After detecting the encoded characters, the MICR converts them into digital data for the computer. Figure 2.36 shows a bank cheque which will be processed using a MICR device.

Figure 2.35 Bar codes

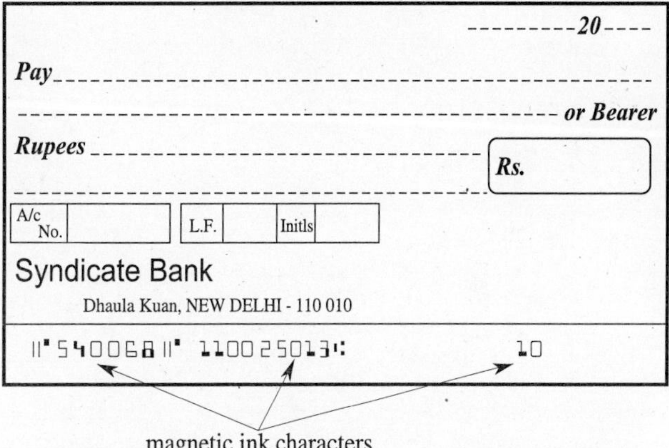

Figure 2.36 A bank cheque that is processed using MICR

Advantages and Limitations of the MICR System

(a) Even roughly handled, folded, smeared and over-stamped cheques can be read with a high degree of accuracy.

(b) MICR devices speed up data input for the banking industry because cheques can be directly fed into the input device.

(c) The characters coded on the cheques using magnetic ink can also be easily read by people.

(d) The main limitation of MICR is that only the 10 digits and 4 special characters needed for bank processing are used. No alphabetic characters are available.

(e) Special type of magnetic ink is required for encoding the characters to be read by the machine.

2.11.13 Optical Character Reader (OCR)

This device is capable of detecting alphabetic and numeric characters on a computer print-out containing complete pages of typed or hand-written text. The characters are examined by passing them under a strong light and a lens system. The inked areas are differentiated from those which are not inked. Once the whole characters are scanned, they are compared with the characters that the machine has been programmed to recognize. If the pattern of both characters matches, the scanned character is accepted for further operations (See Figure 2.37).

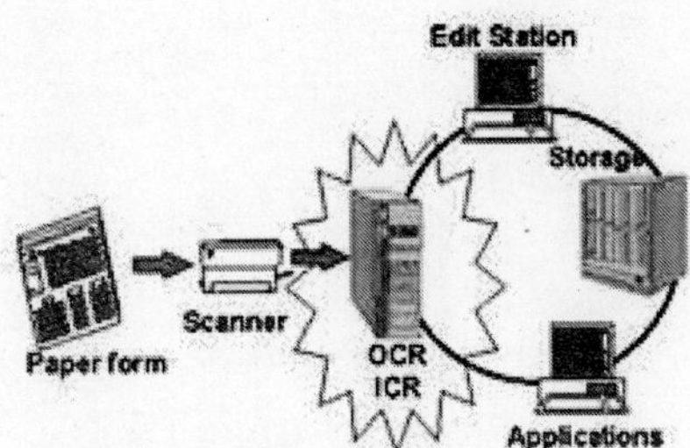

Figure 2.37 An OCR System

Advantages

- It makes data entry simple and faster using scanners.
- It also reduces workload for people who have to feed large amounts of data into computers on a regular basis.

2.11.14 Card Reader

A card reader is a device that reads punched cards. A punched card is a storage medium made of thick paper card that holds data in the form of punched holes. The holes are punched into the card by a key punch machine or card punch peripheral device connected to a computer.

The punched card code is detected by patterns of light passing through the holes in the cards.

Another card reader, called magnetic card reader, is used for reading the magnetic strip on the back of credit cards and transferring data sent through the card (See Figure 2.38).

Figure 2.38 Card Reader

2.11.15 Video Cameras

A video camera takes continuous pictures and generates a digital or analog signal for display on a monitor or for permanent recording. Signals generated by video cameras are traditionally analog, but now-a-days digital video cameras are available. The latter converts analog signals into digital form .

A video camera captures images by breaking down the images into a series of lines. Each line is scanned one at a time and the continuously varying intensities of red, green and blue light across the line are filtered out to convert into a continuously variable (analog) signal. These are then used for sending a picture over a network through computers (See Figure 2.39).

Figure 2.39 Video camera

2.11.16 Web Cameras

A Web camera allows a computer to accept input just by focussing on an object. The camera is focussed on the input object to take a picture of the object. A picture so taken can be transferred over the computer network to a distant place.

The image of the object can be seen on the monitor of the distant computer connected through a network or through the Internet. Voice can also be transmitted over the network. Thus, two or more persons can talk and see each another in this way. This method is used in video conferencing (See Figure 2.40).

Figure 2.40 Web camera

2.11.17 Biometric Sensor

Biometric is the science and technology that usually refers to methodology for measuring and analyzing human body characteristics that is unique to an individual. *Biometric Sensor* is the device that is used to identifies fingerprints, DNA (DeoxyriboNucleic Acid) identification, eye retinas and voice patterns, facial patterns, hand measurements, face shape and signature verification (See Figure 2.41). They are used for security purposes to identify the persons who are permitted to enter the organization.

Figure 2.41 Biometric Sensor

2.11.18 Fingerprint Scanner

A fingerprint scanner can also take the form of one of four different sensors. An optical sensor uses digital imaging to capture the visual image of the fingerprint. A passive capacitance sensor uses pixels to form the image.

When referring to computers and security, a fingerprint refers to any trace of information left by someone. If someone has gained unauthorized access to a computer or network, an administrator or security agent may look for any fingerprints left by the attacker, such as IP (Internet Protocol) addresses, host names, etc. This can be compared to a crime scene detective looking for fingerprints at a crime scene.

When referring to computer hardware, a fingerprint scanner or fingerprint reader is a hardware device that verifies a user or enters password information by scanning their finger. Computers that do not already include a fingerprint scanner can connect devices such as USB ports (See Figure 2.42).

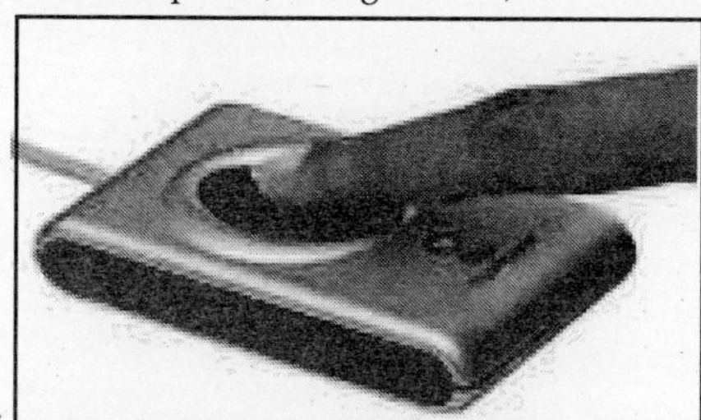

Figure 2.42 Fingerprint scanner

2.12 OUTPUT DEVICES

Output devices supply information or results either in the form of hardcopy (printer) or softcopy (monitor). Some common output devices include:

(a) Monitor
(b Printers
(c) Plotters
(d) Multimedia projector
(e) Speech synthesizer

2.12.1 Monitor

Monitors come in two types:

(a) CRT (Cathode Ray Tube)
(b) TFT-LCD (Thin Film Transistor Liquid Crystal Display)

CRT Monitor

A VDU (Visual Display Unit) or CRT monitor is similar to a television and its size is measured in diagonal length of the screen. Monitors are available in 12", 14", 15", 17", 19" and even in 21" size. It shows text or picture in colour or black and white, depending on the type. Colour monitors are costlier than black and white monitors. Whatever you type on the keyboard, you can see it on the monitor. Figure 2.43 shows a typical CRT monitor.

Figure 2.43 CRT monitor

TFT-LCD Screen/Monitor

Liquid Crystal Display (LCD) monitor is the flat panel type of monitor found on notebook PCs. TFT-LCD is a variant of liquid crystal display which uses thin film transistor technology to improve image quality. TFT-LCD is a type of active matrix LCD. It is used in televisions, flat panel displays, projectors, etc. Figure 2.44 shows a TFT-LCD monitor.

TFT-LCD has a sandwich-like structure with liquid crystal filled between two glass plates. TFT glass has as many TFTs as the number of pixels displayed, while a Colour Filter Glass (CFG) has colour filter which generates colour. Liquid crystals move according to the difference in voltage between the Colour Filter Glass and the TFT Glass. The amount of light supplied by Back light is determined by the amount of movement of the liquid crystals in such a way as to generate colour.

LED and LCD monitors are based on the same basic technology for image displaying, but differ in the kind of backlighting used. While LCD monitors use CCFL (Cold Cathode Fluorescent Lamps) for backlighting, the latter use light emitting diodes. This is the prime difference between the two display technologies.

Figure 2.44 TFT-LCD monitor

Since LED's are built on LCD technology, they have taken this process (manipulating light as it traverses polarized liquid crystals) and have enhanced it, making a higher quality backlight that distinctly affects the quality of the monitor's display.

This means that LED monitors offer more intense lighting and finer colour resolution, meaning that the colours of an LED monitor come closer to the colours one will find in nature. It has a sharper contrast which makes it an excellent choice for those who enjoy quality colour and picture.

Another major difference between LCD monitors and LED monitors is energy consumption. LEDs are unarguably better on power consumption. On average they use 40% less power than their LCD counterparts, a percentage that really starts adding up, especially for computers that are used regularly in a home or office setting.

Differentiate between LCD and CRT

Both LCD and CRT monitors are frequently used types of displays in computers. The difference between these two monitors are:

(a) **Size:** LCD is lightweight and compact, which saves desktop space as compared to a CRT.
(b) **Resolution:** LCD is designed to work in a single resolution while CRT is designed for many resolutions.
(c) **Pixel Density:** Pixel density of LCD is generally not as tight as the dot pitch in CRT but for most applications, the density is suitable.
(d) **Brightness:** The illuminated phosphor of a CRT is not nearly as bright as what the LCD can produce with its florescent backlight.
(e) **Power Consumption:** LCD consumes significantly less power than CRT and has a low emission risk. Typically, a LCD consumes approximately half the power of a CRT.
(f) **Flicker:** With CRT monitors, the aim is to get a faster refresh rate of at least 85 Hz, but LCD monitors are designed to run at a much lower refresh rate and flicker is never as issue.
(g) **Pixel Response Time:** The time taken by a pixel to change its state is called pixel response time. CRT has extremely fast pixel time but LCD can be quite slow. The fastest LCD monitors today have a reaction time of 25 milliseconds which is still only about half the speed of a CRT monitor.
(h) **Viewing Angle:** CRT can be viewed at almost any angle but LCD is best viewed "head on", Even when viewing an LCD head on, narrow viewing angles can appear to have inconsistent colour and brightness.
(i) **Cost:** Prices of LCD screens are quite high. They are much costlier than CRT.

2.12.2 Printers

Printers are the most popular output devices. They provide information in a permanent readable form. They produce printed outputs of results, programs and data. A character printer prints one character of the text at a time. They are low-speed printers, with their speed ranging from 300–600 characters per second. Character printers can be classified as:

(a) Impact printers
(b) Non-impact character printers

Impact printers use an electro-mechanical mechanism that causes hammers or pins to strike against a ribbon and paper to print the text. Two types of impact character printers are available: dot-matrix printers and letter quality printers.

Non-impact printers do not use any electro-mechanical printing head to strike against ribbon and paper. They use thermal, chemical, electrostatic, laser beam or inkjet technology for printing the text. Usually a non-impact type printer is faster than an impact type. The disadvantage of non-impact type printers is that they produce only a single copy of the text whereas impact printers can produce multiple copies of the text.

Dot-Matrix Impact-Type Character Printers

A character is printed with the selected number of dots from a matrix of dots. Figure 2.45 shows a dot-matrix printer. The print head contains a vertical array of 7, 9, 14, 18 or even 24 pins. A character is printed in a number of steps. One dot-column of the dot-matrix is taken up at a time. The selected dots of a column (i.e., the column of dot-matrix) are printed by the print head at a time as it moves across a line.

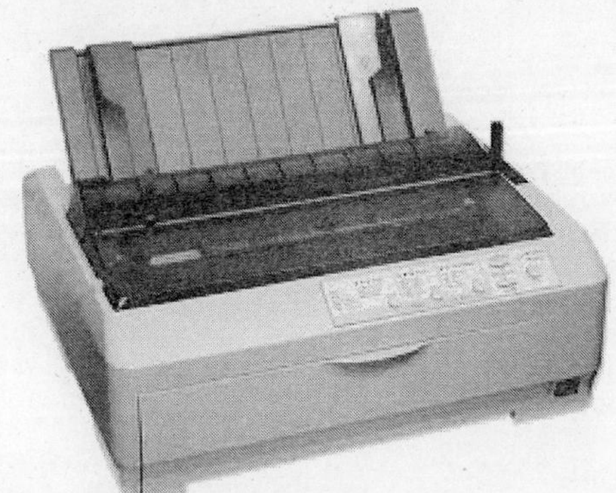

Figure 2.45 Dot-matrix printer

Dot-matrix printers are very flexible. They do not have fixed character fonts. The term font is used to refer to a character set of a printer. As fonts are not fixed, a dot-matrix printer can print any shape of a character by software. This permits printing of many special characters, such as α, β, σ, √, ∫, etc., and various sizes of print, bold or expanded characters, italic characters of any language and also provides the ability to print graphics.

Non-impact Character Printers

This type of printer uses thermal, electrostatic, chemical and ink-jet technologies. The printer type is briefly described as follows:

Dot-Matrix Type Thermal Character Printers

This type of printer uses a special heat-sensitive paper. These papers have a special heat sensitive coating. When a spot on the special paper is heated, it becomes dark. A character is printed with a matrix of dots. A print head consists of 5 × 7 or 7 × 9 matrix of tiny heating elements. The heating element is heated by electric current. To print a character, the printing head is moved first to the correct character position. Then, the heating elements for the desired character are turned on. After a short time they are turned off. Thereafter the print head is moved to the next character position. Such printers have a speed of about 20 characters per second (cps) only.

Inkjet Printers

Inkjet printers are more efficient than dot matrix printers. Just as dot-matrix printers, inkjet printers too have printhead but inkjet's printhead does not have metal pins that come out from the printhead. Instead, the inkjet's printhead has many tiny nozzles that spray ink into the paper. Each nozzle is thinner than human hair.

Inkjet printers use a continuous stream of ink drops to print characters on paper. Droplets of ink are electrically charged after leaving a nozzle. The droplets are then guided to the proper position on the paper by electrically charged deflection plates. The print quality is good because the character is formed by dozens of tiny ink dots. These printers produce better quality of text and graphics and are faster. Almost all inkjets offer a color option as standard, in varying degrees of resolution. Inkjet printers are capable of producing high quality print which almost matches the quality of a laser printer. A standard ink-jet printer has a resolution of 300 dots per inch, although newer models have improved on that. (See Figure 2.46)

☞ *Inkjet printers are ideal for small business, home computers and individual computer office.*

It uses the dot-matrix approach to print text and graphics. One type of an earlier inkjet printer uses one or more nozzles in the print head that emit a steady stream of tiny ink drops. Each droplet is charged when it passes through a valve. Then it passes through horizontal and vertical deflecting plates. These plates deflect the ink drops to direct them to the desired spots on the paper to form the impression of a character. In this type of printers, continuous stream of ink-drops is used. The speed of inkjet printers lies in the range of 40-300 characters per second (cps). The average life of an ink-jet print head is about 10 billion characters which is 5 times more than that of the print head of an impact type dot-matrix printer.

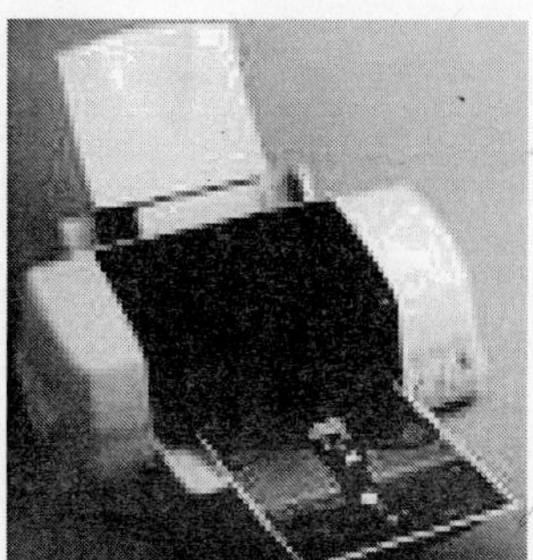

Figure 2.46 Inkjet printer

Laser Printers

Laser printers are non-impact type printers. They print one page at a time. These printers use laser or other light source to produce an image on a photosensitive drum. The computer controls the laser beam to turn it on and off. An image is produced following the raster scan principle. The laser-exposed areas attract the toner (an ink powder). Thereafter, the drum transfers the toner to the paper. The paper then moves to a fusing station where the toner is permanently fused on the paper with heat or pressure. Next, the drum is discharged and cleaned. Now the drum is ready for processing the next page. Figure 2.47 shows a modern, high-speed laser printer.

Figure 2.47 Laser printer

2.12.3 Plotters

Plotters are output devices. They are used to produce precise and good quality graphics and drawings under control of the computer. They use ink pen or inkjet to draw graphics or drawings. Either single colour or multicoloured pens can be employed. The pens are driven by a stepper motor. Drawings can be prepared on paper, vellum or mylar (polyester film). Colour transparencies can also be prepared. Figure 2.48 shows a plotter.

Pen plotters are slow devices. The graphics and drawings produced by pen plotters are uniform and precise and are of very good quality. They are used for low to medium volume jobs. A pen plotter can take from several seconds for simple drawings to several minutes for complex drawings. But it takes much less

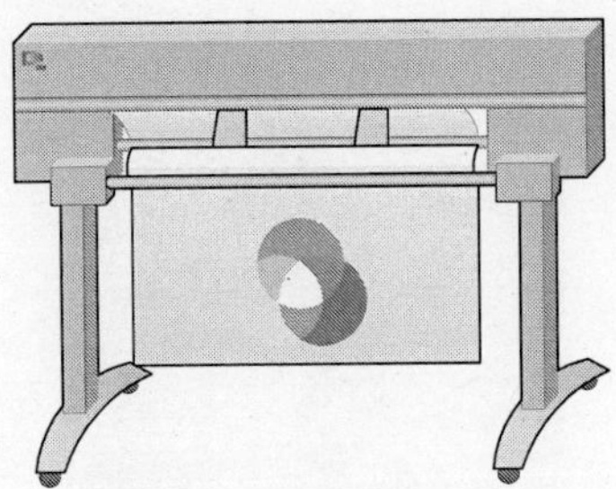

Figure 2.48 Plotter

time as compared to traditional manual methods of producing drawings. Pen plotters may be classified into the following four types:

(a) Drum plotter
(b) Microgrip plotter
(c) Flat-bed plotter
(d) Inkjet plotter

Each type is used depending on the quality of graphic work needed.

Drum Plotter

A drum plotter contains a long cylinder and a pen carriage. The paper is placed over the drum (i.e., cylinder). The drum rotates back-and-forth to give an up-and-down movement. The pen is mounted horizontally on the carriage. The pen moves horizontally along with the carriage left-to-right or right-to-left on the paper to produce drawings. Under computer control, both the drum and the pen move to produce the desired drawings. Several pens with inks of different colours can be mounted on the carriage. Since each pen is program selectable, multicoloured drawings can be produced.

Microgrip Plotters

Such plotters do not use drums. The paper or any other medium is held (gripped) on both sides at the edges by pinch wheels which give back-and-forth movement of the paper. With such printers, high performance is obtained at low cost.

Flat-bed Plotters

Flat-bed plotters use horizontal flat surface on which paper, or any other medium can be fixed. The pen moves along both the axes: the X-axis and the Y-axis. The pen carriage is controlled by the computer in both the axes.

Inkjet Plotters

Some plotters employ inkjets in place of ink pens. The paper is placed on a drum and inkjets with different-coloured inks are mounted on a carriage. Such printers are capable of producing multicoloured large drawings.

Projector

A projector is an image that receives a video signal and projects the corresponding image on a projection screen using a lens system. Projectors are widely used for many applications, such as conference room presentations, classroom training, home theatre and concerts. Projectors are widely used in many schools and other educational settings, sometimes connected to an interactive whiteboard to interactively teach pupils.

There are two types of projectors these are:

(a) **DLP Projectors:** DLP technology is based on an optical semiconductor called a DMD (Digital Micromirror Device) chip, which was invented in 1987 by Texas Instruments. It is a chip made up of millions of tiny mirrors, that can rotate at a 10 degrees angle. These mirrors are capable of switching on and off thousands of times per second and are used to direct light towards and away from a dedicated pixel space. The length of time a pixel is on/off. On is lightest (white) and off is darkest (black) (See Figure 2.49).

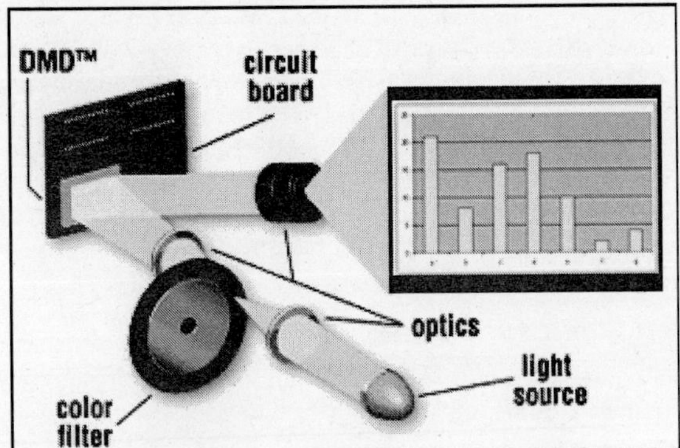

Figure 2.49 DLP Projector display

(b) **LCD Projector:** LCD (Liquid Crystal Display) projectors contain three separate LCD glass panels, one for red, green, and blue components of the image signal being transferred to the projector. As the light passes through the LCD panels, individual pixels can be opened to allow light to pass or closed to block the light. This activity modulates the light and produces the image that is projected onto the screen (See Figure 2.50).

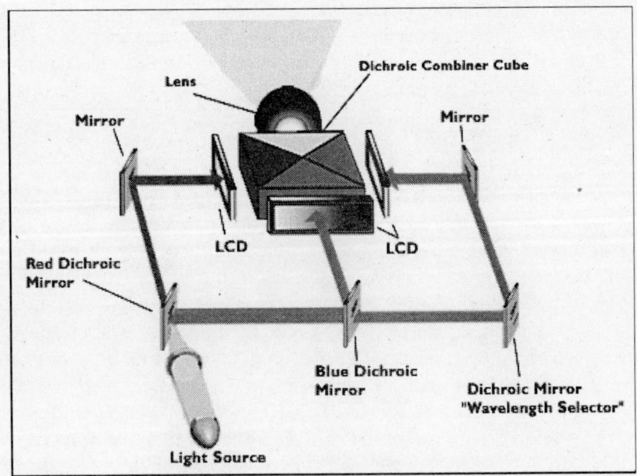

Figure 2.50 LCD Projector display

Visualizer

Visual presenter is a document camera designed to display any object or material onto a screen. It is a powerful presentation tool as one can place documents, such as A4 size printed handouts, books or 3D objects. Once connected to a projector, it becomes an effective tool in the hands of a presenter. It can be used as a part of Interactive classroom or standalone tool to presenting document to a large or small group of audience.

Document cameras replaced overhead projectors, which were formerly used for this purpose. The zoom feature a document camera can enlarge the small print in books and project a printed page. The document in cameras can also send a video signal to a computer via USB cable. Sometimes document cameras are connected to an interactive whiteboard instead of a standard screen.

2.13 PORTS AND INTERFACES

Ports and Interfaces are the rear panel of the system unit of your PC, you will see certain holes found at the back of the computer, using which external devices are connected to the computer motherboard.

A port is a means by which data is transferred between an input device to output device or vice versa. The CPU receives or transfers data from main memory and thus uses the memory addresses to send or receive data. Specialized hardware are used to place data from the devices in the memory addresses and to send data from the memory addresses to the devices. All computer systems have ports for connecting peripheral devices, such as printers, keyboard, mouse and modems.

2.13.1 PS/2 PORT

The PS/2 (Personal System/2) standard was introduced by IBM in 1987. It is an electronic plug which connects mouse or keyboard. Most PCs come with two PS/2 ports. It accepts a PS/2 cable with a mini-DIN connector, and is most often used to plug in a keyboard or mouse. The PS/2 port is female while the mini-DIN cable is male. The connector is small with a diameter of about 1/3 inch (9.5mm). The PS/2 port was initially a large DIN plug used for a keyboard, while the mouse was commonly plugged into a serial port.

The PS/2 mouse connector has replaced the older DE-9 RS-232 "serial mouse" connector, while the keyboard connector has replaced the larger 5-pin DIN used in the IBM PC/AT (Personal Computer/Advanced Technology) design. The keyboard and mouse interfaces are electrically similar with the main difference being that open collector outputs are required on both ends of the keyboard interface to allow bidirectional communication. Normal desktop motherboards will not identify the keyboard and mouse if they are placed on each other's sockets. Female pin connection of the PS/2 from the front is shown in Figure 2.51 and the details of these pins are described in Table 2.2.

Table 2.2 Female Connector from the front

Pin 1	+DATA	Data
Pin 2	Not connected	Not connected
Pin 3	GND	Ground
Pin 4	Vcc	+5 V DC at 100 mA
Pin 5	+CLK	Clock
Pin 6	Not connected	Not connected

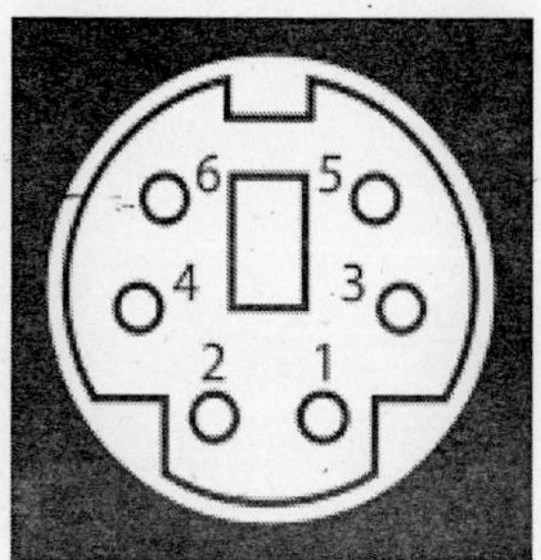

Figure 2.51 PS/2 Port

2.13.2 Serial Port

Serial port is an asynchronous port through which information transfers in or out one bit at a time. Usually referred to as a DB9 or DB25 connection. Where D represents the shape of the connector. The number 9/25 indicating the number of pins found on the connector. DB9 Serial connections are now commonly found on modern PCs and DB9 serial connection is identified first by its 9 pins. The DB9 is shaped like a D (See Figure 2.52). It will generally be a male connector on the back of the computer whereas DB25 is commonly found on older computers.

Following is the list of component that is used with serial port in computer:

(a) Mouse
(b) Keyboard
(c) Modem
(d) Network

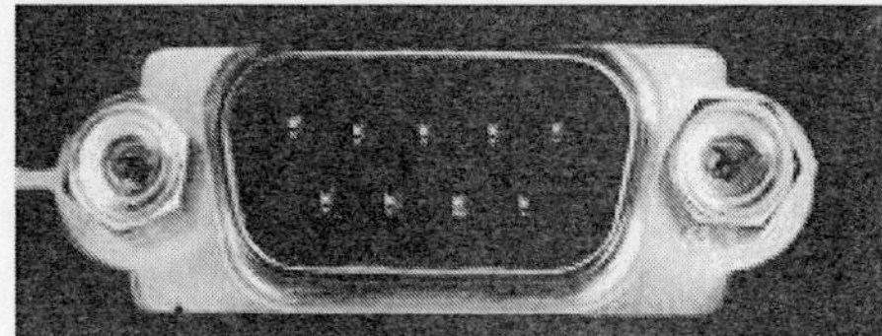

Figure 2.52 COM Port or Serial Port

☞ *In present day PCs, USB interface is used to replace the serial port.*

2.13.3 Parallel Port

LPT (Line Printing Terminal) is the original name of the parallel port interface on IBM PC compatible computers. It was designed to operate a text printer that used IBM's 8-bit extended ASCII (American Standard Code for Information Interchange) character set. A parallel port is a type of socket found on personal computers for interfacing with various peripherals. It is also known as a printer port. LPT port which you might have seen on the back of the PC is shown in Figure 2.53.

Usually, a PC will have 2 LPT ports. You may also find some PCs with 3 LPT ports. These ports are each with their own name LPT1, LPT2 and LPT3. They were designed primarily for printers. However, there is a variety of peripherals that can be connected to these ports.

☞ *Modern printers are connected through USB connection. On many high-end PCs, the parallel port is omitted for cost savings. Printers print at much higher speed when connected with USB port.*

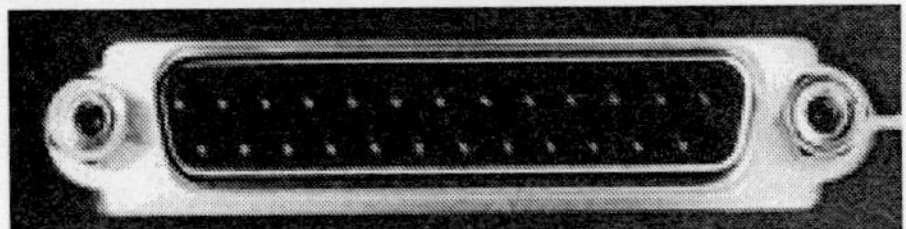

Figure 2.53 LPT Port or Parallel Port

2.13.4 USB Port

Universal Serial Bus (USB) is standardized by the USB Implementers Forum (USB-IF), an industry standards body incorporating leading companies from the computer and electronics industries. USB is a serial bus standard which was designed to allow peripherals to be connected using a single standardized interface socket, to improve plug-and-play capabilities by allowing devices to be connected and disconnected without rebooting the computer (See Figure 2.54). Other convenient features include powering low-consumption devices without the need for an external power supply and allowing some devices to be used without requiring individual device drivers to be installed.

☞ *The Universal Serial Bus (USB) is a single, standardized, easy-to-use way to connect up to 127 devices to a computer.*

Figure 2.54 Commonly used USB Plug

A sample list of USB devices that you can buy today includes:

(a) Printers
(b) Scanners
(c) Mice
(d) Joysticks
(e) Flight yokes
(f) Digital cameras
(g) Webcams
(h) Modems
(i) Speakers
(j) Network connections

2.13.5 SCSI Port

SCSI (pronounced as "scuzzy"), stands for Small Computer System Interface. It is a set of ANSI (American National Standard Institure) standard electronic interfaces that allow personal computers to communicate with peripheral hardware, such as disk drives, tape drives, CD-ROM drives, printers, and scanners faster and more flexibly than previous interfaces. The present set of SCSIs are parallel interfaces in many personal computers today and are supported by all major operating systems.

In addition to faster data rates, SCSI is more flexible than earlier parallel data transfer interfaces. The latest SCSI standard, Ultra-2 SCSI for a 16-bit bus can transfer data at up to 80 megabytes per second (Mbps). SCSI allows up to 7 or 15 devices (depending on the bus width) to be connected to a single SCSI port in daisy-chain fashion. This allows one circuit board or card to accommodate all the peripherals, rather than having a separate card for each device, making it an ideal interface for use with portable and notebook computers.

The latest SCSI standard is Ultra-3 (sometimes spelled "Ultra3") which increases the maximum burst rate from 80 Mbps to 160 Mbps by being able to operate at the full clock rate rather than the half-clock rate of Ultra-2. The standard is also sometimes referred to as Ultra160/m. New disk drives supporting Ultra160/m will offer much faster data transfer rates. Ultra160/m also includes Cyclical Redundancy Checking (CRC) for ensuring the integrity of transferred data and domain validation for testing the SCSI network.

Expansion Cards

The expansion card also known as expansion board or adapter card in circuit board that can provides additional capabilities to the computer system. The cards are plugged into the expansion sockets present on the computer's motherbord to provide the computer an added functionality. However, now-a-days most of the adapters come in-built on the motherboard and no expansion card is required, unless the need for high performance is required.

- **Sound Card:** Sound card is applied to external audio interfaces that use software to generate sound. The use of sound cards include providing the audio component for multimedia applications, such as music composition, editing video or audio, presentation, education and entertainment (games) and video projection. Most sounds cards use a Digital-to-Analog Converter (DAC), which converts digital data into an analog format. The output signal is connected to an amplifier or headphones.
- **Video Card:** A video card also called a video adapter, display card, graphics card. It is an expansion card which generates a feed of output images to a display (such as a computer monitor).
- **Network Interface Card:** A Network Interface Card (NIC) is a circuit board or card that is installed in a computer so that it can be connected to a nework. A network interface card provides the computer with a dedicated, full-time connection to a network. Personal computers and workstations on a local area network typically contain a network interface card specifically designed for the LAN (Local Area Network) transmission technology.

- **Modem:** Modem is an expansion card that allows two computers to communicate over ordinary phone lines. It converts digital data into analog data, transmits over the telephone lines and also converts incoming analog signals back to digital signals for the receiving computer.
- **PC Card:** A PC Card (known as a PCMCIA or Personal Computer Memory Card International Association card) is a credit card-size memory or I/O device that fits into a personal computer. The most common use of a PC Card is the telecommunications modem for notebook computers. There are 16-binary digit and 32-bit (CardBus). The PC Card is based on standards published by the PCMCIA, an industry group organized in 1989 to promote standards for both memory and I/O integrated circuit card.

2.14 CONNECTORS

The part of a cable that plugs into a port or interface to connect one device to another. Most connectors are either male (containing one or more pins) or female (containing holes in which the male connector can be inserted).

2.14.1 DIN Connector

DIN is short for Deutsches Institute for Normung. A DIN connector is an electrical connector that was originally standardized by German national standards organization. DIN connectors are used in personal computers. For example, the keyboard connector is a DIN connector (See Figure 2.55).

A DIN (or DIN5) connectors is a plug with 5 pins, formerly used to connect keyboards to computers.

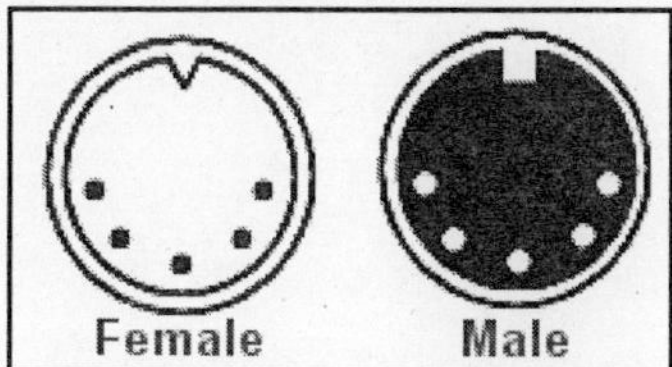

Figure 2.55 DIN connector

The DIN 5 connector has been made by PS/2 and USB connectors.

Pin number	Function
1	Reset (_RST)
2	+ 5 V (power)
3	Data
4	Ground
5	Clock

Mini-DIN connector

Mini-DIN connectors are cylindrical in shape and feature between three and nine pins, each compatible with various audio and/or visual devices. Four-pin mini-DIN connectors are used to carry a separate video (commonly called S-video) signal.

Some examples of standard mini-DIN connectors include:

- Mini-DIN-3 connectors were used in early implementations of Apple LocalTalk.
- Mini-DIN-4 connectors are used for S-video, and were used for Apple Desktop Bus.
- Mini-DIN-6 connectors were used for IBM PC compatible PS/2 keyboard and mouse ports.
- Mini-DIN-8 connectors were used for Apple and Sun Microsystems keyboard and mouse ports, as well as for serial printer, modem, and Apple LocalTalk connections.
- Mini-DIN-7 and Mini-DIN-9 connectors have been used for a variety of audio and video applications.
- Mini-DIN-6 and Mini-DIN-8 connectors are frequently used in ham radio applications to interface with computers for data packet communications and radio programming.

2.14.2 RCA Connector

An RCA (Radio Corporation of America) connector, sometimes called a phono connector or cinch connector, is a type of electrical connector commonly used to carry audio and video signals. The RCA plug is used to send video and audio signals (in mono or stereo) through a two-wire cable, with either an analog or digital transmission method.

The connector's colour indicates how it is meant to be used. For stereo analog audio transmissions, the connectors are red and white as shown in Figure 2.56.

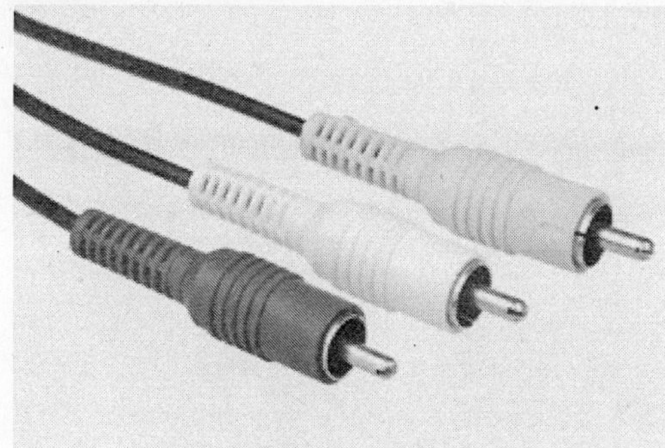

Figure 2.56 RCA connector

For a composite video signal, the connector is yellow (See Figure 2.57).

Figure 2.57 RCA cable in yellow colour

The RCA connector is also used for sending component video, also called YUV or YCrCb, is a color representation model in which Y represents luminance (black and white), and U and V represent the chrominance (information regarding the color). In YUV representation, U is sometimes written as Cr and V is sometimes written as Cb therefore YCrCb notation is also used in color representation. For such a video signal, 3 connectors, colored red, green, and blue, are used (See Figure 2.58).

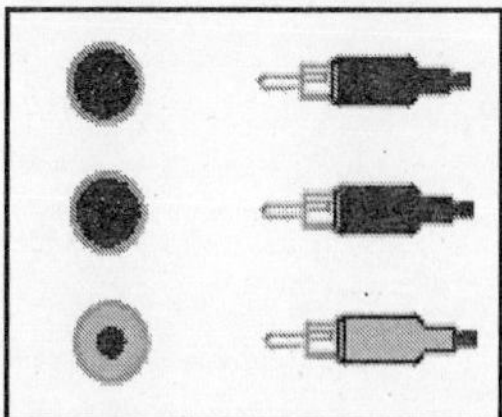

Figure 2.58 Three RCA cables: 1 green, 1 blue and 1 red

2.14.3 AV (Audio Video) Connector

Audio connectors and video connectors are electrical connectors (or optical connectors) for carrying audio signal and video signal. Either analog or digital format. Analog A/V connectors often use shielded cables to inhibit Radio Frequency Interference (RFI) and noise. The most common types of connectors used between your new A/V receiver, video display (with an emphasis on HDTV), DVD/CD player, loudspeakers, and subwoofer.

Audio connectors are electrical connectors designed and used for audio frequencies. They can be analog or digital. Common audio connectors include:

- **Banana Connector:** A banana connector (commonly banana plug for the male, banana socket or banana jack for the female) is a single-wire (one conductor) electrical connector used for joining wires to equipment. The term 4 mm connector is also used in Europe. Although not all banana connectors will mate with 4 mm parts. The plug is a four-leafed spring tip that snaps into the jack. The plugs are frequently used to terminate patch cords for electronic test equipment. They are also often used as the plugs on the cables connecting the amplifier to the loudspeakers in hi-fi (high fidelity) sound systems (See Figure 2.59).

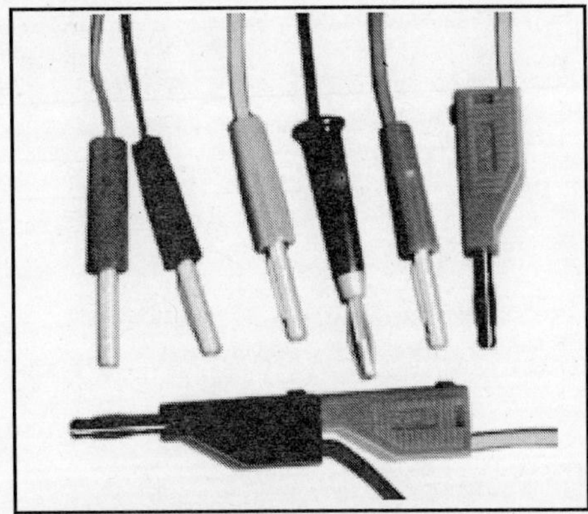

Figure 2.59 Various banana plugs

- **Five-way Binding Posts:** A type of speaker cable input and receiver/amplifier output connector that accepts bare speaker wire when you unscrew the top and push the wire through the hole. It is also used for high-level connections for amplified audio signals from an A/V receiver's speaker outputs to the speakers. Stereo systems with amplifiers or preamps lacking a subwoofer output would also use the amplifier's high-level outputs and the subwoofers hi-level inputs. Signals may be routed through the subwoofer and then to the main speakers, or separately from the amplifier to the main speakers with a second set to the subwoofer (See Figure 2.60).

Figure 2.60 Five-way binding posts

Video connectors carry only video signals. Common video-only connectors include:

- **Component Video:** The most common type of connector used for both standard-quality video and HD video, it uses three coaxial RCA cables and plugs color-coded red, green and blue (the three cables may be wrapped together for convenience) to carry analog standard or high definition video between a set top satellite or cable-TV box to the A/V receiver and TV display or projector (See Figure 2.61).

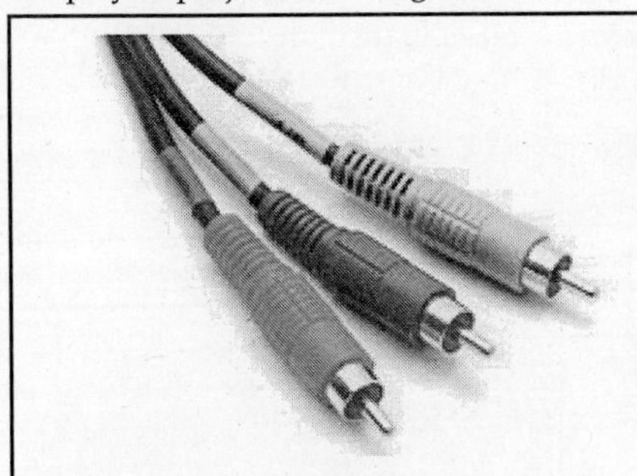

Figure 2.61 Component video cable

- **Composite Video:** A single video connector that combines all the color, brightness, and sync signals into one cable using a single RCA connector. It is the most common type of analog video connection between older VCRs and TVs (except for RF (Radio Frequency) connectors). Use composite video only if your TV, VCR or DVD player lacks S-video or component-video connectors. Composite video will not carry High Def or progressive-scan video signals (See Figure 2.62).

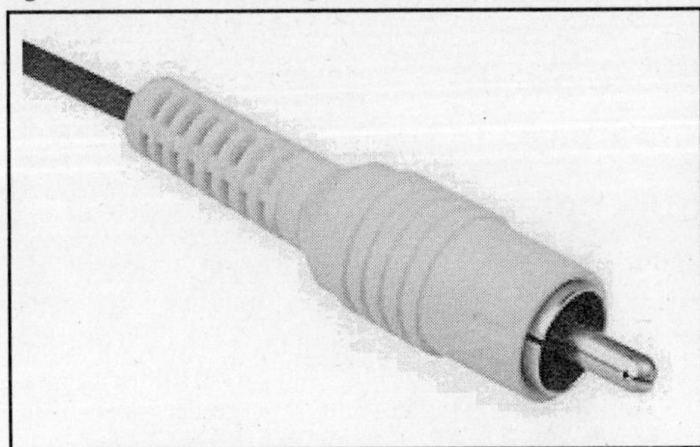

Figure 2.62 Composite video cable

2.14.4 USB Connectors

Most computer users are familiar with USB, which has become the most commonly used way to connect peripheral devices to a computer. For example, mouse, printer, digital camera, scanner, and other devices probably all connect to your computer via a USB port. Many memory storage devices, such as portable hard drives, flash drives, and memory card readers, also connect to a computer via USB.

USB connectors make it possible to connect a device to your computer using USB. A long cable is used to connect the device to your computer. Usually, the connectors on each end of the cable are quite different, making it necessary to know which of them goes to your computer and which gets plugged into the device.

Different types of USB Connectors

There are many types of UBS connector cards you may use depending on the device you are connecting.

Type-A These types of USB connectors are identified by their rectangular shaped plug. The plug is always found in the cable and the receptacle is found in the device. They are commonly used with keyboard, mouse, data cards etc. The image of a type A connector and the pin position are shown in Figures 2.63 and 2.64, respectively.

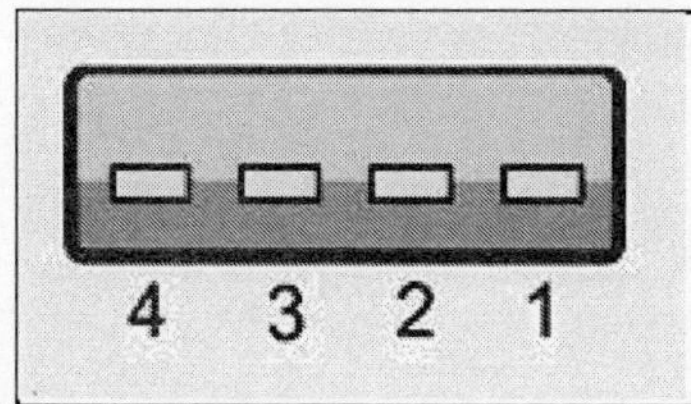

Figure 2.63 The pin-position of Type A USB connector

Figure 2.64 The image of Type A male and female USB connector

The pin-out of the Type A USB Connector.

Pin 1 VBus
Pin 2 D-
Pin 3 D+
Pin 4 Ground

Type-B The Type-B connectors are designed to be used with devices which are meant to be connected with the device having Type-A receptacle. These connectors are square shaped with beveled exterior corners. They are found in USB devices like printers, USB to serial converters, simple USB powered devices like battery chargers, etc. The image of a type B connector and the pin position are shown in Figures 2.65 and 2.66, respectively.

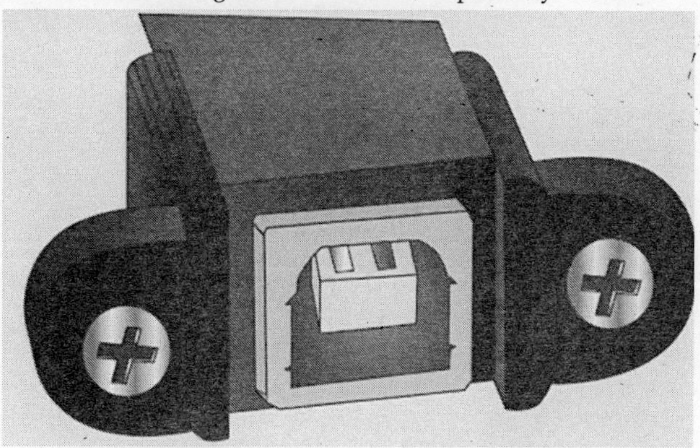

Figure 2.65 Female Type B connector

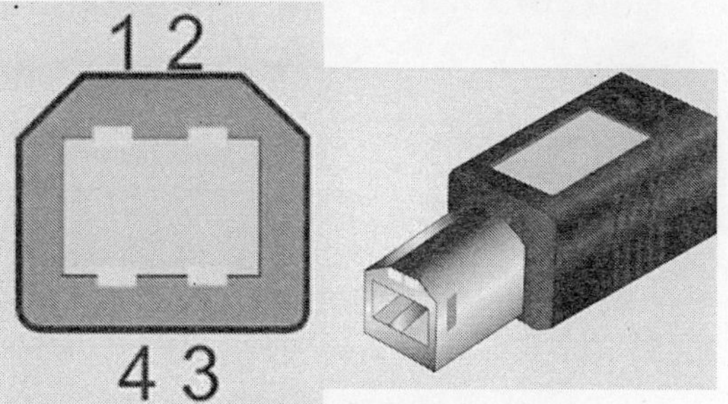

Figure 2.66 Male Type B connector and pin position

Figure 2.67 The image of Mini A and B male USB connector and Pin position

Mini-A and Mini-B The Mini-A and Mini-B connectors are used with USB devices which are meant to be connected to Type A receptacles. But these connectors are smaller than the Type B connector. They are designed to be connected with small sized USB devices like camera, mobile phones, etc. (See Figure 2.67).

The pin-out of the Mini USB Connector

Pin 1	VBus
Pin 2	D-
Pin 3	D+
Pin 4	ID
Pin 5	Ground

Micro-A and Micro-B The Micro-A and B connectors are introduced to replace the Mini-A and Mini-AB connectors. They are smaller in size than the Mini connectors. They have up to 10, 000 mating cycles. The Micro connectors are used with small devices like mobiles, smart phones, PDAs (Personal Digital Assistants), etc. (See Figure 2.68).

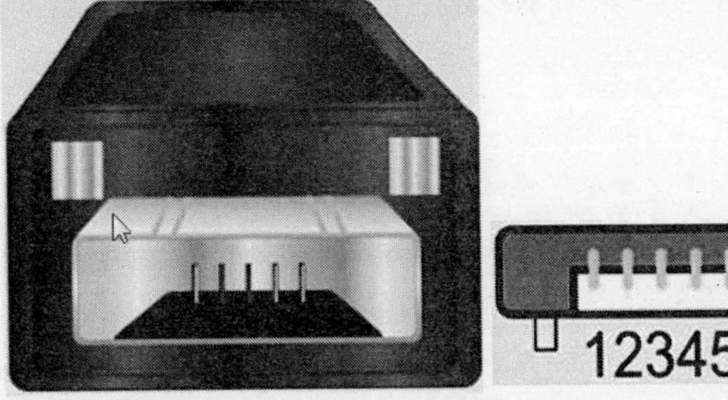

Figure 2.68 The image of Micro B and A male connector and pin position

The pin-out of the Micro USB connector

Pin 1	VBus
Pin 2	D-
Pin 3	D+
Pin 4	ID
Pin 5	Ground

2.14.5 FireWire (IEEE 1394)

IEEE (Institute of Electrical and Electronics Engineers) 1394, also named "FireWire" by Apple, and "i.Link" by Sony, and it was developed by Apple in 1986. It is a standard I/O interface designed to service the demands of the emerging multimedia bus requirements. It includes a plug-and-socket connection with a serial bus interface. Up to 63 devices may be connected at the same time with (relatively) high data transfer speeds.

The IEEE 1394 standard has proved very popular for communication between computers and peripheral devices. IEEE 1394 interface has the following features:

- Real-time data transferring for multimedia applications
- 100-800 Mb/s data transfer rate
- Hot plugging is allowed (at a minimum ratio)
- Line terminators are not required
- Plug-and-play
- Auto-configuration for many peripheral devices
- Same connectors for multiple devices and components

The FireWire system is commonly used to connect digital cameras and other storage devices. FireWire has an edge over USB in terms of power distribution, reliability and data transfer speed. Moreover, FireWire system has adopted the functionalities and characteristics of SCSI.

2.14.6 HDMI

It stands for "High-Definition Multimedia Interface." HDMI is a digital interface for transmitting audio and video data in a single cable. It is supported by most HDTVs and related components, such as DVD and Blu-ray players, cable boxes, and video game systems.

While other types of A/V connections require separate cables for audio and video data, HDMI carries the audio and video streams together, greatly eliminating cable clutter. For example, a component cable connection requires three cables for video and two for audio, totaling five cables in all. The same information can be transmitted using one HDMI cable.

Because HDMI is a digital connection, HDMI cables are less prone to interference and signal noise than analog cables. Also, since most components, such as DVD players and digital cable boxes process information digitally, using HDMI eliminates the analog to digital conversion other interfaces require. Therefore, HDMI often produces the best quality picture and sound compared to other types of connections.

2.15 COMPUTER SOFTWARE

Software is a set of computer programs procedures, and associated documentation related to the effective operation of a computer system. Hardware represents the physical components of the computer, i.e., the components that can be seen and touched. Input devices, output devices, CPU, Floppy disk, etc., are examples of hardware. Computer hardware in itself cannot perform any useful task. It must be complemented with some instructions, which the hardware understands and obeys. A program is the name given to a list of instructions or statements that direct the computer to perform the required task.

Software (Programs) are of the following types:

(a) System software
(b) Application software

2.15.1 System Software

System software, or system packages, are sets of one or more programs that are basically designed to control the operation of a computer system. They are general programs written to assist users in performing tasks, such as controlling hardware, moving data into and out of a computer and all the other steps in executing the application program. In general, system packages control the following :

(a) Running of other software packages.
(b) Communicating with peripheral devices, such as printers, hard disk and tape devices, etc.
(c) Monitoring the use of various hardware resources, such as memory, peripherals, CPU, etc.

System software, thus, make the operation of the computer system more effective and efficient.

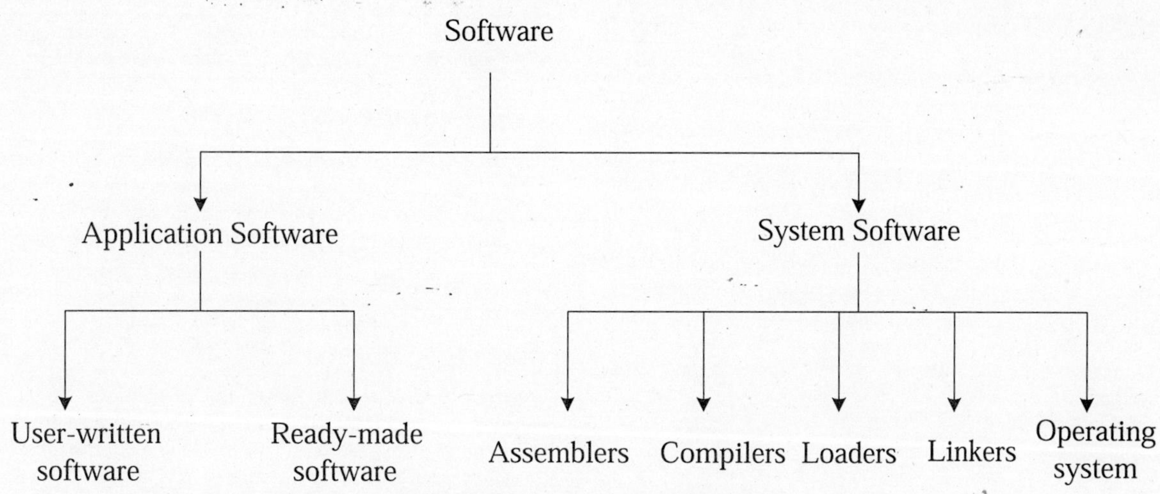

Figure 2.69 Classification of software

2.15.2 Application Software

Application software packages cater to the need of a specific group of users, namely, software for scientists, for inventory control, for school administration, for library management, etc. The System software packages, on the other hand, manage computer hardware and supervise the working of application packages. Such software packages also do input/output device management, file management, storage management, etc.

☞ *System software are the ones which directly talk with the hardware components. The Application software in turn talk with the System software for their execution.*

You as a user would be working mostly with the Application software packages (See Figure 2.69).

☞ *System programming is an activity of designing and implementing system software programs to use hardware efficiently.*

The system software work in the background for effective utilization of computer resources and minimize human effort in programming and debugging. Some examples of system software are *Language Translators, Loaders, Linkers* and *Operating system software*, such as Windows 2000 and Linux, etc.

Differences between System and Application Software Packages

System software packages offer several advantages and conveniences to application programmers and computer users. A good system software allows application packages to be run on the computer with less effort. Without system software, application packages cannot be run on the computer system. However, the production of system software is a complex task that requires extensive knowledge and considerable specialized training in computer science.

System programmers, who prepare system software, are highly trained computer specialists and important members of the computer architecture team. Because of its technical complexity, a system software is rarely developed in-house. System software is normally developed and distributed by the computer manufacturers. The customer who buys or leases a computer system would usually receive, in addition to the hardware, some software needed for the effective operation of his computer. Figure 2.70 depicts the layers that isolate hardware from users.

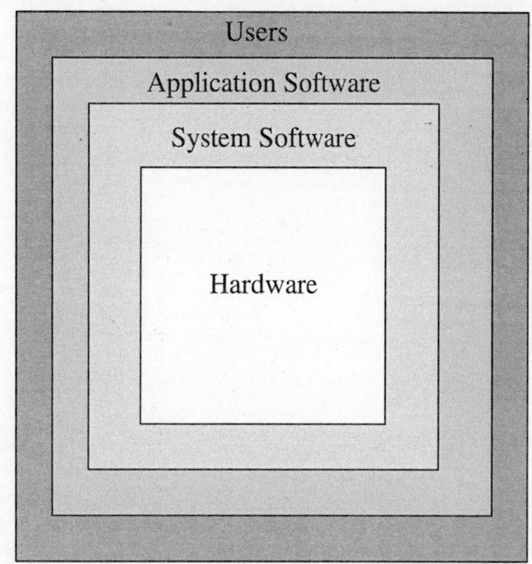

Figure 2.70 Layers that isolate hardware from users

The system software is an indispensable part of a total computer system. Its function is to compensate for the differences that exist between the user needs and the capabilities of the hardware. A computer without system software would be ineffective and impossible to operate.

2.15.3 Relationship between Hardware and Software

Hardware includes every computer-related object that you can physically touch and handle like disks, screens, keyboards, printers, chips, wires, central processing unit, floppies, USB ports, pen drives, etc.

Software includes every computer-related program that you cannot feel with the physical senses for example, system operating system, an anti-virus program, Web browser, memory, all data, reports, etc. All storage devices that keep data safe and store it in some electronic form are hardware while all data in itself is software.

Software is what makes the hardware function properly and to an optimum level. Sometimes, there is confusion between software and hardware because the two terms are so integrally connected. If you buy an anti-virus program you buy software but since it comes on a disk, you have also bought the hardware. The major confusion between software and hardware occurs relating to memory. Software defines the memory capacity of a computer but it depends on the kind of hardware "memory chip" used in the computer.

2.15.4 Assembler

It is a program which translates an assembly language program into a machine language program. An assembler which runs on a computer for which it produces object codes (machine codes) is called a self assembler (or resident assembler). A less powerful and cheaper computer may not have enough software and hardware facilities for program development using conventional assembler. In such a situation, a faster and powerful computer can be used for program development. The programs so developed can be executed on smaller computers. For such program development a cross assembler is required. A *cross assembler* is an assembler that runs on a computer other than that for which it produces the machine codes.

2.15.5 Compiler

A program which translates a high-level language program into a machine language program is known as a compiler. It checks all kinds of limits, ranges, errors etc. But its program execution time is more and occupies a larger part of the memory. It has low-speed and low efficiency of memory utilization. If a compiler runs on a computer for which it produces the object code it is known as a *self* or *resident compiler*. If a compiler runs on a computer other than that for which it produces a object code, it is known as a *cross-compiler*.

2.15.6 Interpreter

An interpreter is a program which translates *one* statement of a high-level language program into machine codes and executes it. In this way it proceeds further till all the statements of the program are translated and executed. On the other hand, a compiler goes through the entire high-level language program once or twice and then translates the entire program into machine codes. A compiler is nearly 5 to 25 times faster than an interpreter. An interpreter is a smaller program as compared to the compiler. It needs less memory space. It can be used in a smaller system which with limited memory space. The object program produced by the compiler is permanently saved for future reference. On the other hand, the object code of the statement produced by an interpreter is not saved. If an instruction is used next time, it must be interpreted once again and translated into machine codes.

☞ *If a compiler runs on a computer other than that for which it produces object code, then it is called a cross-compiler.*

2.15.7 Loader

To run an object program, it must be loaded into the memory of a computer after compilation. A loader is a software that loads the translated or compiled object program into the memory of the computer. The object program will be in one of the following two forms:

(a) *Absolute format*
(b) *Relocatable format*

Absolute Format

In the absolute format, the programmer provides the actual hardware addresses where instructions and operands are to be stored in the main memory. In such a case, the loader loads the binary program into the memory as per the indications.

Relocatable Format

In this format, a programmer does not provide the memory address. It only provides address of modules with respect to each other or relative to the address of the first module.

Another software called *Locater*, assigns the memory address to each line of (binary) machine code of such relocatable programs before the loader loads the binary program into the memory.

☞ *The loader is actually a part of operating system software. It works as per the storage management laws of the operating system.*

The functions of a loader can be summarized as follows:

(a) Allocate memory space for the programs.
(b) Replace address related constants in the programs with the allocated address of the memory.
(c) Physically load the machine instructions and data into memory for execution.

2.15.8 Linker

It is a good and common practice to break a large program into smaller modules for better readability and debugging. These modules are saved in different files. Also subroutines and functions needed by a program are written in separates files, so that these can then be used by one or more programs. Each of these files are compiled separately. But for a program to execute successfully, these compiled files must coordinate and execute as a single unit. The software program that links these files to work together is called *Linker.*

☞ *A linker is a software which puts together the different object modules so as to produce the executable program. Linker also links the program with library functions which a programmer must have called in the program.*

Linker takes as input the translated module programs. These programs contains reference to each other in symbolic form. The Linker's job is to resolve these symbolic references into actual memory addresses.

Linker produces a *Link File* containing the binary code of all the modules. Linker also creates a *Link Map* containing the address information about the linked files.

Figure 2.71 shows a block diagram for the linking and loading process.

Linker is also known as *Binder* or *Linkage Editor*. In most cases, Linker is considered as a part of the Loader. They together are known as *Linking-Loader*.

There is a loading and linking scheme called ***Dynamic Linking-Loader***. In this scheme, the loading and linking to external reference is postponed until execution time. This is done to load into memory only those modules and subroutines which will be executed next. It has the advantage that the memory need not be filled with routines which are referenced in the program but not needed immediately.

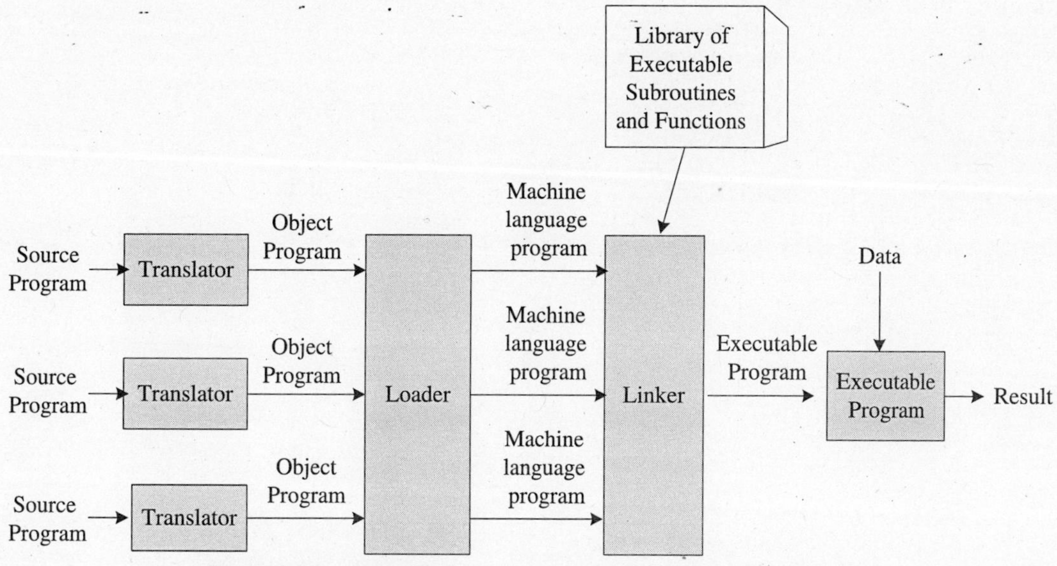

Figure 2.71 Block diagram for the linking and loading of programs

REVIEW QUESTIONS WITH ANSWERS

1. Multiple Choice

1.1 Which of the following devices can be used to input printed text?
a. OCR b. OMR
c. MICR d. All of the above

1.2 CPU reads the information from secondary memory:
a. Directly
b. First, information is transferred to the main memory and from there, the CPU reads it
c. Through registers
d. None of these

1.3 Add, Subtract, Divide, Multiply and Logic operations are performed by:
a. Registers b. Control unit
c. ALU d. None of these

1.4 Main memory stores:
a. Data only
b. Program only
c. Data, program and results or any other kind of information
d. None of these

1.5 A smart terminal is one which:
a. Looks very attractive
b. Has in-built processing capability
c. Must convert input on CRT screen
d. None of these

1.6 A laser printer uses:
a. Photo-sensitive drum b. Camera lens
c. Heat sensitive paper d. None of these

1.7 A plotter is:
a. An input device to produce good quality graphics
b. An output device to produce drawings and graphics
c. A fast output device using camera lens
d. None of these

1.8 In a hard disk, the 0 track is:
a. The outermost b. The innermost
c. Totally machine dependent d. None of these

1.9 Logical operations in a computer are done by:
a. Registers b. Control unit
c. ALU d. None of these

1.10 A CD-ROM is:
a. An optical ROM b. A magnetic ROM
c. An erasable ROM d. None of these

1.11 Software designed for a specific purpose is known as:
a. System software b. Compiler
c. Specific software d. Application software

1.12 Which of the following is not an output device?
a. Plotter b. Printer
c. MICR d. Smart and intelligent terminal

1.13 The best mode of connection between devices which need to send or receive large amounts of data over a short distance is_______.
a. Bus b. Serial port
c. Parallel d. Isochronous port

*1.14 A language translator is best described as:
a. An application software b. A system software
c. A hardware component d. An operating system

1.15 A floppy disk is organized as:
a. Tracks b. Sectors
c. Tracks and sectors d. Heads and sectors

1.16 Optical storage technique is used:
a. Floppy disk drive b. Hard disk drive
c. Magnetic disk drive d. CD-ROM drive

1.17 The errors that can be pointed out by the compiler are:
a. Syntax errors b. Semantic errors
c. Logical errors d. None of these

1.18 Which one of the following is not an output device?
a. Monitor b. Printer
c. Plotter d. Digitizer

1.19 The disadvantage of using parallel mode of communication is ________.
a. It is costly b. Leads to erroneous data transfer
c. Security of data d. All of the above

1.20 Which of the following is an open source operating system?
a. UNIX b. Linux
c. Windows d. None of these

1.21 An optical mark reader is:
a. A scanner b. A printer
c. A video camera d. A CD writer

1.22 The disadvantage of the EPROM chip is:
a. The high cost factor
b. The low efficiency
c. The low speed of operation
d. The need to remove the chip physically to reprogram it.

1.23 Which one of the following is not a hardware?
a. Magnetic tape b. VDU terminal
c. Printer d. Assembler

1.24 Multiple choice examination answer sheets can be evaluated automatically by:
a. OMR b. OCR
c. MICR d. Scanner

1.25 To create large size drawings, architects and engineers often use a device called:
a. Plotter b. Band printer
c. Line printer d. Laser printer

1.26 A program that converts a high-level language program to a set of machine instructions that can run on a computer is called a:
a. Compiler b. Debugger
c. Editor d. None of these

1.27 Indicate which of the following is not true about an interpreter:
a. Interpreter generates an object program from the source program
b. Interpreter is a kind of translator
c. Interpreter analyses each source statement every time it is to be executed
d. None of the above

1.28 Laser printer resolution is specified in terms of:
a. CPI b. API
c. DPI d. LSI

1.29 An operating system is:
a. A collection of hardware components
b. A collection of input output devices
c. A collection of software routines
d. None of these

2. State whether the following statements are True or False

2.1 Printers can be classified by the method of their printing.
2.2 A personal computer is an electronic data processing machine used by one person at a time.
2.3 Now-a-days, mostly digital computers are used.
2.4 Intermediate results of processing are held in a mass storage unit.
2.5 The job of an output unit is just the reverse of the job of an input unit.
2.6 Light pen and joystick are both pointing devices.
2.7 ROM can be used to store system's startup programs (the BIOS).
2.8 Even though the power supply is on, the RAM may lose its stored information, due to virus.
2.9 A smart terminal has in-built processing capability.
2.10 Fetching of an instruction for execution is done by the control unit.
2.11 An assembly language is a third generation, high-level language.
2.12 Partition table is found in hard disks.
2.13 An optical disk is a secondary storage device of the computer system.
2.14 A microsecond is 1000 times longer than a naonsecond.
2.15 A high-level language can be understood by a computer without using a translation.
2.16 A video camera is the most commonly used input device for capturing video data.
2.17 The most complicated part of a computer's sound system is the sound card.
2.18 EEPROM stands for Electrically Erasable Programmable Read Only Memory.
2.19 The machine languages of all computers are identical.
2.20 An object program is created by a compiler, from a source program at run-time.

3. Matching the following:

3.1	I/O devices and secondary storage unit	a. Semiconductor memory
3.2	Mass storage memory	b. Laser technology
3.3	Special memory unit within CPU	c. Secondary memory

3.4	Over all responsible for execution of program	d. Nibble
3.5	Terminal with keyboard and printer	e. RAM
3.6	Continuously variable signals	f. Analog
3.7	1 MB	g. Peripherals
3.8	A low-level language which is directly understandable by the computer system	h. Teleprinter
3.9	A non-volatile memory chip in which data is stored permanently and cannot be altered by the programmer	i. Multimedia
3.10	More than one media for information presentation	j. CPU
		k. 1024 KB
		l. ROM
		m. Machine language

4. Fill in the blanks

a. Inkjet	b. Central nervous system	c. Scanner
d. Memory	e. Sectors	f. Tracks
g. Photo diode	h. Register	i. Store
j. Main	k. Hard	l. Output
m. Laser	n. Assembly	o. Operating system
p. Biometric sensors	q. Flatbed scanner	r. Smart card

4.1 Final results of processing, before releasing, to output unit are held in __________ unit.

4.2 A printer is an __________ device.

4.3 A control unit acts as __________ for all components of a computer.

4.4 A general purpose __________ holds data and intermediate result during the execution of a program.

4.5 The function of the memory is to __________ information.

4.6 The __________ memory is directly addressed by the CPU.

4.7 Magnetic ink character reader is one type of __________.

4.8 Some plotters employ __________ in place of ink pens.

4.9 CD-ROM is read through the use of __________.

4.10 Invisible concentric circles on floppy disk are called __________.

4.11 An organized collection of software that controls the overall operations of a computer is called as __________.

4.12 The __________ printer is used for DTP application.

4.13 An assembler translates __________ language programs into machine language.

4.14 A __________ is like a copy machine.

4.15 __________ is the measuring of unique attributes of a human, such as DNA machine fingerprints, etc.

4.16 A __________ contains a small processor that holds certain information.

Answers

1.

1.1 a	1.2 b	1.3 c	1.4 c	1.5 b	1.6 a
1.7 b	1.8 a	1.9 c	1.10 a	1.11 d	1.12 c
1.13 c	1.14 b	1.15 c	1.16 d	1.17 a	1.18 d
1.19 a	1.20 b	1.21 a	1.22 d	1.23 d	1.24 a
1.25 a	1.26 a	1.27 d	1.28 c	1.29 c	

2.

2.1 T	2.2 T	2.3 F	2.4 F	2.5 T	2.6 T
2.7 T	2.8 T	2.9 T	2.10 T	2.11 F	2.12 T
2.13 T	2.14 T	2.15 F	2.16 T	2.17 T	2.18 T
2.19 F	2.20 T				

3.

3.1 g	3.2 c	3.3 e	3.4 j	3.5 h	3.6 f
3.7 k	3.8 m	3.9 l	3.10 i		

4.

4.1 d	4.2 l	4.3 b	4.4 h	4.5 i	4.6 j
4.7 c	4.8 a	4.9 g	4.10 f	4.11 o	4.12 m
4.13 n	4.14 q	4.15 p	4.16 r		

Short Questions with Answers

1. Define computer architecture.
2. What is optical memory?
3. What is the role of MAR and MDR?
4. What is the role of IR and PC?
5. What are the various units in the computer?
6. What is the function of I/O interface?
7. Name some of the I/O devices.
8. Differentiate between the following;
   a. Compiler and Interpreter
   b. Dot-matrix printer and laser printer
9. What are the functions of the following:
   a. Arithmetic Logic Unit (ALU)
   b. Control Unit (CU)

Answers to Short Questions

1. Computer architecture is defined as the functional operation of the individual hardware unit in a computer system and the flow of information among the control of units.
2. Optical or light based techniques for data storage, such memories usually employ optical disk which resemble magnetic disk in that they store binary information in concentric tracks on an electromechanically rotated disks. The information is read or written optically, however with a laser replacing the read write arm of a magnetic disk drive. Optical memory offers high storage capacities but their access rate is generally less than those of magnetic disk.
3. The MAR (Memory Address Register) is used to hold the address of the location to or from which data are to be transferred and the MDR (Memory Data Register) contains the data to be written into or read out of the addressed location.
4. Instruction Register (IR) contains the instruction being executed. Its output is available to the control circuits, which generate the timing signals for controlling the processing circuits needed to execute the instructions. The Program Counter (PC) register keeps track of the execution of the program. It contains the memory address of the instruction currently being executed. During the execution of the current instruction, the contents of the PC are updated to correspond to the address of the next instructions to be executed.
5. (a) Input unit
   (b) Output unit
   (c) Control unit
   (d) Memory unit
   (e) Arithmetic and logical unit
6. The function is to coordinate the transfer of data between the CPU and external devices.
7. (a) Video terminals
   (b) Video displays
   (c) Alphanumeric displays
   (d) Graphics displays

(e) Flat panel displays
(f) Printers
(g) Plotters

8. a. Compiler and Interpreter
   1. A program which translates high-level language program into machine language program is known as a compiler. A compiler goes through the entire program and then translates the entire program into machine codes.
      An interpreter is a program which translates one statement of a high-level language program into machine code and executes it at a time.
   2. A compiler shows a list of errors along with line numbers at the end of program execution, whereas interpreter shows errors line by line.
   3. An interpreter is smaller program as compared to the compiler.
   4. The compiler is faster than an interpreter.

   The object code program produced by the compiler is permanently saved for future reference, whereas the object code of the statement produced by an interpreter is not saved. Thus, the presence of source program is always required for the interpreter. If the instruction is used next time, it must be interpreted once again and translated into machine code.

   b. Dot-atrix printer and laser printer

   Dot-matrix printer
   1. Dot-matrix printer is a type of impact printer.
   2. These printers print characters on the paper by striking the paper with a print head and using an inked ribbon present between the print head and the paper.
   3. Print quality produced by a dot-matrix printer is not very good but they are low-cost printers.
   4. Printing speed is low and noise level is very high.

   Laser printer
   1. Laser printer is a type of non-impact printer.
   2. These printers print the characters without engaging the print mechanism with the print surface. These printer use laser beam technology.
   3. Laser printers are quiet and produce high-quality output, but they are expensive.
   4. These printers are faster than dot-matrix printers and they print one page at a time.

9. The major components of a central processing unit are:
   Arithmetic Logic Unit: All calculations are performed and all comparisons are made in the ALU. The data and instructions, stored in the primary memory prior to processing, are transferred to the ALU where processing takes place. All processing and manipulation of data is done in the ALU.

   Intermediate results generated in the ALU are temporarily transferred back to the primary memory until needed again. After the completion of processing, the final results available in the primary memory are sent to an output device, such as printer, etc.

   Control Unit: It is responsible for managing and coordinating all the activities of the computer system. CU obtains instructions from the program stored in the main memory, interprets the instructions and issues signals that cause other units of the system to perform their functions. The control unit does not process data but it acts like our central nervous system for the other data-manipulating components of the computer.

DESCRIPTIVE TYPE QUESTIONS

1. How is an OCR device different from an MICR?
2. Compare the advantages and limitations of a mouse and a keyboard as data input devices.
3. What is ROM? Differentiate between EPROM and EEPROM.
4. State the function of a joystick and that of a light pen.
5. What is the difference between an input device and an off-line data entry device?
6. Discuss the roles played by the various components of CPU.
7. The ROM contains the essential information and the hard disk contains all relevant programs. What purpose does the RAM serve?
8. What are expansion cards? How many types of expansion cards can be used in a computer system?
9. What is the difference between a graphical printer and a plotter? Compare the two printers in terms of speed, accuracy or quality of output.
10. What type of keys, other than alphabetic and digits, are available on a keyboard and for what purpose? How is a key pressed on the keyboard interpreted by the computer?
11. What is a compiler? Give the difference between a compiler and an interpreter.
12. Explain primary memory and its properties and types?
13. Discuss advantages of disadvantages of:
    (a) Magnetic disks
    (b) Magnetic tapes
14. With a neat diagram, explain the working of a mouse.
15. Distinguish between static RAM and dynamic RAM
16. State basic units of the computer. Name the sub units that make up the CPU and give the function of each of the units.
17. What is the function of memory? What are its measuring units?
18. Difference between inkjet and laser printer?
19. What is cache memory? How is it different from primary memory?
20. What are registers in a computer system?
21. Discuss the methodology used for creating special effects in movies.
22. Explain the various components of CPU with the help of a sketch diagram.
23. What is function of ALU in a microprocessor?
24. What are the types of memories available in the computer system? How are they organized in a hierarchy?
25. What is pointing device? Name different types of pointing device.

CHAPTER 3

Operating Systems

3.1 INTRODUCTION

An Operating System (OS) is a set of system software programs in a computer that regulates the ways application software programs use the computer hardware and the ways that users control the computer. For hardware functions, such as input/output and memory space allocation, operating system programs act as an intermediary between application programs and the computer hardware. Although application programs are usually executed directly by the hardware. Operating system is also a field of study within Applied Computer Science.

The job of an operating system for a computer is mainly to manage the hardware and software resources of the system. In desktops or laptops, the hardware resources include processes, hard disk, memory, disk space, mouse, printers, other peripherals, etc., whereas the software resources are the various software applications being used on that desktop or laptop. Operating systems also play a very important role in providing a consistent interface for the applications irrespective of the hardware or peripherals used. There may be different drivers used along with the operating systems for this purpose.

3.2 BASIC CONCEPTS OF OS

An operating system is a master control program that runs the computer and acts as a scheduler. It controls the flow of signals from CPU (Central Processing Unit) to various parts of the computer. It is the first program loaded (copied) into the computer's memory after the computer is switched on. Some popular operating systems are Windows XP, Windows 7, OS/2, UNIX, Linux, etc. IBM (International Business Machines) Mainframe computers use MVS (Multiple Virtual Storage), VM (Virtual Memory) or VSE (Virtual Storage Extended) operating systems.

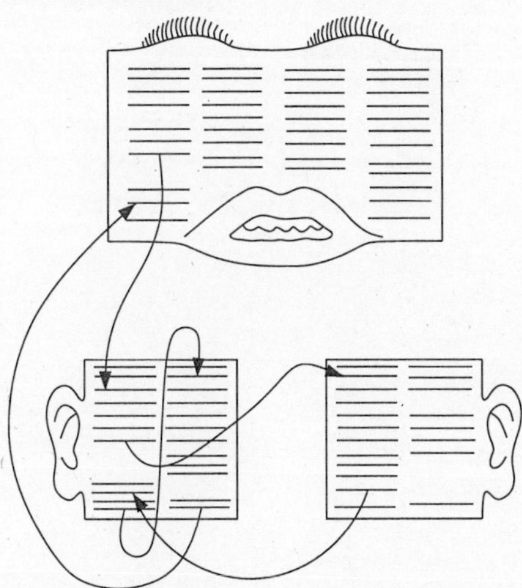

Programs talk to each other

Figure 3.1 Program talks with an Operating System loaded in the main memory of a computer

The operating system is an important component of the computer system, because it sets the standards for the application programs that run on it. All programs must be written to "**talk to**" the operating system (See Figure 3.1).

3.2.1 Need of Operating System

User interacts with the application programs but the application programs do not access the hardware resources directly. Hardware resources include input/output devices, primary memory, secondary memory (like hard disk drives, etc.) and the microprocessor. Therefore, an operating system is required to access and use these resources. The application programs are so created that they talk with the operating system to get access to the resources.

☞ *An Operating System (OS) is the first program that is loaded (copied) into the computer's main memory, when a computer is switched on. The efficiency of any operating system is measured in terms of its throughput, turn around time and the response time.*

The two primary objectives of an operating system are:

(a) To enable running of application programs.
(b) To manage the different computer hardware resources.

3.3 FUNCTIONS OF AN OPERATING SYSTEM

An operating system performs the following functions:

(a) *Processor Management*: The operating system assigns processors (if a computer has more than one processor) to the different tasks that must be performed by the computer.
(b) *Memory Management*: It (OS) allocates the main memory and secondary memory to the system programs, user programs and data.
(c) *Input/Output (I/O) Management*: It carries out input/output management and co-ordinates and assigns different input and output devices.
(d) *File Management*: It manages files on various storage devices and transfers these files from one storage device to another. It also allows the files to be easily changed and modified through the use of text editors or some other file manipulation software packages.
(g) *Security Management*: It establishes data security and integrity. That is, it keeps different programs and data in such a manner that they do not interfere with each other. Moreover, it also protects data from being destroyed by any other user.

The main functions of an operating system, in short, can be categorized as follows:

(a) **Resource Management** (Processor management, memory management, device management).

(b) **Process Management** (Job scheduling, task management).

(c) **Data Management** (File management and Input/Output management).

(d) **Security management.**

☞ *Some of the popular operating systems are MS-DOS (Microsoft Disk Operating System), Windows XP, Vista, UNIX, Linux, Solaris and OS/2.*

All operating systems can be classified into four categories:

(a) ***Single User Operating System*:** Operating system which allows only one user to work on a computer at a time is known as single user operating system. Examples include DOS, Windows XP, etc.

(b) ***Multiuser Operating System*:** A Multiuser operating system allows a number of users to work together on a single computer. Each user will be provided a terminal connected to a single computer. Examples include Linux, UNIX, Windows 2000, etc.

(c) ***Single Tasking Operating System*:** Operating system which can execute only a single job/program at a time is known as single tasking operating system, e.g., MS-DOS.

(d) ***Multitasking Operating System*:** Multitasking operating system supports execution of more than one job at a time. Most of today's operating systems, such as Windows 2000, OS/2, UNIX, Linux, etc., support multitasking.

Windows 7 are the later versions of Windows desktop operating system for the PC (Personal Computer). Windows XP brings a new, more personalized look to the desktop that will also make it easier for users to scan or import images. It is meant to acquire music files on the Web and transfer them to portable devices. Windows 7 allows different family members to use their own desktop and personal set of files. The Start menu has been redesigned to make the most-used programs easiest to find. Windows XP as well as Windows 7 come in a Professional version and a Home Edition version.

3.3.1 Processor Management

The OS assigns processor (if a computer has more than one processor) to different tasks that must be performed by the computer system. Whenever the OS finds any processor idle, one of the processes waiting to be executed is assigned to this idle processor. The objective of the Processor Management module of the OS is to ensure that a process is run on each processor at all times. These can be multitasking or multiprogramming.

Multitasking

The concept of multitasking allows the user to perform more than one job at the same time on a computer. Most of today's operating systems, such as Windows 9X, OS/2, UNIX, Linux, etc., support multitasking. For example, when you open two or more than two software packages at the same time, the Windows operating system does multitasking. The operating system is able to keep track of where you are in each of these applications and switch from one application to another without losing track. All this is done with the help of CPU processor and OS.

Multiprogramming

To increase resource utilization, multiprogramming technique of processing was developed. In multiprogramming, the CPU runs several programs at the 'same time'. The phrase 'same time' is incorrect to use in case of single processor computers, but multiprogramming is implemented in such a way that it appears as if many programs are being executed *concurrently*.

Multiprogramming keeps CPU busy, switching its attention from one program to another. For example, while one program is waiting for some input or output operation, another program can use the processor because of the high speed of processor. This is shown in Figure 3.2.

In Figure 3.2, the CPU's idle time is utilized by the slow input and output devices. Moreover, each program takes necessary share of CPU's time, thus making the system very efficient.

Threads: A thread is a basic unit of CPU utilization. It comprises a thread ID, a program counter, a register set, and a stack. It shares with other threads belonging to the same process its code section, data section, and other operating system resources, such

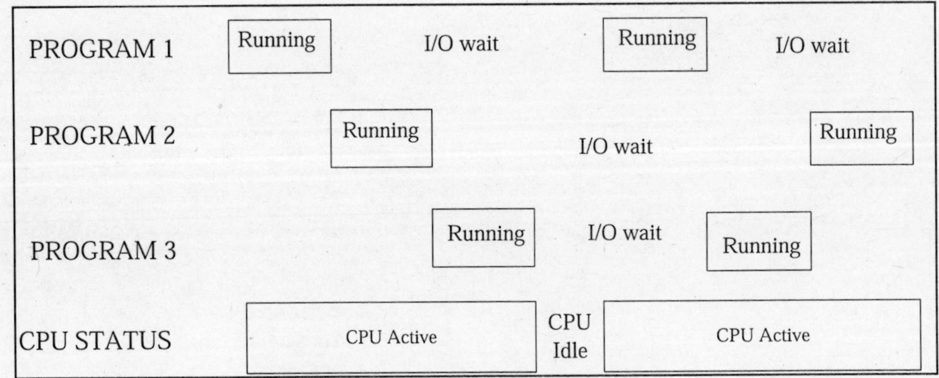

Figure 3.2 Concept of multiprogramming

as open files and signals. A traditional process has a single thread of control. If a process has multiple threads of control, it can perform more than one task at a time.

An application typically is implemented as a separate process with several threads of control. A Web browser might have one thread display images or text while another thread retrieves data from the network. .For example, a word processor may have a thread for displaying graphics, another thread for responding to keystrokes from the user, and a third thread for performing spelling and grammar checking in the background.

Process Scheduling In a single-processor system, only one process can run at a time. Others wait until the CPU is free and can be rescheduled. The objective of multiprogramming is to have some processes running at all times, to maximize CPU utilization.

Multiprogramming operating system allows more than one process to be loaded into the present memory at a time and for the loaded process to share the CPU using time multiplexing. The scheduling mechanism is the part of the process manager that handles the removal of the running process from the CPU and the selection of another process on the basis of particular device.

Scheduling refers to a set of policies and mechanisms built into the operating system that govern the *order* in which all pending works are completed by the computer.

A *Scheduler* is a part of OS that selects the next job to be admitted into the system and the next process to be run. Different OSs use different kinds of scheduling methods. Some such methods are described in what follows:

Scheduling Queues

When the process enters into the system, they are put into a queue. This queue consists of all processes in the system. The OS also has other queues.

Device queue is a queue for which a list of processes waiting for a particular I/O device. Each device has its own device queue. Figure 3.3 shows the queuing diagram of process scheduling. In the Figure 3.3, queue is represented by rectangular box. The circles represent the resources that serve the queues. The arrows indicate the flow of processes in the system.

Queues are of two types : ready queue and set of device queues. The newly arrived process is put in the ready queue. Processes are stay in ready queue for allocating the CPU. Once the CPU is allow to the process, then process will execute. While executing the process, one of the several events are occured

1. The process can issue an I/O request and then place in an I/O queue.
2. The process can create new sub-process and waits for its termination.
3. The process can be removed forcibly from the CPU, as a result of interrupt and put back in the ready queue.

Two State Process Model

Process may be in one of two states:

(a) Running

(b) Not Running

When the process is created by OS, that process enters into the system in the running state.

Processes that are not running are hold in queue, waiting their turn to execute. Each entry in the queue is a printer to a particular process. Queue is implemented by using linked list. Use of dispatcher is as follows:

- When a process interrupted, that process is transferred in the waiting queue. If the process has completed or aborted, the process is discarded.
- In either case, the dispatcher then selects a process from the queue to be executed.

Schedulers

Schedulers are of three types.

(a) Long Term Scheduler

(b) Short Term Scheduler

(b) Medium Term Scheduler

Long Term Scheduler: Long term scheduler determines which programs are admitted to the system for processing. Job scheduler selects processes from the queue and loads them into memory for execution. Process loads into the memory for CPU

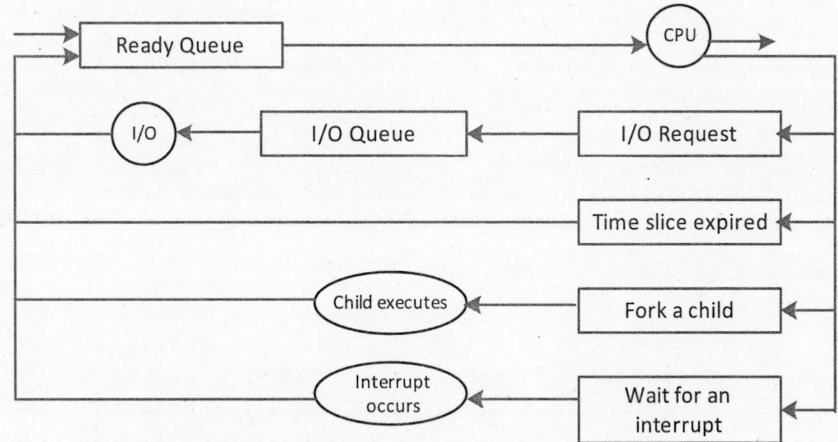

Figure 3.3 Queuing Diagram of Process Scheduling

scheduler. The primary objective of the job scheduler is to provide a balanced mix of jobs, such as I/O bound and processor bound. It also controls the degree of multiprogramming. If the degree of multiprogramming is stable, then the average rate of process creation must be equal to the average departure rate of processes leaving the system.

On same systems, the long term scheduler may be absent. Time sharing operating systems have no long term scheduler. When process changes the state from new to ready, then there is a long term scheduler.

Short Term Scheduler: It is also called CPU scheduler. The main objective is increasing system performance in accordance with the chosen set of criteria. It is the change of Ready state to running state of the process. CPU scheduler selects from the processes that are ready to execute and allocates the CPU to one of them.

Short term scheduler also known as dispatcher, execute most frequently and makes the fine grained decision of which process to execute next. Short term scheduler is faster than long term scheduler.

Medium Term Scheduler: Medium term scheduling is part of the swapping function. It removes the processes from the memory. It reduces the degree of multiprogramming. The medium term scheduler is in charge of handling the swapped out-processes.

Running process may become suspended by making an I/O request. Suspended processes cannot make any progress towards completion. In this condition, remove the process from memory and make space for other process.
Suspended process moves to the secondary storage is called swapping, and the process is said to be swapped out or rolled out. Swapping may be necessary to improve the process mix.

Preemptive Scheduling In this type of scheduling, each process is allocated a priority level. Depending on the priority level, the OS can run a process of high priority. The OS may remove a low priority process in Running state, in order to allow a higher priority process to run. Figure 3.4 shows the different states of a process in preemptive scheduling.

With preemptive scheduling, a running process may be replaced by a higher-priority process at any time. This is accomplished by invoking the scheduler. Scheduler is invoked whenever an event that changes the state of a process is detected. If a higher priority process has changed state from being dormant or suspended to Ready state, the scheduler will choose this process to be the next process to run.

> *If a running process is preempted by a higher-priority process, it remains in the Ready state rather than in the Suspended state, since the only resource it lacks is the processor.*

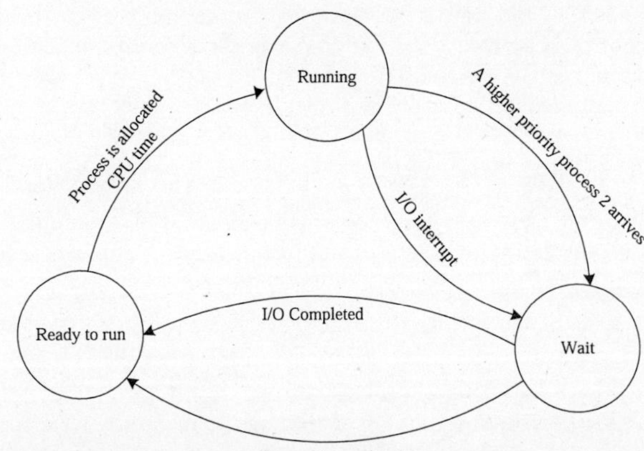

Figure 3.4 States of a process in preemptive scheduling

Non-preemptive Scheduling In this type of scheduling, each process continues to run till it terminates or requires an Input/Output (I/O) or some synchronization signal. Figure 3.5 shows the different states of a process in a non-preemptive scheduling.

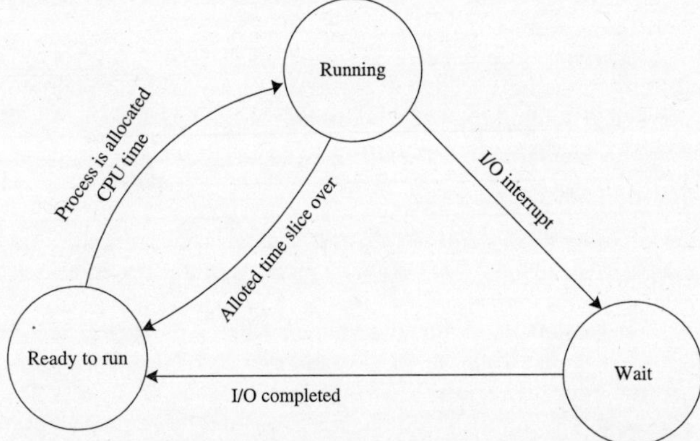

Figure 3.5 States of a process in non-preemptive scheduling

In non-preemptive scheduling, once scheduled, a selected job runs till it is completed. The running process retains ownership of allocated resources, including the processor, until it voluntarily surrenders control to OS. In other words, the running process is not forced to relinquish ownership of the processor when a higher priority process becomes ready for execution. However, when the running process becomes suspended as a result of its own action, say by waiting for an I/O completion, another ready process may be scheduled.

> *In a non-preemptive scheme, each process retains the CPU until it completes its job or awaits for an I/O operation.*

Co-operative Scheduling In this type of scheduling, the responsibility for releasing control is placed in the hands of the application program and not managed by the operating system. That is, each process is expected to relinquish control to other processes periodically. Note that this scheduling is different from the non-preemptive scheduling, because in the latter type of scheduling the control is transferred to OS when the process waits for some I/O operation.

First Come, First Served (FCFS) Scheduling: In this method, the workload is processed in the order of arrival, with *no preemption*. As a consequence of no preemption, component utilization and the system throughput rate may be low. Here, short jobs may suffer delay, especially when one or more long jobs are being executed in the system.

Shortest Remaining Time Next (SRTN) Scheduling: In Shortest Remaining Time Next (SRTN) scheduling policy, whenever an event, that makes a new process ready, occurs, the scheduler is invoked. The scheduler then compares the remaining processor execution time of all the running and ready-to-run processes, including that of the newcomers. The process requiring least time to complete execution is selected as the next process to run. Preferred treatment of short jobs in SRTN scheduling tends to result in an increased waiting time of long jobs as compared with FCFS (First Come First Served) basis scheduling.

Round Robin Scheduling In this type of scheduling, each process is given the CPU's attention for only a fraction of a second. The processes are run in a sequential order. In other words, each active process is given 'time slice' in rotation (See Figure 3.6). None of the processes can run for more than one time slice when there are others waiting in the ready queue. If the process needs more time to complete after exhausting its time slice, it is placed at the end of queue to await for the next allocation. Implementation of Round Robin scheduling requires support of an *interval timer*. The timer is set to interrupt the OS whenever a time slice expires and thus forces the scheduler to be invoked. In case of suicidal termination (a process terminating before completing its execution), resetting of the timer is required.

☞ *Round Robin scheduling is regarded as a fair and disciplined scheduling. It is also one of the best known scheduling disciplines for achieving good and evenly distributed terminal response time.*

3.3.2 Memory Management

Memory Management module of an operating system takes care of allocation and de-allocation of main memory to various processes. It allocates the main memory and secondary memory to the system programs, user programs and data. For executing a program, its copy must be loaded into the main memory. Also, a program would require main memory to hold data from disk files, the contents of which it is reading or manipulating at the execution time.

An operating system manages the memory of a computer so that it can be used efficiently. The tasks of OS along these lines are:

(a) Protecting programs including itself (operating system) from accidental erasure from main memory.

(b) Handling programs that exceed the physical limitations of the main memory, i.e., using the virtual memory (virtual memory is the hard disk space used as a part of main memory by the OS).

(c) Protecting users and programs from one other, i.e., sharing of the single main memory among multiple programs and different users.

(d) Providing memory protection, i.e., preventing programs from interfering with one other. Also users would be prevented from interfering with the work of other users.

Other tasks under memory management are detailed in the following paragraphs.

Protecting Programs from Accidental Erasure

If the operating system is not loaded in a Read Only Memory (ROM) chip, one of its jobs is to protect itself. OS does this by knowing how much memory it would occupy and disabling any writing in this area of main memory. A similar approach enables the operating system to protect other computer programs. When a computer program is first stored in the main memory of the CPU, the operating system assigns it a fixed size of memory space and protects these memory locations from encroachments by any other programs.

Virtual Memory

Application programs can be of a size that needs main memory of a size larger than the main memory available on the computer. In such cases, application programs access hard disks as an extension of the main memory, known as *virtual memory*. Users, thus

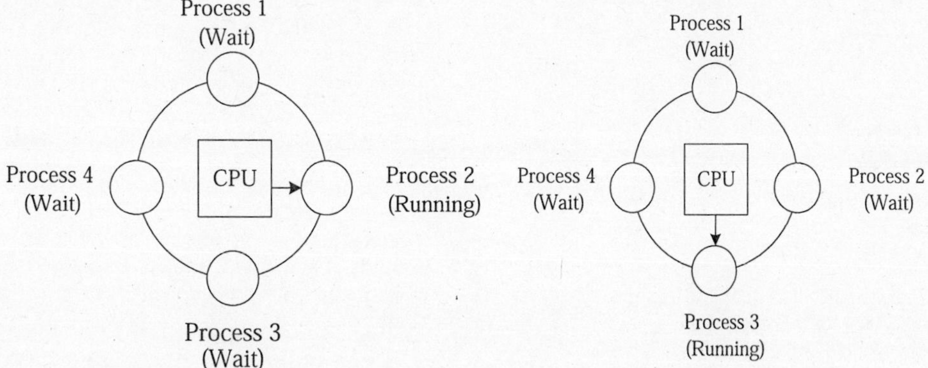

Figure 3.6 CPU attention is switched to adjacent processes in each time slice

can generate programs that need larger main memory-size even though computer has a smaller main memory. This is achieved by treating the memory-addresses of the *hard* disks as a consecutive extension of the memory-addresses of the *main memory*. This technique is called *virtual memory* and is managed by the operating system, in association with the application program.

☞ ***Virtual memory*** *is the auxiliary or secondary memory of the computer system, seen as if it is the main memory by the application program.*

Virtual memory scheme gives users an *illusion* of working with a large block of contiguous memory space (perhaps even larger than real main memory), when in actuality most of their work is done in a small primary memory. In a computer that implements virtual memory system, the user has the option to use part of or more of auxiliary memory. Users can then freely employ much greater memory space than is available in the main memory. The addresses used by the user-generated program refers to a virtual memory which is outside the address of main memory. The *virtual memory system*'s job is to map this virtual address into the real main memory address. This *mapping* is done dynamically at run time of the program.

☞ *The address used by a programmer is called* ***virtual address*** *and a set of such addresses is called the* ***address space.*** *An address in main memory is called a* ***location*** *or* ***physical address*** *and a set of such addresses is called the* ***memory space***.

Paging

Although there are many methods by which the mapping is done but we will learn address mapping using the technique of *paging*. The address space and memory space are divided into equal size groups.

Suppose we have an auxiliary memory of capacity 16K and main memory of capacity of 4K. Then the address field of the instructions in the user-generated program, will have 14 bits (2^{14} = 16K). But the physical memory address of main memory must be specified with 12 bits (2^{12} = 16,384K). The conversion of 14 bits virtual address into 12-bit real physical address is the job of the memory address table.

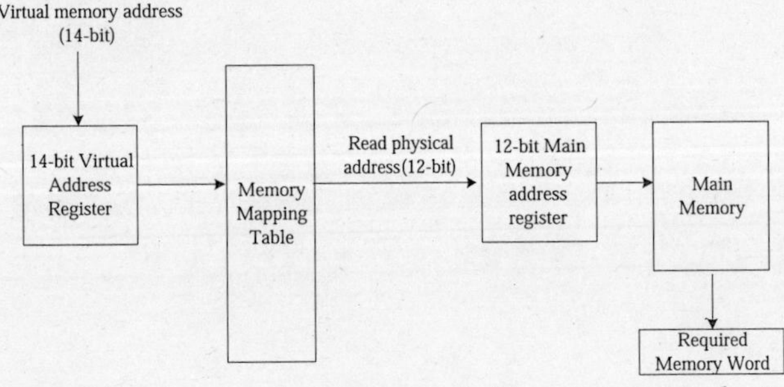

Figure 3.7 Mapping the 14-bit virtual address into 12-bit physical address

As explained above, for execution of user's program, the 14-bit address needs to be mapped into 12-bit main memory address. The mapping is a dynamic operation in the sense that whenever a word is referenced using the 14-bit address, mapping system immediately converts the address into actual 12-bit address.

As shown in Figure 3.7, the virtual address given by the user is mapped into a physical address of main memory and the required word is obtained.

☞ *The fixed size groups of address space are called pages or segments and the fixed size groups of memory space are called blocks.*

In the above example, suppose we decide to divide the address space and memory space into groups having 1K words each, then the 16K virtual memory is divided into 16 *pages* and main memory is divided into 4 *blocks* (See Figure 3.8).

Virtual Memory
Page 0
Page 1
Page 2
-
-
-
-
-
-
-
-
-
-
-
Page 14
Page 15

Virtual Memory
16K = 2^{14}
16 pages each of 1K

Main Memory
Block 0
Block 1
Block 2
Block 3

Main Memory
4K = 2^{12}
4 blocks each of 1K

Figure 3.8 Division of address space and memory space into equal size groups

Fixed-size pages are read into main memory as and when needed. Since, there are 16 pages and only 4 blocks, at a time only 4 pages can remain in the main memory. If the word requested by the CPU is found in the memory space, it is well and good, otherwise the required page is searched in the auxiliary memory, acting as the virtual memory. If found, it is fetched and stored in the main memory replacing another page that previously existed in the main memory space.

A *memory page table* is prepared and kept in the main memory. The memory page table contains the list of all the 16 pages of virtual memory and the block number where the *page* is stored in the main memory. There is also a *presence bit* which indicates whether the *page* is present in the main memory or not. For example, if at a moment the pages 3, 5, 6 and 8 are present in the main memory then the content of memory page table will shown in Figure 3.9.

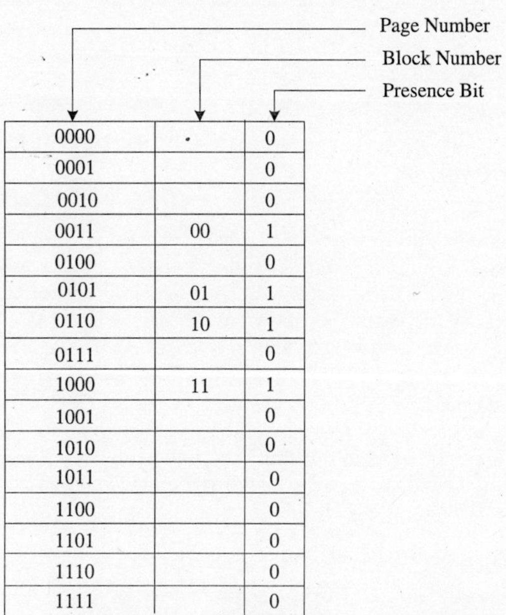

Page Number	Block Number	Presence Bit
0000		0
0001		0
0010		0
0011	00	1
0100		0
0101	01	1
0110	10	1
0111		0
1000	11	1
1001		0
1010		0
1011		0
1100		0
1101		0
1110		0
1111		0

Figure 3.9 Contents of Memory Page Table

The first 4-bits of a virtual memory address will specify the page number where the word is stored. Similarly the first 2 bits of a physical address will specify the block number of the memory where the word is stored.

The 4-bit page number is taken from the virtual address and searched in the memory page table. If the *presence bit* against this page number is 1, then the block number is taken and is written in place of the page number in the address. Thus, a 14-bit virtual address (10 bit word address + 4-bit page number) is mapped into a 12-bit physical address (10-bit word address + 2-bit block number). The block number is searched in the main memory and then the word located at the address is fetched.

The whole process of mapping from virtual address to physical address is shown in Figure 3.10.

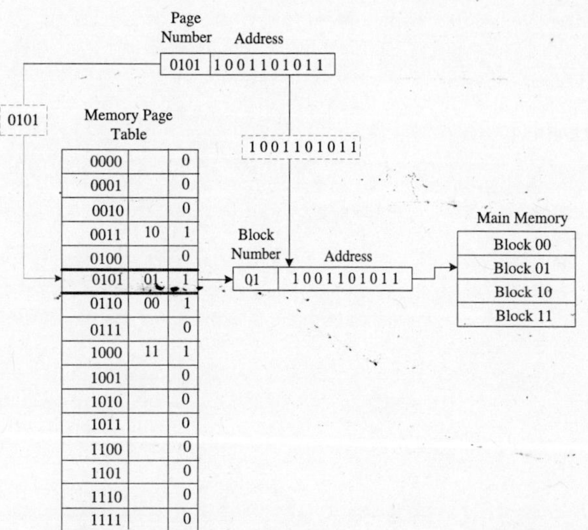

Figure 3.10 Mapping using memory page table

Page Replacement

When a requested page is not present in the main memory, i.e., the *presence bit* against the page number is 0 in the memory page table, then the condition is called a *page fault*. Under this condition, the required page need to be fetched from the auxiliary memory and brought to store it in the main memory. If the main memory has free space to store the page, then it is well and good. But, if the memory is full, one of the pages existing in the memory must be moved to auxiliary memory and the requested page must be shifted to main memory. The method used to decide which page can be removed from main memory can be any of the following:

(a) *First In First Out* (FIFO): In FIFO method, the page which arrived first i.e., the oldest page, is removed when a new page needs to be brought into the main memory. This method is based on the principle that the page which had arrived first is less likely to be referenced now.

Whenever a page is loaded into the main memory its identification number (ID) is pushed into a FIFO stack. Whenver a page needs to be removed the page whose ID is at the top of the stack is removed. FIFO method has the advantage that it is easy to implement.

(b) *Least Recently Used* (LRU): In LRU method, the page which had not been used recently is removed from the main memory. It is based on the principle that the page which had not been used till now is not going to be referenced in near future also. It is better to remove a least recently used page than a least recently loaded page.

In this method, each page in the main memory has a counter associated with them. The counter is incremented by 1 at fixed intervals of time. When a page is referenced, its counter is set to 0. Thus, counter tells the age of a page. Hence this counter is also called *ageing register*. When a page needs to be removed, the page with the highest counter value is removed.

Swapping

Swapping is the process of transferring a block of data from secondary storage (such as hard disk) to main memory and vice versa. The former is known as *swapping in* of data and the latter is known as *swapping out* of data. This is done to accommodate larger size of the program, to be executed, in a small sized main memory of the computer.

3.3.3 File Management

File system is of the most visible aspects of the OS. Data is stored in a computer system as *files*. The File Management module of the operating system would manage files held on various storage devices as well as transfer of files from one storage device to another. Thus, file management takes care of organization, storage, retrieval, naming, sharing and protection of different files. It also allows files to be read and modified by using text editors or some other file manipulation software packages.

The file management system allows the retrieval and storage of files by name, keeps track of the mappings, allocates and frees space, allows the mounting and unmounting of file structures, and provides other functions required to maintain the structures of the file system.

(a) Directory structures for each I/O device in the system and tools to access and move around these structures. The directory structure provisions are made to move easily from one structure to another.

(b) It also protects files and limit file access to authorized users.

File management systems are particularly important in systems in which secondary storage devices are shared in common by multiple users, since they provide a directory system that assures that there is no duplicate use of physical storage.

The basic file system needs only to issue generic commands to the appropriate device driver to read and write physical blocks on the disk.

The file organization module knows about files and their logical blocks, as well as physical blocks. By knowing the type of file allocation used and the location of the file, the file organization module can translate logical block addresses to physical block addresses for the basic file system to transfer.

Each file's logical blocks are numbered from 0 (or 1) through N, whereas the physical blocks containing the data usually do not match the logical numbers, so a translation is needed to locate each block. The file organization module also includes the free-space manager, which tracks unallocated and provides these blocks to the file organization module when requested.

The logical file system uses the directory structure to provide the file organization module with the information the latter needs, given a symbolic file name. The logical file system is also responsible for protection and security. To create a new file, an application program calls the logical file system.

The logical file system knows the format of the directory structures. To create a new file, it reads the appropriate directory into memory, updates it with the new entry, and writes it back to the disk. Once the file is found the associated information, such as size, owner, access permissions and data block locations are generally copied into a table in memory, referred to as the open-file table, consisting of information about all the currently opened files.

The first reference to a file causes the directory structure to be searched and the directory entry for this file to be copied into the table of opened files. The index into this table is returned to the user program, and all further references are made through the index rather than with a symbolic name. The name given to the index varies. UNIX systems refer to it as a file descriptor, Windows/NT as a file handle, and other systems as a file control block.

3.3.4 I/O Device Management

The Input/Output (I/O) Device Management module of the operating system coordinates and assigns different input and output devices, namely terminals, printers, disk drives, tape drives etc. It controls all I/O devices, keeps track of I/O requests, issues commands to these devices and takes measures which would ensure that data is transmitted efficiently and correctly to and from I/O devices.

There are three ways by which data can be sent from the I/O device to the memory by the CPU. These are discussed as follows:

Programmed I/O

In Programmed I/O mode, when an input/output instruction is encountered in a program, the CPU checks the input/output flag. It keeps on checking the flag till the flag is set to 1. When the flag is set to 1, the CPU transfers data from the I/O device to the memory. This method is also known as *polling*.

Polling

Polling is a method of input/output handling by CPU wherein the CPU continuously interrogates devices attached to it to determine if a device wishes to transmit. It a peripheral device is ready to transmit, it sends back an Acknowledgement Code (ACK) and the transmission sequence begins.

Interrupt-initiated I/O

Another method is to let CPU concentrate on some other program and use an *interrupt signal* to inform the CPU that the input/output flag is set to 1.

Direct Memory Access (DMA)

Direct Memory Access (DMA) is a technique for moving data directly between main memory and peripheral equipment without needing CPU's intervention. In other mode of data transfer, CPU was required to work as an intermediate between the I/O devices and the main memory, where data is ultimately stored or read from. But in the DMA method, the input/output devices directly writes or reads information from the main memory without the interference of CPU.

SPOOLING (Simultaneous Peripheral Operations On Lines)

Spooling is a technique used to reduce the speed mismatch between the CPU and input/output devices, such as printers. In this process, data which needs to be sent to an input device or output device, is first place on either a magetic tape or disk. This is illustrated in Figure 3.11. Jobs are read in via a card reader and copied into a disk file. Similarly printable output is writen to another disk file before sending to output device.

☞ *Spooling mecahanism increase system performance cosiderably. This is because, the spooling opertions are run when the CPU is idle. Also the I/O operations are incurred by a much faster disk system.*

3.3.5 Security Management

Security management module of the OS ensures data security and integrity. That is, it protects data and programs stored in the computer system from destruction and unauthorized access. It

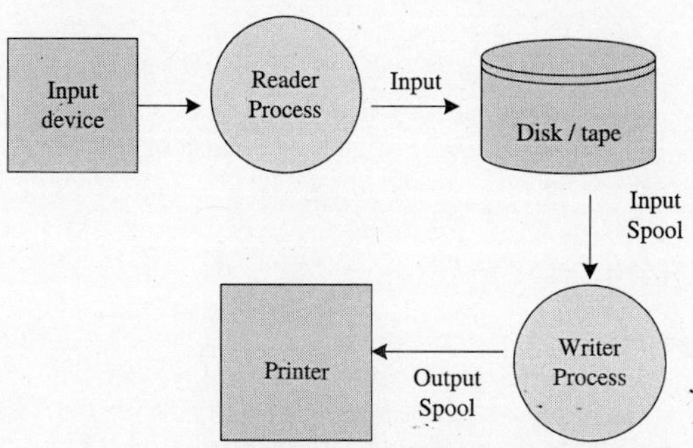

Figure 3.11 Spooling Process

keeps the different programs and data, which are executed concurrently in the memory, in such a manner that they do not interfere with each other. Moreover, it protects files from being accessed or modified by unauthorized users.

Security of operating systems has long been a concern because of highly sensitive data held on computers, both of a commercial and military nature. For a computer to be secure depends on a number of technologies working properly. A modern operating system provides access to a number of resources, which are available to the software running on the system, and to external devices like networks via the kernel.

The operating system must be capable of distinguishing between requests which should be allowed to be processed, and others which should not be allowed. While some systems may simply distinguish between "privileged" and "non-privileged", some have a form of requester identity, such as a *username*. The process of establishing identity is known as *authentication*.

☞ ***Authentication*** *involves quoting of a username and password. Other methods of authentication include magnetic cards, biometric data, etc.*

Once a user is authenticated he may be allowed/disallowed to certain resources of the system using *authorization*. The concept of authorization says that the particular services and resources accessible by the requester once logged into a system are based on either the requester's user account or the variously configured groups of users to which the requester belongs.

In addition to the allow/disallow model of security, a system with a high-level of security will also offer *auditing* options. This would allow tracking of requests (such as, "who has been reading this file?").

Security management can be further classified as follows:

External Security

External requests from outside the computer, such as a login at a connected console or some kind of network connection involves the need for external security. External requests are often passed through device drivers to the operating system's kernel, where they can be passed onto applications, or carried out directly. At the front line of external network security are hardware devices known as firewalls or intrusion detection/prevention systems. At the operating system level, we have internal security.

Internal Security

Internal security, or security from an already running program in the same system is only possible if all possibly harmful requests must be carried out through interrupts to the operating system kernel. If programs can directly access hardware and resources, they cannot be secured. Internal security is especially relevant for multiuser systems wherein each user of the system have private files that the other users should not tamper with or read. Internal security is also vital if auditing is to be of any use, since a program can potentially bypass the operating system, inclusive of bypassing auditing.

There are a number of software firewalls available, as well as intrusion detection/prevention systems. Most modern operating systems include a software firewall, which is enabled by default.

☞ *A software firewall can be configured to allow or deny network traffic to or from a service or application running on the operating system.*

In modern operating systems, there are many in-built security modules to prevent these malicious threats. As an example, with Windows 7 OS, there is a program called Microsoft Security Essentials to prevent all the security holes.

3.4 TYPES OF OPERATING SYSTEMS

Operating Systems may be classified into the following types:

(a) Single-user Operating System
(b) Multiuser Operating System
(c) Single-tasking Operating System
(d) Multitasking Operating System
(e) Time Sharing Operating System
(f) Real-time Operating System
(g) Network Operating System
(h) Distributed Operating System
(i) Interactive (Graphical User Interface or GUI-Based) Operating System

3.4.1 Single-user Operating System

Operating system which allows only one user to work on a computer at a time is known as single user operating system. Examples include Windows XP, Windows 7, etc.

3.4.2 Multiuser Operating System

A Multiuser operating system allows a number of users to work together on a single computer. UNIX is a multiuser operating system. It is not that all users will give instructions to a computer at the same time. Each user will be provided with a terminal and all such terminals will be connected to the single computer system.

☞ *Multiuser operating system running on a computer will manage the work of all the users, without letting them know that they all are actually working on a single computer.*

3.4.3 Single-tasking Operating System

Operating system which can execute a single job at a time is known as single-tasking operating system. For example, MS-DOS

(Microsoft Disk Operating System) is a single tasking operating system because you can open and run only one application in DOS (Disk Operating System), at one time.

3.4.4 Multitasking Operating System

Multitasking operating system allows the user to perform more than one job at the same time on a computer. Most of today's operating systems, such as Windows XP, OS/2 (Operating System/2), UNIX, Linux etc. support multitasking. For example, when you open MS Word and Internet Explorer at the same time, the Windows operating system is doing multitasking. The operating system is able to keep track of where you are in each of these applications and switch from one application package to another without losing track.

3.4.5 Real-time Operating System

Real-time operating systems work towards providing immediate processing and also responding to user's commands in a very short time. Such an operating system is more commonly used in chemical industry for process control and scientific processing like airplane control and space vehicle control operations. Success of a real-time system does not depend only on the correctness of the result, but also on the timeliness of the result. A correct answer obtained after the expiration of time limit is as bad as a wrong answer. Some examples of real time operating systems are HP-RT (Hewlett Packard Real-Time) and VTWorks.

3.4.6 Network Operating System (NOS)

Network Operating System (NOS) is an operating system specifically designed to support interconnection of several computers. NOS provides support for multiuser operations as well as administrative, security and network management functions. Some examples of NOSs are Novell's Netware, Windows 2003, Artisoft's LANtastic etc.

☞ *A network operating system has to acknowledge and respond to requests from many workstations, managing network access, resource allocation and sharing, data protection as well as error control. It provides for printer, file-system, database and application sharing.*

3.4.7 Distributed Operating System

A distributed operating system hides the existence of multiple computers (interconnected by a network) from the user. That is, the user remains unaware of the fact that many computers are being used to process data. These computers may be located at many places around the globe. Distributed operating system provides single-system image to its users. Each computer in a distributed computing system processes a part of the global distributed operating system. All these computers work in close coordination with each other. Processes and system resources are managed globally, and controlled from specific locations. Users view the complete system as a "virtual uniprocessor" and not as a collection of machines. The distributed operating system works towards generating this illusion.

☞ *Degree of autonomy of individual computers in an environment that uses network operating system is very high whereas the degree of autonomy of individual computers in an environment that uses distributed operating system is considerably low.*

3.4.8 Interactive (GUI-Based) Operating System

Interactive (GUI-based) operating system is a graphical user interface for ease of working. These operating systems have come into existence because they are graphical oriented and more user friendly. Windows operating system is graphical user interface

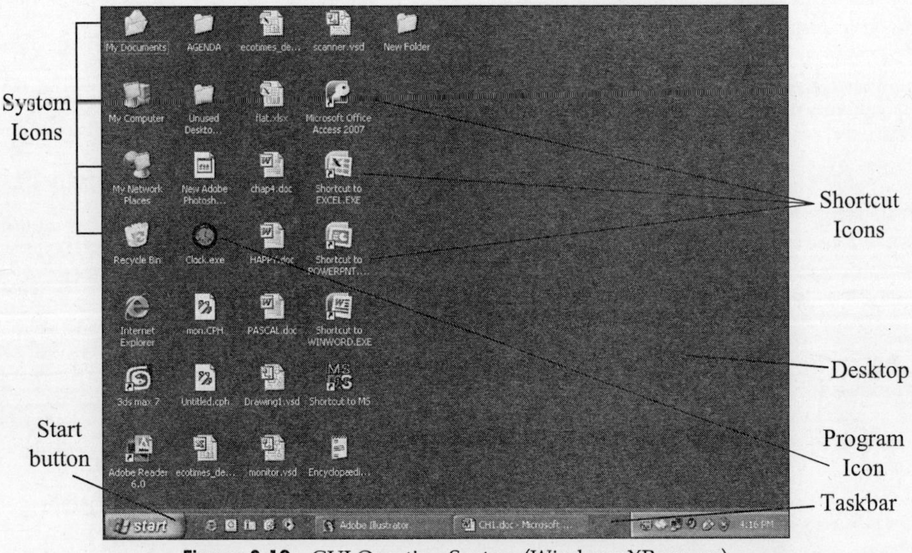

Figure 3.12 GUI Operting System (Windows XP screen)

system (See Figure 3.12). This system establishes interface between user and application program with the help of mouse rather than keyboard. Interactive operating systems contain window, pull-down menus, buttons, scroll bars and many more. With increasing use of multimedia, sound, video, etc; such as GUI OS are likely to become defacto OS for PCs and palmtop computers.

☞ *GUI stands for Graphical User Interface.*

3.5 POWER-UP PROCESS

Booting is a bootstrapping process that starts operating systems when the user turns on a computer. A boot sequence is the initial set of operations that the computer performs when power is switched on. The boot loader loads the main operating system for the computer.

A Bootstrap Loader (BSL) is a small program which can be activated immediately after a micro-controller has been powered up, in order to load and execute another program in a well-defined manner. The bootstrap loader is hard coded into the micro-controller.

After the micro-controller's bootstrap mode has been activated, a loader program can be used to store some routines on the micro-controller. In the next step those routines are used to upload a new firmware and save it in the program memory. This provides an easy way to upload a new firmware.

The most common operating system is Windows XP. It is the world's largest selling operating system for PCs.

Windows belongs to the category of software called GUI (Graphical User Interface). The user interface determines how you interact with your computer. The hardware part of the interface consists of your *screen* monitor, the *keyboard* and the mouse. The software part of the interface determines what things look like on the screen and how you give commands to your PC to get your work done. Before Windows, this was done with *keyboard* commands and, therefore, using an operating system was quite cumbersome. With the advent of Windows environment, many of everyday computer tasks, such as *running programs, opening files, choosing commands,* etc., are done using a graphical approach that is very intuitive to new users of computers. Further, Windows programs use the same command structure and graphical items on the screen. So, if you have mastered one Windows program, learning other programs becomes easy.

When you switch on the power supply, Windows operating system program gets loaded and takes over the PC's control. It provides the communication link between your computer hardware and the software that you use. For example, when you tell your spreadsheet software to save a file, the operating system instructs the computer hardware how and where to store, namely, in hard disk, etc.

☞ *Windows operating system takes care of PC and does many things in the background that are not visible to you. It manages software packages and hardware working.*

Windows also provides functions that let you manage many programs simultaneously, customize a PC and do many of the maintenance tasks associated with a PC. It also comes with many accessories and software programs.

Windows performs the following jobs:

- It provides ways for you to start programs.
- It runs more than one program at a time. This is called multitasking.
- It provides a way for you to manage files, i.e., *copy, move, organize, delete* and *work* on the files.
- It helps you to set up Internet access. The Internet connection wizard will help you set up an account with an Internet Service Provider (ISP) if you do not already have one.
- Windows 7 has Outlook integrated, which is an e-mail program. Use this program to send and receive electronic mail, via Internet.
- It provides a way to customize the desktop and other screen areas of the monitor.

The Windows 7 startup process closely resembles that of a Microsoft Windows NT version 4.0, Microsoft Windows 2000 and Windows Server 2003. All computers running Windows XP Professional share the same startup sequence.

- Power-on Self Test or POST phase
- Initial startup phase
- Boot loader phase
- Detect and configure hardware phase
- Kernel loading phase
- Log on phase

With Windows NT workstation, Windows 2000/XP and Windows 7, there are two types of partitions that are important during the boot process - the system partition and the boot partition. The system partition is the active drive partition that has the files needed to load the operating system. This is normally the C: drive (the active partition). The boot partition is the partition or logical drive where operating system files are located.

The major steps involved in boot process are the following:

- Power on the computer: As soon as you turn on a computer, its Central Processing Unit (CPU) begins to carry out the programming instructions contained in the Basic Input/Output System (BIOS). The BIOS, which is a type of firmware (Read Only Memory) contains the processor-dependent code that starts the computer regardless of the operating system installed.
- POST (Power On Self Test) executes. During POST, the computer checks most of its parts to make sure that they are working normally.

☞ *After POST, check if everything is all right. This will be indicated by a single beep sound.*

- After POST, the settings that are stored in CMOS (Complementary Metal Oxide Semiconductor) memory, such as boot order, determine the devices that the computer can use to start an operating system. BIOS searches CMOS for the boot device order and checks for a boot sector. If the boot device is a hard drive, BIOS reads the boot code instructions locate on the Master Boot Record (MBR). The MBR is the first sector of data on the startup hard disk and contains instructions (boot code) and a table (partition table) that identify primary and extended partitions. The BIOS reads the MBR into memory and transfers control to the code in the MBR.

  The computer then searches the partition table for the active partition. The first sector of the active partition contains the boot code, which enables the computer to do the following.

- Determine the file system used, and
- Locate and start the operating system loader file **Ntldr**.

If an active partition is successfully located, the code in the boot sector locates and starts **Ntldr**. Also, the BIOS releases control to it.

Ntldr loads startup files from the boot partition. It contains the program code that Windows 7 needs to read and write to disks formatted by using NTFs or file allocation table (File Allocation Table or FAT 16 or FAT 32) file systems.

Ntldr parses the Boot.ini file to determine the location of operating system boot partition. For systems that use a single boot configuration, such as Windows XP, Ntldr initiates the hardware-detection phase by starting Ntdetect.com.

Ntdetect.com is a program that performs basic device detection. Ntldr then passes Boot.ini information as well as hardware and software data in the registry, to Ntoskrhl.exe. Ntdetect.com detects hardware profile information and also checks for information stored in Advanced Configuration and Power Interface (ACPI) tables. ACPI-compliant firmware enables Windows XP Professional to detect device power management features and determine device resource requirements.

After processing the Boot.inifile, Ntlder starts Ntdetect.com. Ntdetect.com collects information about installed hardware by using calls to system firmware routines. Ntdetect.com then passes this information back to Ntldr, which organizes the information into internal data structures. Ntldr starts Ntoskrnl.exe and provides it with information obtained from Ntdetect.com. Ntdetect.com collects the following types of hardware and device information:

- system firmware information (time and date)
- Bus and adapter types
- Video adapters
- Keyboard
- Communication ports
- Disks
- Floppy disks
- Input devices (such as mouse devices)
- Parallel ports
- Devices installed on the Industry Standard Architecture (ISA) bus.

Ntldr is responsible for loading the Windows kernel (Ntoskrnl.exe) and the Hardware Abstraction Layer (HAL) into memory. The Hal.dll file that your computer uses can vary. The HAL allows Windows XP to run with different hardware configurations and components without affecting (or crashing) the operating system.

Ntldr reads control set information from the HKEY_LOCAL_MACHINE\SYSTEM registry key, which is created from information in the systemroot/system32\config\system file, so that Ntldr can determine which device drivers need to be loaded during startup. Typically, several control sets exist, with the actual number depending on how often system configuration settings change.

The operating system kernal initializes and Ntldr passes control to it. The start up process bar displays. During this time, a hardware key is created, then the device drivers load and services start.

The Winlogon.exe file executes and log on screen appears. It is then that XP detects plug-and-play devices.

3.5.1 Booting Windows XP/7 System

The different steps involved in the booting process of Windows 7 are listed in Table 3.1. The column "Action" mentions the corresponding action that takes place during each step.

Table 3.1 Booting process steps of Windows 7

s.no.	Step	Action
1.	Power supply is switched on.	The power supply performs a self-test. When all voltages and current levels are acceptable, the supply indicates that the power is stable and sends the Power Good signal to the processor. The time from switch-on to Power Good is usually between 0.1 and 0.5 seconds.
2.	The microprocessor timer chip receives the Power Good signal.	With the arrival of the Power Good signal, the timer chip stops sending reset signals to the processor, thereby allowing the CPU to begin operations.
3.	The CPU starts executing the ROM BIOS (Read Only Memory Basic Input/Output System) code.	The CPU loads the ROM BIOS.
4.	The ROM BIOS performs a basic test of central hardware to verify basic functionality.	Any errors that occur at this point in the boot process are reported by means of 'beep-codes' because the video subsystem has not yet been initialized.
5.	The BIOS searches for adapters that may need to load their own ROM BIOS routines.	Video adapters provide the most common source of adapter ROM BIOS. The start-up BIOS routines scan memory addresses C000:0000 through C780:0000 to find video ROM. An error loading any adapter ROM generates an error, such as: XXXX ROM Error, where XXXX represents the segment address of the failed module.

(*Contd...*)

s.no.	Step	Action
6.	The ROM BIOS checks if this is a 'cold-start' or a 'warm-start'.	To determine whether this is a warm-start or a cold-start, the ROM BIOS startup routines check the value of two bytes located at memory location 0000:0472. Any value other than 1234h indicates that this is a cold-start.
7.	If this is a cold-start, the ROM BIOS executes a full POST (Power On Self Test). If this is a warm-start, the memory test portion of the POST is switched off.	The POST can be broken down into three components: The Video Test initializes the video adapter, tests the video card and video memory, and displays configuration information or any errors. The BIOS Identification displays the BIOS version, manufacturer and date. The Memory Test tests the memory chips and displays a running sum of installed memory. Errors that occur during the POST can be classified as either 'fatal' or 'non-fatal'. A non-fatal error will typically display an error message on screen and allow the system to continue the boot process. A fatal error, on the other hand, stops the booting process and is generally signaled by a series of beep codes.
8.	The BIOS locates and reads the configuration information stored in CMOS.	CMOS (Complementary Metal Oxide Semiconductor) is a small area of memory (64 bytes) which is maintained by the current of a small battery attached to the motherboard. Most importantly for the ROM BIOS startup routines, CMOS indicates the order in which drives should be examined for an operating systems floppy first, CD-ROM (Compact Disk Read Only Memory) first, or fixed disk first.
	Fixed Disk	
9.	If the first bootable disk is a hard fixed disk, the BIOS examines the very first sector of the disk for a Master Boot Record (MBR). For a floppy, the BIOS looks for a boot record in the very first sector.	On a fixed disk, the Master Boot Record occupies the very first sector at cylinder 0, head 0, sector 1. It is 512 bytes in size. If this sector is found, it is loaded into memory at address 0000:7C00 and tested for a valid signature. A valid signature would be the value 55AAh in the last two bytes. Lacking an MBR or a valid signature, the boot process halts with an error message which might read: NO ROM BASIC - SYSTEM HALTED A Master Boot Record is made up of two parts: the partition table which describes the layout of the fixed disk and the partition loader code which includes instructions for continuing the boot process.
MBR	With a valid MBR loaded into memory, the BIOS transfers control of the boot process to the partition loader code that takes up most of the 512 bytes of the MBR.	The process of installing multiple operating systems on a single PC involves replacing the original partition loader code with a Boot Loader program that allows the user to select the specific fixed disk to load in the next step.
Part-ition Table	The partition loader (or Boot Loader) examines the partition table for a partition marked as active. The partition loader then searches the very first sector of that partition for a Boot Record.	The Boot Record is also 512 bytes and contains a table that describes the characteristics of the partition (number of bytes per sector, number of sectors per cluster, etc.) and also the jump code that locates the first of the operating system files (IO.SYS in DOS).
	Operating System	
Boot Record	The active partition's boot record is checked for a valid boot signature and, if found, the boot sector code is executed as a program.	The loading of Windows XP is controlled by the file Ntldr which is a hidden system file that resides in the root directory of the system partition. Ntldr will load XP in four stages: 1) Initial Boot Loader Phase 2) Operating System Selection 3) Hardware Detection 4) Configuration Selection

(*Contd...*)

Function Name	Step	Action
Ntldr Initial Phase	During the initial phase, Ntldr switches the processor from real mode to protected mode which places the processor in 32-bit memory mode and turns memory paging on. It then loads the appropriate mini-file system drivers to allow Ntldr to load files from a partition formatted with any of the files systems supported by XP.	Windows XP supports partitions formatted with either the File Allocation Table or FAT-16, FAT-32, or NTFS (New Technology File System) file system.
NTLDR OS SelectionBOOT. INI	If the file BOOT.INI is located in the root directory, NTLDR (NT Loader) will read contents into memory. If BOOT.INI contains entries for more than one operating system, NTLDR will stop the boot sequence at this point, display a menu of choices and wait for a specified period of time for the user to make a selection.	If the file BOOT.INI is not found in the root directory, NTLDR will continue the boot sequence and attempt to load XP from the first partition of the first disk, typically C:\.
F8	Assuming that the operating system being loaded is Windows NT, 2000, or XP and 7, press F8 function key at this stage of the boot sequence to display various boot options including "Safe Mode" and "Last Known Good Configuration".	After each successful boot sequence, XP makes a copy of the current combination of driver and system settings and stores it as the Last Known Good Configuration. This collection of settings can be used to boot the system subsequently if the installation of some new device has caused a boot failure.
NTLDR Hardware Detection	If the selected operating system is XP, NTLDR will continue the boot process by locating and loading the DOS-based NTDETECT.COM program to perform hardware detection.	NTDETECT.COM collects a list of currently installed hardware components and returns this list for later inclusion in the registry under the HKEY_LOCAL_MACHINE\HARDWARE key.
NTLDR Configuration Selection	If this computer has more than one defined hardware profile, the NTLDR program will stop at this point and display the Hardware Profiles/ Configuration Recovery menu.	Lacking more than one hardware profile, NTLDR will skip this step and will not display this menu.
Kernel Load	After selecting a hardware configuration (if necessary), NTLDR begins loading the XP kernel (NTOSKRNL.EXE).	During the loading of the kernel (but before it is initialized), NTLDR remains in control of the computer. The screen is cleared and a series of white rectangles progress across the bottom of the screen. NTLDR also loads the Hardware Abstraction Layer containing Dynamic Link Library file (HAL.DLL) at this time, which insulates the kernel from hardware. Both files are located in the \system32 directory.
NTLDR Boot Device Drivers	NTLDR now loads device drivers that are marked as boot devices. With the loading of these drivers, NTLDR relinquishes control of the computer.	Every driver has a registry subkey entry under HKEY_LOCAL_MACHINE \SYSTEM\Services. Any driver that has a Start value of SERVICE_BOOT_START is considered a device to start at boot-up. A period is printed to the screen for each loaded file (unless the /SOS switch is used in which case file names are printed).
Kernel Initialization	NTOSKRNL goes through two phases in its boot process: Phase 0 and Phase 1. Phase 0 initializes just enough of the micro kernel and executive subsystems so that basic services required for the completion of initialization become available. At this point, the system displays a graphical screen with a status bar indicating load status.	XP disables interrupts during Phase 0 and enables them before Phase 1. The HAL is called to prepare the interrupt controller; the Memory Manager, Object Manager, Security Reference Monitor and Process Manager are initialized. Phase 1 begins when the HAL is called to prepare the system to accept interrupts from devices. If more than one processor is present, the additional processors are initialized at this point. All executive subsystems are re-initialized in the following order: 1) Object Manager 2) Executive 3) Microkernel 4) Security Reference Monitor

(Contd...)

		5) Memory Manager 6) Cache Manager 7) LPCS (Local Proxy Cache) 8) I/O Manager 9) Process Manager
I/O Manager	The initialization of I/O Manager begins the process of loading all the system driver files. Picking up where NTLDR left off, it first finishes the loading of boot devices. Next, it assembles a prioritized list of drivers and attempts to load each in turn.	The failure of a driver to load may prompt NT to reboot and try to start the system using the values stored in the Last Known Good Configuration.
SMSS	The last task for Phase 1 initialization of the kernel is to launch the session.	SMSS runs in user mode but unlike other user mode applications, SMSS is considered a trusted part of the operating system and is also a native application (it uses only core executive functions). These features allow it to start the graphics subsystem and login processes.
Win32k. sys	SMSS loads the win32k.sys device driver, which implements the Win32 graphics subsystem.	Shortly after win32k.sys starts, it switches the screen into graphics mode. The services subsystem now starts all services mark as Auto Start. Once all devices and services are started, the boot is deemed successful and this configuration is saved as the Last Known Good Configuration.
Log on	The XP boot process is not considered complete until a user has successfully logged onto the system. The process is begun by the WINLOGON.EXE file which is loaded as a service by the kernel and continued by the Local Security Authority (LSASS.EXE) which displays the logon dialog box.	This dialog box appears at approximately the time that the Services Subsystem starts the network service.

3.5.2 Concept of BIOS

The BIOS supports all peripheral technologies including hard disk drive as well as internal services, such as the real-time clock. The CMOS is the memory located on the motherboards that stores the BIOS setting. When the system starts, the BIOS loads the setting from the CMOS.

BIOS-Power On Self Test (Post)

The Power On Self Test (POST) is a built-in diagnostic program that checks PC hardware to ensure that everything is present and functioning properly, before the actual booting begins. The most important job of the BIOS is to give the microprocessor its first instructions and to load the operating system when the computer is switched on. It then performs a POST. This is an inspection to check that everything in the PC is working properly.

If everything is found to be working properly, the BIOS will then try to boot the computer from the hard disk drive. This is the process of launching the operating system.

☞ *Sometimes, errors occur during the booting sequence. For instance, if there is a floppy disk left in the drive when you switch your computer on, you might get an error asking you to remove the disk.*

The booting sequence for PC is as follows:

1. The first thing is BIOS working, as soon as PC is switched on.
2. The BIOS checks the CMOS for the settings that you have specified for operating system (such as background, font, etc.). It is a ROM chip that stores basic information about the PC and configurations. The BIOS will check this to find out the type of hard drive, CD drive, floppy disk drive, etc. in the computer and how much memory is there.
3. The BIOS loads in the main memory, interrupt handlers, which are the program that act like translators. It loads the device drivers, which are software-identifying hardware components like a keyboard, mouse, hard disk and floppy disk. It will check the motherboard ports to make sure that all these devices are working properly.
4. The BIOS also performs the POST to make sure that everything is working properly.
5. It will finally display the system settings.

BIOS Setup Utility

BIOS setup utility enables the user to modify the PC settings and store them in the CMOS. This utility also enables to control the booting sequence. It can be used to change the BIOS to correct any hardware problem, such as floppy disk drive error, etc.

To enter the BIOS setup utility, do the following:

- Start the system

To enter or to modify the CMOS setup, press a key or combination of keys during the initial startup sequence. Most PC systems use "Esc", "Del", "F1", "F2", "Ctrl-Esc" or Ctrl-Alt-Esc keys" to enter setup.

Once you have entered setup, you will see a set of text screens with a number of options. Some of these are standard, while others vary according to the BIOS manufacturer. Common options include the following:

- **System Time/Date** - Set the system time and date.
- **Boot Sequence** - The order in which BIOS will try to load the operating system.
- **Plug-and-Play** - A standard for auto-detecting connected devices. You should set it to "Yes" if your PC and operating system both support it.

- **Mouse/Keyboard** - "Enable Num Lock", "Enable the Keyboard", "Auto-Detect Mouse".
- **Drive Configuration** - Configure hard drives, CD-ROM and floppy disk drives.
- **Memory** - Direct the BIOS to shadow to a specific memory address.
- **Security** - Set a password for accessing the computer if it is needed.
- **Power Management** - Select whether to use power management, as well as set the amount of time for standby and suspend.
- **Exit** - Save your changes, discard your changes or restore default settings.
  After you have finished with the changes, choose "Save Changes" and exit. The BIOS will then restart the PC so that the new settings take effect.

☞ *Press Esc key to exit without saving the new changes. A dialog box appears confirming if you want to exit without saving. Enter "Y" and press the Enter key to exit without saving.*

Upgrading the BIOS

By updating the BIOS, you can add additional functions and fix all errors and bugs. You must also upgrade the BIOS if the software or hardware that you installed needs an updated version of the BIOS. You can get updated BIOS by removing the old motherboard and installing a new one. However, if the BIOS is not permanently soldered on the motherboard, you can remove the BIOS chip and install a newer version of the chip on the PC motherboard.

You can also update the BIOS if your system has an Electronically Erasable Programmable Read Only Memory (EEPROM) for the BIOS. This enables you to change the BIOS using software. You can download the BIOS from the motherboard company's website. Some motherboards have a flash recovery jumper that you can use to restore the system if BIOS upgrade does not work properly.

3.5.3 User Management

A user interface, also called a "UI" or simply an "interface," is the means in which a person controls a software application or hardware device. A good user interface provides a "user-friendly" experience, allowing the user to interact with the software or hardware in a natural and intuitive way.

Command Line Interface

A Command-Line Interface (CLI), also known as command line user interface, is a means of interacting with a computer program where the user give commands to the program in the form of text (See Figure 3.13).

Command line interfaces to computer operating systems are less widely used by users, who favor graphical user interfaces. Command line interfaces are often preferred by more advanced computer users, as they often provide a more concise and powerful means to control a program or operating system.

Alternatives to the command line include, but are not limited to text user interface menus, keyboard shortcuts, and various other desktop metaphors centered on the pointer (usually controlled with a mouse).

Graphical User Interface

Graphical user interface or GUI (pronounced "gooey") is much easier to learn and use than command line interface. Unlike command line interface in which commands are textual, GUI command are graphical, such as pictorial. For example, in case of command line interface, to delete a file named proj.txt we need to type a command like "rm proj.txt". However, with GUI, the same operation can be performed by using a mouse to drag the icon to Recycle Bin and then releasing the mouse button.

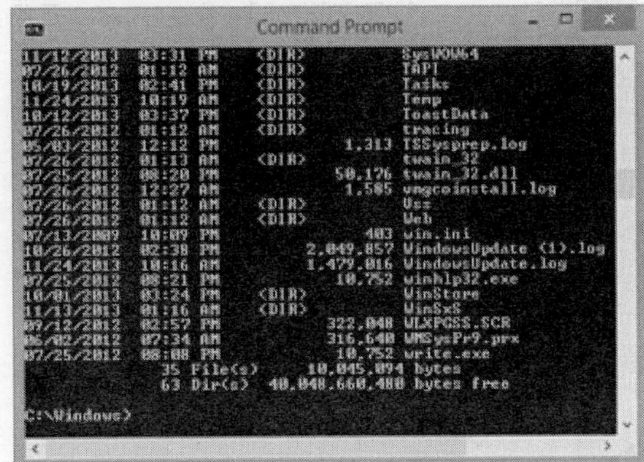

Figure 3.13 Commnd Line Interface

3.6 MICROSOFT WINDOWS

Windows 7 is the latest version of Windows desktop operating system for the PC. It is more advanced and robust operating system than any other operating system of Microsoft Corporation. It is built on the same foundation as on Windows Vista.

3.6.1 Different Versions of Windows 7

Microsoft Corporation of USA provides multiple versions of Windows 7 with a mixture of features and capabilities intended for different hardware platforms, personal preferences and business needs.

Versions of Windows 7 are discussed as follows:

- *Windows 7 Home Premium:* This edition is mostly used in new PCs. It includes entertainment features as its predecessor, Window Vista Home Premium.
- *Windows 7 Professional:* This edition is a superset of Home Premium and includes all features including Windows Media Center.
- *Windows 7 Ultimate/Enterprise:* These editions are identical. Ultimate is available on retails and Original Equipment Manufacturer (OEM) editions. But, Enterprise is distributed only to large-sized customers. This edition contains all features found in the Home Premium and Professional editions with some advance networking features, BitLocker encryption and support for multiple languages.

All of these editions are available in 32-bit and 64-bit options. Today Windows 7 64-bit is commonly installed on new computers, especially on systems with 4 GB or more RAM (Random Access Memory).

☞ *Windows 7 has a good antivirus program. You can download a free antivirus program called Microsoft Security Essentials that works well with any editions of Windows 7.*

Features of Windows 7 Operating System

Windows 7 offers many new features over Windows XP. Some vital features of Windows 7 are as follows:

- *Libraries:* Libraries make it simple to pull documents, music, pictures, etc., from various places (folders) and have them shown up together. Note that while the files are displayed together, they are actually stored in their original folders, so the same file may be in multiple libraries.
- *Windows Aero:* 3D Graphical User Interface (GUI) with translucent "glass-like" window to view a thumbnail of programs when pointed on the Taskbar.
- *Instant Search:* It is much faster and more diligent than other Windows OS. Search is integrated into every folder, making it simple to find a file from anywhere without having to use the Start Menu.
- *Windows Defender and Firewall:* Advanced anti-spyware and two-way firewall have been incorporated within the Windows 7 operating system to protect the OS, services, programs, Internet Explorer, and other parts of the computer from spyware.
- *Internet Explorer 8:* It is an improved Web browser, which is more secure and comes with a tabbed interface.
- *Windows Media Player 12:* Big work is done here with a new interface for the media library, photo display and organization, search-as-you-type capabilities, and music sharing.
- *Windows Live Mail:* A replacement for Outlook Express, this offers better stability, real-time search, junk mail filtering and anti-phishing.
- *Ease of Access Center:* Ease of Access Center is same as Accessibility Options available in earlier versions of Windows. It now comes with several improvements and new features that you can use to get suggestions for accessibility features.
- *Taskbar Improvements:* Taskbar in Windows 7 makes it simple to rearrange icons on the Taskbar and have them to stay where they are placed. It is also easy to review recent documents visited, Websites, playlist, etc.
- *Jump Lists:* With Jump Lists, you can quickly find files that you have recently worked with. With this feature, you can right click the icon and select it from the list.
- *Parental Controls:* Parental Controls option makes it easy for parents to select games for their children to play. Parents can restrict specific game titles, control their children to play the games that are below a certain age level, or block games with certain types of content that they may not want their children to see or hear.
- *BitLocker Drive Encryption:* It encrypts the contents of the computer's system drive (C: drive) or any other internal hard disk or removable hard drive or (USB) flash drive to make it unreadable. Security can further be enhanced by requiring a USB key to be inserted with decryption key.
- *User Account Control:* It asks for permission whenever administrative tasks are requested to make sure that you, rather than a virus or spy-ware application, asked for them. This is true even if you log on with a user name that has administrative rights. It can be customized to be as obtrusive or secure as desired.
- *Home Group:* Home group make it easier to setup a home network and share files, videos, photos, etc., with other using network. A wizard is used to set up the feature and a password is used by other computers wishing to join the group. Home groups are only accessible when the network location is set to "Home" and does not interfere with a domain that the computer may belong to at work.
- *Other Features:* Windows XP mode in Windows 7 provides the ability to run applications with compatibility issues with Windows 7 via a Virtual Machine (VM) running XP SP 3. Application installed in the VM appear in the Windows 7 Start Menu and runs like any other application. It is available as a free download from Microsoft's Website. It requires AMD-V or Intel-VT enabled in the BIOS.

  Battery life has been extended on laptops due to updated drivers, allowing more sleep features for devices and providing Adaptive Display Brightness, which automatically dims the display if the computer has not been used in a while.

  Touch screen support is available via Windows Touch if display supports it, allowing menu selections, scrolling media playing, etc., all possible without using a keyboard or mouse.

3.7 BASIC ELEMENTS OF OPENING SCREEN OF WINDOWS 7

Different parts of the Windows 7 opening screen are as marked in Figure 3.14 and discussed in the following sections.

3.7.1 The Desktop

As you work in Windows 7, you move items on the Desktop, retrieve and put away items and perform many other day-to-day tasks. By default, the only item on the Desktop is the Recycle Bin. Functions of the Desktop icons are explained in the following Table.

System Icon	Function
Computer	This icon lets you browse through the resources connected to your computer.
User's Files	This icon represents the name of the (personal user who logs on to the computer). Its folder contents are unique for every user on the computer. This folder contains files that belong to the user.
Recycle Bin	This icon provides temporary storage for files and folders that you want to delete.
Network	This icon opens a Window displaying the names of each server or computer in your own workgroup.
Control Panel	This icon opens window containing system configuration and management tools.

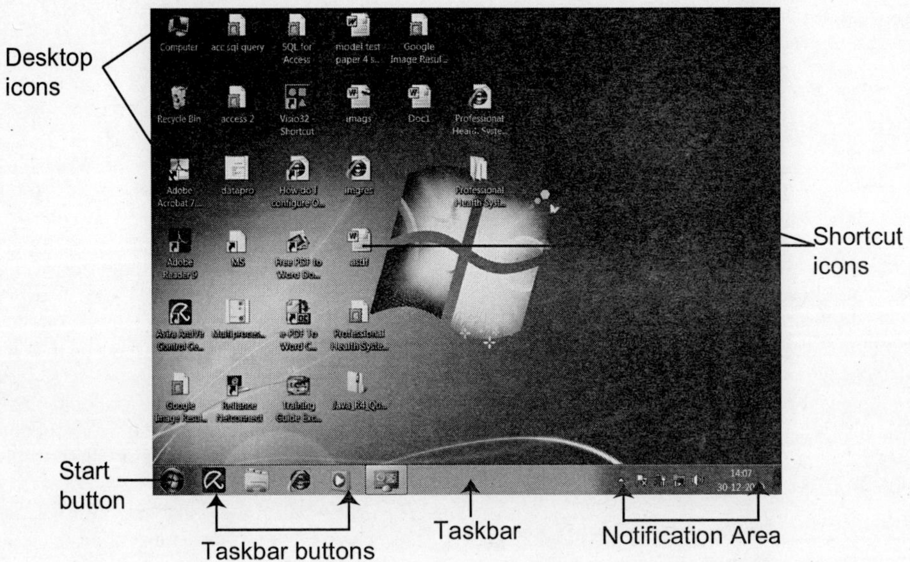

Figure 3.14 Different parts of the Windows 7 screen

Computer Icon

Computer is the gateway to resources stored on your own system. Computer icon on desktop allows you to browse through all the resources attached to your PC. When you click on Computer icon, a window appears as shown in Figure 3.15. The computer's information is divided into three parts: (i) Hard Disk Drives, (ii) Devices with Removable Storage (iii) Network. In fact, the Computer icon is used to see the disk drives and other hardware connected to your computer.

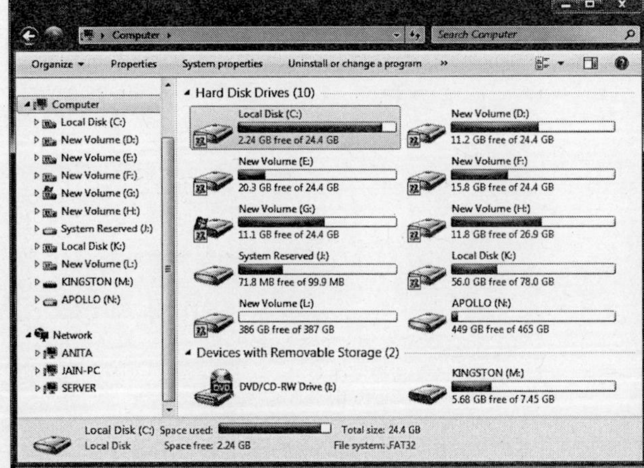

Figure 3.15 Computer window

Network Location: In the left pane of the Computer window, it displays the location of any disk drive or folder which is connected to the computer.

Rest of the features, such as shortcut icons and Recycle Bin will be explained later.

Taskbar

Taskbar is the horizontal bar at the bottom of the screen (See Figure 3.14).

Taskbar Elements	Function
Start button	It is located at the left end of the taskbar. Clicking the start button brings up the Start menu as shown in Figure 3.16.
Taskbar Icons	Taskbar Icons represent a set of icons. It lets you launch programs with single click. When clicked, these buttons or icons activate certain functions or tasks. For example, the Taskbar Icons include icons for launching Internet Explorer, Windows Media Player, Windows Explorer. You can also add your favourite programs in Taskbar. Right click the program that you want to add and then click this program to Taskbar.
Show Desktop button	Show Desktop button is used to temporary hide all the open windows to show the desktop.
Task buttons	Task buttons are displayed in the center portion of the Taskbar. A button appears for each program you have started or each document you have opened. You can click these buttons to move from one open Program or Folder to another (See Figure 3.14).

3.7.2 Elements of a Window

When you start a program, it appears on the Windows 7 desktop. You work with a program by manipulating the various elements of its window. These elements of a program window are shown in Figure 3.17.

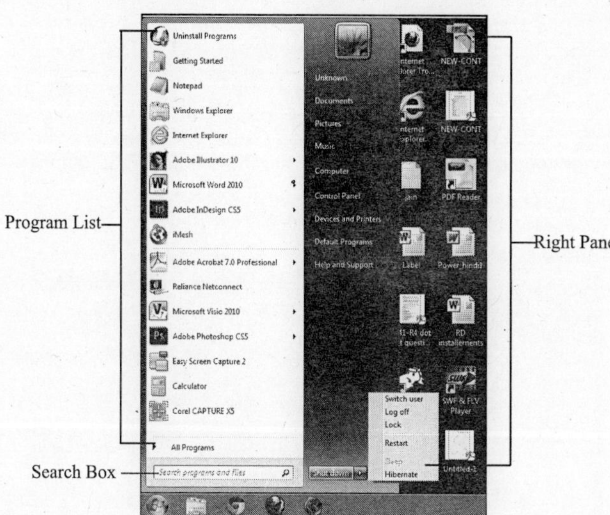

Figure 3.16 Start menu

Borders

The four edges that define the perimeter of a window are known as borders. Borders also give a way to change the size of the window.

Title Bar

Just below the top border of the window is the Title bar. It displays the name of the program or the document. It is also used for moving the window.

System Menu Icon

System menu icon is the small icon located on the left side of the Title bar. The System menu icon performs two functions. These are:

- It opens the menu whenever you click this icon. In most of the programs, the command on a System menu lets you control the size of the window. But some programs may have special items on their menus.
- System menu icon for a program or document will close the window that terminates the program or closes the document when you double-click it.

Close Button

At the right edge of the Title bar is a square containing an × called the Close button. Clicking the Close button closes a *document* or folder, or terminates a program (See Figure 3.17).

Minimize, Maximize and Restore Buttons

The three small buttons at the right end of the Title bar as shown in Figure 3.17 with small graphics are *Minimize* button, *Maximize* or *Restore* button, and the *Close* buttons. These are control buttons with which you can quickly change the size of a window or close it.

- Clicking the *minimize* button reduces the window to a button on the Task bar. Once *minimized*, the window no longer takes space on the desktop but the program in it continues to run.
- Clicking the *maximize* button enlarges the window to occupy the whole desktop. When the window is *maximized*, the *minimizes* and *restore* buttons appear.

Scroll Bars, Scroll Boxes and Scroll Buttons

If a window is not long enough to display its contents completely, you can scroll the *vertical scroll bar* which appears along the right edge. Similarly, if the window is not wide enough, a *horizontal scroll bar* appears along the bottom of the window.

☞ *Scroll bars offer an easy way to navigate through a window with the mouse. They also provide useful information about the contents of the window.*

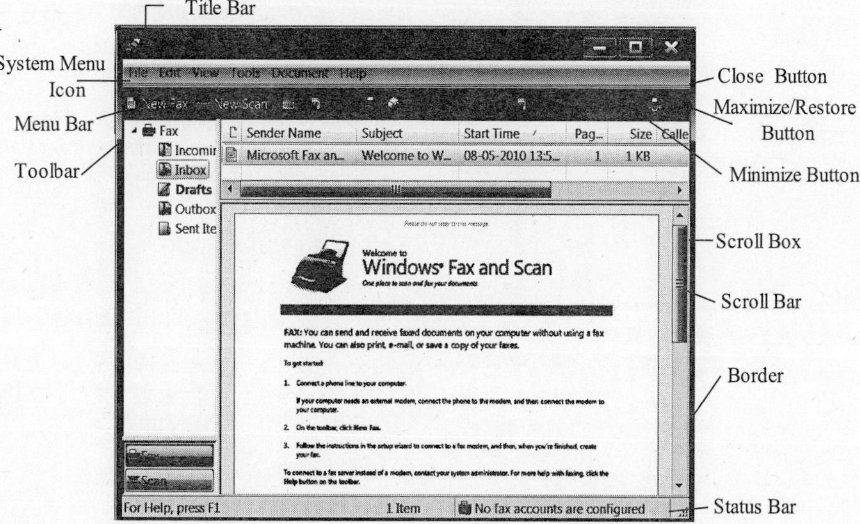

Figure 3.17 Elements of a program window

Scroll bars have small rectangular boxes called scroll box (See Figure 3.17). The position of this box within the scroll bar tells you where you are within the window itself. If the scroll box is at the top of the scroll bar, it means you are at the top of the document.

Scroll buttons appear along the top and bottom edges of the vertical scroll bar, and along the left and right edges of the horizontal scroll bar.

Menu Bar

The row of words just below the Title bar constitute the *Menu bar* (See Figure 3.17). *Menu bar* appears only in an application window and not in a document window. Each word on the Menu bar represents a menu which opens up when you click it (See Figure 3.18). The names of the menus may vary from program to program but they have some common headings, such as File, Edit, Window and Help.

☞ *In Windows 7, Menu bar is hidden by default, such as in Control Panel. To display the menu bar, you have to press Alt key. Menu bar is displayed above the toolbar. If you want to permanently display the Menu bar, Select Layout from the Organize tab of that window and then select Menu bar. Menu bar appears on the screen.*

Choosing Menu Commands

Choosing a menu command involves two steps:

- Click to open it.
- Selecting the required command from the menu.

➜ To open a menu, do this:

1. Using the mouse click on the menu name. Or using the keyboard, press Alt+(underlined letter in the menu name). For example, to open the Edit menu press Alt+E keys together (See Figure 3.18).

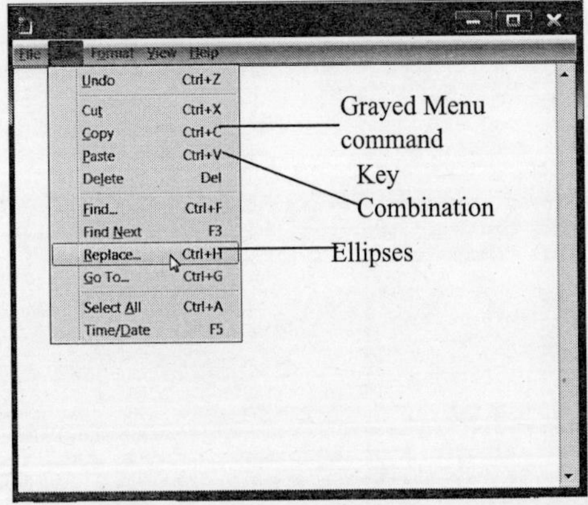

Figure 3.18 Edit menu open

After a menu is opened, you can select a menu command either one of the following ways:

- By typing the underlined letter in the command name (e.g. **P** for Paste in Figure 3.18). Or
- By clicking on a command's name.
- By pressing the ↓ arrow or ↑ arrow keys to highlight the desired command name and then pressing Enter key.

To close a menu without selecting any command, press the Esc key or click anywhere outside the menu.

Special Indicators in Menus

When you open a menu you would notice that many of the commands have additional words or symbols next to the command name (See Figure 3.19).

These additional words or symbols next to the command name indicate the following:

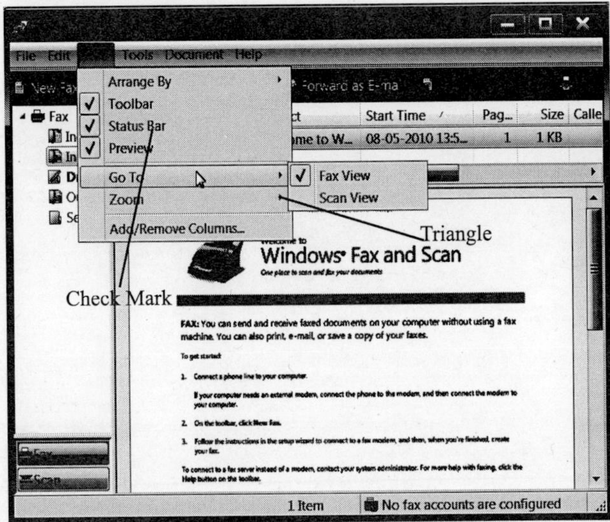

Figure 3.19 Special Indicators in Menu

Grayed (Dimmed) Command Name

When a command is displayed as grayed, or dimmed as shown in Figure 3.18, it means that this choice is not currently available for selection. A command can be dimmed for many reasons. For example, if a window is already Maximized, the Maximize command on the System menu will be dimmed because this choice does not make sense.

Ellipses(...)

Ellipses as shown in Figure 3.18 next to a command means that you will be asked for additional information before it is executed on selecting, such command. A dialog box appears on the screen, asking you to provide additional information.

Check Mark (✓)

A check mark preceding a command as shown in Figure 3.19 means the command is a toggle that is activated (turned on). A toggle is a command that is alternately turned *Off* and *On* each time you select it. Each time you select one of these commands, it switches from *On* to *Off* or *Off* to *On*. If there is no check mark, then the command or setting is *Off*.

Triangle (▸)

A triangle to the right of a menu command as shown in Figure 3.19 means that the command has additional choices to choose from. This is also called a *cascading menu*. You can make selections from a cascaded menu in the same way as you would select from a normal menu.

A Key Combination

Some menu commands list keystrokes that can be used for opening the menu and choosing that command (See Figure 3.18). These are also called *shortcut keys*.

Shortcut Menus

Pressing the right mouse button brings up a small menu related to the currently selected object or the one the mouse is pointing to. This menu is also referred to as *popup* menu. For example, if you right click the Taskbar, you will get a menu of commands relating only to the Taskbar (See Figure 3.20).

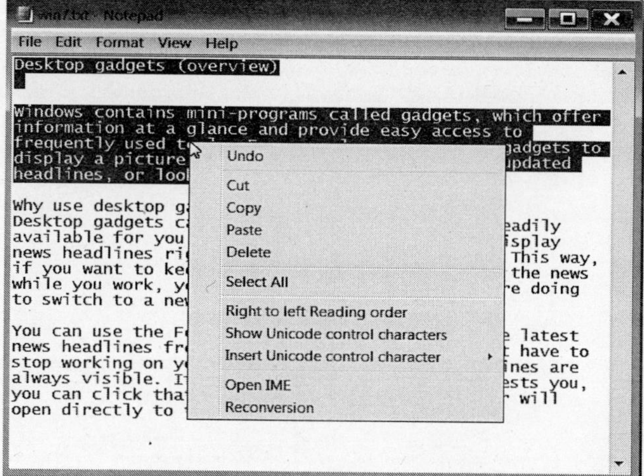

Figure 3.20 Shortcut/Popup menu

Dialog Boxes

A dialog box as shown in Figure 3.21 is a special type of window that asks you a question, allows you to select options to perform a task, or provides information. A dialog box will appear when you select a command with ellipsis (...) after it. Dialog boxes appear when Windows or its application program needs more information to execute the command. The various dialog box elements are as follows:

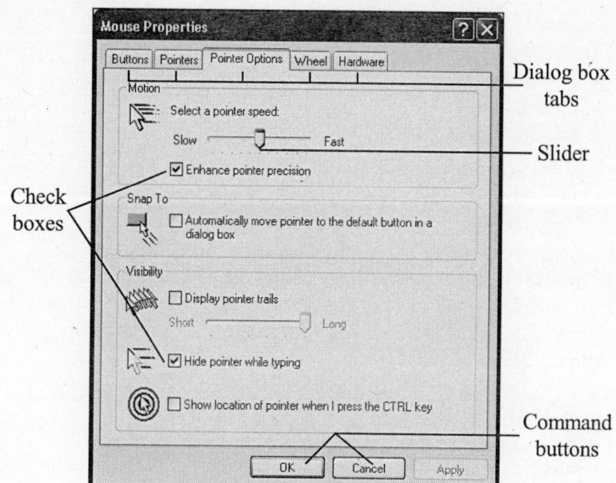

Figure 3.21 Dialog box Tabs

Dialog Box Tabs

Some of the dialog boxes have multiple option pages (See Figure 3.22). You need to select the page of your choice by clicking its icon at the top of the dialog box. Using the keyboard, press Ctrl+tab to flip through the option pages.

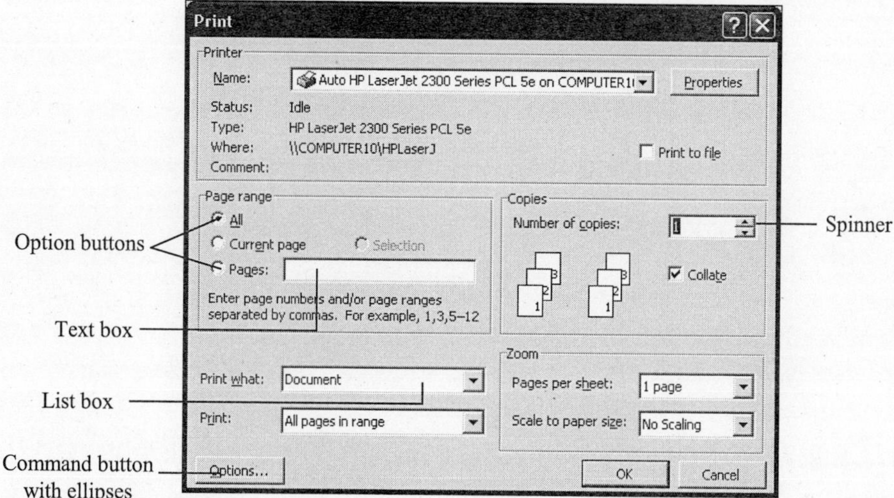

Figure 3.22 Dialog box elements

Moving between Dialog Box Elements

Dialog boxes often have several sections in them as seen in Figure 3.22. You can move between the sections in two ways:

- By clicking on the section that you want to change.
- Using the keyboard, you can press the Tab key to move between sections and press the Spacebar to select them.

Entering Information in a Dialog Box

The dialog boxes have following eight different types of sections where you need to enter information (See Figures 3.21 and 3.22).

- Text boxes
- Check boxes
- Option buttons
- Command buttons
- List boxes
- Sliders
- Spinners

Text Boxes

Text box is also called an *Edit box* and it is where you type in the information (See Figure 3.22). To enter information on the text box, click the text box. The insertion point appears in the text box. The insertion point indicates the place where the character you type will appear.

- If the text box is empty, the insertion point appears at the left side of the box.
- If the box already contains text, the insertion point appears at the point where you clicked the mouse.

Check Boxes

Check boxes are small square boxes (See Figure 3.22). Each check box is independent of all other check boxes in the dialog box. To select a check box item, click the box or anywhere in the text next to the box and similarly, to deselect repeat the same procedure. A check box when selected displays an (×) or (✓) within the box. Some check boxes have three states — *checked, unchecked,* and *partly checked*. A gray (in place of a black) check mark means that certain condition applies to it and some of the selections do not apply.

Option Buttons

Option buttons are also called *radio buttons* and present a set of mutually exclusive options (See Figure 3.22). Option buttons are always present in groups of two or more and may either be round or diamond shaped. You may select any one option from the group, but not more than one. To select the option click the button or any where in the text next to the button.

Command Buttons

Command buttons are like option buttons and are used to execute a command immediately. They are rectangular and not square or circular in shape. An example of a command button is the OK button found on almost every dialog box (See Figure 3.22).

Drop-Down List Boxes

A Drop-down List box presents a list of options or items from which you can select. To make a selection from a list box, using the mouse, click on it or using the keyboard highlight the desired option and then press Enter to choose it (See Figure 3.22).

Sliders

A slider works like a sliding control. Moving it in one direction increases some value, moving it in the other direction decreases the same value (See Figure 3.21).

Spinners

A spinner is a pair of arrows used to increase or decrease the value in a text box (See Figure 3.23). To increase the value in the text box, click up arrow and to decrease the value click down arrow.

3.7.3 Switching between Two Windows

You may have different Application windows open at the same time. In such a case, the window on the top is called the *active window*, i.e., window in which you are working and it is also called the foreground window. Active window's title bar is normally displayed in one color, while the title bars of all inactive windows are displayed in another color. In addition, Taskbar button for the active window appears to be pressed in the taskbar.

➜ **To change the active window, use any one of the following methods:**

1. Click the *Taskbar* button for the window you want to switch to. Or
2. Press and hold the Alt key. Then press Tab key to bring up the *Taskbar Switcher window* (See Figure 3.23).

Figure 3.23 Taskbar Switcher window

3. The *Task Switcher window* displays an icon for each running program and draws a box around the icon of the active window. Continue holding Alt key and pressing Tab key until the window that you want to keep active.
4. Windows 7 brings the program's window to the foreground.

➜ **To see the thumbnail preview of the open window, do this:**

1. Move the mouse pointer to the Taskbar button of the window you want to see the preview.
2. A small picture of the window called *thumbnail* appears as seen in Figure 3.24.

➜ **To see the Windows Aero 3D Flip view of the open windows, do this:**

1. Press the *Windows logo* key + Tab key to open Aero Flip 3D (See Figure 3.25).
2. While holding down the *Windows logo* key, press Tab key repeatedly or rotate the mouse wheel to cycle through open windows.

☞ *Aero Flip 3D and thumbnail preview would not work in the computer unless your computer is running Windows Aero.*

Figure 3.24 Thumbnail preview of window

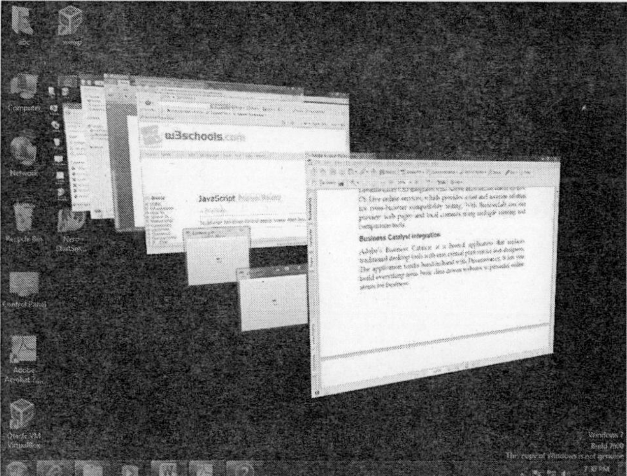

Figure 3.25 Aero 3D Flip view of the open windows

Following are the hardware requirement for the Windows Aero:

(a) 1-GHz 32-bit (x86) or 64-bit (x64) processor
(b) 1 gigabyte (GB) of Random Access Memory (RAM)
(c) 128-MB graphics card
(d) A DirectX 9 class graphics processor that supports a Windows Display Driver Model Driver, Pixel Shader 2.0 in hardware, and 32 bits per pixel.

☞ *Aero is not included in Windows 7 Home Basic. This aero desktop experience will work only with the Enterprise, Home Premium, Professional and Ultimate editions of Windows 7.*

3.8 FILE MANAGEMENT IN WINDOWS 7

Files and folders are two of the most fundamental concepts of Windows operating system. You can create and organize files and folders as soon as you save your work in a PC (Personal Computer).

3.8.1 Windows Explorer

Windows Explorer is a file manager application and also a navigation tool that is included with releases of the Microsoft Windows operating system from Windows 95 onwards. It provides a graphical user interface for accessing the file systems.

When you open Windows Explorer from the Taskbar in Windows 7, it defaults to the Libraries view. One way of opening Windows Explorer is to press **Windows Key + E**. Windows Explorer in Windows 7 has many new features, such as libraries, File list, search box, address bar and buttons to toggle the preview pane.

Earlier, Windows Explorer was a simple file browser in which a full pathname begins with a disk drive name followed by a colon (:) followed by a backslash (\). If the file resides in the disk drive's top folder (called the root directory), you then type the filename. However, if the file resides in another folder, you must list the folder after the backslash. If the file resides in several nested folder, you must list each folder in order, from the outermost to the innermost, and separate each folder name with a backslash.

For example,
c:\autoexec.bat
d:\Sherry\WordProc\Home\Insure\Fire and Casualty.exe
The first filename is autoexec.bat located in the root directory.
The second filename is Fire and Casualty located within a series of nested directories.

But, over the years, Windows Explorer has changed significantly. Today, Windows Explorer is a full-featured shell that helps you manage practically every aspect of the operating system. It still functions like a file manager, but the drive letters and folder trees are highlighted in Windows 7 instead of tress out on a new file-organizing feature called **libraries**.

A library is a virtual folder that contains links to actual folders located on your system or on a network. When you view a library in Windows Explorer, the contents pane displays every file and folder contained in the locations that are a part of that library. You can browse your files the same way you would in a folder or you can view your files arranged by properties like date, type, and author. By default, Windows 7 displays four libraries (See Figure 3.26).

These are:

(a) **Documents:** This library is used to organize and arrange word-processing documents, spreadsheet, presentations, and other text-related files.
(b) **Pictures:** This library is used to organize and arrange digital pictures of camera, scanner, or e mail.
(c) **Music:** This library is used to organize and arrange digital music whether it open from an audio CD or downloaded from the Internet.
(d) **Videos:** This library is used to organize and arrange videos which are clips from digital camera, camcorder, or video files downloaded from the Internet.

The other major change in Windows Explorer is its outstanding support for indexed searches that can work magically while you are looking for one particular document on a hard drive.

➜ **To start Windows Explorer, do this:**

1. Click **Start** button, highlight **All Programs** and then highlight **Accessories**.

2. Then click **Windows Explorer**. Or Alternatively, click on the Windows Explorer button from the Taskbar.
3. Windows Explorer window will appear as shown in Figure 3.26.

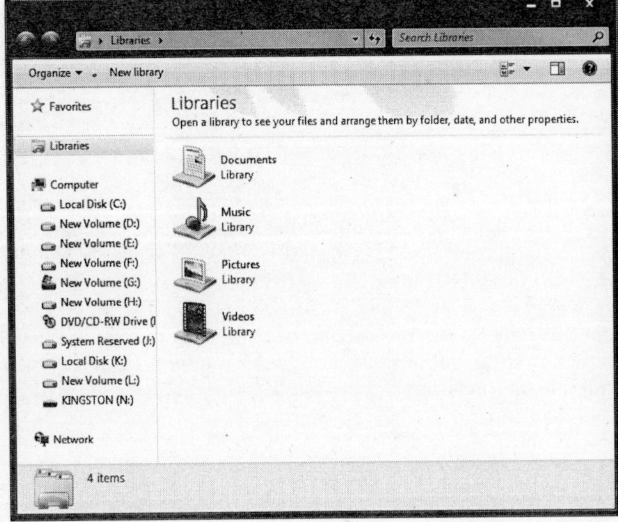

Figure 3.26 Libaries folder in Windows 7

The various elements of this window are designed to help you navigate around Windows or work with files, folders, and libraries more easily (See Figure 3.27). These elements are explained below.

3.8.2 Elements of Folder or Library Window

When you open a folder or library, you see it in a window. The various elements of this window are designed to help you navigate around Windows or work with files, folders, and libraries more easily. Elements of folder or library window are marked in Figure 3.27 which are explained below.

Navigation Pane

Navigation pane appears at the left side of window. It shows four or five nodes, such as **Favorites**, **Libraries**, **Computer**, **Network** and **HomeGroup** (visible only if the network location is set to Home). You can hide the *navigation pane*, adjust its width, or change its content to include only the Favorites node and hierarchical folders list. You can also use the navigation pane to access *libraries, folders, saved searches*, and *even entire hard disks*.

Address Bar

Address bar is used to navigate to a different folder or library or to go back to a previous one (See Figure 3.27). It also shows you where you are and helps you get where you want to go.

Back and Forward buttons are used to navigate to other folders or libraries you have already opened without closing the current window.

History drop-down list lets you revisit addresses you entered in previous sessions.

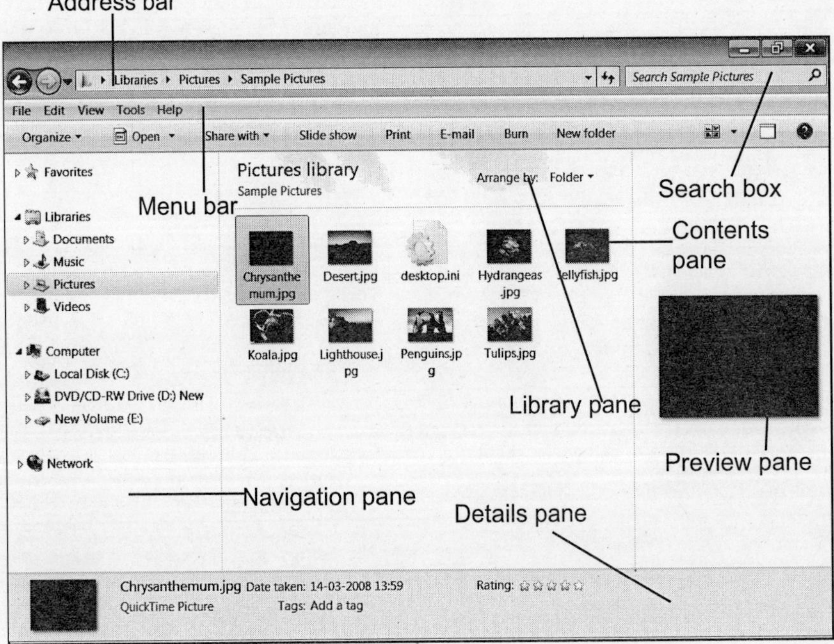

Figure 3.27 Elements of folder or library window in Windows 7

The *new breadcrumb trail feature* is used to help you in navigating to the *address bar*. To use this feature, click any folder name to move straight to that location or click down arrow next to the folder to display other subfolders at the same level (See Figure 3.28).

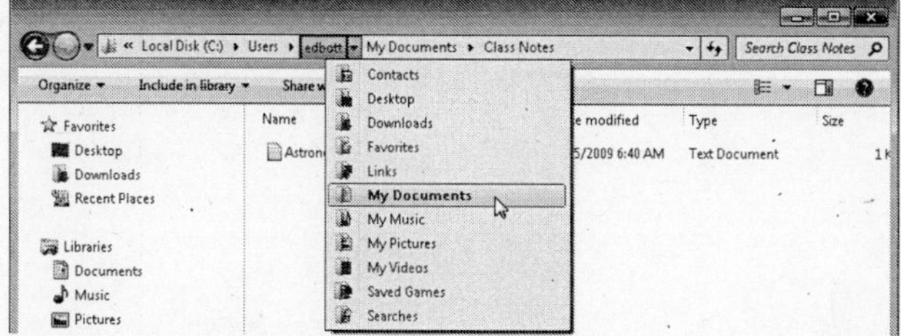

Figure 3.28 Breadcrumb trail feature to navigate in the address bar

Toolbar

Toolbar is used to perform common tasks, such as changing the appearance of your files and folders, burning files to a CD, or starting a digital picture slide show. A few elements on the toolbar are always available, including the Organize menu on left and three buttons on the far right, which change views, show or hide the preview pane, and open a Help window (See Figure 3.27). But, the other buttons on the toolbar vary depending on the current selection.

Library Pane

Library pane appears only when you are in a library, such as Pictures library (See Figure 3.27). It is used to customize the library or arrange the files by different properties.

Search Box

Type a word or phrase in the search box to look for an item in the current folder or library (See Figure 3.27). The scope of search is restricted to the current location and displays search results immediately in the contents pane. The width of the search box can be adjusted by dragging its left edge in either direction.

Details Pane

Details pane displays the properties associated with the selected file (See Figure 3.27). File properties are information about a file, such as author, date you last changed the file, and any descriptive tags you might have added to the file. You can adjust the height of Details pane by dragging the top border up or down.

Preview Pane

Use the preview pane to see the contents of most files. If you select an e-mail message, text file, or picture, for example you can see its contents without opening it in a program (See Figure 3.27). If you do not see the *Preview pane*, click the *Preview* pane button in the toolbar to turn it on.

Menu Bar

By default, Menu bar is hidden. If it is seen, it is placed above the toolbar shown in Figure 3.27. If the menu bar is not displayed, you can make it appear temporarily.

➔ **To display menu bar, do this:**

1. Click the Organize menu, choose Layout and then select Menu bar. Or alternatively, press Alt or F10 keys.

Selecting Files and Folders in Windows 7

➔ **To select a single file, do this:**

1. Open the folder or Windows Explorer window containing the file.
2. Click the file.

➔ **To select multiple files, do this:**

1. Open the folder or Windows Explorer window containing the file.
2. Click the first file.
3. Then press and hold down Ctrl key and then click the other files you want to select (See Figure 3.29).

➔ **To select a group of files, do this:**

1. Open the folder or **Windows Explorer window** containing the file.

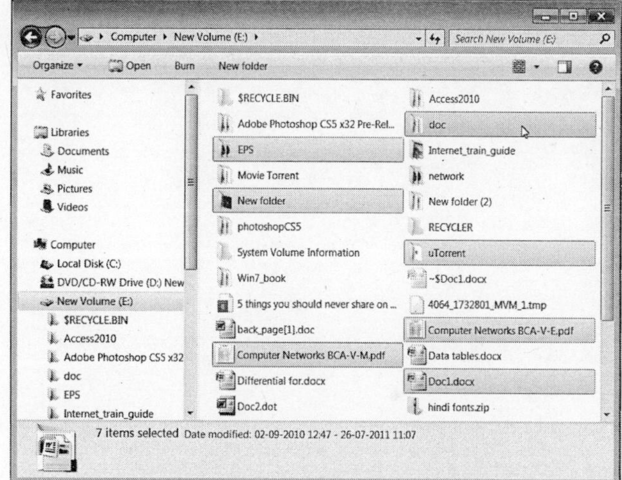

Figure 3.29 Selecting multiple files

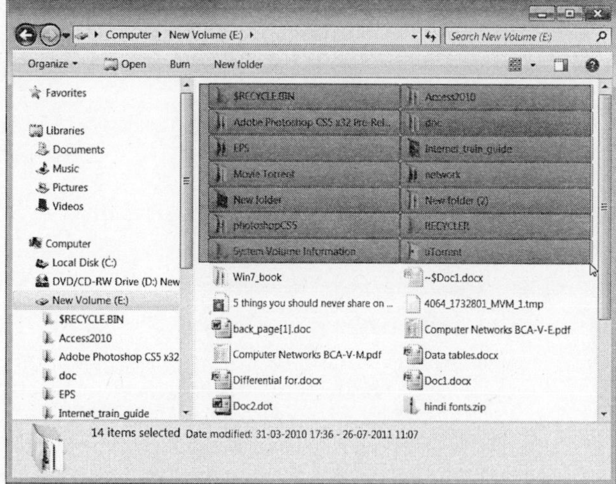

Figure 3.30 Selecting group of files

2. Move and position the mouse to the left of the first file you want to select.
3. Then click and drag mouse to the right until all the files you want are selected (See Figure 3.30).

➜ **To select all the items in a folder do this:**

1. Open the folder or **Windows Explorer window** containing file.
2. Click the **Organize** menu and choose **Select all**. Or press **Ctrl + A** keys together.
3. Windows Explorer selects all the files in the folder.

Creating Files and Folders in Windows 7

➜ **To create a new File/Folder do this:**

1. In the **Folder window**, click the **File** menu and choose **New** or right click an empty area of folder window and choose **New**.

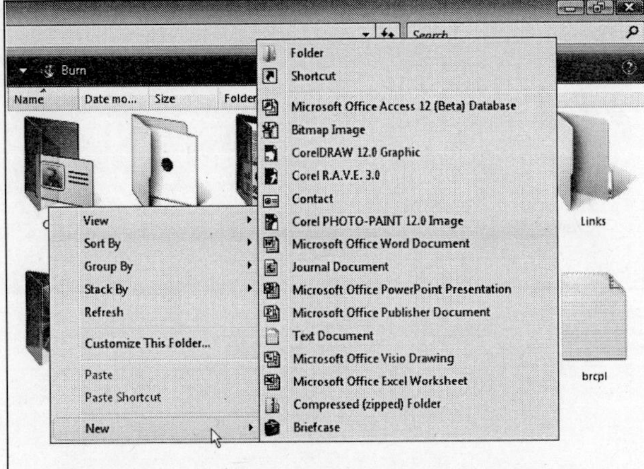

Figure 3.31 Creating new file or folder

2. In both cases, a submenu lists the new objects you can create: *folders, shortcuts,* and a variety of types of files (See Figure 3.31).
3. Select an element out of the list. Windows 7 creates the selected object.

☞ *If you click **Folder button** from the **Toolbar**, Windows 7 creates a new folder.*

Naming and Renaming Files and Folders in Windows 7

➜ **To rename a file or folder, do this:**

1. Select the file/folder you want to rename.
2. Click the **Organize menu** and choose **Rename**. Or press F2 key (See Figure 3.32). Or *alternatively,* right click the file/folder and choose **Rename** from the context menu.
3. A box appears around current name, with its details is selected. Type the new name in the box and press **Enter** key (See Figure 3.31).

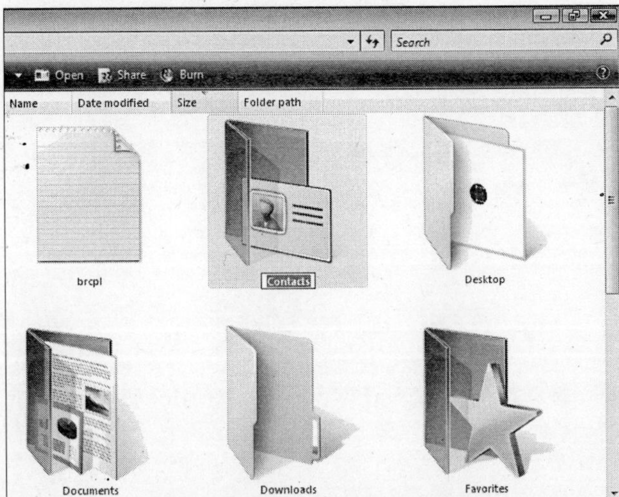

Figure 3.32 Renaming a folder

Opening File and Folder in Windows 7

1. You have to **double-click a file** or **folder** in this pane to open it (Figure 3.33).

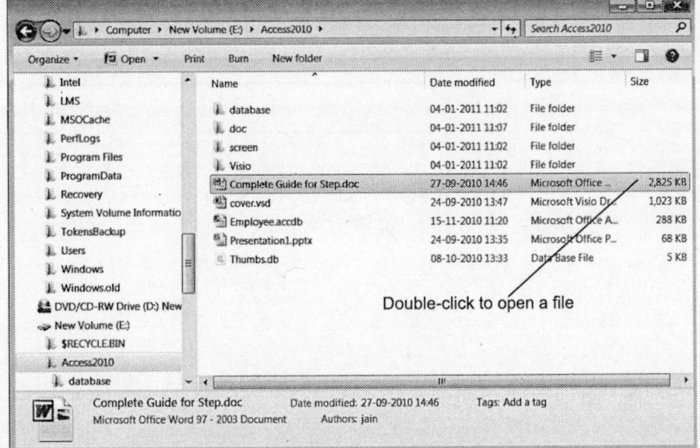

Figure 3.33 Opening a file

Moving or Copying Folder and File

Moving/copying a file or folder to another drive or folder is easy. Just drag a file/folder from the right pane to another disk drive (or a folder on another drive) to copy/move it there.

➜ **To move a file or folder to another drive or folder, do this:**

1. Select the file or folder you want to move.
2. Point to the selected file or folder, and then press and hold down the left mouse button.
3. Drag the file/folder from the right pane to the left pane and drop it into the selected folder or drive where you want (See Figure 3.34).
4. A Move button as shown in Figure 3.34 indicates where the file or folder will be moved.
5. Release the mouse button to move the file/folder into desired place.

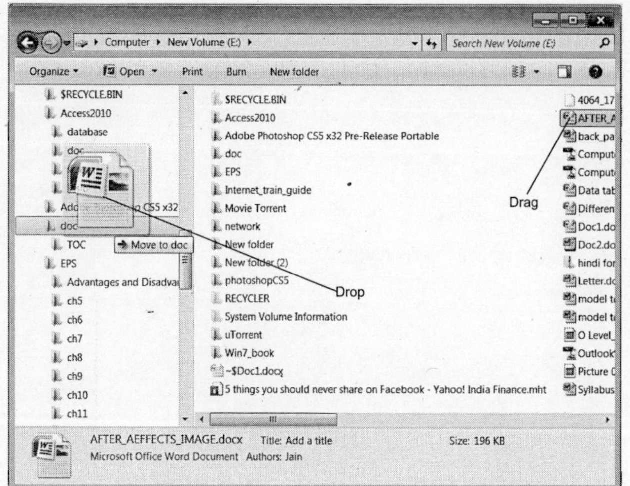

Figure 3.34 Moving a file or folder from one location to another

➜ To copy a file or folder to another drive or folder, do this:

1. Select the file or folder which you want to copy.
2. Point to the selected file or folder, and then press and hold down the left mouse button.
3. Press Ctrl key while dragging the file/folder from the right pane to the left pane and drop it into the selected folder or drive where you want (See Figure 3.35).
4. A **Copy** button as shown in the Figure 3.35 indicates where the file or folder will be copied.
5. Release the mouse button to copy the file/folder into desired place.

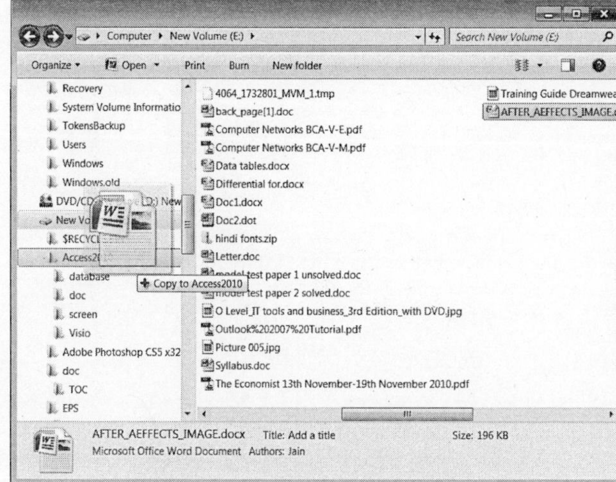

Figure 3.35 Copy a file or folder

Deleting Files and Folders in Windows 7

➜ To delete file(s) and folder(s), do this:

1. Select the file or folder that you want to delete.
2. Click the **Organize** menu and choose **Delete** . Or *alternatively*, right click the file/folder and choose **Delete** from the context menu.
3. The **Delete File** dialog box appears. Click **Yes** in this dialog box.
4. The selected file is deleted from the folder.

☞ *Objects deleted from your computer are sent to the Recycle Bin. You can recover them by double-clicking the Recycle Bin folder, if desired.*

3.9 START MENU IN WINDOWS 7

Start menu appears when you click on the Start button on the Taskbar. The Start menu provides you more customization options. It shows you who is logged on. It automatically adds the most frequently used programs to the top-level menu. It enables you to move any which programs you want to be in the Start menu. Start menu is divided into three basic parts. These are:

(a) Program List
(b) Search Box
(c) Right Pane

3.9.1 Program List (Left Pane)

Left pane of the Start menu shows recently used programs and those programs that have been pinned to Start menu. Program list shows up to eight recently used programs. If you want to see the complete list of programs installed in your computer, then click on the All Programs.

3.9.2 Search Box (Lower Left Pane)

Lower left pane of the Start menu is the search box allows computer to search files, folders, programs or computer that are connected to your computer. To search any files or folder, type the name of the file or folder in search box and then press Enter key. To clear the search result, click on the Clear button [X].

3.9.3 Right Pane

Right Pane of the start menu gives access to commonly used folders. These are discussed below.

Current User

It opens the folder of the user who is currently logged on to Windows. This folder contains files, such as Documents, Pictures, etc.

Documents

It opens the Document Folder where you can store files.

Pictures

It opens Picture Folder where you can store pictures and graphic files.

Music

It opens the Music Folder where you store and play the music files.

Games

It opens the Game Folder from where you can access the games which are installed in your computer.

Computer

It opens a computer from where you can access hard disk drives, printers, scanner, CD drive and other hardware connected to your computer.

Control Panel

It opens window that allows you to install software and change different setting of Windows, such as Date, Time, Keyboard, Mouse, Password, Display, Sound settings, etc.

Devices and Printers

It opens a window where you can see information about the printer, mouse, and other devices installed on your computer.

Default Programs

It opens a window where you can see information about the printer, mouse, and other devices installed in your computer.

Help and Support

It displays help which is a set of screens of information about Windows itself where you can browse and search Help topics using Windows and your computer.

At the bottom of the right pane is the Shut down button. Click the Shut down button to turn off your computer. Clicking the arrow next to Shut down button displays a menu with additional options for switching users, logging off, restarting, Sleep, or shutting down.

☞ *If you want Windows 7 to automatically reopen all the programs and documents currently on your screen, click the power button arrow from the Start menu and then click Sleep.*

3.10 SHORTCUTS

A shortcut is a small file that is linked to a *program, document, folder* or an *Internet address*. The file is represented by an icon with an arrow in its lower left corner.

Shortcut is linked to a file or folder, which can be located anywhere on a local hard disk or CD-ROM drive or on a floppy disk.

3.10.1 Creating a Shortcut

A shortcut can be created in the following two ways:

- By using cut and paste or
- By using the Create Shortcut wizard.

☞ *A shortcut is a pointer to an object, and not the object itself. This means that you can create and delete shortcuts without affecting the object which is linked to a file.*

➜ To create a shortcut using copy and paste, do the following:

1. Right click the items for which you want to create a shortcut.
2. From the **context** menu, choose **Copy**.
3. Now right click on the desktop and choose **Paste** from the context menu.

➜ To create a shortcut using the create shortcut wizard, do this:

1. Right-click the desktop, from the **Context** menu choose **New**, and then choose **Shortcut** as seen in Figure 3.36.

Figure 3.36 Creating Shortcut

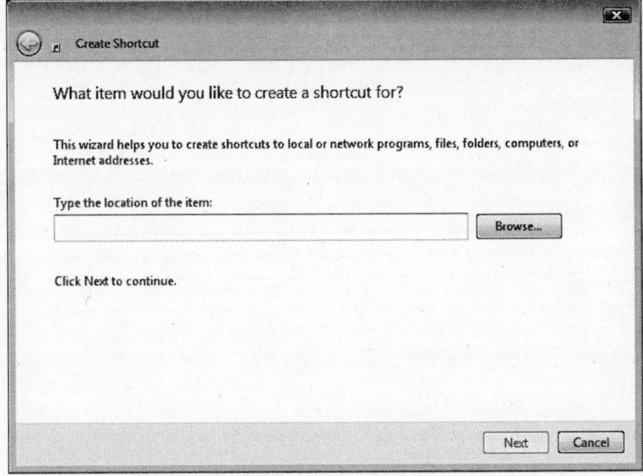

Figure 3.37 Creating Shortcut wizard

2. The wizard for **Create Shortcut** appears as shown in Figure 3.37.
3. Click the **Browse...** button. In the Browse for Folder dialog box, locate the item for which you want to create a shortcut.
4. Click Next > type a name for your shortcut, click **Finish**, and your shortcut will appear on the desktop.

3.10.2 Renaming a Shortcut

When you create a shortcut, Windows gives it a default name based on the underlying object.

➜ To change the shortcut name, do this:

1. Right-click the shortcut.
2. From the context menu, choose **Rename**.
3. Type the name that you want to use.

3.10.3 Deleting a Shortcut

➜ To delete a shortcut, do this:

1. Select the icon and press the Del key. *Alternatively*, right click the shortcut to be deleted and choose **Delete** from the context menu.

2. Windows prompt you for conformation before deletion.

3.11 ESSENTIAL WINDOWS ACCESSORIES

Windows 7 provides some utility software packages, such as Calculator, Notepad, Paint, Entertainment, Snipping Tool, Sound Recorder, WordPad, and System tools, such as Disk Cleanup, Disk defragmenter, Task Scheduler, Tablet PC, and many more in Accessories group.

3.11.1 System Tools

System Tools option is found under Accessories. It provides a set of tools for Computer System Management. It includes Disk Defragmenter, Disk Cleanup, Backup, Scheduling, etc.

Disk Defragmenter

Disk Defragmenter consolidates fragmented files and folders on your computer's hard disk, so that each file occupies a single, contiguous space on the volume. As a result, your system can gain access to your files and folders and save new ones more efficiently. By consolidating your files and folders, *Disk Defragmenter* also consolidates the volume's free space, making it less likely for new files to be fragmented.

➜ **To open Disk Defragmenter, do this:**

1. Click **Start** button, Choose **All Programs**, highlight **Accessories**, highlight **System Tools**, and then choose **Disk Defragmenter**. Disk Defragmenter window will open up as shown in Figure 3.38.

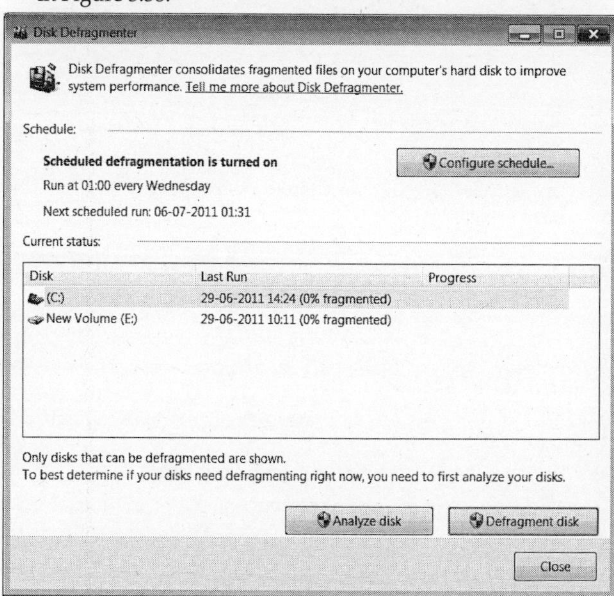

Figure 3.38 Disk Defragmenter window

2. To start defragmentation, under **Current status**, select the disk you want to defragment.
3. Click **Defragment** disk.

Disk CleanUp

You can use Disk CleanUp to free up space on your hard disk by removing temporary Internet files, removing installed components and programs that you no longer use, and emptying the Recycle Bin.

➜ **To open Disk Cleanup, do this:**

1. Click **Start** button, Choose **All Programs**, highlight **Accessories**, highlight **System Tools**, and then choose **Disk Cleanup**.
2. **Disk Cleanup: Drive Selection** dialog box appears as shown in Figure 3.39.
3. Choose the drive which you want to clean and then click OK.
4. The **Disk Cleanup** dialog box appears for the drive which you have selected (See Figure 3.40).

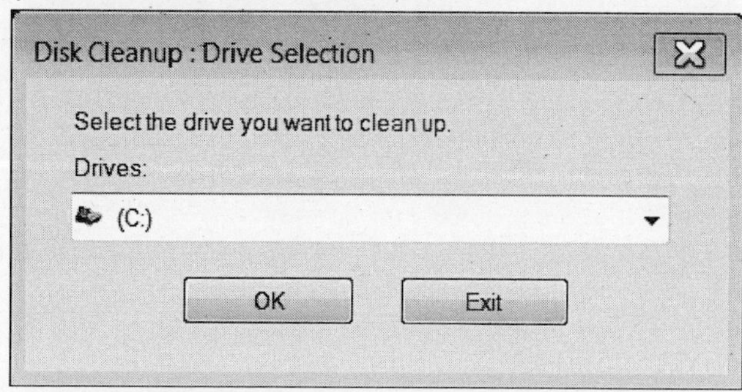

Figure 3.39 Disk Cleanup: Drive Selection dialog box

Figure 3.40 Disk Cleanup dialog box

☞ *Disk Cleanup helps to free up space on your hard drive. Disk Cleanup searches your drive, and then shows you temporary files, cache files, and unnecessary program files that you can safely delete. You can direct Disk Cleanup to delete some or all of those files.*

5. Under **Files to delete:** list, click the check box for each file that you want to delete.
6. Then click OK button.

Task Scheduler

It is a tool that enables you to schedule tasks (such as Disk Defragmenter) to run regularly, at a time most convenient for you. The Task Scheduler starts each time you start Windows 7 and runs in the background.

➜ **To add scheduled task, do this:**

1. Click **Start** button, Choose **All Programs**, highlight **Accessories**, highlight **System Tools** and then choose **Task Scheduler**.
2. **Task Scheduler** window appears as seen in Figure 3.41.
3. In this Window, Click the **Action** menu and then click **Create Basic Task** (See Figure 3.41).

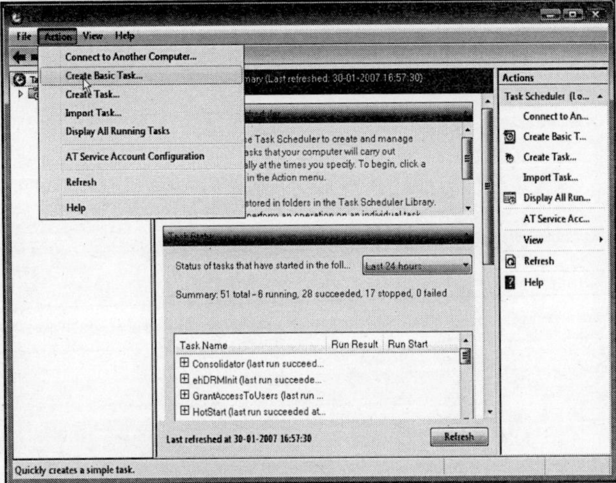

Figure 3.41 Task Scheduler window

4. In **Create Basic Task Wizard**, type a name for the task and give description, and then click **Next**.
5. In the next step, select an option from *When do you want the task to start?*, i.e., *Daily*, *Weekly*, etc., and then click **Next**.
6. In Next dialog box, specify the schedule which you want to use, and then click Next.
7. To schedule a program to start automatically, click **Start** a program, and then click **Next**.
8. Select a program from the list, or browse to the program you want to start, and then click **Next**.
9. Click **Finish**.

3.12 OPERATING SYSTEM SIMPLE SETTING

To use Windows 7 effectively, you have to configure or reshape Windows and the other programs that you run to work with your computer's hardware. You do this using the following features:

Feature	Function
Properties	These are the settings for many different objects in your computer's hardware and software.
Control Panel	This lets you see and change many properties and other settings.

3.12.1 Properties

Every object in Windows 7-the hardware components of your computer, software programs, files, and icons—has *properties.* These properties are settings that determine how that object works. For example, a file has properties, such as *filename, size* and *the date* the file was last modified.

➜ **To change the properties of an object, do this:**

1. Right click the object, the shortcut menu is displayed as shown in Figure 3.42.

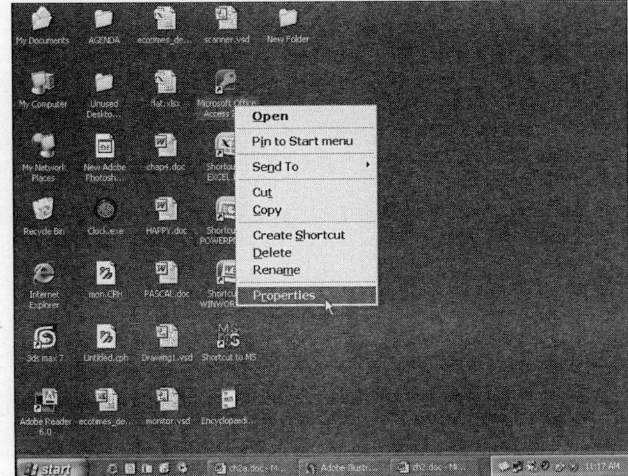

Figure 3.42 Shortcut Menu to change the property of an object

2. From the shortcut menu click **Properties**. The **Properties** dialog box appears.

The properties that you can change will depend upon the object you have selected.

3.13 PERSONALIZING YOUR COMPUTER

The Personalization window is one of the most powerful and useful features of Windows 7. The settings which are related with computer or desktop is the personalize properties. These properties include desktop background, screen saver, color, font etc. Personalize properties can be set through Personalization window.

➜ **To show the Personalization window, do this:**

Click on the **Start** button then click on **Control Panel**. In Control Panel window, double click on **Personalization** icon to open it. *Alternatively*, right click at an empty space on the desktop and then choose **Personalize**. This will show the Personalization window on the screen.

3.13.1 Desktop Background or Wallpaper

Wallpaper is the background pattern or picture against which desktop menus, icons and other elements are displayed and moved around. A wallpaper image can be in **jpeg** (Joint Photographic Expert Group) format or a **gif** (Graphics Interchange Format) format. A wallpaper image may be centered, stretched, or tiled.

Windows 7 comes with more than three dozen desktop background images, such as scenes of nature, architectural photos, and much more. If none of the built-in images appeal to you then you can use one of your own photos as desktop background.

➜ **To set the background on the desktop, do this:**

1. In Personalization window, click on Desktop Background link. The Desktop Background window will appear as shown in Figure 3.43. In this window select the picture or any solid colour from the Picture Location drop-down list box which you want to use.

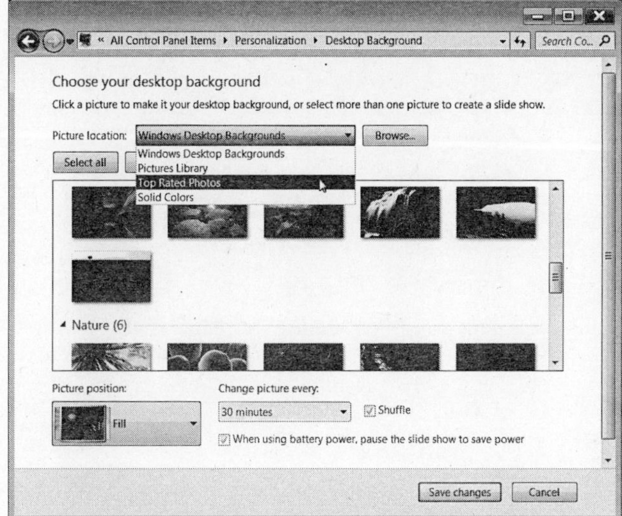

Figure 3.43 Setting the wallpaper in Desktop

2. Click on the Browse... button if you want to use your own image from the different drives.
3. Select the position of the wallpaper from the Picture position drop-down list.
4. Then click Save changes to accept the changes and close the window.
5. The picture or colour you select will be applied as desktop background.

Screen Saver

Screen saver is an animated image that is activated on the PC monitor when user walks away from the computer and leaves the monitor on. The main purpose of the screen saver is to prevent the burning of an image into the phosphorus material inside the monitor.

➜ **To set the screen saver, do this:**

1. In **Personalization** window, click on select **Screen Saver** link (Figure 3.44).
2. Select the desired screen saver from the drop-down list from the Screen Saver group.
3. You can also set the time in **Wait:** section under the **Screen Saver** group.
4. To see the preview of the selected screen saver click on the **Preview** button.

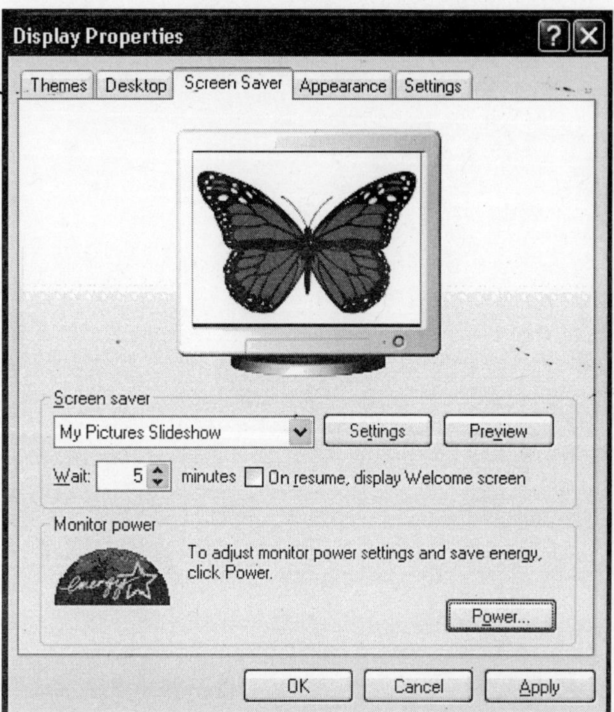

Figure 3.44 Display properties with Screen Saver Tab

5. Click the On resume, display logon screen check to ensure that anyone who interrupts the screen saver can see your work only if he/she know your password.
6. To apply all the settings, click on the **Apply** button and then click on the **OK** button to close the dialog box.

☞ *In Windows 7, you can also use personal pictures as a screen saver. For this, you have to select Photos from Screen Saver group.*

3.13.2 Adding and Removing Printers

Windows 7 provides Add a printer feature to simplify installing printers. The Printers folder for running the wizard and for managing printing processes. You can open the Printers folder in the following ways.

➜ **To add a printer, do this:**

1. Click **Start** menu and choose **Control Panel** or click **Devices and Printers**.
2. Click **Add a printer** from the **Devices and Printers** dialog box.
3. Select the option that describes the printer you want to use.
   - Click Local printer.
   - A network printer, wireless or Bluetooth printer.
4. Select the port you want your printer to use.
   - Create a new port. Or,
   - Click Local port and then click next.
5. Follow the instructions on the screen to finish adding a printer with the Add printer wizard.

☞ *The only difference between installing a network printer and a local printer with the Add Printer Wizard is that you must specify the path to the network printer or browser to find its network location.*

➜ **To remove a printer, do this:**

1. If you will not longer be using a printer, you can remove it from the **Devices and Printers** folder.
2. Click to open **Devices and Printers**.
3. Rigth-click the printer that you want to remove, click **Remove device**, and then click **Yes**.

☞ *If you can not delete the printer, right-click it again, click Run as administrator, click Remove device, and then click Yes.*

3.13.3 Working with Desktop Gadgets

Windows 7 contains mini-programs called Desktop gadgets. It keeps information and tools readily available for you to use. Gadgets are used to display a picture slide show, view continuously updated headlines, or look up contacts. For example, you can use the Headline gadgets to show the latest news headlines. You do not have to stop working on your document, because the headlines are always visible. If you see a headline that interests you, you can click that headline, and your Web browser will open that headline.

Adding Gadgets

By default, gadgets are not displayed on the desktop. But, you can easily add or remove gadgets whenever you feel the need for something new on your computer screen. The gadget gallery that comes with Windows 7 includes about a dozen offerings but has a handy link to a much larger online gallery.

➜ **To add a gadget on the desktop, do this:**

1. Right click an empty area on the desktop and then choose **Gadgets**.
2. The **Windows Gadgets Gallery** window opens, displaying various gadgets as shown in Figure 3.45.

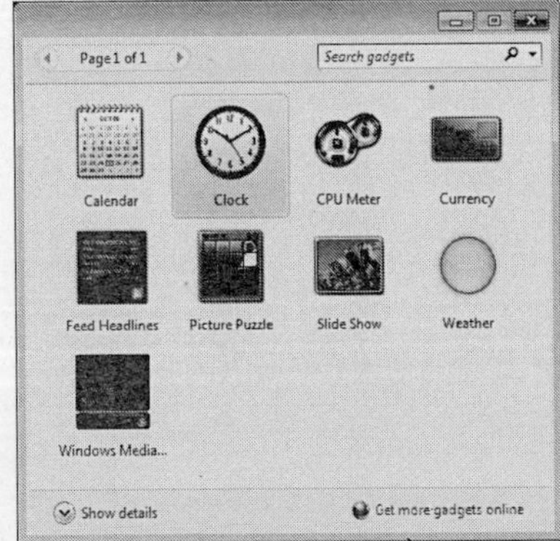

Figure 3.45 Windows gadgets gallery dialog box

3. Double-click the selected gadget that you want to add to the Desktop or right click the gadget and then click **Add** button.
4. The Clock gadget appears on the desktop as shown in Figure 3.46.

Figure 3.46 Adding gadgets on the desktop

5. After adding the gadgets, you can close the **Windows Gadgets Gallery** window by clicking the **Close** button.

3.14 LINUX OPERATING SYSTEM

3.14.1 Overview of Linux

Linux is a multiuser, multitasking operating system first developed by Linus Benedict Torvalds in the year 1991. Linux is a 32-bit operating system. It runs on a wide variety of platforms, such as Intel, Sparc, Alpha, etc. It can be considered in every sense as a full-blown implementation of UNIX. But it cannot be called as UNIX because UNIX is a registered trademark product owned by American Telephone and Telegraph Company (AT&T). Linux is distributed as a free software under a free software licence called the GNU General Public License (GPL).

Linux is known as an open source operating system and also called free software because everything about Linux is accessible to the public and is freely available to anyone. Since the Linux source code is available, anyone can copy, modify, and distribute this software. This allows for various companies, such as SuSE, Red Hat, Caldera and others to sell and distribute Linux.

3.14.2 Types of Linux Operating Systems

Linux is an popular operating system that is proving to be a viable alternative to Microsoft's Windows and Apple's Mac operating systems. There are many different types of Linux operating systems available to users. These are called "distributions." Each distribution has a different main goal and is tailor-made for that function.

Ubuntu

The most popular and widely used Linux distribution is called "Ubuntu." Ubuntu is aimed at bringing Linux to casual computer users and is comparable in features to Microsoft's Windows operating system. It is estimated that 30 percent of all Linux users use the Ubuntu distribution.

Kubuntu

Kubuntu is similar to Ubuntu in operation. The main difference is that Kubuntu uses a different type of file system than Ubuntu. They both perform the same basic functions, and both are easily accessible to casual computer users.

Debian

Debian is a more complicated version of the Linux operating system. It is what the distributions Ubuntu and Kubuntu are based on, though it is not nearly as accessible to casual computer users. Debian has the ability to operate as a standard desktop computer operating system, as well as an operating system used to run computer servers.

Fedora

Fedora is another example of a Linux distribution. In appearance, Fedora's desktop and standard operations are similar to those of Ubuntu and Kubuntu. Fedora is used primarily for older PCs due to its limited system requirements.

Linux Mint

Linux Mint is a Linux distribution that was modeled after Ubuntu. As opposed to Ubuntu, which has limited functionality when first installed and requires users to pick and choose which applications to install based on their needs, Linux Mint's focus is providing all programs and drivers a user would need immediately after installation.

Components of Linux System

Linux operating system has primarily three components:

- **Kernel**–Kernel is the core part of Linux. It is dependable for all major activities of this operating system. It consists of various modules and it interacts directly with the hardware. Kernel provides the required abstraction to hide low-level hardware details to system or application programs.
- **System Library**–System libraries are special functions or programs using which application programs or system utilities accesses Kernel's features. These libraries implements most of the functionalities of the operating system and do not requires kernel module's code access rights.
- **System Utility**–Its programs are responsible to do specialized, individual level tasks.

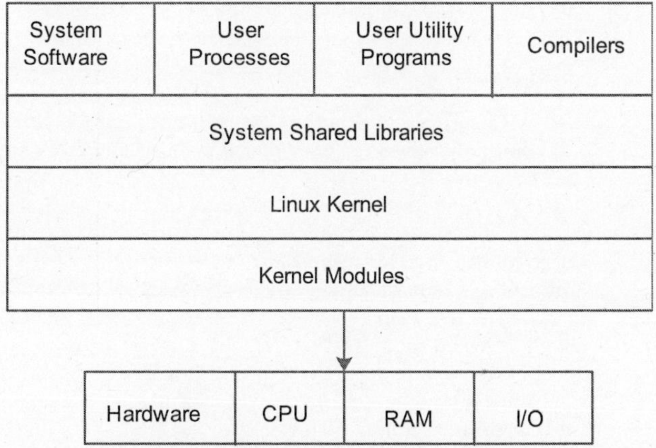

Figure 3.47 Components of Linux

Figure 3.47 illustrates the various components that make up a full Linux system. The most important distinction between the kernel and everything else. All the kernel code executes in the processor's privileged mode with full access to all the physical resources of the computer. Linux refers to this as **kernel** mode. Under Linux, no user code is built into the kernel. Any operating system support code that does not need to run in kernel mode is placed into the system libraries and runs in **user** mode.

Unlike kernel mode, user mode has access only to a controlled subset of the system's resources.

3.14.3 Basic Features of Operating System

Following are some of the important features of Linux operating system.

- **Portable**–Portability means software can work on different types of hardware in same way. Linux kernel and application programs support their installation on any kind of hardware platform.
- **Open Source**–Linux source code is freely available and it is community-based development project. Multiple teams works in collaboration to enhance the capability of Linux operating system and it is continuously evolving.
- **Multi-User**–Linux is a multiuser system means multiple users can access system resources like memory/ram/application programs at same time.
- **Multiprogramming**–Linux is a multiprogramming system means multiple applications can run at same time.
- **Hierarchical File System**–Linux provides a standard file structure in which system files/user files are arranged.
- **Shell**–Linux provides a special interpreter program which can be used to execute commands of the operating system. It can be used to do various types of operations, call application programs, etc.
- **Security**–Linux provides user security using authentication features like password protection/controlled access to specific files/encryption of data.

3.14.4 Basic Linux Elements

The basic elements of Linux are discussed in the following subsections:

Kernel

The kernel is at the core of Linux system and is loaded into the memory as soon as the system starts up. It manages main memory, files and peripheral devices. Maintaining the time and date, launching applications, and allocating system resources are also functions of this part of the operating system.

Shell

Shell is a program which interprets commands given by the user. The command can be either typed in through the command line or contained in a file called *'shell script'*. Commands in 'shell script' files are interpreted by the shell.

File System

Linux treats everything as file. Even a directory is treated as a file that contains entries for several other files. All the hardware devices, such as I/O devices, storage devices, etc., are all treated as files.

The Linux file system is organized in an hierarchy which starts with the *root* directory. The root is represented by a forward slash (/). Under the root directory are several system directories and the home directory. Figure 3.48 lists the standard system directories in Linux.

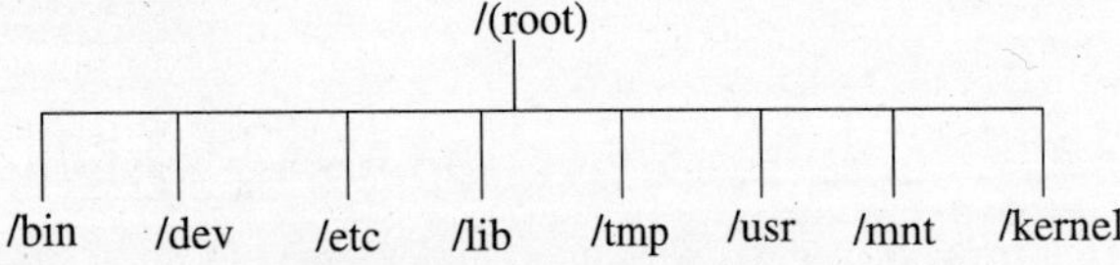

Figure 3.48 Linux file system

Linux uses forward slash (/) as a separator (Windows or DOS uses backslash (\) as a separator). For example, a subdirectory *mydir* of the directory *usr*, will be shown as /usr/mydir. The slash (/) before the *usr* represents the root directory.

/bin This directory contains executable program files (**bin**ary files). In this directory, one can find the files for the Linux commands. (Similar to command.com file in DOS).

/dev This directory contains the special **dev**ice files. For example, the printer may be a file known as *prn* in this directory, the hard disk may be *hda* file and its first partition would be *hda0*.

/etc This directory contains all the system-wide configuration information as text files.

/lib This directory contains the **lib**rary files. Library files contain the reusable functions and routines for the programmer to use.

/tmp This directory contains all the **temp**orary files, which will eventually be deleted from the system. This is similar to the `C:\windows\temp directory` in Windows XP.

/usr This directory contains the home directories of the users, source text for the online manual (man) pages, games and other directories. There is one home directory for each user. For example, for a user called mini, there will be a directory with the same name in **usr** directory. The directory *mini* will contain all the files and sub-directories created by the user 'mini'.

/kernel This directory contains all the **kernel** specific code. Kernel is the heart of the Linux system. It is responsible for resource allocation, security and low-level hardware interfaces.

/mnt This is the directory where the storage devices other than hard disks (floppy disks and CD disks) are mounted. This directory contains the sub-directories 'floppy' and 'cdrom' which when these devices are mounted show the contents of the CD-ROM or floppy disk, respectively.

Linux transparently supports many different filesystems, such as MS-DOS (Microsoft Disk Operating System), Minix, VFAT (Virtual File Allocation Table), PROC, ISO9660, EXT2, etc. Transparently, it means all of the mounted file systems and files appear as a single hierarchical *virtual file system* to the user. Users need not know what type of file or file system they are using. The files in floppy disks, compact disks, etc., all form part of this virtual file system.

Commands

A Linux command is a series of characters that you type. These characters consist of words which are separated by white spaces. The first word is the command itself and the rest are the command's arguments. These arguments provide information that the command may need for its execution. Linux commands are case-sensitive. That is, cp is different from CP and cP.

☞ *You must type all Linux commands in lowercase letters.*

Commands are issued to the shell at the command line. A command line comprises of commands, the line of instructions, options and any command line arguments that you may provide. For example, the following is a command line:

```
$ man cp
```

Commands are entered at the shell prompt ($, #). Prompt is merely a symbol that appears at the start of a command line. This lets the operator know that Linux is ready and waiting for your command.

Device Drivers

Device drivers are software packages that form a major part of the kernel. They control the interaction between the hardware devices and the operating system.

Utilities

Utilities are software tools that are included with the Linux operating system and lets you do miscellaneous jobs, such as text editing, programming and communications.

3.14.5 System Features

Linux supports features found in other implementations of UNIX, and many which are not found elsewhere. In this section, we will discuss the features of the Linux kernel.

- Linux is a complete multitasking, multiuser operating system, as are all other versions of UNIX. This means that many users can log into and run programs on the same machine simultaneously.
- The Linux system is mostly compatible with several UNIX standards at the source level including IEEE (Institute of Electrical and Electronics Engineers) POSIX.1, UNIX System V, and Berkely System Distribution UNIX. Linux was developed with source code portability in mind, and it's easy to find commonly used features that are shared by more than one platform.
- Other specific internal features of Linux include POSIX (Portable Operating System Interface) job control (used by shells like csh and bash), pseudoterminals (pty devices), and support for dynamically loadable national or customized keyboard drivers. Linux supports virtual consoles that let you switch between login sessions on the same system console. Users of the screen program will find the Linux virtual console implementation familiar.
- Linux supports various file systems for storing data, like the ext2 file system, which was developed specifically for Linux. The Xenix and UNIX System V file systems are also supported, as well as the Microsoft MS-DOS and Windows 95

VFAT file systems on a hard drive or floppy. The ISO (International Standards Organization) 9660 CD-ROM file system is also supported.

- Linux provides a complete implementation of TCP/IP (Transmission Control Protocol/Internet Protocol) networking software. This includes device drivers for many popular Ethernet cards, SLIP (Serial Line Internet Protocol) and PPP (Point-to-Point Protocol), which provide access to a TCP/IP network via a serial connection, PLIP (Parallel Line Internet Protocol), and NFS (Network File System). The complete range of TCP/IP clients and services is also supported, which includes FTP, telnet, NNTP (Network News Transfer Protocol), and SMTP (Simple Mail Transfer Protocol).
- The Linux kernel is developed to use protected-mode features of Intel 80386 and better processors. In particular, Linux uses the protected-mode, descriptor based, memory management paradigm, and other advanced features.
- The kernel supports demand-paged, loaded executables. Only those segments of a program which are actually in use are read into memory from disk. Also, copy-on-write pages are shared among executables. If several instances of a program are running at once, they share physical memory, which reduces overall usage.
- In order to increase the amount of available memory, Linux also implements disk paging. Up to 1 GB of swap space may be allocated on disk (upt to 8 partitions of 128 megabytes each). However, swapping data to disk is no substitute for physical RAM, which is much faster.
- The Linux kernel also implements a unified memory pool for user programs and disk cache. All free memory is used by the cache, which is reduced when running large programs.
- Executables use dynamically linked, shared libraries code from a single library on disk. Executable files occupy less disk space, especially those which use many library functions. There are also statically linked libraries for object debugging and maintaining "complete" binary files when shared libraries are not installed. The libraries are dynamically linked at run time, and the programmer can use his or her own routines in place of the standard library routines.

3.14.6 Software Features

- Virtually every utility one would expect of a standard UNIX implementation has been ported to Linux, including basic commands like ls, awk, tr, sed, bc, and more. The familiar working environment of other UNIX systems is duplicated on Linux. All standard commands and utilities are included.
- Many text editors are available, including vi, ex, pico, jove, and GNU emacs, and variants like Lucid emacs, which incorporates extensions of the X Window System, and joe. The text editor you are accustomed to using has more than likely been ported to Linux.
- The choice of a text editor is an interesting one. Many UNIX users prefer "simple" editors like vi. But vi has many limitations due to its age, and modern editors like emacs have gained popularity. emacs supports a complete, Lisp-based macro language and interpreter, powerful command syntax, and other extensions. There are emacs macro packages which let you read electronic mail and News, edit directory contents,
- Most of the basic Linux utilities are GNU software. GNU utilities support advanced features that are not found in the standard versions of BSD and UNIX System Vprograms. For example, the GNU vi clone, elvis, includes a structured macro language that differs from the original implementation. However, GNU utilities are intended to remain compatible with their BSD and System V counterparts.
- A shell is a program which reads and executes commands from the user. In addition, many shells provide features like job control, managing several processes at once, input and output redirection, and a command language for writing shell scripts. A shell script is a program in the shell's command language and is analogous to a MS-DOS batch file.
- Many types of shells are available for Linux. The most important difference between shells is the command language. For example, the C SHell (csh) uses a command language similar to the C programming language. The classic Bourne SHell sh uses another command language. The choice of a shell is often based on the command language it provides, and determines, to a large extent, the qualities of working environment under Linux.
- The GNU Bourne Again Shell (bash) is a variation of the Bourne Shell which includes many advanced features like job control, command history, command and filename completion, an emacs-like interface for editing command lines, and other powerful extensions to the standard Bourne Shell language. Another popular shell is tcsh, a version of the C Shell with advanced functionality similar to that found in bash. Other shells include zsh, a small Bourne-like shell; the Korn Shell (ksh); BSD's ash; and rc, the Plan 9 shell.

3.14.7 File Handling in Linux

Each directory or file in Linux is referred to, by using its pathname beginning from the root directory. For example, the directory **usr** is referred to as /usr (/ or root is its parent directory); mini is referred to as /usr/mini, where usr is the parent directory of mini directory.

There are two types of pathnames. These are:

(a) Absolute Pathname
(b) Relative Pathname

An absolute pathname tells you the complete path of a directory starting from the root, as explained above. Root is represented by a forward slash (/). For example, absolute pathname of "Delhi" directory is /usr/mini/sales/north/Delhi.

Relative pathname gives location of a directory, relative to the current working directory. For example, suppose your current working directory is /usr/mini/sales/north. Then the relative pathname to the "Delhi" directory is Delhi. Relative pathnames do not start with a "/".

☞ *If you do not start a pathname with "/", Linux assumes that you are using relative pathname.*

Identifying the Current Working Directory

To find out which directory you are currently working in, type the following command.

$ pwd Enter

The pwd command prints the absolute pathname of your current working directory. It takes no arguments. For example, in Figure 3.49[1], the user "mini" got the result as /usr/mini.

Making New Directories (mkdir)

To create a new directory, use the mkdir command followed by the directory name. For example, suppose user mini (who is currently in the home directory /usr/mini) wants to create a directory named "sales", she should give the following command (See Figure 3.49).

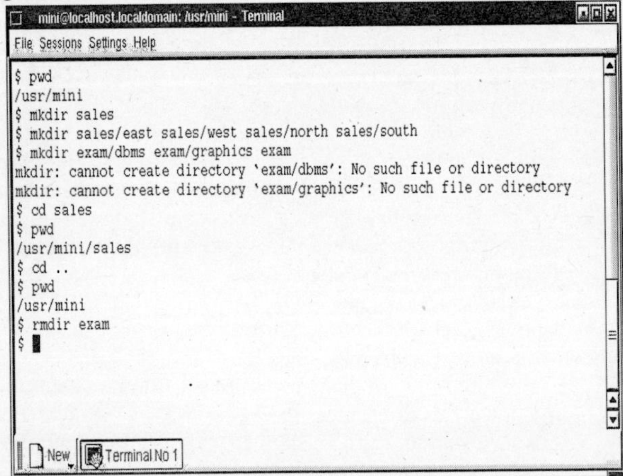

Figure 3.49 A sample Linux session using commands discussed till now

`$ mkdir sales`

The sub-directory "sales" is created under the current directory (i.e., /usr/mini).

To create a number of directories with one mkdir command, separate the directory names with spaces. For example, the following command creates various directories (See Figure 3.49).

`$ mkdir sales/east sales/west sales/north sales/south` Enter

The above command will create four directories under the sales directory.

☞ *The order of specifying the arguments is important. Note that we cannot create a sub-directory before creating its parent directory.*

If we enter the command as:

`$ mkdir exam/dbms exam/graphics exam` Enter

In this case, the system will fail to create the two sub-directories dbms and graphics, but it will create the exam directory.

Moving to a Different Directory (cd)

You can change your working directory using the cd command followed by the pathname (absolute or relative) to which you want to move.

For example, to move to the sales directory, type the following command:

`$ cd sales` Enter

Note that in the above command, we have made use of the relative pathname. After giving the above command, if you give the pwd command, you will see the result as /usr/mini/sales (See Figure 3.49).

☞ *The cd command without any following pathname always takes the user back to the user's HOME directory.*

Linux uses a single dot (.) to represent the current working directory and double dots (..) to represent the parent directory of the current working directory. For example, typing cd.. will take user "mini" to her HOME directory (/usr/mini), since that is the parent directory of sales.

Removing a Directory (rmdir)

The command rmdir is used for deleting a directory. The directory to be deleted must be empty for this command to work. For example, to remove the "exam" directory, type the following command (See Figure 3.49):

$ rmdir exam Enter

☞ *We can also delete more than one directory by separating the multiple directory names with spaces:*

☞ *You cannot remove a directory if you are placed in one of its sub-directories.*

Listing the Contents of Directories (ls)

To list the files and sub-directories of the current directory, **ls** command is used. Its function is equivalent to the DIR command of DOS. For example, to list the contents of her current directory, user "mini" should type the following:

`$ ls`

She will get the following result:

east
north
south
west

The order of display is numerals→uppercase characters→lowercase characters. That is, the list is displayed with numerals having precedence over alphabets and in alphabets, uppercase has precedence over lower case.

If the names of files and directories under a specified directory (say north) are to be listed out, then we need to specify the directory name with ls command, as follows:

`$ ls north`

The above command will give the result as shown in Figure 3.49.

Usually, a directory contains many files, and user may be interested in knowing whether a particular file is available or not. In that case, he/she just has to use **ls** with the filename, as follows:

`$ ls March`

The above command will prompt – File Not Found error, since there is no file called "March" in our current directory. Had the file existed, *ls* would have displayed the filename.

1 The screens shown in this book are taken from a Linux terminal.

The command *ls* can be used along with a number of *options*. Options are nothing but predetermined arguments used along with a minus sign (-). The different options forces the command to work differently.

For example, the following command will display file and directory names in multiple columns.

```
$ ls -x
east      north      south      west
```

Table 3.2 lists the different options of **ls** and their uses.

Table 3.2 Options of the command ls

Option	Used to
-x	Get multi-columnar output.
-r	List files and sub-directories in reverse order.
-t	List files and sub-directories with time order.
-a	List all files, including the normally hidden files.
-A	List all files excluding . and .. .
-c	List files by inode modification time.
-i	List the inode for each file.
-l	Display permissions, owner, size, modification time, etc., along with file and directory names.

Creating Files (using cat)

To create a file, type the command **cat** at the shell prompt, followed by > character and the filename. For example, to create a file called January, enter the following command.

$ cat > January Enter

After you press Enter key, you will be prompted to enter the contents of the file. Type the data and press Ctrl + D keys together to terminate the command line (See Figure 3.50).

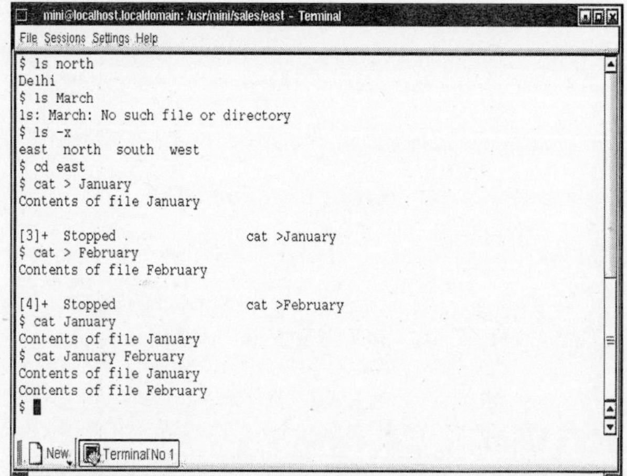

Figure 3.50 A sample Linux session using commands discussed till now

Listing the Contents of Files (cat)

To list the contents of a file, use the command **cat** followed by the filename. DOS has TYPE command for this.

For example, to list the contents of file January type the following:

$ cat January Enter

Absolute pathname can be given to display a file in another directory. The cat command can also display more than one file by separating different filenames with spaces, as shown in the following command:

$ cat January February Enter

The above command will display the contents of the two files in different rows. Use of cat method to create and display the contents of files is shown in Figure 3.50.

Copying Files (cp)

The command cp is used to copy a file into another. DOS equivalent for cp is the COPY command. Like in DOS, the cp command requires two arguments – a source filename, the contents of which are to be copied and a target filename, to which the contents are to be copied.

For example, to copy the file February into another file, say March, type the following (See Figure 3.51):

$ cp January March Enter

Note that the *ls* command will now show three files, namely January, February and March.

☞ *Use cp with -i option if you want the system to ask for confirmation before copying the files.*

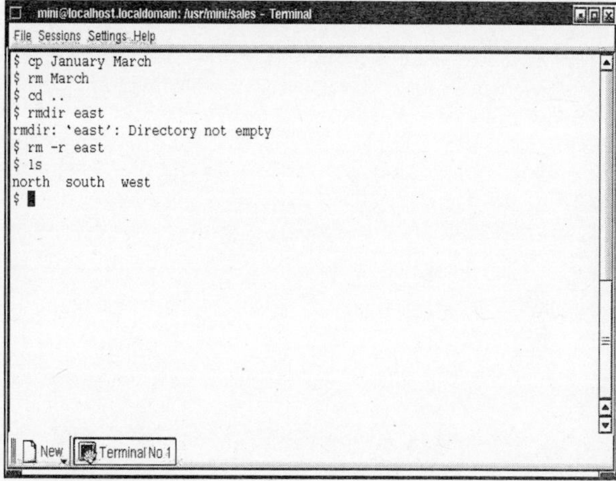

Figure 3.51 A sample Linux session using cp and rm commands

Here, the file January is copied to a new file called March.

☞ *If March file already exists, its contents will be destroyed and replaced by contents of January file.*

If you want to give more than one options along with command, you can use either of the following:

$ ls -l -a -t

$ ls -lat

Both the above methods will work.

Deleting Files (rm)

To delete or remove a file, the rm command is used. This is equivalent to the DEL command in DOS.

For example, to remove the file March, type the following command:

$ rm March Enter

This is shown in Figure 3.51.

☞ *Use rm with -i option if you want the system to ask for confirmation, like in cp.*

To remove a directory, use rm with -r option. Here -r stands for recursive deletion. For example, the following command will remove the directory accounts.

$ rm -r accounts Enter

☞ *Unlike rmdir, rm -r will remove directories even if they are not empty.*

In Figure 3.51, the system did not delete the directory "east" when *rmdir* command was given, but did so with the *rm -r* command.

Moving Files (mv)

A file can be moved, using the mv command. Equivalent command in DOS is MOVE. The following command will displace the directory north from "sales" directory to the directory "/usr/mini".

$ mv north /usr/mini/north Enter

The above command does not create a copy of "north" but displaces it.

Now if you type the ls command, you will only see two directories, south and west (See Figure 3.52). The directory "east" was removed using *rm -r* command and "north" is moved to a different directory. The directory "/usr/mini" now contains the north directory and all its sub-directories and files as shown by the ls command in Figure 3.52.

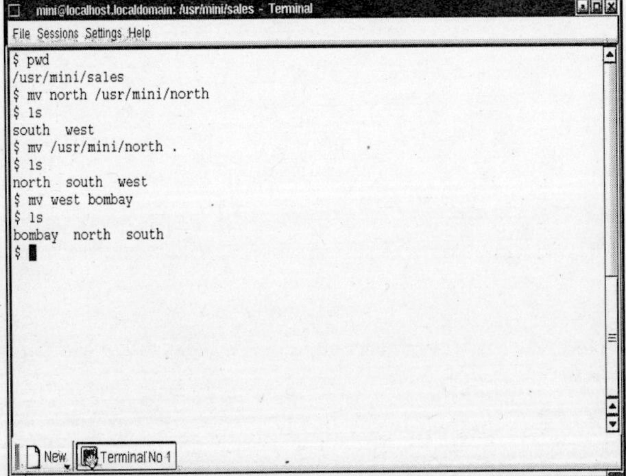

Figure 3.52 A sample Linux session using commands discussed till now

Perform mv operation again to bring back the directory.

$ mv /usr/mini/north.

Note that the dot (.) represents current directory.

Files and directory can also be renamed using the **mv** command. For example, the following command will rename the directory "west" as "bombay" (See Figure 3.52):

$ mv west bombay Enter

Files can also be renamed in the same way. If the destination exists, it will be overwritten and if it does not exist, it will be created.

☞ *mv also has the -i option like cp and rm commands and works in the same way.*

Installation of Linux

We will be discussing about the installation of popular Red Hat Linux 7.2 in this section. Before listing the procedures to follow for installing the Linux operating system, let us see what are the hardware and software requirements of Linux.

Hardware Requirements

Red Hat Linux can be installed if the following basic hardware requirements are met:

(a) x86 platform namely 80386, 80486 etc.
(b) Intel, Sparc, Alpha or Advanced Micro Devices (AMD) processor
(c) x386 CPU family or above
(d) Minimum 128 MB RAM
(e) Minimum 2 GB free hard disk space
(f) Input devices, such as keyboard, mouse etc.
(g) Controller cards, such as Small Computer System Interface
(h) (SCSI), Integrated Development Environment (IDE), Firewire, etc.
A Network card, such as Internet Security and Acceleration (ISA), Peripheral Component Interconnect (PCI) or Universal Serial Bus (USB), etc.
(i) Sound card compatible to Linux

Software Requirements

Software requirements for Linux installation are listed as follows:

(a) A partitioning program, such as fdisk or disk druid supplied by Red Hat.
(b) Linux Software package.

Preliminary steps before Installation

The first step is to create an installation disk.

➜ **To create the installation disk, do this:**

1. Copy the "boot.img" file from the Red Hat CD-ROM disk into a floppy disk. This file can be found in the /images directory of the CD. The file can be created using either the DOS rewrite command (in a DOS/Windows system) or the Linux dd command (in an existing Linux or UNIX system). For example, to create an installation diskette using the dd command, do the following:
   (a) Insert and mount the CD-ROM and then insert a blank floppy into the floppy drive of your computer.
   (b) Now give the following command:
   # dd if=mnt/cdrom/images/boot.img of=/dev/fd0 bs=1440k Enter
   The above command will copy from the input file ("if") mnt/cdrom/boot.img onto the output file ("of") /dev/fd0. It is assumed that floppy drive is accessible from /dev/fd0.

To create an installation diskette using the rawrite program, give the following command (it is assumed that CD-ROM is accessible as drive D):

D:>cd images dosutils\rawrite Enter

For the source file enter "D:\boot.img" and for destination enter "A:".

The bootable installation disk is now ready and you can use it to install your Linux system.

Red Hat Linux can also be installed by booting using any of the following methods:

(a) Booting using a floppy diskette (created as explained above).
(b) Booting directly from the CD-ROM (your BIOS should support this).
(c) Using a hard drive partition to hold the installation software.
(d) Booting from a DOS command line.
(d) Booting from across a network using HTTP (Hypertext Transfer Protocol) or FTP (File Transfer Protocol) protocols.
(e) Booting from an NFS (Network File System) mounted hard drive.

2. The next step is to plan a partitioning strategy. This step is based on the knowledge of existing hardware. The planning process should also take into consideration the future expansion of the system. Knowing how to allocate the hard disk space for each of the Linux software is a real big challenge every Linux system administrator has to take. He should find answers to the following questions:
   (a) How much of the disk is required presently and in future?
   (b) Is any other operating system also required?
   (c) How many application software packages are expected to be installed in future?
   (d) How much data needs to be backed up?
   (e) How many users will the system have?
3. If you require that the system should boot any other operating system also along with Linux, the next step is to choose a boot loader. Boot loader is a software that is responsible for booting Linux along with any other operating system. Examples include LILO (LInux LOader) and GRUB (GRand Unified Boot loader).
4. Now insert the floppy disk (the installation diskette you have created if you are using floppy to boot your system) into a floppy drive and power-on your system. After a few moments, the Red Hat installation program screen will appear.

Hard Drive Partitioning

A hard disk must be partitioned taking into consideration the present and future requirements. For example, let us consider that we have a given hard disk of 40 GB capacity. The different partitions can be as follows:

/swap directory	About double the main memory size. For example, a system having 128 MB memory should get 256 MB swap space.
/ directory (root)	About 60% of the available space.
/bin directory	About 20% of the available space.
/usr directory	Remaining space

The size of /usr should be the largest one. This is because all the users' directories and files, installed application software, Web pages, log files etc. will be stored here only.

Booting a Linux system

The general booting procedure involves checking of the basic subsystems of your computer, such as amount and validity of Read Only Memory or ROM, Central Processing Unit or CPU time and speed, presence of floppy, CD-ROM or hard drive, keyboard and other attributes. The Linux may fail to boot if it detects a hardware failure, missing hardware or hardware mis-configuration.

Next the BIOS will look for the bootable disk, in the order given in the settings (such as search floppy first, then CD-ROM and then the hard drive). Following this, it will look for the boot code in the *Master Boot Record* (*MBR*) of the first hard disk. This area of the disk (MBR) contains the boot sector which loads the boot loader (viz. LILO, GRUB or BootMagic).

When the Linux kernel is loaded, the kernel will carry out the following:

(a) Initialize and load a RAM disk image.
(b) Perform timing tests.
(c) Parse for any boot time kernel arguments.
(d) Recognize, set-up and initialize the CPU.
(e) Set up kernel memory and process handling.
(f) Open a console for displaying kernel boot messages.
(g) Initialize configured system devices.
(h) Start memory handling (paging etc.).
(i) Set up and mount the file system.
(j) Start the init command.

The entire sequence of events that take place when the Linux kernel is loaded can be found in the file usr/src/linux/init/main.c.

☞ *If all goes well, you will see a "login" prompt. You can now login using your username and password.*

3.15 OVERVIEW OF MAC OS

Mac OS is a series of graphical user interface-based operating systems developed by Apple. It is designed a line of Personal Computers (PCs). Steve Jobs Introduced the Macintosh 128K on January 24, 1984. This was the first personal computer featuring a graphical user interface. The integral system software first introduced in 1984 with the original Macitosh. The System was renamed to Mac OS in 1996 with version 7.6.

Macintosh released in two major series. The major changeover in 9 realesed in 1984 to 2000, it is historically known as *Classic Mac OS*. And changeover in 10 released in 2001 to present. The Mac OS X now known as OS X. Both series share a general interface design and application frameworks for compatibility.

3.15.1 Different versions of Mac

The first version was released in 1984. The classical desktop designed used as a single user operating system. The interface is very easy to use and does not need the mouse button for user interaction. Mac OS does not include a command line interface.

Starting with version 3.0, the used filesystem HFS (Hierarchical File System) was used officially, which does not different between uppercase and lowercase letters. Version 5.0 was the first release to run several programs with the integrated MultiFinder at the same time. The operating system was programmed up to version 6.0 mostly in assembler and partially in Pascal and used a 24-bit addressing mode. version 7.0 first supported 32-bit addressing. Thus allow the operating system can use more memory and more powerful programs. Since 1994 version 7.5 supported for the first time the PowerPC architecture and is optimized with the following Mac OS versions further on this architecture. With version 7.6 the name was changed to Mac OS in January 1997.

System 6 (MAC OS)

Mac system software 6 came onto the market in 1988. It requires 1 MB RAM and can address up to 8 MB. The file system can organize hard disks up to 2 GB with 65,536 files. Optionally applications run with the multi Finder in cooperative multitasking. For word processing are programs, such as WriteNow, MacWrite II, and Microsoft Word 4.0 available.

System 7 (Mac OS)

The system 7 was first available in May 1991. The new operating system needed 2 MB RAM, optionally it can be switched to 32-bit depending from the used hardware. Cooperative multitasking is now enabled by default, the addressable memory is no longer limited to 8 MB. In addition virtual memory can be enabled.

The System Software 7.5 appeared in 1994 and requires at least 4 MB RAM. It was running both on 68k-Macs and Power Macintosh. In September 1996, the update System 7.5.5 includes all available bug fixes, Open Transport 1.1.2, current Ethernet driver and support for storage drive volumes up to 4 GB. With release 7.6 the company Apple changed the name for the operating system from System Software to Mac OS in 1997. At the 31. January 1999 Apple gave the Mac system software 7.5.3 public as free download.

Mac OS 7.6 can be installed on every Mac compatible computer, which contains at least a 68030 processor and supports 32-bit addressing. The 24-bit addressing is no longer supported. Performance is improved in the area of virtual memory and memory management. QuickTime version 2.5 offers better image quality and benefits of multiple processors.

On systems with 68040 or PowerPC processors partitions can be used of up to 2 TB, systems with 68030 processor remain limited to 4 GB.

Mac OS 8

Mac OS 8 by Apple appeared in July 1997. As minimum requirements are specified a 68040 or PowerPC processor, 32 MB RAM and 120 MB of free disk space. The Ctrl key is used to display a specific context menu for different actions. Finder in version 8 is now multithreaded and other applications during the copy of files. The starting time of the operating system and applications is been reduced. As standard the browser software Microsoft Internet Explorer 3.0 and Netscape Navigator 3.0 are included. Inside of a TCP/IP (Transmission Control Protocol/Internet Protocol) network can shared files and printers accessed.

With Mac OS 8.1 the file system HFS+ is included by default. Now informations are stored more efficiently on the file system and does less waste disk space in comparison of HFS. The limit of the partition size is depending on your hardware, the maximum size is now 2 TB for all Quadra and PowerMac systems. The file system can handle up to 2 billion files with a current file size of up to 2 GB. PC Exchange 2.2 allows users the mount of DOS and Windows drives on your desktop. The supported file systems include FAT12, FAT16, FAT32, VFAT.

Mac OS 8.5 further optimized the stability and speed of the operating system, Sherlock is extended for full-text search in local files and Internet search wizard for the first time. Mac systems with 68k processors are no longer compatible with this version. The throughput in Ethernet networks has been increased, AppleScript is now up to 5 x faster than the previous version. The graphical display is accelerated by new QuickDraw routines. Copying files has become faster and increase the disk throughput. A tool for system maintaining detects and fixes errors on the file system automated. The "Apple System Profiler" creates comprehensive reports about the used hardware and software.

Following applications are included in current version: Finder 8.5 QuickTime Pro 3, Open Transport 2, Internet Explorer 4.01, Outlook Express 4.01, Netscape Navigator 4.0.5, Mac OS Runtime for Java 2.0 and File Exchange 3.

Mac OS 8.6 requires 250 MB free disk space and 24 MB RAM. A new kernel is included which improves performance and added support for the PowerPC G4 processor. The ability of multitasking and multiprocessing has been optimized further and enhanced with new features.

Mac OS 9

The operating system Mac OS 9 has been developed under the name Sonata and released to the 23. October 1999. The installation requires 32 MB RAM with virtual memory and a PowerPC 601 processor or higher. For models with G3 processor are at least 64 MB RAM recommended for optimal performance. The first G4 and iMac systems until summer 2000 are supported. The free disk storage should be 150 up to 400 MB depending on the installation type.

Fifty new features are added in comparison to the previous version. This includes support for multiple users with password and access management for files and settings. The operating system can automatically update itself via the Internet. You can back up all personal passwords with a password. The search engine Sherlock 2 is extended with language and search templates. The first version "Carbon" API (Application Programming Interface) is available for new applications.

The following applications are included in current version: Finder 9.0, Mac OS Runtime for Java 2.1.4, Apple data security 2.0 and Open Transport 2.5.

Mac OS X

Different technologies like the Mach Kernel, NEXTSTEP and tools from NetBSD and FreeBSD found in Mac OS X to merge the previous Apple technology with UNIX features. The operating system core Darwin is open source and can be used also on x86 computers. Mac OS X works with preemptive multi-tasking and includes beside the new GUI Aqua the classic GUI from Mac OS 9.

Mac OS X 10.0 came out in March 2001. To install are 128 MB RAM (256 MB RAM starting from Mac OS X 10.3.9) and 1.5 GB hard disk space (3.0 GB starting from Mac OS X 10.2) provided. Mac OS X 10.5 requires at least 512 MB RAM and 9 GB of free disk space.

- 32-bit or 64-bit processing
- SMP or Symmetric Multi Processor with up to 32 CPUs
- needs a PowerPC G3, G4 or G5
- POSIX compatible
- HFS+ file system

Field of Application

- digital photography
- 2-D and 3-D animations
- video processing, streaming
- audio processing
- platform for DTP (Desktop Publishing), web design
- office applications

Structure Information

- supports QuickTime/VR
- monolithic Kernel
- Read/Write FAT, FAT32, ISO9660, UDF
- well proven TCP/IP Stack
- graphical user interaction with the finder
- graphical representation by Quickdraw
- central password administration (Keychain)

Mac OS X 10.3 has now a GUI in metallic scheme and the optimized Finder. The use and access in heterogeneous networks was further simplified. Files can be provided with etiquettes, the compression format ZIP is now directly supported. 12 million MacOS X user were counted in October 2004.

According to Apple Mac OS X 10.4 more than 200 new features. Features are the fast, system-wide and index-based search function named Spotlight, the Dashboard for easy access to small programms (Widgets), the Automator for the simplified composition of Applescripts for the automation of tasks. The Web browser Safari in version 2.0 now contained RSS (Really Simple Syndication) support, the QuickTime software was updated to version 7 with support for the H.264 video codec.

First since the 10th January 2006 is Mac OS X 10.4.4 next to the PowerPC version available for Intel based Macs. On 6 June 2005 Steve jobs announced at the WWDC (World Wide Developers Conference) the switch to Intel processors. Apple had developed Mac OS X since 2000 internally also for the Intel platform.

Apple released the successor MacOS X 10.5, Leopard at the 2007. With more than 300 innovations Mac OS offers enhanced user interface with virtual desktops, a fast file preview and Dock with 3D effect. For the surfing on the Internet the Apple Safari 3 Web browser is included. Backups can be made, managed and restored in a simple way with "Time Machine". Time Machine makes every hour the day automatically a file backup and every day a snapshot for the duration of a complete month. Lost files are recovered easily over the display of a dynamic time line of those snapshot.

Mac OS X 10.6 is a Mac computer with Intel Core 2 Duo processor with at least 1 GB memory and 5 GB free space. This operating system no longer exists as PowerPC execution. It supports up to 16 TB memory, it is optimized for multi core processors, and is a pure 64-bit operating system. With the technology OpenCL graphics processor can speed up in specific applications calculations.

3.15.2 Features of the Mac OS

With Mac OS X Lion, Apple introduced some new features. These are discussed below:

ActiveSync and Exchange 2007: Following in the footsteps of the iPhone, Snow Leopard makes these Microsoft technologies to the OS. It means Apple's e-mail, calendar, and contacts apps work with Exchange 2007 server.

The way Exchange support works in Snow Leopard is pretty simple. Once you add an Exchange account in Mail, you will start receiving e-mail messages in Mail. You will be able to view Exchange contacts in Address Book, and Exchange calendars and tasks will appear in iCal. iCal will even perform tricky tasks like scheduling meetings based on the free/busy status of invitees; you can accept or decline meeting invitations from Mail. If you are syncing your iPhone to the Exchange server, all those calendar events will sync up automatically.

Expose integration in the Dock: The Mac OS X Dock makes it easy to access applications, open documents, and common folders. Open documents are easily accessed in Snow Leopard. Now, when you click and hold an app icon in the Dock, you get preview windows for each of its open documents, allowing you to switch easily among them or to close them, all without having to clutter your screen with document windows. The Dock-integrated Expos functionality that Snow Leopard adds.

Automatic location detection: When you travel, you have to mentally calculate the current time when looking at the calendar or clock. You can change the time zone in the Date & Time system preference, but it is easy to forget. Snow Leopard changes the time zone for you automatically, using Wi-Fi (Wireless Fidelity) mapping to figure out where you are -- you will need to be connected to a Wi-Fi access point or router. iCal can also be set to adjust the times to the current time zone automatically, so your calendar always reflects the current times.

New Preview is like Adobe Reader: In other words, it works a lot like Adobe Reader. You can open multiple PDF (Portable Document Format) documents, display their contents as contact sheets, and show thumbnails of pages in a sidebar for easy navigation.

Movie and screencast recording: Snow Leopard takes the formerly QuickTime Pro makes it a standard, free app in Mac OS X. It means you can record movies and screencasts from your Mac with no additional software.

Finder: The Finder, the central point for managing files and folders in Mac OS X, has been completely rewritten in Snow Leopard. This new version, which was written using the Cocoa frameworks required for any 64-bit application, looks more or less identical to the older version. Apple says that this new Finder is much more responsive than the older model due to the complete rewrite, support for 64-bit mode, and increased threading using the new Grand Central Dispatch technologies.

Smart Eject: Snow Leopard's new eject manager improves on the old method in two ways. When you first attempt to eject a disk. The eject manager actually sends out a signal to its own subsystems and other programs, asking them to relinquish their hold on the volume if possible. But it fails because a program really is using the drive. Snow Leopard will bring up a window telling you which program does not want to let you eject the disk. You can then switch to that program, quit out of it, and eject the disk.
Substitutions: Many programs autocorrect what you type, for example, changing teh into the. Mac utilities built autosubstitution of text into OS X. Programs have to be modified to specifically support it; but once they are, they are all share the same substitution list, which you can see in the Text tab of the Language & Text pane in System Preferences. A few common substitutions are enabled by default into the copyright symbol and the aforementioned teh into the. But you can add your own as well. To see substitutions in action, open TextEdit and choose Edit → Substitutions → Text Replacement. When the Text Replacement box is checked, TextEdit will follow the system wide substitutions list. You can also enable smart quotes, links, and dashes, which replace commonly typed symbols.
Preview: Snow Leopard's Preview app, now exceedingly useful fixes and refinements. The first and most obvious of these is enhanced text selections. The program now accurately detects and lets you select horizontal and vertical columns in page layouts, making for cleaner, more accurate cutting, copying, and pasting. This is a vast improvement over the previous version, which could not detect columns accurately. (Apple credits artificial intelligence algorithms now built into the core of the operating system). This improved column detection also extends to Safari.

Selecting text in a multi-column document is much more accurate in Snow Leopard's Preview. The new Preview features imaging enhancements. It can now detect images from a Universal Serial Bus or USB-connected digital camera or scanner. A new Import From Scanner menu item replaces the Import Image command of the previous version and lets you scan, view, and correct your images in Preview; it even detects where the images are placed on the scanning bed. The new Preview will also detect a connected camera and let you import images from it. However it does not work with every camera. It did not recognize a Canon PowerShot G2, for example, but it did detect a Canon Digital Rebel XSi.

The Annotate button is paired with a new Annotations Toolbar that appears at the bottom of your document when you click on the button. It shows you the following tools: Arrow, Oval, Rectangle, Text, Note, Link, Highlight, Strikethrough, Underline, Color Menu, Line Width Menu, and Show Font Panel. Text and Arrow are new in this version.
Accessibility: Apple has been gradually bringing Mac OS X up to speed in terms of accessibility features for users with physical disabilities. Tiger was a big leap forward, and Leopard added more improvements. Snow Leopard takes accessibility features in Mac OS X. The new additions are improvements to VoiceOver, support for trackpad gestures for the vision impaired, and support for Braille displays.
Safari 4: Safari 4 offers a couple of new features when running in Snow Leopard. Safari 4 includes Top Sites for viewing all your favorite sites as thumbnails for easy access and full history search, which lets you view your history in a Cover Flow-like interface. But in Snow Leopard, Safari is now crash resistant. This means that if a plug-in crashes, it will not crash the whole browser. Simply refresh the page to try to load the plug-in again. Also, Safari checks to see if a site you are visiting is known to be corrupt, or is known to be a phishing site, and then warns you if it is.
QuickTime X: QuickTime X, Apple's media player, got some major tweaks in Snow Leopard. Now, when you play a movie and move your mouse outside the window, the interface fades away quickly to give you a more immersive video-viewing experience. When watching a movie, you can click the new Share button to convert your movie for iPod, iPhone, or Apple TV. QuickTime converts the video to work best on your chosen device. You also can now record video from your Webcam, audio, or just the action on your screen with a few clicks.

QuickTime X probably received the most interface tweaks in the Snow Leopard. The cleaned-up interface and autofade features look great. The recording features for video, audio, and screencast capturing are used in QuickTime Pro. It is good to see these features will be able to be used by a audience in Snow Leopard.

3.15.3 File and User Management

In Mac OS, you use the Finder to organize and manage your files. These are:

- View the contents of your disks in windows in a variety of ways.
- Automatically sort items by name, kind, creation date, or other criteria in ascending or descending order.
- Rename items.
- Create folders to store related items.
- Move items stored on disk to organize them so they are easy to find and back up.
- Copy items to other disks to back them up or share them with others.
- Delete items you no longer need.
- Mount and eject disks.
- Write to, or "burn," CD-ROMs.

Mac OS X Disk Organization

Mac OS and most other computer operating systems, Mac OS X uses a Hierarchical File System (HFS) to organize and store files, including system files, applications, and documents.

The top level of the filing system is the computer level. You can view the computer level window as shown in Figure 3.53 by clicking the **Computer** icon in the toolbar of any **Go** window. This level shows the computer's internal hard disk, any other disks the computer has access to, and the Network icon.

The next level down is the computer's hard disk level. You can view this level by opening the hard disk icon in the computer level window or on the desktop.

A typical hard disk window, such as:

- Applications contains Mac OS X applications.
- System and Library contain the Mac OS X system files.
- Users contains individual folders for each of the computer's users, as well as a Shared folder.

The Users folder contains a home folder for each user, as well as a Shared folder.

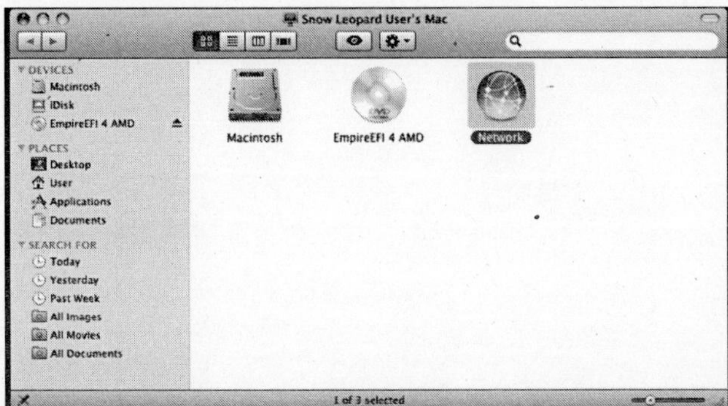

Figure 3.53 The top level of your computer shows disks and network icon

- System Folder contains the Mac OS system files.
- Documents contain documents you saved on your hard disk.
- Desktop contains items that appear on the desktop.

By default, a Mac OS X hard disk is organized for multiple users. Each user has his or her own "home" folder, which is stored in the Users folder as shown in Figure 3.54. You can view the items inside your home folder by opening the house icon with your name on it inside the Users folder or by clicking the Home icon in the toolbar of any Go window.

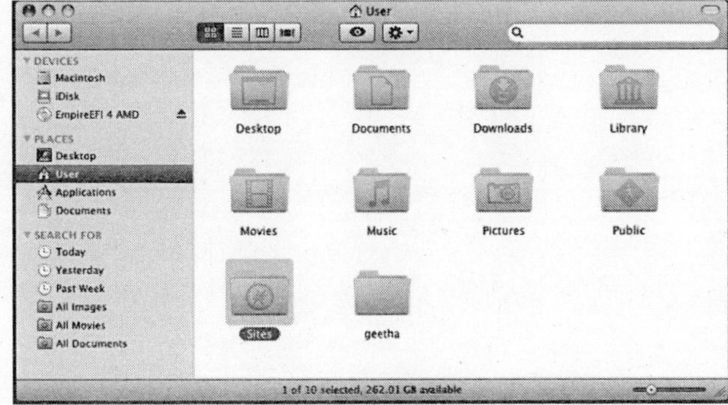

Figure 3.54 Home folder for stroing a variety of item types

Pathnames

A path or pathname is a kind of address for a file on disk. It includes the name of the disk on which the file resides, the names of the folders the file is stored within, and the name of the file itself. For example, the path name for a file named Letter.rtf or Rich Text Format in the Documents folder of the mlanger folder, for example Macintosh HD/Users/mlanger/Documents/Letter.rtf.

When entering a pathname from a specific folder, you do not have to enter the entire path name. Instead, enter the path as it relates to the current folder. For example, the path to the above-mentioned file from the mlanger folder would be: Documents/Letter.rtf.

To indicate a specific user folder, use the tilde (~) character followed by the name of the user account. So the path to the mlanger folder it would be as ~mlanger.

The Go Menu

The Go menu as shown in Figure 3.55 offers a quick way to open specific locations on your computer:

The Go menu has the following options. These are:

- **Back**–Press ⇧ ⌘ [opens the parent folder for the active window's folder. This command is only available if a window is active and if it has been used to display the contents of a folder.
- **Forward**– Press ⇧ ⌘] displays the contents of the window you were viewing before you clicked the Back button. This command is only available if a window is active and if the Back button has been clicked.
- **Enclosing**– Press ⌘ ↑ displays currently inside a folder, you can return to the parent folder by clicking Enclosing Folder.
- **Computer**– Press ⇧ ⌘ **C** opens the top level window for your computer.
- **Home**– Press ⇧ ⌘ **H** opens your home directory for the user currently logged in.
- **iDisk**–This window displays the contents of your Internet iDisk storage.
- **Network**–It displays a window with all your network's servers.
- **Applications**– Press ⇧ ⌘ **A** opens all the applications that appear in your Mac OS X Applications folder.
- **Documents**– Press ⇧ ⌘ **O** This window displays the contents of your Document folder.
- **Utilities**–Press ⇧ ⌘ **U** to open Utilities Window. This window displays a submenu that allows you to choose among the folder that you have recently opend.
- **Recent Folders**–It displays a submenu of recently opened folders.
- **Go to Folder**–Press ⇧ ⌘ **G** to open any folder your computer has access to.
- **Connect to Server**– Press ⌘ **K** enables you to open a server accessible via network.

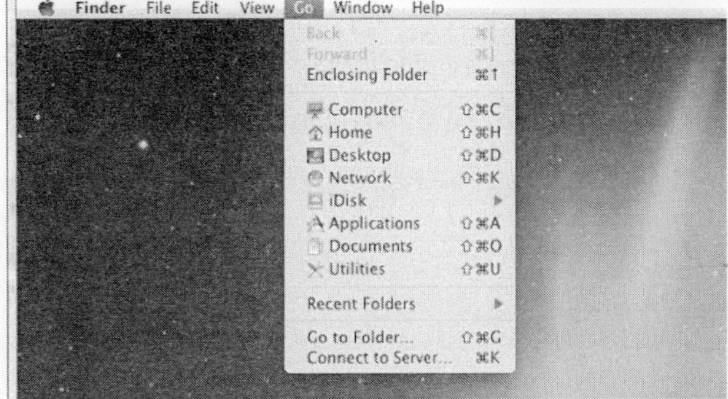

Figure 3.55 Go Menu commands

➜ To go to a folder, do this:

1. Click **Go** menu and choose **Go to Folder...** or press ⇧ ⌘ **G**. The **Go to Folder** dialog box appears as shown in Figure 3.56.
2. Enter the pathname for the folder you want to open.
3. Click Go. If you entered a valid pathname, the folder opens in a Finder window.

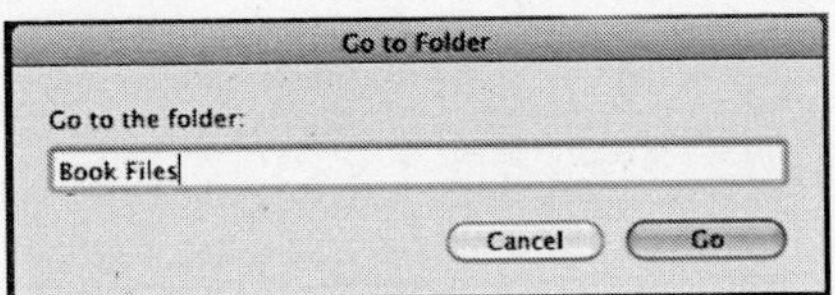

Figure 3.56 Go to Folder dialog box

☞ *If you do not enter a valid pathname, an error message appears in the Go To Folder dialog box.*

Different Views

A Finder window's contents can be displayed using three different views.

- Icon displays the window's contents as small or large icons.
- List displays the window's contents as a displays the window's contents as a sorted list.
- Column displays the window's contents with a multiple-column format that shows the currently selected disk or folder and the items within it.

➜ **To change the window's view, do this:**

1. Click the window whose view you want to change.
2. Choose the desired view option you want from the view menu, or press the corresponding shortcut key ⌘ **1** as shown in Figure 3.57.

Figure 3.57 View menu offers a variety of options for changing a window's view

3. The View menu offers a variety of options for changing a window's view, along with three new commands key equivalent for switching from one view to another. Or
4. Click the toolbar's view button for the view you want. The view of the window changes as shown in Figure 3.58.

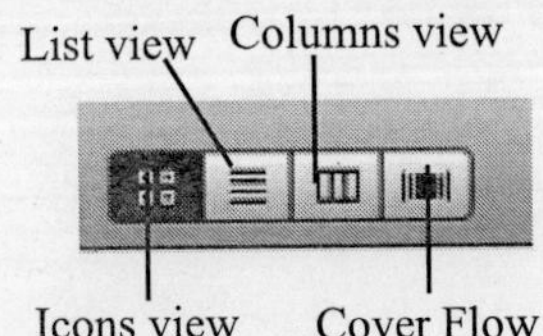

Figure 3.58 View buttons in the toolbar

➜ **To neatly arrange icons in icon view, do this:**

1. Activate the window that you want to clean up with disordered window as shown in Figure 3.59.

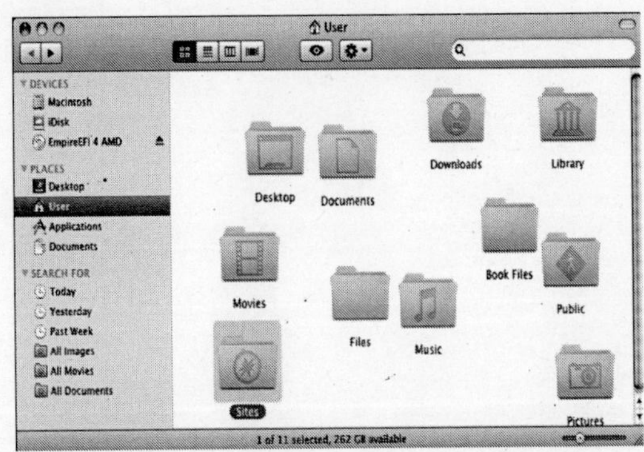

Figure 3.59 window shows disorder list

2. Click **View** menu and choose **Clean Up**. The icons are neatly arranged in window's invisible grid as shown in Figure 3.60. Or

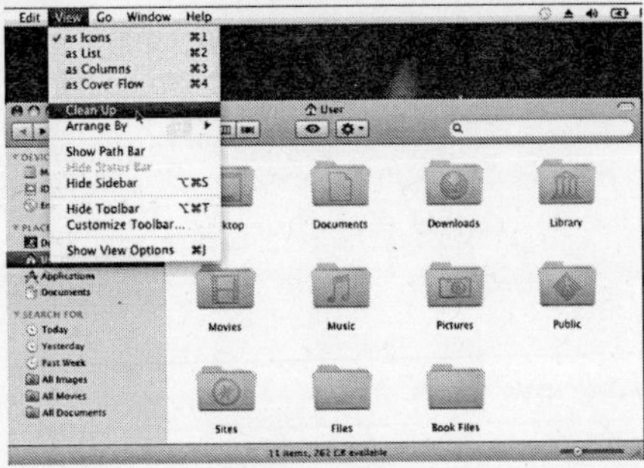

Figure 3.60

3. Choose one of the commands from the **Arrange** submenu under the **View** menu as shown in Figure 3.61.
   - By Name arranges the icons alphabetically by name.
   - By Date Modified arranges the icons sequential by the date they were last modified. With the most recently modified item last.
   - By Date Created arranges the icons sequential by the date created, with the most recently created item list.
   - By Size arranges the icons in size order, with the largest item last.
   - By Kind arranges the icons sequential by the kind of file.

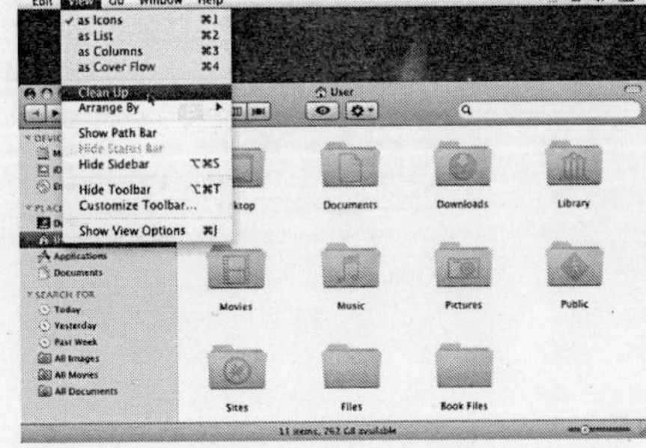

Figure 3.61 The Arrange submenu offers several options for arranging icons

Icons Names

Mac OS is very flexible when it comes to names for files, folders and disks.

- A file or folder name can be up to 255 characters long. A disk name can be up to 27 characters long.
- A name can contain any character except a colon(:). This makes it easy to give your files, folders, and disks names that make sense to you.

➜ To rename an icon, do this:

1. Click the icon to select it.
2. Click and point to the name of the icon. A box appears around the name becomes active.
3. Type a new name. The text you type automatically overwrites the selected text.
4. Press *Return*, or click anywhere else. The icon is renamed as shown in Figure 3.62.

Figure 3.62 To rename an icon

Folders

Mac OS uses folder to organize files and other folder on disk. You can create a folder, give it a name that makes sense to you, and move files and folders into it.

➜ To create a folder, do this:

1. Click **File** menu and choose **New Folder** or press ⌘N. A new untitled folder appears in the active window as shown in Figure 3.63.
2. The icon box around the new untitled folder's name appears. Type a name for it and press **Return** as shown in Figure 3.64.

Figure 3.63 Choose New Folder from the File menu

Moving and Copying Items

You can move or copy items to other locations on the same disk or to other disks by dragging them.

- When you drag an item to a location on the disk, the item is moved to that location.

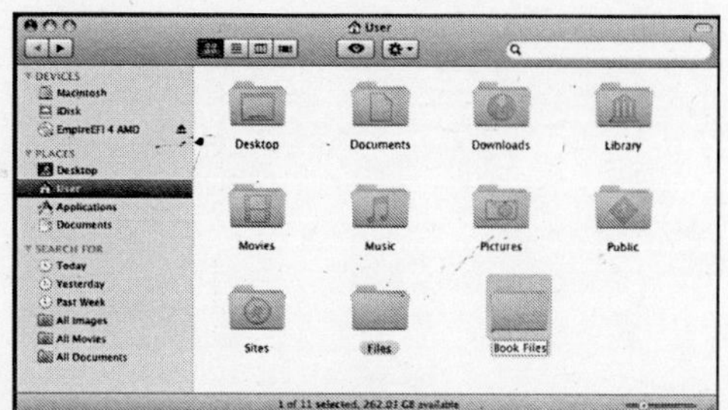

Figure 3.64 Enter the name for the folder in the edit box appears around it

- When you drag an item to a location on another disk, the item is copied to that location.
- When you hold down **Option** while dragging an item to a location on the disk, the item is copied to that location.

➜ To move an item to another location on the disk, do this:

1. Drag the icon for the item that you want to move do as follows:
    - To move the item into a specific folder on the disk, drag the icon onto the icon for the folder. The destination folder icon becomes selected when the mouse pointer mover over it as shown in Figure 3.65.

Figure 3.65 Drag the icon onto the icon for the folder to which you want to move it

    - To move the item into a specific window on the disk, drag the icon into the window. A border appears around the inside of the destination window as shown in Figure 3.66.
2. Release the mouse button. The selected item moves.

➜ To copy an item to another disk, do this:

1. Drag the icon for the item that you want to copy and do as follows:
    - To copy the item to the top root level of a disk, drag the icon to the icon for the destination disk as shown in Figure 3.67.

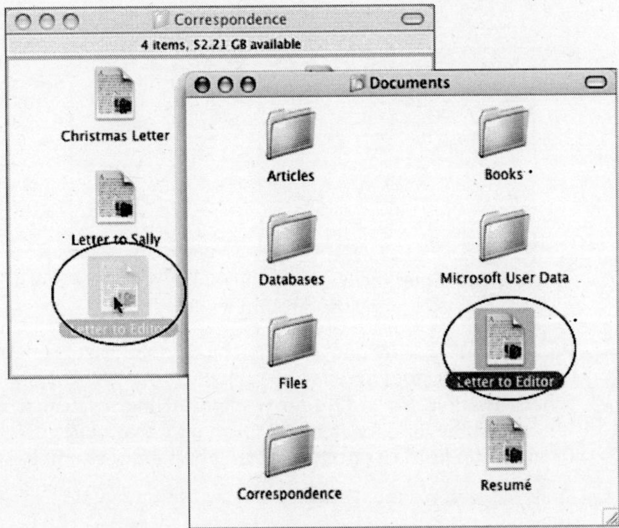

Figure 3.66 Drag the icon into the window in which you want to move it

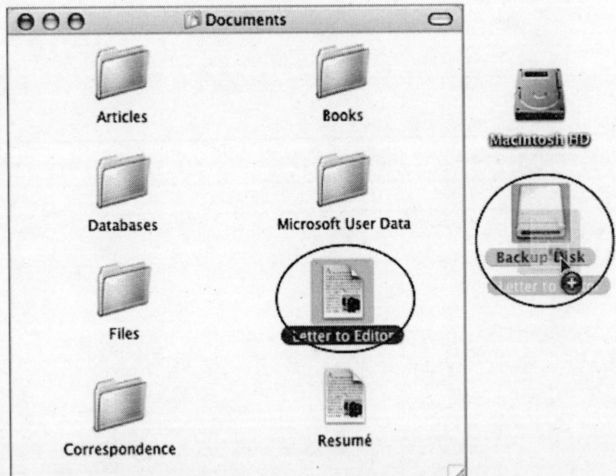

Figure 3.67 Drag the icon to the destination disk's icon

- To copy the item into a folder on the disk, drag the icon for the folder on the destination disk as shown in Figure 3.68.
- To copy the item into a specific window on the disk, drag the icon into the window as shown in Figure 3.69. When the item you are dragging moves on top of the destination location, a plus sign in a green circle appears beneath the mouse pointer. If the destination is an icon, the icon becomes selected.

2. Release the mouse button. A Copy window appears as shown in Figure 3.70. When it disappears, the copy is complete.

➜ **To duplicate an item, do this:**

1. Select the item you want to duplicate.

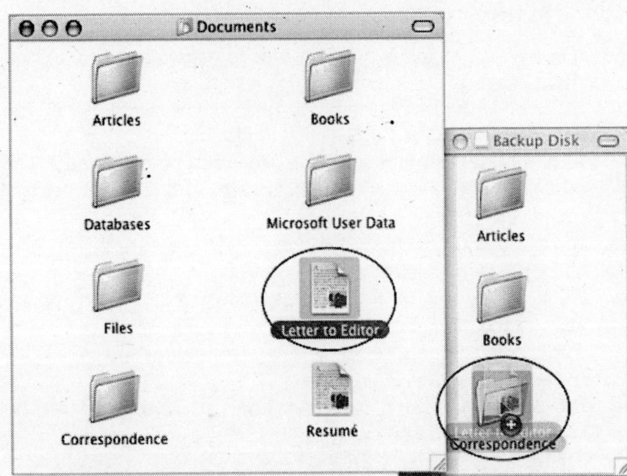

Figure 3.68 Drag the folder icon in a window on the destination disk

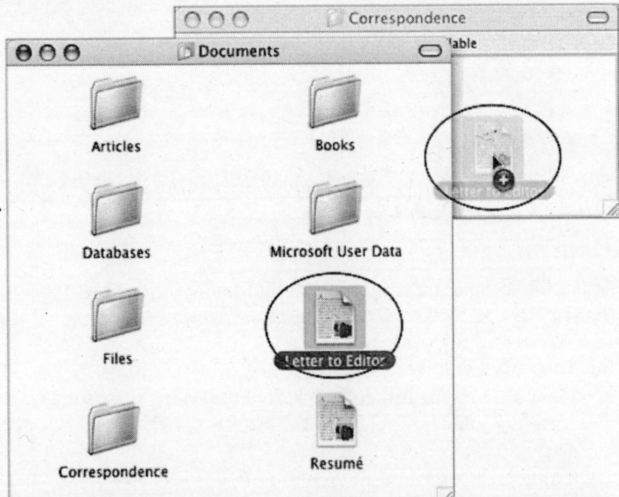

Figure 3.69 Copying the folder into a specific window

Figure 3.70 Copy dialog box indicates copy progress

2. Choose **File** menu and choose **Duplicate** or press ⌘ **D** as shown in Figure 3.71. Or
3. Hold down Option while dragging the item that you want to duplicate to a different location in the same window.
4. A copy of the item you duplicated appears beside the original. The word copy is added to the file name as shown in Figure 3.72.

Figure 3.71 Choose Duplicate from the File menu

Figure 3.72 A duplicate appears beside the original

The Trash and Deleting Items

The Trash is a specific place on your hard disk where you place items you want to delete. Items in the Trash remain there, until you empty the Trash, which premanently deleted. In Mac OS X, the trash appears as an icon in the Dock.

➜ **To move an item to the Trash, do this:**

1. Drag the icon for the item you want to delete to the Trash icon in the Dock.
2. When the mouse pointer moves over the Trash icon, the Trash icon becomes selected as shown in Figure 3.73. Release the mouse button. Or
3. Select the item that you want to delete.
4. Click **File** menu and choose **Move to Trash** or press ⌘ **Delete**.

➜ **To move an item out of the Trash, do this:**

1. Click the **Trash** icon on the **Dock** to open the **Trash** window as shown in Figure 3.74.
2. Drag the item from the Trash window to the Desktop or to another window on your hard disk. The item is moved from the Trash to the window you dragged it to. Or
3. Choose **Edit** menu and choose **Undo Move** of **'Name of Item'**, i.e., (Letter to Editor copy) or press ⌘ **Z**. The item is moved back to where it was before you moved it to the Trash.

☞ *The Undo command will only take an item out of the Trash if the last thing you did was put in the Trash.*

➜ **To empty the Trash, do this:**

1. Click the **Finder** menu and choose **Empty Trash** or press **Shift** ⌘ **Delete** keys together as shown in Figure 3.75.

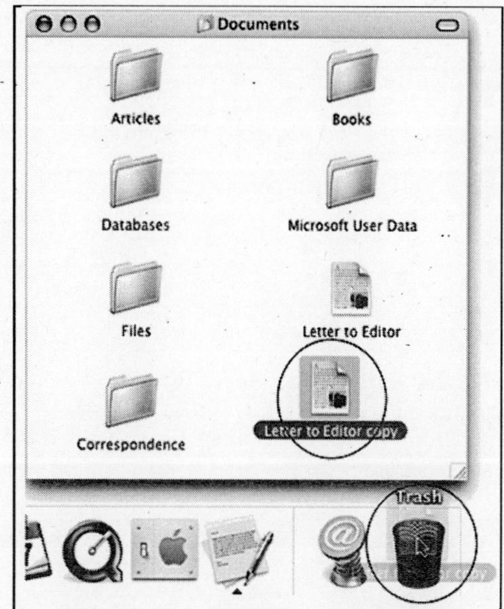

Figure 3.73 Move an item to the Trash

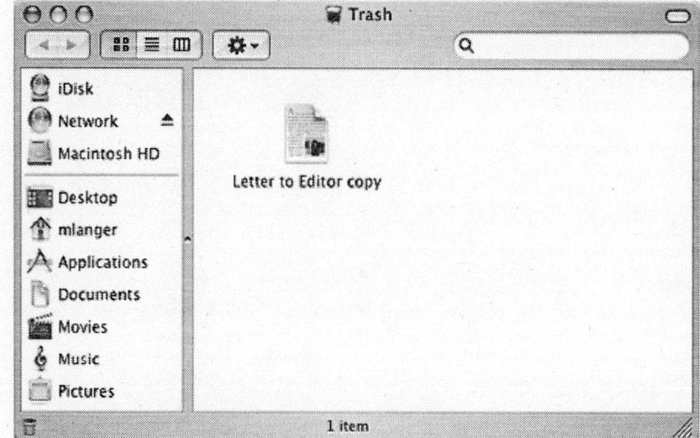

Figure 3.74 Trash window

Figure 3.75 Empty Trash in Finder menu

2. A **Trash warning** dialog box appears as shown in Figure 3.76. Click OK to delete all items that are in the Trash. Or

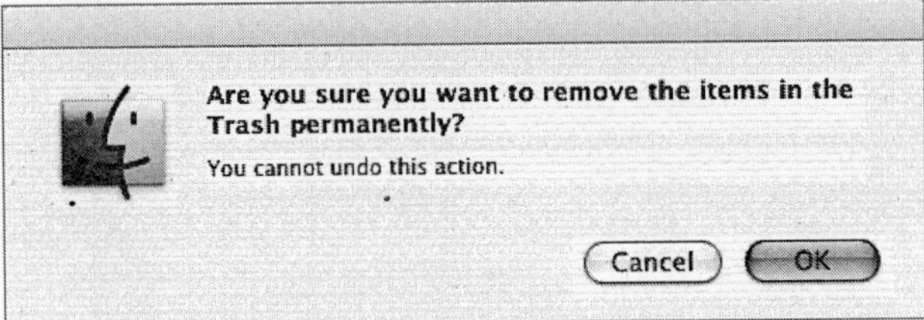

Figure 3.76 The Trash warning dialog box asks you to confirm that you want to delete the items in the Trash

3. Point to the Trash icon, press the mouse button, and hold it down until a menu appears as shown in Figure 3.77.
4. Choose **Empty Trash**. The contents of the Trash are deleted.

Figure 3.77 Selecting Trash icon on the Dock

➜ **To permanently remove items Trash from your disk, do this:**

1. Click **Finder** menu and choose **Secure Empty Trash**.
2. A Trash warning dialog box appears as shown in Figure 3.78. Click OK to permanently remove all the items that are in the Trash.

Figure 3.78 Using the Secure Empty Trash command displays a warning dialog box

Storage Media

A Macintosh computer can read data from, or write data to, a wide range of storage media, including:

- Hard disk, such as high capacity magnetic media.
- CD-ROM, CD-R, DVD, and DVD-R discs–high capacity, removable optical media.
- Zip, Jaz, or other disks–high capacity magnetic media.
- Floppy disks or diskettes–low capacity, removable magnetic media.

Points to Remember

- Do not confuse storage media with memory. The term memory usually refers to the amount of RAM in your computer, not disk space.
- At a minimum, all new Macintosh computers include a hard disk and CD-ROM drives.
- Storage devices can be internal (inside your computer) or external (attached to your computer by a cable).
- Some external storage devices must be properly connected and turned on before you start your computer or your computer may not recognized the device.

Mounting Disks

You mount a disk by inserting it in the disk drive so it appears on the Mac OS desktop as shown in Figure 3.79.

Figure 3.79

➜ **To mount a CD or DVD disk, do this:**

1. Place the CD or DVD disk in the tray or caddy, label side up.
2. Gently push the tray or caddy into the drive. After a moment, the disc icon appears on the desktop as shown in Figure 3.79.

➜ **To mount a Zip or Jaz disk, do this:**

1. Insert the disk in the Zip or Jaz drive. After a moment, the disk icon appears on the desktop.

Ejecting Disks

When you eject a disk, the disk is removed from the disk drive and its icon disappears from the desktop.

➜ **To eject a disk, do this:**

1. Select the disk's icon fron the desktop as shown in Figure 3.80.
2. Click **File** menu and choose **Eject** or press ⌘ **F** keys together. Or
3. Drag the disk's icon to the Trash as shown in Figure 3.80. As you drag, the Trash icon turns into a rectangle with a triangle on top.
4. Press the Eject key on the keyboard.

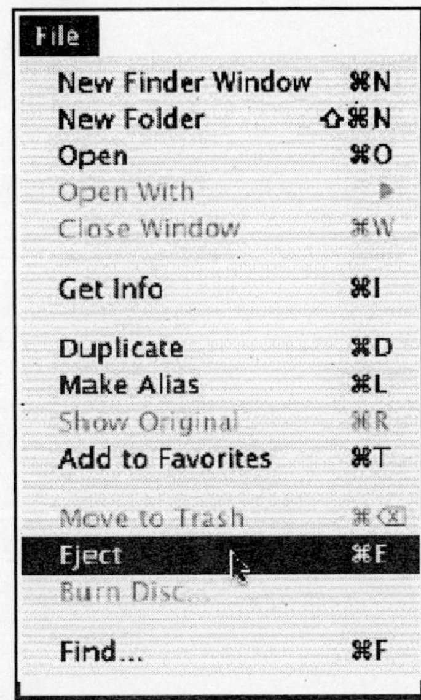

Figure 3.80 Selecting Eject from the File menu

Burning CDs

If the Macintosh includes a CD-R/CD-RW drive or SuperDrive, you can write or burn, files onto blank CD-R media. This is the way to archive important files that you do not need on your computers hard disk and to share files with other computer users.

➜ **To burn a CD, do this:**

1. Insert a blank CD-R disk into your computer's CD-R drive or SuperDrive.

Figure 3.81 Drag the disk icon to eject the disk

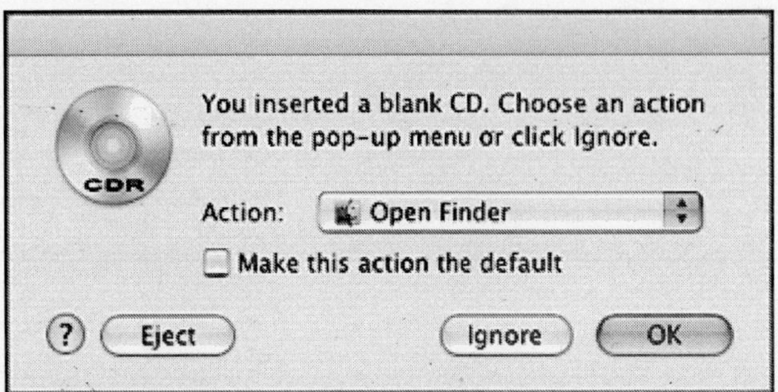

Figure 3.82 When you insert a blank CD-R disk, Mac opens a dialog box

Figure 3.83 A Pop-up menu enables you to choose the application you want to use to burn the CD

Figure 3.84

2. A dialog box appears as shown in Figure 3.81. Make sure Open Finder is chosen from the Action pop-up menu as shown in Figure 3.82.
3. Wait while your computer prepares the disc. When it is finished, a CD disk icon appears on the desktop as shown in Figure 3.83.
4. Drag the files you want to write on the disk onto the disk icon or into the open disk window.
5. Wait while your computer copies the files.
6. Repeat Steps 4 and 5 until all files you want on the disk have been copied.
7. Click **File** menu and choose **Burn Disc...** as shown in Figure 3.85.
8. A confirmation dialog box appears as shown in Figure 3.86. Choose a speed from the **Burn Speed:** pop-up menu and then click **Burn** button.
9. Wait while your computer prepares, burns, and verifies the disk. A Burn disk window reports its progress as shown in Figure 3.87. When it disappears, the disk is ready to burn the files in the disk.

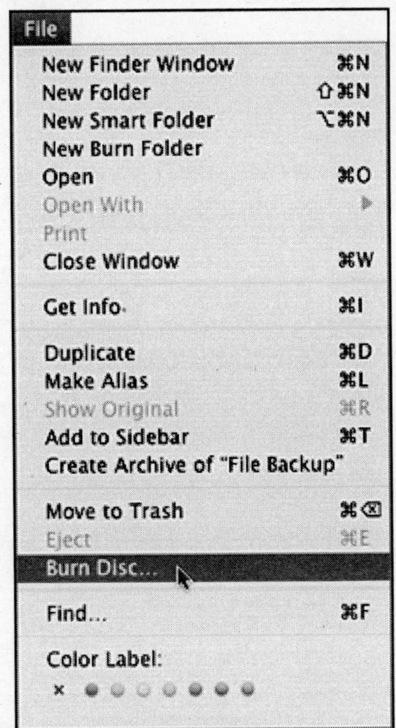

Figure 3.85

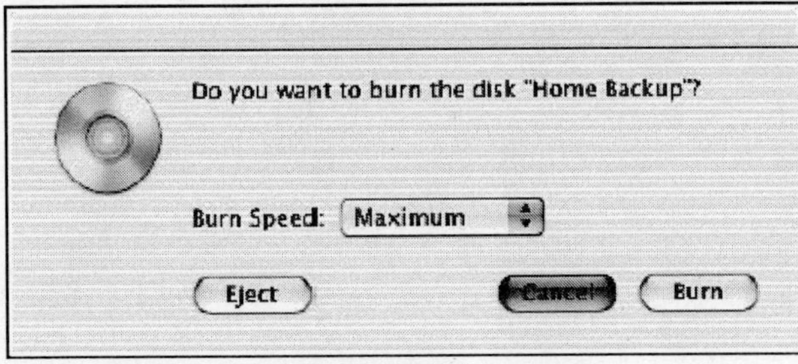

Figure 3.86

Figure 3.87

User Management

User management contains everything from setting up accounts for network access and creating home folders to the user by managing preferences and settings for users, groups, computers, and computer groups.

User management tools and technologies in Mac OS X Server include Workgroup Manager, Server Admin, Server Preferences, and command line tools.

Workgroup Manager

Workgroup Manager is a powerful tool that delivers features for comprehensive management of Macintosh clients. You can use Workgroup Manager on a computer with Mac OS X or Mac OS X Server. Workgroup Manager included with Mac OS X Server v10.6 can manage client computers running Mac OS X v10.4 or later.

You use Workgroup Manager to create user accounts and set up groups to provide convenient access to resources. You can:

- Use account settings and managed preferences to achieve the level of administrative control.
- Manage Finder, login, media access, and print settings.
- Control access to computers and restrict the applications allowed to run on them.

Server Admin

The Server Admin application provides access to various tools and services that play a role in server management.

After installing the Mac OS X Server software, use Server Admin to set up directory services and establish your network. Then use Workgroup Manager to create and manage accounts. After that, use Server Admin to set up additional services to provide mail service, host Websites, share printers, and create share points (which allow users to share folders and files).

Server Preferences

You can use Server Preferences to configure key features of collaboration and file services. You can also configure user and group accounts (such as setting passwords, enabling services, and assigning group membership), but not computer or computer group accounts.

Command Line Tools

Mac OS X Server includes several client-management command-line tools. For example, the dscltool allows you to view and edit account settings and manage preferences, while the mcxquerytool reports the managed preferences that are effective for a particular user.

Use the mcxquerytool to review how combined and managed preferences interact at the user, group, computer, or computer group level. The tool also determines which directory domain stores those managed preference settings.

Accounts

To manage accounts, you use an administrator account. With an administrator account, you can set up and manage the following account types:

- User accounts
- Group accounts

When creating a user account, you must specify a user name and password, which are needed to prove the user's identity. You can also specify a user identification number (user ID or UID), which is used for folder and file permissions.

Where User Accounts Are Stored

User accounts, group accounts, computer accounts, and computer groups are stored in a directory domain, available to any Mac OS X computer. A directory domain can reside on a Mac OS X computer (for example, in an Open Directory domain or other read/write directory domain), or it can reside on a non-Apple server (for example, on a non-Apple LDAP or Active Directory server).

Creating User Accounts

To create a user account in a directory domain, you must have administrator privileges for the domain. To create users in an Active Directory domain, use Active Directory administration tools on a Windows computer. You can not use Workgroup Manager to create user accounts, group accounts, computer accounts, or computer groups in a standard Active Directory domain.

If you create user accounts in a server's local directory domain, you can only authenticate for services provided by that server. You can not use these accounts to log in to a Mac OS X client computer or to perform Windows domain login. However, Windows users can authenticate with Windows file service, mail service, and other platform-neutral services.

➜ **To create a user account, do this:**

1. In Workgroup Manager, click Accounts.
2. Make sure the directory services of the Mac OS X Server computer you are using configured to access the directory domain.
3. Click the globe icon and then choose the domain where you want the user's account to reside. For Mac OS X Server v10.5 or later, Local and /Local/Default refer to the local directory domain.
4. To authenticate, click the lock and enter the name and password of a directory administrator.
5. Choose Server → New User or click New User in the toolbar.
6. In the panes provided, specify settings for the user.

Deleting a User Account

You can use Workgroup Manager to delete a user account stored in an Open Directory domain, the local directory domain, or from any other read/write directory domain.

➜ **To delete a user account using Workgroup Manager, do this:**

1. In Workgroup Manager, click Accounts.
2. Select the user account you want to delete.
3. To authenticate, click the lock and enter the name and password of a directory administrator.
4. Choose Server → Delete Selected User or click the Delete icon in the toolbar.

About Group Accounts

A group account stores the identities of users who belong to the group, as well as information that lets you customize the working environment for members of the group. When you define preferences for a group, the group is known as a workgroup.

Where Group Accounts are Stored

Group accounts can be stored in any Open Directory domain. A directory domain can reside on a Mac OS X computer (for example, an Open Directory domain) or it can reside on a non-Apple server (for example, an LDAP or Active Directory server). Workgroup Manager can work with accounts stored in any of these directory domains.

Creating Group Accounts

To create a group account in a directory domain, you must have directory administrator privileges.

➜ **To create a group account, do this:**

1. In Workgroup Manager, click Accounts.
2. Make sure the directory services of the Mac OS X Server computer you are using are configured to access the directory domain.
3. Click the globe icon and choose the domain where you want the group account to reside.
4. To authenticate, click the lock and enter the name and password of a directory administrator.
5. Click the Groups button.
6. Click New Group and then specify settings for the group in the panes provided.

Deleting a Group

You can use Workgroup Manager to delete a group account stored in an Open Directory domain, the local directory domain, or other read/write directory domain.

➜ **To delete a group using Workgroup Manager, do this:**

1. In Workgroup Manager, click Accounts.
2. Select the group account you want to delete. To select the account, click the globe icon, choose the directory domain where the account resides, click the Groups button, and then select the group.
3. To authenticate, click the lock and enter the name and password of a directory administrator.
4. Choose Server menu and choose Delete Selected Group or click the Delete icon in the toolbar.

3.15.4 GUI and Mac Devices and Tools

A GUI is a graphical user interface to a computer. The first interactive user interfaces to computers were not graphical. They were text-and-keyboard oriented and usually consisted of commands. The command interface of the DOS operating system (which you can still get to from your Windows operating system) is an example of the typical user-computer interface before GUIs arrived. An intermediate step in user interfaces between the command line interface and the GUI was the non-graphical menu-based interface, which let you interact by using a mouse rather than by having to type in keyboard commands.

The GUI familiar to most of us today in either the Mac or the Windows operating systems and their applications. Apple used it in their first Macintosh computers. Later, Microsoft used many of the same ideas in their first version of the Windows operating system for International Business Machines or IBM-compatible PCs.

Today's major operating systems provide a graphical user interface are:

Fonts

In a GUI, text is treated as a graphic, not as a fixed set of characters like in a typewriter. So they can differ in design, size, and even character spacing. The original Mac fonts were bitmaps, rendered by an OS service called QuickDraw in a similar to dot-matrix printers. But in 1985's Mac OS and LaserWriter printer, Apple adopted Adobe's PostScript technology, which treats fonts like drawings so that they can be manipulated in all sorts of visual ways.

Mouse– The Mac's GUI required something more than a keyboard to manipulate and a pointing device was that "something more." Apple, features like multiple buttons and scroll wheels found in PCs, insisting on a "pure" one-button experience that made sense in the large screens and Web pages. Today, all modern computers use mice or similar pointing devices. Tablets and smartphones also use the same fundamental concept, though in the form of your own fingers.

CD-ROM drive– The Apple's Mac was the first personal computer to come with a CD-ROM drive for use with both data and music. Apple long had a love affair with music, supporting the MIDI (Musical Instrument Digital Interface) protocol as far back as the Apple II Plus, and musicians took to the Mac because it both supported MIDI and could display music graphically. But the CD-ROM's in a Mac (1992's Mac IIvx) was the first step to marry music and computing for the masses.

Windows– The new window top carries the "gumdrop" buttons for closing, resizing and hiding the window. A mouseover function only makes the symbol visible when rolling over the area. The symbols used are equal to the ones used in MS Windows for zooming, for hiding, X for closing the window. Gumdrop buttons are color-coded in non-mouseover mode. The user learns which color stands for which functionality. The buttons appear in yellow, green and red.

Menus, Dialog Boxes– Pull-down menus have some transparency and fade out if they are not needed. Dialog boxes, such as "Save As ..." are attached to the relevant window. Like system menus, they have some transparency. Instead of simply appearing and disappearing, they are animated to scroll down out of and up into the window's title bar. The readability of messages can be restricted by the window's transparency.

Menu-bar– The Apple-icon has moved to the center of the menu bar. It represents the new "light source" for the desktop. It seems to originated in the top center, but some elements on the desktop, such as topmost windows, cast a shadow as though the light source were in its traditional, upper-left position. The centered position appears unusual and disturbing, as all menus have to be arranged around it. Its position restricts the consistency of left-aligning all Apple-Menus.

Finder– One of the most important features of the Mac GUI is the desktop-finder. All documents are represented in a filing system at the bottom of the screen called the "dock". The finder is a useful tool which provides a spatial orientation for the user. Enabling navigation is done through any amount of files and folders. It is now possible to navigate through lists of file-structures in the finder-browser. The multi-windows mode could cause screen-clatter for the user, but it was always possible to find a way around this problem. Instead of improving this, Apple now decided to allow only one open window at a time.

Dock– The Dock is always centered along the bottom of the screen and can accept any window or document. As the Dock grows full, individual "tiles" shrink. A user option called the "genie mode" magnifies tiles as the cursor moves over them. The Dock represents another equivalent to the Microsoft world: the taskbar. It displays a resized version of any open document, and also contains the trash-can. The finder-icon is always the first on the left side, the trash-can is always the last icon at the right end of the Dock.

The more documents have to be displayed in the Dock, the smaller the icons shrink. The Dock can display up to 128 documents at once, making recognition of a special document nearly impossible. There is no possibility to see document names in the dock.

The Dock holds as many things as you want to keep there. As you add items, the Dock expands until it reaches the edge of the screen. Once it reaches that point, the icons in the Dock shrink proportionately to accommodate additional items. To make the smaller icons more legible, however, it included a great new feature called magnification: just pass your mouse over the icons, and they magnify to your preset maximum resolution.

MAC Devices and Tools - Mac OS X used icons to represent the various hardware devices of your computer, including your hardware, DVD (Digital Versatile/Video Disk) Drive and iPod. Just double click a hardware icon to display the folders and files that it contains in your hare drive and a disk loaded in the DVD drive. The hardware icons only on Desktop or in Finder windows or within a device or source list in applications, such as iTunes and iPhoto.

Apple's Mac OS X operating system is included in all of the company's personal computers and laptops. The operating system includes several built-in applications and tools that are meant to improve productivity. These tools are are explained in the following sections:

Bean– Bean is a simple word processor for Mac OS X systems that is free to download and use. The rich text editor can be used to create simple documents and reports. It provides a live word count and in-depth statistics for your document. Additionally, the application provides an AutoSave Feature and Date-stamped Backups. Bean is partially compatible with Microsoft Word's .doc and .docx file formats. Because it is not full-featured, Bean does not serve as a replacement for Word or other powerful word processors.

Burn– Burn is an open-source Mac OS X tool that allows users to burn several types of discs, including audio CDs, MP3 compilations, videos, DVDs, normal disk images, cue/bin images and toc images. The Burns Inspector feature allows people to change advanced settings, such as file permissions, the disk icon and file dates. Additionally, Burn can copy disks or use disk images to recreate previous disks. The application also automatically converts video and audio files into the correct format for playback on multiple devices.

SuperDuper– SuperDuper is a tool used to back up and recover files. In the event that the computer fails to boot, crashes or simply fails. It allows you to recover files that may have been lost. The application can make a full backup in minutes, duplicate the boot drive to another drive or update an existing clone with the latest data. It also includes a streamlined interface that allows users to complete any of the actions.

The Unarchiver– The Unarchiver is a free tool that is meant to replace Mac OS X's Achive Utility application. The Unarchiver supports many formats, including Zip, Rar, 7z, ISO / BIN, Cab and Tar. The application can be used to extract files from an archive that was downloaded. Files also can be compressed and added to an archive using the program. Additionally, The Unarchiver supports other popular Mac OS X applications, such as Squeeze, Zoo, StuffIt X and DiskDoubler.

REVIEW QUESTIONS WITH ANSWERS

1. Multiple Choice

1.1 Which of the following is the most famous example of open source software?
a. Mac OS X b. UNIX
c. Linux d. None of the above

1.2 A _________ is a collection of buttons which represent various operations that can be carried out within an application.
a. Buttons b. Menu
c. Toolbar d. None

1.3 The topmost bar in any application window is the _________. It displays the name of the document or application.
a. Menu bar b. Toolbar
c. Status bar d. Title bar

1.4 What happens when you boot up a PC?
a. Portions of the operating system are copied from disk into memory.
b. Portions of the operating system are copied from memory onto disk.
c. Portions of the operating system are compiled.
d. None of the above

1.5 Device drivers are:
a. Small, special-purpose programs.
b. The innermost part of the operating system.
c. Tiny power cards for external storage devices.
d. None of the above

1.6 An application can be opened through shortcut on desktop by:
a. Double clicking on its shortcut.
b. Right clicking and choosing "Open" option.
c. Selecting the icon and pressing Enter key.
d. All of the above

1.7 What is the main folder on a storage device called?
a. Platform b. Interface
c. Root directory d. Device driver

1.8 Windows Explorer is a file management program that you can use to:
a. View and change the folder/file structures of your disks.
b. View and change the contents of your folder and files.
c. Move, copy, rename create and delete folders and files.
d. All of the above

1.9 Process State is a part of:
a. Process Control back b. Inode
c. File allocation table d. None of the above

1.10 Linux components include:
a. Kernel b. File system and user programs
c. Shell d. All of the above

1.11 One of the following is a system tools in Windows:
a. Notepad b. Disk defragmeter
c. Disk fragmenter d. Disk operating system

1.12 Which of the following program your personal computer uses to get the computer system started after you turn it on?
a. Boot b. Source code
c. Initialization d. BIOS

1.13 A program at the time executing is called __________.
a. Dynamic program b. Static program
c. Binded program d. Process A

1.14 Paging _______.
a. Solves the memory fragmentation problem A
b. Allows modular programming
c. Allows structured programming
d. None of the above

1.15 Recycle Bin is a:
a. Folder that contains deleted files and folders
b. Folder that contains the files used for backup
c. File that contains information of files on the disk
d. None of the above

1.16 A thread is a ________ process.
a. Heavy weight b. Multiprocess
c. Inter Thread d. Light weight

1.17 Functions of operating system are:
a. Processor management b. Memory management
c. I/O management d. All of the above

1.18 Which file extensions indicate only graphics files?
a. BMP and DOC b. JPEG and TXT
c. TXT and STK d. BMP and GIF

1.19 Which of the following is the most famous example of open source software?
a. Microsoft Windows b. Mac OS X
c. UNIX d. Linux

1.20 ________ begins at the root and follows a path down to the specified file
a. Relative path name b. Absolute path name
c. Standalone path name d. All of the above

1.21 What happens when you boot up a PC?

a. Portions of the OS are copied from disk into memory
b. Portions of the OS are copied from memory onto disk
c. Portions of the OS are compiled
d. None of the above

1.22 Round robin scheduling is essentially the preemptive version of _______.
a. FIFO b. Shortest job first
c. Longest time first d. None of the above

1.23 Which feature of Windows 7 allows the desktop backgrounds to change automatically after some specified time interval?
a. Gadget b. Aero theme
c. Desktop Slide show d. Jump List

1.24 Which of the followng applications in no longer a part of Windows 7?
a. Windows Media Player b. Windows Media Centre
c. Windows Photo Gallery d. None of the above

1.25 The ________ snipping tool enables to select a window like dialog box or browser window that you want to capture.
a. Window A b. Rectangular
c. Free-form d. Full-screen

1.26 Which feature allows you to arrange two open windows side-by-side on the screen?
a. Aero Snap b. Aero Peek
c. Aero Shake d. None of the above

1.27 An Aero Theme is the combination of one or more desktop backgrounds, _____, ________, and screen savers.
a. Sounds, Gadgets b. Desktop icons, Gadgets
c. Window color, Sounds d. Window colour, Gadgets

1.28 In the multi-programming environment, the main memory consisting of __________ number of process.
a. Greater than 100 b. Only one
c. Greater than 50 d. More than one

1.29 The purpose of co-operating process is __________.
a. Information Sharing b. Convenience
c. Computation Speed-up d. All of the above

1.30 ________ allocates the largest hole available in the memory.
a. Best-Fit b. Worst-Fit
c. First-Fit d. None of the above

1.31 Number of CPU registers in a system depends on _________.
a. Operating System b. Computer Architecture
c. Computer Organization d. None of the above

1.32 The operating system of a computer serves as a software interface between the user and the __________.
a. Hardware b. Peripheral
c. Memory d. Screen

1.33 In Interactive environments, such as time-sharing systems, the primary requirements is to provide reasonably good response time and in general, to share system resource equitably. In such situations, the scheduling algorithm that is most popularly applied is ___________.
a. Shortest Remaining Time Next Scheduling
b. Priority Based Preemptive Scheduling
c. Round Robin Scheduling
d. None of the above

2. State whether the following statements are True or False

2.1 To use a computer, you need an operating system.

2.2 Linux is quite suitable for priority oriented multitasking operations but not suitable for multiuser tasks.

2.3 Deleted objects can be recovered from the Recycle Bin folder in Windows.

2.4 Another term for time-sharing is multitasking.

2.5 Formatting of all the partitions or mount points is a must for Linux installation.

2.6 Internal commands are stored on the disk in the form of a file.

2.7 When a folder is copied to another place, the subfolders in the folder also get copied.

2.8 The DATE command in DOS displays the current date as well as time.

2.9 Check boxes are used to present options requiring individual on/off decisions in Message boxes.

2.10 The FILES command is used at command prompt.

2.11 MS Word operating system was developed by Microsoft to overcome the limitation of its MS-DOS operating system.

2.12 The kernal performs the basic functions of an operating system.

2.13 grep command in Linux is used to search for lines that contain a specified pattern in a specified file.

2.14 Linux is a multi-user time-sharing system.

2.15 You can delete files by dragging them to the Recycle Bin.

2.16 The job of splitting the primary memory into segments as the memory is allocated and de-allocated to the proces is known as fragmentation.

2.17 A document printing process uses spooling.

2.18 Round robin is a non-preemptive scheduling technique.

2.19 Microsoft Windows 7 is a GUI-based OS.

2.20 In Windows 7, the Show desktop button is placed at the left-most corner of the taskbar.

2.21 You can make any open window active by clicking on its thumbnail.

2.22 Using the Aero Shake feature, dialog boxes can be minimized.

2.23 The taskbar in Window 7 is smaller than it was in previous versions of Windows.

2.24 Windows 7 Home baisc edition includes features like touch-screen support, Aero effects, etc.

2.25 You can view the Jump list for a program on the taskbar by right-clicking on the program icon.

2.26 CPU Scheduling is the basis of real-time operating system.

2.27 The operating system keeps the information of files in a table called file folder table.

2.28 A shell is a command interpreter.

2.29 The state of a process after it encounters an I/O instruction is called blocked/waiting.

2.30 The mechanism that bring a page into memory only when it is needed is called page replacement.

3. Match the following:

3.1	Screen background and main area of windows where you can open and manage files and programs	a.	Multimedia
3.2	A multipurpose window used by Windows Operating System to display everything	b.	COPY file1.txt + file2.txt file3.txt
3.3	A generic term for such computer applications and files that combine standard computer capabilities with other media, such as video and sound	c.	Desktop
3.4	To remove a directory with a large number of files and subdirectories	d.	Process control block
3.5	A command to create a directory	e.	DELTREE mydir
3.6	To rename a file available on drive A to another filename	f.	Memory allocation opposite to Best-fit
3.7	A switch that will display the name of the file before being deleted	g.	rm -r
3.8	To copy several files into one file	h.	The act to hold down the mouse button while moving the mouse.
3.9	Embedded	i.	REN A:\oldfile A:\newfile
3.10	Drag	j.	This is to insert an object, which is not linked on its originating document, into a destination document.
3.11	Process state is a part of	k.	Windows Explorer
3.12	Virtual memory	l.	MD mydir
3.13	FIFO	m.	Interleaved execution of two or more programs
3.14	Paging	n.	Page replacement algorithms suffers from Belady's anamoly
3.15	Thread	o.	An illusion of extremely large main memory
3.16	Worst fit	p.	Solves the memory fragmentation problem
3.17	Multiprogramming	q.	Smallest sequence of programmed instructions lightweight process
3.18	Throughout	r.	Basis of CPU scheduling
3.19	Files	s.	CPU performance is measured
3.20	Device drivers	t.	Data (information) is stored in computer
		u.	Small, special purpose program
		v.	Root directory

4. Fill in the blanks

a.	Edit	b.	Alt + Delete	c.	Move
d.	Recycle Bin	e.	Cls	f.	Desktop
g.	Operating system	h.	Task bar	i.	Folder
j.	Attrib	k.	My Computer	l.	Recover
m.	My Documents	n.	Icon	o.	Multi-programming
p.	Notification area	q.	Windows 7 Starter	r.	start, Windows logo
s.	FIFO	t.	Internet Explorer, Windows Explorer	u.	Aero
v.	Process control block				

4.1 The ________ can be used to transfer files from one directory to another command.

4.2 _________ is represented by a computer icon and it contains information regarding your computer system.

4.3 The name of the text editor included in DOS is _______.

4.4 Device drivers control the interaction between the input/output devices and _________.

4.5 The _______ command is normally used to recover readable information from bad or defective disks.

4.6 A _________ can contain files as well as sub-folders.

4.7 The _______ command clears the screen.

4.8 The screen that you see once Windows 2000 is loaded is called the _________.

4.9 The ___________ command displays or changes the file attributes.

4.10 The _________ allows you to easily recover deleted files and folders in Windows.

4.11 In Windows, you store all your files in a __________ folder.

4.12 A small graphic image that represents an application file command or a tool is called as _________.

4.13 A general operating system related technique that allows two or more programs to execute concurrently on the same computer is called __________.

4.14 You can open the Start menu by clicking the _________ button on the taskbar or by pressing the _________ key on the keyboard.

4.15 ________ edition usually comes pre-installed on computers by the computer maufactures.

4.16 By default, the taskbar displays only three buttons corresponding to _____________ Media Player, and ___________ program.

4.17 The ___________ interface of Windows 7 takes advantage of latest graphics hardware and provides smoother window handling, enhanced animations and glass visual effects.

4.18 The kernel keeps track of the state of each task by using a data structure called _____________

4.19 _________ contains a group of icons that indicated the status of certain programs installed on the computer.

4.20 Page replacement algorithm suffers from Belady's anamoly is known as ___________.

Answers

1. | | | | | | | | | | | | |
|---|---|---|---|---|---|---|---|---|---|---|---|
| 1.1 | c | 1.2 | d | 1.3 | d | 1.4 | a | 1.5 | c | 1.6 | d |
| 1.7 | d | 1.8 | d | 1.9 | c | 1.10 | d | 1.11 | b | 1.12 | a |
| 1.13 | c | 1.14 | b | 1.15 | a | 1.16 | b | 1.17 | d | 1.18 | d |
| 1.19 | d | 1.20 | b | 1.21 | a | 1.22 | a | 1.23 | c | 1.24 | c |
| 1.25 | a | 1.26 | a | 1.27 | c | 1.28 | d | 1.29 | d | 1.30 | b |
| 1.31 | b | 1.32 | a | 1.33 | c. | | | | | | |

2. | | | | | | | | | | | | |
|---|---|---|---|---|---|---|---|---|---|---|---|
| 2.1 | T | 2.2 | F | 2.3 | T | 2.4 | F | 2.5 | T | 2.6 | F |
| 2.7 | T | 2.8 | F | 2.9 | F | 2.10 | F | 2.11 | F | 2.12 | T |
| 2.13 | T | 2.14 | T | 2.15 | T | 2.16 | T | 2.17 | T | 2.18 | F |
| 2.19 | T | 2.20 | F | 2.21 | T | 2.22 | F | 2.23 | F | 2.24 | F |
| 2.25 | T | 2.26 | F | 2.27 | F | 2.28 | T | 2.29 | T | 2.30 | F |

3. | | | | | | | | | | | | |
|---|---|---|---|---|---|---|---|---|---|---|---|
| 3.1 | c | 3.2 | k | 3.3 | a | 3.4 | g | 3.5 | l | 3.6 | i |
| 3.7 | e | 3.8 | b | 3.9 | j | 3.10 | h | 3.11 | d | 3.12 | o |
| 3.13 | n | 3.14 | p | 3.15 | q | 3.16 | f | 3.17 | m | 3.18 | s |
| 3.19 | t | 3.20 | u | | | | | | | | |

4. | | | | | | | | | | | | |
|---|---|---|---|---|---|---|---|---|---|---|---|
| 4.1 | c | 4.2 | k | 4.3 | a | 4.4 | g | 4.5 | l | 4.6 | i |
| 4.7 | e | 4.8 | f | 4.9 | j | 4.10 | d | 4.11 | m | 4.12 | n |
| 4.13 | o | 4.14 | r | 4.15 | q | 4.16 | t | 4.17 | u | 4.18 | v |
| 4.19 | p | 4.20 | s | | | | | | | | |

Short Questions with Answers

1. When and how Linux developed?
2. Name any four operating systems commonly used in personal computers.
3. How will you delete files or folders permanently in Windows operating system?
4. Explain the functions of an operating system in computer.
5. Write short notes on:
   a. Disk Defragmenter
   b. Disk Cleanup
6. What the commond used for List the contents of your home directory, current directory and ALL subdirectories.
7. How you will Create new folder/directories and how to remove file and folder in linux?
8. Differentiate between a 32-bit and 64-bit CPU.
9. What is a file?
10. What is virtual memory?
11. What is the difference between hard and soft real-time systems?
12. What is a real-time system?
13. What are demand-paging and pre-paging?

Answers to Short Questions

1. The Linux operating system was conceived and implemented in 1969 at AT&T's Bell Laboratories in the United States by Ken Thompson, Dennis Ritchie, and Douglas McIlroy. It was first released in 1971 and was initially entirely written in assembly language, a common practice at the time. Later in 1973, UNIX was re-written in the programming language C by Dennis Ritchie. The availability of an operating system written in a high-level language allowed easier portability to different computer platforms.
2. Four operating systems are:
   1. MS-DOS 2. UNIX 3. Linux 4. Windows XP
3. To delete files or folders permanently press shift + Del key together. This will permanently delete files or folders.
4. *Refer 3.3 section.*
5. a. *Refer 3.11.1 section.*
   b. *Refer 3.11.1 section.*
6. A word List formed a command LS that show contents of home directory like below
   $ ls ~
   To show everything in a vertical column used like below
   $ ls -al
   it will show like below
   drwxr-xr-x 5 root root 3090 Jun 19 20:39 boot/
   drwxr-xr-x 8 root root 4509 Jul 21 09:56 dev/
   drwxr-xr-x 94 root root 4096 Jul 12 10:35 etc/
   show directories in the current directory
   $ ls -d */
   show ALL subdirectories
   $ ls *
7. Create new folder or directory, if they do not already exist already
   syntex like below
   mkdir [Options] directories
   OPTIONS
   -m, --mode=MODE set permission mode (as in chmod), not rwxrwxrwx - umask -p, --parents no error if existing, make parent folder as needed
   mkdir creates the standard entries . (dot) for the current folder and .. (dot dot) for its parent
   cd used for Change Directory
   rm To Remove files
   rmdir To Remove folder(s)
8. The two main categories of processors are 32-bit and 64-bit. The type of processor a computer has not only affects it's overall performance, but it can also dictate what type of software it uses.
   Differences between a 32-bit and 64-bit CPU
   The main difference between 32-bit processors and 64-bit processors is the speed they operate. 64-bit processors can come in dual core and quad core. Multiple cores allow for increase processing power and faster computer operation. Software programs that require many calculations to function operate faster on the multi-core 64-bit processors. It is important to note that 64-bit computers can still use 32-bit based software programs, even when the Windows operating system is a 64-bit version.

   Another big difference between 32-bit processors and 64-bit processors is the maximum amount of memory (RAM) that is supported. 32-bit computers support a maximum of 3-4GB of memory, whereas a 64-bit computer can support memory amounts over 4 GB. This is important for software programs that are used for graphical design, engineering design or video editing,
9. A file is an object on a computer that stores data, information, settings, or commands that are used with a computer program. In a graphical user interface (GUI), such as Microsoft Windows, files are shown as unique icons that relate to the program that opens the file. For example, the picture is an example of the icon associated with Adobe Acrobat PDF files. Double-clicking this icon in Windows would open that file in Adobe Acrobat or the PDF reader installed on the computer.
10. Virtual memory is hardware technique where the system appears to have more memory that it actually does. This is done by time-sharing, the physical memory and storage parts of the memory one disk when they are not actively being used.

11. A hard real-time system assurance that critical tasks complete on time. This goal requires that all delays in the system be bounded from the retrieval of the stored data to the time that it takes the operating system to finish any request made of it. A soft real time system where a critical real-time task gets priority over other tasks and retains that priority until it completes.
12. A real time process is a process that must respond to the events within a certain time period. A real time operating system is an operating system that can run real time processes successfully.
13. With demand paging, a page is brought into memory only when a location on that page is actually referenced during execution. With pre-paging, pages other than the one demanded by a page fault are brought in. The selection of such pages is done based on common access patterns, especially for secondary memory devices.

DESCRIPTIVE TYPE QUESTIONS

1. What is multi tasking, multi programming, multi threading?
2. Discuss the function of the following:
   a. My Computer b. Recycle Bin e. Help
   c. Start Menu d. Taskbar
3. (a) Explain the usage of /, /usr, /bin, /lib and /mnt directories.
   (b) How does linking a file differ from embedding a file in Windows?
4. What are the advantages of disk partitioning?
5. What is fragmentation? Different types of fragmentation?
6. What is a Notepad and how does it differ from WordPad? How does it compare with a word processing package, such as Microsoft Word?
7. (a) Describe in detail the usage of COPY command. Give the process of combining two or more files into another file using the COPY command.
   (b) Explain the use of DEL command.
8. What is LILO? How is it useful in Linux?
9. Describe the different components of a Windows Desktop.
10. What are short, long and medium-term scheduling?
11. What are the internal tasks or activities involved during booting of a computer?
12. In MS Windows environment, what is the difference in using "My Computer" from "Windows Explorer" for exploring contents of a computer.
13. When is a disk said to be fragmented? Write one disadvantage of a fragmented disk.
14. What are the various types of operating systems?
15. What are the three types of user interface?
16. Explain the functions of operating system in computer.
17. What is the role of "Control Panel" in Windows?
18. What is the role of "Disk Cleanup" and "Disk Defragmenter" in Windows?
19. Explain what are the key advantages of Linux over Windows? What are its deficiencies?
20. What is an operating system? What are the three main purposes of an operating system?
21. Explain various components of Windows disktop.

CHAPTER 4

Word Processing

4.1 INTRODUCTION

Word processing is the most common applications packages to create, edit, and print documents using a computer. To perform word processing, you need a computer, a special program called a word processor, and a printer. A word processor enables you to create a document, store it electronically on a disk, display it on a screen, modify it by entering commands and characters from the keyboard, and print it on a printer.

The great advantage of word processing over using a typewriter is that you can make changes without retyping the entire document. If you make a typing mistake, you simply back up the cursor and correct your mistake. If you want to delete a paragraph, you simply remove it, without leaving a trace. It is equally easy to insert a word, sentence, or paragraph in the middle of a document. Word processor also makes it easy to move sections of text from one place to another within a document, or between documents. When you have made all the changes you want, you can send the file to a printer to get a hardcopy. You can also mail it electronically to the addressee.

4.2 WORD PROCESSING BASICS

Word processing package, such as Word 2010 helps enter text and manipulate words and phrases. You can change typed letter, document and report easily and store them for future use. You can even print these documents as and when desired. Thus, documents created on a word processor can be made accurately giving better look and printed for use.

☞ *A word processor allows you to function more effectively and efficiently with minimum effort.*

Word 2010 is a Word Processor that operates under Windows Operating System. When you use a computer program to create, and edit text documents, you are using word processing. Word 2010 is one of the most sophisticated word processing programs available to day. With Word 2010, it is easier than ever to efficiently create a wide range of business and personal documents, from a simples letter to the most complex project report. Word 2010 includes many desktop features that you can use to enhance the appearance of documents so that they are easy to read.

4.2.1 Opening Word Processing Package (MS Word 2010)

➜ **To start Word 2010, do this:**

1. Click **Start** button, highlight **All Programs** and click **Microsoft Office**. Select **Microsoft Office Word 2010** (See Figure 4.1).

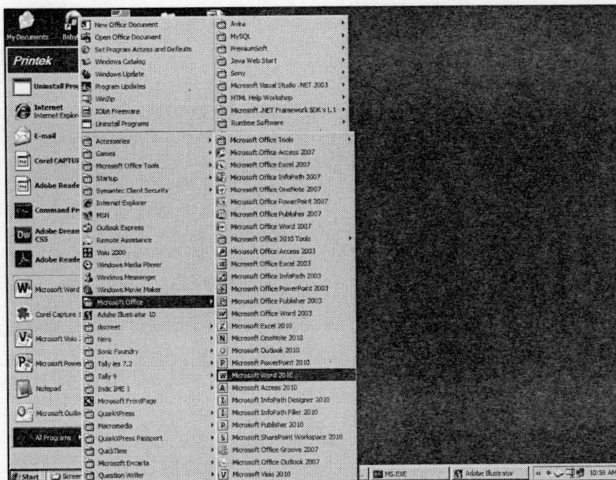

Figure 4.1 Starting MS Word 2010

4.2.2 Using Word 2010 Interface

User interfaces of MS Word 2010 is similar to MS Word 2007. MS Word 2010 has introduced several new features, such as improved WordArt, improved themes, background removal, and other image editing features. The new user interface that replaces menus, toolbars, and most of the task panes from previous versions of MS Word have been replaced by the File tab and Ribbon. It is designed to help you to be more productive. You can find the right features of various tasks more easily, discover new functionality and be more efficient. Figure 4.2 shows the elements of Word 2010 application window and an open Word 2010 document in detail.

4.2.3 File Tab

File tab is the colored tab which is located in the upper-left corner of Microsoft Office 2010 programs and below the Quick Access Toolbar (See Figure 4.2). When you click the File tab, you can see the Backstage view. File Tab replaces the office button in Word 2007. It contains commands like New, Open, Save, Save As, Print, etc.

4.2.4 Quick Access Toolbar

This toolbar is located by default at the top of Word 2010 window. By default, this toolbar displays the Save, Undo and Repeat buttons.

4.2.5 Dialog Box Launcher

Dialog box launchers are small icons that appear in some groups. Clicking a Dialog Box Launcher opens a related dialog box or task pane, providing more options related to that group.

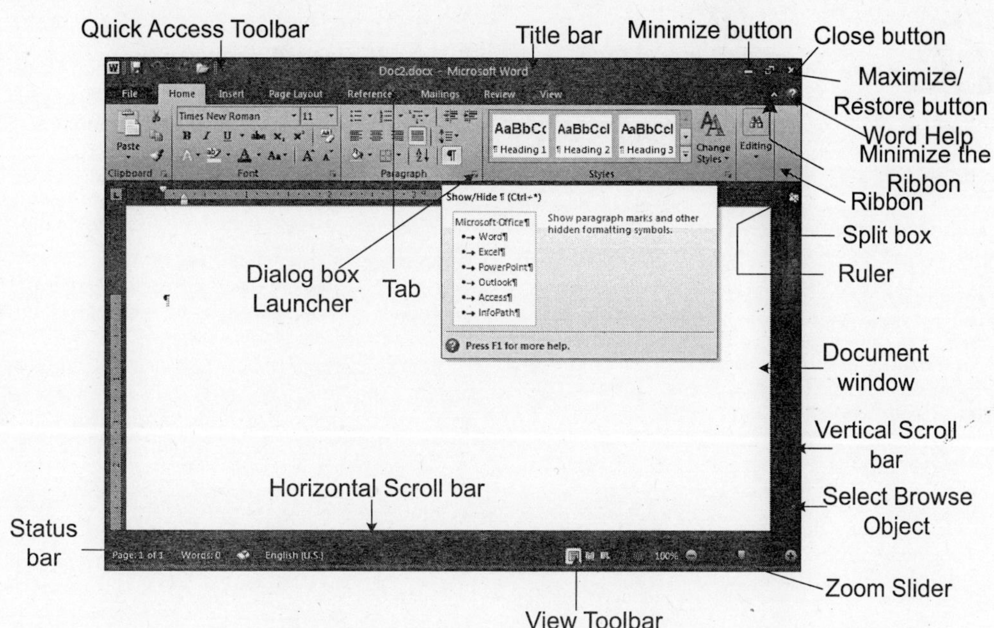

Figure 4.2 Elements of Word 2010 window

4.2.6 Terminology

Following terminologies for Word 2010 are used in this book.
Select–Highlight or mark a section of text, menu name, command, dialog box option, or graphical object with the keyboard or with mouse actions.
Choose–Execute and complete a command. You may execute some commands when you select the command on the Ribbon tabs. Other commands are executed when you choose OK from a dialog box.
Active–Bring an application or document window to the foreground. When you are working with more than one application or more than one document within Word 2010, the active window is the window you are working in.

4.2.7 Word 2010 Document Window

Title Bar

It is at the top of an open window and is called Title bar (See Figure 4.2).

Minimize button

An underscore (_) at the right of a title bar which stores an application programme at the bottom of the screen.

Maximize button

A box at the right of a title bar that fills available space with the document or application.

Close button

A box at the right of a title bar marked as (X) that closes the window or dialog box, when you click it with a mouse pointer.

Restore button

A double box at the right of a title bar that restores an application or document into a sizable window.

Help button

It appears at the right end of the Ribbon. When the mouse pointer is over any button for a few seconds (called hovering), it displays a ScreenTip with not only the button's name but also its function.

Status bar

At the bottom of the window, the Status bar gives you information about the current document. You can turn off the display of an item of information by right-clicking the Status bar and then clicking that item.

View toolbar

At the right end of the Status bar is the view toolbar. It provides tools for adjusting the view of document.

Mouse pointer

The on-screen arrow, I-beam, or drawing button indicates the current location affected by mouse actions.

Select Browse Object

The toolbar that enables you to browse through an active document by field, endnote, footnote, comment, section, page, edits, heading, graphic, or by table. Go To and Find functions are also part of this toolbar.

Ruler

A bar containing a scale that indicates *tabs, paragraph indents,* and margins in the paragraph where the insertion point (cursor) is located. The ruler can be used with the mouse to format paragraphs quickly.

Split box

Light gray bar at the top of the vertical scroll bar that you can drag down to split a window into two views of the same document.

ScreenTips

ScreenTips show the name of the command button shown in ribbon. ScreenTips appear as soon as you position the mouse pointer on the selected tabs command.

4.2.8 Ribbon Command

Ribbon is displayed just below the title bar. In Ribbon, Commands are organized in logical groups, which are collected together under tabs (See Figure 4.2). You can hide the Ribbon by double-clicking the active tab. Different types of Tabs are available in Word 2010.

Home Tab: This button related to working with document, such as *clipboard, font, paragraph, styles,* and *editing.*

Insert Tab: This button for related items you can insert *tables, header* and *footer,* and *symbols.*

Page Layout Tab: This button for related items to the appearance of the document, such as *Page Setup, Page Background, Paragraph* and *Arrange.*

References Tab: This button that are related to items you can add to long documents, such as *Tables of Contents, Footnotes, Bibliography, Captions, Index* and *Table of Authorities.*

Mailings Tab: This button contains commands related to creating mass mailings. It contains *create, start mail merge, write* & *insert fields, preview results* and *finish.*

Review Tab: This button related to *proofing, language comments, tracking, changes, compare* and *protect.*

View Tab: This button contains commands related to changing the view or the display of documents.

Scroll Bar

The scroll bar appears at the *left* for vertical scrolling and at the *bottom* for horizontal scrolling as shown in Figure 4.2.

In Word 2010, you can work simultaneously with more than one document.

Using Quick Access Toolbar

You can add buttons to the Quick Access Toolbar which expands to accommodate them. If you add many buttons, it might become difficult to view the text in the title bar or all the buttons might not be visible. To resolve this problem, you can move the Quick Access Toolbar below the Ribbon by clicking the Customize Quick Access Toolbar button and then clicking Show Below the Ribbon.

1. At the right end of the **Quick Access Toolbar**, click the **Customize Quick Access** Toolbar button.

   By default, the Save, Undo, and Repeat buttons appear on the Quick Access Toolbar (See Figure 4.2).

4.2.9 Using Quick Access Icons by Ribbon Command

If you click the Save icon in the Quick Access toolbar, Word 2010 saves your current file. If you are saving a new file, a dialog box pops-up, asking you to choose a name for your file. If you click the Print icon, it immediately prints your entire file through the default printer.

The Redo icon reverses the last Undo command you choose. For example, if you delete a paragraph, it disappears. Then if you immediately click the Undo icon, the paragraph reappears. If you immediately click the Redo icon, the Redo command reverses the Undo command and deletes the paragraph once more.

The Undo icon is unique. It offers two ways to use it. First, you can click the Undo icon to undo the last action you chose. Second, you can click the downward-pointing arrow that appears to the right of the Undo icon to display a list of one or more of your previous actions as shown in Figure 4.3.

Figure 4.3 The Undo icon displays a list of actions

Rulers

The ruler helps you to control the *margins, paragraph indentation,* and *tab* settings for a document.

☞ *The horizontal ruler is always displayed at the top of the document window. The vertical ruler is displayed only in the Page Layout view or in Print Preview.*

Displaying or Hiding Rulers

Word 2010 gives you the flexibility to hide or display ruler according to your working needs.

➜ **To display the ruler, do this:**

1. On the **View** tab, in the **Show** group, select the **Ruler** check box (See Figure 4.4).
2. Horizontal and vertical rulers appear above and to the left of the page.

Reading the Horizontal Ruler

Margin settings are managed by the upward facing pointers at the bottom edge of the ruler. Dragging these pointers adjust the position of the right or left margin. However, if you drag these pointers, Word 2010 displays a vertical line showing the position of the margin in the document.

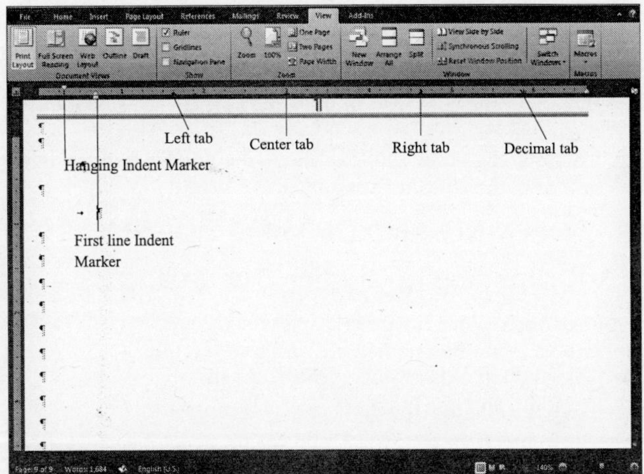

Figure 4.4 Word 2010 horizontal ruler including tabs marking

☞ *The indent markers and the tab stops on the horizontal ruler reflect the settings for the paragraph that contains the insertion point.*

The paragraph indentation setting is managed by the downward-facing pointer at the top edge of the ruler. Dragging this pointer adjusts the indentation of the first line of a paragraph. However, if you drag the pointer, Word 2010 shows a vertical line so that you can see the exact position of the new indentation setting.

Note that you can adjust tab settings by double-clicking on the ruler. There are four types of tab with details given in Table 4.1.

Table 4.1 Different types of tab

Tab	Function
Left-aligned	Characters appear to the right of the tab as you type; indicated by an L-shaped angle in the box.
Centre-aligned	Characters are centred at the tab position; indicated by an angle with the vertical bar centred over the base line.
Right-aligned	Characters extend to the left of the tab as you type; indicated by a reverse L-shaped angle.
Decimal	The decimal point aligns with the tab position; indicated by the symbol for a centre-aligned tab with a decimal point to the right of the vertical member.

The Status Bar

The Status bar, seen at the bottom of Word 2010 Window shows information about the active document or the work you are processing.

Displaying Status Bar

The location of the insertion point is displayed on the Status bar. By default, Status bar tells you which page the insertion point is, on, but you can also display its location by section, line, and column and in inches from the top of the page. Simply right-click the Status bar, and then click the option you want to display. After selecting the options, the screen appears as shown in Figure 4.5.

➜ **To hide the items on the status bar, do this:**

1. Right click the mouse on the Status Bar, Customize Status Bar pop menus appears. Select the options you want to hide the items in the Status bar.

Reading the Status Bar

The status bar shows the information about the text visible on the screen. Table 4.2 explains the message appearing in the status bar (See Figure 4.5).

Table 4.2 Message in the Status Bar

Message	Explanation
Page 6	You are in page 6 of the document.
Sec 1	In section 1 of the document.
6/6	On page 6 of 6 pages in the document. This page number is based on the actual number of pages in the document, not on the printed page number. If you have started numbering pages from a number other than 1, this will not match the printed page number.
At 8.4"	A line of text that is vertical position from the top of the page.
Ln 6	The six line of the text on this page.
Word count	Number of words in the document.
Col 1	Beginning of the line character position within the line of the text.
Over/Insert	Indicates with overtype mode is *on* or *off*.
View tabs	Different view of the document.
Zoom	Click the Zoom slider. If you move Zoom In (i.e.,+ icon) moves to increases. If you move Zoom Out (i.e., - icon) it moves to decrease.

4.2.10 Getting Help

You can use the Word Help system to get assistance on any Word topic or task. This system is a combination of tools and files that were stored on your computer when Word 2010 was installed. If your computer is connected to the Internet, you can also access resources from Office.com.

➜ **To get help, do this:**

1. Click the Word Help button located at the right end of the Ribbon. Or, press the **F1** key. The Word Help window opens displaying a list of general help topics as shown in Figure 4.6.

Figure 4.5 Word 2010 Status Bar elements

2. Click any topic to display the corresponding information (See Figure 4.6).
3. To find help on a specific topic, type a word or phrase related to the topic in the **Search** box, and then press the **Enter** key. For example, we have type the word, such as **SmartArt graphics** in the Search box (See Figure 4.7).

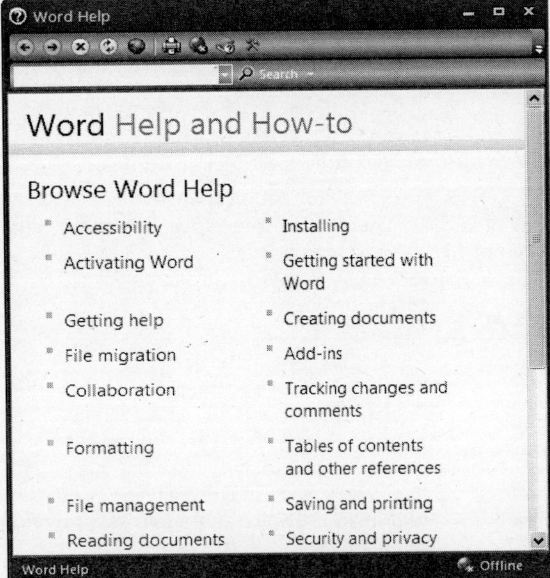

Figure 4.6 Word Help dialog box

4. The Help window displays a list of topics, i.e., searched for *Alignment text*. Choose the selected list topic you want (See Figure 4.7).
5. The Help window displays step-by-step explanations.
6. Click the **Close** button to close the Help window in the upper-right corner of the window.

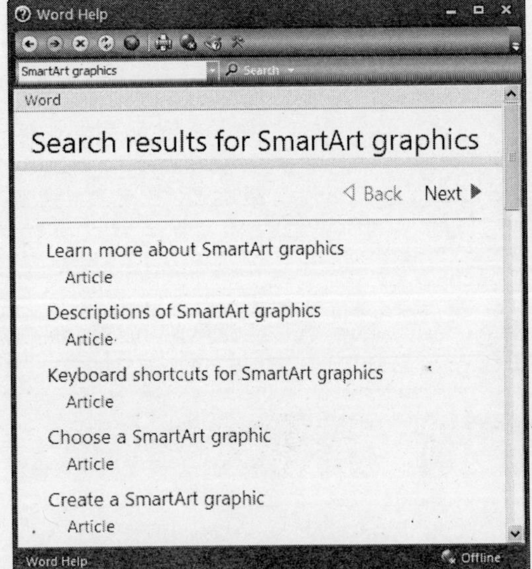

Figure 4.7 Type a word in the search box

➜ **To resize or reposition the help, do this:**

1. To resize the Help Window, move the pointer over a corner of the Help window until you see the double-headed arrow and then drag the corner until the window is of the size that you want it to be.
2. To move the Help window, move the pointer to the title bar and drag the window as you want to keep it.

4.3 OPENING AND CLOSING DOCUMENTS

4.3.1 Opening an Existing Documents

You can open Word document that you can make modifications and save it in another name with different location.

➜ **To open an existing document, do this:**

1. Click the **File** tab, the Backstage view appears.
2. Click the **Open** tab. The **Open** dialog box appears as shown in Figure 4.8.

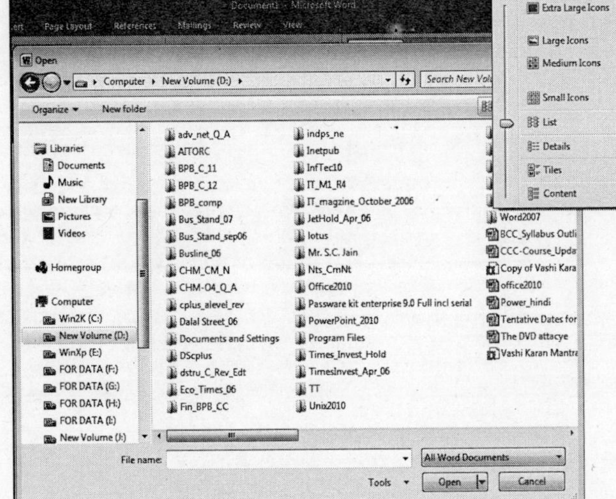

Figure 4.8 Open dialog box

3. In the Look in: drop-down list choose the location of the file you want to open.
4. Click the drop-down triangle views button to change the way the folder and file list is displayed in the Table below.

Button	Function
Thumbnails	It displays icons in Thumbnails. When you click a folder name, a thick highlighted border appear.
Tiles	It displays icons in medium size.
Icons	It displays icons in smaller size.
List	Displays a list of commands.
Details	Displays the details the size type, last modified, etc.
Properties	Displays the properties of the file.
Preview	Displays a preview of the file.

5. Select the document from the list, and then click the Open button.
6. The selected Word 2010 document is opened.

Moving around in a Document

Scroll through a document

You can scroll through a document by using the mouse or the keyboard. If you split the document window, you can display two different parts of a document.

Scrolling through a document using the mouse

To	Do this
Scroll up one line	Click the up scroll arrow
Scroll down one line	Click the down scroll arrow
Scroll up one screen	Click above the scroll box
Scroll down one screen	Click below the scroll box
Scroll to a specific page	Drag the scroll box
Scroll left	Click the left scroll arrow
Scroll right	Click the right scroll arrow
Scroll left, beyond the margin, in normal view	Hold down Shift key and click the left scroll arrow

For a quick way to scroll up or down one page, click Select Browse Object on the vertical scroll bar, and then click the desired option (See Figure 4.2).

Typing and Editing a Document

You can start typing in a document without worrying about the end of the right margin. The words at the end of the line will automatically wrap text to the next line. You may correct the text by pressing Backspace key. The editing of documents is based on the windows principle, that is *select* and *do*.

4.3.2 Save and Save As

The first time you save a file, you need to specify three items:

1. The drive and folder in which you want to store your file.
2. The name of the file.
3. The format to save the file.

➜ **To save a document, do this:**

1. Click **File** tab and then select **Save** tab. *Alternatively*, choose the save button on the Quick Access toolbar.
2. When you save a document for the first time, Word 2010 displays the Save As... dialog box, so that you can type a name for the document (See Figure 4.9).
3. Click Save in: drop-down, to specify a drive and folder to save your file.
4. Click in the File name: text box and type a name of the file.
5. Click Save button.

Naming a Document

In Windows, a filename can be from 1 to 255 characters long, followed by a period and upto three character filename extension. (In most cases, it is best to let Word supply the default extension for Word documents, which is **.docx**). You can use any characters except the following characters for naming the files:

* ? : [] + = \ / : / <>

You cannot use a period (.) except to separate the filename from the extension.

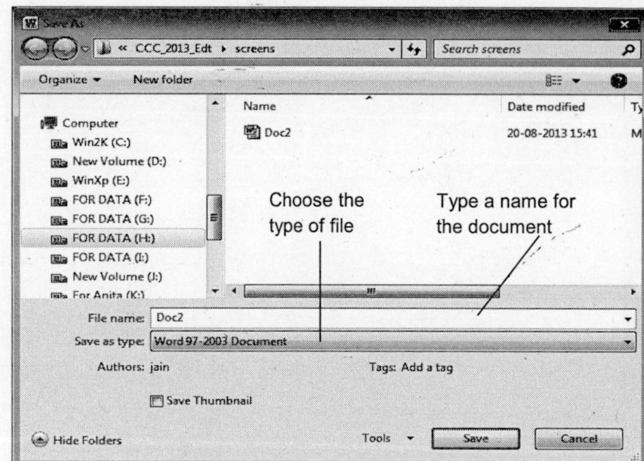

Figure 4.9 Save As dialog box

☞ *You should preview a document before printing it. This will help you to know exactly where the page break will occur. You can change page break if required.*

4.3.3 Page Setup Options

Word 2010 default margins are 1 inch at the *top* and *bottom* each and 1 inch on the *left* and *right*. You can change the margins for the entire document or for different parts of the document (if you divide the document into sections).

Note that in Draft and Outline view, you do not see the margins. However, you can see the space between them in Print Layout view, and you can see the page as it will print. Always select the Print Layout view if you want to see *headers, footers, page numbers, footnotes*, etc.

You can also select one of the two types of page orientations namely, portrait (*vertical*) and landscape (*horizontal*). You can change the paper size and page orientation for a section or for the entire document.

☞ *Indents are added to margin settings. That is, if you specify a 1.0" left margin and a 1/2" left indent, your text will print 1 1/2 from the left margin. If you set a 1.0" right margin and indent the right edge of a paragraph 1.0", the text will stop 2.0" from the right edge of the page* (See Figure 4.10).

A *page* can have only one user-defined left margins setting and only one user-defined right margin setting, but each *paragraph* on the page can have different left and right indentation.

Setting Document Margins

There are two methods to set margins. These are:

- Page Setup command in the Page Layout tab.
- Adjust the margin using the rulers in the Print Layout View.

➜ **To set margins with the page setup command, do this:**

1. Select the sections for which you want to change margins. *Alternatively*, position the insertion point in the section whose margins you want to change.

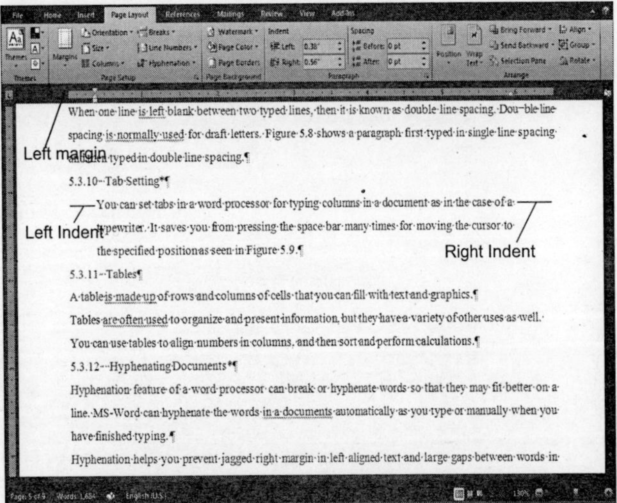

Figure 4.10 Page margins and indents

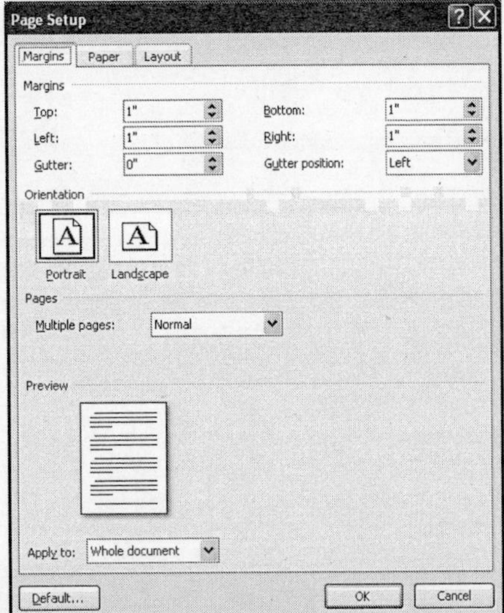

Figure 4.11 Page Setup dialog box

2. Click **Page Layout** tab and click the right corner arrow of **Page setup**. The **Page Setup** dialog box appears. Click the **Margins** tab property sheet as shown in Figure 4.11 appears.
3. Margins Property sheet has the following options:

Option	Description
Top:	Select or type out the desired margin from the top of the page.
Bottom:	Select or type out the desired margins from the bottom of the page.
Left:	Select or type out the desired margin from the left edge of the page.
Right:	Select or type out the desired margin from the right edge of the page.

(Contd...)

Option	Description
Gutter:	Select or type out the gutter space as required. Gutter is the extra space added to the margins to leave the space for binding the documents.
Orientation	Select between Portrait (vertical) or Landscape (horizontal) page setting.

4. In the Pages area, select the **Multiple pages:** list.
   Mirror margins—This option adjusts left and right margins so that when you print on both sides of the page the inside and outside margins of the facing pages are of the same width.
   The Preview box displays the effect of the settings you select.
5. In the Apply to: choose the portion of the document from where you want to apply the new settings.
6. Click OK.

➜ **To set the margins using the ruler, do this:**

1. Switch to Print Layout view.
2. If the ruler is not displayed, click **View** tab. In the **Show** group, click the **Ruler** check box.
3. Point to the transition area on the ruler that is where *gray becomes white.*
4. The mouse pointer will become a two-headed arrow.
5. Drag the margin to the desired position with a mouse. The ruler's dimensions change as you drag (See Figure 4.12).

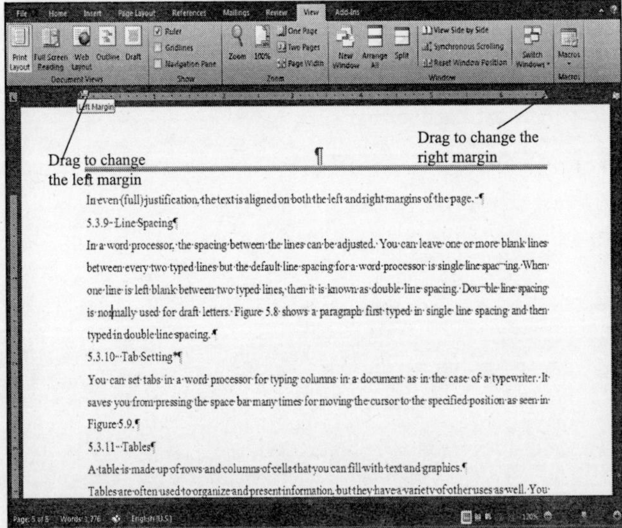

Figure 4.12 Drag ruler ends in print Layout to change the margins

Paper Size

Page margins are usually set in according to paper size you use.

➜ **To select paper size, do this:**

1. Select the text, in the section you want to change.
2. In the **Page Setup** dialog box click **Paper** tab. The property sheet as shown in Figure 4.13 appears.

3. The options are as follows:

Option	Function
Paper size:	The list in the form of drop-down offers different standard paper size. Select from the standard sizes or specify the width and height as the case may be. The commonly used paper size is A4 and legal.
Width:	Type or select the width of the paper you are using.
Height:	Type or select the height of the paper you are using.

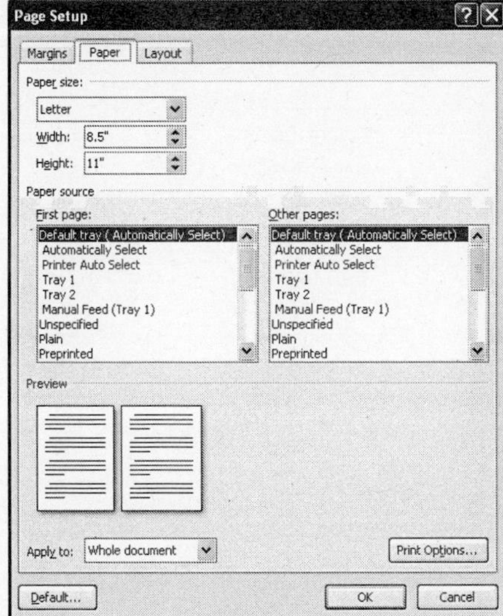

Figure 4.13 Paper size property sheet tab

4. In the Apply to: select the portion of the document you want to print on the selected paper size.
5. Click the Default... buttons if you want to save these settings as default settings, so that they can apply to all pages printed hereafter.
6. Click OK.

4.3.4 Previewing and Printing a Document

When you are ready to print a document, you can click the **File** tab, point to print. The Backstage view appears then click **Print** icon. Word then uses your computer's default printer and the settings specified in the **Print** Backstage view. You can also use a different printer or change the printer settings on the File tab Backstage view. You can then specify which printer to use, what to print, and how many copies. You can also make other changes to the settings.

☞ *Before you print a document, you may want to check how it will look on paper by previewing it. Previewing is essential for multi-page documents but is helpful even for one-page documents also.*

Setting Printer Properties Options

Windows manages details of setting up a printer. However, Windows leaves three tasks for you:

- Selecting the printer you want to use in Word 2010.
- Installing the printers if not available in the list of Windows printers.
- Changing the printer setup for special printing needs.

☞ *Most of the printer options are set by Word 2010 depending upon the printer selected by you. All the same, many options are available to you so that you can customize the printing options as per your requirement.*

➜ **To set printer specific options, do this:**

1. Click the **File** tab, the Backstage view appears as shown in Figure 4.14.
2. Under the **Printer** drop-down list select the printer.
3. Click the **Printer Properties** in the **File** Backstage view as shown in Figure 4.14.

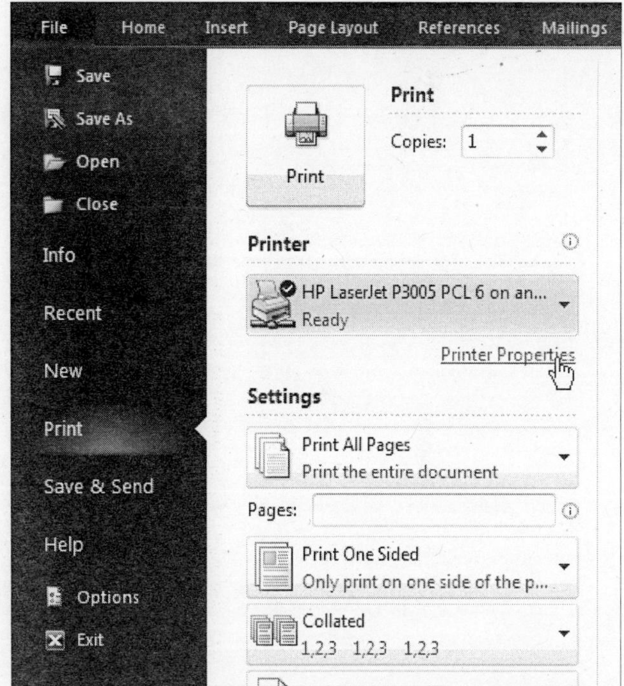

Figure 4.14 Selecting Printer Properties in the File tab

4. The **Printer Properties** dialog box appears as shown in Figure 4.15.
5. The **Properties** dialog box generally has the following tabs.

Tab	Options
Advanced	Additional features, such as page protection, copies, paper size and postscript options may be found on the Advanced tab.
Paper/ Quality	Sets the option for the paper and the quality of printing.

(Contd...)

Tab	Options
Finishing	Select the quality of printing that you desire. This options can vary from printer to printer.
Effects	It shows prints of your document on a paper size that is different from the one for which it is formatted. It also specifies the percentage of normal size.

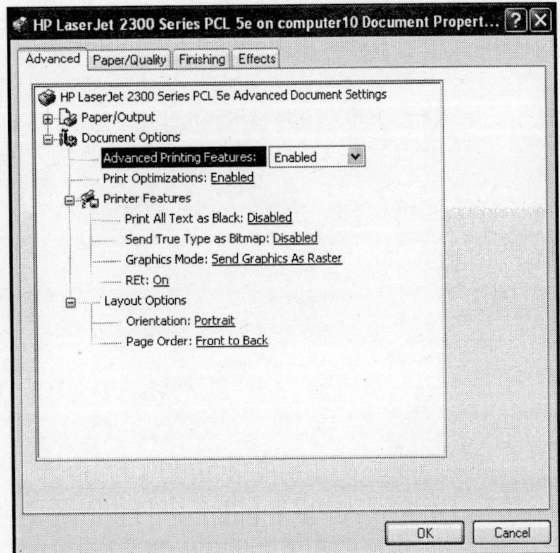

Figure 4.15 Selecting Printer Properties in the File tab

6. Click the **Advanced** tab. The options are:
   In the page order section
   - If you choose Front to Back, it specifies the order in which the pages of your document will be printed. It starts printing from page 1 to end.
   - If you choose Back to Front, it prints the document from end to first page.
7. Click the Paper/Quality tab as shown in Figure 4.16 the options are:
   In the paper options
   - Click use different paper to enable settings that allow you to select a different paper source and type settings for the first page, other pages and back cover in the print job.
   - Click the Source is: drop-down list and choose the desired option where the paper is located in the printer.
   - Type is: option is used to select the kind of paper you want to use.
8. Click OK.
9. In the **Print** dialog box, again click OK.

Printing the Current Document

The simplest way to print is to open a document, click **File** tab, choose Print tab. The Backstage view appears choose **Print** icon. *Alternately*, click the Print button on the Quick Access toolbar. By default, Word 2010 prints one copy of all pages of the currently open document on the selected printer without printing hidden text.

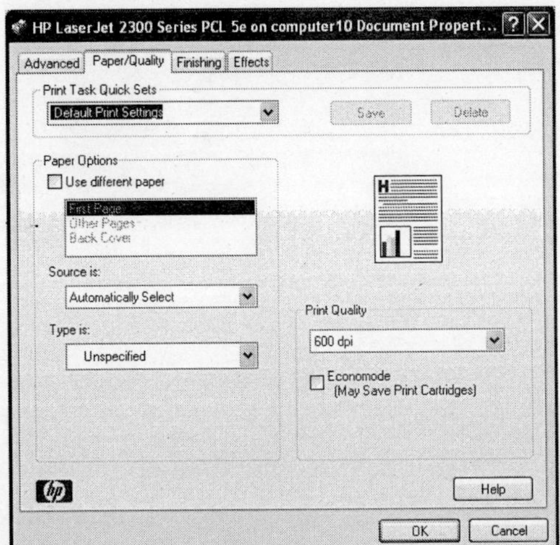

Figure 4.16 Properties options of Paper/Quality tab property sheet

To print a copy of the document, do this:

1. Open the document you want to print.
2. Click the **File** tab and then choose **Print** command. The Print Backstage view appears then click Print icon or press Ctrl+Shift+F12 keys together (See Figure 4.17).

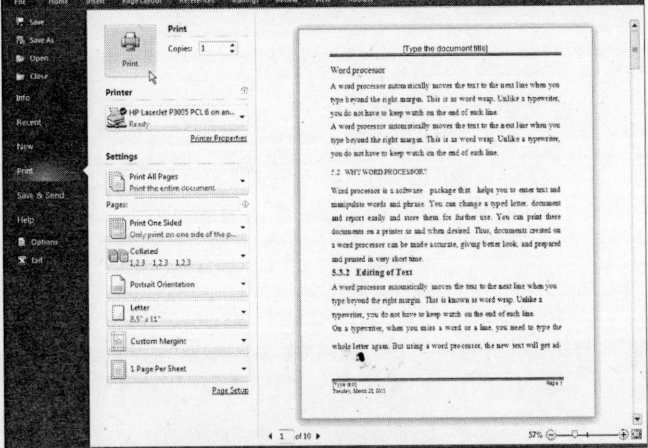

Figure 4.17 Print Backstage view

3. The Print Backstage view closes and in the Status bar displays the process of the print job (See Figure 4.18).

Page Range Options

- To print the entire document, click All button.
- To print just the page in your document currently containing the insertion point, click on the Current Page button.
- To print the selected text, first select it, then in the Print dialog box, use the Selection button in the Page Range area. This choice will be dimmed unless you have selected something in your document.
- To print a range of pages, say, pages **6-10** in a 50 page document, type the first page number and the last desired page

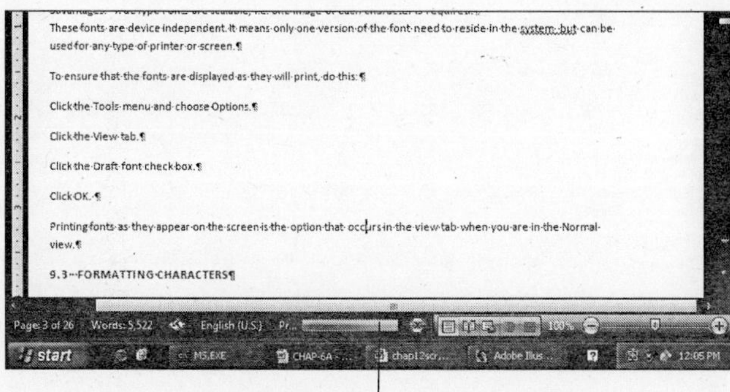

The process of print job in the status bar

Figure 4.18 Displaying the print process in the Status bar

number in the Pages: text box. Separate the numbers with hyphens like **6-10**.

- You can also print pages in a certain section. To print the second section in your document, type **s2** in the Pages box. If you want to print from page 7 in the second section to page 10 in the third section, type **p7s2-p10s3** in the Pages box.
- The Print: drop-down list has the option which allows you to select the pages you want to print.

Option	Description
All pages	This is the default option and Word 2010 prints all pages in the range.
Odd pages	This option when selected prints the odd numbered pages in the range.
Even pages	This option when selected prints the even numbered pages in the range.

Odd and Even pages option is very useful when you want to do double-sided printing.

Copies: In the number of Copies: box, specify the number of copies of the document you want to print.

Collate: This option determines how multiple copies are printed. Say, you print five copies of a 10-page document without the Collate option, Word 2010 will first print all five copies of page 1 then all five copies of page 2 and so on. You will need to arrange them manually to make the sets. With the Collate option Word 2010 prints five sets, each one complete and in order.

➜ To cancel printing, do this:

1. Click the Start button and then click **Printers and Faxes**.
2. In the **Printers and Faxes** dialog box, open the printer that you are using by double-clicking the printer's icon (See Figure 4.19).
3. Select the document you want to cancel printing, and then choose **Document Name**, right click and choose Cancel Printing.

Previewing a Document

Previewing a document allows you to visualize the document in its printable format before actually executing the Print command. The preview of a document displays the document in a printable format and shows how the document will appear after taking a printout.

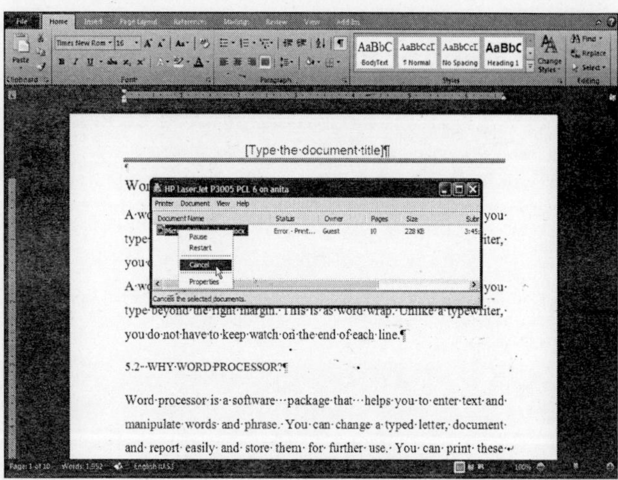

Figure 4.19 Printer folder open

➜ To preview the document, do this:

1. Open the document whose print preview you want to view.
2. Click the **File** tab and then choose **Print** option from the **File** tab. The **Print** options are visible in the Backstage view as shown in Figure 4.20.

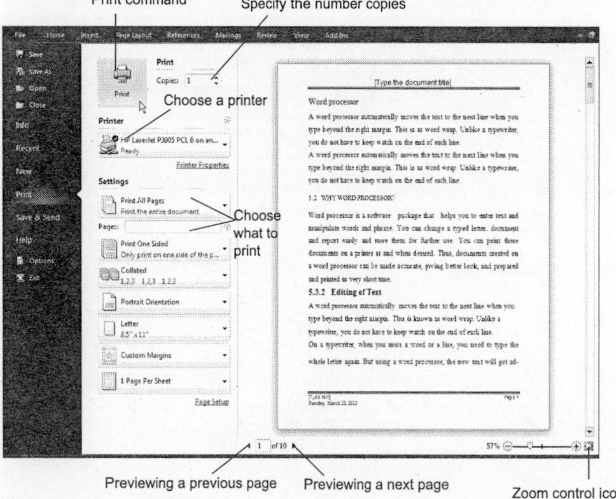

Figure 4.20 Print preview in the Backstage view

3. The Backstage view consists of three panes. The left pane contains several options, such as Save, Save As, Open, Close, Info, Recent, etc. In the middle pane, print options and its related printer settings are shown. In the right pane, the preview document is seen. In the bottom of the right pane, the Zoom control button is available. The + (plus) button is used to increase the document and the – (minus) button is used to decrease the preview document. The Next button goes to next page of document and the previous button to move to the pervious page of document.

4.3.5 Closing, and Quitting Word 2010

After finishing a document, you should close the window to remove it from the screen and to free computer's main memory.

➜ **To close a document and exit Word 2010, do this:**

1. Click the **File** tab, and then choose **Close** tab.
2. The window closes if no changes have been made to the document since the last save. However, if you made changes since the last time you saved the document, Word 2010 displays an Alert dialog box, asking whether you want to save your work before closing (See Figure 4.21).
3. After you have saved the contents of the document, the window is closed.

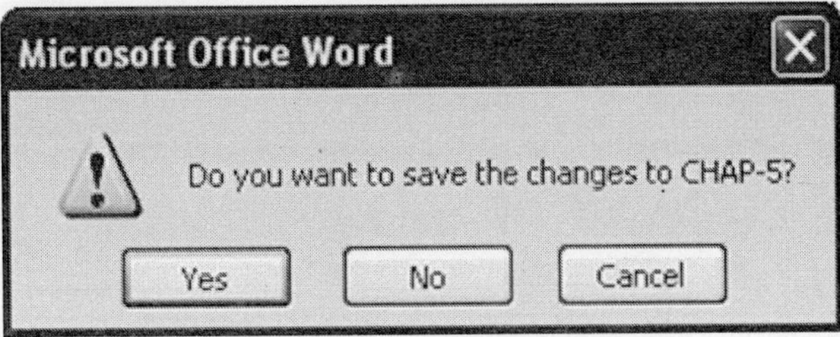

Figure 4.21 Alert dialog box

➜ **To quit Word 2010, do this:**

1. Click **File** tab, and then choose **Exit**. Word 2010 window closes, and the application is terminated (See Figure 4.22).

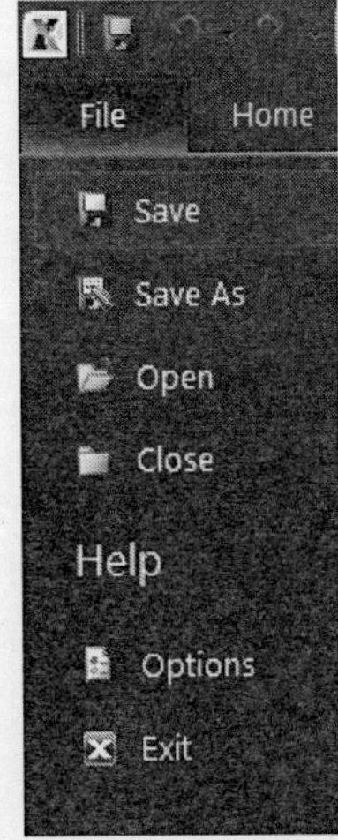

Figure 4.22 Selecting Exit from the File tab

4.4 TEXT CREATION AND MANIPULATION

When you open a new document in Word 2010, the insertion point is at the top left corner of the screen. You can start typing in this document. You can make changes at any time by editing the document.

You can click the Show/Hide button on the Paragraph group to display or hide all non-printing characters, such as *paragraph marks, tab characters*, and *spaces*. These characters are *not printed*, even if they are shown on the screen (See Figure 4.23).

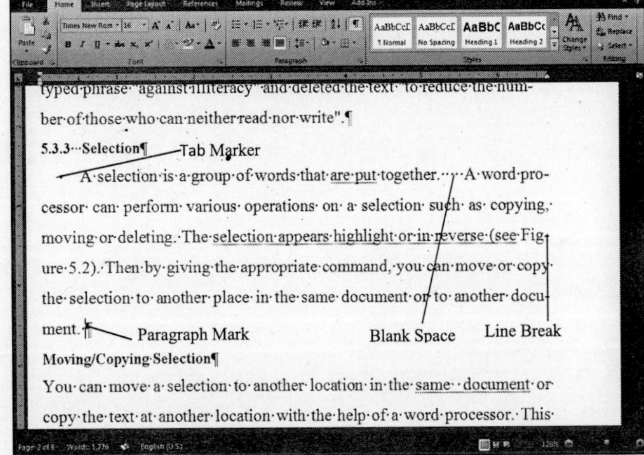

Figure 4.23 A screen displaying non-printing characters

4.4.1 Creating a Blank Document

If you are creating a document, such as *memo, letter, report,* or *resume, Brochures, Calendars, Card,* etc., you can save time by using one of the wizards or templates that come with Word 2010.

You can also create a blank document which is based on the blank template of Word 2010. The blank template offers you the flexibility to create a edit documents according to your requirements.

➜ **To create a new document, do this:**

1. Click **File** tab, a Backstage view appears, click the **New** tab in the Backstage view as shown in Figure 4.24.
2. Select the **Blank document** option under **Available templates** as shown in Figure 4.24.
3. Click the **Create** button as shown in Figure 4.24. The new blank document is created as shown in Figure 4.25.

Starting a New Paragraph

In Word 2010, a paragraph is any amount of text or graphics followed by a paragraph mark. A paragraph ends whenever

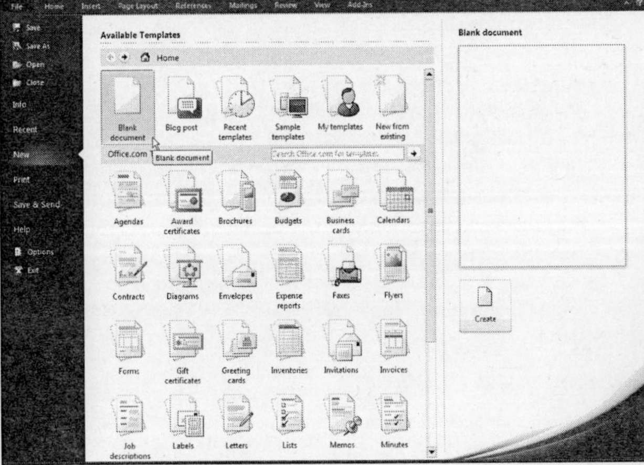

Figure 4.24 New tab Backstage view

Figure 4.25 Word blank document

you press the Enter key. Even if you have not typed any text but press Enter key, Word 2010 inserts a paragraph mark (¶). In Word 2010, many types of formatting (for example, justification and line spacing) are applied to paragraphs as a whole.

➜ **To start a new paragraph, do this:**

1. Position the insertion point where you want to start the new paragraph, and press the Enter key.

When you press Enter key, Word 2010 inserts a paragraph mark and moves the insertion point to the first line of the new paragraph.

Starting a New Line

Word 2010 automatically wraps text to the next line when the typed text reaches the end of the right margin.

➜ **To start a new line within the same paragraph, do this:**

1. Position the insertion point where you want to start the new line, and then press Shift+Enter keys together.
2. Word inserts a line break character and moves the insertion point to the beginning of the next line.
3. To see the line breaks, click the Show/Hide command on the **paragraph** group of **Home** tab.

4.4.2 Editing Text

On a typewriter, when you miss a word or a line, you need to type the whole letter again. But using a Word 2010, you can insert new words, new sentences or paragraphs anywhere in the text typed earlier. The new text will get adjusted automatically.

Similarly, you can delete any portion of the text and the remaining part of the matter will get adjusted automatically.

In Figure 4.26, you can see the highlighted text is newly inserted and rest of the text gets deleted.

Inserting Text

If you notice that some text has been left out of the document, you can move the Insertion pointer to that position and type it in. This method is called *Inserting*.

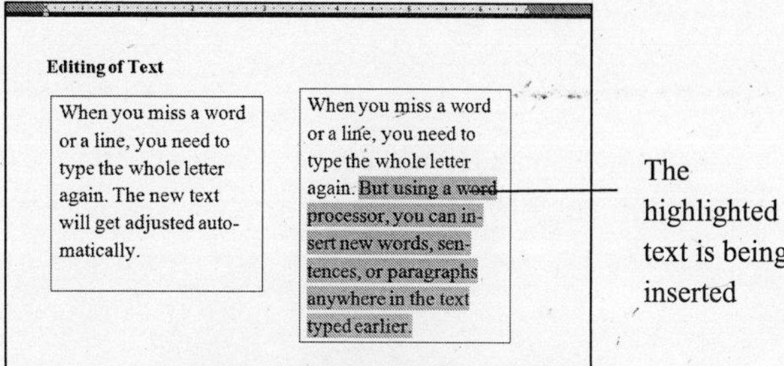

Figure 4.26 Adding/deleting text

Typing over the Existing Text

By default, Word moves the existing text to the right as you insert new characters. If you want the new text to replace the existing text, character-by-character, switch to *overtype* mode. Again clicking the *overtype* mode in the status bar will automatically replace the *insert* mode.

➜ **To type over the existing text, do this:**

1. Click the **File** tab and then chooose **Options**.
2. The **Word Options** dialog box, click **Advanced** tab in the left pane and then under **Editing options**, select *use the Insert key to control overtype mode* check box.
3. Click OK.

Applying Corrections in the Typed Text

To correct simple typing mistakes, press Backspace or Del keys. To delete more characters, *first select the text you* want to delete and then press the Backspace or Del key. Table 4.3 lists different methods for deleting texts and graphics.

Table 4.3 Key Combinations for deleting Text or Graphics

To delete	Key combination
Selected text	Press Backspace or Del
Characters before the insertion point	Press Backspace key
Characters after the insertion point	Press Del key
A word before the insertion point	Ctrl+Backspace
A word after the insertion point	Ctrl+Del

➜ **To restore the deleted text, do this:**

1. On the Quick Access toolbar, click the Undo button. *Alternatively*, click the Ctrl+Z keys together.

➜ **To replace a selection with a new text, do this:**

1. Select the text you want to replace.
2. Type the new text.

The text you type replaces the entire selection.

Undoing Mistakes

If you make a mistake in Word 2010, you can apply "Undo" command. For example, if you accidentally delete a word, you can bring it back with the Undo command. To reverse the action of undo use the "Redo" command. There are certain actions you cannot undo, such as saving or printing a document.

➜ To undo or redo changes do this:

1. To undo or redo the most recent action, click the Undo (press Ctrl+Z) or Redo button (press Ctrl+Y) on the Quick Access toolbar.
2. To undo or redo multiple actions, click the down arrow next to either the Undo or the Redo button, and then select the actions you want to undo or redo (See Figure 4.27).

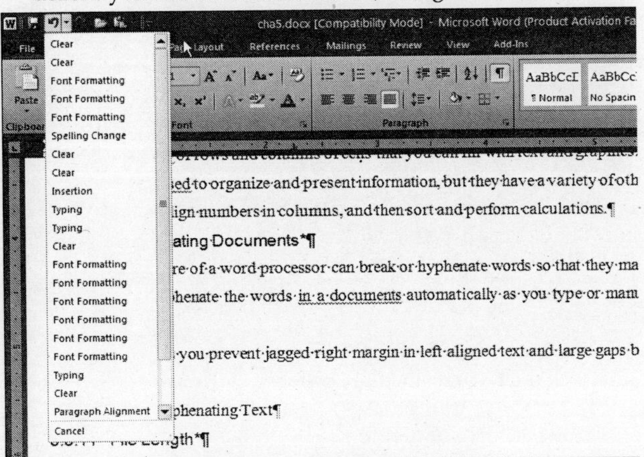

Figure 4.27 Selecting Undo list

Select the Text with the Pop-up Toolbar

Word 2010 displays a pop-up toolbar. For example, select the text you want to apply formatting, such as *bold, font size*, etc., a pop-up toolbar appears to the upper right of the selected text as a faint image. The closer you move the mouse towards this pop-up toolbar, the darker and sharper the toolbar appears as shown in Figure 4.28.

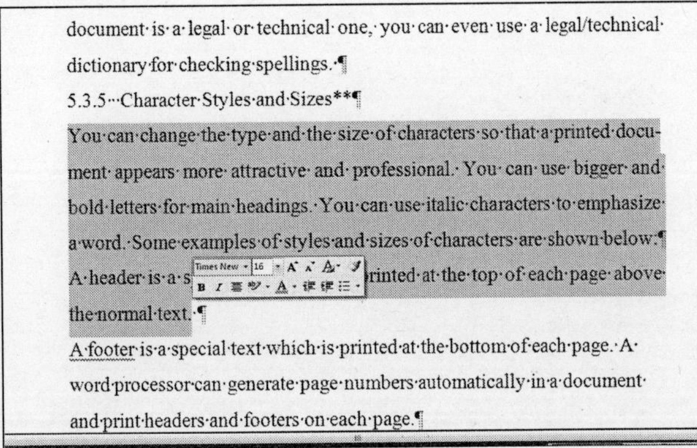
document·is·a·legal·or·technical·one,·you·can·even·use·a·legal/technical·dictionary·for·checking·spellings.·¶

5.3.5···Character·Styles·and·Sizes**¶

You·can·change·the·type·and·the·size·of·characters·so·that·a·printed·document·appears·more·attractive·and·professional.·You·can·use·bigger·and·bold·letters·for·main·headings.·You·can·use·italic·characters·to·emphasize·a·word.·Some·examples·of·styles·and·sizes·of·characters·are·shown·below.¶

A·header·is·a·s ... printed·at·the·top·of·each·page·above·the·normal·text.·¶

A·footer·is·a·special·text·which·is·printed·at·the·bottom·of·each·page.·A·word·processor·can·generate·page·numbers·automatically·in·a·document·and·print·headers·and·footers·on·each·page.¶

Figure 4.28 Selecting text and displaying pop-up toolbar

Displaying Different Views of a Document

The type of work that you do will help you to determine the best screen view as per your needs. There are different views available in Word 2010. These are:

- Print Layout View
- Full screen Reading View
- Web Layout View
- Outline View
- Draft View

There are two ways so that you can change the view. These are:

- Click the View tab, in the Document views group, and switch to any view you wish to see the document.
- Click view buttons that are found on the right side of the status (See Figure 4.29).

Editing text in Print Layout View

This is the default view. Print Layout view is used to see how text, graphics and other elements, such as header, footer, etc., will look on the printed output. This view is useful for editing headers and footers, for adjusting margins and for working with columns and drawing objects.

➜ To work in Print Layout view, do this:

1. Click the **View** tab, in the Document views group and click Print Layout command. Alternatively click from the status bar icons (See Figure 4.29).

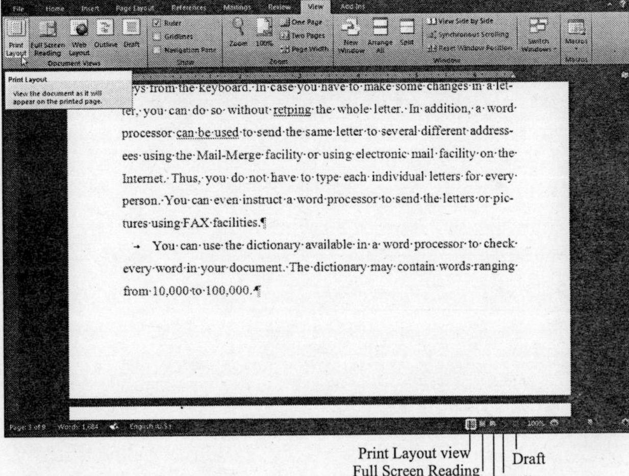

Figure 4.29 Editing a document in Print Layout view

Editing text in Full Screen Reading View

Full screen view displays as much of the typing area of the document as will fit on the screen at a size that is comfortable for reading. In this view, the Ribbon is replaced by a single toolbar at the top of the screen. You can print the document, highlight text and write comments. You can also move from page-to-page and adjust the view.

➜ To switch to full screen view, do this:

1. Click the **View** tab, in the **Document Views** group and click Full Screen Reading command as in Figure 4.30. *Alternatively,* click from the Status bar icons.
2. In Full reading screen, click the View Options, a drop-down menu appears. You can make the text larger or smaller for reading by clicking Increase Text Size or Decrease Text Size. This will temporarily change as to how text fits on a page. It does not affect the original document.
3. You can read one page at a time by clicking Show one page, or you can read two pages at a time by clicking Show Two pages.
4. While reading in full screen view, you can edit document by clicking Allow Typing.

5. To go to the *previous screen* or to the *next screen*, click jump to a screen at the top of the Title bar in the full screen view (See Figure 4.30).
6. To exit Full Screen Reading view, click (Esc) button or click Print Layout button.

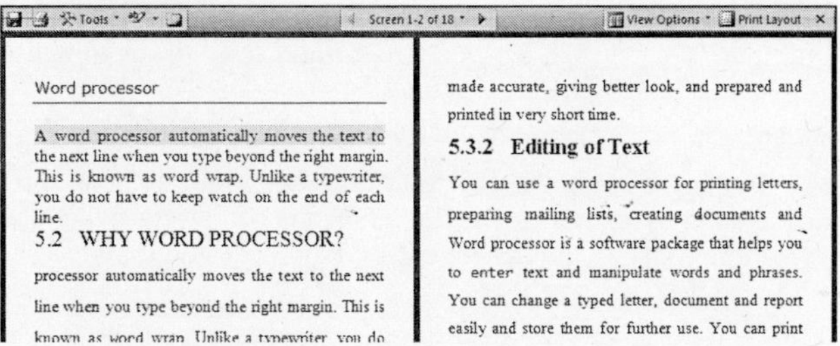

Figure 4.30 Editing a document in Print Layout view

Editing in Web Layout View

While creating a Web page in Word 2010, you should work in Web Layout view. In Web Layout view, you can see that background text is wrapped to fit the window. Graphics are positioned at proper places, so that the page will look just as it would look in a Web browser (See Figure 4.31).

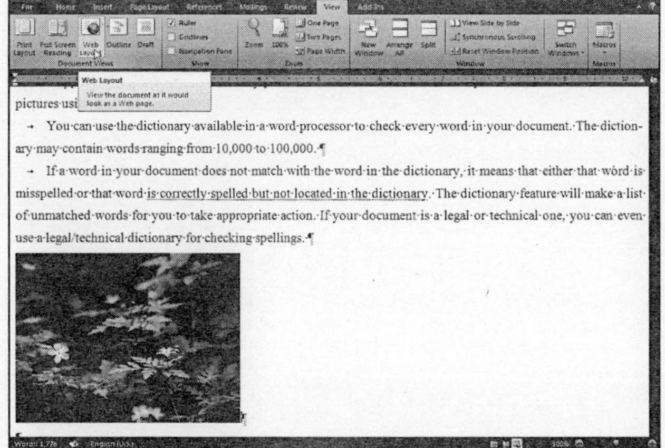

Figure 4.31 Document seen in Web Layout view

➜ To switch to Web Layout view, do this:

1. Click the **View** tab, in the **Document views** group and click **Web Layout** view command as in Figure 4.31. *Alternatively*, click from the Status bar icons.

Editing text in Outline View

In the Outline View, you can collapse a document to see only the main headings or expand it to see the entire document. In this view, it is easy to scroll or move text to a longer distance or to change the hierarchy of topics (See Figure 4.32).

➜ To switch to Outline View, do this:

1. Click the **View** tab, in the **Document views** group and click **Outline** view command as shown in Figure 4.31. *Alternatively*, click from the Status bar icons.

In the Outline view, the outline toolbar appears as shown in Figure 4.32. Word 2010 indents the formatting headings and body

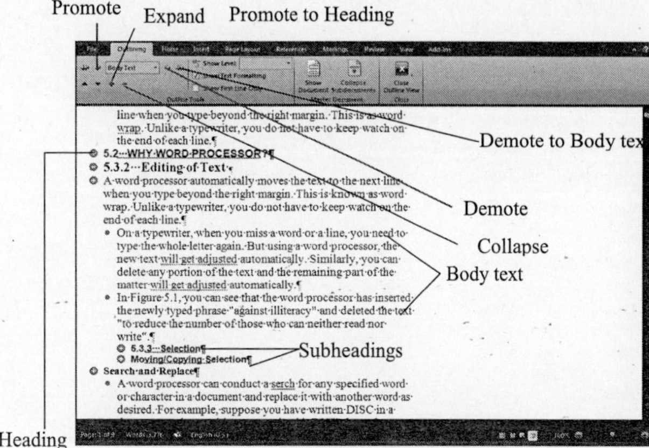

Figure 4.32 Document in Outline view

text paragraphs to different levels. Note that (+) or (–) sign appears to the left of each heading.

- A plus sign (+) indicates that sub-heading or paragraphs of the body text are associated with the heading.
- A minus sign (–) indicates that no headings or paragraphs are beneath the heading.

☞ *In the outline view you will also get the options of viewing headings at different levels or of viewing entire document, including the body text.*

Editing in Draft View

Draft view is the best view for most of your typing and editing as can be seen in Figure 4.32. In this view, you can see character and paragraph formatting as they will be printed. Line and page breaks, tab stops and alignments are accurate. The area outside the text body – the area containing *headers, footers, footnotes, page numbers, margin spacing*, etc., do not appear. Images are also not shown in Draft view.

☞ *Note that the cursor movement is very fast in Draft view.*

➜ To switch to Draft view, do this:

1. Click the **View** tab, in the **Document** views group and click **Draft** view command as in Figure 4.33. *Alternatively*, click from the Status bar icons.

4.4.3 Text Selection

Before you can *move, format, delete*, or otherwise change text or a graphic picture, you must select the items. You can select the item using a mouse or keyboard. Note that the selected text or graphics are highlighted. To cancel the selection, click outside the selection, or use the arrow keys to move the insertion point.

➜ To select text, do this:

1. Position the insertion point from where you want to select text.
2. Now press the left mouse button and select the text by moving mouse pointer. *Alternatively*, you can also select text and graphics by positioning the insertion point at the

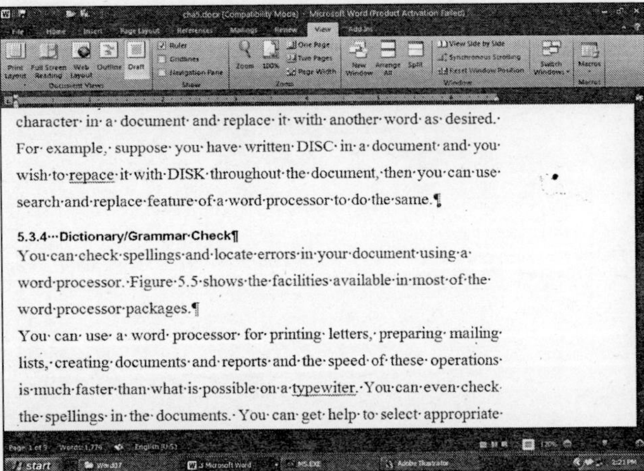

Figure 4.33 Document in Draft view

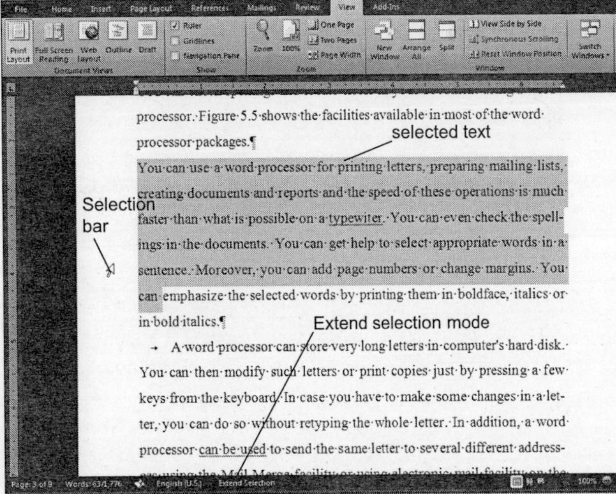

Figure 4.34 Using selection bar to select text

beginning of the text or graphic you want to select, holding down the Shift key, and then clicking where you want the selection to end. The selected text highlighted appears as shown in Figure 4.34.

Selecting Text with a Mouse

You can select a piece of text, or a single character or an entire document. You can also combine mouse and keyboard selection techniques.

➜ **To select a small amount of text with the mouse, do this:**

1. Click and hold the mouse button at the beginning of the text you want to select.
2. Drag the pointer in any direction across the text you want to select.

☞ *If the pointer touches the edge of the window as you are dragging, the window scrolls in that direction if more text exists.*

You can select text using one of the methods given in Table 4.4.

Table 4.4 Method for Selecting Text

Text to select	Mouse Action
A word	Double-click the word.
A line	Click selection bar (blank margin to left of a line of text).
Multiple lines	Click selection bar and drag up or down till the end of lines.
A paragraph	Double-click selection bar.
Document	Press Ctrl key and click in selection bar.
Rectangular block or column (not within a table)	Click the top left of the column to be selected and then hold Alt key while you drag to select the text.

Selecting Text with a Keyboard

The method for selecting text is to hold down the Shift key as you move the insertion point. You can select text by using Shift in combination with any move key. Some of these key combinations are listed in Table 4.5.

Table 4.5 Key Combination for Selecting Text

To Select	Press
A word	Shift+Ctrl + ← or → arrow key
To the beginning of a line	Shift+Home
To the end of a line	Shift+End
To the end of a paragraph	Ctrl+Shift+↓
To the beginning of a paragraph	Ctrl+Shift+↑
One line at a time	Shift+↑ or Shift+↓
To the beginning of a document	Shift+Ctrl+Home
To the end of a document	Shift+Ctrl+End

➜ **To select from the insertion point to a distant location, do this:**

1. Move the insertion point to the beginning of the text you want to select.
2. Press F8 (Extend Selection).

☞ *While you are in Extend Selection mode, the word appears on the Status bar at the bottom of the screen.*

3. Press one of the keys listed in the Table 4.6. And finally press Esc key.

Table 4.6 Selecting Text from the Insertion Point

To Select	Press
Next or previous character	← or → arrow key
The end of a line	End key
The beginning of a line	Home key
The top of the previous screen	PgUp key
The bottom of the next screen	PgDn key
The beginning of a document	Ctrl+Home keys
The end of a document	Ctrl+End keys

4.4.4 Cut, Copy and Paste

"Copying" means to make a copy of the selected text or graphic and insert it in another location, leaving the original document unchanged.

➔ **To copy text from one location to another in the same document, do this:**

1. Select the text you want to copy.
2. Click **Copy** option from the **Clipboard** group. The selected text will be placed on the Clipboard which is an accessory in Word (See Figure 4.35).
3. Now position the insertion point at the location you want to place the text.
4. Click the **Paste** option from the **Clipboard** group as shown in Figure 4.36. The selected text will be pasted.

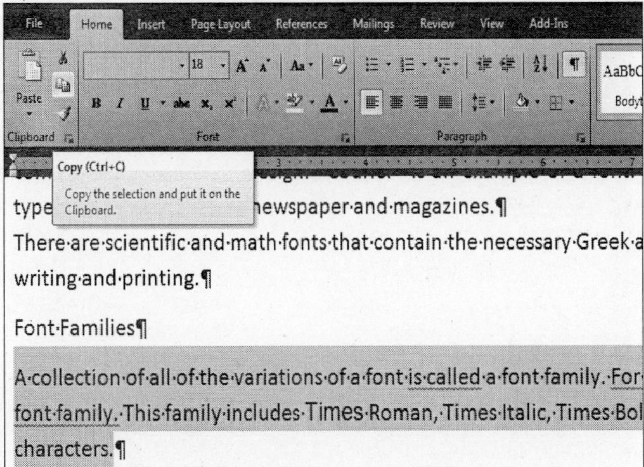

Figure 4.35 Select the text to be copied

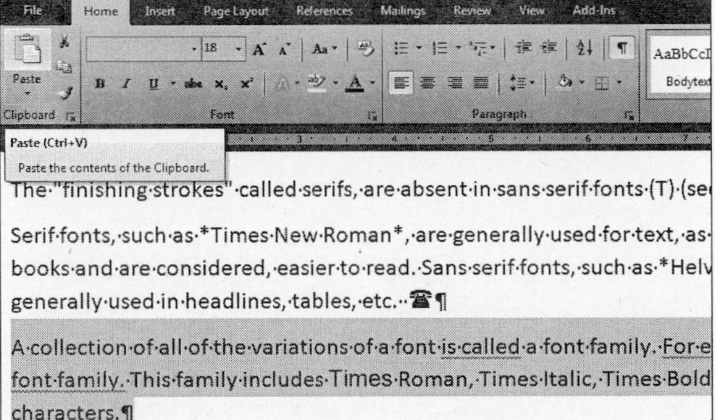

Figure 4.36 Selected text has been pasted

Moving Text

"*Moving*" means to remove (cut) the selected text or graphic from one location and insert it in another location in the same document.

➔ **To move text from one location to another in the same document, do this:**

1. Select the text you want to move (See Figure 4.37).

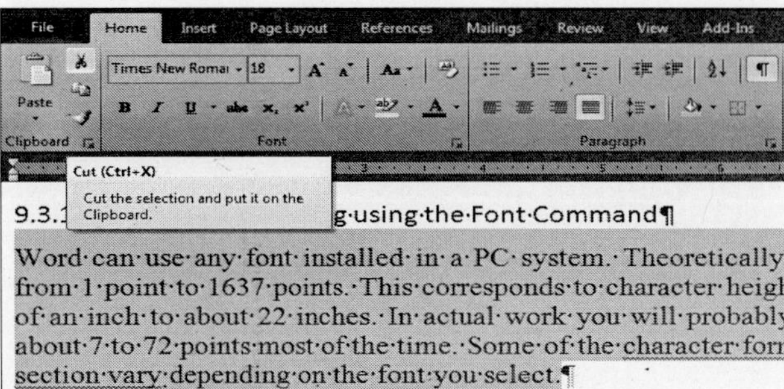

Figure 4.37 Highlight the text to move

2. Click the **Cut** option from the **Clipboard** group. The selected text will disappear from the screen and will be placed on the Clipboard.
3. Now position the insertion point at the location you want to paste the text.
4. Click the **Paste** option from the **Clipboard** group. The selected text will be moved (See Figure 4.38).

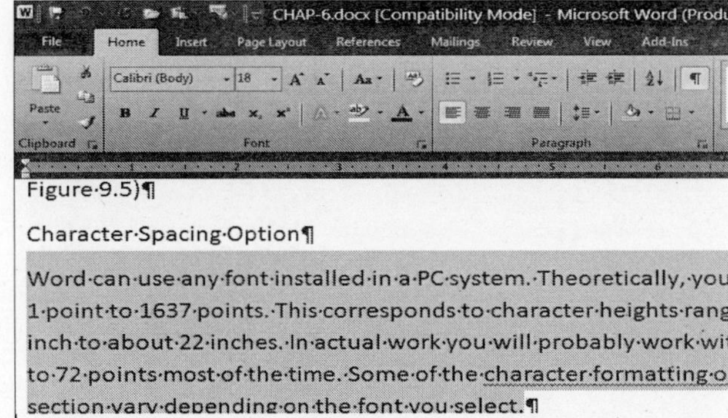

Figure 4.38 Highlighted text pasted in the new location

Moving and Copying using Drag and Drop Technique

Drag-and-drop editing is an easy way to move or copy a selection with in a short distance of a document. You can *drag* and *drop* items between documents. However, to move or copy a selection to a longer distance in a document or to a different document, you should use the Cut, Copy, and Paste commands.

➔ **To move text using drag-and-drop editing, do this:**

1. Select the text or the graphics you want to move.
2. Point to the selected text or graphics, and then press and hold down the left mouse button. When the drag-and-drop pointer appears as shown in Figure 4.39, drag the dotted insertion point to the new location.
3. Release the mouse button to drop the text into desired place.

➔ **To copy text/graphics using drag-and-drop editing, do this:**

1. Select the text or the graphics you want to copy.
2. Press and hold down Ctrl key, point to the selected text or the graphics, and then press and hold down the left mouse button while you drag the dotted insertion point to the new location.

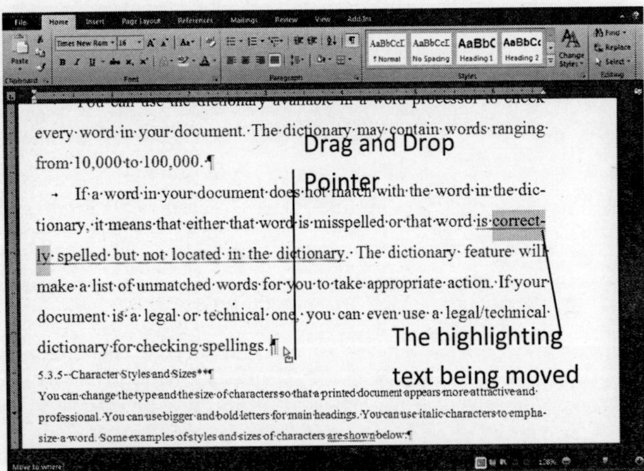

Figure 4.39 Drag-and-Drop mouse pointer

➜ **To move or copy the text/graphics using the toolbar, do this:**

1. Select the text or the graphics you want to move or copy.
2. Do one of the following:
   - To move the selection, click the Cut button on the Home tab of Clipboard group.
   - To copy the selection, click the Copy button on the Home tab of Clipboard group.

   Word places the selected text to the Clipboard.
3. Position the insertion point in the new location, where you want to insert the new text or the graphics. Now click the Paste command on the Home tab of Clipboard group.

Using Keyboard Shortcuts for Moving and Copying

Word 2010 has many keyboard shortcuts, i.e., combination of keys for moving and copying text and graphics. Table 4.7 lists different methods for cutting, copying and moving text or graphics using the keyboard shortcuts.

Table 4.7 Keyboard Shortcuts for Moving and Copying Text or Graphics

Action	Key combination
Copy the selected text or the graphics to the Clipboard	Ctrl+C keys pressed together.
Move the selected text or the graphics to the Clipboard	Ctrl+X or Shift+Del keys pressed together.
Paste Clipboard contents into a document	Ctrl+V or Shift+Ins keys pressed together.
Move a paragraph up	Alt+Shift + ↑ arrow keys pressed together.
Move a paragraph down	Alt+Shift + ↓ arrow keys pressed together.

Deleting Text

To delete characters to the right of insertion point press Del key but to delete characters to left of insertion point use Backspace key. However, when you have to delete number of lines, deleting one letter at a time becomes a lengthy process. It would be better if you select or highlight all the lines to be deleted as a block.

➜ **To delete text do this:**

1. Select the text to be deleted by pressing the left mouse button.
2. Now press Del key from the keyboard.

4.4.5 Font and Size Selection

To modify character appearance, you can also use the commands in Ribbon or when you select the text, a mini toolbar appears.

➜ **To change the font using Ribbon, do this:**

1. Select the text that you want to change the font. Click the down arrow to the right of the font list box (See Figure 4.40).

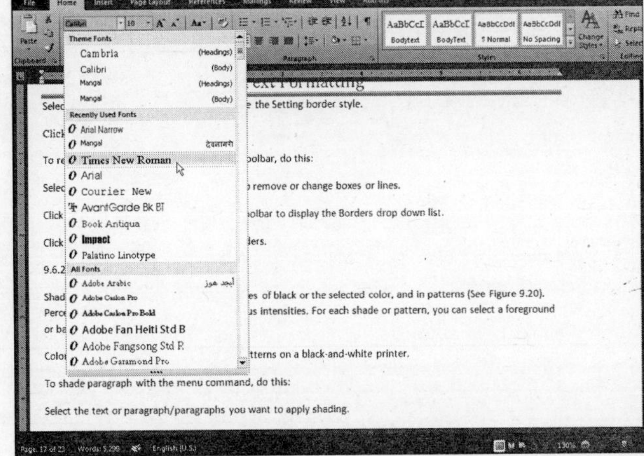

Figure 4.40 Font drop-down list

2. The drop-down list shows all the available fonts. Use the scroll arrow on the right of the drop-down list to scroll through the list. When you move the cursor over the font you can see the changes in the appearance of text.
3. To change the size, enter the desired font size in Font size list box and press Enter. Or you can select from the mini toolbar (See Figure 4.41).

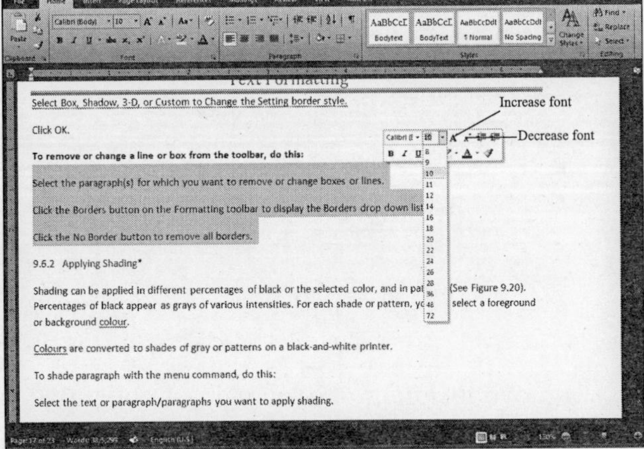

Figure 4.41 Font size drop-down list on the mini toolbar

4. To make a character *Regular, Bold, Italic* click the corresponding button on the mini toolbar (See Figure 4.41). These are toggle buttons clicking them once switches *on* the option and clicking them the second time switches *off* the option.

Applying Character Formatting using Keyboard

Most of the character formatting can also be applied using the keyboard shortcut as discussed in the following sections:

➜ **To format using shortcut keys, do this:**

1. Select the text you want to format and use the shortcut key combinations for the desired formatting effect.

Format	Shortcut
Bold	Ctrl + B
Italic	Ctrl + I
Single underline	Ctrl + U
Word underline	Ctrl + Shift + W
Double underline	Ctrl + Shift + D
SMALL CPAS	Ctrl + Shift + K
ALL CAPS	Ctrl + Shift + A
Hidden text	Ctrl + Shift + H
Superscript	Ctrl + Shift + =
Subscript	Ctrl + =
Copy formatting	Ctrl + Shift + C
Paste formatting	Ctrl + Shift + V
Remove formatting	Ctrl + Spacebar
Change case of letter	Shift + F3
Font	Ctrl + Shift + F. This command activates the Font dialog box. Type a new font name or use the arrow keys to highlight the desired font. (See Figure 7.3)
Symbol font	Ctrl + Shift + Q
Next larger point size available for selected fonts	Ctrl + Shift + >
Next smaller point size available for selected fonts	Ctrl + Shift + <
Up one point size	Ctrl +]
Down one point size	Ctrl + [

4.4.6 Alignment of Text

The attribute Alignment of a paragraph refers to the position of the main document text on the page. Different alignment options in Word 2010 are given in Table 4.8 and shown in Figure 4.42.

Table 4.8 Different Alignment Options for a Paragraph

Left Alignment	Aligns the text at the left margin and makes a zig-zag right margin.
Right Alignment	Aligns the text to the right margin and makes a zig-zag left margin.
Centre Alignment	Centres text between the left and right margins on the centre line. In this case both the margins are zig-zag.
Justify	Aligns the text at both the margins by increasing the spacing between the words.

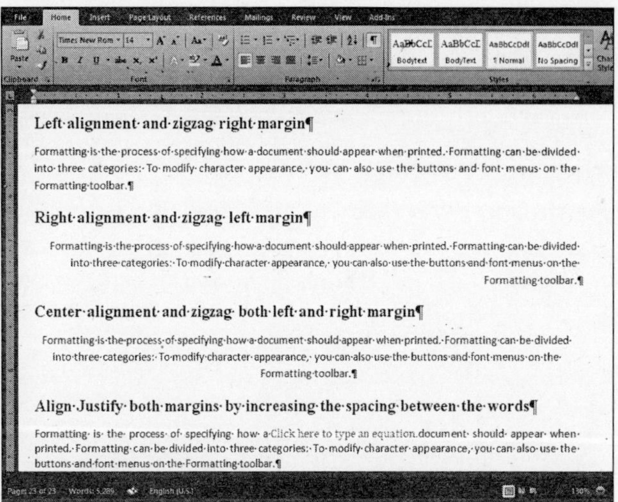

Figure 4.42 Paragraph alignment options

4.5 FORMATTING THE TEXT

The Paragraph formatting involves controlling the appearance of text in a paragrpah as a whole. The Paragraph formatting options are: *text alignment, paragraph indentation, line spacing, spacing before and after the paragraph,* and *border and shading,* etc.

4.5.1 Paragraph Indenting

Indents are the white space added to the margins, and thus decreasing the text area for paragraphs. So, when you have a "right margin and you want to add a right indent of 1.0", your text will be printed 2.0" from the right edge of the paper.

☞ *The first line of each paragraph can be indented differently from other lines in the paragraph. The first line can be shorter than the others, creating a regular indent, or longer than the others creating a hanging indent.*

Once you change the indent, each new paragraph you start by pressing the Enter key will maintain the same indentation setting until you change it.

Line Spacing

Line spacing in a paragraph means the amount of space between the lines. Word 2010 offers the line spacing options as given in Table 4.9.

Table 4.9 Different Options of Line Spacing

Option	Description
Single spacing	No blank line space appears between the lines of text.
Double spacing	A blank line space appears between the lines of text.
1 1/2 spacing	Half the height of one line space of text appears between the lines of text.
Exact line height	Specify the space you want between the lines.

Space before and after Paragraphs

There is a spacing box in the Paragraph dialog box which lets you define the amount of white space that Word 2010 must place before and after paragraphs. Space settings can be entered in *points* (pts), *inches* (in), *centimetres* (cm), or *lines* (li). Thus, 12 points would be entered as **12 pt**.

Formatting Paragraphs using Dialog Box Launcher

➜ **To format paragraphs, do this:**

1. Position the insertion point anywhere in the paragraph to be formatted or select multiple paragraphs.

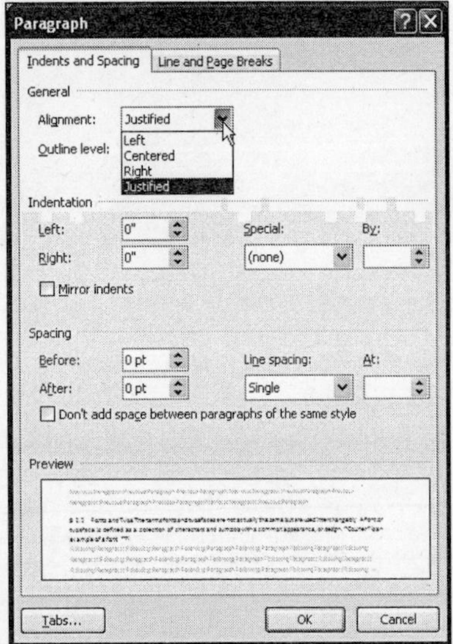

Figure 4.43 Paragraph dialog box with Indents and Spacing Property sheet

2. Click the **Home** tab of **Paragraph** group. Click **Paragraph launcher** dialog box. The **Paragraph** dialog box appears as shown in Figure 4.43 appears.
3. Click the **Indents and Spacing** tab, the property sheet as in Figure 3.44 appears.

   General Options:
4. The Alignment list box show the current alignment.
5. Change the current alignment, if need be. For this, click the down arrow next to the list box. Open it to show the list. From the list, click alignment option as required.

   Paragraph Indent Options:
6. The Indents and Spacing tab to displays line spacing/indentation options (See Figure 4.44).
7. The Left text box shows the current left indentation. Enter the new value for indentation or use the up and down arrow keys to change the indentation.
8. The Right text box displays the current right indentation. Enter the new value for indentation or use the up and down arrow keys to change the indentation.
9. To apply the first line indent or the hanging indent use the Special: list box. Click the down arrow key of the Special: list box to display the options as given below:

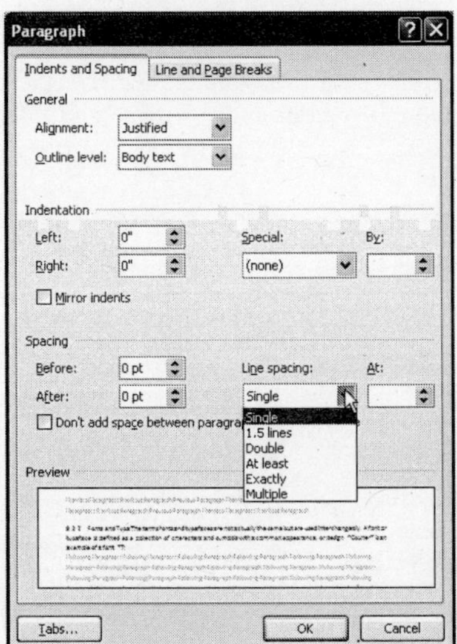

Figure 4.44 Indents and Spacing tab with line spacing options

Option	Effect
First line	This indents only the first line of the paragraph.
Hanging indent	This indents all except the first line of the paragraph.

Click the option as needed to select it.

10. In the By: text box, enter the indention or use the up and down arrow to give the required indentation. The Preview box displays the effect of the selected indentation.

    Line Spacing Options:
11. Line spacing text box has the options for controlling the line spacing. Click the down arrow in the spacing box. The options are given below:

Option	Explanation
Single	Default value.
Double	Places a blank line between successive lines.
1.5 Lines	Leaves half the line space between the lines.
At Least	Indicates the minimum space between lines.
Exactly	Gives the exact space between lines.

Space Before/After Paragraphs Options:

12. Type the space or select the space required in the Before: text box for adding space before the paragraph.
13. Type the space or select the space required in the After: text box for adding space after the paragraph.
14. Click OK or press the (Enter) key to close the paragraph dialog box.

Formatting Paragraphs using Ruler

➜ **To format paragraphs using ruler, do this:**

1. Position the insertion point anywhere in the paragraph you want to format or select multiple paragraphs to align.

2. Click the appropriate alignment button, e.g., *left, centre, right, justified* alignment on the **Home** tab of **Paragraph** group.

➜ **To indent paragraphs using mouse, do this:**

1. Position the insertion point in the paragraph to be indented or select as many paragraphs, as you want to indent.
2. On the **Home** tab of **paragraph** group click the indentation button.
3. The *increase* Indent button moves the indent marker to the right by one tab stop and the *decrease* indent moves it back by one tab stop.

➜ **To indent paragraphs using the ruler, do this:**

1. Position the insertion point in a paragraph or select multiple paragraphs, that you want to indent.
2. Indent markers appear on the ruler.
3. Drag the appropriate triangular indent markers to the desired location.
4. As you drag the marker, the rulers scale shows the position of the indent mark in relation to its respective margin (See Figure 4.45).

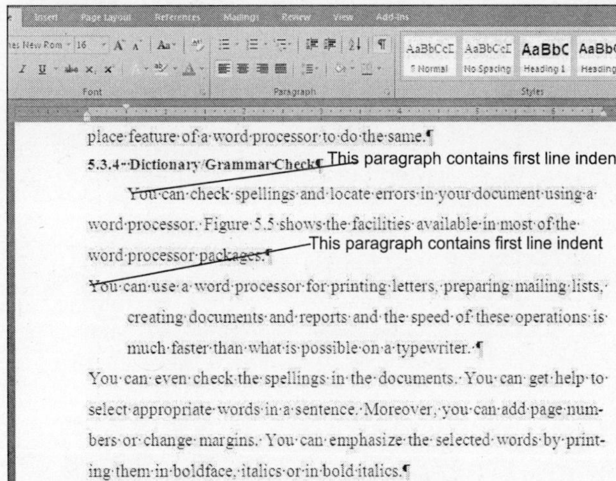

Figure 4.45 Indentation buttons on the paragraph group

5. When you release the mouse button after positioning it, the text in selected paragraphs moves accordingly.

Formatting Paragraphs using Shortcut Keys

➜ **To format paragraphs using the shortcut keys, do this:**

1. Position the insertion point anywhere in the paragraph to be aligned or select multiple paragraphs.
2. Use one of the keyboard shortcuts given below:

Alignment	Key combinations
Left	Ctrl+L keys together.
Right	Ctrl+R keys together.
Centre	Ctrl+E keys together.
Justify	Ctrl+J keys together.

➜ **To indent paragraphs using the keyboard shortcuts, do this:**

1. Position the insertion point in a paragraph or select multiple paragraphs to be indented.
2. Use the shortcut key combination explained below:

Key combination	Effect
Ctrl+M	Left indent.
Ctrl+Shift+M	Remove left indent.
Ctrl+T	Create hanging indent.
Ctrl+Shift+T	Reduce hanging indent.
Ctrl+Q	Remove paragraphs formatting.

➜ **To change the line spacing using the keyboard shortcuts, do this:**

1. Position the insertion point in a paragraph or select the paragraphs for which you want to change the line spacing.
2. Use one of the keyboard shortcuts given below:

Key combination	Effect
Ctrl+1	Creates single spaced lines.
Ctrl+2	Creates double spaced lines.
Ctrl+5	Creates one and half spaced lines.
Ctrl+0 (zero)	Add or remove one line space preceding a paragraph

➜ **To add a single line of space before a paragraph, do this:**

1. Position the insertion point in a paragraph or select the paragraph before which you want to add single line of space.
2. Press Ctrl+0 (zero) keys together.
3. To remove the single line of space added before the paragraph, add Ctrl+0 (zero) a second time.

4.5.2 Bullets and Numbering

Word 2010 provides the ability to create bulleted, numbered and multilevel lists. A bulleted list is a list with a graphic character, a very small picture or a bullet at the beginning of each paragraph in the list. A numbered list is similar, except each paragraph is numbered or lettered. The style of each list type can be changed and different bullets can be used.

➜ **To create a bulleted list, do this:**

1. Select the text to be bulleted or the location of the new list to be created.
2. To use the last style of bullets for the list, press the Bullets or Numbering button as shown in Figure 4.46. Press it again to end the list. Or
3. Right-click in the selected text and select Bullets or Numbering from the shortcut menu to view a gallery of available styles.

☞ *The bullet or number appears at the beginning of a line of text when the Enter key is pressed at the end of the preceding line of text.*

Use of Tab and Tab Setting

Tabs are used for creating relatively simple lists of items. Each

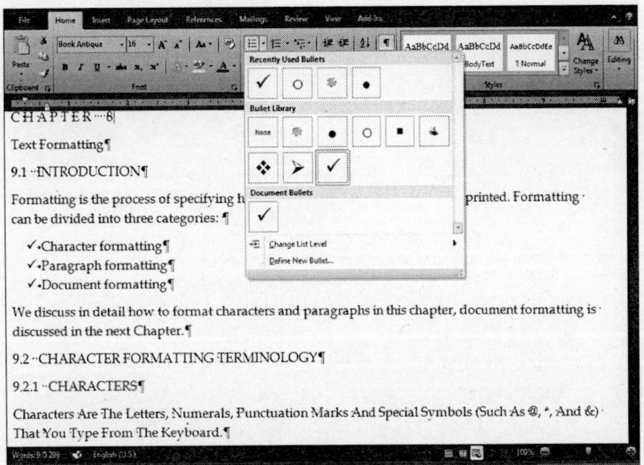

Figure 4.46 Bullets and numbering dialog box

paragraph in a Word 2010 document can take several different tab settings. It offers four types of tab settings (See Figure 4.47). Each tab is meant to align text. Tabs are particularly useful for making columnar lists. The different tabs and their functions are as given below.

Tab	Function
Left Tab	Text typed at these tabs aligns against the left edge of the stop.
Centre Tab	A centre tab stop, centres your text around the tab stop.
Right Tab	Right tab stop, positions whatever you type to the left of the tab.
Decimal Tab	Decimal tab stops, align columns of numbers on the decimal point. This is mainly used for financial reports.

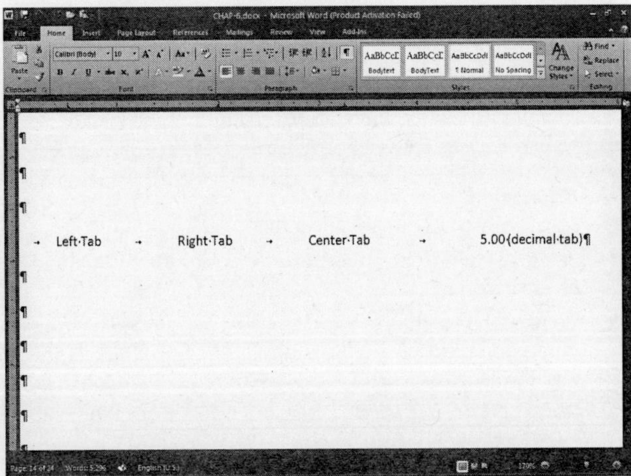

Figure 4.47 Tabs available in Word 2010

Setting Tab Stops with the Tabs Dialog Box

➧ **To set tabs using the tabs dialog box, do this:**

1. Position the insertion point in paragraph for which you want to insert tab.
2. Click the **Home** tab. Click **Paragraph Launcher** dialog box.
3. The **Paragraph** dialog box appears, click **Tabs...** button. **Tabs** dialog box appears as shown in Figure 4.48.
4. In the Tab stop position box, enter the position where you want to insert the tab stop.
5. In the alignment area, select the type of tab you want to insert.

☞ *Measurements in the Tabs dialog box are in inches as default, unless you type another one (cm for centimeter, pt for point, or pi for pica). As an example, 5 cm would position the left tab stop five centimetres from the left margin.*

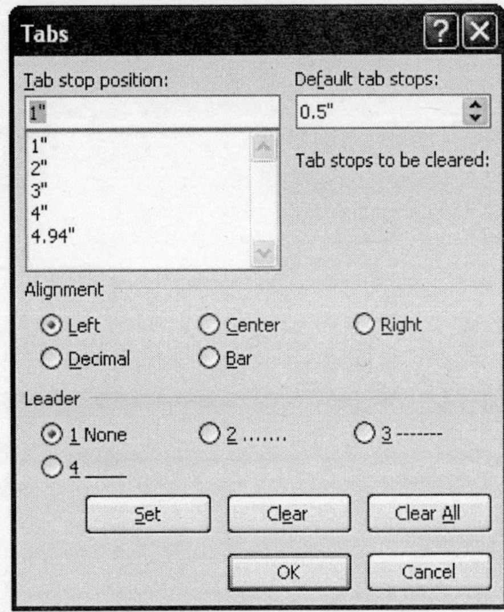

Figure 4.48 The Tabs dialog box

4.5.3 Using the Change Case Command

Word provides facilities to change to capital letters of any text by using the Change Case command.

➧ **To apply capitalization, do this:**

1. Select the text for which you want to change capitalization.
2. Click the **Home** tab of **Font** group. Click **Change Case** command (See Figure 4.49).
3. The options offered by the Change case dialog box are as follows:

Option	Description
Sentence case	The first character of the first word is capitalized.
lower case	All the characters are in lowercase.
UPPER CASE	All the characters are in uppercase.
Capitalize Each Word	The first letter of each word is capitalized.
tOGGLE cASE	The first letter of each selected word is in lowercase, the rest are in uppercase.

4. The above options are applied in the text and shown in Figure 4.49.

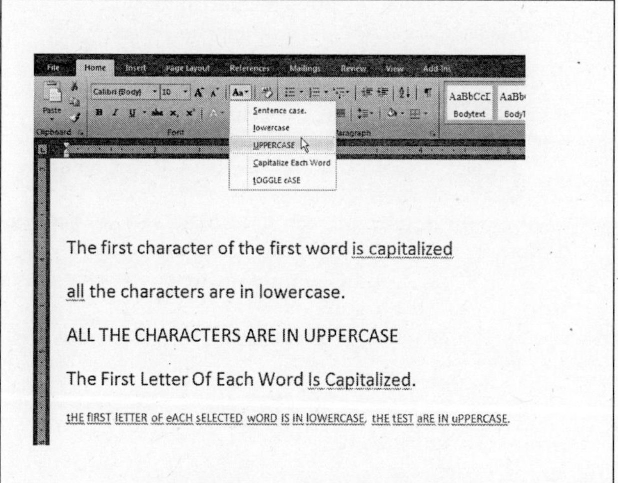

Figure 4.49 Change Case options

4.6 USING SPELLING CHECKER

Spelling checker is a flexible and powerful tool that will automatically check spelling in a paragraph or the entire document. It finds and corrects the spelling errors but does not consider the context of words. For example, it cannot check the improper usage of various words, namely *farm* in place of *form* or *no* in place of *know*.

The spelling checker compares each word in the document with the correct spelling stored in its electronic dictionary. If it does not find a word, then it asks you to verify the spelling of that word.

When automatic spell checking is on, Word 2010 uses a *red wavy line* to underline words it thinks are not spelled correctly, so that you can spot them on the screen. An icon of an open book with a red cross also appears at the right in the status bar to indicate that the current document has spelling mistakes.

Spell checking begins at the insertion point in your document and works throughout your document, checking its entire contents.

☞ *You can check spelling in a smaller selection of text by first selecting that area of text and then checking the spelling.*

4.6.1 Checking a Document's Spelling Automatically

Spell checking and underlining occur as you type the text in Word 2010 document. However, automatic spell checking works only when this feature is enabled.

➜ **To switch on automatic spelling check, do this:**

1. Click the **File** tab on the ribbon. The Backstage view appears Select **Options**.
2. The **Word Options** dialog box appears. In the left side pane options, select **Proofing** as shown in Figure 4.50.

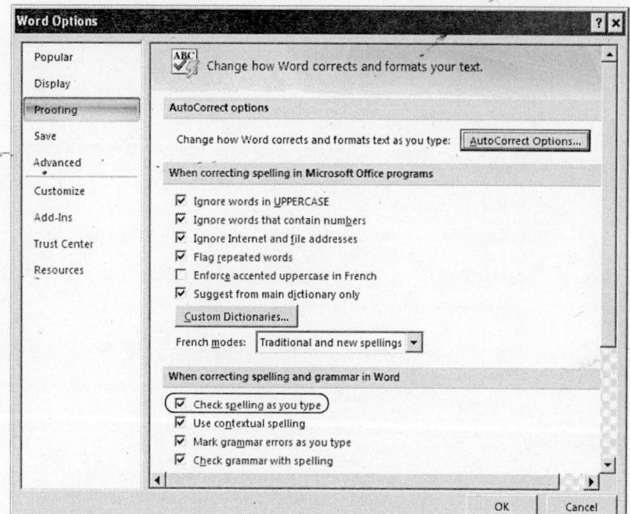

Figure 4.50 Word Options displaying Proofing Options

3. In Proofing page options, right side pane, under **When correcting spelling and grammar in Word**, select *Check spelling as you type* check box. Then click OK.

➜ **To check spelling of words with a wavy underline, do this:**

1. Right-click an underlined word. A pop-up menu appears (See Figure 4.51). It displays a list of suggested words and additional options.

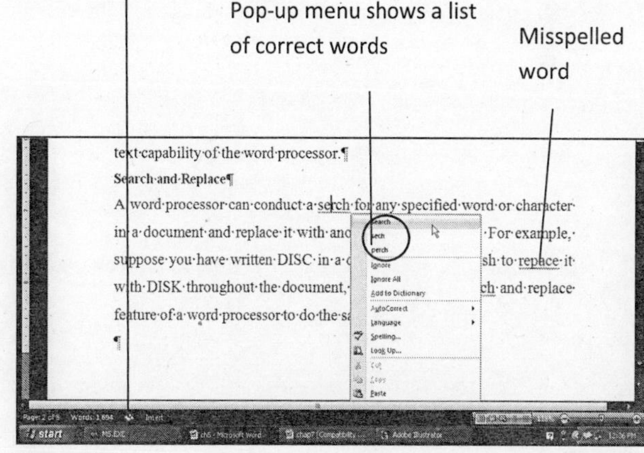

Figure 4.51 Pop-up Menu showing a list of suggested words

2. You have five choices for correcting the misspelled word. These are:
   - Select a word from the list shown in the pop-up menu.
   - Select Ignore to leave the word as it is.
   - Select Ignore All to ignore all occurrences of the word in your document.

- Select Add to Dictionary to add the word to the selected dictionary displayed in the Custom Dictionary in the Spelling dialog box.
- Select AutoCorrect and choose the correct spelling to automatically correct the misspelled word.

To go to the next word, double-click the open book icon in the Status bar at the bottom of the screen to find the next underlined word in the document.

3. Repeat Step 2 for each word you want to check spelling.

4.6.2 Spelling Command for Checking Spelling

➔ To check spelling with spelling command, do this:

1. Select the word or select a document that you want to check for spelling. If you select nothing, Word 2010 checks the entire document.
2. Click the **Review** tab. Click **Spelling & Grammar** icon or press F7 key in the **Proofing** group. Word 2010 scrolls through your document and selects words that it does not recognize. The misspelled word is highlighted in the text and displayed in the **Not in Dictionary:** box (See Figure 4.52).
3. Select the correct word from the Suggestions: list and then choose any one from the following list:
   - Click Ignore Once to leave the word as it is.
   - Click Ignore All to ignore all occurrences of the word in the document.
   - Click the Add to Dictionary button to add this word to the Word 2010 dictionary. The selected word will be added to the dictionary.
   - Click the Change button to change the word.
   - Click Change All to change all occurrences of the misspelled word in the document.
4. If none of the words in the **Suggestions:** list are correct, you can edit the word from within the **Not in Dictionary:** box.

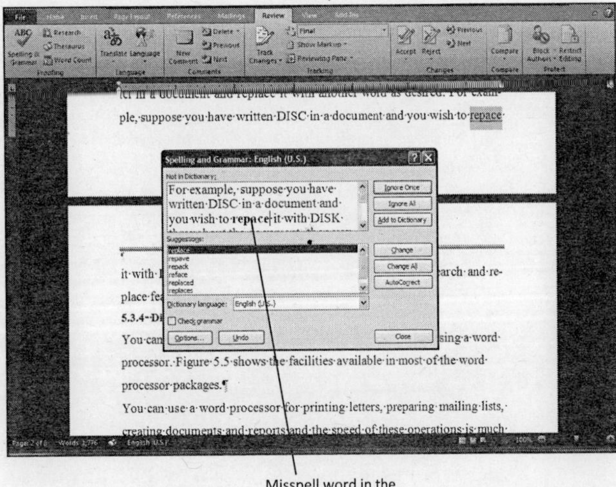

Figure 4.52 Spelling and Grammar dialog box

5. After the editing the word do one of the following:
   - Click the Change button to update the document window.
   - Click the Undo Edit button to undo the spelling change.
6. Word will now continue searching misspelled word. Click **Cancel** to stop the spell checking if so desired.
7. If you are checking a selected portion of a document, then after reaching the end of the selection, a dialog box asks whether you want to check the remaining portion of the document. Click Yes to check the remaining document or No to exit the spell checker.

➔ To edit your document without closing the spelling and grammar dialog box, do this:

1. Drag the Spelling and Grammar dialog box away from the area that you want to edit.
2. Click in the document or press Ctrl+Tab keys to activate the document window.
3. After editing the document, click the Resume button in the Spelling and Grammar dialog box or press Ctrl+Tab keys to resume checking spelling, where you had stopped.

Double Words Correction

When Word spelling checker detects double words, (say the the) then the Not in Dictionary: box changes to the **Repeated Word:** box, as shown in Figure 4.53 and the repeated word is highlighted in red.

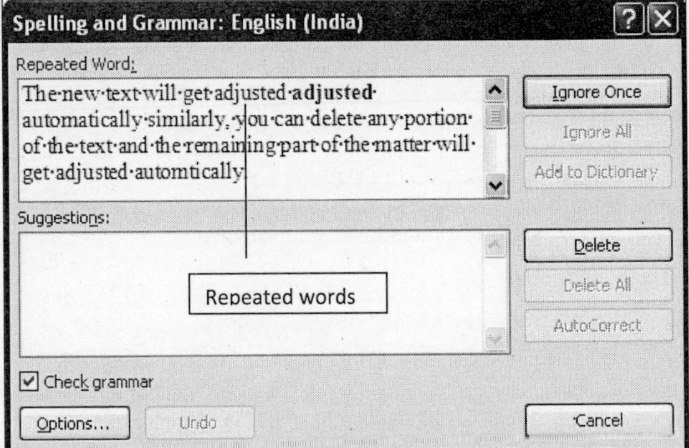

Figure 4.53 Repeated word indicated

To delete the repeated word, click the Delete button.

4.6.3 Setting Options for Checking Spelling

The Spelling and Grammar dialog box has the Options... button. Clicking this button opens up the Word Options with Proofing page options dialog box appears. In this page, you can select different options to customize the spell checking operations.

➔ To set spelling check options, do this:

1. In the Spelling and Grammar dialog box click Options... button. Word Options dialog box appears.
2. Various options available are as follows:

Option	Function
When correcting spelling in MS Office programs	
Ignore words in UPPERCASE	Ignores words in all uppercase letters namely proper nouns.

(Contd...)

Option	Function
Ignore words that contain numbers	Ignores words that include numbers.
Ignore Internet and file addresses	Ignores Internet addresses and file names.
Flag repeated words	Ignores the repeated words in the document.
Suggest from main dictionary only	Suggestions will come from the Main dictionary only, not from any open custom dictionaries.
When correcting spelling and grammar in Word 2010	
Check spelling as you type	Automatically identifies words not found in the dictionary by placing a red wavy line under each word.
Use Contextual spelling	It suggests related spelling.

3. Click OK.

4.7 WORKING WITH GRAMMAR CHECKER

The grammar checker evaluates a document for grammatical errors. Word 2010 uses collections of rules while reading a document. It also gives you the flexibility of deciding which rule you want to follow.

➜ **To check a document's grammar, do this:**

1. Word 2010 may underline one or more words with a green wavy line to highlight some possible grammar errors.
2. Click the **Review** tab and then choose **Spelling & Grammar** icon or press F7 key in the **Proofing** group.
3. The **Spelling and Grammar** dialog box appears on the screen. Click Check grammar check box. Word 2010 finds a sentence with a grammatical error, i.e., a sentence appears in green line. The mistaken words are highlighted in the upper text box. (Figure 4.54)

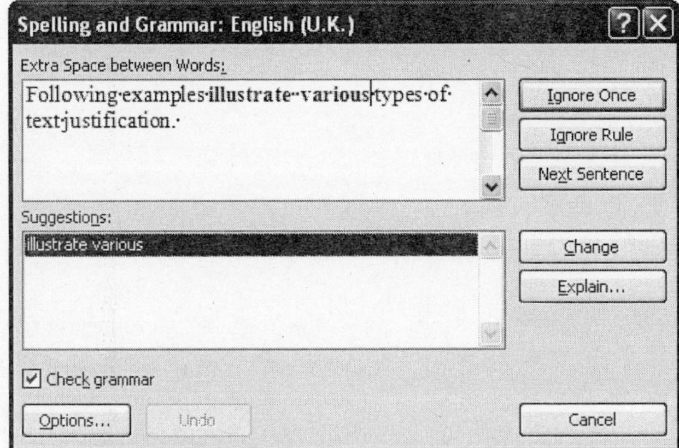

Figure 4.54 Spelling and Grammar dialog box

4. Word 2010 lists the suggestions in the **Suggestions:** text box if it finds error. If you click the **Explain...** button, Word 2010 provides more information about the error.
5. Correct the sentence by selecting a suggestion in the **Suggestions:** box and then clicking the **Change** button. Or correct the sentence by editing it in the upper text box and then click the Change button. Or
6. Right click the underlined green wavy line. A pop-up menu appears.
   Choose one of the following:
   1. Click the correct grammar that appears in bold in the pop-up menu.
   2. Click Ignore Once, to ignore the type of grammatical error throughout your document.

The options of the Spelling and Grammar box are given below.

Option	Function
Ignore Once	Ignores the questioned word or phrase.
Ignore Rule	Skips other similar occurrences that break the same grammar or style rule.
Undo Edit	Undoes all edits made in the upper text box. It appears when you edit the sentence.
Next Sentence	Leaves the sentence unchanged and moves to the next sentence.
Explain	Provides more information about the error. A window appears describing the relevant grammar or style rule. After you read the information, click the window's X button to clear the window and return to the Spelling and Grammar dialog box.

4.8 USING THESAURUS

Thesaurus is a Word 2010 electronic database, that contains English words with similar meaning. It defines selected words and offers alternative terms. When you are not sure of a particular word's meaning, or you think you are using a particular word too often, or when you cannot come up with the right word, use thesaurus. The Thesaurus is one of a set of research services provided by Word 2010.

➜ **To use the thesaurus, do this:**

1. Select the word for which you want to locate a synonym (similar meaning word).
2. Click the **Review** tab on the ribbon in the **Proofing** group. Click the **Thesaurus** button or press Shift+F7 keys together.
3. The **Research** task pane opens. For example, type the word *appropriate* in the **Search for:** box. Click the arrow to the right of the box. A listing of synonyms for the word *appropriate* appears (See Figure 4.55).
4. Synonyms for *appropriate* are now listed in the task pane.
5. For example, select the word **proper**. Click the arrow next to accurate and then click **Insert**.
6. The word *proper* replaces *appropriate* in the document.
7. Close the **Research** task pane.

4.9 USING AUTOCORRECT FEATURE

The AutoCorrect feature in Word 2010 recognizes typing mistakes and automatically corrects them. AutoCorrect feature can also be used to type long words from an abbreviation automatically. For example, to automatically type the phrase *not applicable*, when you type the abbreviation *na*.

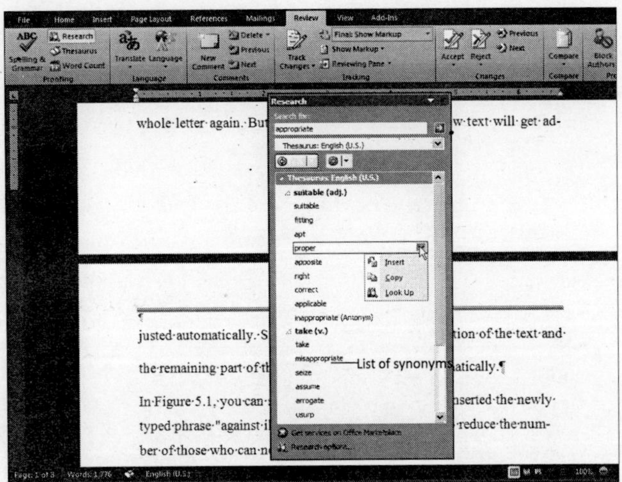

Figure 4.55 List of synonyms in Research dialog box

4.9.1 Creating AutoCorrect Entries

➜ **To add an autocorrect entry with the commands, do this:**

1. Click **File** tab on the button. The Backstage view appears click **Options**.
2. The **Word Options** dialog box appears. In the left side pane options, select **Proofing**.
3. In **Proofing** page options, right side pane, under **AutoCorrect options**, click **AutoCorrect Options...** .
4. The **AutoCorrect** dialog box opens, displaying with **AutoCorrect** tab as shown in Figure 4.56.

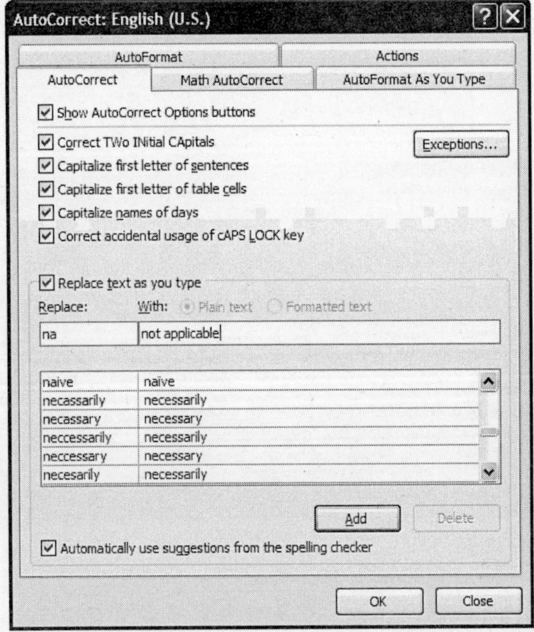

Figure 4.56 The AutoCorrect dialog box

5. In the **R**eplace: text box, type misspelled words or abbreviations that you wish to get corrected by Word 2010 automatically.
6. In the **W**ith: text box, type the correct spelling of the word or phrase.
7. Click **A**dd to add these selected entries to the list of AutoCorrect list.
8. Click OK.

Word 2010 will insert the phrase and then return(s) into the **W**ith text box.

4.10 INSERTING AND REMOVING COMMENTS

When you review or edit a document, you may want to make a comment instead of or in addition to making a change. To insert a comment, you select the text to which the comment refers, click the New Comment button in the Comments group on the Review tab, and type what to say in the balloon that appears. In Print Layout view, Word highlights the associated text in the document in the same color as the balloon and adds your initials and a sequential number to the balloon itself.

➜ **To insert comments in a document, do this:**

1. Select a word or sentence in which you want to insert a comment. For example, we have selected Removing as shown in Figure 4.57.

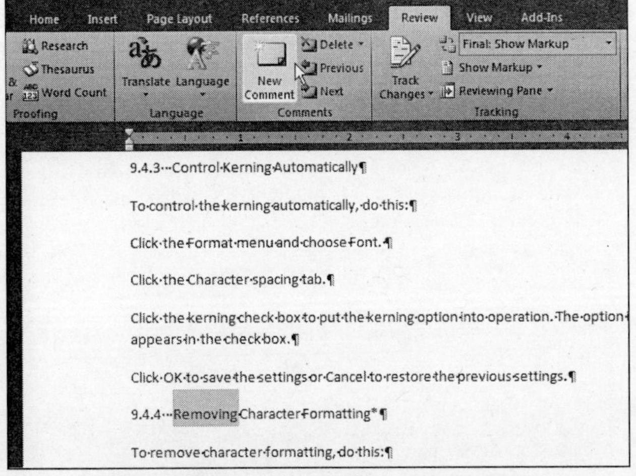

Figure 4.57 Select the word to insert comment

2. Click the **Review** tab on the Ribbon.
3. Select the **New Comment** button under the **Comments** group of the **Review** tab as shown in Figure 4.57.
4. A new balloon appears on the right-hand side of the document where you can enter a comment as shown in Figure 4.58.
5. Click inside the comment and then type the comment inside the balloon. For example, remove character formatting as shown in Figure 4.58.

➜ **To delete the comment in a document, do this:**

1. Select the comment that you want to delete.
2. Click the **Review** button on the Ribbon.

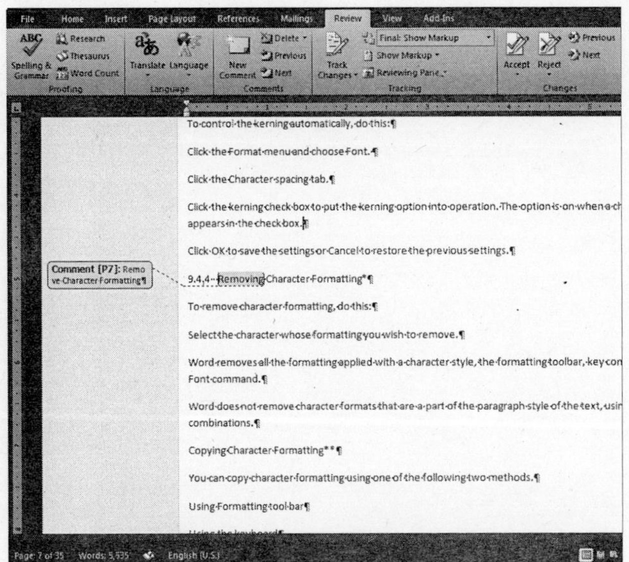

Figure 4.58 Type the comment inside the balloon

3. Click the **Delete** button under the **Comments** group of the **Review** tab.
4. The select comment gets deleted in the document.

4.11 USING GO TO COMMAND

You can move quickly to a location in a document using the Go To command. For this command, you specify, a *page, section, line, footnote, table headings,* etc. For example, you can use the Go To command with page numbers to move back and forth between pages in a document.

☞ *You can press* Ctrl+G *or double-click Page on the Status bar to display the Go To tab of the Find and Replace dialog box.*

➜ To move forward 5 pages from your current location in the document do this:

1. Click the **Home** tab and choose Editing command. A drop-down menu appears. Click the **Go To...** or press Ctrl+G to display the Go To tab of the **Find and Replace** dialog box (See Figure 4.59).

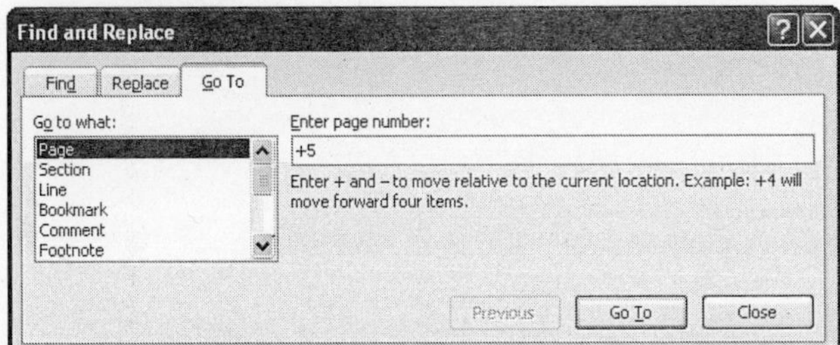

Figure 4.59 Go To tab of Find and Replace dialog box

2. In the Go to what: list box, select Page in the Enter page number: text box.
3. Enter page number namely enter + 5 to move forward 5 pages and –5 to move back 5 pages.
4. Click Go To button to see the result.

5. Click **Close** or press Esc key to close the Find and Replace dialog box.

4.11.1 Moving to a Previous Location

Word 2010 remembers the last three locations where you typed or edited text. Pressing Shift+F5 (Go Back key combination) returns the insertion point to each of the previous locations in turn, then returns the insertion point to its original position.

➜ To return to a previous editing location, do this:

1. Press Shift+F5 keys together until you reach the location you want.

4.12 USING FIND AND REPLACE

Word 2010 has a very powerful, *Find* and *Replace* feature which *greatly* simplifies editing of text. The **Editing** command is in **Home** tab for Finding and Replacing text. You can use this command to search for *text, footnotes, graphics,* etc. To replace these items, you can then use the Replace command.

4.12.1 Finding Text

With the Find feature in Word 2010, you can locate a specific text. You can also search for special characters, such as *tabs, page breaks, extra spaces, line numbers, footnotes,* etc., within a document.

☞ *If you want to search for or replace text in only a portion of a document, then select the portion of the text and then follow the general instructions for finding or replacing text.*

➜ To find specific text do this:

1. Click the **Home** tab and choose **Editing** group. Click a drop-down arrow and choose **Find** command or press Ctrl+F keys together. The **Navigation** pane appears (See Figure 4.60).

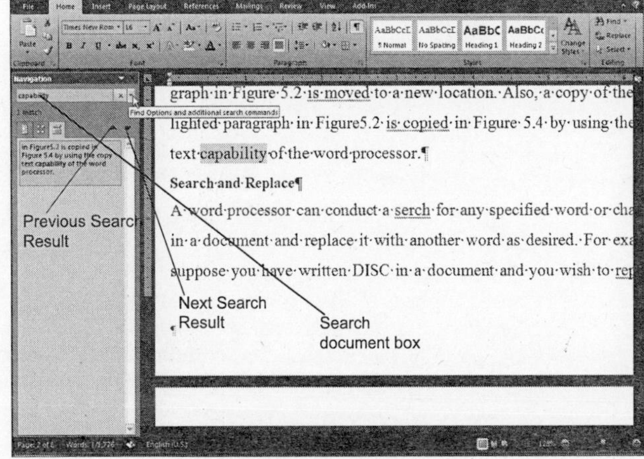

Figure 4.60 Navigation pane

2. In the Search Document box, type the text that you want to find.
3. Word 2010 shows all occurrences of that text in the document. Click the text at the point in the document you want to display.

☞ *If you make a change in your document and the search result disappear, click the down arrow in the Navigation pane to view the list of results.*

Search and Find Objects

Click the magnifying glass tool in the Search Document box to display a list of additional choices, as described in the following Table 4.10.

Table 4.10 Search and find objects options

Choose	To Do This
Options	Displays the Find Options dialog box so that you can enter your preferences for the search operation.
Find	Displays the Find tab of the Find and Replace dialog box so that you can enter Find choices.
Replace	Displays the Replace tab of the Find and Replace dialog box so that you can move directly to a page or object you specify.
Go To	Displays the Go To tab of the Find and Replace dialog box so that you can move directly to a page or object you specify.
Graphics	Moves to the next graphic in the document.
Tables	Moves to the next table in the document.
Equations	Find the next equation in the document.
Footnotes	Moves to the next footnote.
Comments	Displays the next comment in the document.

4.12.2 Replacing Text

You can replace searched text automatically using replacing text facility in Word 2010. You can use the Replace command to search for every occurrence of the incorrect spelling and replace it with the correct version. For example, replace incorrect word *dcument* by *document*.

➜ **To replace text, do this:**

1. Click the **Home** tab and choose **Editing** group. Click a drop-down arrow and choose **Replace** command or press Ctrl+H keys together. The Find and Replace dialog box appears with the Replace tab selected (See Figure 4.61).
2. In the Find what: text box, type the misspelled word, i.e., dcument.
3. In the Replace with: text box, type correct spell word, i.e., document.
4. Choose the Find Next or Replace All button.
5. Click **Cancel** or press Esc key to return to the document.
6. Click **More** to display all the search options. After you click it, the dialog box displays more options and the button changes to Less.
7. Click **Format** button to specify the formatting of the text you are searching for.
8. To replace nontext items, click **Special** button to specify any element that is associated with the text.

☞ *If you want to confirm each change, click Find Next. When Word finds an occurrence of the text, click the Replace button to change the text. To change all occurrences of the specified text without confirmation, click the Replace All button.*

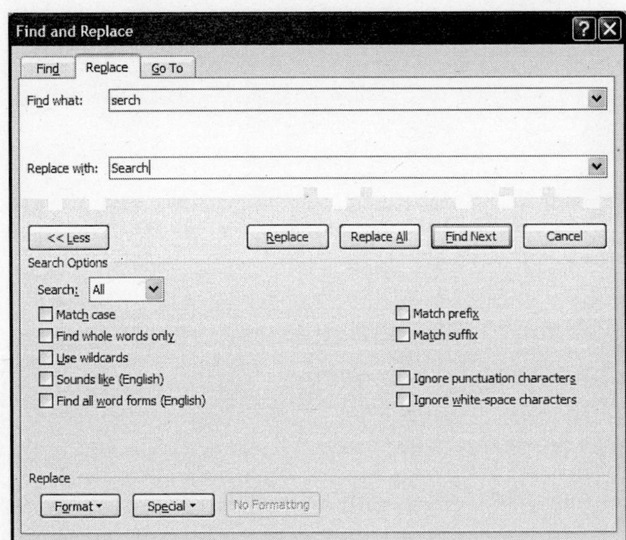

Figure 4.61 Find and Replace dialog box with Replace tab selected

4.13 APPLYING A STYLE

Applying a style to a selection of text is easy as clicking a button in the Styles Gallery.

➜ **To apply a style from Quick Styles gallery, do this:**

1. Select the text to which you want to apply a style.
2. For example, you can select text that you want to make into a heading 1.
3. On the **Home** tab of **Styles** group, click **Quick Styles** drop-down menu. A list of styles gallery options appears as shown in Figure 4.62.

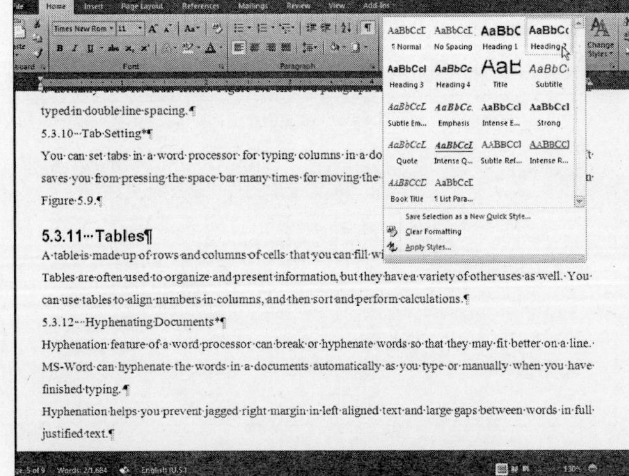

Figure 4.62 Select Style Heading 2 in Style Gallery

4. Select the style called Heading 2 in the Style Gallery.

4.13.1 Adding a New Style to the Styles Gallery

You might want to create a new style and add it to the Styles Gallery.

➜ **To create a style and add to Style Gallery, do this:**

1. Select the text to which you want to create a new style.
2. For example, if you want the selected paragraph to be justified and font size to be 11 pt New Times Roman.
3. Select the paragraph, above the selection, the Mini toolbar appears. Click the **Font** type and **Size** to format the text.
4. Right-click the selection, choose Styles. A sub menu appears. Click Save Selection as a New Quick Style... .

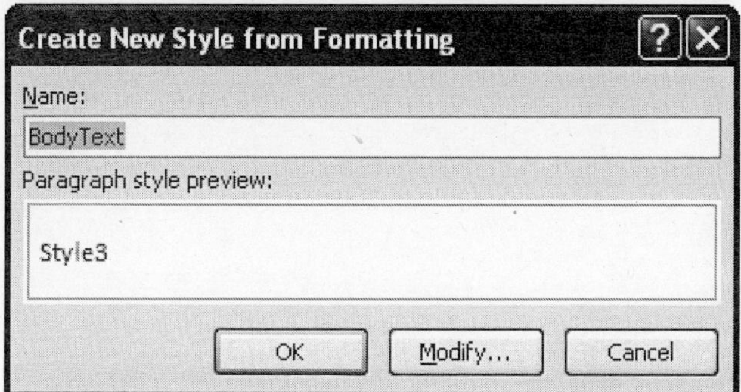

Figure 4.63 Create New Style form Formatting dialog box

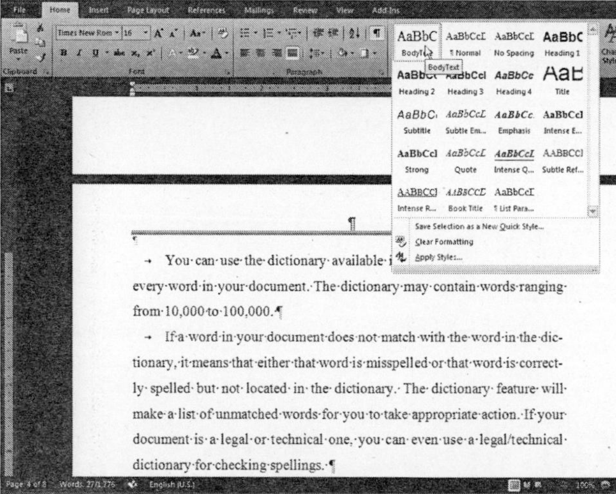

Figure 4.64 BodyText name given to Quick Style Gallery

5. **Create New Style from Formatting** dialog box appears as shown in Figure 4.63.
6. In the Name: box, give the style name to format. For example BodyText and then click OK.
7. The style you created appears in the **Quick Style Gallery** with the name you gave it, whenever you want to format a paragraph (See Figure 4.64).

4.13.2 Removing a Style from the Styles Gallery

➜ **To remove a style from Style Gallery, do this:**

1. Select the style you want to remove from the Style Gallery.
2. On the **Home** tab on **Styles** group, right-click the style that you want to remove from the gallery.
3. Click Remove from Quick Styles Gallery.

4.14 INSERTING FOOTNOTES AND ENDNOTES

Word 2010 footnote feature enables you to *enter, edit,* and *view* footnotes/endnotes in a variety of formats. The only difference between footnotes and endnotes is that, the *footnotes appear at the bottom of the page* and *endnotes appear at the end of the section or document.*

Creating footnotes and endnotes involves two steps:

1. Insert the note reference to mark the location in the document where a footnote or endnote is referred to. The note reference is usually a number.
2. After Word 2010 inserts the note reference, type the note entry. The note entry is the text information that appears in the footnote or endnote.

Several options are available for specifying where footnotes and endnotes appear, the type of separator line that is used as well as the style of numbering used for the reference numbers. These are further discussed in the following sections:

4.14.1 Entering Footnotes/Endnotes

When you insert a footnote or endnote, Word 2010 inserts a reference mark in the text at the current insertion point. The reference mark is a sequential number that identifies the note you are adding. You are then given the opportunity to type the text to which the reference mark would refer to.

In the Web and Draft view, a pane opens at the bottom of the window. In that pane, you can type either a footnote/endnote, depending on the type of note you select. If you click **Show Notes** in **References** tab, Word 2010 moves the insertion point to the bottom of the page for footnotes or to the end of the document for endnotes.

➜ **To enter a footnote/endnote, do this:**

1. Position the insertion point after the text where you want to insert a reference mark. Word 2010 inserts the reference mark at the insertion point, unless you have selected text, in which case it positions the mark after the selection.
2. Click **References** tab. Click the arrow at the right corner of **Footnotes** group. The **Footnote** and **Endnote** dialog box appears (See Figure 4.65). *Alternatively,* press Alt+Ctrl+F keys together for footnote and press Alt+Ctrl+D keys together for endnote.
3. Select either the Footnote or the Endnote option.
4. Select the desired format in the **Number format:** drop-down list.
5. To customize the numbering, click **Custom mark:** now click the **Symbol...** button. The **Symbol** dialog box opens. In the symbol box select the symbol you want to use for numbering and then click OK. The selected character appears in the **Custom mark:** text box.

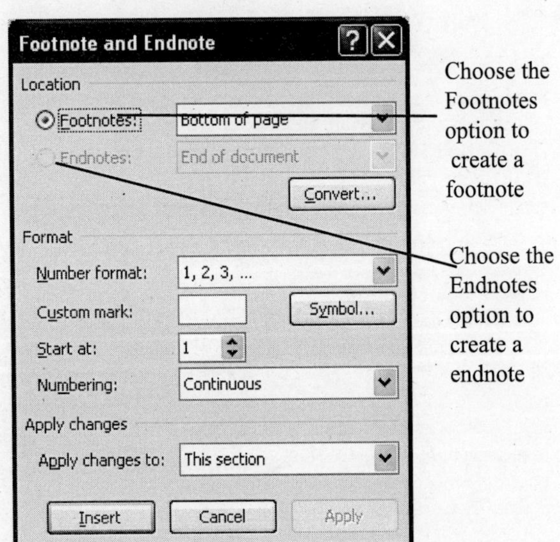

Figure 4.65 Footnote and Endnote dialog box

6. In **Start at:** spinner box, select the format according to, in Number format.
   Select the desired changes in the **Apply Changes to:** drop-down box.
   Click **Insert** button to insert the footnote and then click OK.
7. Word 2010 displays the note pane in the *Draft* view (See Figure 4.66). Or the bottom margin in *Print Layout* view, so that you can type the footnote (See Figure 4.67).
8. Type the text in footnote or endnote.
9. If you are in Draft view, leave the note pane visible and press Show Notes in the **Footnotes** group.

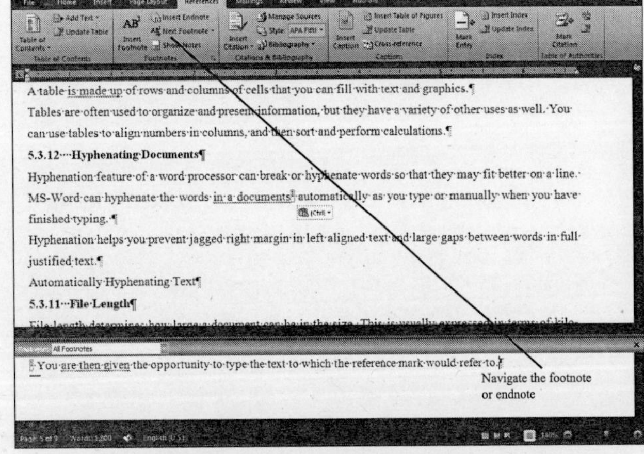

Figure 4.66 Entering Footnote in Draft view

If you are in Page Layout View, you can Navigate next or previous footnote in the document.

4.15 TABLE MANIPULATION

You can use tables to create documents, such as *forms*, *financial reports*, *catalogs* and *biodata*. Word tables consist of horizontal *rows* and vertical *columns*. You type in the areas called cells formed by intersection of rows and columns. Cells can contain *text*, *numbers*, or *graphics*.

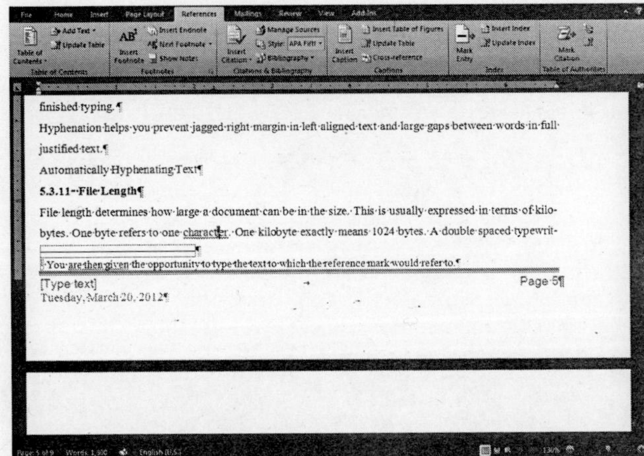

Figure 4.67 Entering Footnote in Print Layout view

You can even control the size, shape, and appearance of the cells, and use border and shading features. You can insert and delete rows and columns in a table.

☞ *A new feature called the Table Wizard helps you to automate table creation.*

4.15.1 Concept of Table

A table is made of rows and columns of cells that you can fill with text and graphics. You can use tables to align numbers in columns, and then sort and perform calculation on them. You can also use tables to create page layouts, and arrange text and graphics.

Rows

A row is a horizontal block of cells that runs through the entire width of the table.

Column

A column is a vertical block of cells that runs through the table.

Cell

A cell is the intersection of a row and a column.

4.15.2 Draw Table

Word 2010 allows you to draw a table selecting the Insert Table grid on the **Insert** tab or Insert Table... using the Table options in the Table groups.

➜ **To draw a table using the mouse, do this:**

1. Position the insertion point where you want to insert a table.
2. Click the **Insert** tab of **Tables** group. Click down arrow and choose the Insert table grid as shown in Figure 4.68 appears. Drag the mouse button to highlight the desired number of *rows* and *columns*.
3. The displayed grid represents the required number of rows and columns. Click the mouse button after getting the right number in the grid.

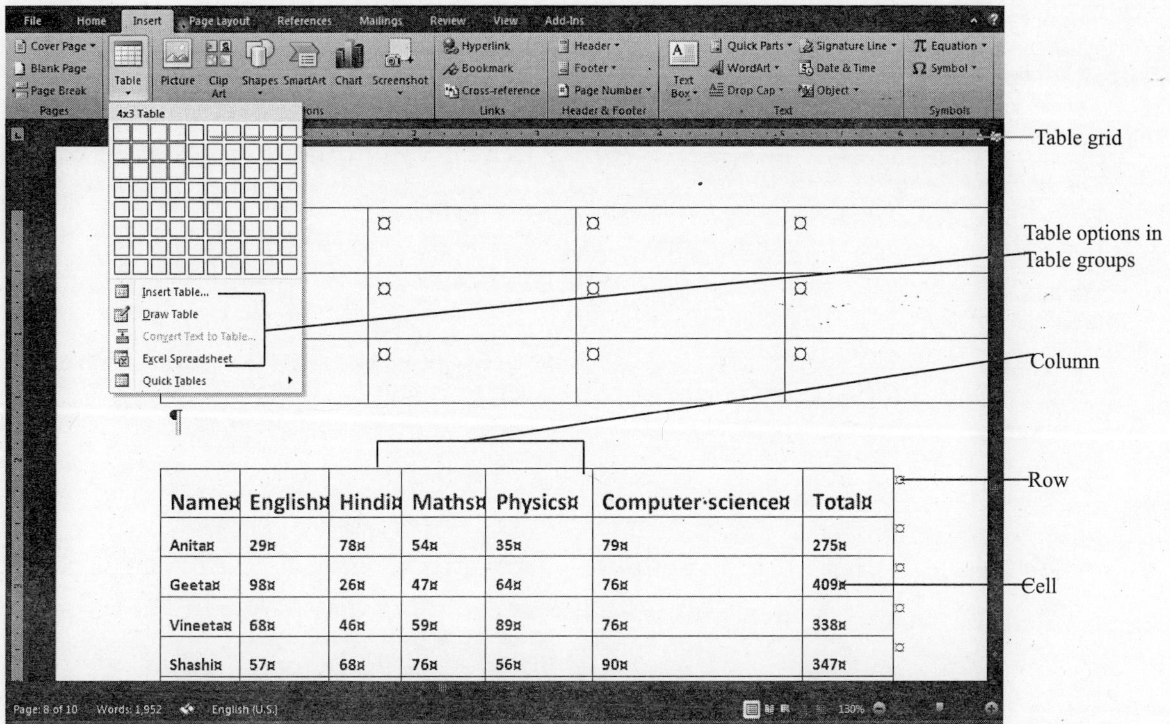

Figure 4.68 Table grid

4. Word inserts an empty table when you release the mouse button (See Figure 4.68).

➜ **To create a table using the table option, do this:**

1. Position the insertion point where you want to insert the table.
2. In **Insert** tab of **Tables** group, click the **Table** down arrow highlight **Insert Table...** options. The **Insert Table** dialog box appears as shown in Figure 4.69.
3. Enter the desired number of rows and columns as required in the table.
4. Click OK.

Entering and Editing Text in a Table

You can move, enter and edit text in a table just as you do with other types of text matter. Use mouse or arrow keys to position the insertion point, then type the text. The cell borders work as margins. Word 2010 automatically wraps text within the cell as you reach the right edge.

➜ **To move within a table using the mouse, do this:**

1. Position the pointer in the cell you want to move and click.

➜ **To move within a table using the keyboard, do this:**

1. The insertion point will move *left* and *down* to the next row when you press Tab key in the last column on the right side of a table.
2. It will move right and up one row when you press Shift+Tab past the last column on the left.

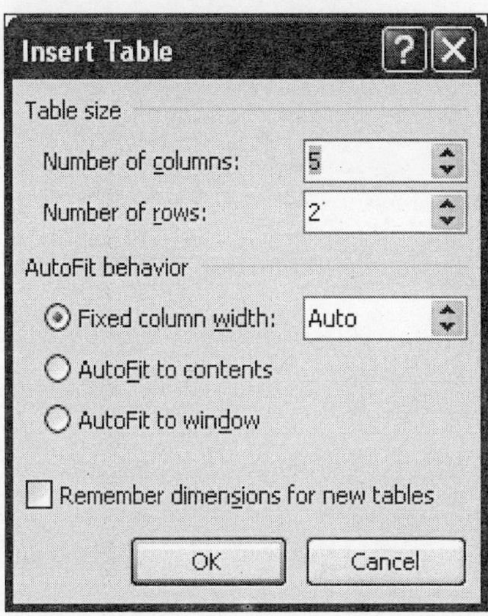

Figure 4.69 Insert Table dialog box

You can apply all of Word 2010 paragraph and character formats to the text in cells. Cells can contain multiple paragraphs as well as multiple paragraph formats.

4.14.3 Changing Cell Width and Height

Changing Row Heights

Word 2010 sets the height of each row automatically in order to accommodate the cell containing the tallest entry. For example, if one cell in a row needs 2" to accommodate the text or graphics, then all the cells in that particular row will be 2" high.

➜ **To adjust the height of a row, do this:**

1. Click anywhere in the row where you want to change its height.
2. Move the pointer to the vertical ruler at the left edge of the screen or to the top of the row. The pointer changes to an up-and-down arrow. Use it to drag the row to the desired height (See Figure 4.70).
3. Release the mouse button. Or
4. Click **Table Row Height** scroll box, to change the height of row in the **cell size** group in the **Table Tools** contextual tab of **Layout** tab.

Changing the height of row

Name	English	Hindi	Maths	Physics	Computer science	Total
Anita	29	78	54	35	79	275
Geeta	98	26	47	64	76	409
Vineeta	68	46	59	89	76	338
Shashi	57	68	76	56	90	347
Sunita	55	60	50	79	87	331
Bindya	49	52	73	84	92	350

Figure 4.70 Changing table height

Changing Column Width

➜ **To change the width of column using mouse, do this:**

1. Point to a column boundary.
2. The pointer will change shape to a double arrow (See Figure 4.71). Drag the column width marker. Watch the dotted line as well as the ruler settings, then release the mouse button when it reaches the desired width. Or

Changing Column Width

Name	English	Hindi	Maths	Physics	Computer science	Total
Anita	29	78	54	35	79	275
Geeta	98	26	47	64	76	409
Vineeta	68	46	59	89	76	338
Shashi	57	68	76	56	90	347
Sunita	55	60	50	79	87	331
Bindya	49	52	73	84	92	350

Figure 4.71 Adjusting column width

3. Click **Table Column Width** scroll box, to change the Table Column Width in the **cell size** group.

- If you hold down the Shift key while dragging, the column to the right does not changes size while the table's overall width increases.
- If you hold down Ctrl key while dragging mouse, all columns to the right changes size, but the table's overall width will not change. Thus, the width of the columns on the right will only change.

4.15.4 Delete/Insertion of Row and Column

Inserting Rows

To add a new row at the end of an existing table, position the insertion point anywhere in the last cell and press the Tab key. Word 2010 inserts a new row using the styles of the cells that are immediately above it.

➜ **To insert a single row in the middle of a table, do this:**

1. Position the insertion point below the row where you want the new row to be inserted.
2. Click the **Layout** contextual tab, click **Insert Above or Below** in the **Rows & Columns** group. The new row is inserted below or above the selected row.

   Alternatively, right click and select Insert, click the small triangle, a sub menu option appears as shown in Figure 4.72. Select the Insert Rows Above or Below option.

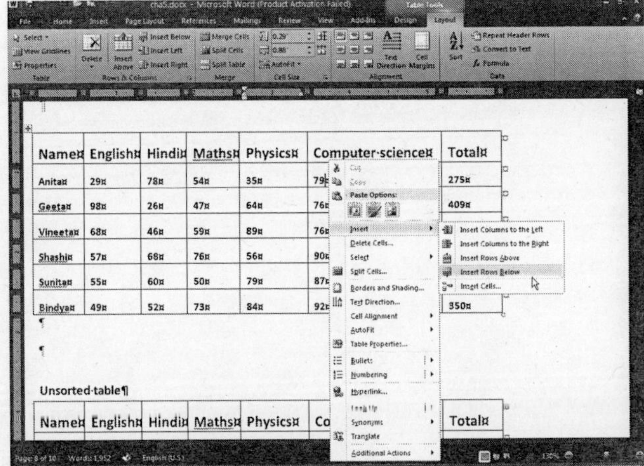

Figure 4.72 Inserting rows

3. To add multiple rows, either repeat the Insert Rows command by clicking right mouse button or select as many existing rows as you want to insert. Word 2010 inserts as many rows as you have selected.

Inserting Columns

➜ **To insert a single column in the middle of a table, do this:**

1. Select the column to the right of which you wish the *new* column to be appeared.
2. Click the **Layout** contextual tab, click **Insert Left** or **Right** in the **Rows & Columns** group. The new column is inserted left or right to the selected column.

   Alternatively, right click and select **Insert** option. Click the small triangle. A sub menu appears. Select the **Insert Columns to Left** or **Right** option from the sub menu list.

3. Word 2010 will add a new column but it will not change the width of the earlier columns to accommodate this new inserted column. In order to make the enlarged table fit on your page, you will have to adjust *margins, column widths* or change *page orientation*.

☞ *New column retains the format of the column, adjacent to which it is inserted but borders will not change.*

To insert multiple columns, select as many existing columns as you want to insert new ones to the right of the desired location of the new columns. If you want to add three columns, select the three existing columns to the right of the desired insertion point, then click on the Insert columns to the Left button.

➜ **To insert a column at the right edge of a table, do this:**

1. Select an end of row marker (See Figure 4.73).
2. Right click and select Insert. A small triangle, a sub menu option appears. Select **Insert Columns to Right** option.

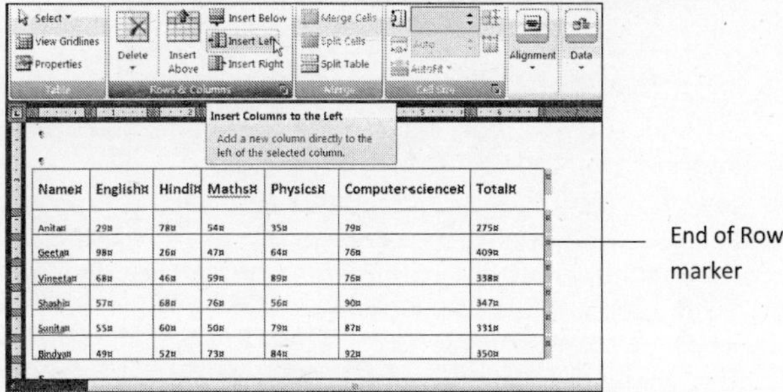

Figure 4.73 End of row marker

Deleting Rows

➜ **To delete a row or rows of cells, do this:**

1. Select the row(s) to be deleted.
2. Click the **Layout** contextual tab, click **Rows & Columns** group. Click down arrow and choose Delete Rows. This will delete the rows and their contents.
3. To delete the *contents* of cells only, leave the cells intact, select text or graphic and press the Del key.

Deleting Columns

➜ **To delete columns, do this:**

1. Select the column or columns to be deleted.
2. Click the **Layout** contextual tab. Click Table down arrow and choose Delete Columns.
3. Click OK.

4.15.5 Alignment of Text in Cell

You can align text in a table cell in nine different ways: Top Left (the default alignment), Top center, Top Right, Centre Left, Centre Right, Bottom Left, Bottom Centre, and Bottom Right as shown in Figure 4.74.

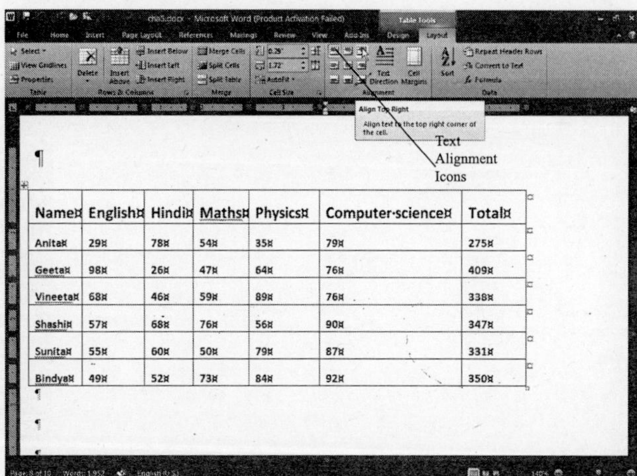

Figure 4.74 Tables can align text within cells in nine different ways

4.15.6 Border and Shading

A *border* may be a box around a paragraph (or paragraphs) from all sides. It could be a line that sets a paragraph off on one or more sides. A border can include *shading*, which fills a paragraph with a pattern. Boxes and lines can be solid black and shading can be gray or in color.

If a group of paragraphs is formatted with a box around them and you press Enter key at the end of the last paragraph, your new paragraph falls within the box. However, if you want to create a new paragraph outside the border, then move the insertion point outside the border before you press Enter key.

Applying Borders

➜ **To apply borders to a paragraph, or group of paragraphs, do this:**

1. Position the insertion point anywhere in the paragraph to be enclosed in a border or select multiple paragraphs or select the text to be enclosed (See Figure 4.75).
2. In **Paragraph** group, click **Borders and Shading**. A drop-down menu appears. Choose the selected border you want to apply for paragraph as shown in Figure 4.75.
3. In **Paragraph** group, select **Borders and Shading...** option. The **Borders and Shading** dialog box appears as shown in Figure 4.76.
4. Choose from the options given below:

Option	Effect
None	No box.
Box	A box with identical lines on all four sides, of the selected text or paragraphs.
Shadow	A box with a drop shadow on the bottom right corner.
3-D	A "Picture frame" box.
Custom	Custom design borders on one or more sides of the selected paragraph(s).

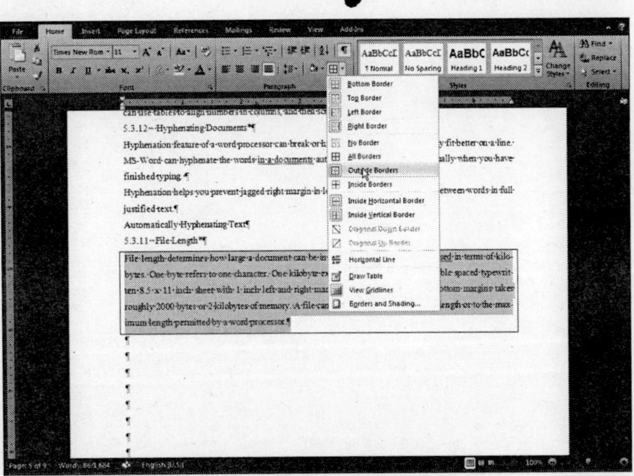

Figure 4.75 Paragraphs enclosed in border

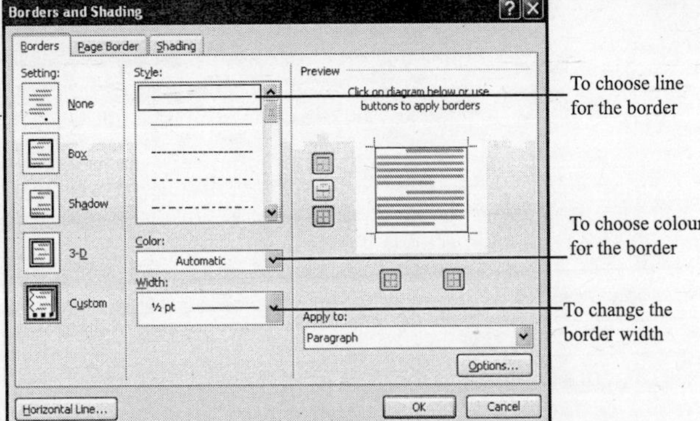

Figure 4.76 Borders and Shading dialog box

5. After selecting the setting, choose the St<u>y</u>le: in the style scroll list. Style determines the type of line used for border.
6. In the <u>C</u>olor: drop-down list, choose the color you want the border to be in. If you choose Auto option, the default color for text is used.
7. In the <u>**W**</u>idth: drop-down list specify the width for the border.
8. The Preview box shows how the borders are applied to the selected text.
9. In App<u>l</u>y to: choose width you want to apply border to a selected text or paragraph.
10. Click <u>O</u>ptions... to bring up dialog box as shown in Figure 4.77.
    In the dialog box specify the gap between the border and the text if need be.
11. Click OK or press Enter.

When paragraphs extend exactly to the margins of your page (as they always do if you do not indent the paragraphs), borders extend slightly outside the margins. If you want borders to fall within or exactly on the margins, you must indent the paragraph. To make borders fall on the margins, indent the paragraph by the width of the border.

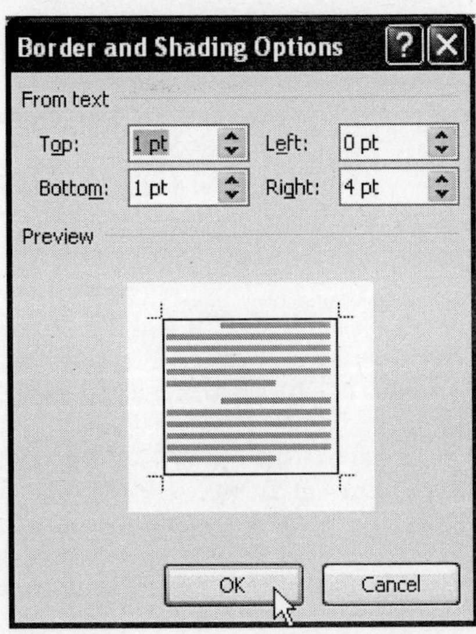

Figure 4.77 Border and Shading Options

➔ **To remove or change a box or line from the dialog box launcher command, do this:**

1. Select the paragraph or paragraphs for which you want to remove or change boxes or lines.
2. In **Paragraph** group, select **Borders and Shading...** option.
3. The **Border and Shading Options** dialog box appears. Select the <u>B</u>orders tab.
4. Select the <u>N</u>one option in the Setting: group to remove all borders.
5. Select the line you want to change and choose a different option from the **Style:** box. You also can select a different line color from the Color: list box.
6. Select Bo<u>x</u>, Sh<u>a</u>dow, 3-D, or Custom to Change the Setting border style.
7. Click OK.

➔ **To remove or change a line or box, do this:**

1. Select the paragraph(s) for which you want to remove or change boxes or lines.
2. Click the **Borders and Shading** option on the **Home** tab of **Paragraph** group. A list of options appears.
3. Select the <u>N</u>o Border option to remove all borders.

Applying Shading

Shading can be applied in different percentages of black or the selected color, and in patterns (See Figure 4.78). Percentages of black appear as grays of various intensities. For each shade or pattern, you can select a foreground or background colour.

Colors are converted to shades of gray or patterns on a black-and-white printer.

➔ **To shade paragraph with the mouse, do this:**

1. Select the text or paragraph/paragraphs you want to apply shading.
2. In **Paragraph** group click **Border** down arrow and choose B<u>o</u>rders and Shading... . In the Borders and Shading dialog box click the **Shading** tab property sheet as shown in Figure 4.78 appears.

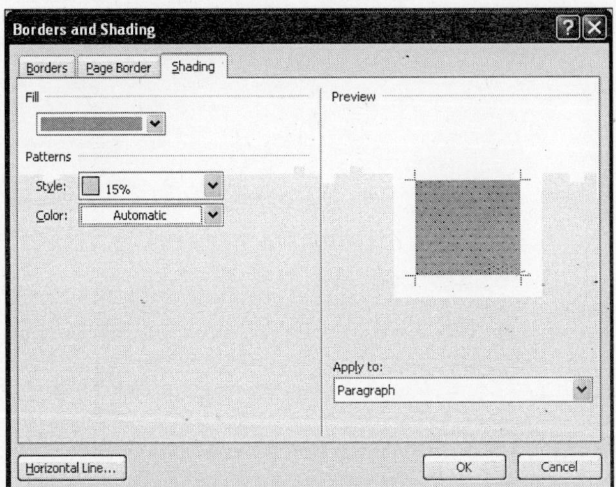

Figure 4.78 Shading tab of Borders and Shading dialog box

3. In Fill: box click the fill color you want for the shading or click None to remove shading color.
4. Style: In this drop-down list click the shading style you want to apply "over" this fill color.
5. In Color: drop-down list, click a color for the line and dots in the selected shading pattern. The Color: box is not visible if you click color in the style: box.
6. Select a color from the Fill list to color a percentage pattern or a pattern background. The effect of the selection option appears in the Preview box.
7. Click OK.
8. The selected shading style option is applied in the paragraph as shown in Figure 4.79.

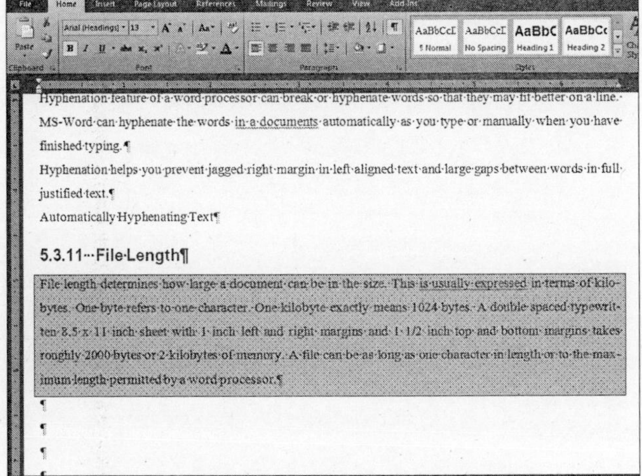

Figure 4.79 Paragraph with shading effects

➜ **To remove shading using mouse, do this:**

1. Select the paragraph or paragraphs from which you want to remove shading.
2. In Borders and Shading dialog box, select the Shading tab.
3. Choose No fill from the Fill group and also clear Style from the Patterns group.
4. Click OK.

4.16 MAIL MERGE

Mail Merge is a mass-mailing facility that takes names, addresses and pertinent facts about recipients and merges the information into the form of a letter. Mail Merge printing (merge printing in short) uses two files: a data file that contains a listing of data items (or fields) arranged in some specific order and a master file that contains the standard text as well as the data variables which are replaced with specific data items from the data file during the merge operation performed by Word 2010.

4.16.1 Creating a Mail Merge Letter

The best way to learn how to create and print a merged document is to consider a practical example. This is described in the following sections.

Creating a Document for Mail Merge

For mail merge, you need to do the following:

- Create a data source.
- Create main document.
- Insert fields into the main document.
- Check for design and data entry errors.
- Merge the data source document and the main document and finally, print merged documents.

Planning Data Source

Designing a data source document is one of the most important parts of using the mail merge feature. To begin with, you may want to create a data source document which has one field for the *name of your friend*; *one field for the address* and *one field each for the city and pincode*. It is always good if you read data into multiple fields. That is you should use two fields namely, *Last name* and *First name* for name field. Similarly, keep separate fields for *house number*, *colony*, *city* and *pin*. For example, if you want to deliver an invitation through a messenger, you may need to sort the addresses on the basis of *colony* field in the address, so that invitations belonging to one colony can be sent together through a messenger.

Starting Mail Merge

Word 2010 has a step-by-step Mail Merge Wizard that guides you through the steps for creating merged documents.

➜ **To use the mail merge helper, do this:**

1. First create a blank document.
2. Click the **Mailings** tab in the **Start Mail Merge** group and click, down pointing arrow list appears as shown in Figure 4.80 offering five options – *Letters, E-Mail Messages, Envelopes, Labels* and *Directory*.

   The first step in the mail merge process is to Create the Main document, because the type of main document governs the subsequent choices you can make in the Mail Merge Helper. Note that *Letters, E-Mail Messages, Envelopes, Labels,* and *Catalog* are various types of documents you can produce using Mail Merge Wizard. Hence, the Helper offers you different choices of data source.

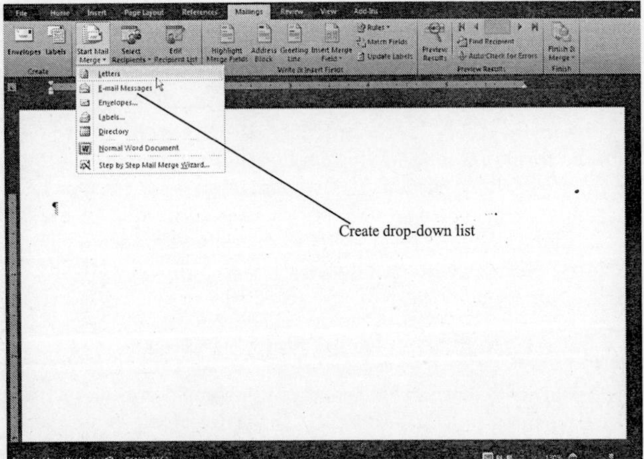

Figure 4.80 Create data source drop down list

Creating Main Document

Word 2010 has a step-by-step Mail Merge Wizard that guides you through the steps for creating merged documents.

➜ **To create main document, do this:**

1. Click the **Mailings** tab in the **Start Mail Merge** group and click down pointing arrow and select **Step by Step Mail Merge Wizard...** .

Figure 4.81 Step 1 of Mail Merge task pane

2. On the right hand side the Mail Merge task pane box appears as shown in Figure 4.81 showing Step 1 of the Wizard's six steps.
3. Under the **Select document type**, click Letters radio button.
4. Click **Next: Starting document.**
   The wizard guides you through the rest of the mail process. The following are more details, listed in step-by-step order.
5. There are three options under **Select starting document**, click **Use the current document** radio button, which specifies *how do you want to set up your letters*? (See Figure 4.82).
6. Click **Next: Select recipients**.
7. Under **Select recipients**, click **Type a new list** radio button (See Figure 4.83).

Figure 4.82 Step 2 of Mail Merge task pane

8. Click **Create...** under Type a new list section.

Specifying Data Source

It contains the fields you specified in the data source. You can enter as many data records as are required. After entering data, click the close button to save the Address list (See Figure 4.84).

9. A **New Address List** dialog box appears as shown in Figure 4.84. Type the information you want to include for the data source.

Adding and Removing Field Names

As you may not require all the field names in the **New Address List** dialog box, so for each of the following field names, first select the field and then click the **Customize Columns...** button. The Customize Address list dialog box appears as shown in Figure 4.85.

Figure 4.83 Step 3 of Mail Merge task pane

10. Select the Field names order appears in the **Customize Address list** dialog box, then click OK.
11. The Selected Field names are: *Title, First Name, Last Name, Address Line 1, City, Zip Code.*

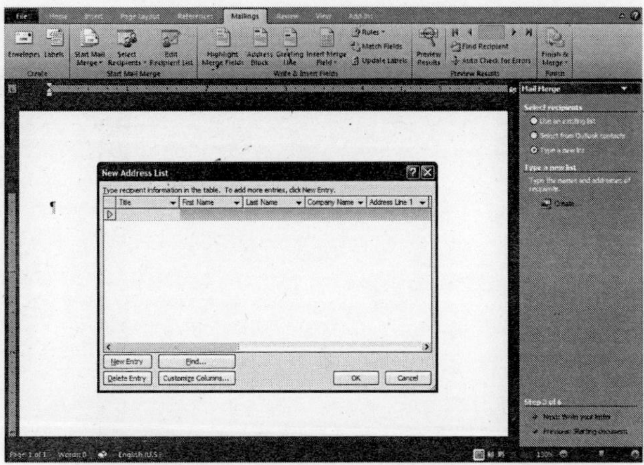

Figure 4.84 New Address List dialog box

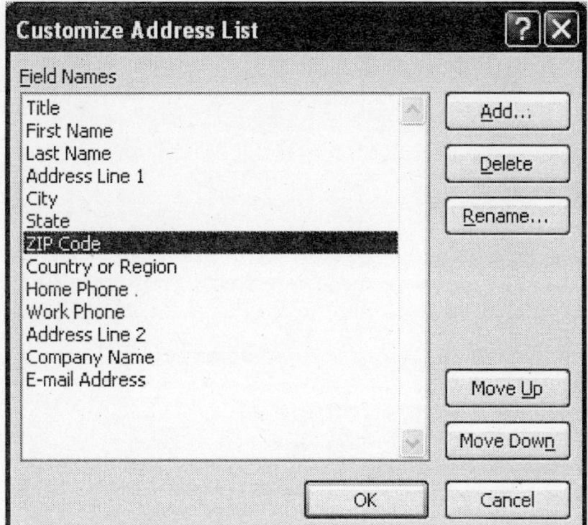

Figure 4.85 Customize Address list dialog box

12. Under Field names: type (use tab key to go next field)
    Title: Mr.
    First Name: Rahul
    Last Name: Verma
    Address Line 1: 120-A, Vikaspuri
    City: New Delhi
    Pin: 110 018

    After completing the First entry, click New Entry to enter another data records as follows:
    Title: Ms.
    First Name: Urvashi
    Last Name: Batra
    Address Line 1: A-3, Janakpuri
    City: New Delhi
    Pin: 110 049

    Title: Mr.
    First Name: Ravi
    Last Name: Kumar
    Address Line 1: D2/4, Model Town
    City: New Delhi
    Pin: 110 009

Saving Data Source

When you have finished adding, removing and arranging fields, click OK to save your data source.

13. The **Save Address List** dialog box appears as shown in Figure 4.86. Enter a name and location for your data source file, say, **Data.doc** and click **Save** button to save the file.

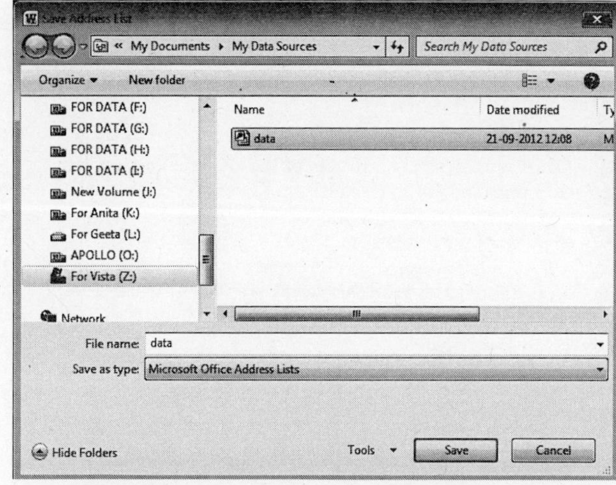

Figure 4.86 Save Address List dialog box

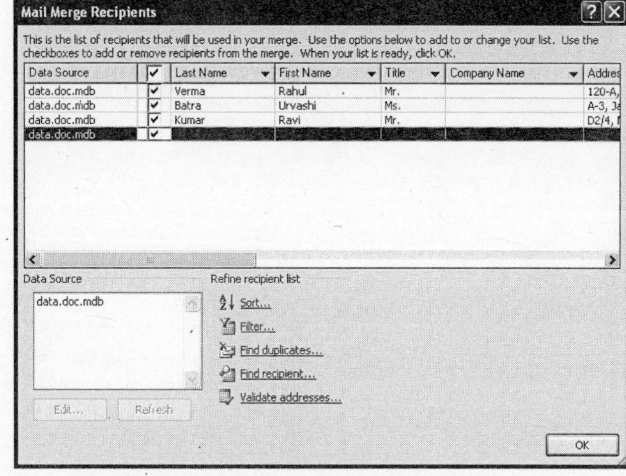

Figure 4.87 Mail Merge Recipients dialog box

14. The Mail Merge Recipients dialog box appears as shown in Figure 4.87. Select the receipients that will be used in your merge process.
15. Click OK.
16. Click **Next: Write your letter.**

Typing Letter

Now type the following letter.

Rohini
New Delhi-110 056
Ref.Rahul/Comm/20

Dated: 3rd May, 2014

To

<<Title>> <<FirstName>>
<<LastName>>
<<Address1>>
<<City>>-<<Pin>>

Dear <<Title>> <<LastName>>

I have to inform you that the meeting of the club committee will be held at the Club House, 36-N, Chanakyapuri, Vinay Marg on Tuesday 25th June, 2014 at 8.30 p.m. I hope you will make it convenient to attend the conference.

The agenda for the conference is as under:

1. **Confirmation of the minutes of the last meeting (enclosed).**
2. **Accounts and Internal Auditors Report for the months of Feb and March 2007 (enclosed).**
3. **Election of new members.**
4. **List of outstanding.**
5. **Any other matter with the permission of the Chairman.**

Yours faithfully,

P.K. Verma
(Secretary)

Inserting Fields Names in the Master Document

When you place the merge field names into a master document, you are essentially telling Word 2010 where you desire the variable information from the *data source* file to appear. You will see that Word 2010 encloses each *field name* in chevrons, i.e., the marks represented as << >>.

➜ **To insert a field, do this:**

1. In the **Mailing** tab, click **Insert Merge Field** in the **Write & Insert Fields** group. Click the down pointing arrow and choose the field names that you can insert in your master document appears. You select field names from this list (See Figure 4.88).
2. Click the Title from merge field name to insert it into the document.
3. Press the Spacebar key to insert a blank space between the Title and the FirstName.
4. Click the Insert Merge Field button to insert the next field name and select FirstName.
5. Press the Spacebar key to insert a blank space between the fields FirstName and LastName.
6. Click the Insert Merge Field button and select LastName.
7. Press the Enter key to move to the next line.
8. Place the cursor below the **<<Title>>**. Click the Insert Merge Field button. Select **<<Address1>>** and press the Enter key.
9. Again place the cursor below **<<Address1>>**. Click the Insert Merge Field button. Select **<<City>>** type a hyphen and select **<<Pin>>** from the merge field button and press Enter key.
10. Press the Enter key twice to leave a blank line.

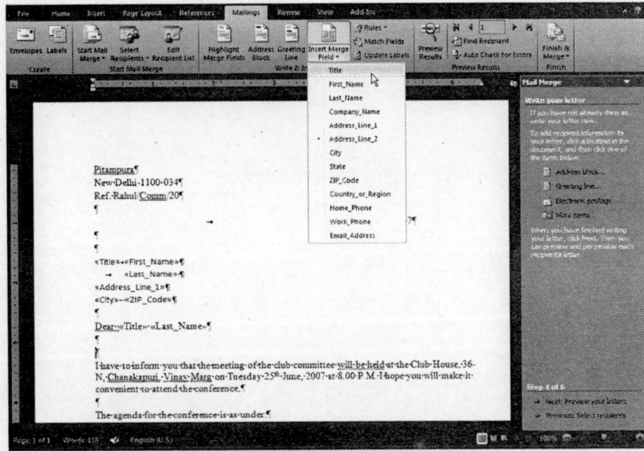

Figure 4.88 Step 4 of Mail Merge task pane

11. Type *Dear* and press the Spacebar key.
12. Click the Insert Merge Field button and select **<<Title>>**.
13. Press the Spacebar to leave a space between the Title and the LastName.
14. Click the Insert Merge Field button and select **<<LastName>>**.
15. Type a comma, and then press the Enter key twice to leave a blank line.
16. After completing the above Steps, your screen will be as shown in Figure 4.89.
17. Now type the remaining part of the letter.

Saving the Master Document

18. After you have completed the main document and inserted all of the merge fields, click Save As on the Office button.
19. Give the name of the document, and then click Save button.
20. Click **Next: Preview your letters.**
21. In the Preview your letters, click arrow button, i.e., (<<) to show the first record, and to go the second record click (>>) arrow button (See Figure 4.89).
22. Click **Next: Complete the merge** (See Figure 4.90).
23. To personalize individual documents, you actually complete the merge, and then edit the information you want in the resulting merged document.
24. Click **Edit individual letters....** under **Merge** section. The Merge to New Document dialog box appears as shown in Figure 4.91.
25. In the Merge records area, select the records you want to merge.
26. Click All radio button and then click OK.
Word 2010 creates and opens a new merged documents. Your main document also remains open. You can switch back to it if you want to make a change to all the documents and then save all the merged documents. Click Office button and save the file.

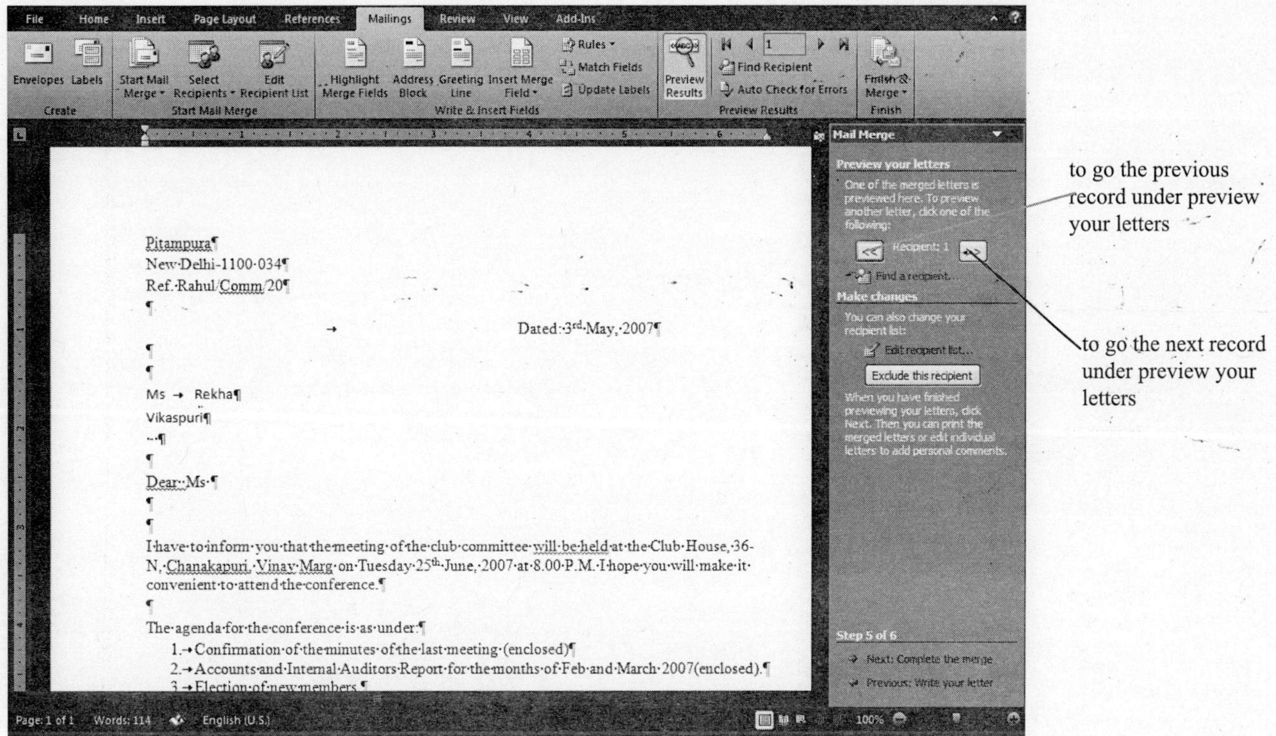

Figure 4.89 Step 5 of partially completed screen

Printing the Merged Letters

If you want to print the letters, make sure that the printer is switched on and is in ready to print. Then click **Finish & Merge** in **Finish** group. Click down pointing arrow and choose **Print Documents...** . The **Merge to Printer** dialog box appears. Select the records and click OK.

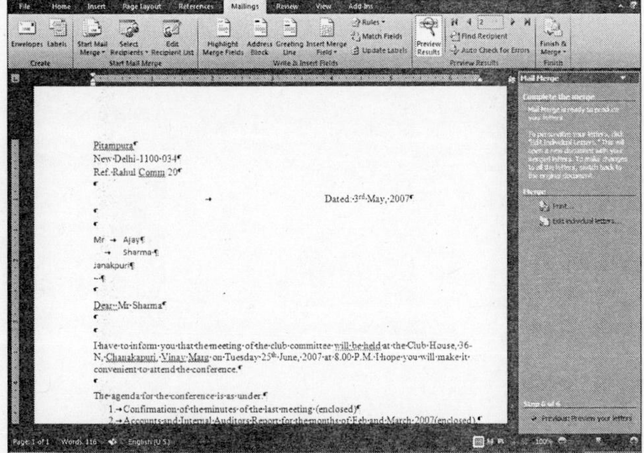

Figure 4.90 Step 6 of partially completed screen

4.17 WORKING WITH GRAPHICS

Graphics can include a wide variety of images, including pictures and drawing objects. Pictures and graphics that have been created outside Word 2010-a scanned photograph, clip art, that are created within Word-a shape, a diagram, a line, or WordArt text. You can use the buttons on the Insert tab to insert pictures and draw different kinds of objects. Word 2010 lets you draw, place, resize, reposition and format graphics.

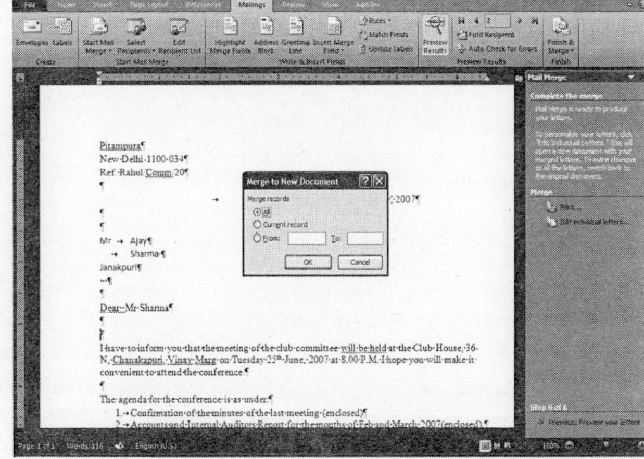

Figure 4.91 Merge to New Document dialog box

4.17.1 Insert Picture Command

You can insert scanned photographs or pictures created in any program into a Word 2010 document. Two buttons in the illustrations group on the Insert tab can be used to specify the source of the picture as follows:

- **Picture:** Click this button to insert a picture from a file. Or you an also insert a picture directly from the camera.
- **Clip Art:** Click this button to insert one of the hundreds of Clip Art images that come with Word 2010, such as photos and drawings of people, places and things etc.

➔ To insert a picture, do this:

1. Open the document in which you want to insert the graphics.
2. Position the insertion point where you want the graphics to be appeared.
3. Click the **Insert** tab and choose **Picture** icon in the **Illustrations** group. Insert Picture dialog box of Word 2010 appears as shown in Figure 4.92.

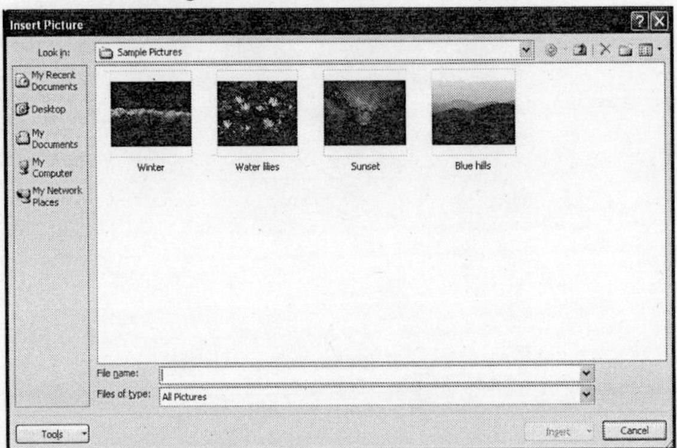

Figure 4.92 Insert Picture dialog box

4. In Insert Picture dialog box, displaying the contents of your **Sample Pictures** folder.
5. Select the desired picture you want to insert in the document.
6. On the **Format** contextual tab, in the **Adjust** group, choose the desired option you want to apply in the picture.
   Click **Corrections** down-arrow button. A list of brightness and contrast options appears. Select the desired type of brightness and contrast under the Brightness and Contrast category from the list.
   Color: You can adjust the color intensity and color tone of a picture.
   Artistic Effects: You can apply artistic effects to a picture to make the picture look like a sketch, drawing and painting.
7. In the **Picture Styles** group, click the **More** button. The picture Styles Gallery opens as shown in Figure 4.93.
8. In the gallery, point to each thumbnail in turn to see its effect. Then, click the desired style you want to apply.

➔ To insert a Clip Art, do this:

1. Open the document in which you want to insert the graphic.
2. Position the insertion point where you want the graphic to appeared.
3. Click the **Insert** tab and choose **Clip Art** icon in the **Illustrations** group.
4. In the Clip Art task pane, select the graphics you want to insert in the document.
5. Click the arrow right side of the picture. A pop-up menu appears. Click Insert as shown in Figure 4.94.

4.17.2 Customizing Graphics

Resizing Graphics

➔ To resize the graphics, do this:

1. Click the graphic you want to select. The picture is surrounded by a box containing eight handles (See Figure 4.94). You will find one in each corner and one on each side of the outline box.

   When you position the mouse pointer on a handle, it turns into a two-headed arrow.

2. To increase or decrease the size of the entire graphic proportionally (*height* and *width* increase proportionally), drag a *corner* handle diagonally, releasing it when the image is of proposed size.

3. To distort a dimension, use the handles on the edges of the graphics.

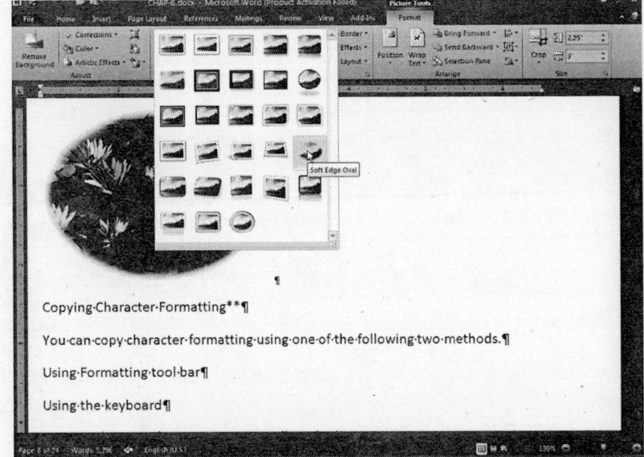

Figure 4.93 Picture styles gallery

Figure 4.94 Insert graphics in the Clip Art task pane

4.18 CREATING A DRAWING IN WORD 2010

➜ **To draw an object, do this:**

1. In the **Illustrations** group, click **Shapes** button. Click the down pointing arrow and choose different shapes, such as *lines, Basic shapes, flowchart, Block arrows, callouts*, etc.

   For example, to draw rectangle, under Basic shapes: click a *rectangle* button, click on the page to set the rectangle's upper left corner, and drag with your mouse to create a rectangle of the desired shape and size. Hold the Shift key until you create squares as shown in Figure 4.95.

4.18.1 Applying Styles to Objects

➜ **To apply style to objects, do this:**

1. Click the Object you want to apply style. The selected objects are surrounded by small handles.
2. Click **Format** contextual tab, click **Shape Styles** group. Click **More** button. A list of styles appears as shown in Figure 4.96. Click the desired style you want to apply.

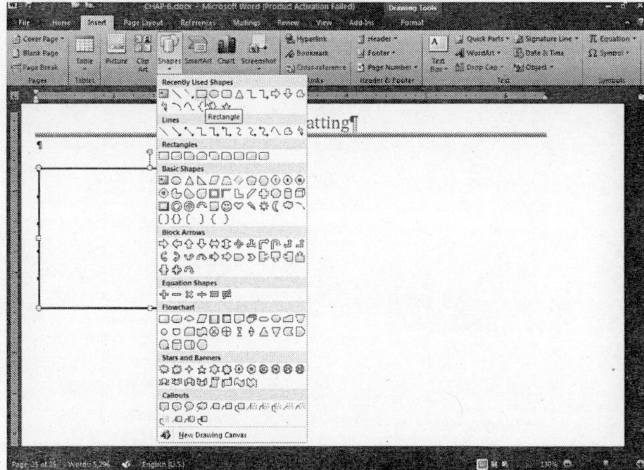

Figure 4.95 Drawing a rectangle Object

Figure 4.96 Applying style to Object

Text in Drawings

You can create text for drawings in *text boxes*.

➜ **To insert text in drawing position, do this:**

1. Click on the **Text Box** button in the **Text** group.
2. Drag the text box to its desired size and shape. Text box is inserted as shown in Figure 4.97.

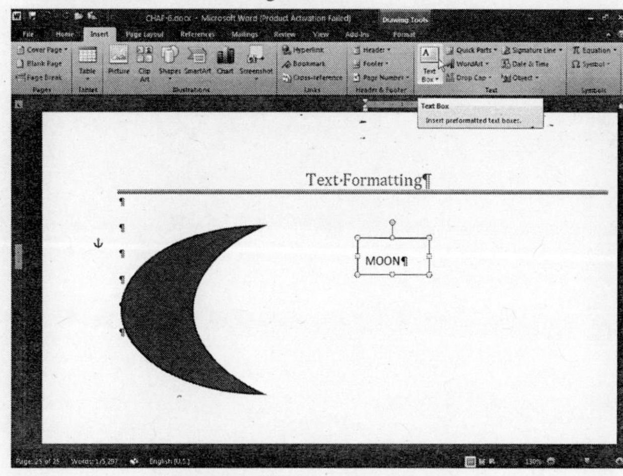

Figure 4.97 Inserting Text box

3. Type the text.
4. If necessary, you can increase the size of the text box by dragging, just as if it were any other graphic object.

Delete a Text Box

1. Click the border of the text box that you want to delete, and then press **Delete** key.

☞ *Make sure that the mouse pointer is not inside the text box, but rather on the border of the text box. If the pointer is not on the border, pressing Delete key will delete the text inside the text box and not the text box.*

Moving Objects

➜ **To move objects, do this:**

1. Select the item or items to be moved.
2. Point to one of the selected items with your mouse pointer, avoiding the object's handles.
3. The pointer will change, to an arrow with four heads.
4. While the pointer has this shape, drag it with your mouse and watch as an outline of the object(s) proposed a new location.
5. Releasing the mouse button completes the move.

Wrapping Text

Wrapping text around a picture requires positioning a picture independently of the text on a page, which is called 'absolute positioning'. You can also wrap the text around an object to improve visual appearance in a document.

➜ **To wrap text around an object, do this:**

1. Click the picture to select it. For example, we have inserted the (Tulips) picture.

2. Select the picture in which you want to wrap text. A Picture Tools contextual tab appears as shown in Figure 4.98.

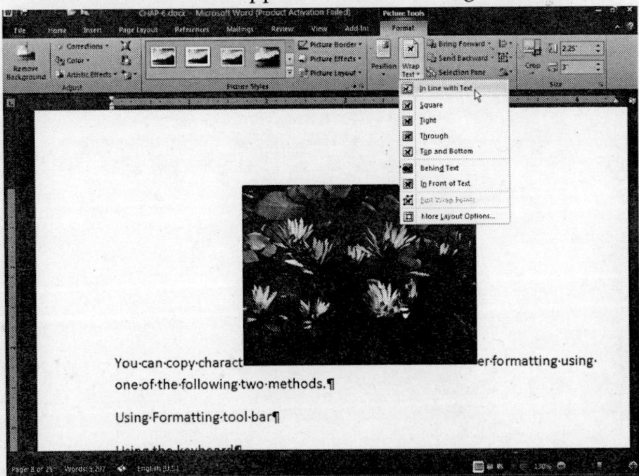

Figure 4.98 Select the picture to wrap text

Inserting a WordArt

Office 2010 enables you to create special effect with text by using WordArt. You can use vibrant color, 3-D effects and outline effects.

➔ **To insert WordArt in a document, do this:**

1. Open the document in which you want to insert the WordArt.
2. Click the **Insert** tab, in the **Text** group.
3. Click **WordArt** drop-down arrow. A list of WordArt sytles appears as shown in Figure 4.99.

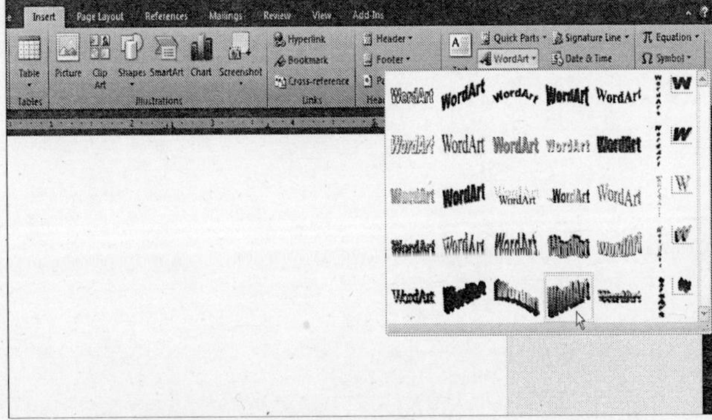

Figure 4.99 Selecting WordArt from the Insert tab

4. Select the desired style you want to apply.
5. A WordArt graphic displays an **Edit WordArt Text** dialog box that appears as shown in Figure 4.100.
6. Type the text that you want to insert in the WordArt **Text:** box.
7. Click the **Font:** drop-down arrow and choose the desired font.
8. Click the **Size:** drop-down arrow and choose the desired font size.
9. Click a text style button if desired.
10. Click OK to return to the document window.
11. The WordArt graphic placeholder is inserted in the document as shown in Figure 4.101.

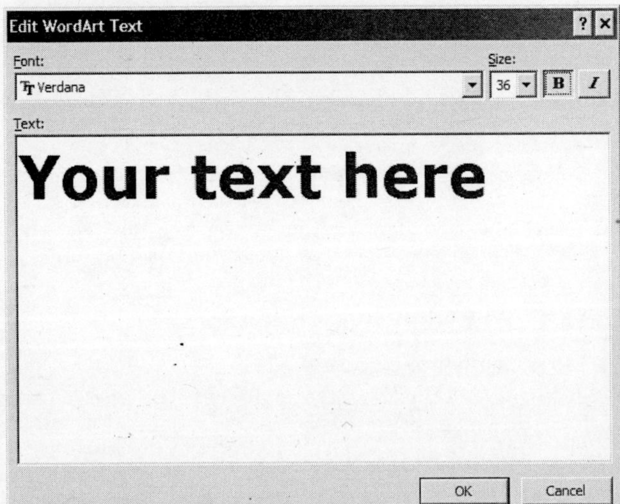

Figure 4.100 Edit WordArt Text dialog box

Figure 4.101 WordArt graphic is inserted in the document

REVIEW QUESTIONS WITH ANSWERS

1. Multiple Choice

1.1 When Word gets loaded, the opening screen displays a document named:

a. Document1 b. Document
c. Doc1 d. No document name is displayed

1.2 You specify the save details of your file in the:

a. Save As... dialog box
b. Save the File As... dialog box
c. File Save dialog box
d. None of the above

1.3 Word offers certain ways by which you can move around in a document

a. By scrolling b. By moving to a specific page
c. Both a and b d. None of the above

1.4 The contents of the Clipboard remain the same until:

a. You cut other text b. You shut down your computer
c. You copy other text d. All of the above

1.5 Word text can be made Italic by:

a. Ctrl+I c. Ctrl+B
b. Ctrl+U d. None of the above

1.6 In Word you can align the selected paragraph to its right by pressing:
a. Ctrl+E b. Ctrl+L
c. Ctrl+R d. None of the above

1.7 Word automatically places a default left aligned tab stop at every:
a. 0.2" b. 0.4"
c. 0.3" d. 0.5"

1.8 What is the term used for the word processing programs that show you directly on the PC screen the appearance of your final document as you might expect when the document is printed on the paper?
a. Search & Replace b. Pagination
c. Soft Copy d. WYSIWYG

1.9 When you insert a table in a document?
a. Word outlines each cell with continuous lines so that you see the cells when you work in a table.
b. Word outlines each cell with dotted gridlines so that you see the cells when you work in a table.
c. No line is drawn.
d. None of the above

1.10 After a table has been created, which of the following operations cannot be performed?
a. Insert rows in a table b. Delete and insert columns
c. Split the table into two tables d. None of the above

1.11 How many scroll bars can be visible on the text area if your document is over 200%?
a. Four b. Two
c. One d. Three

1.12 What Ribbon will you find where you can add a chart?
a. View b. Reference
c. Insert d. Page Layout

1.13 What Ribbon do you use to change margins?
a. Page Layout b. View
c. Insert d. Home

1.14 What can be shown on the Status bar?
a. Name of document, insert button, spell check
b. Number of spellings errors, page number, document name
c. Size of Margins, word count, Web layout
d. Number of pages in the document, word count, spelling/grammar check

1.15 Which Ribbon shows what fonts are available for use?
a. View b. Page Layout
c. Reference d. Home

1.16 What Ribbon do you need to be on to see the document views that are available?
a. Insert b. View
c. Page Layout d. Home

1.17 What page view can you use to see what it will look like when printed?
a. Outline view b. Draft view
c. Reading view d. Print view

1.18 What is NOT a new feature in Word 2010?
a. Ribbon b. Button
c. Charts d. Drop-down menu

1.19 What is the name of the small toolbar at the top that can show the save disk?
a. My Documents b. Quick Access
c. Title bar d. Find Me

1.20 What is NOT on the Insert Ribbon?
a. Shapes b. Clip Art
c. Page Numbers d. Thesaurus

2. State whether the following statements are True or False

2.1 To highlight the paragraph, double-click in the selection bar next to the paragraph.

2.2 To select an entire document, you will double-click the mouse in the selection bar.

2.3 Right justification makes the ends of lines uneven.

2.4 Italic character is slanted than regular characters.

2.5 Margins are the distances between the text and the edges of the paper.

2.6 Microsoft operating system was developed by Microsoft to overcome the limitations of its own MS-DOS operating system.

2.7 In order to save a file, on the Standard toolbar, click on the Save button.

2.8 The Page Break button in Pages Group is used to start the next page at the current position.

2.9 You cannot undo certain operations like saving, printing, opening and creating documents.

2.10 Print button on the Quick Access toolbar will print the entire document using the default settings.

2.11 Using Home tab you can perform editing functions, such as Cut, Copy, Paste, Find and Replace, etc.

2.12 Using Insert menu you can insert various objects, such as page numbers, headers and footers, picture etc.

2.13 Using Review tab you can access to various utilities of word, such as spell check, macros and mail merge etc.

2.14 In MS Word, every command is available in Ribbon.

2.15 Formula bar is available in MS Word 2010.

3. Match the following:

3.1	Margin	a.	The distance between text boundaries and page margins.
3.2	Indent	b.	The text layout within a paragraph with respect to document margins.
3.3	Text alignment	c.	Preset column position of text.
3.4	Tab stop	d.	Placement of text going past the right margin to the next line.
3.5	Line spacing	e.	The distance between the text and the paper edge.
3.6	Word wrap	f.	Total height of line including space above or below it.
3.7	Ruler	g.	It is a graphical bar displayed across the top of the document window.
3.8	Quick Style gallery	h.	It is a family of type styles.
3.9	header	i.	Applying a style to a selection of text in Word 2010 is a easy to clicking a button.
3.10	Font	j.	Text that displays at the top of every page.

3.11	Main document	k.	It refers to a combination of one or more sources of text into a single document.
3.12	Merge	l.	It contains text and graphics.
3.13	Merge field	m.	It refers to a document that is made up of text to be merged into a main document.
3.14	Data source	n.	Create letters, e-mail messages, labels, envelopes, etc.
3.15	Mail Merge	o.	Directs Word 2010 where to insert a specific information from the data source.
3.16	Highlight Merge fields	p.	It contains lines, basic geometric shapes, arrows, equations shapes, flowchart shapes, etc.
3.17	Shapes	q.	Resizing an object
3.18	Sizing handle	r.	It is easy to see what part of your form letter will be replaced by information from the recipient list you have chosen.
3.19	Extension of bitmap file	s.	To place a database field in a document.
3.20	Insert Merge Field button	t.	**.bmp**

4. Fill in the blanks

a. Print Preview	b. Printed	c. Show/Hide
d. 255	e. Change Case	f. Orientations
g. Cell	h. Border and Shading	i. Start Mail Merge
j. Endnote	k. Top	l. Thesaurus
m. Illustrations	n. WordArt	o. Document

4.1 The toolbar is located by default at the ________ of the Word 2010 window.

4.2 The two types of page ________ namely, portrait (vertical) and landscape (horizontal).

4.3 In Windows, a filename can be from 1 to ________ characters long.

4.4 The _______ option is used to preview and make changes to pages before printing.

4.5 The _______ button in Paragraph group is used to show paragraph marks and other hidden formatting symbols.

4.6 The Print Layout view in Document Views group is used to view the document as it will appear on the _______ page.

4.7 The ______ button in Font group is used to change all the selected text to UPPERCASE, lowercase, or other capitalizations, such as Sentence case., tOGGLE cASE, Capitalize Each Word.

4.8 _______ suggests other words with a similar meaning to the word which has been selected.

4.9 The Change Styles button in Styles group is used to change the set of styles, colors, and fonts used in the current ________.

4.10 A ________ is the intersection of a row and a column.

4.11 The ________ button on the Home tab of Paragraph tab containing three tabs, namely Borders, Page Border and Shading is used to customize the borders of the selected cells or text.

4.12 Press Alt+Ctrl+D keys together to insert __________.

4.13 The Select Recipients button in ________ group is used to choose the list of contacts you intend to send the letter to.

4.14 The Insert Picture from File option is available in ________ group.

4.15 _________ button in Text group is used to insert decorative text in the document.

Answers

1.	1.1	a	1.2	a	1.3	c	1.4	d	1.5	a	1.6	c
	1.7	d	1.8	d	1.9	b	1.10	c	1.11	b	1.12	c
	1.13	a	1.14	d	1.15	d	1.16	b	1.17	d	1.18	d
	1.19	b	1.20	d								
2.	2.1	T	2.2	F	2.3	T	2.4	T	2.5	T	2.6	T
	2.7	T	2.8	T	2.9	T	2.10	T	2.11	T	2.12	T
	2.13	F	2.14	T	2.15	F						
3.	3.1	e	3.2	a	3.3	b	3.4	c	3.5	f	3.6	d
	3.7	g	3.8	i	3.9	j	3.10	h	3.11	l	3.12	k
	3.13	o	3.14	m	3.15	n	3.16	r	3.17	p	3.18	q
	3.19	t	3.20	s								
4.	4.1	k	4.2	f	4.3	d	4.4	a	4.5	c	4.6	b
	4.7	e	4.8	l	4.9	o	4.10	g	4.11	h	4.12	j
	4.13	i	4.14	m	4.15	n						

Short Questions with Answers

1. Why are "text wrapping breaks" used? Explain with an example.
2. How to insert an optional hyphen in Word document?
3. Why is the Ribbon minimized?
4. Word provides six views: Print Layout, Full Screen Reading, Web Layout, Outline, Draft. Explain with the help of examples.
5. How to set Default Font Formatting?
6. How do you modify a style so it always starts on a new page?
7. Define and explain how to adjust "Line spacing" and "Paragraph spacing" in Word document.
8. How to convert text to a table?

Answers to Short Questions

1. Text wrapping breaks are used to separate the text around objects on Web pages. For example, you can use a text wrapping break to separate caption text from body text. Text wrapping breaks are formatting marks that are not visible in the Word document. If you want to view these breaks, click Show/Hide button in the Paragraph group on the Home tab.
2. An optional hyphen is a hyphen that is used to control where a word or phrase breaks if it falls at the end of a line. For example, you can specify that the word "non-printing" breaks as "non-printing" instead of "nonprint-ing". When you insert an optional hyphen in a word that is not at the end of a line, the hyphen will be visible only if you turn on Show/Hide button.
   To insert an optional hyphen in Word document, do this:
   1. On the Home tab, in the Paragraph group, click Show/Hide.
   2. Click in the word where you want to insert the optional hyphen.
      You can also press Ctrl+Hyphen(-).
3. The Ribbon is designed to find quickly the commands that you need to complete a task. Commands are organized in logical groups and arranged under tabs. Each tab relates to a type of activity, such as writing or laying out a page. Some tabs are shown only when the are needed. Therefore, you can minimize the Ribbon to make more space available on your screen.

4. Word provides six view these are: Print layout, Full Screen Reading, Web Layout, Outline, Draft.
Print Preview: In print preview, you can display multiple pages of a document in a reduced size. In this view, you can see page break, hidden text, watermarks, etc. In Print preview, you can access to the Normal, Page Layout, and Outline icons at the left corner of the horizontal scroll bar. Clicking any of these buttons closes the preview screen and displays the document in the view mode you selected.
Full Screen Reading view: Full screen view displays as much of the typing area of the document as will fit on the screen at a size that is comfortable for reading. In this view, the Ribbon is replaced by a single toolbar at the top of the screen. You can print the document, highlight text and write comments. You can also move from page-to-page and adjust the view.
Web Layout view: Work in Web layout view when you are creating a Web page or document that is viewed on the screen. In Web layout view, you can see background, text is wrapped to fit the window, and graphics are positioned at proper places, so that the page will look just as it would look in a Web browser.
Outline view: Work in outline view to look at the structure of a document and to move, copy and reorganize the text by dragging the headings. In the outline view, you can collapse a document to see only the main headings or expand it to see the entire document. In this view it is easy to scroll or move text to a longer distance or to change the hierarchy of topics. In outline view, page boundaries, graphics, headers and footers do not appear.
Draft view: Draft view is the best view for most of your typing, editing. Draft view shows text formatting but simplifies the layout of the page, so that you can type and edit quickly. In Draft view line and page breaks, tab stops, and alignments are accurate but the area outside the text body, i.e., the area containing headers, footers, page numbers, etc., do not appear.
Document Map: The Document Map is a separate window pane that displays a list of headings in the document. Use the Document Map to quickly navigate through the document and keep track of your location in it. When you click a heading in the document map, Word jumps to the corresponding heading in the document. It displays at the top of the window, and highlight the headings in the Document Map.

5. To set the default font in MS Word 2010 do the following steps:
   a. Highlight some text in your open document or create a new document and enter some text.
   b. On the Home tab in the Font group, click the Font launcher icon to open the Font dialog box.
   c. Style the text font as desired (Font-family, size, color, etc.).
   d. A dialog box opens. "Do you want this change to affect all new documents based on the NORMAL template?" Click Yes. (If you click No, it will save the new default font to the current document only).
   e. In Word 2010, select All New Documents based on the Normal.dotm Template, then click OK.

6. In your document, place your cursor within any of the instances of Heading 1, then follow these steps:
   a. In the Styles pane, click the down arrow next to Heading 1, the select modify.
   b. Click Format, then select Paragraph.

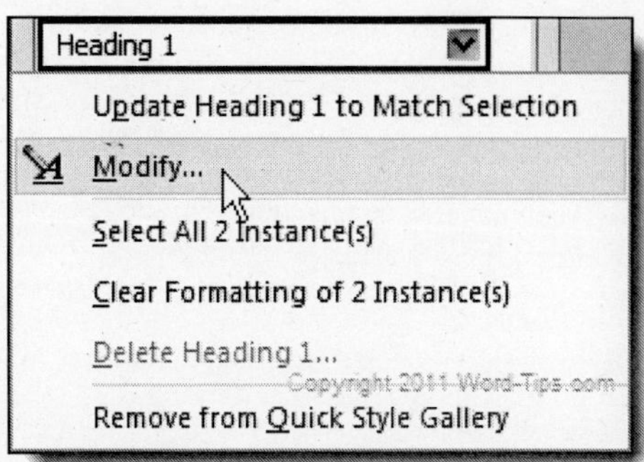

   c. The Paragraph dialog box appears, click the Line and Page Breaks tab.
   d. Select first Page break, then click OK.
   e. Click OK.

Each instance of Heading 1 will now start on a new page.

7. Line spacing: The amount of space from the bottom of one line of text to the bottom of the next line. Line spacing determines the amount of vertical space between lines of text. Microsoft Word uses single line spacing by default. The line spacing you select will affect all lines of text in the selected paragraph.
   1. Select the paragraphs in which you want to change the line spacing.
   2. On the Format menu, click paragraph and then click the Indents and spacing tab.
      Under spacing do one of the following:
   3. To change line spacing, select the options you want in the line spacing box.
      Single spacing: No blank line space between the lines of text.
      Double spacing: A blank line space between the lines of text.
      1 1/2 spacing: Half the height of one line space of text between the lines of text.
      Exactly: Give fixed line space between lines.
      Multiple: Line spacing that is increased or decreased by a percentage that you specified. In the At box, enter or select the line spacing you want. The default is three lines.

Paragraph spacing: The definition of the term paragraph in English language is "a series of related sentences". In Microsoft Word, a paragraph is a distinct unit of information that has its own formatting characteristics, such as alignment, spacing and styles. A paragraph is always followed by a paragraph mark. The way you format paragraphs in a document depends on how you intend to use the document and how you want it to look.
   1. Select the paragraph(s) in which you want to change paragraph spacing.
   2. On the Format menu, click paragraph and choose Indents and Spacing tab.
   3. There is a spacing box, in Indents and Spacing tab, which lets you define the amount of white space that word must place before and after paragraphs.
   4. Select the space required in the Before: text box for adding space before the paragraph.
   5. Select the space required in the After: text box, for adding space after the paragraph.
   6. Click OK.

8. To insert separator characters, such as commas (,) or tabs in Word document is used where you want to arrange the text into columns. For example, in a list with two word groups in a sentence separated by a comma (Software Engineering, Computer Fundamental) or a tab can be converted into two-column table. Following steps are required to convert text to a table:
   (a) Select the text that you want to convert. On the Insert tab, in the Tables group, click Table and then click Convert Text to Table.
   (b) In the Convert Text to Table dialog box, under Separate text at section, select separator character option like comma or tab that has been used as a separator in the text.

DESCRIPTIVE TYPE QUESTIONS

1. Differentiate between line spacing before and after the paragraph.
2. Explain the difference between Left, Centre, Right and Justified alignments. When do you think Left Justification is preferable over Justified alignment?
3. What is meant by Page Margins? Which option in Word will you choose to set the left margins in your document?
4. Which command is used to save a file in Word 2007?
5. a. Briefly explain the use of Quick Access Toolbar in Word 2010.
   b. What is the function of the Status bar in Word 2010? List down the information that is displayed in the Status bar.
6. What is an insertion point in Word 2010? How will you correct the mistakes you commit while typing in text?
7. What is smart cutting and pasting? How do you control the option in Word?
8. How many types of breaks like page break, etc., are available in Word 2010? Explain each one.
9. What is meant by editing a document? What is the difference between editing and formatting a document?
10. While selecting text, what is use of Extend Selection mode.
11. Briefly explain how you will search for a particular word in the document and replace it with a new word.
12. Explain the features of the spelling check facility in Word 2007. How do you add new words to a dictionary?
13. What is the difference between Replace and Replace All in Find and Replace operation in Word 2010?
14. Differentiate between the following:
    a. Moving text and copying text
    b. Special characters and other characters
    c. Web and Print Layout view
    d. Draft and Outline view
    e. Paragraph and line break
15. Explain the features of the spelling check facility in Word 2007. How do you add new words to a dictionary?
16. Briefly explain how you will search for a particular word in the document and replace it with a new word.
17. How can you check spellings in Word? What are the various options available to correct the wrong spellings?
18. Differentiate between paragraph formatting and character formatting.
19. What are the important features of page formatting in Word 2010?
20. What is page break? What are soft and hard page breaks?
21. How do you setup headers and footers in Word? Discuss briefly.
22. You may prefer your Word documents or multiple page letters to be printed without any numbering on the first page. How it is achieved?
23. What do you mean by a column? What is meant by two column text?
24. How do you insert a picture in Word document?
25. What is mail merge? Explain the steps to mail merge two documents using Word?

CHAPTER 5

Spreadsheet

5.1 INTRODUCTION TO SPREADSHEET

Spreadsheet applications (sometimes referred to simply as spreadsheets) are computer programs that let you create and manipulate spreadsheets electronically. In a spreadsheet application, each value sits in a cell. You can define what type of data is in each cell and how different cells depend on one another. The relationships between cells are called formulas, and the names of the cells are called labels.

A table of values are arranged in rows and columns. Each value can have a predefined relationship to the other values. If you change one value, therefore, you may need to change other values as well, or they will change automatically.

Once you have defined the cells and the formulas for linking them together, you can enter your data. You can then modify selected values to see how all the other values change accordingly. This enables you to study various what-if scenarios.

Excel 2010 is a popular spreadsheet program, where you design worksheets using this software package. Excel 2010 uses a workbook-style presentation which is made up of several worksheets, like pages in a notebook.

5.2 ELEMENTS OF ELECTRONIC SPREADSHEET

When you are working with a spreadsheet package, such as MS Excel 2010 you have to know some spreadsheet terminologies. Some such terms are given in the following paragraphs:

Workbook

A workbook is a collection of many worksheets. In a single workbook, you can store information in an organized manner. By default, a workbook is open with three worksheets and it can contain a maximum of 255 worksheets.

Worksheet

A worksheet is a sheet made up of rows and columns. It is used for planning a project or financial documents of an organization. Worksheet refers to the actual document you create by using the spreadsheet program. A worksheet is always stored in a workbook.

☞ *Excel is a popular spreadsheet program, where you design worksheets using this program.*

Chartsheet

Chartsheet is a separate sheet in a workbook that contains only graphs or charts. It is useful when you want to see a chart or tabular data separated from other type of data.

Row

A row is a horizontal block of cells that runs through the entire width of the worksheet. The rows are numbered from top to bottom along the left edge of the worksheet. The first row is numbered 1, the second 2, and so on. There can be a maximum of 1,048,576 rows and 16,384 columns in an Excel 2010 worksheet.

Column

A column is a vertical block of cells that runs through the entire worksheet. A worksheet contains 16,384 (A to XFD) columns. The first column is **A**, the second is **B** and so on until you reach **Z**. Then comes column **AA** through **XFD**. The last (or rightmost) column of the worksheet, **XFD** is the 16,384th column.

Cell

A cell is the intersection of a row and a column. For example, the uppermost cell is A1 (column A, row 1). Cell G9 is the intersection of column G, row 9. When you select a cell by clicking it with the mouse, or moving to it using the keyboard, it becomes the active cell.

Formula

Formulas are equations that perform calculations on values in your worksheet. It is an order of values, names, cell references, functions and operators in a cell that together give a new values. A formula always begins with = (equal) sign.

Function

Functions are pre-defined formulas or programs that perform calculations in Excel on specific values, called arguments. Each function takes specific types of arguments, such as numbers, references, text, or logical values.

5.2.1 Working with Spreadsheet

In Excel 2010, each workbook can contain many worksheets. These sheets may also contain *charts*, *macros*, etc. Sheets may contain different types of information but all data or information is related to each other.

☞ *Generally, spreadsheet is a software tool and worksheet is a work file created with spreadsheet software. But sometimes, worksheet is also called a spreadsheet.*

Each worksheet contains 16,384 columns and 1,048,576 rows. The intersection of a row and a column forms a cell in which you can enter data or a formula. Column headings start at **A** and as they reach the letter **Z** column, headings restart with **AA**, **AB**, and so on till **XFD**. Row headings, down the left side of a sheet, go from **1** to **1,048,576**. It is equally easy for formulas to refer to information in another worksheet of the same workbook as it is in the same worksheet.

Advantages of Spreadsheet

The advantages of using spreadsheets are as follows:

- Many built-in function do the complex calculations easily.
- Large volume of data can be handled easily.
- A graphical representation of data is possible. With the help of graph and charts data can be interpreted easily.
- Useful information can be imported or exported from/to other software packages, such as Word and PowerPoint.
- If entries are changed, then formulas automatically calculate the new results.

Disadvantages of Spreadsheet

The disadvantages of using spreadsheets are as follows:

- It requires very large memory of a computer to perform complicated calculations and to plot graphs.
- It has limited number of rows and columns in one worksheet. If user has more data to enter then he/she has to shift data in another worksheet that may create confusion.
- It requires skilled user because small mistake in formula will give absurd results.

Terminologies used in MS Excel

The following terminologies should be kept in mind, while using MS Excel.

Select Highlight a cell or group of cells, dialog box option, or graphical object with the keyboard or mouse action.

Choose Execute and complete a command.

Active Bring an application or document window to the foreground.

Table 5.1 gives the details of the terminology for the mouse operations.

Table 5.1 Terminologies for Mouse Function

Action	Function
Position	Position the mouse pointer on an item.
Click	Point to an item and then quickly press and release the mouse left button.
Double click	Point to an item and quickly press and release the mouse left button two times.
Drag	Point to an item, press and hold the mouse left button as you move the mouse pointer to a new location, then release the mouse button.
Right click	Point to an item and click the right mouse button.

5.3 STARTING EXCEL 2010

MS Excel 2010 needs *Windows 7* as operating system to run on an IBM-PC. However, Excel 2010 can also be run on *Windows XP* operating system, if *Service Pack 3* is installed on *Windows XP*.

➔ **To start Excel 2010 in Windows 7, do this:**

1. Click the **Start** button on the taskbar, highlight **All Programs**, click **Microsoft Office** and then click **Microsoft Excel 2010** (See Figure 5.1).

Figure 5.1 Starting Excel 2010 in Windows 7

5.4 EXCEL 2010 INTERFACE

Excel 2010 includes the Microsoft Office Fluent interface, which consists of a customizable visual system of tools and commands. Figure 5.2 shows the elements of Excel 2010 application window and an open Excel 2010 workbook in detail.

Title Bar

At the top of an Excel 2010 window, there is the title bar. The left edge of this bar has the Office button next to which the name of the open document is displayed. On the right edge of the title bar, the *Minimize*, *Restore/Maximize* and *Close* button are placed (Figure 5.2).

Application Window

The window within which Excel 2010 runs.

Quick Access Toolbar

The Quick Access Toolbar is a customizable toolbar that contains a set of commands that are independent of the tab that is currently displayed. You can add buttons that represent commands to the Quick Access Toolbar. You can move the Quick Access Toolbar from one of the two possible locations. This toolbar is located by default at the top of Excel 2010 window. It provides tools that you use frequently, such as Save, Undo and Repeat buttons (See Figure 5.2). You can customize the Quick Access Toolbar by adding commands to it.

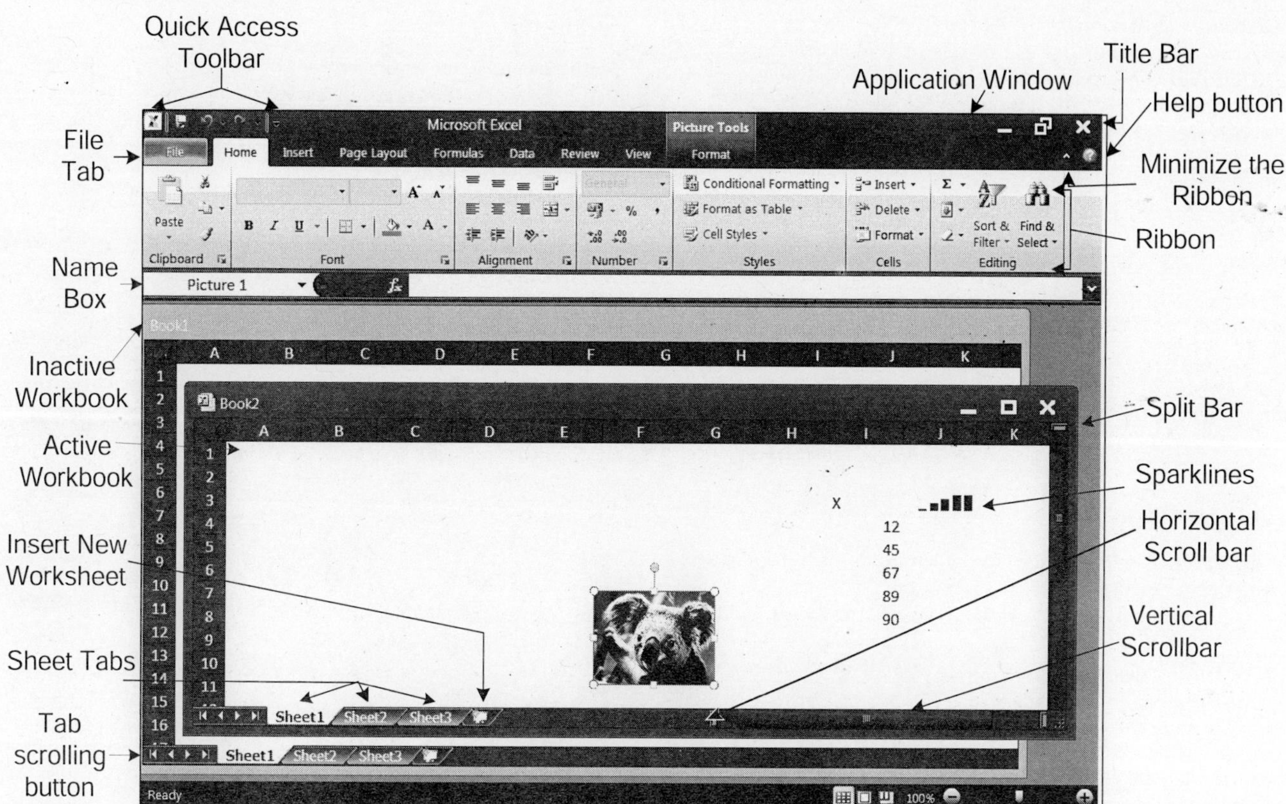

Figure 5.2 Elements of Excel 2010 window

Workbook Window

A window within the Excel 2010 application window in which a worksheet, chart, or dialog box is shown.

File Tab

File tab is the colored tab which is located in the upper-left corner of Microsoft Office 2010 programs and below the Quick Access Toolbar (See Figure 5.2). When you click the File tab, you can see the Backstage view. File tab replaces the Office button in Excel 2007. It contains commands like New, Open, Save, Save As, Print, etc.

Active Workbook

The Excel 2010 workbook window that accepts entries and commands.

Inactive Workbook

A window that contains Excel 2010 information. It is not affected by commands. Such a window has a gray Title bar and is behind the active workbook window.

Ribbon

Ribbon is displayed just below the Title bar (See Figure 5.2). In Ribbon, *Commands* are organized in logical *groups*, which are collected together under *tabs*. You can hide the Ribbon by double-clicking the active tab. Different types of Tabs described hereunder are available in the Ribbon of Excel 2010.

Home Tab: When you open Excel 2010, Home Tab is active. It contains the buttons related to the worksheet contents, such as entering, editing, and formatting data. It is divided into seven groups, i.e., Clipboard, Font, Alignment, Number, Style, Cells and Editing.

Insert Tab: Insert tab contains the button related to the items which you can insert in your worksheet. Groups of this tab are Tables, Illustrations (picture, clipart) Charts, Sparklines, Filter, Links, Text and Symbols.

Page Layout Tab: It includes the buttons related to the appearance of the worksheet. This tab is divided into five groups, i.e., Themes, Page Setup, Scale to Fit, Sheet Options, and Arrange.

Formulas Tab: It contains the button related to functions. Group of this tab are Function Library, Defined Names, Formula Auditing and Calculation.

Data Tab: It contains the button related to data analysis. Get External Data, Connections, Sort & Filter, Data Tools, Outline and Analysis are the group of this tab.

Review Tab: It contains the button related to security and accurate data. Proofing, Language Comments and Changes are the group of this Tab.

View Tab: It contains the button related to view of the worksheet, i.e., how you want to view the worksheet. Workbook view, Show/Hide, Zoom, Window are the group of this tab.

Developer Tab: It contains the button related to create, run and edit macros. It also includes commands or buttons to import XML (eXtensible Markup Language) view of the worksheet, i.e., how you want to view the worksheet. Code Controls, XML and Modify are the groups of this tab.

Scroll Bar

The scroll bar appears at the *left* for vertical scrolling and at the *bottom right* for horizontal scrolling as shown in Figure 5.2.

- To scroll one cell at a time, click the scroll button with arrows at the corners of the scroll bars.
- To scroll more, drag the scroll button in the scroll bar.

Split Bar

The split bar is located at the top of the *vertical* scroll bar and to the right of the *horizontal* scroll bar (See Figure 5.2). Double click the split button on the vertical scroll bar. It splits the sheet horizontally.

Tab Scrolling Buttons

These are the arrow buttons to the left of the sheet tabs for scrolling the worksheet (See Figure 5.2).

- To scroll between sheet tabs, click an arrow for the direction you want to scroll.
- To scroll one sheet tab at a time in left or right direction, click the middle tab scrolling buttons.
- To scroll through a group of sheet tabs in left or right direction, click the tab scroll buttons at the left and right corner.
- To display a list of the sheets in the workbook right click a tab scrolling button to display the menu.

Sheet Tabs

A tab is near to the bottom of a work book window that displays the name of a sheet (See Figure 5.2). Click the sheet tab to move to the next sheet. To display the shortcut menu, right click the sheet tab. To scroll through the sheet tabs, use the tab scrolling button.

Name Box

The *name box* is at the left end of the formula bar (See Figure 5.2). It identifies the selected *cell, chart item* or *drawing object.*

Formula Bar

The *formula bar* displays the constant value or formula used in the active cell. The formula bar is also used for editing the cell contents (See Figure 5.2).

Shortcut Menus

Shortcut menus are meant to display frequently used commands relating to the selected *item* or *object.*

ScreenTips

ScreenTips show the name of the command button shown in ribbon. ScreenTips are shown in small windows appearing as soon as you position the mouse pointer on the toolbar button. Enhanced ScreenTips are larger windows that display more descriptive text than a ScreenTip and can take a link to a Help topic.

Status Bar

Status bar appears at the bottom of the Excel 2010 window. It displays information regarding a selected command or an operation in progress. Note that the right side of the Status bar shows zoom slider, different views tool, such as Normal, Page Layout and Page Break view.

5.4.1 Creating a New Workbook

➜ To create a new workbook, do this:

1. Click the **File** Tab as shown in Figure 5.3. Here, Select **New**. Under **Available Templates**, click **Blank Workbook** and then click **Create** button or *alternatively,* press Ctrl + N keys together.

☞ *You can create a blank workbook or create new workbook based on an existing workbook, the default workbook template, or any other template.*

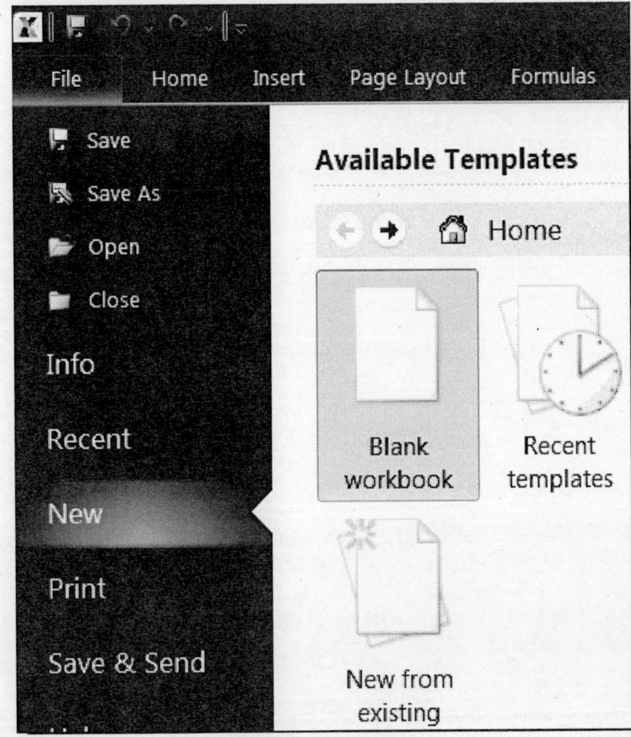

Figure 5.3 File Tab

5.4.2 Opening a Workbook

➜ To open a workbook, do this:

1. Click the **File** Tab as shown in Figure 5.3. Here, choose **Open** or *alternatively*, press Ctrl + O keys together. The Open dialog box appears as shown in Figure 5.4.
2. In dialog box, choose the drive, folder name that contains the workbooks. After finding the required workbook, select it.
3. Then click OK.

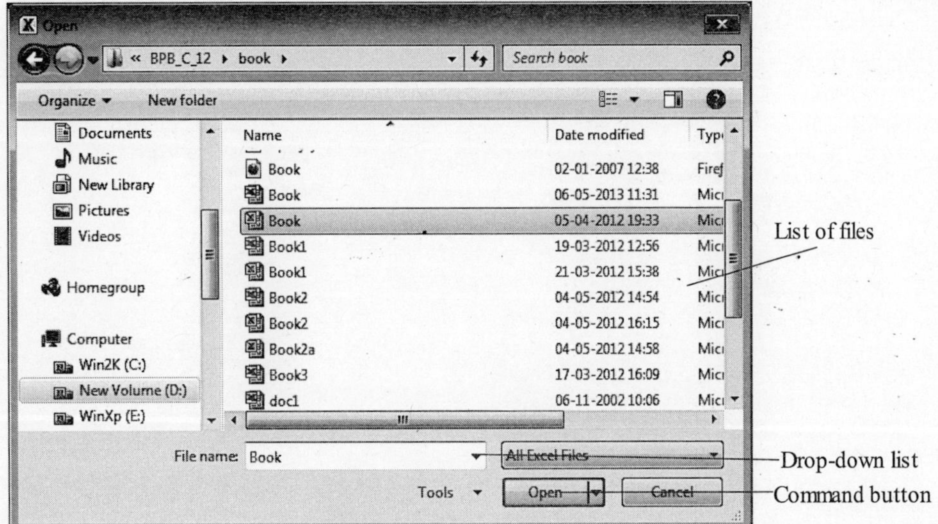

Figure 5.4 Open dialog box

➜ **To Open more than one workbook simultaneously, do this:**

1. Repeat Steps 1. and 2. of opening a single workbook.
2. Click the name of one file and then hold down Ctrl key and click another file name and then press Enter key.

5.4.3 Saving a Workbook

Excel has two commands for saving workbooks. *Save* command is used to save an existing workbook; *Save As* command is used to save the workbook when you save it for the first time or save the workbook under a new name.

➜ **To save the workbook for the first time, do this:**

1. Click on the **File** Tab as shown in Figure 5.3. Here, choose **Save As**. The *Save As* dialog box appears as shown in Figure 5.5.
   You can also specify the location where you want to save the file in the Save in: box.
2. In the File name: box give the name of the file.
3. In the Save as type: box give the type of file.
4. Click Save button.

☞ *Excel 2010 worksheet is saved with .xlsx extension indicating that it uses the XML-based file format.*

5.4.4 Closing a Workbook Window

When you finish using worksheet or chart, you close its window. If you have made any changes since the last time you saved the workbook, Excel 2010 displays an alert dialog box, as shown in Figure 5.6, asking whether you want to save your work before closing.

➜ **To close a file in a workbook, do this:**

1. Click on the **File** Tab as shown in Figure 5.3. Here, choose **Close**. The window closes provided no change has been made to the workbook since it was saved last.
2. If you have made changes to the workbook since the last save, the Alert dialog box appears. In the dialog box, choose *Don't Save* if you do not want to save a changed version of the file, or choose *Save* if you do want to save changes (See Figure 5.6). Type a new file name and choose **Save** button.

Figure 5.5 Save As dialog box

Figure 5.6 Alert dialog box

5.4.5 Quitting Excel 2010 Program

➜ To quit Excel 2010, do this:

1. Click on the **File** Tab and then choose **Exit.** *Alternatively*, click the Close button (x) in the top-right corner or press Alt+F4 or double-click the Control icon at the left of the title bar.
2. When all workbooks are closed, Excel 2010 window closes, and the application is terminated.

5.4.6 Printing a Spreadsheet

The simplest way to print any open worksheet is to choose **Print** option from the Backstage view or *alternately*, click the **Print Preview and Print** button from the **Quick Access toolbar**. In Excel 2010, you can print entire or partial worksheets and workbooks, one at a time, or several at once. And if the data that you want to print is in a Microsoft Excel table, you can also print just the Excel table by setting the print area.

☞ *You can also print a workbook to a file instead of to a printer. This is useful when you need to print the workbook on a different type of printer from the one that you originally used to print it.*

➜ To print a spreadsheet, do this:

1. Open the worksheet that you want to print.
2. Click the **File** tab and then choose **Print** command (See Figure 5.7) or *Alternatively*, press Ctrl+Shift+F12 keys together.

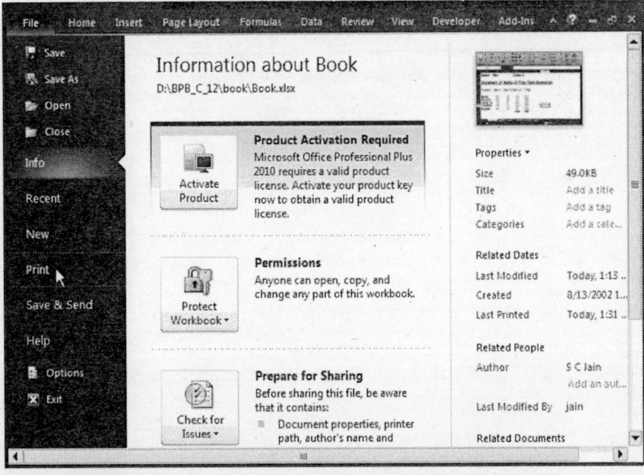

Figure 5.7 Print command in Backstage view

3. The Backstage view appears. Here, click **Print** icon.
4. The Backstage view closes and in the Status bar displays the process of the print job.

Backstage Print Options shown in Figure 5.8, are described in Table below.

Option	Function
Print Section:	
Copies	Specify the number of copies to be printed.
Printer Section:	This section shows selected printer from a drop-down list, print queue status, type, printer port being used, and whether the printer is busy or idle is also shown below the print selection. Select the desired printer from the Printer drop-down list.
Print to File	Select this option to create a disk file for the selected printer.
Settings:	This section shows the Page Setup options, such as page orientation, paper size, and page margins. These options are described below:
Print what option:	
Print Active Sheets	Prints only selected worksheet.
Print Entire Workbook	Prints currently open workbook
Print Selection	Prints selected cells.
Ignore Print Area	Select this option if you want to ignore the print area you have selected.
Page(s) From:/To:	Select this option to print pages you wish to print.
Collate	Select this option to collate multiple copies.
Page Orientation	Allows you to change the page orientation, i.e., portrait (vertically) or landscape (horizontally).
Page Size	Allows you to select the paper size.
Margin	Allows you to set the margin of the pages.
Scaling	Allows you to adjust the size of the worksheet.

(Contd...)

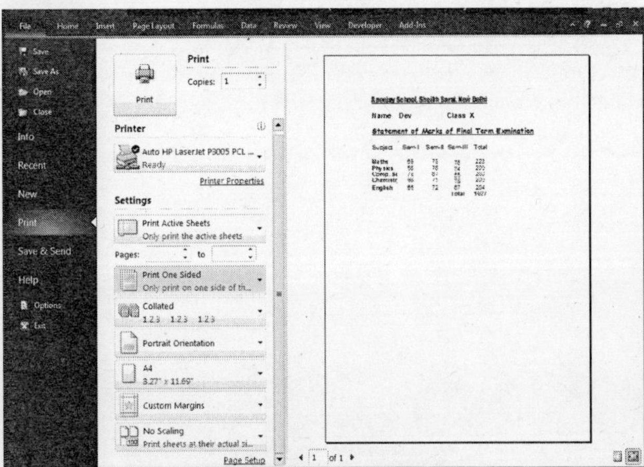

Figure 5.8 Print Options

Printing Sections of a Worksheet or Multiple Worksheets

Suppose you have a year's worth of data accumulated in a given worksheet, but you want to print just one month's worksheet data, then you use this method.

➜ To print a section of a worksheet, do this:

1. Select the range of cells to print.
2. In the **Print Backstage** window, under **Setting** section, in the **Print what drop-down list**, select **Print Selection** to print the selected cells (See Figure 5.8). Excel 2010 ignores any Print Area that has been set and prints the selected range.

➜ **To print several worksheets with one command, do this:**

1. Select all the sheets (the worksheets must be within the same workbook) you want to print.
2. In the **Print Backstage** window, under **Setting** section, in the **Print what drop-down list**, select **Print Active Sheets**.

5.5 MOVING BETWEEN WORKBOOKS

When you open an Excel 2010 file, you really open a workbook that contains *multiple* sheets. In Excel 2010, you can also get multiple workbooks open, each in its own document window. To work on a workbook you need to *activate* it. Bring to the top, the workbook in which you want to work presently.

5.5.1 Switching between Workbook Windows

➜ **To switch between the open workbook windows, do this:**

1. Click on the **View** Tab, in the **Window** group, click arrow next to the **Switch Windows** and select the workbook window you want to switch from the list of open windows (See Figure 5.9).
2. Or *alternatively*, you can cycle between workbook windows by pressing Ctrl+F6 keys together.

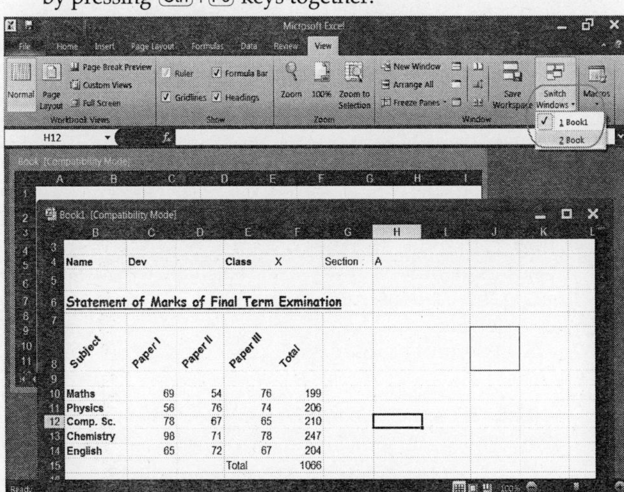

Figure 5.9 Switching between workbook windows

Changing Default Number of Sheets in New Workbooks

➜ **To change the number of sheets in new workbooks, do this:**

1. Click the **File** Tab and then click **Options**. Excel Options dialog box appears with **General** properties as shown in Figure 5.10.
2. Enter the number of sheets in **Include this many sheets:** spinner box under the **When creating new workbooks** section.
3. Click OK to accept the settings.

☞ *A default workbook opens with 3 worksheets. However, you can change the number of sheets depending upon your needs. The maximum being 255.*

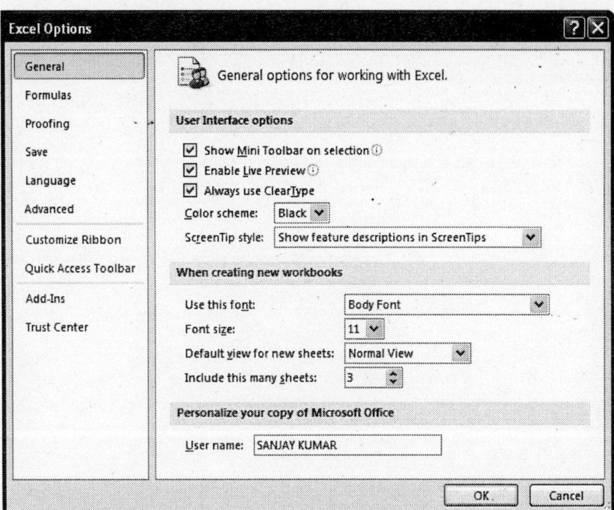

Figure 5.10 Change the number of sheets in a workbook

5.5.2 Inserting and Deleting Sheets

If you revise workbooks, you will want to *insert/delete* sheets from the workbook. Excel 2010 gives you the flexibility to easily insert and remove sheets.

Example 1

How will you insert a sheet in a workbook?

Solution

1. Activate the workbook into which you want to insert the sheet.
2. Select the existing sheet before which you want to insert the new sheet by clicking its sheet tab or by pressing Ctrl+PgUp or Ctrl+PgDn as the case may be.

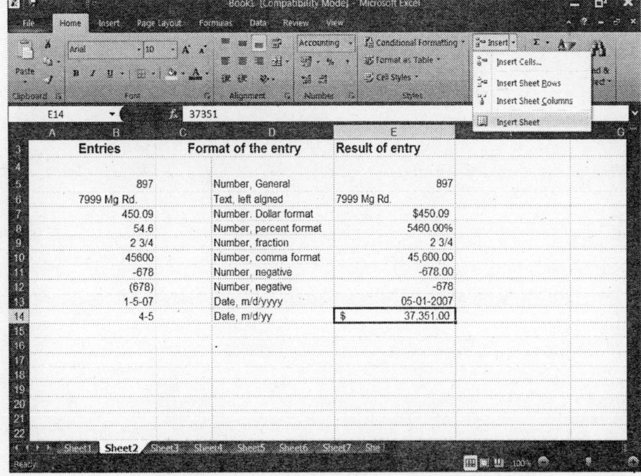

Figure 5.11 Inserting a worksheet

3. Click the **Insert Worksheet** button at the bottom of the screen (See Figure 5.11). *Alternatively*, position the mouse pointer on the tab of any sheet, click the right mouse button and then choose <u>I</u>nsert... . A dialog box appears. In this dialog box, click Worksheet and then click OK button. *Or*, Press Alt+ Shift+F1 keys together to insert a new worksheet. *Or* Select In<u>s</u>ert Sheet option from **Insert** drop-down list of the **Cells** group of the **Home** Tab (Figure 5.11).

☞ *You can also insert a new sheet in the workbook at any location you desire.*

Example 2

How will you delete a sheet in a workbook?

Solution

1. Select the sheet you want to delete.
2. Click on the **Home** tab, in the **Cells** group. Select Delete <u>S</u>heet from the **Delete** drop-down list (See Figure 5.12). *Alternatively*, position the mouse pointer on the tab of the sheet to be deleted, click the right mouse button and then choose <u>D</u>elete.

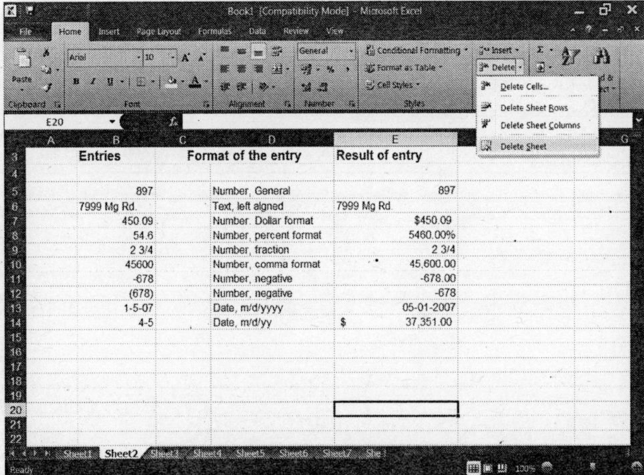

Figure 5.12 Deleting a worksheet

☞ *You cannot undo or get back a worksheet after deletion. Therefore, you should be very careful before you delete a worksheet.*

Copying and Moving Worksheets in a Workbook

Suppose that you use a budget worksheet in one workbook and the same worksheet is also required for another workbook. You could re-create the worksheet in the new workbook or copy the data from one workbook to another, but it would be much easier if you just copy the entire worksheet of other workbook.

Further, you can also move worksheets to new locations. In case you copy the worksheet from the old location to a new location, then a copy of the worksheet is left at the old location.

➜ **To copy/move a worksheet, within the workbook using mouse, do this:**

1. Select the sheet you want to *copy* or *move*.
2. If you want to ***copy*** within the same workbook, press and hold down Ctrl key and drag the sheet tab to its new location.
3. However, if you want to ***move*** the sheet within the original workbook, drag the sheet tab to the location where you want to move the worksheet.

➜ **To copy/move worksheet between workbooks, do this:**

1. Open both the workbooks.
2. In **Window** group of the **View** tab, click **Arrange All** button. **Arrange Windows** dialog box appears as shwon in Figure 5.13. Select the desired arrangement.

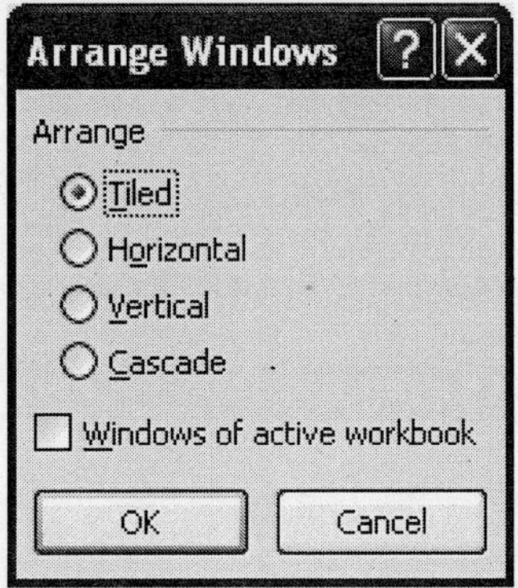

Figure 5.13 Arrange Windows dialog box

3. ***To copy***: Press and hold down Ctrl key and drag the sheet tab from one workbook onto the tabs in the other workbook.
4. ***To move***: In order to move one sheet in one workbook to another workbook, drag the sheet tab onto the tabs at the bottom of the other workbook.
5. A black triangle appears above the receiving tabs, to show the location for the insertion. Figure 5.14 shows the triangle above the tabs.
6. Finally, release the mouse button.

☞ *If you want to add a sheet to the end of the workbook, you need to first insert it before an existing sheet and then move the new sheet to the end.*

When a sheet is inserted at the new location, then name of the copied sheet will be that of the original sheet name. If a sheet with the same name is already in the workbook, the name is followed by a number in parentheses indicating its *copy number*.

➜ **To create a new workbook and copy the sheet, do this:**

1. Open the worksheet you want to copy.
2. Right click on the sheet tab and then and choose <u>M</u>ove or Copy.
3. From the <u>T</u>o <u>b</u>ook: drop-down list, select (Book1).
4. In <u>B</u>efore sheet: section select one of the given options as sheet1, sheet2, sheet3 and (move to end).
5. Click OK.

5.5.3 Renaming a Sheet

The names assigned to worksheets in a workbook by default are Sheet 1, Sheet 2, etc. However, you can also name the sheets as per your needs.

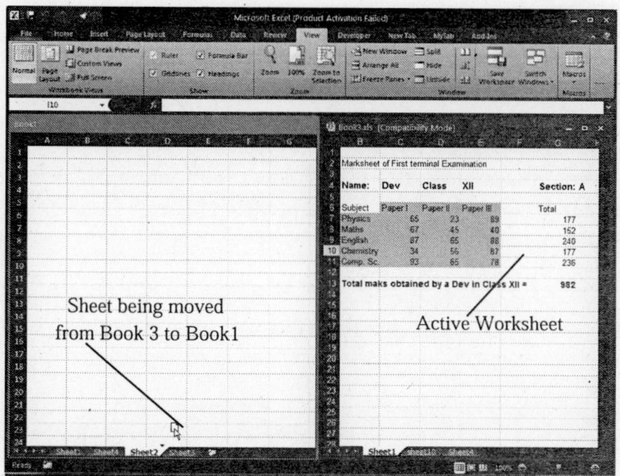

Figure 5.14 Copying a worksheet between workbooks

Example 3

Explain step-by-step procedure to rename a sheet.

Solution

1. Select the sheet you want to rename.
2. In **Home** Tab, under the **Cells** group, from the **Format** drop down list, select Rename. *Alternatively*, double-click the sheet tab. *Or* click the right mouse button on the sheet tab whose name you want to rename, then choose Rename. The sheet name is highlighted, as shown in Figure 5.15.
3. Type the new sheet name, using up to 31 characters including spaces.
4. Press Enter.

The new sheet name appears on the sheet tab.

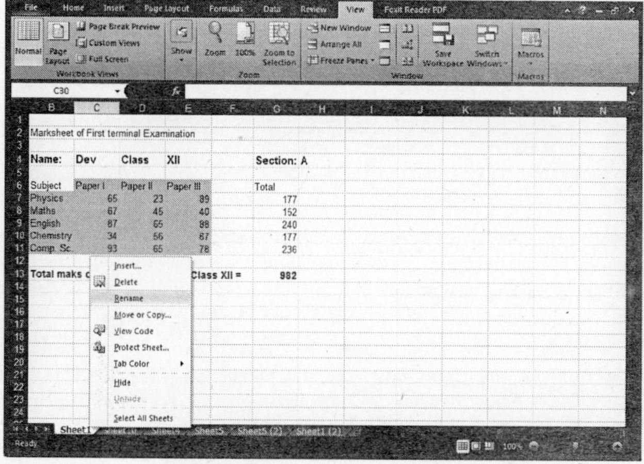

Figure 5.15 Renaming a Sheet

Selecting and Moving between the Sheets

If you have multiple sheets in a workbook then you need a quick and easy way to select or move between the sheets. For this, when you select a single sheet, that sheet moves to the top of the window and you can work there. Similarly, as shown in Figure 5.16 you can also select multiple sheets. Selecting multiple sheets is useful if you want to insert or delete many sheets at the same time.

How to move between Worksheets in a Workbook?

If you want to work within a specific worksheet, then activate first the workbook that contains the worksheet and then activate the *worksheet* in which you want to work. The name on the tab of the active sheet is in bold letters. You can switch between worksheets by using either the keyboard or a mouse.

☞ *An active sheet is the sheet in which you can operate.*

➜ **To move to a worksheet using the keyboard, do this:**

Press Ctrl + PgUp to activate previous sheet.
Press Ctrl + PgDn to activate next sheet.

➜ **To move to a worksheet in a workbook using a mouse, do this:**

1. Click the tab scrolling buttons to scroll through the workbook until you can see the name of the worksheet in which you want to work.
2. Click the tab containing the name of the worksheet you want to activate.

Grouping Sheets for Editing, Formatting and Reorganizing

You can perform operations on several sheets at one time by creating a *group selection*. This group selection is useful to edit or format a group of sheets *identically* or to reorganize a group of sheets. You can group the worksheets and then add text or format them all at once. You may begin by grouping the sheets that you want to work with.

➜ **To select a group of adjacent sheets, do this:**

1. Select the first sheet tab.
2. Press and hold down Shift key, while selecting the last sheet tab in the group. All sheets in between, including the first and last sheet you clicked are selected.

➜ **To select a group of non-adjacent sheets, do this:**

1. Select the first sheet tab.
2. Hold down Ctrl key and click the next sheet tab you want to select. Do this for each sheet tab you want to select.

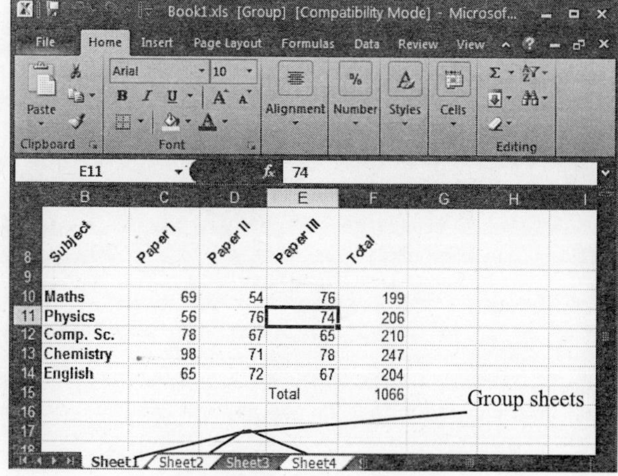

Figure 5.16 Grouped sheets

☞ *When you select a group of sheets, the word [Group] is displayed in the Title bar which indicates that a group of sheets is selected.*

Example 4

How can you select all sheets in a workbook?

Solution

1. Point to any sheet tab.
2. Click the right mouse button to open the sheet tab shortcut menu and then choose Select All Sheets.
3. After you create a group selection, [Group] appears in the title bar of the workbook. (Figure 5.16)

☞ *To deselect the group, click any sheet tab that is not selected.*

5.6 WORKING IN A WORKSHEET

An Excel 2010 worksheet may have a large number of filled cells. In order to find data on a worksheet, you need to know how to move in a worksheet. You can scroll a worksheet with a mouse or a keyboard.

5.6.1 Scrolling with Mouse

To scroll the window with the mouse, use the scroll bars located at the right and bottom of each worksheet. The arrows in the scroll bars show the direction the window moves over the worksheet. Click the arrow to scroll in that direction.

☞ *The vertical and the horizontal scroll boxes give you the position in the worksheet. You can also drag the scroll box to move the relative distance in the worksheet.*

5.6.2 Scrolling with Keyboard

When you scroll using a keyboard, the cell selected by you changes as you scroll. Table 5.1 lists the keys and their combination to scroll the window.

Table 5.1 Keys that Scroll the window

Key	Movement
↑	Scrolls up one row.
↓	Scrolls down one row.
←	Scrolls left one column.
→	Scrolls right one column.
PgUp	Scrolls up one screen.
PgDn	Scrolls down one screen.
Alt+PgUp	Scrolls right one window.
Alt+PgDn	Scrolls left one window.
Home	Moves to the beginning of the row.
Ctrl+Home	Moves to the beginning of the worksheet.

5.6.3 Selecting Cells and Ranges of Cells

Before you can *enter*, *edit* or *modify* the contents of a cell, you must select or activate the cell or cells you want to change.

Selecting a Single Cell

➜ **To select a cell using mouse, do this:**

1. Move the mouse pointer over the cell and click the cell.

➜ **To select a cell using keyboard, do this:**

1. Press the appropriate key as given in Table 5.2 to select the cell.

Table 5.2 Keys that Move the active cell

Key	Movement
↑	Moves the active cell up one cell.
↓	Moves the active cell down one cell.
→	Moves the active cell right one cell.
←	Moves the active cell left one cell.
Tab	Enters data and moves the active cell right.
Shift+Tab	Enters data and moves the active cell left.
Enter	Enters data and moves the active cell down.
Shift+Enter	Enters data and moves the active cell up in the selected range.
Ctrl+ arrow	Moves the active cell in the direction indicated by arrow until the edge of a block of data is reached.
Home	Moves the active cell to column A of the current row.
Ctrl+Home	Moves the active cell to the first cell in the worksheet (cell A1).
Ctrl+End	Moves the active cell to the last cell in the used portion of the worksheet.
PgUp	Moves the active cell up one full window.
PgDn	Moves the active cell down one full window.
Alt+PgUp	Moves the active cell one screen left.
Alt+PgDn	Moves the active cell one screen right.

☞ *The single cell that receives the data or formula you enter is the active cell. A selection of multiple cells is referred to as a range.*

Selecting a Range of cells

Selecting a range of cells will be very helpful when you want to apply a command to all the selected cells or want to enter data into the cells in the range.

➜ **To select a range of cells using the mouse, do this:**

1. Click the cell at one corner of the range.
2. Drag to the opposite corner of the range and release the mouse button. The number box displays the number of rows and columns selected.
3. A rectangular range of cells is selected, as shown in Figure 5.17. Make sure that the pointer is on the correct cell when you release the mouse button.

- If a corner of the range is not displayed, drag the mouse pointer against the document window's edge in the direction you want to move. The window scrolls over the worksheet.

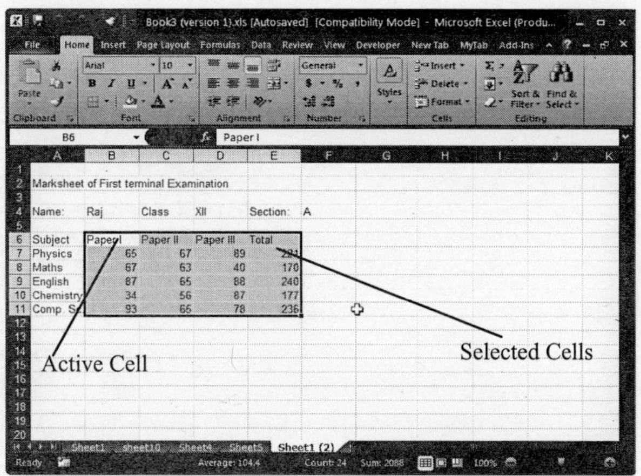

Figure 5.17 Selected Cells

Selecting Range of Cells using Keyboard

Table 5.3 shows some keyboard shortcut for selecting ranges of cells.

Table 5.3 Keyboard shortcut for selecting ranges of cells

Key	Extend Selection from Active Cell to
F8	Activate extend.
Shift+Arrow key	Next cell selected.
Shift+Home	Beginning of row.
Shift+Ctrl+Home	Beginning of worksheet (A1).
Shift+Ctrl+End	End of screen.
Shift+Spacebar	Entire row of active cell.
Ctrl+Spacebar	Entire column of active cell.
Shift+Ctrl+Spacebar	Entire worksheet.
Shift+Ctrl+PgUp	Cell in same row one window right.
Shift+Ctrl+PgDn	Cell in same row one window left arrow.
Shift+Ctrl+Arrow key	Edge of the next block of data in key the direction of the arrow key.

Selecting more than one Ranges of cells

Excel 2010 has the capability to select multiple non-adjacent ranges at a time. This feature helps you to format multiple ranges with a single command. You may even print different parts of the worksheet with a single print command. Similarly, you can erase multiple data-entry cells with one keystroke.

➔ **To select multiple ranges of cells with the mouse, do this:**

1. Select the first range of cell.
2. Press and hold down Ctrl key as you select each additional range of cells.
3. Release Ctrl key.

Figure 5.18 shows an example of selecting multiple ranges of cells.

5.6.4 Selecting Rows and Columns with Mouse

Some operations are quicker if you select an entire row or column at one time. For example, formatting is simple and more efficient if you select and format the entire row or column instead of formatting each cell in the row or a column (See Figure 5.19).

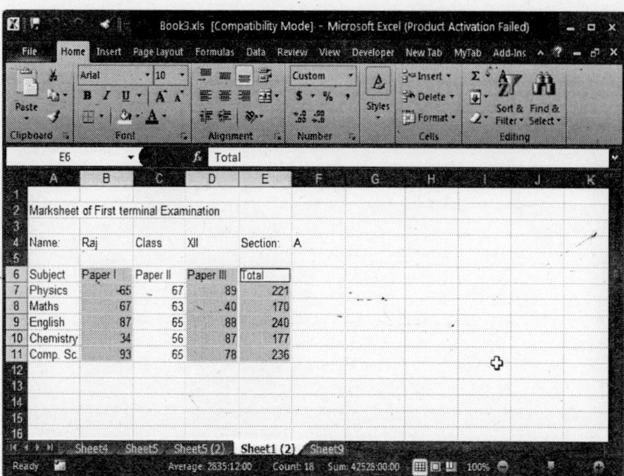

Figure 5.18 Multiple Ranges of cells selected

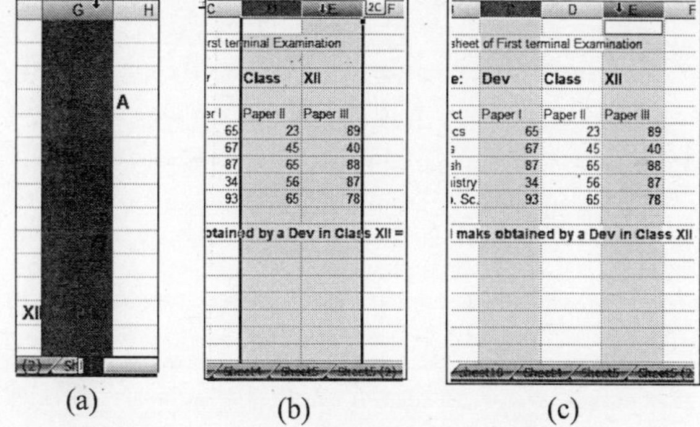

(a) (b) (c)

Figure 5.19 Selecting Column with mouse

➔ **To select an entire row/column with a mouse, do this:**

1. Click the *row* or *column's* heading. The complete row or column is selected (See Figure 5.19(a)).
2. You can select adjacent rows or columns by dragging across the headings or by clicking the first row and pressing the Shift+clicking the last row or column (See Figure 5.19(b)).
3. To select multiple non-adjacent rows and columns, hold down the Ctrl key as you click each heading (See Figure 5.19(c)).

5.7 ADDRESSING OF CELLS

A spreadsheet consists of rows and columns which combine to form cells. A cell is a box where you can enter data. Columns form the vertical lines of cells while rows form the horizontal lines of cells. Cell is an intersection of rows and columns. To describe the location or address of a cell, we have to write the names of the column and the row whose intersection has created this cell. Figure 5.20, the intersection of the Column C and the Row 3 is C3. Here C3 is called as a cell and C3 is its address.

Cells can have two types of data in a worksheet.

Constant value: A constant value is data that you type directly into a cell. It can be a number, a date, time, currency, percentage, fraction or text. Constant values do not change unless we edit them.

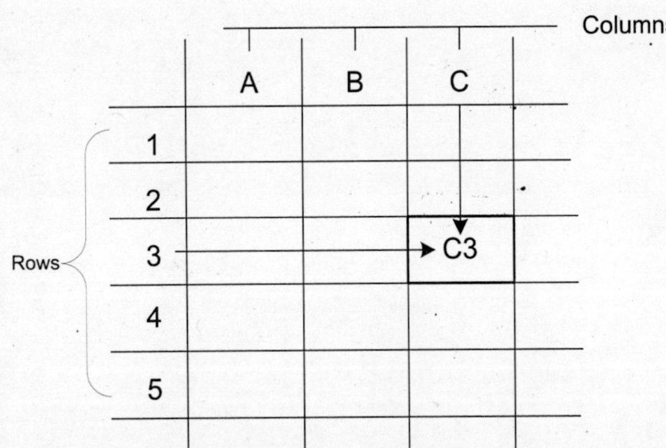

Figure 5.20 Addressing of cells

Formula: A formula is a sequence of values, cell references, names, functions or operators that produce a new value from the existing values. Formulas always start with the equal sign (=). A value that is produced as the result of the formula changes automatically when other values involved in the formula in the worksheet change.

MS Excel helps you perform calculations on numerical data. For example, you need to find the sum of some data or calculate through a complex set of formulas and Excel can quickly provide the answer. By using formulas, you can efficiently keep track of your business or personal finances.

To find the sum of numbers from cell address A1 to A10 the formula would be as follows:

= +Al+A2+A3+A4+A5+A6+A7+A8+A9+A10

A function is a shortcut for a formula. For example, to calculate the sum of numbers from cell address Al to A10, the function used would be as follows:

= Sum(A1:A10)

Colon (:) symbol indicates a group of cell addresses. It is easier to write a function as compared to a formula.

5.7.1 Formulas using Cell Addresses

A formula can also contain cell addresses instead of values or numbers. In that case, the formula is applied on the contents of cell address included in it. Cell addresses could be included in a formula by typing or highlighting them. In a formula, the cell addresses can be used along with numbers, mathematical operators and functions. For example, if the contents of cell address B20 have to be added to that of cell address D13, then type the following formula:

= B20+D13

If a formula contains various operators then Excel performs calculations in a preset order, i.e., multiplication is done before addition. For example, in the formula 2*3+4, it will multiply 2 and 3 first. And then, 4 will be added to their product. So, the result will be 10 and not 14.

5.8 MANIPULATION OF CELLS

The power of Excel lies in storing, manipulating, and displaying data items. Before you can manipulate and display data, you must enter it correctly. This Chapter discusses the types of data you can enter in a cell of the Excel worksheet.

5.8.1 Types of Data Entered in a Cell

There are four distinct types of data that can reside in a cell (See Figure 5.21). These types of data are:

a. Text
b. Numerals
c. Logical values
d. Error

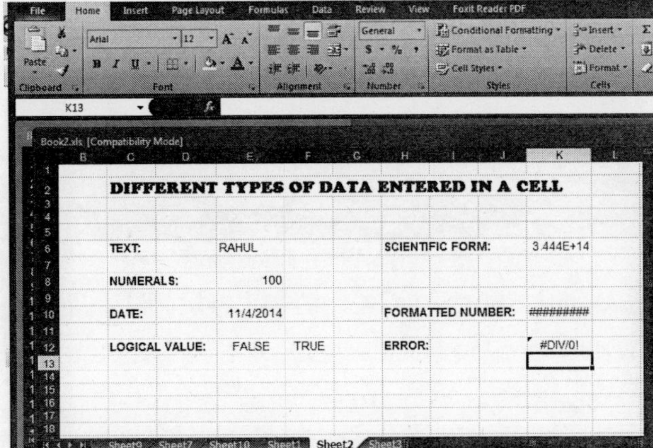

Figure 5.21 Different types of data entered in cells

Text

Text in a cell can include any combination of *letters, numbers* and *keyboard symbols*.

- A cell can contain up to 32,000 characters.
- If column width prevents a text string from fitting visually in a cell, the display extends over neighboring cells. However, if the neighboring cells are occupied, the display is truncated.

Numerals

Numerals contain all the decimal digits, such as 0 to 9 on which you can do *addition, subtraction, multiplication*, and other mathematical or statistical operations. Numeric calculations is the most common thing that is done with Excel 2010. Therefore, it is important to known how Excel understands numerals.

- A number may be displayed using *commas, scientific notation*, or one of many built-in numeric formats. The number's in Excel have two aspects *displaying format* and the *underlying value*. The *display format* is what you see in the cell and the *underlying value* is the calculated value (which you can see in the formula bar).
- *Date* and *time* are numbers, but with special formatting. If you try to enter 1-9 as a text string. Excel 2010 will interpret this as 9th January as a date and display it as 9-Jan.
- When an unformatted number does not fit in a cell, it is displayed in scientific notation (See Figure 5.21).
- When a formatted number does not fit in a cell, number signs like hash (####) are displayed.

Logical Values

You can enter the logical values namely, TRUE or FALSE into cells. Logical values are often used in writing conditional formulas. Also, there are many formulas that give the calculated result in terms of logical values. Thus, if you say 3 > 4, the result is FALSE because 3 is not greater than 4.

Error

An error value is a distinct type of data. For example, if a formula attempts to divide a number by zero, the result is the # DIV/0! Error value.

5.8.2 Entering Text, Numbers and Dates in a Worksheet

When you see the message *Ready* as shown in Figure 5.21 in the Status bar then you can enter data items in a worksheet. Entering data in Excel 2010 worksheet actually consists of three steps:

1. Activate the cell in which you want to enter data.
2. Type the data you want to enter.
3. Finalize the data entry by pressing Enter key, Tab, or anyone of the arrow keys.

Example 5

How do you enter data item in a cell?

Solution

1. Click on the desired cell where you want to enter data, just to make it active. The active cell appears with a dark border and its row and column headings appear to be raised to easily identify the cell address.
2. Type your data in the active cell. Two buttons appear in the formula bar: ***Enter*** button and ***Cancel*** button. The Status bar shows *Enter* to indicate that you are in the process of entering data (See Figure 5.22).

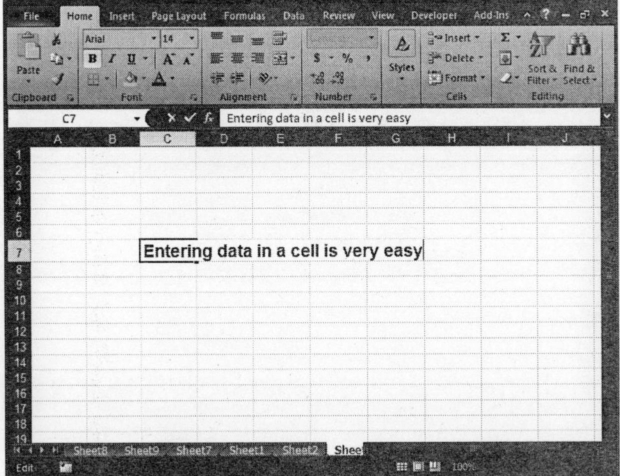

Figure 5.22 Entering data in a cell

3. Click the ***Enter*** button to indicate that you have completed the data typing. You can also press Enter key, Tab key or any one of the arrow keys to complete the data entry.
4. If you make a mistake before finalizing your data entry, press the Backspace key to delete the character to the left of the insertion point. To erase every thing that you have typed, click the Cancel button or press Esc key.
5. Repeat the above Steps to complete the data entry.

Excel provides you with the following two options to enter and edit data:

- You can enter data in the formula bar.
- You can also enter and edit data directly in the cell.

To enter and edit data directly in the cell you need to turn on the in-cell editing option, if not done already.

> *If the Edit directly in-cell feature is turned off, the entry you type appears in the cell but the cursor appears in the formula bar.*

To turn on in-cell editing option, do this:

1. Click the **File** Tab and then click **Options**. **Excel Options** dialog box appears. In this dialog box, click on **Advanced** button on the left side. **Excel Options** dialog box appears with **Advanced** properties as shown in Figure 5.23.
2. Click on the check box, i.e., Allow editing directly in cells under the **Editing options** group as shown in Figure 5.23. The option is *on* when a check mark appears.
3. Click OK to accept the settings you change.

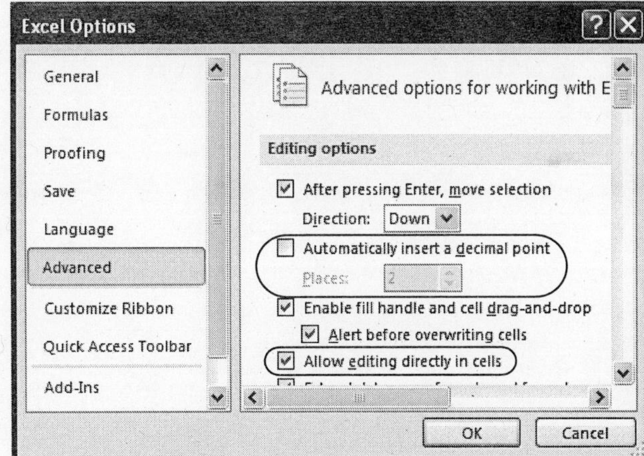

Figure 5.23 Excel Options with Advanced Properties

Entering Text

Text entries can include *alphabetical characters, numbers* and *symbols.*

To enter text in a cell, do this:

1. Select the cell, type the text entry, and then enter the text by clicking the **Enter** button in the formula bar or by pressing Enter key.

- To enter numbers as text, type an apostrophe (') followed by the number, for example, '45,000. *Alternatively*, place an equal sign in front of the numbers and enclose the number in quotation marks. For example, to enter the number 45,000 as text, type ="45,000".
- Notice that in a cell with the General format, numbers entered as text will align on the left like text. When you enter a number as text, you can still use the number if it is needed in a numeric formula.

Example 6

How do you quickly format a range of numbers as text in your worksheet by using the Text numeric format?

Solution

1. Select the range of cells containing the numbers.
2. Select the **Text** option from the drop-down list of the **Number** group from the **Home** Tab (See Figure 5.24). *Alternatively,* press Ctrl+1 keys or click on the **Home** tab and then in the **Number** group, click the **Dialog Box Launcher**. In this dialog box, click on the Number tab, and select the Text from the Category list: and click OK.

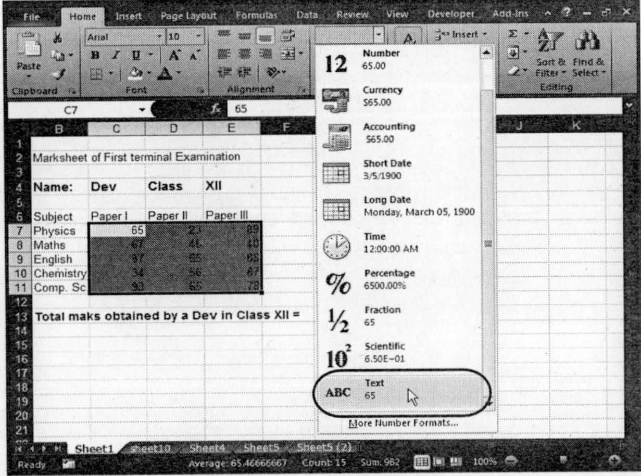

Figure 5.24 Drop-down list

Entering Numbers

Numbers are having constant values and contain the following characters given in Table 5.2.

Table 5.2 Special Characters for Numeric Entries

Character	Function
0 through 9	Any combination of numerals.
+	Indicates exponents when used in conjunction with E, such as 3E+3 means $3x10^3$.
–	Indicates negative number.
()	Indicates negative number.
, (comma)	Thousands marker.
/	Fraction indicator (when fraction is preceded by a space) or date separator.
$	Currency indicator.
%	Percentage indicator.
. (period)	Decimal indicator.
E	Exponent indicator.
e	Exponent indicator.
:	Time separator.
(single space)	Separators of compound fractions (e.g 4 1/2); and date time entries (e.g 1/2/94 5:00).

➔ To enter a number, do this:

1. Select the cell, type the number, and then press Enter key or click the Enter button in the Formula bar.
2. You can enter *integers*, such as 145; *decimal fractions*, such as 145.437; *integer fractions*, such as 1 1/2; or *scientific notation*, such as 1.45437E+2.

☞ *Entering a number as text enables the number display to exceed the cell's width. If you enter a number in the normal way and the cell is not wide enough to display it, the cell fills with # signs or in some cases may display the number in scientific notation.*

Excel 2010 stores the numbers typed into a cell as well as the format or appearance in which the numbers should be shown. When you enter a number into a cell, Excel tries to establish how the number should be formatted. For example, it accepts and displays the entries listed in Table 5.3 with the formats indicated. The entries of the Table 5.3 are displayed in Figure 5.25, as entry would appear in an Excel 2010 worksheet.

Table 5.3 Excel's Automatic Formats

Typed Entry	Chosen Format	Result
897	Number, General	897
7999 Mg Rd.	Text, left aligned	7999 Mg Rd
450.09	Number, dollar format	$450.09
54.6%	Number, percent format	5460.00%
(678)	Number, negative	-678
2 3/4	Number, fraction	2 3/4
45600	Number, comma format	45,600.00
-678	Number, negative, decimal	-678.00
1/5/07	Date, m/d/yyyy	01/05/2014
4/5	Date, m/d/yy (current year assumed)	05-Apr

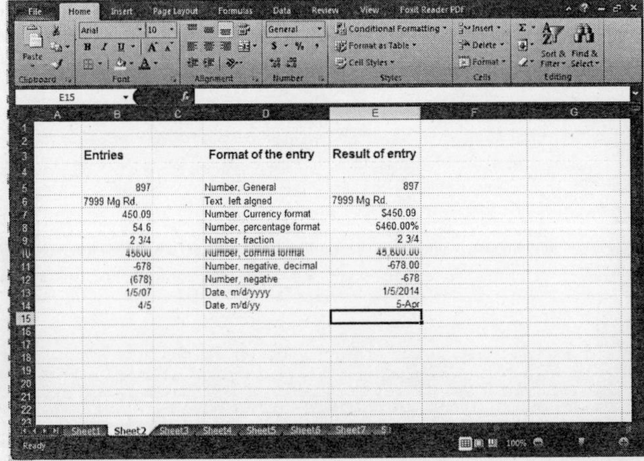

Figure 5.25 Automatic formats done for data given in Table 5.3

☞ *Entering a number as text enables the number display to exceed the cell's width. If you enter a number in normal way and cell is not wide enough to display it, the cell gets fills with # signs or in some cases may display the number in scientific notation.*

➔ To control fixed decimal option, do this:

1. Click the **File** Tab and then click **Options**. Excel Options dialog box appears. In this dialog box, click on **Advanced** button on the left side. **Excel Options** dialog box appears with **Advanced** properties as shown in Figure 5.23.

2. Click the Automatically insert decimal point: check box under the **Editing options** group so that the check mark does not appear (See Figure 5.23).
3. Click OK.

☞ *Using fixed decimal representation feature of Excel 2010, you can automatically add decimals to every value entered in a worksheet.*

Entering Date and Time in a Worksheet

Excel 2010 automatically understands date and time typed in most of the common ways. When you type a *date* or *time*, Excel converts your entry to a serial number. The serial number represents the number of days from the beginning of the century until the date you type. Time is recorded as a decimal fraction of a 24-hour day.

If your entry is recognized as a valid date or time format, you see the date or time on-screen. Correctly entered dates appear in the formula bar with the format **mm/dd/yyyy**, regardless of how the cell is formatted. Here, **mm** for month, **dd** for day and **yyyy** is for year.

For example, if you type 2 March 14 in a cell formatted to show numbers with a comma and two decimal places (#,##0.00), you will see that date as **41,700.00.**

If Excel 2010 does not recognize the entry as a valid date or time format and you type a text date, such as Apr 5 14, Excel treats the entry as text. It aligns it to the left in the cell.

Example 7

Explain the step to be followed to enter date in different formats.

Solution

1. Select the cell in which you want to enter the date.
2. Type the date into the cell with any of the following formats. For example to enter 7th March 2014 type:
   3/7/14
   7-Mar-14
   7-Mar (The year from the system date is used)
   Mar-14 (Only the month and year are shown)
   3/7/14 0:00

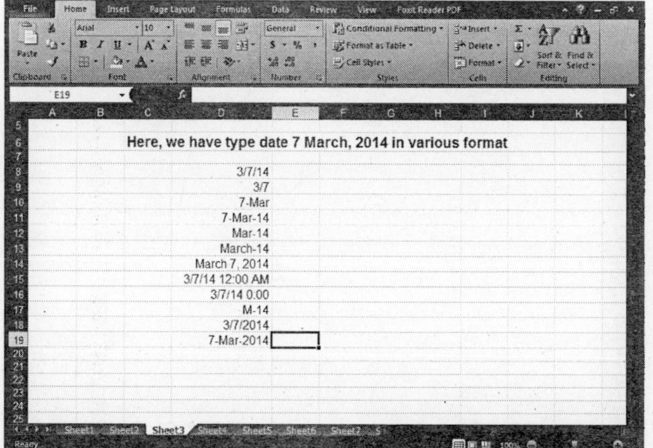

Figure 5.26 Various ways to enter date in a worksheet

You can also enter the dates as **3/7, 03/07/14, Mar-14**, or **March 7, 2014** (See Figure 5.26). In any of these date formats, you can use either /, -, or space to separate different elements.

Example 8

How do you enter time in an Excel 2010 worksheet?

Solution

1. Select the cell in which you want to enter the time.
2. Type the time in any of the following formats. For example to enter **1:32 PM**, type:
   13:32
   13:32:45
   1:32 PM
   1:32:45 PM
   3/7/14 13:32

The first two examples are from a 24-hour clock. If you use a 12-hour clock, follow the time with a space and A, AM, P, or PM (in either upper or lowercase letters).

☞ *Leave a space before the AM or PM. Do not mix a 24-hour clock time with an AM or PM. As the last format shows, you can combine the date or time during entry.*

➜ **To enter the current date/time in a cell, do this:**

1. To enter the current date select the cell and press Ctrl+; keys together.
2. To enter the current time select the cell and press Ctrl+: keys together.

☞ *To format a date in the default date format, press* Ctrl+# *keys together. To format a time in the default time format, press* Ctrl+@ *keys together.*

5.8.3 Creating Text, Number and Data Series

Creating Text

To create text in a cell, position the cell pointer at the desired cell address and then type the entry from the keyboard. For example, to enter text **Entering text** in cell address A1, do the following steps:

1. Move the mouse-pointer to cell address **Al** and click the left mouse button just once. Instantly, the cell pointer changes like rectangle shape at cell address **Al** (See Figure 5.27).
2. Now type entering text in a cell.
3. Then press the Enter key from the keyboard. Your workbook will look like as shown in Figure 5.27.
4. Text entries are normally used as row and column headings, for entering phone numbers, addresses, etc. All texts are left aligned. And a formula cannot be applied over text entries.

Each cell has a default width of 9-10 characters, i.e., each cell can hold up to 9-10 characters. In case, the entry of cell address is more than its default width, its display gets extended to the next cell. This does not mean that it has occupied the space of the next cell. It has just got displayed over it.

For example, entering text in a cell at cell address A1. You will observe that the type text gets extended to the next cell B1 (See Figure 5.27).

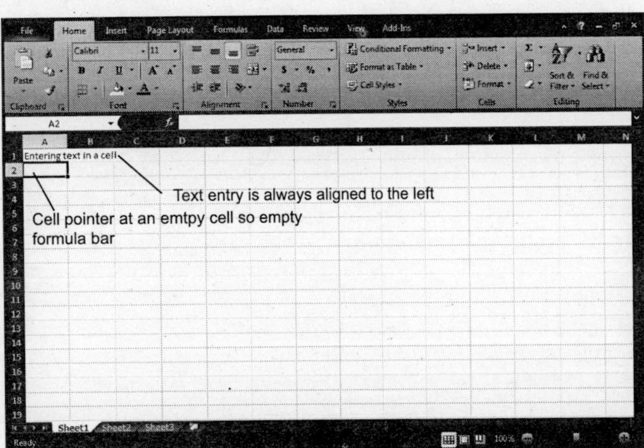

Figure 5.27 Creating text in a cell

Although the label occupying two cell addresses (Al and B1) it is normally in cell address A1. To find out cell, in which the text is actually displayed, do this:

- Click the left mouse button over the cell address B1. You will see that the Formula bar does not display the text entry.
- Now, click the left mouse-button over the cell address A1. You will see that the Formula bar displays the text Entering text in a cell.

Using Number and Date Series

Excel 2010 makes it very easy to enter a series of dates, number or text. For example, you can insert column heading like *Jan, Feb, Mar*, etc., or enter number at equal intervals, such as 2, 4, 6, 8, etc., very easily.
You can enter the above type of series in two ways:

1. Using the mouse to drag the fill handle.
2. Using a command that gives you the capability to create many types of series.

☞ *Dragging the fill handle to the right and down fills the series in increasing order; dragging the fill handle up or left fills the series in decreasing order.*

Creating a Linear Series

➜ To create a linear series, do this:

1. Enter the first two elements of data in the series in adjacent cells, namely 1 and 3 in cells B6 and C6 (See Figure 5.28). Excel uses these two data items to determine the amount of increment in each step and the starting number for the series.
2. Select these two cells and then drag the fill handle *down* or *right* to fill in increasing and drag the fill handle *up* or *left* to fill in decreasing order. The fill handle is the small square located at the lower right corner of a selection (See Figure 5.28).
3. Release the mouse button.

☞ *The area enclosed with the gray border fills with a series of numbers determined by the first two cells you selected.*

Example 9

Create a series of linear data with the help of AutoFill command.

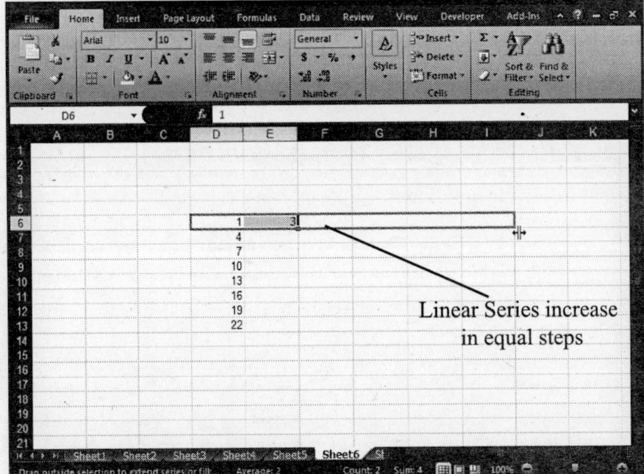

Figure 5.28 Creating a Linear series

Solution

1. In the first cell, enter the starting *number*, if you want the range to be filled with values that increment by one. If you want the range filled with values that increment differently, fill the first cell in the range with the initial value and the second cell in the range with the second value that increases or decreases as you want the series to be increased or decreased.
2. Select the range of cells containing numbers used as starting values for the series. At the lower-right corner of the selection is the square fill handle.
3. Select the range to be filled by dragging the fill handle with the *right mouse button*. Release the right mouse button to display the shortcut fill menu as shown in Figure 5.29.

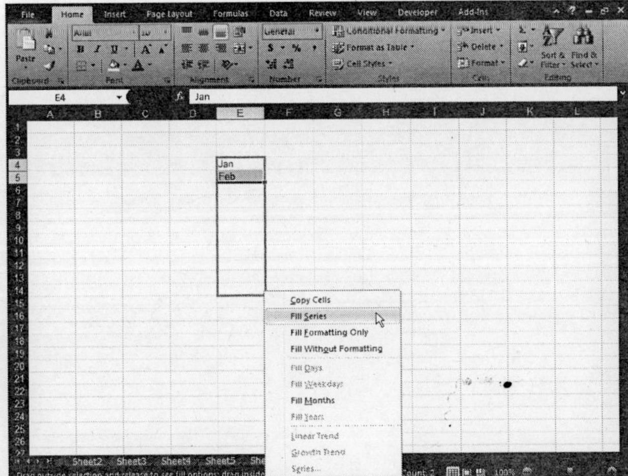

Figure 5.29 Shortcut Fill menu

Some of the options of shortcut menu are as follows:

Command	Description
Fill Series	Fills the selection with values that is increased by one from the value in the first cell.
Fill Days	Fills the selection with days that is increased by one starting from the day in the first cell.
Fill Weekdays	Fills the selection with weekdays that is increased by one beginning with the day in the first cell.
Fill Months	Fills the selection with months that is increased by one beginning with the year in the first cell.
Linear Trend	Fills the blank cells in the selection with linear regression (best fit) values. Starting values are not overwritten. This command is only available when more than one cell is filled with a starting value.
Growth Trend	Fills the blank cells in the selection with values calculated from growth (exponential) regression. Starting values are not overwritten. This command is only available when more than one cell is filled with a starting value.
Series	Displays the Series dialog box.

4. Select the option as shown in the Table given above that you want.

Example 10

Create a number series with the help of Fill Series dialog box.

Solution

1. In the first cell, enter the *first number* or *date*.
2. Select the range of cells you want to be filled.
3. Click on **Home** Tab and then in **Editing** group, click on the **Fill** drop-down list and then choose Series... to display the Series dialog box (See Figure 5.30).
4. Click the Rows or Columns option that matches the type of range you want filled. This is automatically selected to match the orientation of the cells you choose.
5. Select the Trend check box if you want selected values to be replaced by values for a linear or exponential best-fit. This selection limits Step 6 to Linear or Growth options.
6. Select one of the following Type options:

Option	Description
Linear	Adds the Step Value to the preceding number in the series.
Growth	Multiplies the Step Value by the preceding number in the series.
Date	Enables the Date Unit group so that the increment applies to a Day, Weekday, Month, or Year.
AutoFill	Creates automatic series that may include text dates and labels.

7. Depending on the kind of series you want to create, use one of the following sets of steps.

➜ To create a Linear or Growth, do this:

1. In the Step value: box enter the step value. This number is the constant amount by which the series changes from cell to cell. The Step Value may be positive or negative.
2. In the Stop value: box enter a value at which you want to stop the fill. This is required only if you think that you highlighted too many cells when you selected the range to fill.
3. Click OK.

➜ To create Date Series, do this:

1. Click the Date unit area of the Series dialog box (See Figure 5.30).
   Select either Day, Weekday, Month or Year to designate the date increment. Note that *Weekday* gives you dates without *Saturdays* and *Sundays*.
2. To specify the increment amount, enter the Step value in the Step value box. If the starting value is **12/1/2013**, and you choose Month as the Date Unit and 2 as the Step Value, the second date in the series becomes **2/1/2014**.

☞ *When the series reaches either the end of the selected range or the Stop Value, Excel stops filling the cell. If you use a negative Step Value, the Stop value must be less than the starting value.*

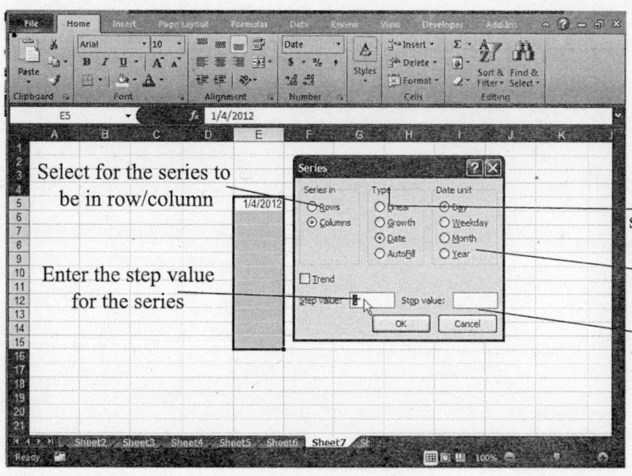

Figure 5.30 Series dialog box

3. To stop the series enter the Stop value in the Stop value: box (e.g. **12/1/2014**). The stop value indicates the last date in the series.
4. Click OK.

Creating Series of Text and Headings

Excel can extend series of headings which are not dates or numbers. For example, there may be a text headings that includes a number, such as *Trend, Quarter, Task*, etc., (See Figure 5.31).

The text series that Excel recognizes includes the text shown in Table 5.4.

Table 5.4 Text Series Recognized by Excel

Type	Example
Day	Tuesday, Wednesday, or Tue, Wed
Month	September, October, or Sep, Oct
Text	Project, Task
Text number	Task 1, Task 2, Paragraph 1.2, Paragraph 1.3
Quarterly	Quarter 1, Quarter 2, Qtr 2, Qtr 3, Q1, Q2

The AutoFill feature in Excel recognizes key words, such as days of the *week*, *month* names, and *Quarterly* abbreviations. Excel extends a series to repeat correctly, namely, Qtr1 follows Qtr4 and then the series continues.

➜ **To type in a custom list for use with AutoFill, do this:**

1. Click the **File** Tab and then click **Options**. Excel Options dialog box appears. In this dialog box, Click on **Advanced** button on the left side. Excel Options dialog box appears with Advanced properties. In this dialog box, under the **General** group, click on the Edit Custom Lists... Custom Lists dialog box appears as shown in Figure 5.32.
2. Select NEW LIST in the Custom lists: box.
3. Select the List entries: list box, and type each item you want in the list. Press Enter to separate items.

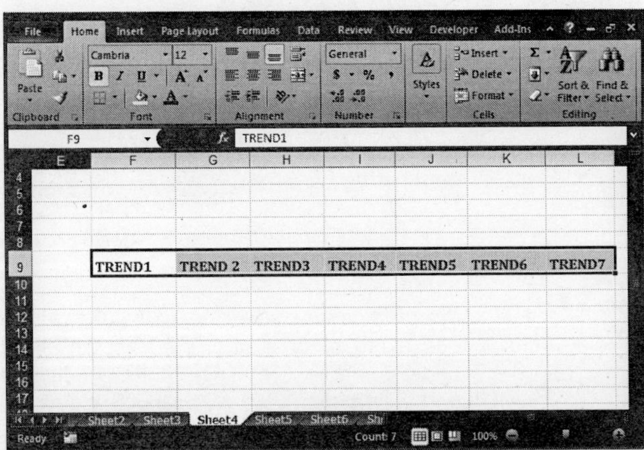

Figure 5.31 Headings that are not Dates or Numbers in a Series

4. To add the list to the Custom lists: list box, click Add. Your list appears in the Custom lists: list box.
5. Click OK if you have no more lists to enter. If you have additional lists to enter, select NEW LIST from the Custom Lists list box, and then begin typing your list in the List entries: list box.

➜ **To add a list that is in a range of cells on the worksheet, do this:**

1. Select the cells that contain the list you want to create. Now follow the Step 1 as given above.
2. The selection range appears in the **Import list from cells:** box you can reselect the list by clicking the arrow on the right.
3. After the selection is final, click Import, and then click **OK**.

The list you create is stored in Excel file. The list can then be used in any other worksheet also.

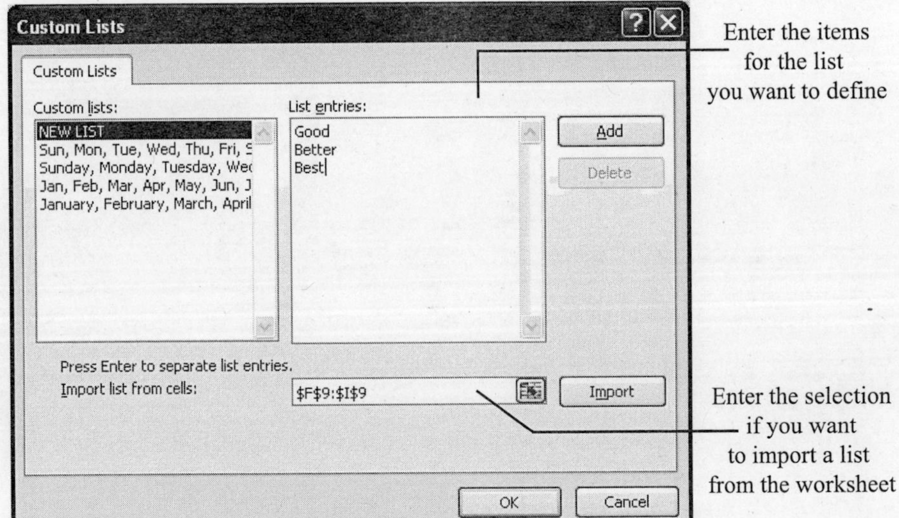

Figure 5.32 Custom Lists Dialog box

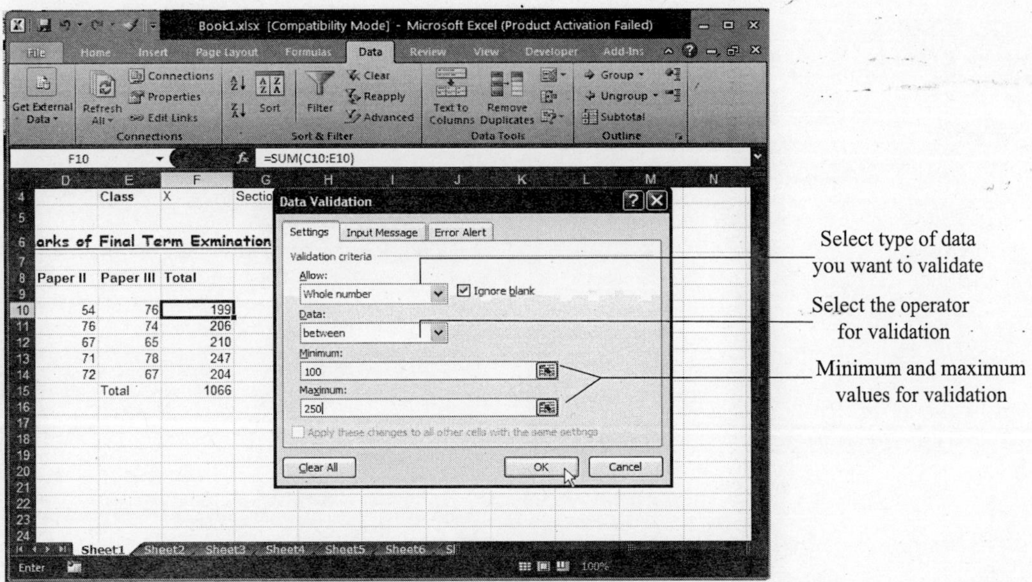

Figure 5.33 Data Validation dialog box with Setting tab Selected

5.8.4 Validation of Data

Validate Data feature of Excel 2010 controls the creation of input criteria for a cell or range of cells. It can either prompt the user for the correct information or can display an error message if the data entered does not match the criteria.

☞ *Data validity is a check to determine whether data entered into a cell is valid, defined by a set of criteria that you may set.*

➜ **To specify the data validation settings, do this:**

1. Select a cell or range of cells for which you want to validate data.
2. Click on the **Data** Tab and then click arrow next to **Data Validation** button under the **Data Tools.** Then select the Data Validation from the drop-down list to open the Data Validation dialog box.
3. In the Data Validation dialog box, click the **Settings** tab property sheet (See Figure 5.33).
4. Select the type of data to be validated from the **Allow** drop-down list.
5. Select an operator for validation from the **Data:** drop-down list.
6. Enter the appropriate values in **Minimum:** and **Maximum:** collapsable box.

➜ **To specify an input message, do this:**

1. Click the **Input Message** tab in **Data Validation** dialog box after specifying the settings property sheet (See Figure 5.34).
2. Click the **Show** input message when cell is selected so that the check box is ticked.
3. In the **Title:** box enter a title for the message. This is displayed in Bold in the message box (See Figure 5.34).
4. Type the text of the message in the **Input message:** box. This message is displayed below the title (See Figure 5.34). The message can be upto 255 character long. Press Enter key to start a new text in the message.

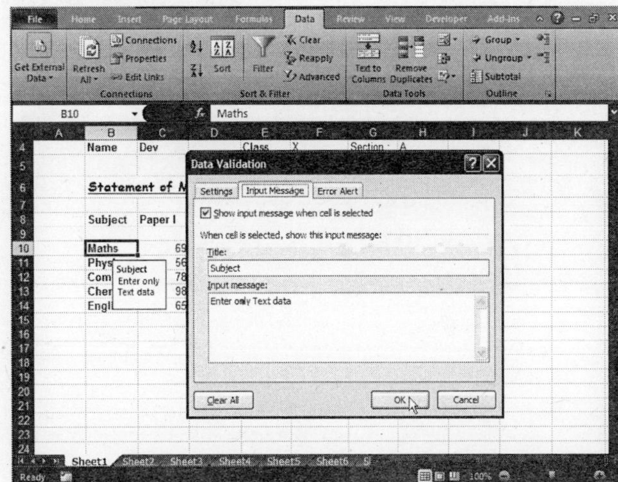

Figure 5.34 Data Validation dialog box with Input Message box Selected

5. Click OK to save settings.

➜ **To specify an error alert, do this:**

1. Click the **Error Alert** tab in the Data Validation dialog box after specifying your settings property sheet (Figure 5.35).
2. Click the **Show** error alert after invalid data is entered, so that the check box is checked.
3. Select a **Style:** for the message from the drop-down list.
4. Enter a Title for the message in the **Title:** box.
5. Enter the text for the error message in the **Error message:** box.
6. Click OK to save your settings.

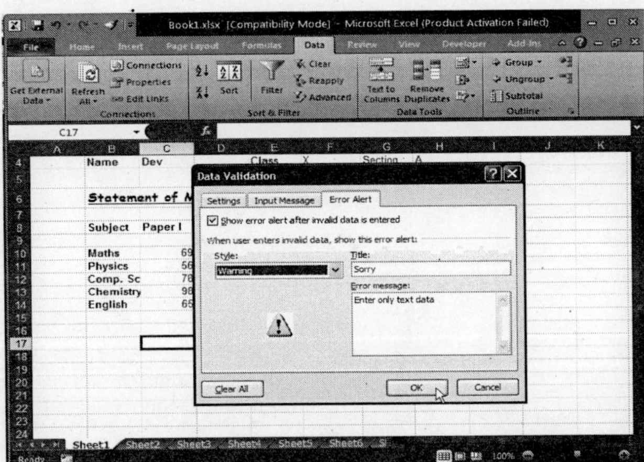

Figure 5.35 Data Validation Dialog Box with Error Alert tab Selected

5.8.5 Editing Worksheet Data

While editing a cell entry, you can edit the text either in the formula bar or in the cell itself.

Editing Cell Entry in the Formula Bar

➜ **To edit cell entry in the formula bar, do this:**

1. Select the cell containing the data you want to edit.
2. Move the insertion point into the text in the formula bar. Position the pointer in the text you want to edit, and then click. A flashing insertion point indicates where typing and editing take place.
3. Edit the cell entry or type new text.

Editing Directly in a Cell

➜ **To edit an entry directly in a cell, do this:**

1. Double-click the selected cell or press F2 key.
2. Press the arrow keys to move the I-beam that marks the insertion point to where you want to edit.
3. Make the desired changes to the cell entry.
4. Press Enter key to change the text. Alternatively, press Esc key to leave the contents unchanged.

5.9 MOVING AND COPYING DATA AND FORMULAS

5.9.1 Moving and Copying Cell Contents

Cutting and pasting is a valuable function for reorganizing a worksheet. You may *cut out* a range of cells to *paste* them elsewhere. This operation can move cell contents, the format, and any note attached to the moved cells. You can also copy a range of cells and paste it into another location. This will copy cell contents which you want to copy and paste.

Moving and Copying Cell Contents by Dragging and Dropping

The easiest and most intuitive way to move or copy a cell or range of cells is to drag the cell or the range of cells to the new location and drop it.

Example 11

How do you move range of cells using drag-and-drop?

Solution

1. Select the cell or range of cells you want to move.
2. Move the mouse pointer over the selection's border. The pointer changes to an arrow.
3. Drag the pointer and the gray outline of the selection to the new location. Drag past the edge of a window to make the window scroll. Figure 5.36 shows the wide gray border that encloses the area to be moved.

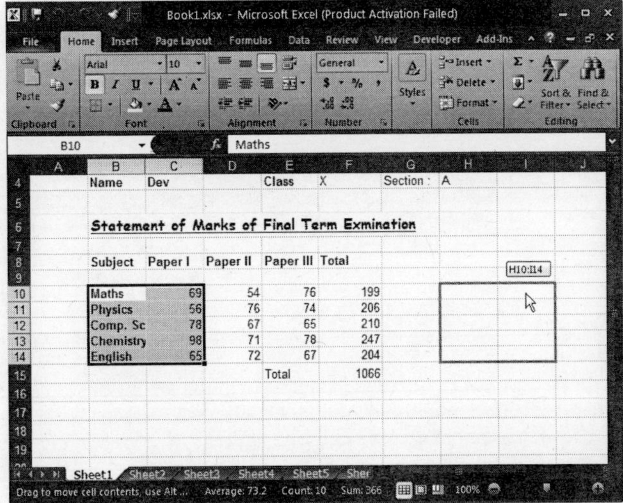

Figure 5.36 Wide Gray Border Enclosing the area to be moved

Notice that as you move, you see the range reference where the selection will be pasted.

4. Release the mouse button when the gray outline is where you want to place the selected range.

Example 12

How do you copy range of cells using drag-and-drop?

Solution

1. Select the range of cells you want to copy.
2. Hold down the Ctrl key and move the pointer over an edge of the selection. The pointer becomes an arrow with a + (plus) sign.
3. Continue holding down Ctrl key as you drag the edge of the selection to where you want to copy. The copy's location appears enclosed by a wide gray border, as shown in Figure 5.37.

☞ *Using the drag-and-drop method, you can make only a single copy. You cannot copy to multiple locations.*

If you release the Ctrl key before you release the mouse button, the copy operation becomes a move operation. The plus sign next to the arrow disappears. You can press Ctrl key again to switch back to copy operation.

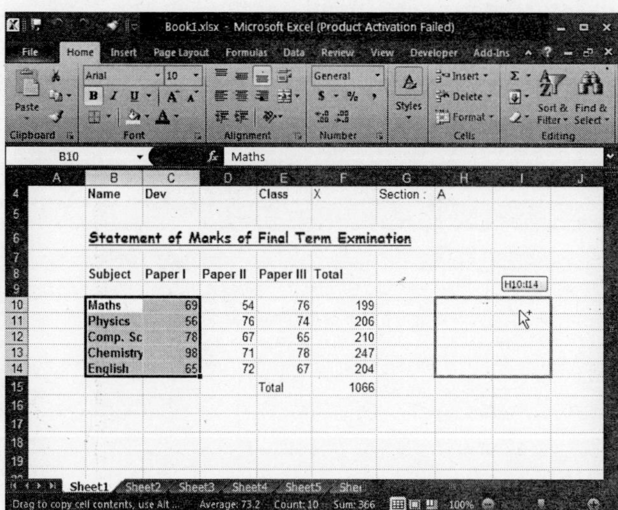

Figure 5.37 Selecting a portion of data to be copied to another place

Moving and Copying Cells with Ribbon

You can use drag-and-drop technique only when you want to move or copy data between different worksheets, or between panes in a split worksheet. But, when you want to move or copy data to another application, such as MS Word, you cannot use drag-and-drop technique. For this, you can use ribbon commands or shortcut keys as explained below.

➜ To move cell's contents using ribbon command, do this:

1. Select the cell or range of cells you want to move.
2. Click on the **Home** Tab and then click **Cut** button under the **Clipboard** group, or press Ctrl+X keys together. The cells you selected appear surrounded by a marquee – a moving dashed line.
3. Select the *cell* at the upper-left corner, where you want to paste the selected cells.
4. Click **Paste** button under the **Clipboard** group, or press Ctrl+V keys together to paste and retain the copy in memory. Press Enter key to paste only one time.

☞ *To copy a picture of the selected cell (s) instead of actual contents, click the down arrow of Copy button and then select Copy as Picture... option as shown below:*

➜ To copy cell's contents using ribbon command, do this:

1. Select the cell or range of cells you want to copy.
2. Click on the **Home** Tab and then click **Copy** button under the **Clipboard** group, or press Ctrl+C keys together. The cells to copy are surrounded by a marquee a moving dashed line.
3. Select the cell at the top-left corner, where you want the duplicate to appear. Check to see whether other cell contents will be overwritten.
4. Click **Paste** button under the **Clipboard** group, or press Ctrl+V keys together to paste and retain the copy in memory. Press Enter key to paste only one time.

Dragging and Inserting Cells

You can drag and insert a cell or range of cells so that existing cells can move aside. With this procedure, you do not have to insert cells to make room for new data.

☞ *This method would be used, if you want to retain the existing data and move it for inserting new data items.*

➜ To move and insert data, do this:

1. Select the cell or range of cells you want to move.
2. Move the mouse pointer over the selection's border. The pointer changes to an arrow.
3. Press and hold down the Shift key and drag the pointer to where you want the data inserted. The location where the data is inserted appears as a grayed partial cell boundary, as shown in Figure 5.38. As you drag, you also see the range reference where the selection will be inserted.

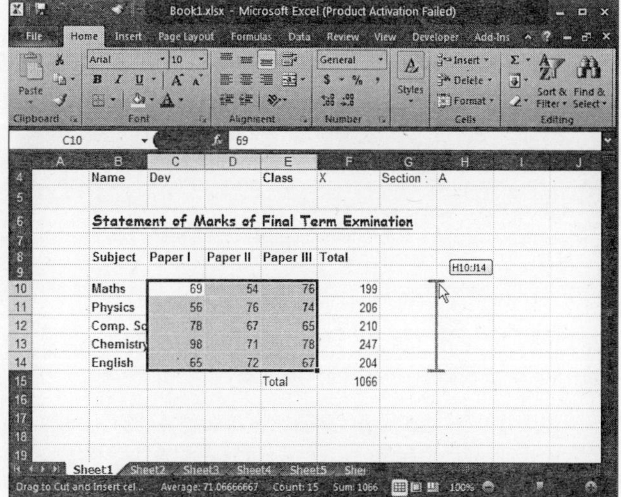

Figure 5.38 Dragging and Inserting cells

4. Continue holding down the Shift key as you release the mouse button.
5. Release the Shift key.

The cells you dragged are inserted at the location of the grayed boundary.

Inserting Cells with Copy Command

Pasted cell contents replace the cell contents they paste over. In some cases, you may want to copy and paste to insert the copied material into the worksheet so that *existing cell contents* are moved aside. You can do so by the following method.

➜ To copy and insert cells, do this:

1. Select the cell or range of cells you want to copy.

2. Click on the **Home** Tab and then click **Copy** button under the **Clipboard** group, or press Ctrl+C keys together. The copied cells are surrounded by a marquee.
3. Right-click the top-left cell of the paste area and then click **Insert Copied Cells** from the shortcut menu.
   Excel 2010 needs information about shifting of existing cells, therefore, it displays the Insert Paste dialog box shown in Figure 5.39.

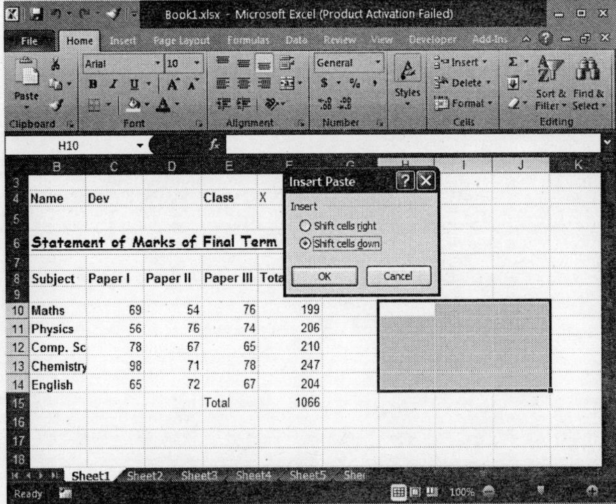

Figure 5.39 Insert Paste dialog box

4. Select from the following options:
   Shift cells right if you want cells being pasted over to move right.
   Shift cells down if you want cells being pasted over to move down.
5. Click OK.

Filling or Copying cell contents with Fill Handle

You can save a great deal of data-entry time with Excel 2010's Copy and Fill commands and many other shortcuts that copy or fill. Rather than typing each formula in a worksheet, you can type a few formulas and copy or fill them into other cells. You can also copy the formulas and format at the same time.

☞ *To fill multiple rows or columns at one time, select all the original cells and then use the Ctrl+drag procedure to fill the cells at one time.*

Using the Fill Handle

If you use a mouse and you need to fill data or formulas into adjacent cells then use the fill handle which is a black square at the lower-right corner of the selected cell or a range of cells. Dragging the fill handle across cells can fill the cells with copies or a series of data items.

☞ *Data series is a series of data items that contain a repeating pattern.*

➔ **To fill adjacent cells, do this:**

1. Select the cell or range of cells that contains the data or formulas.
2. Drag the fill handle so that the wide gray border encloses all cells to fill (See Figure 5.40).
3. Release the mouse button.

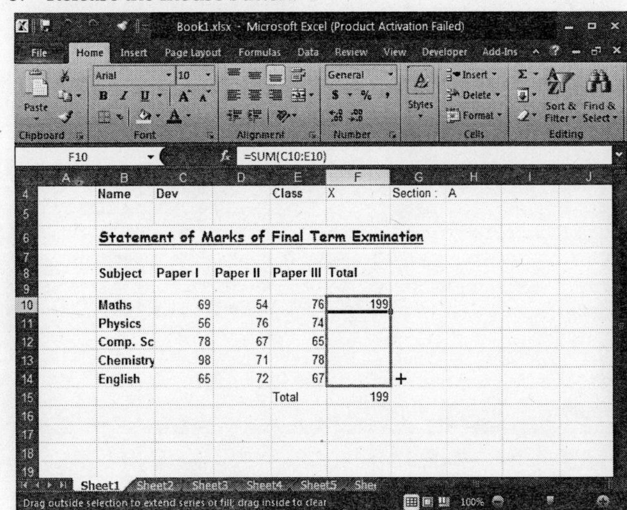

Figure 5.40 Using Fill Handle

Filling formulas into an area produces the same result as copying and pasting. Relative reference formulas adjust as though they were copied. Even if the formula references other spreadsheets, appropriate adjustments will *automatically* be made by Excel 2010.

Using Ctrl+Enter Keys to Fill Cells

You can fill cells as you enter data or formulas if you first select the adjacent cells or range of cells to fill. Next, type the formula or value in the active cell. Rather than pressing Enter key, press Ctrl+Enter keys. Formulas and values fill into all selected cells just as though you used a Fill or Copy and Paste command.

Fill Cells Using Command Button

You can also fill cells by first selecting the adjacent cells or range

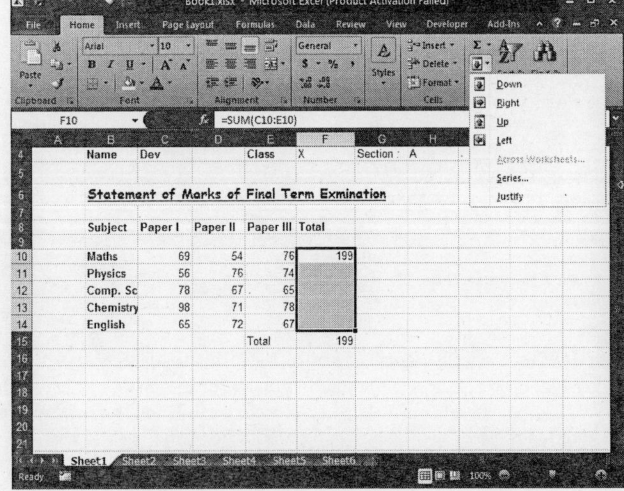

Figure 5.41 Fill Cells using Command button

of cell to fill and then clicking on the **Home** Tab, **Editing** group and click arrow next to **Fill** command, and then click **Down**, **Right**, **Up**, or **Left** option whatever you want (See Figure 5.41).

5.9.2 Using Paste Special Feature

Paste Special feature is very useful to copy and paste part of a cell's attributes, such as the format or value, but not both. With this command, you can reorient database layouts into worksheet layouts and vice versa. This command also enables you to combine the attributes of cells by pasting them together.

☞ ***Paste button of the Clipboard group places the contents of the Clipboard where the cursor is. The drop-down arrow of the Paste button called Paste Preview (shown below). It describes various ways to paste data. Point to an option for a description, click to select it.***

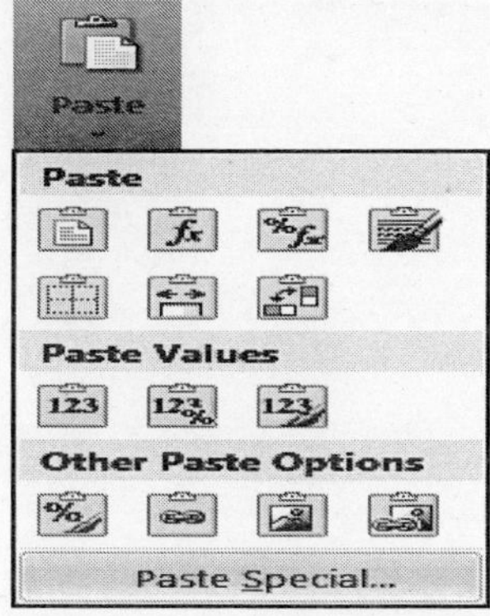

➜ To use Paste Special Feature, do this:

1. Select the cell or range of cells.
2. Click on the **Home** Tab and then click **Copy** button under the **Clipboard** group, or press Ctrl+C keys together.
3. Select the upper-left corner of the worksheet where you want to paste. When transporting (flipping) rows and columns, be sure to consider which cells are covered when the pasted area is rotated 90 degrees.
4. Click the arrow next to **Paste** button under the **Clipboard** group and then select **Paste Special...** to display Paste Special dialog box (See Figure 5.42).
5. Select the characteristics you want to be transferred as explained in the following Table:

Option	Function
All	Paste all the original contents and characteristics.
Formulas	Paste only the formulas.
Values	Paste only the values and formula results.
Formats	Paste only the cell formats.
Comments	Paste only note contents.
Validation	Paste data validation rules.
All using Source theme	Paste all cell contents and formatting using the theme.

(*Contd...*)

Option	Function
All except border	Paste everything except any borders applied to the selected range.
Column widths	Paste the width of one column to another.
Formulas and number formats	Paste formulas but not values with their number format.
Values and number formats	Paste only values with their number format.

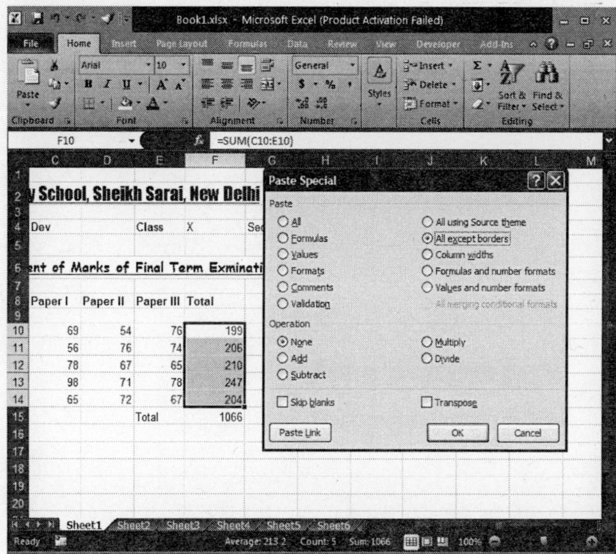

Figure 5.42 Paste Special dialog box

6. Select from the dialog box how you want the transferred characteristics or information combined with the cells being pastes into.

   Table below gives the different options and their functions.

Option	Function
None	Replaces the receiving cell.
Add	Adds to the receiving cell into which they are being pasted.
Subtract	Subtracts from the receiving cell into which they are being pasted.
Multiply	Multiplies by the receiving cell into which they are being pasted.
Divide	Divides into the receiving cell into which they are being pasted.

7. Select the Skip **B**lanks check box if you do not want to paste blank cells which you have selected when you copy a range.
8. Select the Transpos**e** check box to change rows to columns or to change columns to rows.
9. Click OK.

5.9.3 Inserting and Deleting Rows, Columns

With Excel 2010, you can delete or insert entire *rows* or *columns*. You can also easily delete or insert cells, leaving the surrounding rows and columns unaffected. This technique enables you to add or remove cells without having to change entire rows or columns.

Inserting Cells, Rows, or Columns

Sometimes you may need to insert cells, rows, or columns to make room for new formulas or data. You can insert cells, rows, or columns as easily as you can delete them.

➜ **To insert cells, do this:**

1. Select a cell or range of cells where new cells are to be inserted. Or, select cells in the rows or columns where you want to insert new rows or columns.
2. Select **Insert Cells...** option from **Insert** drop-down list of the **Cells** group of the **Home** Tab. *Alternatively*, press Ctrl + + (plus) keys or click the right mouse button and select **Insert...** . The Insert dialog box appears as shown in Figure 5.43.

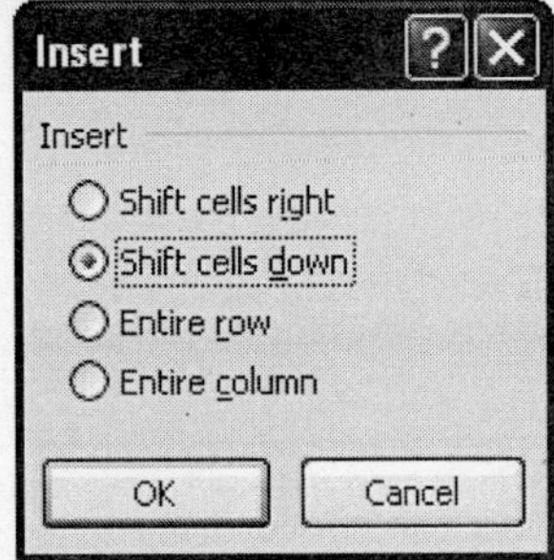

Figure 5.43 Insert dialog box

3. To insert cells, select the direction you want selected cells to be inserted.

The various options to insert cells are summarized in Table below.

Option	Function
Shift cells right	Selected cells move right.
Shift cells down	Selected cells move down.
Entire row	Insert a row at each selected cell.
Entire column	Insert a column at each selected cell.

4. Click OK.

➜ **To insert *rows* or *columns*, do this:**

1. Select cells in the *rows* or *columns* where you want to insert **new** rows or columns.
2. Select Insert Sheet Rows from **Insert** drop-down list of the **Cells** group of the **Home** Tab to insert rows (See Figure 5.11).
3. Select Insert Sheet Columns from **Insert** drop-down list of the **Cells** group of the **Home** Tab to insert columns.

Deleting Cells, Rows or Columns

The Delete command completely removes *cells*, *rows*, or *columns* from the worksheet. This is different from the **Clear** command in the **Editing** Group. The **Clear** command removes a cell's *contents*, *format*, or **comments**, but it leaves the cell intact.

➜ **To delete cells, rows or columns, do this:**

1. Select the cells or range of cells to be deleted, or select cells in the rows and columns to be deleted.
2. Click on the **Home** Tab and then click arrow next to **Delete** button under the **Cells** group and then select **Delete Cells...** as shown in Figure 5.44, or press Ctrl + - (minus) keys together, or click the right mouse button and select Delete... . The **Delete** dialog box appears (See Figure 5.45).

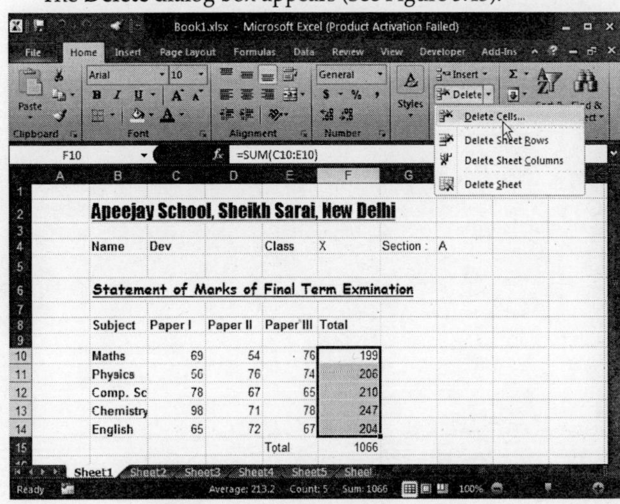

Figure 5.44 Selected group of cells

3. To delete cells, select the direction in which you want remaining cells to be moved.
4. Click OK.

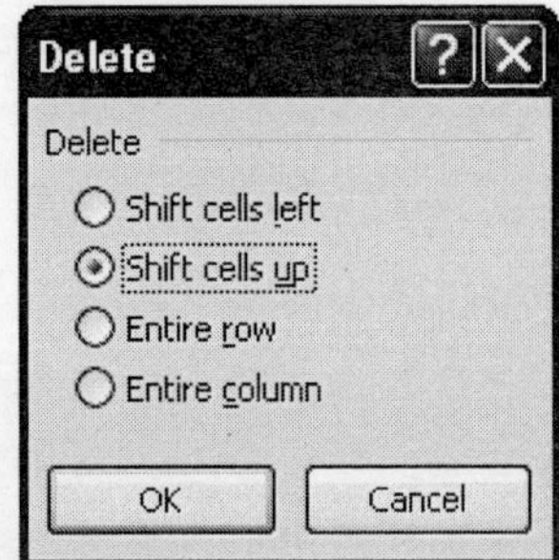

Figure 5.45 Delete dialog box

Option	Description
Shift cells left	Cells to right of the deleted cells move left.
Shift cells up	Cells below the deleted cells move up.
Entire row	Deletes entire row containing a selected cell.
Entire column	Deletes entire column containing a selected cell.

Clearing, Inserting or Deleting Cells in a Worksheet

After you have drafted and tested the worksheet, you may find that you need to reorganize or restructure the layout of the worksheet. When you restructure, you may need to insert or delete cells, rows or columns.

Shortcuts keys that are very helpful in reorganizing the worksheet layout are given in Table 5.5.

Table 5.5 Shortcut Keys for Changing the Worksheet Layout

key(s)	Action
Del	Clears selected formulas or contents; same as the **Home**, Tab, **Editing** Group and then Clear Contents.
Backspace	Clears the formulas bar; activates and clears the formula bar's contents.
Ctrl+C	Copies the selection so that it can be pasted; same as the the **Home** Tab, **Clipboard** Group and then **Copy** Command.
Ctrl+X	Cuts the selection so it can be pasted; same as the **Home** Tab, **Clipboard** Group and then **Cut** Command.
Ctrl+V	Paste at the selected cell; same as the **Home** Tab, **Clipboard** Group and then **Paste** Command.
Ctrl+Z	Undoes last command.
Ctrl+ Backspace	Repositions the worksheet so that the active cell is in view.

5.9.4 Changing Cell Height and Width

In order to improve the appearance of a worksheet or table in it, you can adjust *columns width* and *row height*. Thus, you can fit more data on a page. If need be, you can even hide confidential data.

How to adjust Column Width?

You can adjust the width of one or more columns to get better look in a worksheet. If a column is not wide enough to display a *number*, *date*, or *time*, Excel 2010 displays it using # characters in the cell. Therefore, you may need to adjust columns width to show complete information.

Example 13

Describe the ways by which you can adjust columns width.

Solution

Adjust column width with mouse

1. Select the columns for which you need to change the width.
2. Move the pointer onto the column separator to the right of the column heading (See Figure 5.46). Pointer changes to a two-headed, horizontal arrow.
3. Drag the column left or right until the column is of the required width. Then release the mouse button. The Width box that appears as you drag the column, displaying the numeric value for the column width.

Adjust column width using Ribbon

1. Select the columns that you want to change the width.
2. Under **Home** Tab, click **Cells** group and then click arrow next to **Format**. It pops up the menu (See Figure 5.47).
3. Use one of the following options to adjust column width.

Option	Description
Column Width...	The Column Width dialog box appears (See Figure 5.48). Type the width, and then click OK.
AutoFit Selection	This option adjusts the column width automatically.
Default Width...	This option would adjust to the default column width for all the selected columns.

4. Click OK.

➜ **To copy a column width, do this:**

1. Select cells in the columns that you want to copy the column width.
2. Click **Copy** button on **Clipboard** group of the **Home** Tab.
3. Select the cells where you want to apply this width.
4. Under the **Home** Tab, click the arrow next to the **Paste** button in the **Clipboard** group and then click **Keep Source Column Widths** button as shown in Figure 5.49 or choose Paste Special... . **Paste Special** dialog box appears .

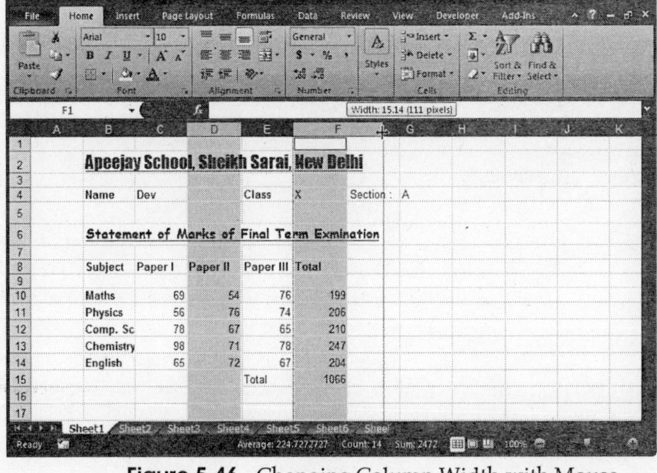

Figure 5.46 Changing Column Width with Mouse

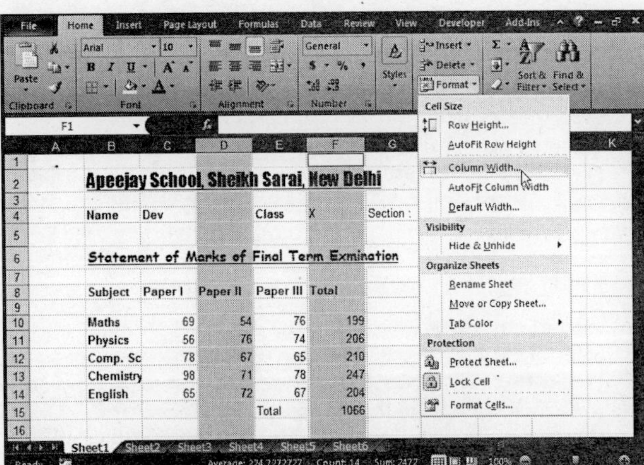

Figure 5.47 Format Column option

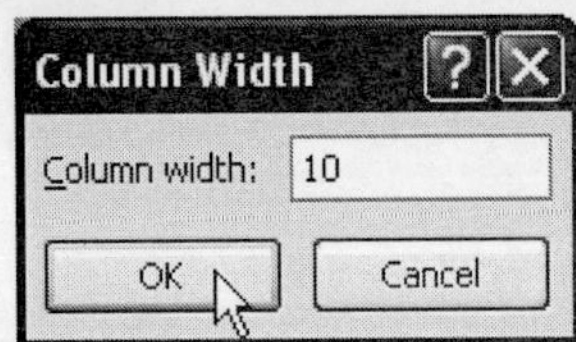

Figure 5.48 Column Width dialog box

Keep Source Column Widths button

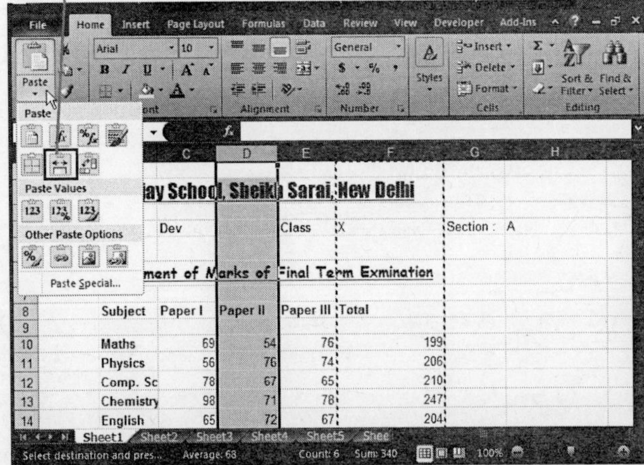

Figure 5.49 Copy column width using Paste options

5. In this dialog box, choose Column widths from Paste group.
6. Click OK.

5.9.5 Hide and Unhide Columns in a Worksheet

If you work on a large worksheet, you may not require to print or view the whole worksheet at one time. For this reason, you can hide columns temporarily so that they do not print or appear on the screen.

Example 14

(a) If you want to hide the confidential data in Excel 2010. How can you do this?
(b) Write the steps to unhide the data in Excel 2010.

Solution (a)

To hide confidential data, you have to hide the column(s). For this you have to follow the undermentioned steps:

1. Select the columns you want to hide.
2. *Using the mouse*: Move the mouse pointer over the column separator line that is on the right of the column you want to hide. The mouse pointer changes to a two-headed pointer. Drag the column separator left until crosses the separator on its left.
3. *Using the Ribbon*: Select the cells (or columns). Under **Home** Tab, click **Cells** group and then click arrow next to **Format**. Here, select Hide & Unhide from the **Visibility** Section. It pops up menu as shown in Figure 5.50. Here, select Hide Columns.

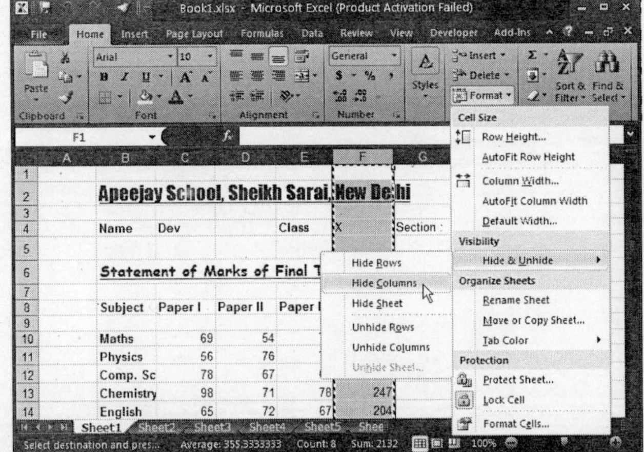

Figure 5.50 Hiding a column using Ribbon

Solution (b)

1. *Using the mouse*: Move the pointer over the column separator on the right of a hidden column. The mouse pointer changes to a two-headed pointer with space between the two heads (See Figure 5.51). Move the pointer so that its left tip touches the column separator. Drag the column separator to the right, and then release it.
2. *Using the Command button*: Select the cells (or columns) between which hidden columns appear. Under **Home** Tab, click **Cells** group and then click arrow next to **Format**. Here, select Hide & Unhide from the **Visibility** Section. It pops up menu as shown in Figure 5.50. Here, select Unhide Columns.

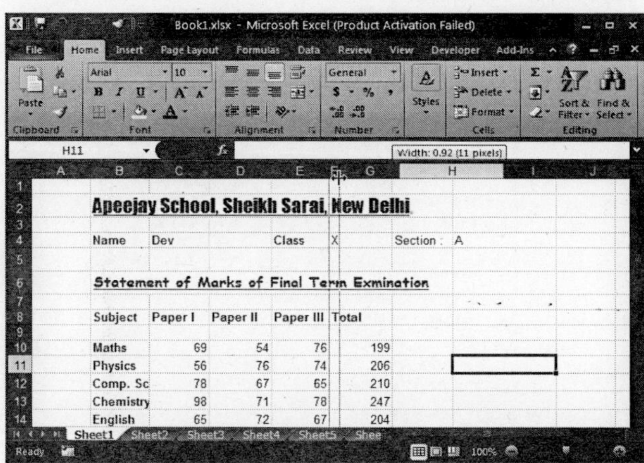

Figure 5.51 Unhiding a column using Mouse

How to adjust Row Height?

You can adjust row height in a worksheet to create enough space for *titles, subtotals, grand totals,* etc.

Example 15

How would you adjust row height?
(a) Using mouse
(b) Ribbon

Solution (a)

1. Select the rows for which you want to adjust the height.
2. Move the mouse pointer to the line directly under the header of the row you want to change. The mouse pointer changes to a two headed vertical arrow (See Figure 5.52).
3. Drag the two-headed arrow pointer up or down until the row is of the required height. Then release the mouse button. The screen tip displays the numeric value for the row height.

Solution (b)

1. Select a cell in each row you want to change.
2. Under **Home** Tab, click **Cells** group and then click arrow next to **Format**. It pops up menu (See Figure 5.47).

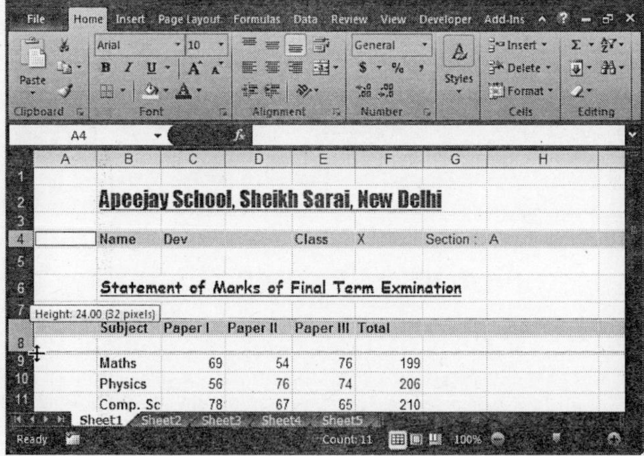

Figure 5.52 Changing row height with a mouse

3. Click from one of the following options.

Option	Description
Row Height...	To display the Row Height dialog box. Here, type the row height and click OK (See Figure 5.53).
AutoFit Row Height	Excel 2010 adjusts rows height automatically.

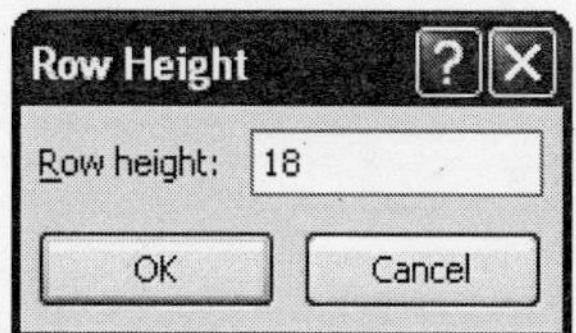

Figure 5.53 Row Height dialog box

5.9.6 Hide and Unhide Rows in a Worksheet

➜ To hide rows, do this:

1. Select a row or rows which you want to hide, in a worksheet.
2. *Using the mouse*: Move the mouse pointer over the row to separate, till it *changes* to double arrow. Now drag till the row is hidden or all the selected rows are hidden.
3. *Using the Ribbon*: Select the cells (or rows). Under **Home** Tab, click **Cells** group and then click arrow next to **Format**. Here, select Hide & Unhide from the **Visibility** Section. It pops up menu as shown in Figure 5.50. Here, select Hide Rows.

➜ To unhide rows, do this:

1. *Using the mouse*: Move the pointer over the row number that is under the hidden rows. Move the pointer up slowly until it changes to a double-headed pointer with space in between the two headings. Drag the line down to display the hidden rows.
2. *Using the Command button*: Select the cells (or rows) between which hidden rows appear. Under **Home** Tab, click **Cells** group and then click arrow next to **Format**. Here, select Hide & Unhide from the **Visibility** Section. It pops up menu as shown in Figure 5.50. Here, select Unhide Rows.
3. The hidden rows are displayed.

5.10 PROTECTING WORKBOOK

With Excel 2010, you can protect cells, graphical objects, sheets, windows and even an entire workbook. To prevent unauthorized people from changing the protection status or the display of hidden information, you can also use the password facility.

The procedure for protecting a worksheet and its contents involves two commands:

- The first command formats the cells or objects that you want protected.
- The second command turns on protection for a sheet or the entire workbook.

5.10.1 Protecting and Unprotecting Sheets

➜ To protect cell's content, do this:

1. Select the cell or range of cells that you want to protect or whose contents you want to hide from the formula bar.

2. Under **Home** Tab, click **Cells** group and then click arrow next to **Format**. Here, select Format Cells... or *alternatively*, press Ctrl+1 keys together and then click on the **Protection** Tab (See Figure 5.54).

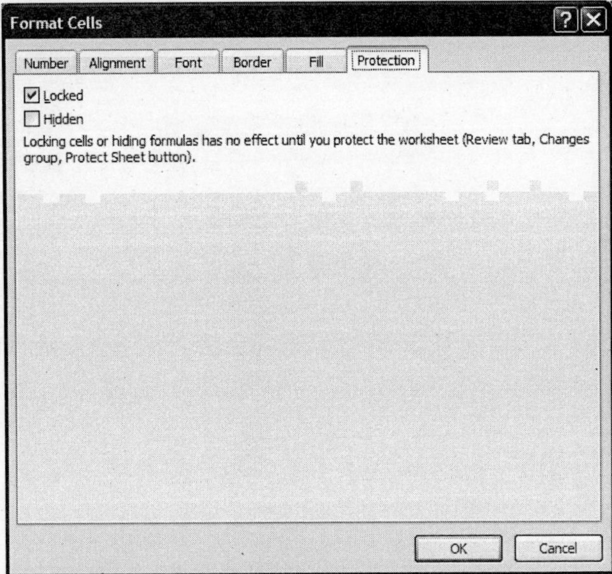

Figure 5.54 Protection tab of the Format Cells dialog box

3. Select the check box whichever you want.
4. Click OK.

☞ *Protecting cell is not useful unless you turn on the Protect Sheet Feature.*

➜ **To unprotect a cell's contents, do this:**

1. Select the cell or range of cells that you want to unprotect or whose contents you want to hide from the formula bar.
2. Under **Home** Tab, click **Cells** group and then click arrow next to **Format**. Here, select Format Cells... or *alternatively*, press Ctrl+1 keys together and then click on the **Protection** Tab (See Figure 5.54).
3. Clear the check box according to the requirement.
4. Click OK.

➜ **To turn on protection for a sheet, do this:**

1. Under **Review** Tab, click **Changes** group and then click **Protect Sheet**: It will display Protect Sheet dialog box (Figure 5.55).
2. Here, **In Allow all user of this worksheet to:** list box, select the elements that you want users to be able to change.
3. If you prefer, enter a password in the **Password to unprotect sheet:** text box.
4. Click OK.

➜ **To unprotect the sheet, do this:**

1. Under **Review** Tab, click **Changes** group and then click **Unprotect Sheet.** It will display Unprotect Sheet dialog box.
2. In this dialog box, type the password, if you give any to unprotect the sheet and then click OK.

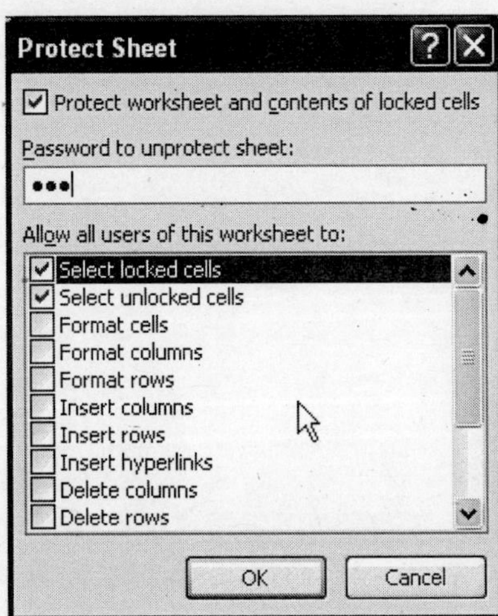

Figure 5.55 Protect Sheet dialog box

➜ **To protect the workbook, do this:**

1. Under **Review** Tab, click **Changes** group and then click arrow next to **Protect Sheet**. It will display Protect Structure and Windows dialog box (SeeFigure 5.56).
2. In this dialog box, click on the Structure check box if you want to protect the structure.
   Click on Windows check box if you want to keep workbook windows in the same size and position each time you open the workbook.
3. If you prefer, enter a password in the Password (optional): text box.
4. Click OK.

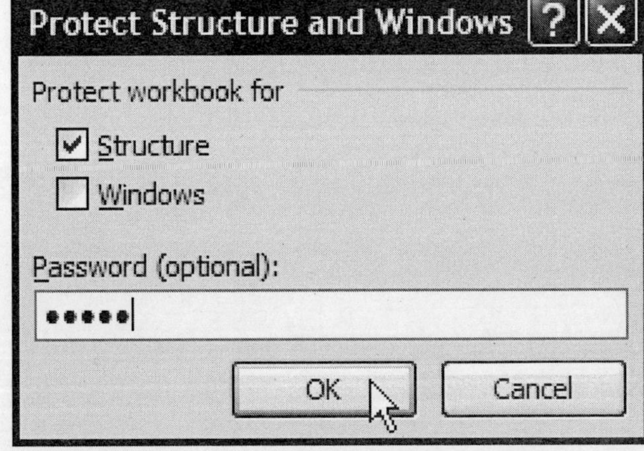

Figure 5.56 Protect Structure and Windows dialog box

5.11 FUNCTION AND CHARTS

5.11.1 Using Formulas

A formula is entered into a cell. It performs a calculation of some type and returns a result, which is displayed in the cell. Formulas in Excel always begin with an equal sign (=) and can include following types of data items:

a. *Numeric* and text values (constants)
b. Arithmetic operator, comparison operators, text operators, functions, parentheses
c. Cell references, and names

☞ *By combining these components, you can calculate the result you want by using the information in the worksheet.*

Excel also gives you the option to display formulas on a worksheet, or the results of the formulas.

➜ To control the display of formula result, do this:

1. Click the **File** Tab and then click **Options**.
   Excel Options dialog box appears. In this dialog box, click on **Advanced** button on the left side. Excel Options dialog box appears with **Advanced** properties as shown in Figure 5.57.

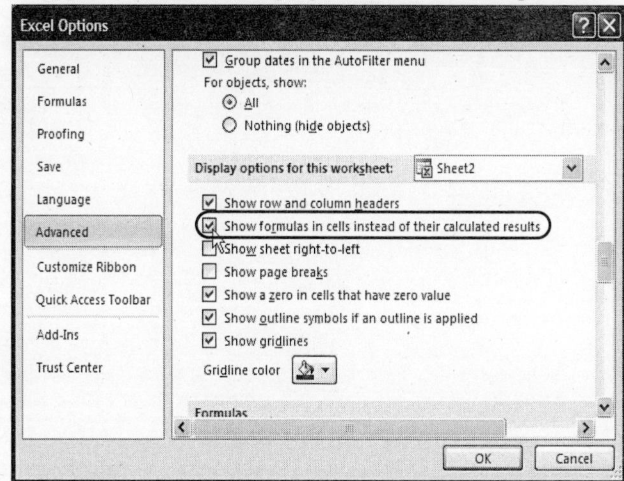

Figure 5.57 Excel Options with Advanced Properties

2. Click on the Show formulas in cells instead of their calculated results check box so that it appears under the **Display options for this worksheet:** group.
3. Click OK.

☞ *To switch between viewing formulas and the results of formulas, click Show Formulas button from the Formula Auditing group of Formulas Tab or alternatively, click* Ctrl + ` *keys pressed together* (See Figure 5.58).

When you display formulas, Excel automatically doubles the width of all columns (See Figure 5.58). The column widths will return to their original settings when you return to displaying the formula results. Formulas automatically recalculate and produce current results after you update data used by the formulas.

☞ *Make sure that you start the formula with an equal sign (=). If you forget an equal sign, Excel 2010 does not interpret the entry as a formula. For example, if you enter B12*D15 (with no equal sign), the B12*D15 is actually entered into the cell as text.*

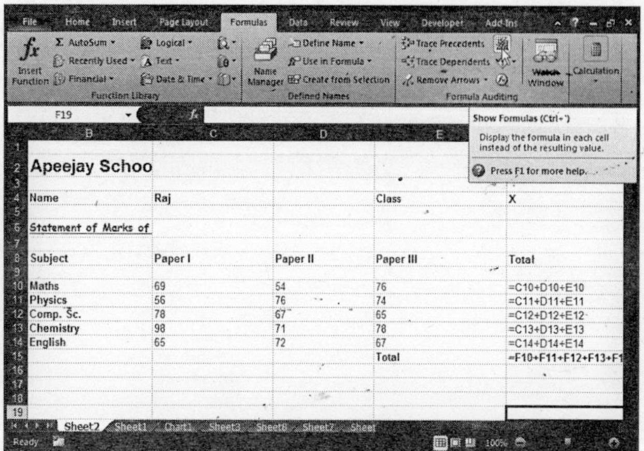

Figure 5.58 Formula displayed in cells

How to Enter Formulas?

To enter a formula, start a formula with an equal sign (=) and then construct the formula using *values, operators, cell references, functions,* and *names* to calculate the required result.

You can enter formulas either in the formula bar or in the cell. You can enter a formula using the formula bar by simply typing in it and pressing Enter. You can also enter a formula directly in the cell and bypass the formula bar.

☞ *Make sure you remember to start the formula with an equal sign (=). If you forget the equal sign, Excel 2010 does not interpret the entry as a formula. If you enter B12*D15 (no equal sign), then B12*D15 is actually entered into the cell as text.*

➜ To enter a formula in the formula bar, do this:

1. Select the cell in which you want to enter the formula.
2. Then click on the Formula bar and then type an equal sign (=).
3. Type a *value, cell reference, function,* or *name.*
4. If the formula is complete, press Enter or click the Enter box (a check mark) in the formula bar. If the formula is incomplete, go to Step 5.
5. Type an operator. There are many types of operators. The most common operators are math symbols, such as + (plus) and – (minus).
6. Return to Step 3.

➜ To enter a formula in a cell, do this:

1. Double-click the cell or select the cell and press F2 key in which you want to enter the formula and type an equal sign (=) (See Figure 5.59).
2. Type a value, cell reference, function, or name.
3. If the formula is complete, press Enter key. If the formula is incomplete, go to Step 4.
4. Type an operator.
5. Return to Step 2.

Always separate terms in a formula with operators or parentheses.

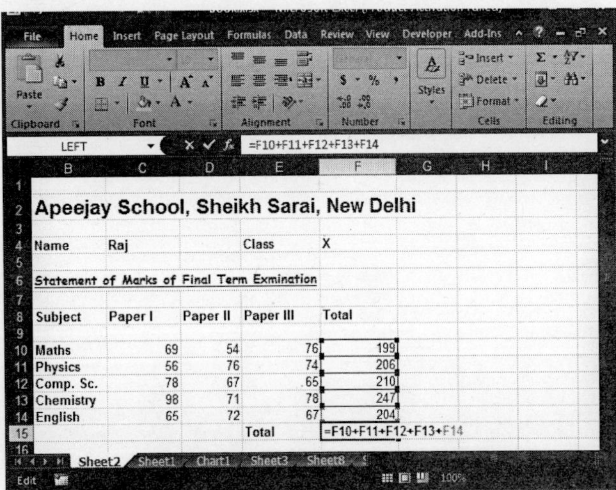

Figure 5.59 Entering a formula in Excel

Use the SUM function to Sum Several Ranges

To sum several ranges, simply refer to each of them, separated by a comma, using the SUM function.

➜ **To sum several ranges, do this:**

1. In cells A20:A26 enter prices from Rupee 1 to 100.
2. Select cells B20:B26 and type the formula = A20*8% to calculate the tax amount.
3. Press Ctrl+Enter keys together.
4. In Cells C20:C26 type some discount values from -1 to -3.
5. In Cell C28, sum all three columns with the following functions (See Figure 5.60).
   =SUM(A20:A26, B20:B26,C20:C26) (Figure 5.60).

	A	B	C
19	Price	Tax	Discount
20	56	4.48	-1
21	80	6.4	-1.5
22	82	6.56	-1.75
23	36	2.88	-2
24	57	4.56	-1.25
25	64	5.12	-1.75
26	26	2.08	-2
28		Total	=SUM(A20:A26,B20:B26,C20:C26)

Figure 5.60 Entering Sum function to several ranges

6. Press Enter key.

Moving or Copying Formula

When you move a formula from one cell to other, the cell references within the formula do not change. But when you copy a formula, then

- Absolute cell references do not change.
- Relative cell references will change when you copy a formula.

➜ **To move or copy a formula, do this:**

1. Select the cell that contains the formula you want to move or copy.
2. Point to the border of the selection.
3. To move the cell, drag the selection to the upper-left cell of the paste area. Excel 2010 replaces any existing data in the pasted area.
4. To copy the cell, hold down Ctrl key as you drag the mouse.

☞ *You can also copy formulas into adjacent cells by using the fill handle. Select the cell that contains the formula and then drag the fill handle over the range you want to fill.*

Entering Cell References

Cell references allow you to use values from different parts of a worksheet and execute and enables you to do the desired calculation. You can use any cell or group of cells in a formula.

☞ *The reference of the active cell is displayed in the name box at the left end of the formula bar.*

Entering the Cell References by Pointing

The easiest method of entering cell references in a formula is by pointing to the cell you want to include in a formula. Although you can type an entire formula, you often can make a typing error or misread the row or column headings. Say for example, you may end up with D52 in a formula when it should be E52.

☞ *When you point to a cell to include it in a formula, you actually move the pointer to the cell you want in the formula. It is found out only when you select the correct cells.*

➜ **To enter a cell reference into a formula by pointing, do this:**

1. Select the cell for the formula.
2. Type an equal sign (=).
3. Point to the cell you want it in the formula and click, or press the arrow keys to move the dashed marquee to the cell you want in the formula. The address of the cell you point to appears at the cursor location in the formula bar.
4. Enter an operator, such as the + symbol.
5. Point to the next cell.
6. Repeat the steps from Step 4 to continue the formula, or enter the formula by clicking the Enter box or pressing Enter key.

☞ *The cell reference in a formula changes after you copy the formula to a new location or after you fill a range with a formula. You would usually want formulas to use relative cell references, only.*

Using Cell References in Formulas

You refer to a cell's location with a *relative* reference or an *absolute* reference. Let us understand the difference in the two types of cell references.

Suppose that you are in your office, and you want someone to take a letter to the post office. Using a relative reference, you tell the person. "*Go out the front door; turn left cross the road and move two building then turn right and go to the second building.*" These directions are relative to your office location at the time you give the instructions. If you move to a different location, these directions are no longer valid.

To make sure that the letter gets to the mailbox no matter where you are then you give different set of directions. You must say something like this. *"Take this letter to the I.P. Estate post office."* No matter where you are when you speak, the post office is at one absolute location: I.P Estate.

☞ *Thus, the difference between relative and absolute reference is that in absolute reference, the cell is fixed once for all. In the relative reference it depends on the location where your pointer is.*

Using Relative References

A relative cell reference in a formula, is based on the relative position of the cell that contains the formula and the cell the reference refers to. If the position of the cell that contains the formula changes, the reference is changed. If you copy or fill the formula across rows or down columns, the reference automatically adjusts.

Excel uses relative referencing for cell addresses when you enter a formula.

In Figure 5.61, the formula in cell F10 is =C10+D10+E10. All these references are relative. The formula, translated into English, would read as follows:

F10 =C10+D10+E10

Apeejay School, Sheikh Sarai, New Delhi

Name	Raj		Class	X
Statement of Marks of Final Term Exmination				
Subject	Sem-I	Sem-II	Sem-III	Total
Maths	69	54	76	199
Physics	56	76	74	206
Comp. Sc.	78	67	65	210
Chemistry	98	71	78	247
English	65	72	67	204
			Total	1066

Figure 5.61 Formula entered with relative reference

"In cell F10, add the number in the 10th column to the left (C10), second column to the left (D10) and the adjacent column on the left (E10)" in the same row.

Suppose you copy formula across Column G, the formulas adjust their cell references to their new positions. The copied formulas are as follows:

Cell Containing Formula	A1 Format
G10	= D10+E10+F10
G11	= D11+E11+F11
G12	= D12+E12+F12

You will notice that the formulas change to give the cell references with relative position from the cell that contains the formula.

Using Absolute References

You use absolute references only to keep the cell reference values from changing as and when you copy a formula to a new location in a worksheets.

➜ **To enter an absolute reference by using the F4 key, do this:**

1. Type an equal sign (=) and the cell reference you want to be absolute.
2. Press F4, the absolute reference key, until the correct combination of dollar signs appears.

☞ *Indicate absolute references by putting a dollar sign ($) in front of the column letter or row number that you want to freeze or both (See Figure 5.62).*

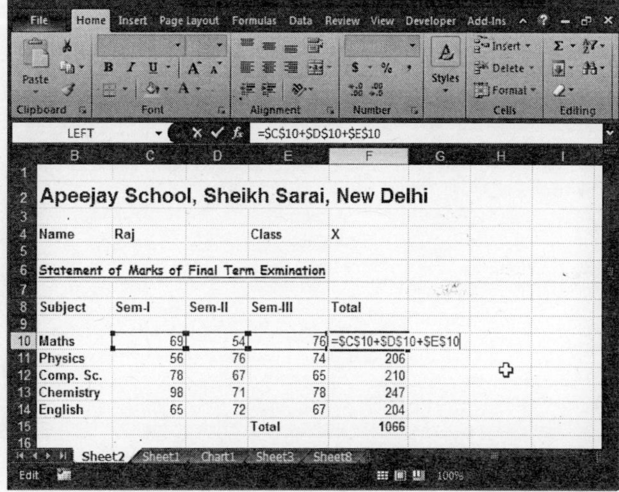
LEFT =$C$10+$D$10+$E$10

Apeejay School, Sheikh Sarai, New Delhi

Name	Raj		Class	X
Statement of Marks of Final Term Exmination				
Subject	Sem-I	Sem-II	Sem-III	Total
Maths	69	54	76	=$C$10+$D$10+$E$10
Physics	56	76	74	206
Comp. Sc.	78	67	65	210
Chemistry	98	71	78	247
English	65	72	67	204
		Total		1066

Figure 5.62 Formula with absolute reference

3. Type the next operator and continue to enter the formula, also.

You can use the F4 key when editing an existing formula.

Using Mixed References

In some cases, you may want either the row to stay fixed or the column to stay fixed when copying the cells from one place to other in a worksheet. In such cases, use a mixed reference. Such references contain both absolute and relative reference. For example, the reference $B5 prevents the column from changing, but the row changes relative to a new copied location. The dollar sign prevents the column from changing. In B$5, just the opposite occurs. The column adjusts to a new location but the row always stays fixed at 5 because the dollar sign prevents the row from changing.

You can create mixed references the same way as you can create absolute references. Type the dollar signs or specific row and column numbers without brackets or press F4 key. Each press of F4 cycles the cell reference to a new combination.

☞ *Each time you press F4, Excel 2010 cycles through all combinations of relative and absolute references. Press F4 four times, for example, and you cycle from B22 through $B$22, B$22, $B22, and B22.*

Referring to Other Sheets in a Workbook

You can also refer to other sheets in a workbook by including a sheet reference as well as a cell reference in a formula. For example, to refer to cell A1 on Sheet6, you would enter Sheet6!A1 in the formula.

You can use the mouse to enter a reference to a cell or range of cells on another worksheet in a workbook.

➜ To refer to cell or range in a different worksheet, do this:

1. Start entering the formula in the cell where you want the result to be appeared.
2. Click the sheet tab for the worksheet you want to refer to.
3. Select the cell or range that you want to refer to. The complete reference, including the sheet reference, appears in the formula bar (See Figure 5.63).

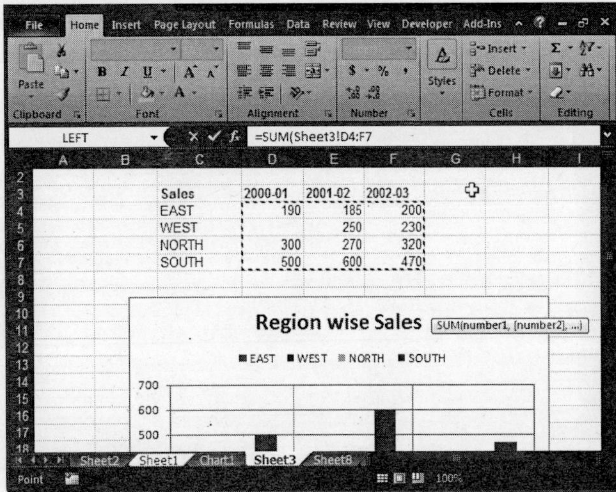

Figure 5.63 Referring a cell or range of cells in another worksheet

4. If the sheet name includes spaces, Excel surrounds the sheet reference with single quotation marks.
5. Finish the formula and press Enter key.

Entering 3-D References

You can use 3-D references to refer to a cell range that includes two or more sheets in a workbook. A 3-D reference consists of a sheet range specifying the beginning and ending sheets, and a cell range specifying the cells being referred to. Let us see an example of a 3-D reference:

=SUM(Sheet1:Sheet6!$E$1:$E$6)

This reference sums up the values in the range of cells $E$1:$E$6 in each of the sheets from Sheet1 to Sheet6, and adds the sums together resulting in a grand total.

➜ To use the mouse to enter the reference, do this:

1. Click for entering the formula in the cell where you want the result to appear.
2. Click the sheet tab for the first worksheet you want to include in the reference. Hold down the Shift key and click the last worksheet you want to include in the reference and then select the cells you want to refer to.
3. Finish the formula and press Enter key.

☞ *Notice the exclamation mark (!) that separates the sheet reference from the cell reference. If you have named the sheet, simply use the sheet name and then cell reference. If the sheet name included spaces, then surround the sheet reference with single quotation marks.*

5.11.2 Using Operators in Formulas

Operators are used in formulas to execute operations on the values taken by formulas. Excel uses four types of operations. These are given below.

Operators	Signs
Arithmetic	+, –, *, /, %, ^
Text	&
Comparative	=, <, <=, >, >=, <>
Reference	Colon (:), comma(,), space ()

Arithmetic Operator

How to use each of the arithmetic operators in formulas explained in the following example?

Example 16

Solution

Figure 5.64 shows the result of the use of arithmetic operator used in the following Table:

Operator	Formula	Result	Type of Operation
+	=5+2	7	Addition of 5 with 2
–	=5–2	3	Subtraction of 2 from 5
–	–5	–5	Negation (negative of the number)
*	=5*2	10	Multiplication of 5 with 2
/	=5/2	2.5	Division of 5 by 2
%	5%	.05	Percentage
^	=5^2	25	Exponentiation (to the power of)

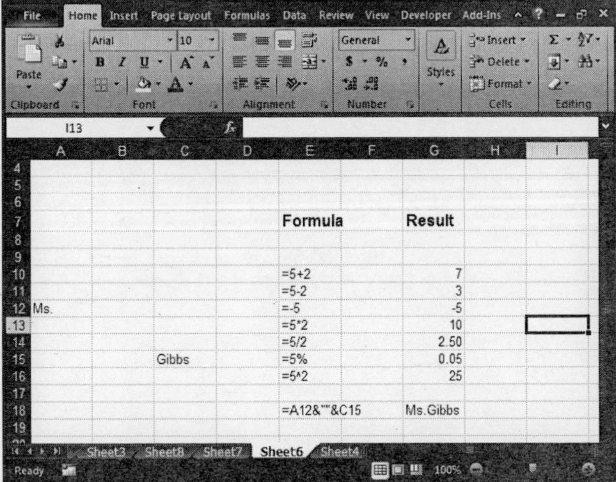

Figure 5.64 Arithmetic and text operators

Text Concatenation Operator

The ampersand (&) operator, joins text within quotation marks or text contained in referenced cells. Joining text is known as *concatenation*, as explained in the following example.

Example 17

Figure 5.65 shows the result of the concatenation operator used in the following table.

Solution

Operator	Formula	Result	Type of Operation
&	=A12&""&C15	Ms.Gibbs	Text in A12 and C15 is joined

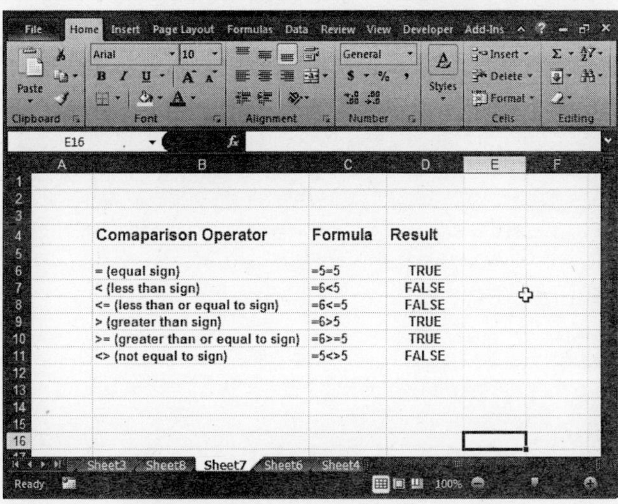

Figure 5.65 Comparison operators

Comparison Operators

To compare values, you can create formulas using comparison operators. These operators return a TRUE or FALSE result, depending on how the formula evaluate the condition. Subsequent Table formulates some Comparison operators and Figure 5.65 shows the use of such comparison operators.

Operator	Type
=	Equal to
<	Less than
<=	Less than or equal to
>	Greater than
>=	Greater than or equal to
<>	Not equal to

The following are examples of comparative operators in formulas:

Formula	Result
=A12<15	TRUE if the contents of cell A12 is less than 15; FALSE if the contents of cell A12 is 15 or more.
=B36>=15	TRUE if the contents of cell B36 is 15 or more; FALSE if the contents of cell B36 is less than 15.

Reference Operator

Reference operators make no changes to constants or cell contents as summarized in Table 5.6. Instead, they control how a formula groups the cells and ranges of cells when the formula is made to calculate. The examples of Reference operators are shown in Figure 5.66.

Table 5.6 Reference Operators

Operator	Example	Type	Result
:	SUM(A7:A11)	Range	Evaluates as a single reference the cells in the rectangular area between the two corners.
,	SUM (A7:A11,B11)	Union	Evaluates two references as a single reference.
space	SUM(A9:A11 A7:A11)	Intersect	Evaluates the cells common to both references (if no cells are common to both, then #NULL results).
space	=Yr99 Sales	Intersect	Cell contents at the intersect of the column named Yr99 and the row named Sales.

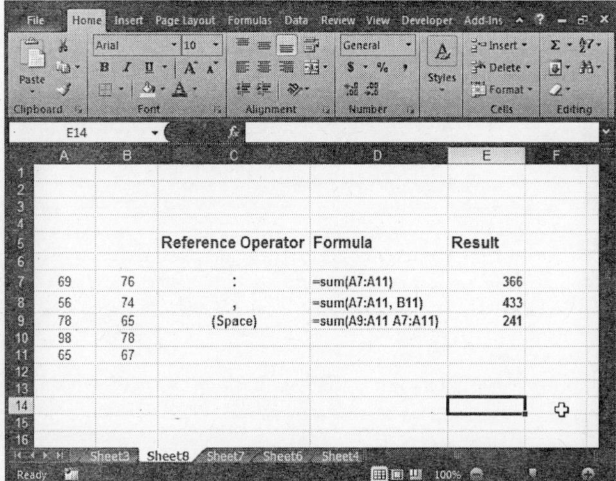

Figure 5.66 Reference operators

☞ *Reference operators enable you to combine absolute and relative references and named ranges. Reference operators are valuable for joining cells (union) or referring to a common area shared between different ranges (intersect).*

Range Operator

Use the range operator (:) to reduce your work in formulas. If you want a formula to refer to all cells in column B, type B:B. Similarly, the range that includes all cells in rows 5 through 12 is entered as 5:12.

Evaluation (Precedence) of Formulas

Excel 2010 follows a set of rules when applying operators in a formula. Working from the first calculation to the last, Excel 2010 evaluates operators in the order shown in Table 5.7.

Table 5.7 Order in which Excel 2010 Evaluates Operators

Operator	Definition
()	Parentheses
:	Range
space	Intersect
,	Union
–	Negation
%	Percentage
^	Exponentiation
* and /	Multiplication and division
+ and –	Addition and subtraction
&	Text joining
=, <, and <= >, >=, and <>	Comparisons

If you want to change the order in which calculations are performed then enclose in parentheses the terms you want Excel 2010 to be calculated first.

For example, you will notice the difference between the results of the following formulas:

Formula	Result
=6+21/3	**13**
=(6+21)/3	**9**

Entering Text, Date and Time in Formulas

You can use *text, dates,* and *times* in formulas by including the data in quotation marks. For example.

="The Total Budget is" &TOTAL_BUDGET

shows the Total Budget and the value in the cell named TOTAL_BUDGET.

If you want to perform date math on explicit dates, which are the dates that are not in cells, then:

="4/14/2014" - "4/14/2013"

or

="14April14" - "14April13"

These formulas produce the number of days between the two dates.

5.11.3 Other Basic Functions

Functions are the predefined formulas that perform calculations on specific values, called arguments. Each function takes specific types of arguments, such as *numbers, references, text,* or *logical values*. You can enter the arguments, enclosing them in parentheses, i.e., ( ), after the function name. Functions use these arguments in the same way that algebraic equations use variables. For example, the SUM function adds values or range of values, and the PMT function calculates the loan payments based on an interest rate, the period of loan, and the principal amount of loan. Excel includes many functions that can be divided into the following categories:

Mathematical Functions

Excel 2010 includes many math and trigonometry functions. Mathematical functions are used to perform a wide variety of simple or complex calculations, such as totaling the value for a range of cells, rounding of a number.

SUM( )

Adds all the numbers in a range of cells (See Figure 5.67).

Syntax

SUM(number1,number2,...)

Where **number1, number2,...** are upto 255 arguments for which you want the total value or the sum of numbers.

- Numbers, logical values, and text representations of numbers that you type directly into the list of arguments are counted.
- If an argument is an array or reference, only numbers in that array or reference are counted. Empty cells, logical values, text, or error values in the array or reference are ignored.
- Arguments that are error values or text that cannot be translated into numbers would cause errors.

Example 18

SUM (3, 2) equal 5

SUM ("3", 2, TRUE) equals 6 because the text values are translated into numbers, and the logical value TRUE is translated into the number 1 (See Figure 5.67).

Unlike the previous example, if A8 contains "text" and A9 contains "text1", then:

SUM(A8,A9,2) equals 2 because references to non-numeric values in references are not translated (See Figure 5.67).

If cells A2:E2 contain, 5, 15, 30, 40 and 50, then

SUM (A2:C2) equals 50

SUM (B2:E2, 15) equals 150

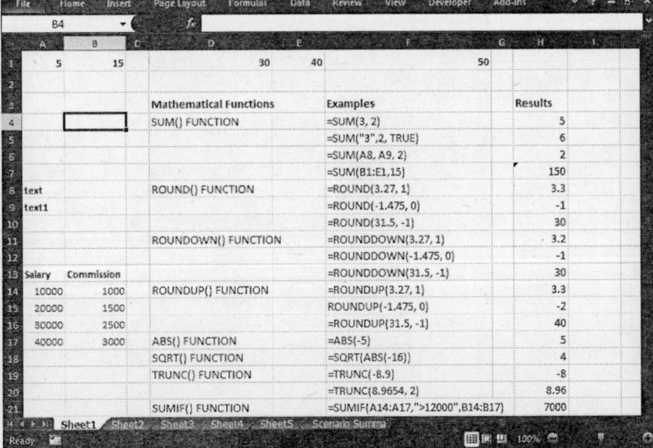

Figure 5.67 Mathematical functions and their results

Round( )

ROUND() function rounds a number to a specified number of digits (See Figure 5.67).

Syntax

ROUND(number,num_digits)
Where **number**– is the number you want to round.
Num_digits specifies the number of digits to which you want to round off a number.

- If num_digits is greater than 0 (zero), then number is rounded to the specified number of decimal places.
- If num_digits is 0, then number is rounded to the nearest integer.
- If num_digits is less than 0, then number is rounded to the left of the decimal point.

Example 19

ROUND (3.27, 1) equals **3.3** (See Figure 5.67)
ROUND (–1.475, 0) equals **–1**
ROUND (31.5, –1) equals **30**

Rounddown( )

ROUNDDOWN() function rounds a number down towards zero (See Figure 5.67).

Syntax

ROUNDDOWN(number, num_digits)
Where **number**– is the number you want to round.
Num_digits specifies the number of digits to which you want to round a number.

- If num_digits is greater than 0 (zero), then number is rounded down to the specified number of decimal places.
- If num_digits is 0, then number is rounded down to the nearest integer.
- If num_digits is less than 0, then number is rounded down to the left of the decimal point.

Example 20

ROUNDDOWN (3.27, 1) equals **3.2** (See Figure 5.67)
ROUNDDOWN (–1.475, 0) equals **–1**
ROUNDDOWN (31.5, –1) equals **30**

Roundup( )

ROUNDUP() function rounds a number up away from 0 (zero) (See Figure 5.67).

Syntax

ROUNDUP(number,num_digits)
Where **number**– is the number you want to keep round.
Num_digits specifies the number of digits to which you want to round a number.

- If num_digits is greater than 0 (zero), then number is rounded up to the specified number of decimal places.
- If num_digits is 0, then number is rounded up to the nearest integer.
- If num_digits is less than 0, then number is rounded up to the left of the decimal point.

Example 21

ROUNDUP (3.27, 1) equals **3.3** (See Figure 5.67)
ROUNDUP (–1.475, 0) equals **–2**
ROUNDUP (31.5, –1) equals **40**

Example 22

ABS( )

ABS( ) function returns the absolute value of a number. The absolute value of a number is the number without any + or – sign.

Syntax

ABS(num)
Where **num** is the real number of which you want to get the absolute value.

Example 23

ABS(5) equals **5**
ABS(-5) equals **5** (See Figure 5.67)

SQRT( )

SQRT( ) returns a positive square root of a number (See Figure 5.67).

Syntax

SQRT(num)
Where **num** is the number for which you want the square root. If number is negative, SQRT returns the #NUM! Error value because square root of a negative number is not defined.

Example 24

SQRT(16) equals **±4**
SQRT(-16) equals **#NUM!**, i.e., error.

But if you want to find the square root of negative number then you have to give function like this:
SQRT(ABS(-16)) equals **4** (See Figure 5.67)

TRUNC( )

TRUNC( ) function truncates a number to an integer value by removing the fractional part of the number (See Figure 5.67).

Syntax

TRUNC(num,num_digits)
Where **num** is the number you want to truncate.
Num_digits is a number specifying the precision of the truncation. The default value for num_digits is 0 (zero).

Example 25

TRUNC(8.9) equals **8**
TRUNC(-8.9) equals **–8**
TRUNC(8.9654, 2) equals **8.96**

5.11.4 Logical Functions

Logical functions are used when we want to check whether a given condition is true or false.

IF( )

IF( ) function used to determine whether a condition specified with in braces is true or false. It returns one value if a specified condition evaluates to TRUE and another value if it evaluates to FALSE (See Figure 5.68).

Syntax

IF(logical_test,value_if_true,value_if_false)

Where

Logical_test is a value or expression that can be evaluated to TRUE or FALSE. For example, A10 = 100 is a logical expression.

Value_if_true is the value that is returned if logical_test is TRUE. For example, if the value in cell A10 is equal to 100, the expression evaluates to TRUE.

Value_if_false is the value that is returned if logical_test is FALSE. For example, if the value in cell A10 is not equal to 100, the expression evaluates to FALSE.

☞ *In Excel 2010, up to 64 IF() functions can be nested to construct more elaborate tests.*

Example 26

On a Marksheet, cell A10 contains a formula to calculate the result. If the result of the formula in A10 is greater than 50, then the following function displays "Pass". Otherwise, the function displays "Fail" (See Figure 5.68).

IF(A10>=50,"Pass","Fail")

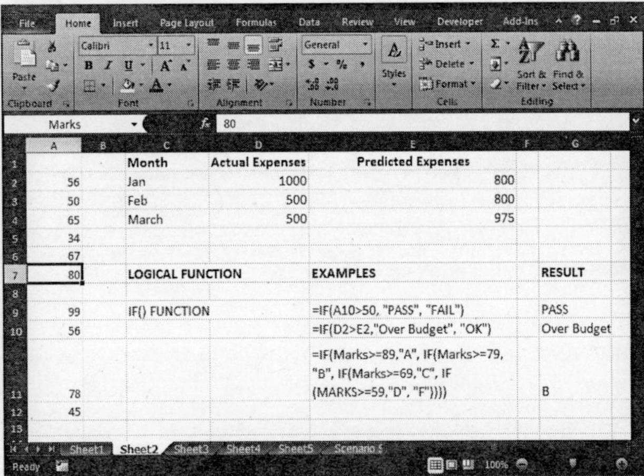

Figure 5.68 Logical functions

Suppose an expense worksheet in D2:D4 contains the following data for "Actual Expenses" for January, February, and March: 1000, 500, 500. E2:E4 contains the following data for "Predicted Expenses" for the same periods: 800, 800, 975.

You can write a formula to check whether you are over budget for a particular month, generating text for a message with the following formulas:

IF(D2>E2,"Over Budget","OK") equals "Over Budget"

IF(D3>E3,"Over Budget","OK") equals "OK"

We can also use nested IF function:

IF(Marks>89,"A",IF(Marks>79,"B",

IF(Marks>69,"C",IF(Marks>59,"D","F"))))

In the above example, **Marks** in the name of the cell **A7** if the first logical_test (Marks>=89) is TRUE, "A" is returned (See Figure 5.68). If the first logical_test is FALSE, the second IF statement is evaluated, and so on.

☞ *When averaging cells, keep in mind the difference between empty cells and those containing the value zero, especially if you have cleared the Zero values check box from the Advanced properties of the Excel Options. Empty cells are not counted, but zero values are counted and evaluated.*

TRUE( )

TRUE( ) returns the logical value TRUE and it takes no arguments.

Syntax

TRUE( )

FALSE( )

FALSE( ) function is same as TRUE( ) but it returns the logical value FALSE.

Syntax

FALSE( )

5.11.5 Statistical Function

Statistical functions are used to perform statistical analysis on ranges of data. Excel 2010 includes simple as well as complex statistical functions, such as *average, min, max, standard deviation, slopes,* etc. Apart from this, it also includes a set of more accurate statistical and other functions. Certain existing functions have also been renamed to better describe what they do.

MAX( )

MAX function returns the largest value in a set of values stored in a cells.

Syntax

MAX(number1,number2,...)

Where **number1,number2,...** are upto 255 numbers for which you want to find the maximum value.

- You can specify arguments that are *numbers, empty cells, logical values,* or *text representations of numbers*. Arguments that are error values or text that cannot be translated into numbers cause errors.
- If the arguments contain no numbers, MAX returns 0 (zero).

Example 27

If A1:A5 contains the numbers 34, 45, 7, 21, and 6, then:

MAX (A1:A5) equals **45** (See Figure 5.69)

MAX (A1:A5, 30) equals **75**

MIN( )

MIN function returns the smallest number in a set of values.

Syntax

MIN(number1,number2, ...)

Where **number1,number2,...** are upto 255 numbers for which you want to find the minimum value.

- You can specify arguments that are *numbers, empty cells, logical values,* or *text representations of numbers*. Arguments that are error values or text that cannot be translated into numbers cause errors.
- If the arguments contain no numbers, MIN returns 0, i.e., zero.

Example 28

If A1:A5 contains the numbers 34, 45, 7, 21 and 6 then:

MIN (A1:A5) equals **6** (See Figure 5.69)

MIN (A1:A5, 0) equals **0**

Average( )

The Average function returns the average (arithmetic mean) of the arguments which are passed in function as an argument (See Figure 5.69).

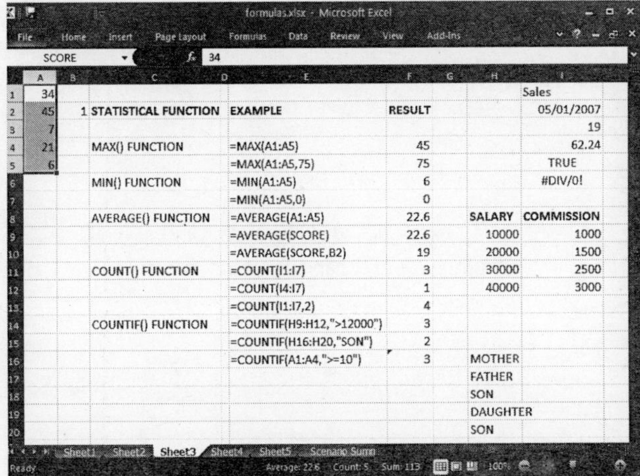

formulas.xlsx - Microsoft Excel

SCORE | 34

	A	B	C	D	E	F	G	H	I
1	34								Sales
2	45	1	STATISTICAL FUNCTION	EXAMPLE		RESULT			05/01/2007
3	7								19
4	21		MAX() FUNCTION	=MAX(A1:A5)		45			62.24
5	6			=MAX(A1:A5,75)		75			TRUE
6			MIN() FUNCTION	=MIN(A1:A5)		6			#DIV/0!
7				=MIN(A1:A5,0)		0			
8			AVERAGE() FUNCTION	=AVERAGE(A1:A5)		22.6		SALARY	COMMISSION
9				=AVERAGE(SCORE)		22.6		10000	1000
10				=AVERAGE(SCORE,B2)		19		20000	1500
11			COUNT() FUNCTION	=COUNT(I1:I7)		3		30000	2500
12				=COUNT(I4:I7)		1		40000	3000
13				=COUNT(I1:I7,2)		4			
14			COUNTIF() FUNCTION	=COUNTIF(H9:H12,">12000")		3			
15				=COUNTIF(H16:H20,"SON")		2			
16				=COUNTIF(A1:A4,">=10")		3		MOTHER	
17								FATHER	
18								SON	
19								DAUGHTER	
20								SON	

Figure 5.69 Statistical functions

Syntax

AVERAGE(number1,number2,...)

Where **number1, number2,...** are upto 255 numeric arguments for which you want to get the average.

Notes

- The arguments must be either numbers or names, or references that contain numbers.
- If an array or reference argument containing text, logical values, or empty cells, such values are ignored; however, cells with the value zero are included.

Example 29

If A1:A5 is named Score and contains the numbers, 34, 45, 7, 21 and 6 then:

AVERAGE (A1:A5) equals **22.6** (See Figure 5.69)

AVERAGE (Score) equals **22.6**. Here **Scores** is the name of range (See Figure 5.69).

AVERAGE (A1:A5, 5) equals **19.667**

AVERAGE (Score, B2) equals 19

If C1:C3 is named OtherScores and contain the numbers 4, 18, and 7, then:

AVERAGE (Scores, OtherScores) equals **10.5**

Count( )

COUNT function counts the number of cells that contain numbers and numbers within the list of arguments. Use COUNT to get the number of entries in a number field in a range or array of numbers (See Figure 5.69).

Syntax

COUNT(value1,value2,...)

Where **value1, value2,...** are upto 255 arguments that can contain or refer to a variety of different types of data, but only numbers are counted.

- Arguments that are *numbers, dates,* or *text* representations of numbers are counted. Arguments that are error values or text that cannot be translated into numbers are ignored.
- If an argument is an array or reference, only numbers in that array or reference are counted. Empty cells, logical values, text, or error values in the array or reference are ignored. If you need to count logical values, text, or error values, use the COUNT function.

Example 30

In the following example, the column I1 to I6 contain the following values (See Figure 5.69):

I1	**Sales**
I2	**5/1/2007**
I3	**19**
I4	**62.24**
I5	**TRUE**
I6	**#DIV/0!**
I7	**Blank**

COUNT (I1:I7) equals **3** (See Figure 5.69)

COUNT (I4:I7) equals **1**

COUNT (I1:I7, 2) equals **4**

5.11.6 Date and Time Function

With date and time functions, you can analyze and work with date and time values in formulas. For example, if you need to use the current date in a formula, you can use the TODAY ( ) function, which returns the current date.

Today ( )

It returns the current date of the system (See Figure 5.70).

Syntax

TODAY( )

Now()

Returns the current date and time (See Figure 5.70).

Syntax

NOW( )

Day()

It returns the day of a date passed as an argument. The day is given as an integer ranging from 1 to 31 (See Figure 5.70).

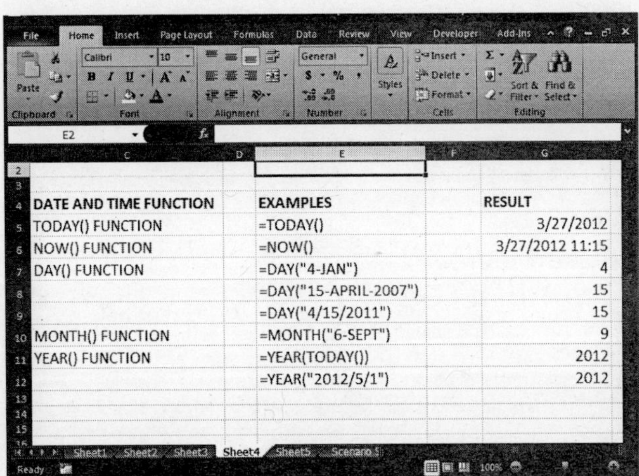

DATE AND TIME FUNCTION	EXAMPLES	RESULT
TODAY() FUNCTION	=TODAY()	3/27/2012
NOW() FUNCTION	=NOW()	3/27/2012 11:15
DAY() FUNCTION	=DAY("4-JAN")	4
	=DAY("15-APRIL-2007")	15
	=DAY("4/15/2011")	15
MONTH() FUNCTION	=MONTH("6-SEPT")	9
YEAR() FUNCTION	=YEAR(TODAY())	2012
	=YEAR("2012/5/1")	2012

Figure 5.70 Date and Time functions

Syntax

DAY(serial_number)

Where **serial_number** is the date of the day you are trying to find. Dates may be entered as text strings within quotation marks.

Example 31

DAY("4-Jan") equals **4**
DAY("15-Apr-2007") equals **15**
DAY("4/15/2011") equals **15**

Month()

It returns the month of a date which is passed as argument. The month is given as an integer, ranging from 1 (January) to 12 (December) (See Figure 5.70).

Syntax

MONTH(serial_number)

Where **serial_number** is the date of the month you are trying to find

Example 32

MONTH("6-Sept") equals **9**
MONTH("2012/04/01") equals **4**

Year()

Returns the year corresponding year to a date (See Figure 5.70).

Syntax

YEAR(serial_number)

Where **serial_number** is the date of the year you want to find.

Example 33

YEAR(TODay()) equals **2012**
YEAR("2012/05/01") equals **2012** (See Figure 5.70)

5.11.7 Text Function

With text functions, you can use text strings in formulas. You can also change the case of the string, find out the length of a text string or you can join two strings, etc.

Concatenate( )

Joins two or more text strings into one text string (See Figure 5.71).

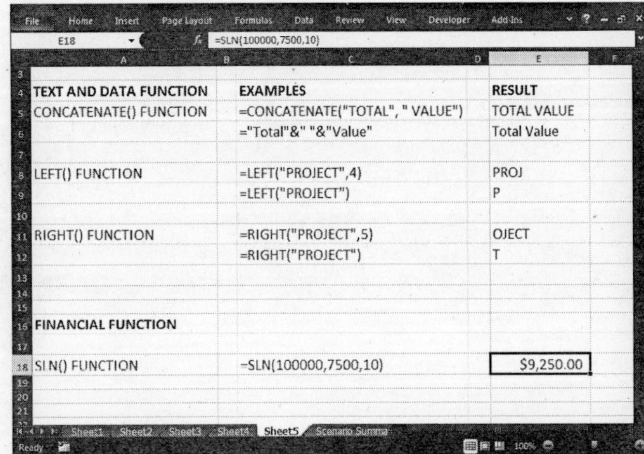

TEXT AND DATA FUNCTION	EXAMPLES	RESULT
CONCATENATE() FUNCTION	=CONCATENATE("TOTAL", " VALUE")	TOTAL VALUE
	="Total"&" "&"Value"	Total Value
LEFT() FUNCTION	=LEFT("PROJECT",4)	PROJ
	=LEFT("PROJECT")	P
RIGHT() FUNCTION	=RIGHT("PROJECT",5)	OJECT
	=RIGHT("PROJECT")	T
FINANCIAL FUNCTION		
SLN() FUNCTION	=SLN(100000,7500,10)	$9,250.00

Figure 5.71 Text and Financial functions

Syntax

CONCATENATE (text1,text2,...)
Where **text1, text2,...** are 2 to 255 text items to be joined into a single text item.
The "&" operator can also be used to join text items.

Example 34

CONCATENATE("Total"," Value") equals "Total Value".
If you use '&' operator to join strings then
"Total"&" "&"Value"

LEFT( )

LEFT returns the first character or characters in a text string, based on the number of characters specified as arguments (See Figure 5.71).

Syntax

LEFT(text,num_chars)
Where **text** is the text string.
num_chars specifies the number of characters to be extracted. By default, it is assumed to be 1.

Example 35

LEFT("PROJECT",4) equals **"PROJ"** (See Figure 5.71)
If A1 contains "SUBJECT", then:
LEFT(A1) equals **"S"**
Because **S** is the left most character and by default it will be left most character value.

RIGHT( )

It is same as LEFT but it returns the last character or characters in a text string, based on the number of characters specified as a arguments (See Figure 5.71).

Syntax

RIGHT(text,num_chars)

Where **text** is the text string.

num_chars specifies the number of characters to be extracted.

Example 36

RIGHT("PROJECT",5) equals **"OJECT"** (See Figure 5.71)

RIGHT("PROJECT") equals **"T"**

5.11.8 Financial Function

Financial functions perform common business calculations For example, determination of the payment for a loan.

SLN( )

Returns the straight-line depreciation of an asset for one period (See Figure 5.71).

Syntax

SLN(cost,Last_value,life)

Where **Cost** is the initial cost of the asset.

Last_value is the value at the end of the depreciation.

Life is the number of year in which the asset is being depreciated (the useful life of the asset).

Example 37

Suppose you purchased a Car for **1,00,000** that has a useful life of 10 years and a salvage value of **7,500**. The depreciation allowance for each year is:

SLN(100000, 7500, 10) equals **9,250** (See Figure 5.71)

PMT( )

Suppose you want to buy a car and you want to calculate your monthly installment you can use the **PMT()** function built in Excel 2010.

Example 38

1. Activate a cell.
2. Under the **Formulas** tab, click on the **Insert Function**. *Alternatively*, click on the **Insert Function** button on the center of the formula bar, i.e., *fx* or press Shift+F3 keys together. It will display the Insert Function Dialog box as shown in Figure 5.72.
3. Select a Financial category from the select a category: drop-down list.
4. Click on PMT Function from the Select a function: list box.
5. Click OK. It will display a Function Arguments dialog box as shown in Figure 5.73.

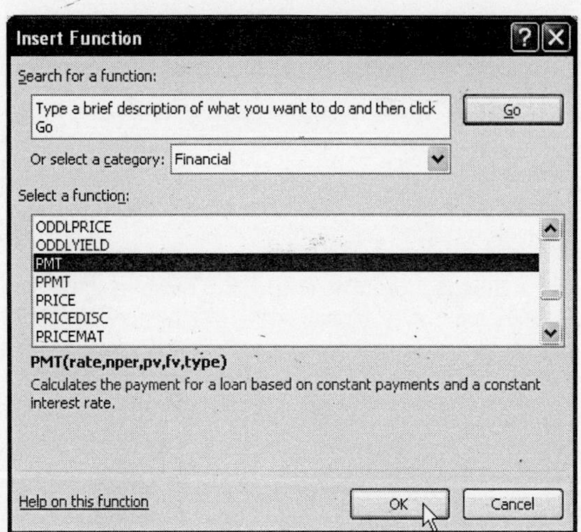

Figure 5.72 Insert Function dialog box

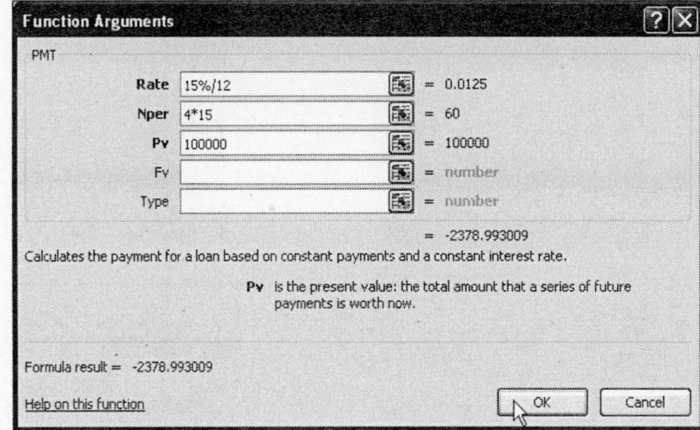

Figure 5.73 Function Arguments dialog box

The arguments required by the function are as follows:

Argument	Description
Rate	Is the *interest rate* for the loan.
Nper	Is the total number of payments for the loan.
Pv	Is the present value, or the total amount that a series of future payments is worth now; also known as the principal amount which is 100000 in our case.
Fv	Is the future value, or a cash balance you want to attain after the last payment is made. If Fv is omitted, it is assumed to be 0 (zero), that is, the future value of a loan is 0.
Type	Is the number 0 (zero) or 1 and indicated when payments are due.

Set type equal to	If payments are due
0 or omitted	At the end of the period
1	At the beginning of the period

Notes

a. The payment returned by PMT includes principal amount and interest.

b. Make sure that you use specific units for *rate* and *Nper*. If you make monthly payments on a four-year loan at an annual interest rate of **15** percent, use **15%/12** for rate and **4*15** for Nper. If you make annual payments on the same loan, use 15 percent for rate and **4** for Nper.

The following formula returns the monthly payment on a 1,00,000 loan at an annual rate of 15 percent that you must pay off in 60 months:

PMT (15%/12, 60, 1,00,000) equals 2378.99

For the same loan, if payments are due at the beginning of the period, the payment is:

PMT (15%/12, 60, 1,00,000, 0, 1) equals 2349.62

The following formula returns the amount someone must pay to you each month if you loan that person 5,000 at 12 percent and want to be paid back in 5 months:

PMT (12%/12, 5, –5000) equals 1,030.20

You can use PMT for in your PPF account to determine payments to annuities other than loans. For example, if you want to save Rupee 5,00,000 in 18 years by saving a constant amount each month, you can use PMT to determine how much you must save. If you assume you will be able to earn 12 percent interest on your savings, you can use PMT to determine how much to save each month.

PMT (12%/12, 18*12, 0, 5,00,000) equals Rs 659.75

that is if you pay Rupee 659.75 per month in 18 years you will get Rupee 5,00,000 after 18 years.

The above examples illustrate the use of financial functions. There are many more complex functions which are very useful for accountants, engineers and other professionals.

5.11.9 Charts in Excel

You can create different types of charts using Excel 2010 that will help you to analyze data in a worksheet and give you a visual presentation of results. You can even customize the chart by adding *text, arrows, titles,* and *legends*, etc. If you print a chart on a laser printer or plotter, the quality of charts is as good as that of a chart created by a professional artist.

☞ *With Excel 2010, you can instantly access formatting options by double-clicking a chart element.*

How to Create a Chart?

You can create two types of charts namely, *embedded charts* and charts that appear in a *chart sheet*.

Embedded Chart

An *embedded chart* appears in a worksheet next to tables or text. Figure 5.74 shows an embedded chart.

☞ *Embedded charts are required when you want a chart side-by-side with the data for the chart, such as in a report.*

Chart in a Chart Sheet

A chart can be created by itself in its own chart sheet within a workbook (See Figure 5.75). Thus, you are able to work with the chart sheet separately from the worksheet containing data. If you insert a chart in a sheet, you add the chart to the active workbook and save it along with the workbook.

☞ *If you need to print a chart on its own, creating the chart on a chart sheet is the best approach.*

To quickly create a chart, select data and press F11 key then Excel 2010 inserts a chart in a chart sheet, using the default chart type. But, when you press Alt + F1 keys together, the chart is displayed as an embedded chart (See Figure 5.74).

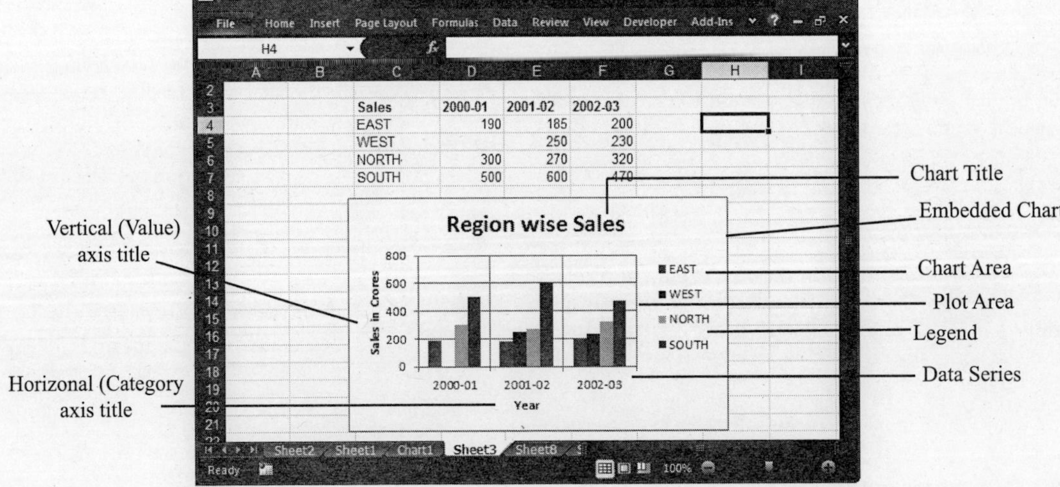

Figure 5.74 Embedded Chart with data Elements in the same worksheet

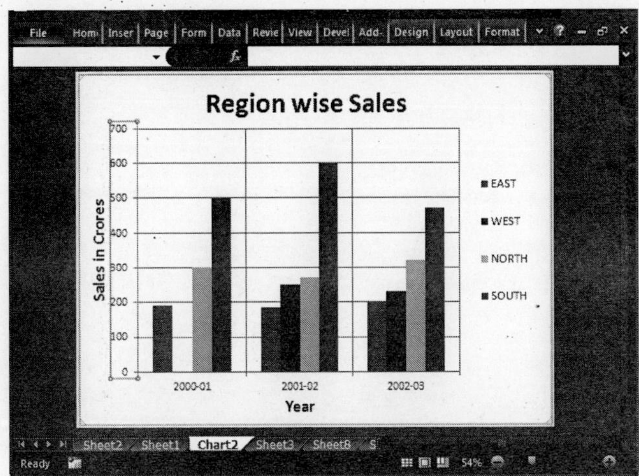

Figure 5.75 Chart in a Chart Sheet

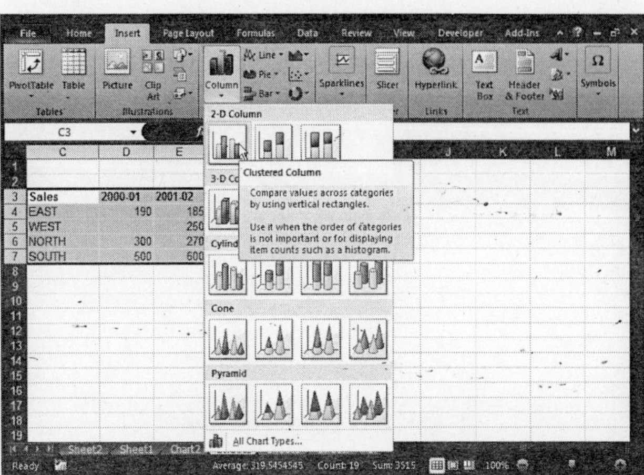

Figure 5.76 Creating Chart

☞ *When you create a chart, chart tools become available and the Design, Layout and Format tabs are displayed as shown in Figure 4.51. You can use command on these tabs to modify the chart so that data is presented the way you want.*

3. Chart will appear as shown in Figure 5.74.

Chart Terminology

An Excel 2010 chart may contain objects that you may like to modify individually. Figure 5.74 showed some of these objects. Table 5.7 describes each object. Note that if you move mouse pointer over an object in a chart, a tip appears to give the description of the chart object.

Table 5.7 Parts of an Excel Chart

Object	Description
Axis (*X-axis* and *Y-axis*)	The horizontal or X-axis along the bottom of most charts is also referred to as *category* axis. The vertical or Y-axis against which data points are measured is also referred to as *value* axis. This axis contains the scale against which data is plotted.
Data point	A single piece of data.
Data series	A collection of data points.
Legend	The name of each data series is used as a legend title.
Marker	An object that represents a data point in a chart, such as bars, pie and symbols. Markers that belong to the same data series appear as the same shape, symbol and color.
Plot area	The Rectangular area is bounded by the two axes.
Text	Text associated with data points or free-floating text that can be moved easily. The box containing the text can be resized.

Creating a Chart

➜ To create a chart, do this:

1. Select the data items you want to be appeared as chart.
2. Under the **Insert** tab, in **Charts** group, click arrow next to that chart which you want to insert and then select the chart from the chart subtype (Here, we select Column chart sub type) (See Figure 5.76).

Changing the Type of Chart

Excel 2010 offers you eleven different chart types and within each of these general types, you can select any sub-types. The easiest way to create chart is to select a chart type and sub-type you want. Thereafter, you may customize this chart according to your requirement.

☞ *In Excel 2010, you can use the macro recorder to record formatting changes to charts and other objects.*

Example 39

How will you change to a different type of chart?

Solution

1. Activate the chart you want to change by positioning the mouse pointer on the tab and clicking the tab for the *chart sheet*. In case, the *chart is embedded*, then click the chart itself.
2. Under the **Design** tab, in **Type** group, click **Change Chart Type**. A Change Chart Type dialog box showing different chart types appear as shown in Figure 5.77.
3. Select a chart type from the left side's list.
4. Select a sub-type from the right side's list.
5. Click OK to close the Change Chart Type dialog box.

Changing Data Source

You can add data to an existing chart. You can even add new data series or data points to existing series or change the range of data used by a chart.

Example 40

How will you change the data source of a chart?

Solution

1. Activate the embedded chart or activate the chart sheet for the chart to which you want to add data.
2. Under the **Design** tab, in **Data** group, click **Select Data**. The Data Source dialog box appears as shown in Figure 5.78.

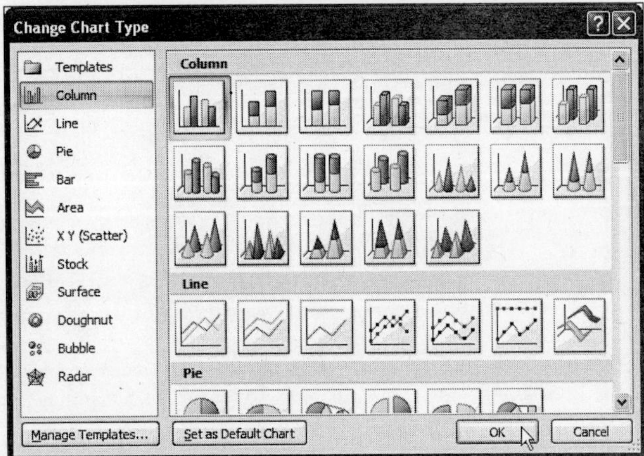

Figure 5.77 Change Chart Type dialog box

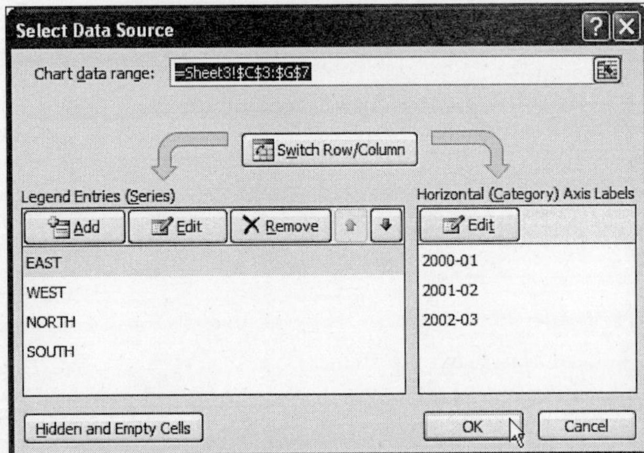

Figure 5.78 Select Data Source dialog box

3. In this dialog box, make the following changes according to your need:

   Chart data range: This box displays the range of data that is plotted in the chart. If you want to change the range, click on the Collapse Dialog button at the right end of this box. It will temporarily minimize. Now select the new range and click this button again after you select the range.

   Switch Row/Column: It switches the rows of worksheet from rows to the columns and vice versa.

   Legend Entries (Series): It displays existing data series names.

   Add: Click to add a new data series to the chart.

   Edit: If you want to edit the existing range, click in this button to make changes to the data series.

   Remove: Click to remove the data series that you select in the Legend Entries (Series) box from the chart.

   Horizontal (Category) Axis Labels: Lists existing horizontal (category) axis labels.

   Edit: Click to modify the horizontal (category) labels.
4. After making changes, click OK.

Inserting Text

When you create a chart, Excel 2010 automatically includes labels along the category and value axes. This happens only if you had selected data and included cells containing labels.

There are two types of text you can add. These are as follows:

1. Text associated with specific objects in a chart, such as the *title*, *axes*, or *data points*. After you insert this type of text, you can select it and revise it whenever you want. You can also reposition it.
2. Text not associated with objects in the chart are known is *floating text*. Such unattached text appears in a box which can be resized and repositioned anywhere on the chart.

Example 41

Write down the procedure to

(a) Insert the title in a chart.

(b) Edit a title.

Solution (a)

1. Activate the Chart to which you want to add a title..
2. Under the **Layout** tab, in **Labels** group, click arrow next to **Chart Title**. Select the option whichever you want as shown in Figure 5.79.

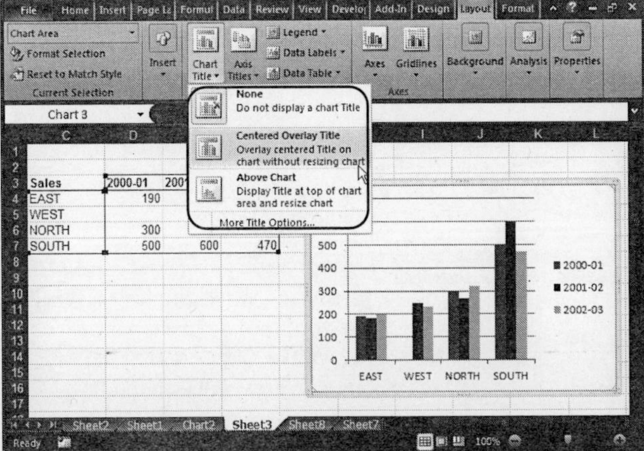

Figure 5.79 Insert Chart Title

3. In the Chart Title text box that appears in the chart, type the text that you want.

Solution (b)

1. Click the *title* to select it and then click inside the box that contains the text.
2. The insertion point appears where you click. You can then use the arrow keys to move around the text or the Backspace and Delete keys to delete characters. You can press letter keys on the keyboard to enter the new text.

Modifying the Axes

Excel 2010 creates a Category (X) axis and Value (Y) axis at the time of creating a chart. But you can modify any one of the axes using the **Axes** group of **Layout** tab.

Example 42

How will you remove an axis from the chart?

Solution

1. Activate the chart where you want to remove an axis.
2. Under the **Layout** tab, in the **Axes** group, click arrow next to **Axes** and then click **Primary Vertical Axis** or **Primary Horizontal Axis** and then click **None** (See Figure 5.80).

Figure 5.80 Modifying the Axes

Inserting Data Labels

You can insert a label that can either be the value for that data point, or the category axis label associated with the data point. You can also attach labels to many data points. This would help a viewer to interpret data in a chart easily.

Example 43

Write down the steps to insert data labels in a chart?

Solution

1. Activate the chart to which you want to add data labels.
2. Under the **Layout** tab, in the **Labels** group, click arrow next to **Data Labels** and then select the display option where you want to insert the data labels (See Figure 5.81).

☞ *To add data label to an individual data series, right-click the data series and choose Add Data Labels.*

Inserting Legends

Legend describes the symbols used in a chart. Excel 2010 creates legends from the labels on the shorter side of the worksheet data series.

➜ **To insert a legend, do this:**

1. Activate the chart.

Figure 5.81 Add Data Labels

Figure 5.82 Add Legends in chart

2. Under the **Layout** tab, in the **Labels** group, click arrow next to **Legend** and select the display option where you want to insert the legends (See Figure 5.82).

Inserting Gridlines

Gridlines help you to compare markers and in reading values accurately.

➜ **To add gridlines to a chart, do this:**

1. Activate the chart you want to add gridlines to.
2. Under the **Layout** tab, in the **Axes** group, click arrow next to **Axes** and then click **Primary Vertical Gridlines** or **Primary Horizontal Gridlines** and then click the option according to your requirement (See Figure 5.83).

☞ *Drawing gridlines in a chart helps you to compare values more easily.*

5.11.10 Previewing Charts

After creating a chart and before printing, it is a good practice to see the full page view (preview) of the chart.

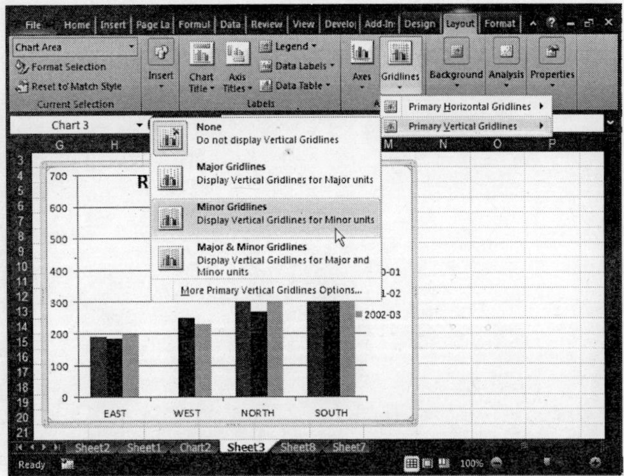

Figure 5.83 Inserting Gridlines

☞ *In Excel 2010, you can preview and print your Excel files in one location – on the Print tab in the Microsoft Office Backstage view. To go back to your workbook and make changes before you print it, click the File tab.*

Example 44

How will you preview a chart if

(a) Chart is in a Chart sheet?

(b) Chart is Embedded on a worksheet?

Solution (a)

1. Activate the chart sheet.
2. Click on the **File** Tab. Menu appears. Here, click on **Print** Option.
3. In this view, the properties of the default printer automatically appears in the left section and the preview of the chart sheet automatically appears in the right section (See Figure 5.84).

Solution (b)

1. Activate the sheet containing the chart.
2. Click on the **File** Tab. Menu appears. Here, click on **Print** Option or click on the **Print Preview and Print** button from the **Quick Launch Toolbar**.
3. A window containing the preview of the chart along with data appears as shown in Figure 5.85.

☞ *Positioning a chart along with data items helps you to analyze data easily. By making changes in the data items, you can immediately preview the effects in the chart.*

5.12 PIVOTTABLE

A PivotTable is an *interactive* table that lets you analyze and view large size of data in a list or database form so that it can be easily understood and analyzed. You can rotate its rows and columns to see different summaries, details and views of the source data as per your need. You can use PivotTable report when you want to do sorting, totaling or to compare related items. In Excel 2010, multithreading help speed up data retrieval, sorting, and filtering in PivotTables.

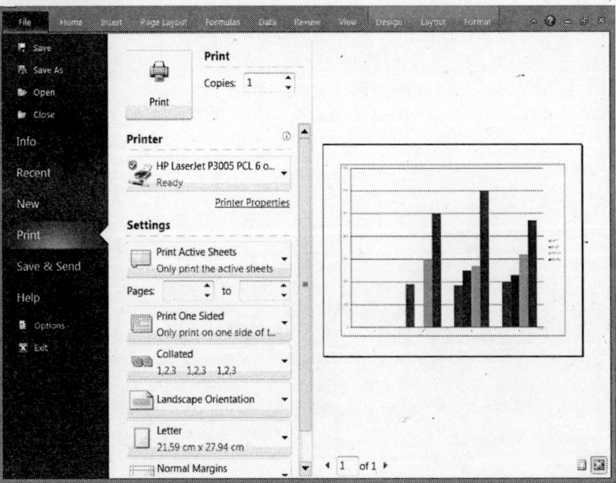

Figure 5.84 Preview of Chart sheet

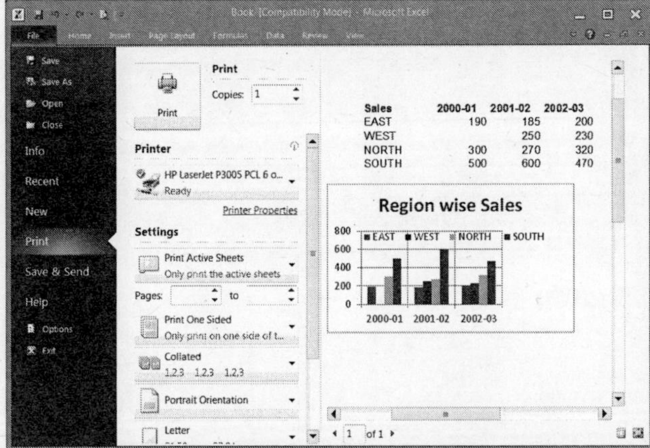

Figure 5.85 Preview of the Embedded chart

☞ *In Excel 2010, it is possible to fill down labels in a PivotTable so that you can more easily use the PivotTable. You can also repeat labels in PivotTables to display item captions of nested fields in all rows and columns.*

Example 45

(a) How will you create PivotTable report?

(b) How will you filter a PivotTable?

Solution (a)

1. Select the cells (including column labels) that you want to include in the PivotTable.
2. Under the **Insert** Tab and in the **Tables** group, click arrow next to **PivotTable** and then choose **PivotTable** (See Figure 5.86). The Create PivotTable dialog box appears (See Figure 5.87).
3. In this dialog box, Select a table or range: if you want to select the cells.

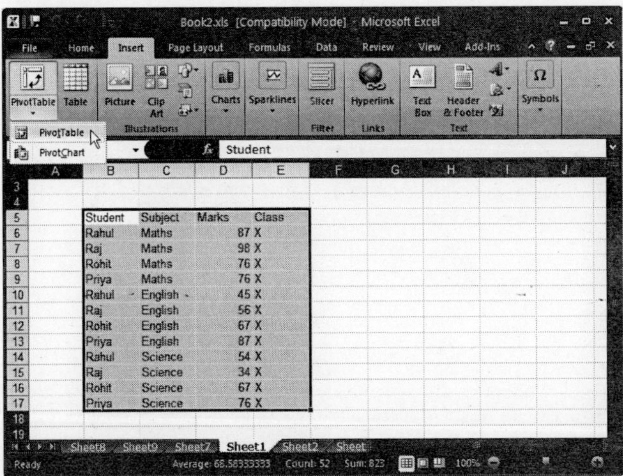

Figure 5.86 Selected Cells

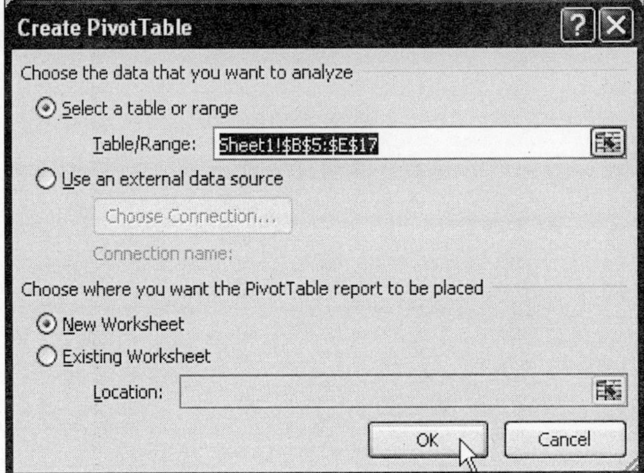

Figure 5.87 Create PivotTable Dialog Box

Use an external data source: option when you want to select range from external source.

New Worksheet: option puts the PivotTable on the new worksheet.

Existing Worksheet: option puts the PivotTable on an existing worksheet.

4. Click OK.
5. After that, an empty PivotTable report is added (**PivotTable Tools** are also displayed with **Options Tab** as shown in Figure 5.88) to the location that you entered with the PivotTable field list so that you can start adding fields (See Figure 5.88).
6. Mark one or more check boxes inside the PivotTable Field List pane. Each time you select another check box, Excel 2010 modifies how data appears in your PivotTable (See Figures 5.89 and 5.90).

Solution (b)

1. Click on the PivotTable you want to filter. The PivotTable list pane appears as shown in Figure 5.91.

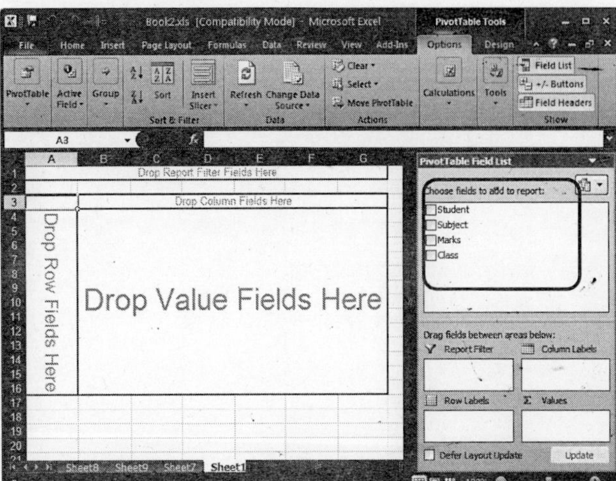

Figure 5.88 PivotTable field list pane to choose data

Click a heading in the **Row Labels** or **Column Labels** group in the PivotTable field list pane. A pop-up menu appears as seen in Figure 5.92.

Select **Move to Report Filter**. Now Excel 2010 moves your chosen label into the **Report Filter** group in the Pivot Table Field List pane and displays a filter list box at the top of your PivotTable (Here, we have selected **Subject** from Row Label and moved it to the Report Filter) as shown in Figure 5.92. Now your report will show only **Student**, **Marks** and **Class** fields. **Subject** field is removed from the Report (Figure 5.92).

In Excel 2010, it is now easier to filter data directly in a PivotChart report and to reorganize the chart's layout by adding and removing fields. Similarly, with a single click, you can hide all field buttons on the PivotChart.

5.13 USING SLICERS

In regular PivotTable report filter, you have to open a drop-down list to find the filtering details. But, with the help of slicers (new in Excel 2010), you can filter data in a PivotTable with the click of a button and to quickly see which filters are applied without open additional menus. A slicer clearly labels the filter that is applied and provides details so that you can easily understand the data that is displayed in the filtered PivotTable report.

Slicers are easy-to-use filtering components that contain a set of buttons that enable you to quickly filter the data in a PivotTable report, without the need to open drop-down lists to find the items that you want to filter. Slicers are typically associated with the PivotTable in which they are created. However, you can also create stand-alone slicers that are referenced from Online Analytical Processing (OLAP).

A PivotTable can have both local and shared slicers. Slicers that are used in one PivotTable only are called local slicers. Slicers that are connected to and used in more than one PivotTable are called shared slicers.

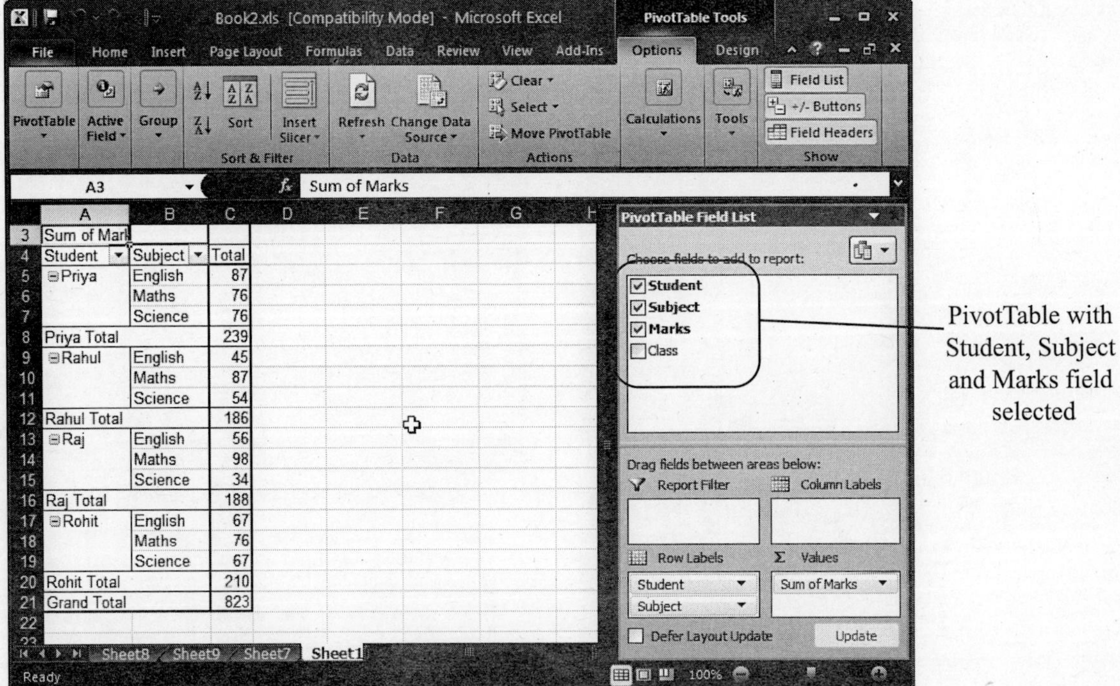

Figure 5.89 PivotTable with Student, Subject and Marks fields selected

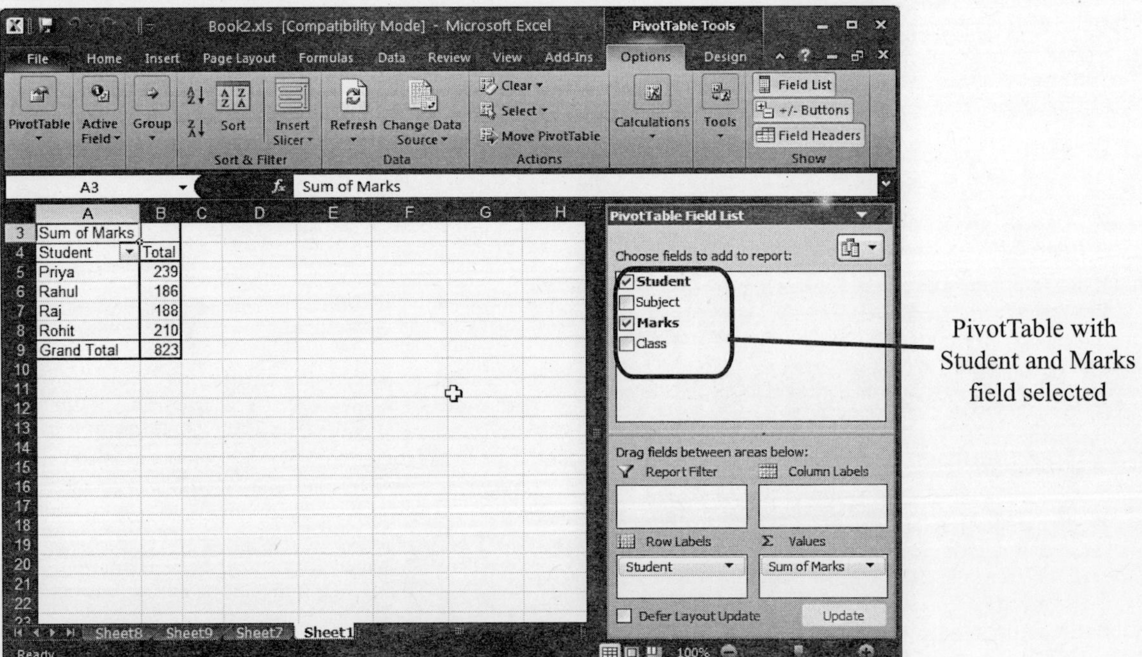

Figure 5.90 PivotTable with Student and Marks fields selected

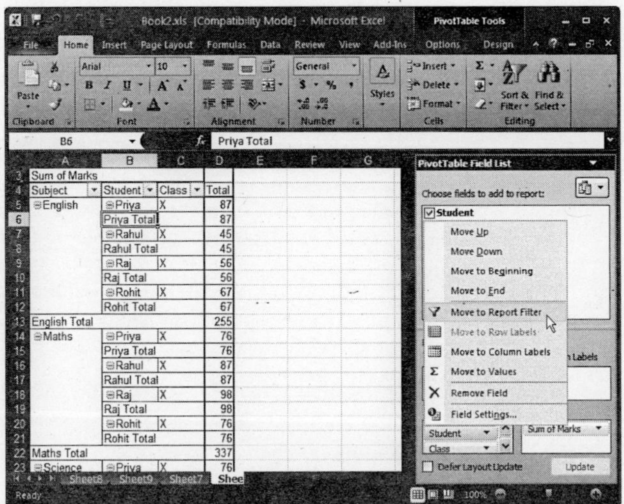

Figure 5.91 Pop-up menu

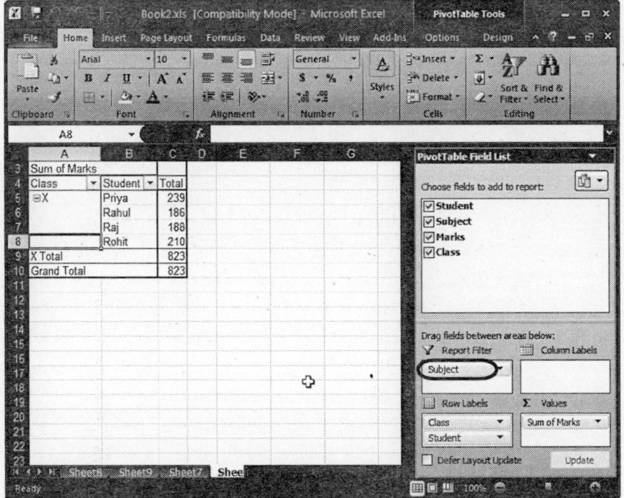

Figure 5.92 Subject field is moved in Report Filter

➜ To create a Slicer in an existing PivotTable, do this:

1. Click anywhere in the PivotTable report. When you click on the PivotTable, it will display the **PivotTable Tools**, adding an **Options** and a **Design** tab.
2. Under the **Options** Tab, in the **Sort & Filter** group, click arrow next to **Insert Slicer** and then select **Insert Slicer...** . It will display Insert Slicers dialog box as shown in Figure 5.93.
3. In this dialog box, select the check box of the PivotTable fields for which you want to create a slicer and then click OK button.
4. As soon as you press OK button, a slicer is displayed for every field that you selected (See Figure 5.94). (Here we select Student and Marks field in the Insert Slicer dialog box).

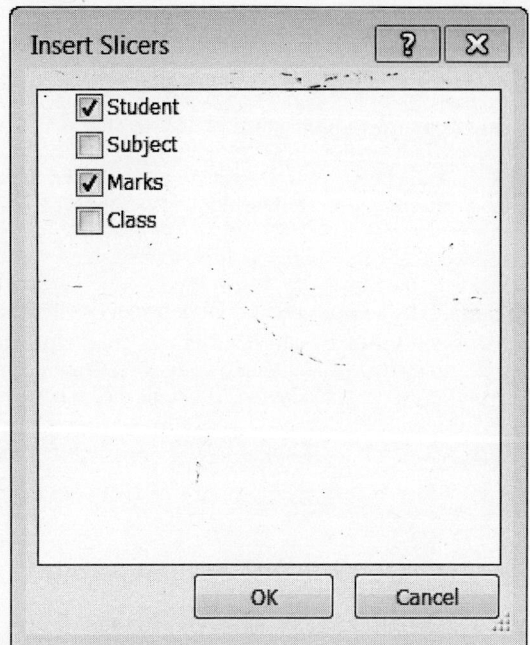

Figure 5.93 Insert Slicers dialog box

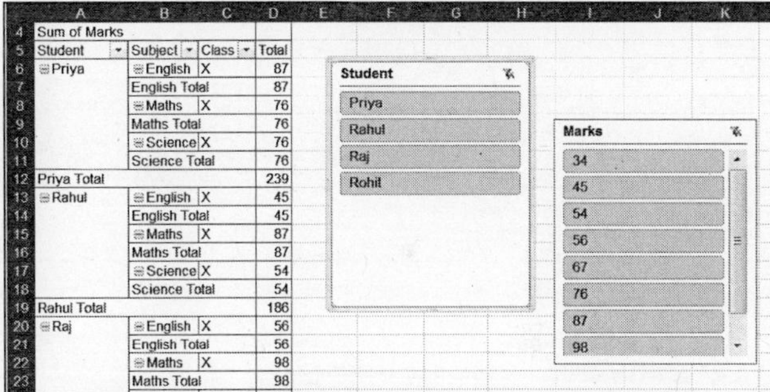

Figure 5.94 Slicer is displayed as per selected Fields

5. In each slicer, click the items on which you want to filter (See Figure 5.95). To select more than one item in a slicer to filter, hold down Ctrl key and then click the items on which you want to filter.

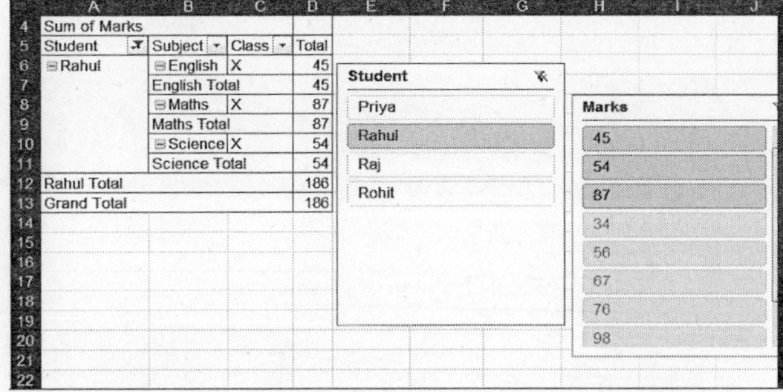

Figure 5.95 Filter Feature has been used for a Slicer

5.14 MACRO IN EXCEL 2010

A macro is the recording of each command and action you perform to complete a task. Whenever you need to carry out that task repeatedly in a spreadsheet, you just run the macro. Complex macros are usually created in Excel with the Macro editor. Simpler macros can, however, be created using the Excel macro recorder. You will need the **Developer tab** for using macros. Therefore, make sure that Developed Tab is available on the ribbon. If it is not there, then perform the following steps to add it in the Ribbon:

➜ **To add the Developer Tab on the Ribbon, do this:**

1. Click the **File** Tab and then click **Options. Excel Options** dialog box appears. In this dialog box, click on **Customize Ribbon** button on the left side. Excel Options dialog box appears with **Customize Ribbon** properties as shown in Figure 5.96.

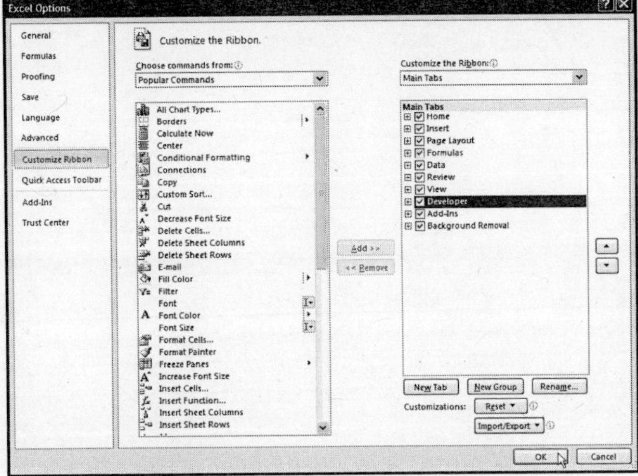

Figure 5.96 Excel Options dialog box

2. In this dialog box, under **Customize the Ribbon**, in the **Main Tabs list**, click **Developer** check box.
3. Click OK.
4. The **Developer** tab should now be visible in the ribbon (See Figure 5.97).

5.14.1 The Excel Macro Recorder

Before we start recording our macro, we need to add the worksheet title we will be formatting. Since, the title of each worksheet is usually unique to that worksheet, we do not want to include the title in the macro. Therefore, we will add it to the worksheet before starting the macro recorder.

1. Click on cell A1 in the worksheet.
2. Type the title, such as "Priintek India".
3. Press the Enter key on the keyboard.

➜ **To record a macro, do this:**

1. Under the **Developer** Tab and in the **Code** group, click **Record Macro** to open the **Record Macro** dialog box (See Figure 5.98).
2. In **Record Macro** dialog box, under the Macro name: field give macro a descriptive name. The name must begin with a letter. Spaces are not allowed. Only letters, numbers and the underscore characters are permitted.
   In the Shortcut key: field (optional) fill a letter, number, or other characters in the available space. This will allow you to run the macro by holding down the Ctrl key and pressing the chosen key on the keyboard.
   In Store macro in: field, select the following options according to your choice.
   (a) **This workbook** - The macro is available only in this file.
   (b) **New workbook** - This option opens a new Excel file. The macro is available only in this new file.
   (c) **Personal macro workbook** - This option creates a hidden file Personal.xls which stores macros and makes them available to you in all Excel files.
3. In Description: field (optional), enter a description of the macro.
4. Click the OK button in the **Record Macro** dialog box to start the macro recorder.

For example, to perform the actions that you want to record

(a) Click on the **Home** Tab of the ribbon.
(b) Drag select cells A1 to F1 in the worksheet to highlight them.
(c) Click on the **Merge and Center** button from the **Alignment** group to center the title between cells A1 and F1.
(d) Click on the **Font Size** button to open the font size drop-down list and choose 16 from the list to change the size the text in the selected cells to 16 point.
(e) After that click on the **Developer** tab of the ribbon.
(f) Click the **Stop Recording** button from the **Code** group to stop the macro recording.

Figure 5.97 Developer Tab in the Ribbon

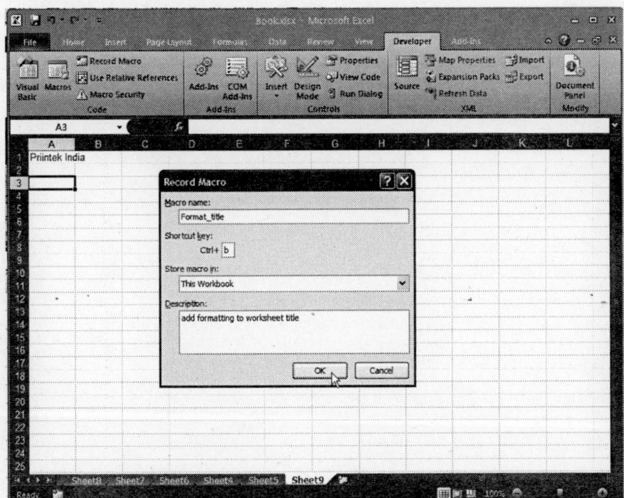

Figure 5.98 Record Macro dialog box

➔ To run a macro, do this:

1. Click on another sheet tab to open the another sheet.
2. Click on cell A1 in the worksheet.
3. Type the title whichever you want to type.
4. Press the Enter key on the keyboard.
5. Click on the **Developer** Tab of the ribbon.
6. Click on the **Macros** from the **Code** group to bring up the **Macro** dialog box (See Figure 5.99).

Figure 5.99 Macro dialog box

7. In **Macro** dialog box, under the Macro name: field, select the macro which you want to run. (Here, we have selected **Format_title** macro name).
8. Then click **Run** button.
9. The steps of the macro should run automatically and the same formatting steps applied to the title of another worksheet.

REVIEW QUESTIONS WITH ANSWERS

1. Multiple Choice

1.1 In Excel the intersection of a row and column is called:

a. Square b. Cell
c. Cubicle d. Worksheet

1.2 By default, Excel sheet displays the following font style:

a. Strikethorugh b. Italic
c. Bold d. None of the above

1.3 Extension of Excel file is:

a. .TMT b. .XXL
c. .xls d. None of the above

1.4 The first electronic worksheet was known as

a. VisiCalc b. Microsoft Excel
c. Lotus 1-2-3 d. None of the above

1.5 A worksheet can be opened by clicking on the:

a. Start button c. Both a and b
b. Open button d. None of the above

1.6 The Formatting toolbar:

a. Is placed just below the Standard toolbar
b. Is used to apply common formats to the worksheet text selection, like making it bold, italics, underlined or changing the font style and size
c. Both a and b
d. None of the above

1.7 To change the cell reference B2:B9 to an absolute row and column reference, you would enter it as:

a. B2:B9 b. \$B\$2:\$B\$9
c. B\$2:B\$9 d. none of the above

1.8 A function in Excel:

a. Is a ready made formula b. Is a shortcut formula
c. Can be built using Function Wizard d. All of the above

1.9 Which of the following is not a financial function?

a. FV() c. SUM()
b. NPV() d. PMT()

1.10 Which of the following is not a text function?

a. CHAR() c. VAR()
b. LEN() d. ABS()

1.11 The number of rows in a worksheet is:

a. 36500 c. 65536
b. 1,048,576 d. 256

1.12 When a formatted number does not fit within a cell, it displays:

a. ##### c. #DIV@

b. #DIV/0 d. None of these

1.13 What symbol is used to enter number as text?

a. = c. '

b. " d. +

1.14 Which of the following is concantenating operator?

a. Apostrophe (') c. Exclamation (!)

b. Ampersand (&) d. Hash (#)

1.15 To select multiple non-adjecent cells in a worksheet you will click and then holding:

a. ALT key c. Ctrl+Shift key combination

b. Shift Key d. Ctrl key

1.16 What does the Now() function return?

a. It returns the serial number of the current date and time

b. It returns the serial number of the current date

c. It returns the serial number of the current time

d. None of the above

1.17 What is shortcut key to insert current date in a cell?

a. Ctrl + D c. Ctrl + T

b. Ctrl + ; d. Ctrl + /

1.18 Which Chart can be created in Excel?

a. Area c. Line

b. Pie d. All of the above

1.19 What will be the output if you format the cell containing 5436.8 as '#,##0.00'?

a. 5,430.00 c. 5,436.8

b. 5,436.80 d. 6.8

1.20 In the formula, which symbol specifies the fixed columns or rows?

a. $ c. %

b. * d. @

1.21 What is the correct way to refer the cell A10 on sheet3 from sheet1?

a. sheet1!A10 c. sheet3!A10

b. sheet3.A10 d. A10

1.22 An Excel 2010 Workbook is a collection ________.

a. Workbooks c. Charts

b. Worksheets d. Worksheets and Charts

1.23 In Excel 2010, you can sum a large range of data by simply selecting a tool button called _______.

a. AutoFill c. Auto Format

b. AutoCorrect d. AutoSum

1.24 Which function is used to calculate depreciation, rates of return, future values and loan payment amounts?

a. Logical c. Statistical

b. Math & Trigonometry d. Financial

1.25 To keep specific rows and columns from scrolling off the screen you first must

a. To the right of the column you want to remain on the screen

b. Below the row you want to remain on the screen

c. On the row you want to remain on the screen

d. Both below and right of the row and column you want to remain on the screen

1.26 Which command will you choose to convert a column of data into row?

a. Home → Paste → Transpose

b. Home → Paste → Paste Special...

c. Home → Paste → Paste as Hyperlink

d. Home → Paste → Paste Link

2. State whether the following statements are True or False

2.1 To create a new worksheet, select Worksheet from the File menu.

2.2 Cells are named by their positions either by rows or columns.

2.3 If the Bold and Underline buttons are appearing lighter than before, it means that they are currently in use.

2.4 Standard width of a column is 18.43.

2.5 To open a file quickly from the Open dialog box, double click the file's icon.

2.6 You cannot move the active cell within a selected range.

2.7 You can simultaneously select an entire row and an entire column.

2.8 Sheet tab is displayed when you split a sheet.

2.9 Last column of the worksheet window is XFD.

2.10 Using the undo command you can undo multiple actions.

2.11 Receives the data the user enters is known as active cell.

2.12 A Workbook is a grid with labeled columns and rows.

2.13 Tabs that appear at the bottom of each workbook is called sheet tabs.

2.14 The first cell in Excel 2010 worksheet is labeled as A0.

2.15 Excel 2010 is a powerful communication software package.

2.16 B7:B9 it indicates cells B7 through B9.

2.17 The Cancel and Enter buttons appear in the Formula bar.

2.18 A21 is an example of a cell address.

2.19 The box on the chart that contains the name of each individual record is called the axis.

2.20 Character type is not a valid data type in Excel.

3. Match the following

3.1	Sheet tab	a.	A collection of Excel worksheet
3.2	Workbook	b.	It is a tab at the bottom of the screen that represents a sheet in a workbook.
3.3	Sort & Filter	c.	Two rows will be inserted after Row 4
3.4	Hide entire Row	d.	Data can be arranged in ascending or descending order by using
3.5	To insert current data in a cell	e.	Ctrl+9
3.6	Getting data from a cell located in a different sheet is called	f.	Cell Tip

3.7	Comments put in cells are called	g.	Apostrophe (')
3.8	Selecting the Rows 5 & 6 then choose Insert sheet rows in the cells group of Home tab	h.	Ctrl+;
3.9	A numeric value can be treated as label value if precedes it	i.	Character
3.10	It is not a valid data type in Excel	j.	Referencing
3.11	Concatenation of text can be done using	k.	Updating
3.12	In Excel window allows entering values and formulas	l.	Ampersand (&)
3.13	To insert a new line in the same cell	m.	Formula bar
3.14	A function inside another function is called	n.	Alt+ Enter
3.15	AutoFill	o.	Nested
		p.	Cells
		q.	Creates a series

4. Fill in the blanks

a. 31	b. Tool Tips	c. Shift+F11
d. Fill handle	e. Range	f. Paste Link
g. Password	h. Currency style	i. Relative references
j. Active cell	k. DAY()	l. Sign
m. average()	o. LEFT()	p. COUNT()

4.1. When you select a cell with the mouse, the cell becomes ________.

4.2. A feature known as ________ provides working of the tool button when you moves the mouse pointer on it.

4.3 To insert a new sheet in a workbook, press ________.

4.4 The name of a sheet can be upto ________ characters long.

4.5 ________ is an area on the worksheet, which is rectangular and contains two or more cells.

4.6 ________ creates a series automatically.

4.7 The ________ button in the Paste Special dialog box enables you to link the pasted data to the original source.

4.8 A worksheet can be protected with a ________.

4.9 ________ button adds a currency sign, a decimal point and two decimal places in your numbers.

4.10 References that change automatically when you copy them to a new cell are called ________.

4.11 The ________ function returns the day of the month from the date serial number.

4.12 To find the average value in a row or a column you will use ________ function.

4.13 ABS() function returns the absolute value without its ________.

4.14 ________ function tells how many cells contain numeric values.

4.15 ________ function extract the left side of character(s).

Answers

1. 1.1 b 1.2 d 1.3 c 1.4 a 1.5 b 1.6 c
1.7 c 1.8 d 1.9 c 1.10 d 1.11 b 1.12 a
1.13 c 1.14 b 1.15 d 1.16 a 1.17 b 1.18 d
1.19 b 1.20 a 1.21 d 1.22 d 1.23 d 1.24 c
1.25 d 1.26 a

2. 2.1 F 2.2 F 2.3 F 2.4 F 2.5 T 2.6 F
2.7 F 2.8 T 2.9 T 2.10 T 2.11 T 2.12 F
2.13 T 2.14 F 2.15 F 2.16 T 2.17 T 2.18 T
2.19 F 2.20 T

3. 3.1 b 3.2 a 3.3 d 3.4 e 3.5 h 3.6 j
3.7 f 3.8 c 3.9 g 3.10 i 3.11 l 3.12 m
3.13 n 3.14 o 3.15 q

4. 4.1 j 4.2 b 4.3 c 4.4 a 4.5 e 4.6 d
4.7 f 4.8 g 4.9 h 4.10 i 4.11 k 4.12 m
4.13 l 4.14 p 4.15 o

Short Questions with Answers

1. How to select a cell or range? Make a list of options.
2. How to rename a worksheet?
3. How do I resize Columns and Rows to better fit the data in MS Excel?
4. How can I dentify which cells in my spreadsheets have a formula and which do not in MS Excel?
5. Is it possible to change the color and font of the sheet tabs?
6. How can I enter the current date into a cell so it does not change from day-to-day? When I use the Now() function, it always shows the current date?
7. What is Excel Spreadsheet Number Format?
8. How do you use the Sum and AutoSum functions in Excel?
9. How do you use the IF functions in Excel?
10. What are slicers? Why they are used in Excel 2010?

Answers to Short Questions

1. The options used to select a cell or range in Excel are summarized in Table below.

To be Selected	Perform this
A single cell	Click the cell, or press the arrow keys to move to the cell.
A range of cells	Click the first cell in the range, and then drag to the last cell, or hold down Shift while you press the arrow keys to extend the selection.
All cells on a worksheet	Click the Select All button. To select the entire worksheet, you can also press Ctrl+A key combination.

Other options of selection are as follows:

- If the row or column contains data, Ctrl+Shift+Arrow key combination selects the row or column to the last used cell.
- Pressing Ctrl+Shift+Arrow key combination a second time selects the entire row or column.

2. To rename a worksheet, do this:

On the Sheet tab bar, right-click the sheet tab that you want to rename, for example Sheet2. Select Rename. Type the new name for Active sheet.
You can also include the name of the sheet while printing the worksheet.

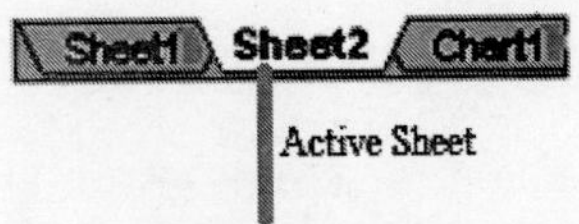

3. a. Move the mouse in between any two labels (Rows/numbers or Columns/letters)
   b. The pointer will turn into a vertical or horizontal line with arrows on both ends
   c. Simply drag the column or row to the desired size.
4. a. Choose View tab in the Show group.
   b. Click 'Formulas' check box.
5. Yes, we can change the color of sheet tabs. By right clicking on sheet tabs and you will get shortcut menu where you can change color of the sheet tab.
6. The easiest way to enter the current date into a cell is to use the Ctrl + ; key combination (press the Ctrl key and type a semicolon). Similarly, you can enter the current time by pressing Ctrl + Shift + ; (press the Ctrl and Shift keys and type a semicolon). Both of these key combinations enter the information as a volatile value, not as a formula.
7. Number formatting in Excel spreadsheet is used to change the look of the numbers in the cell. The most formatting options are currency, comma, date, accounting and percent, although there are more options available.
8. The Excel SUM function is most likely used function in Excel spreadsheets. The AutoSUM button on the Standard toolbar makes it easy to quickly sum columns or rows of adjacent data without actually typing in the cell references.
9. One of the most useful functions in Excel is the IF function. The value in a specific cell to see if that value meets a certain condition. If it does, one result will happen, if not, a different action can occur.
10. Slicers are easy-to-use filtering components that contain a set of buttons that enable you to quickly filter the data in a PivotTable report, without the need to open drop-down lists to find the items that you want to filter.

    In Excel 2010, you have the option to use slicers to filter the data. Slicers provide buttons that you can click to filter PivotTable data. In addition to quick filtering, slicers also indicate the current filtering state, which makes it easy to understand what exactly is shown in a filtered PivotTable report.

DESCRIPTIVE TYPE QUESTIONS

1. Differentiate between workbook and worksheet.
2. How can you insert and delete a sheet from your workbook?
3. What is the procedure to select multiple non-adjacent ranges of cells?
4. How can a worksheet be renamed?
5. How will you copy some data from a worksheet to another worksheet in same workbook or in a different workbook?
6. How to move and copy data and formulas in MS Excel? Explain.
7. What is protection? How do you secure a group of worksheets in Excel 2010?
8. How do you hide columns in a worksheet? How do we adjust row height in MS Excel?
9. Discuss merge cell feature, wrap text feature, fill in cell feature available in Excel 2010.
10. How can you hide or unhide columns and rows? Describe the process:
    a. Using mouse
    b. Using keyboard
11. Explain how range name is defined and used with spreadsheet.
12. In Excel, we have three functions named a ROUND(), ROUNDDOWN(), ROUNDUP(), how these are different? Explain with examples.
13. Differentiate between embedded charts and charts in separate chartsheet. What are the advantages of each chart?
14. What is a PivotTable. How does it help in data analysis?
15. What is macro? How will you record and run macro in Excel 2010?

CHAPTER 6

Presentation Tools

6.1 INTRODUCTION

PowerPoint 2010 is a presentation program developed for the Windows and Mac OS computer operating systems. Being widely used by business people, educators, and trainers, it is among the most prevalent forms of persuasion technology. According to its vendor, Microsoft Corporation, some 30 million presentations are made with PowerPoint everyday.

In Microsoft PowerPoint, as in most other presentation software, text, graphics, movies, and other objects are positioned on individual pages or "slides". The "slide" is a reference to the slide projector, a device which has become somewhat obsolete due to the use of PowerPoint and other presentation software. Slides can be printed, or displayed on-screen and navigated through at the command of the presenter. Transitions between slides can be animated in a variety of ways, as can the emergence of elements on a slide itself. The overall design of a presentation can be controlled with a master slide. The overall structure, extending to the text on each slide, can be edited using an outliner. Presentations can be saved and run in many types of file formats.

6.2 BASICS OF POWERPOINT

PowerPoint is the largest selling presentation graphics software package by Microsoft Corporation of USA and since its introduction in 1987, PowerPoint has set new standards for the working of presentation graphics.

PowerPoint 2010 helps you bringing *ideas* and *information* that you want to convey to your audience with no difficulty. With PowerPoint 2010, you can:

- Quickly create *paper for Overhead Projector (OHP), 35mm slide,* or *on-screen* presentations.
- Supplement your presentations with *speaker's notes.*
- Use material you have created in other application packages, such as Word 2010 and Excel 2010.

6.2.1 Using PowerPoint

Presentations

You can make presentation in the form of *slides, handouts* or *speaker's notes.*

Slides

Slides are individual "*pages*" of a presentation. It may contain *text, graphs, clipart,* etc. You can even print slides for overhead projector transparencies.

Handouts

Handouts consist of printed versions of your slides – either two, three, or six slides per page.

6.2.2 Opening PowerPoint 2010 for Presentation

➜ **To start PowerPoint 2010, do this:**

1. Click the **Start** button on the Taskbar.
2. Highlight **All Programs** menu item and click **Microsoft Office** and choose **MS Office PowerPoint 2010** (See Figure 6.1).

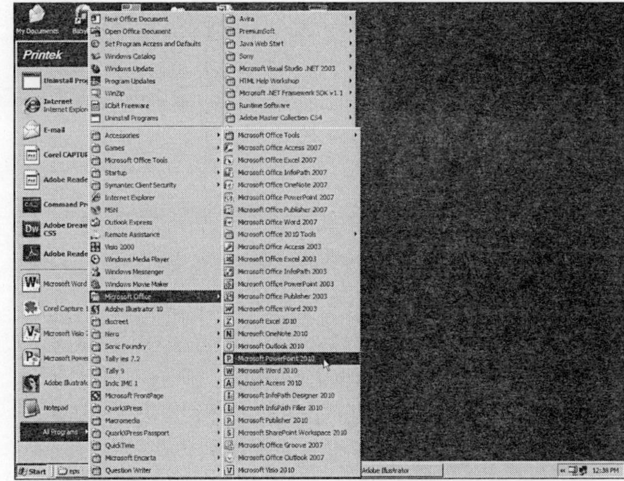

Figure 6.1 Starting Powerpoint with the Start Button

When you first start PowerPoint 2010, it displays a blank presentation with a single slide showing. The layout is simple, with a title at the top and a subtitle below (See Figure 6.2).

Understanding the Screen Elements

You will notice a close resemblance of the PowerPoint 2010 opening screen with the opening screens of Word 2007 and Excel 2007. The main elements of the PowerPoint window are as shown in Figure 6.2.

Title bar: The *Title bar* is at the top of the screen (See Figure 6.2). It shows the title PowerPoint and the name of presentation. If you have not yet saved any presentation then it displays the default name for the presentation which is *Presentation1*.

Ribbon: Ribbon is displayed just below the title bar. In Ribbon, Commands are organized in logical groups, which are collected together under tabs (See Figure 6.2).

Quick Access Toolbar: This toolbar is located by default at the top of PowerPoint 2010 window. By default, this toolbar

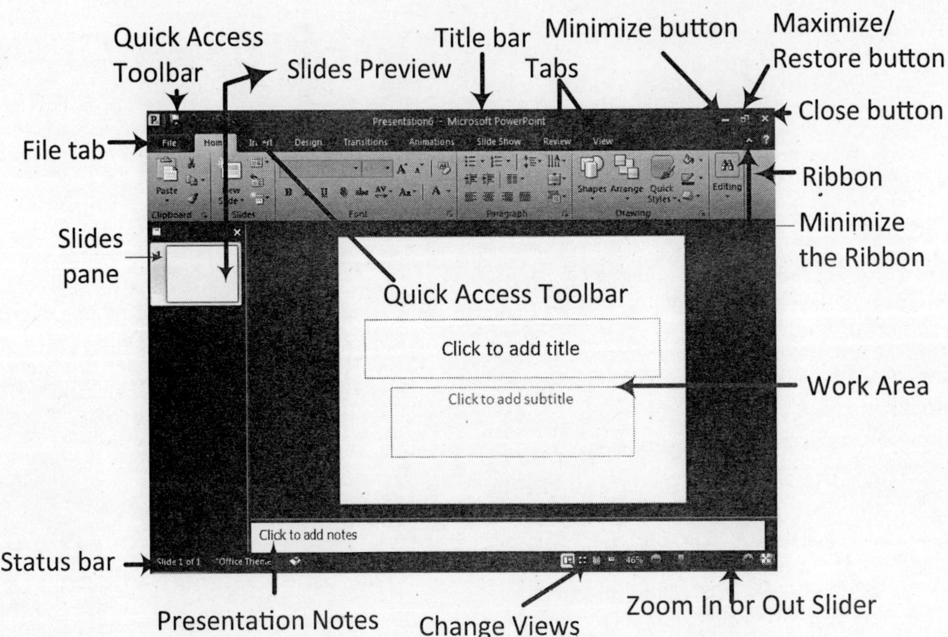

Figure 6.2 A blank presentation displayed by PowerPoint

displays the Save, Undo and Repeat buttons.

Minimize button: Shrinks the application window to a bar on the Taskbar, you can click its button on the Taskbar to reopen it.

Restore button: A double box at the right of a Title bar that restores an application or document into a sizable window.

Close button: A box at the right of a Title bar (X) that closes the window or dialog box.

Work area: Where active PowerPoint slide(s) appear. Figure 6.2 shows it in Normal view, but other views are available that make the work area appear differently.

Status bar: It gives the information about the presentation and provides shortcuts for changing the view and the zoom.

Exploring PowerPoint 2010 Interface

There is a new look for PowerPoint 2010. There is also a new user interface that replaces menus, toolbars, and most of the task panes from previous versions of PowerPoint. The new user interface is designed to help you to be more productive in PowerPoint; more easily find the right features for various tasks and also be more efficient.

The PowerPoint 2010 interface consists of various components, which are as follows:

Minimize/Maximize/Restore and Close Buttons

The Minimize, Maximize and Close buttons are located on the top right corner of the MS PowerPoint window. The Minimize button is used to minimize the MS PowerPoint window over the Task bar whereas the Maximize button helps to restore or maximize the window. The Close button is used to close the document (See Figure 6.2).

File Tab

File tab is the colored tab which is located in the upper-left corner of Microsoft Office 2010 programs and below the Quick Access Toolbar. When you click the File tab, you can see the Backstage view. File tab replaces the Office button in PowerPoint 2010. It contains commands like New, Open, Save, Save As, Print, etc.

Quick Access Toolbar

The Quick Access Toolbar is a customizable toolbar that contains a set of commands that are independent of the tab that is currently displayed. You can add buttons that represent commands to the Quick Access Toolbar. You can move the Quick Access Toolbar from one of the two possible locations. This toolbar is located by default at the top of PowerPoint 2010 window. It provides tools that you use frequently, such as Save, Undo and Repeat buttons (See Figure 6.2). You can customize the Quick Access Toolbar by adding commands to it.

➔ **To add command to Quick Access Toolbar, do this:**

1. Right click the appropriate command that you want to add to the Quick Access Toolbar (See Figure 6.3).
2. Then click **Add Group to Quick Access Toolbar** from the context menu as shown in Figure 6.3.

Dialog Box Launchers

The dialog box launchers are small icons that appear in some groups on the Ribbon. Clicking a Dialog Box Launcher opens a related dialog box or task pane, providing more options related to that group.

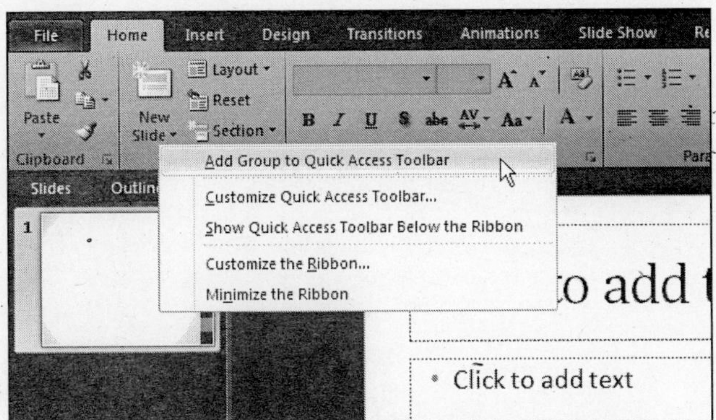

Figure 6.3 Add command to Quick Access toolbar

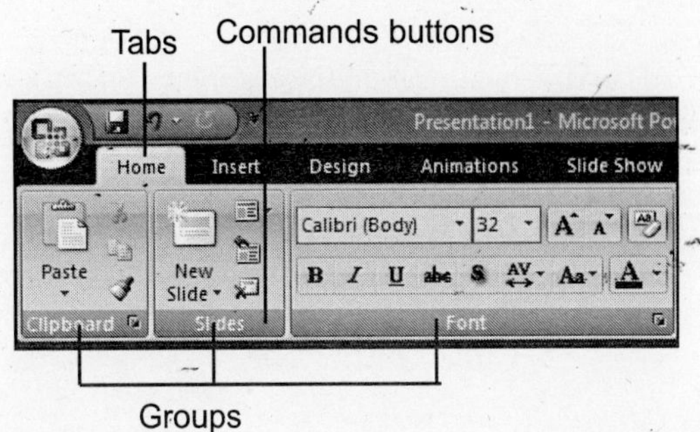

Figure 6.4 Ribbon containing Tab, Command Buttons and Groups

Ribbon

The primary replacement for menus and toolbars in PowerPoint 2010 is the Ribbon. Designed for easy browsing, the Ribbon consists of tabs that are organized around specific scenarios or objects. The controls on each tab are further organized into several groups. The Ribbon can host richer content than menus and toolbars can, including buttons, galleries, and dialog box contents (See Figure 6.4).

1. Tabs are designed to be task-oriented.
2. Groups within each tab break a task into subtasks.
3. Command buttons in each group carry out a command or display a menu of commands.

Contextual Tools

Contextual tools enable you to work with an object that you select on the page, such as table, picture, or drawing. When you click the object, the pertinent set of contextual tabs appear in color next to the standard tabs (See Figure 6.5).

Scroll Bar

The Scroll bar appears at the right side of the PowerPoint. You can also scroll between different slides by using the up and down arrow buttons present in the scroll bar.

Work Area

Where active PowerPoint slide(s) appears. It shows it in Normal view, but other views are available that make the work area different.

Status Bar

It gives the information about the presentation and provides about the current slide, such as slide number and theme name. The slide number displays the currently selected slide with the total number of the slides present in the presentations; whereas, the theme name represents the name of the theme applied to the presentation.

Slides Pane

In the upper-right section of the PowerPoint window, the Slide pane displays a large view of the current slide. With the current slide shown in this view, you can add text and insert pictures (picture: A file (such as a metafile) that you can ungroup and manipulate as two or more objects, or a file that stays as a single object, such as bitmaps, tables, SmartArt graphics, charts, drawing objects, text boxes, movies, sounds, hyperlinks, and animations.

Notes Pane

In the Notes pane below the Slide pane, you can type notes that

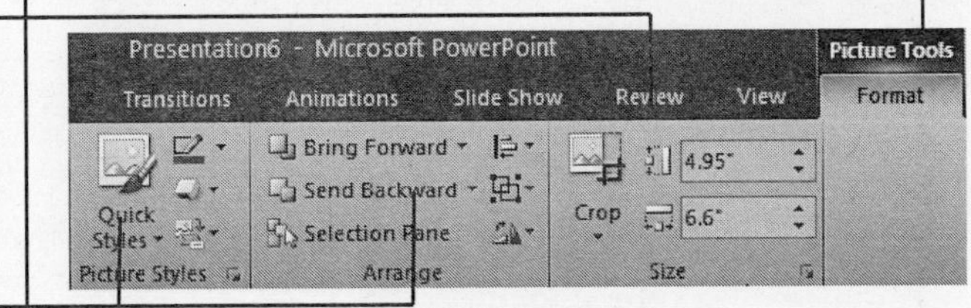

Figure 6.5 Contextual Tools

apply to the current slide. Later, you can print your notes and refer to them when you give your presentation. You can also print notes to handout to your audience or include the notes in a presentation that you send to the audience or post on a Web page.

Zoom Control

You can use Zoom controls to get a larger or smaller view of your presentation by drag the Zoom slider from right to left. You can click the Zoom In (+ plus) button to get a larger view of the presentation and the Out (- minus) button to get a smaller view of the presentation.

Exploring the Tabs

Ribbon in PowerPoint 2010 is a group of tabs. This tab consists of two types, command tabs and contextual tabs. A command tab is a collection of commands of a specific category. Commands in a command tab are placed into different group. Each command set representing a subcategory of commands. Contextual tabs appear on the Ribbon when you add or select some object, such as image, a table, or a chart on a PowerPoint slide. An example of a contextual tab is the Format tab. Some of the tabs are discussed in the following sections:

Home Tab: When you click it, this tab is active. Buttons related to working with document contents are organized in this tab. It has six groups: Clipboard, Slides, Font, Paragraph, Drawing and Editing. Only the button representing commands that can be performed on the currently selected document element are active (See Figure 6.6).

The groups for the Home Tab are:

(a) ***Clipboard:*** This contains the Cut, Copy, and Paste commands.

(b) ***Slides:*** This section allows you to insert new slides (clicking on the 'New Slide' button allows you to select the slide type you wish), as well as adjust the layout of your individual slides, reset slides to default, and delete slides.

(c) ***Font:*** Select the font here. Adjust the font type and size. Make it bold, italic, or underline. Change the color or highlighting. Using the tab, you can also change case of selected text to uppercase or lowercase.

(d) ***Paragraph:*** Bullets or numbered lists. It also changes the alignment of text and change the spacing between lines.

(e) ***Drawing:*** Insert shapes. Arrange objects on a given slide. It also applies fill color in the selected shape and add effect to the shapes.

(f) ***Editing:*** Find, edit, select, and replace text.

Insert Tab: Click this button for related items you can insert. These are organizing on this tab. It has seven groups: *Tables, Images, Illustrations, links, Text, Symbols* and *Media* (See Figure 6.7). When you need to insert anything into your slide show, this is where you come to do it. The groups available to you are:

(a) ***Tables:*** Insert tables into the slide. These can be pre-made, or you can make them as you like.

(b) ***Images:*** It allows you to insert pictures from a file as well as from the Clip Art in a slide. You can also create photo album and apply visual effects to pictures. Screenshot which allows you take screenshot of all currently opened windows on the computer.

(c) ***Illustrations:*** It allows you to insert pre-defined shapes, Smart Arts and charts in the presentation.

(d) ***Links:*** Add a hyperlink, to take you out of your slideshow to a Web resource. Add an action to cause something to happen in the slide-show if you point to an object with the mouse.

(e) ***Text:*** It is not just about typing text into a slide. Insert text boxes, which allow you to play with the location and orientation of words. Insert headers and footers. Turn your text into "***Word Art***". Insert date, times, slide numbers and other embedded objects.

(f) ***Symbols:*** It allows you to insert and edit equations and insert symbols in the presentation.

(g) ***Media:*** Insert video and sound into your slide, to create a truly vibrant presentation.

Design tab: Click this tab which will show buttons that are related to items. You can give design to your slides. They are organized on this tab. It has three groups: *Page Setup, Themes, Background* (See Figure 6.8).

Adjust the look of individual slides with the contents of the design tab. Change just one slide, or apply your changes to the whole presentation:

(a) ***Page Setup:*** Adjust margins, page size, and orientation (portrait or landscape).

(b) ***Themes:*** PowerPoint 2007 comes with 20 built-in themes (combinations of color, layout, and font). You can browse the Web for more themes, or create your own custom ones.

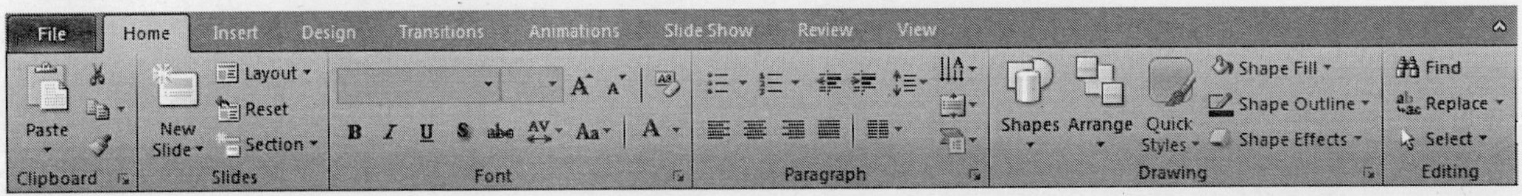

Figure 6.6 Home tab

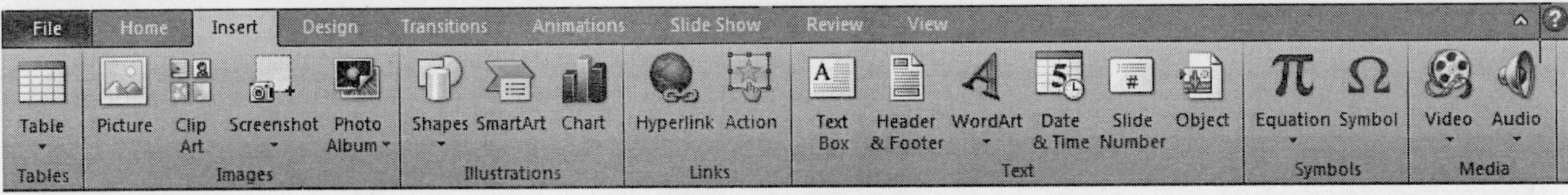

Figure 6.7 Insert tab

(c) ***Background:*** It adjust the background look of your slides by changing the color, or adding special images like watermarks.

Transitions: The transitions tab let you preview the presentation after applying effects, add transitions to a slide, and set the timing for the slide show of the presentation. It has three groups: *Preview, Transition to this slide, timing* (See Figure 6.9).

(a) ***Preview:*** It helps to view the slide after the transition effect is applied.

(b) ***Transition to this slide:*** It allows you to apply transition to a slide and set the effect option specific to a transition.

(c) ***Timing:*** It allows you to add transition sound and set the time to move to the next slide.

Animations tab: Click this tab which will show buttons that are related to items. You can give animations to your slides. For example, you can animate individual objects on the slide. They are organized on this tab. It has three groups: *Preview, Animation, Advance Animation* and *Timing* (See Figure 6.10).

(a) ***Preview:*** To preview the animation applied in the slide, include transition effect and animation applied on objects and text.

(b) ***Animation:*** It allows you to apply animation to a slide and the effect based on the animation type.

(c) ***Advanced Animation:*** It allows you to apply advanced features to the applied animation and apply trigger effect.

(d) ***Timings:*** To set the duration of the slides and delay between the slides. You can reorder the animation.

Slide Show: Click this tab which will show buttons that are related to items. In this tab, you can view; take up the full computer screen, like an actual presentation. For example, you can see how your graphics animated effects will look during the presentation. It has three groups: *Start Slide Show, Set Up* and *Monitors* (See Figure 6.11).

(a) ***Start Slide Show:*** Run it from the beginning or from a selected slide. Or, create a second slide show using only those slides in the presentation you want to use.

(b) ***Set Up:*** Record narration for your slide show. Practice your timing as you speak while the show's slides transition automatically.

(c) ***Monitors:*** It allows you to select a screen resolution or a presenter view.

Review tab: Click this tab which will show buttons that are related to items. In this tab, you can view and add comments to your presentation and you might prefer to check spelling all at once when you finish your document. It has four groups: *Proofing, Language, Comments* and *Compare* (See Figure 6.12).

(a) ***Proofing:*** Check the spelling, open research task pane to references for more information; find synonyms so you do not use the same word repeatedly, check the grammar, etc.

(b) ***Language:*** It allows you to translate the text in other languages.

(c) ***Comments:*** Add or edit comments about a given slide, or about a specific bit of content on a slide. Helpful when planning narration.

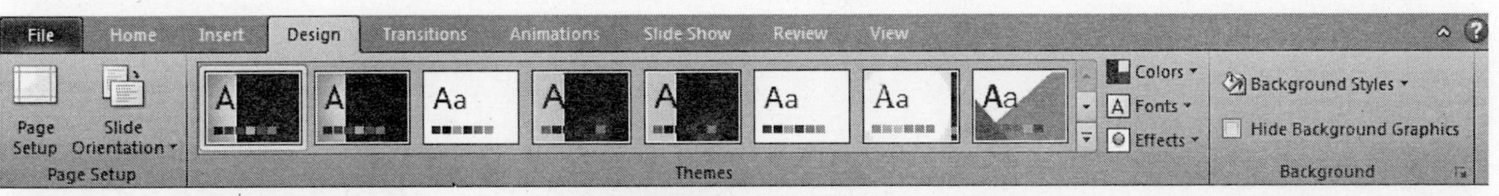

Figure 6.8 Design tab

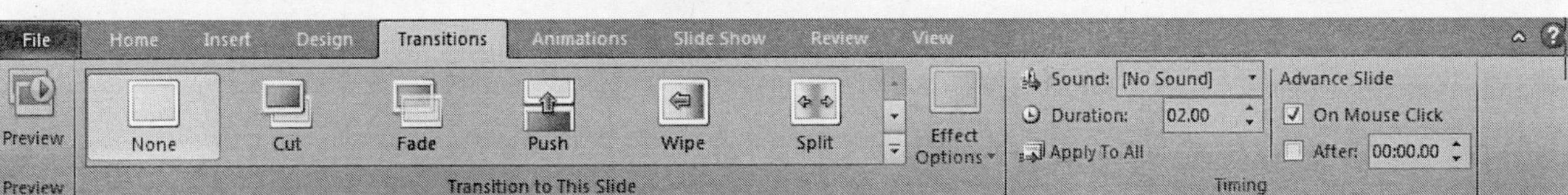

Figure 6.9 Transitions tab

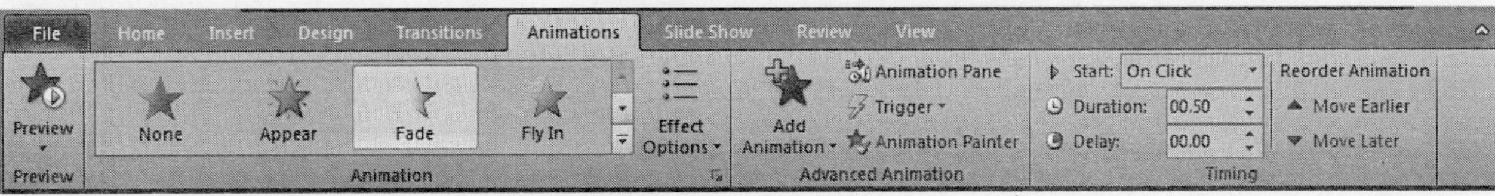

Figure 6.10 Animations tab

Figure 6.11 Slide Show tab

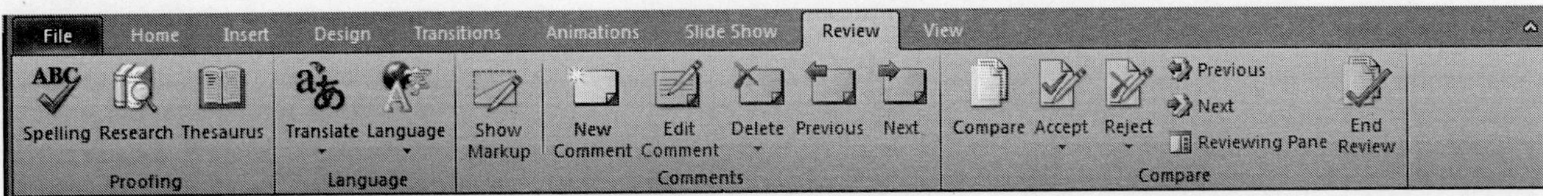

Figure 6.12 Review tab

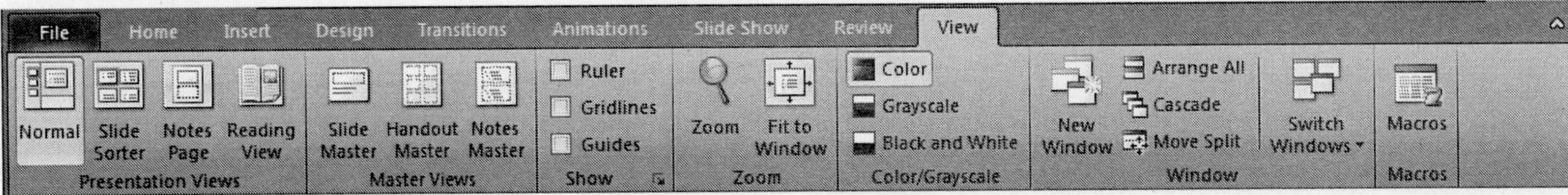

Figure 6.13 View tab

(d) ***Compare:*** To compare different presentations, accept or reject the changes, and show the review pane.

View tab: Click this tab which will show buttons that are related to changing the view during presentation. It has six groups: *Presentation views, Master Views, Show/Hide, Zoom, Color/Grayscale, Window* and *Macros* (See Figure 6.13).

(a) ***Presentation View:*** Choose from normal, slide sorter, notes view, handout view, and other options, either for on screen viewing, or printouts.

(b) ***Master Views:*** To view the presentation in slide master view, handout master view and notes master view.

(c) ***Show/Hide:*** It displays, gridlines, rulers and other tools to help you place objects into the slides exactly where you want them.

(d) ***Zoom:*** Zoom In or Out to change the size of the slide window.

(e) ***Color/Grayscale:*** View the presentation in color, grayscale or even black and white.

(f) ***Window:*** Arrange the windows in which you are working to help you be more productive.

(g) ***Macros:*** Create and use custom macros to do complex tasks with just a click or two.

Figure 6.14 Selecting Open option from the File tab

6.2.3 Opening an Existing Presentation

PowerPoint 2010 opens files in any of the several format, such as (.pptx, .pptm, .potx, .ppt, .pot, etc.).

➜ **To open an existing presentation, do this:**

1. Open the **File** tab on the Ribbon. The Backstage view appears. Alternatively, press Ctrl+O (See Figure 6.14).
2. Click the **Open** option from the Backstage view (See Figure 6.15).
3. The **Open** dialog box appears as shown in Figure 6.15.

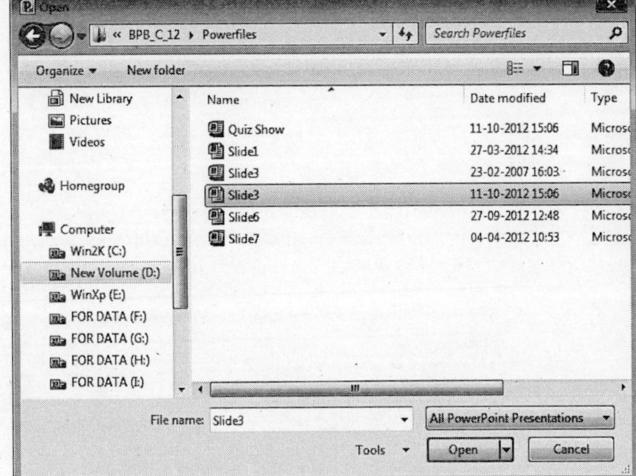

Figure 6.15 PowerPoint's Open dialog box

4. Choose the files and folders in the **Look in:** drop-down list.
5. Select the name of the file you want to open from the list.
6. Click Open button to open the presentation.

6.2.4 Saving the Presentation

When working on a presentation, it is very important that you save it at regular intervals so that in case there is system failure you do not loose much of your work.

PowerPoint has two commands to save your file – Save and Save As command.

- The Save command is used to save the presentation.
- The Save As command is used when you want to save an existing presentation under a new name or you are saving your presentation for the first time.

➜ **To save a presentation, do this:**

1. Click the **File** tab and on the Ribbon. The Backstage view will appear. Select the **Save** option from the **File** tab. Or click the **Save** button on the Quick Access toolbar or from the keyboard press Ctrl+S.
2. If you have already saved the file then PowerPoint updates the earlier saved file. If you have not saved the file before, the **Save As** dialog box appears as shown in Figure 6.16 .

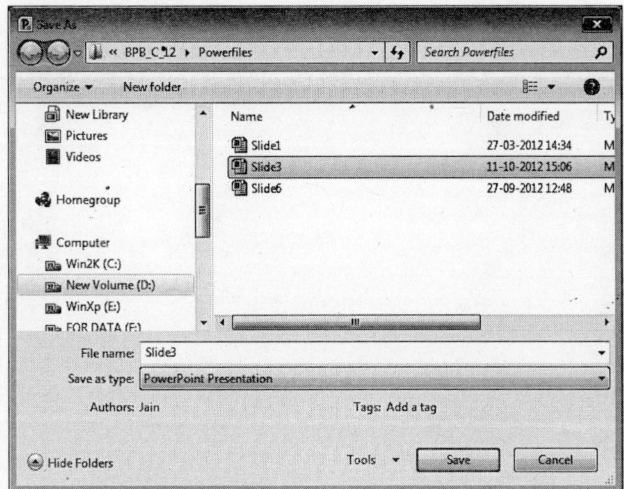

Figure 6.16 PowerPoint's Save As dialog box

3. In the **Save As** list box specify the location where you want to save the file in the **Save in:** drop-down list. (Choose PowerPoint Template). It adds the template to your list of available templates.
4. Type the desired file name which you want to save the presentation in the **File Name:** list box.
5. Click **Save** button.

➜ **To save a presentation using Save As command, do this:**

1. Click the **File** tab and choose **Save As...** . The **Save As** dialog box appears as shown in Figure 6.16 . Now follow Step 1 through 5 in the save procedure.

6.3 CREATION OF PRESENTATION

PowerPoint is designed to give your slide presentations a consistent look. There are four ways that PowerPoint helps you control the look of your slides – with design related elements, Visual elements, color schemes, and layouts of slides.

6.3.1 Creating a Presentation using an Installed Template

A template is a file that contains many types of documents, including resumes, cover letters, business plans, business cards, etc. Microsoft provided templates and presentations that are preinstalled with PowerPoint. These templates offer various layouts, visual elements, and other design-related elements to create presentations.

➜ **To create a presentation by using an installed template, do this:**

1. Click the **File** tab. The Backstage view appears as shown in Figure 6.17.
2. Select the **New** option from the Backstage view. It displays the list of all available templates appears in the middle pane as shown in Figure 6.17.
3. Under the **Available Templates and Themes** category, select the **Sample templates** option.

Figure 6.17 Select Sample templates under the available templates themes

4. In the Sample templates, you can see a different types of templates, with all formatting, such as background, themes colors, font, etc., (See Figure 6.18).

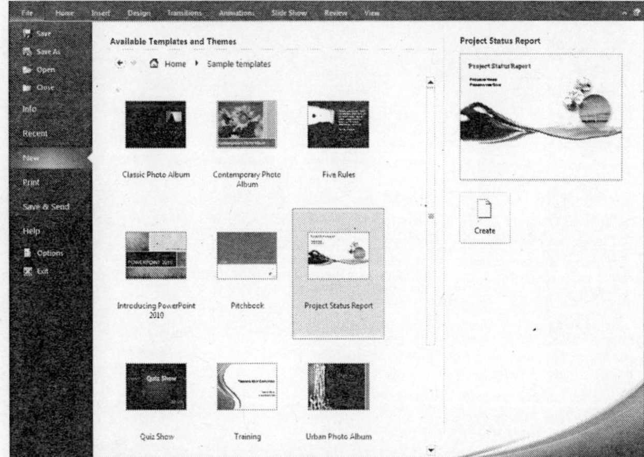

Figure 6.18 Select desired template from the sample templates

5. Select the desired template you want to apply. For example, we have selected, **Project Status Report** (See Figure 6.18).
6. In the **Preview** box, you see a sample presentation for which the template is designed.
7. Click **Create** button.
8. You can see the selected template as default presentation title name (See Figure 6.19).

6.3.2 Creating a Blank Presentation

When you start PowerPoint 2010, the program displays a blank title slide by default. You can begin to add text and pictures on that slide choose a different slide layout, apply a design, etc.

If you want to create a PowerPoint presentation on your own, you can use the blank template in PowerPoint 2010. The blank template offers only the basic visual elements of a presentation, such as placeholder to add a title to a slide.

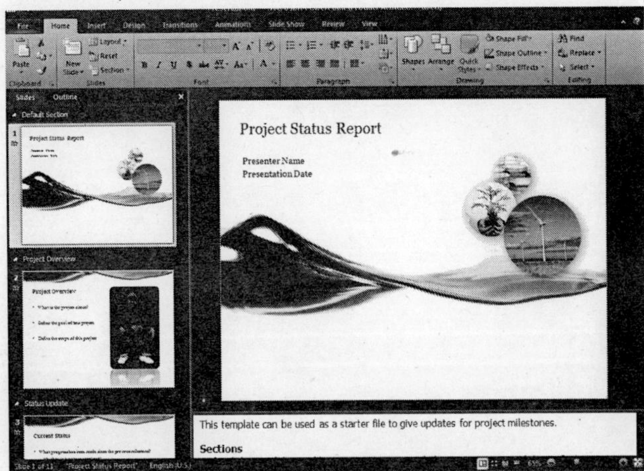

Figure 6.19 PowerPoint opens the selected template

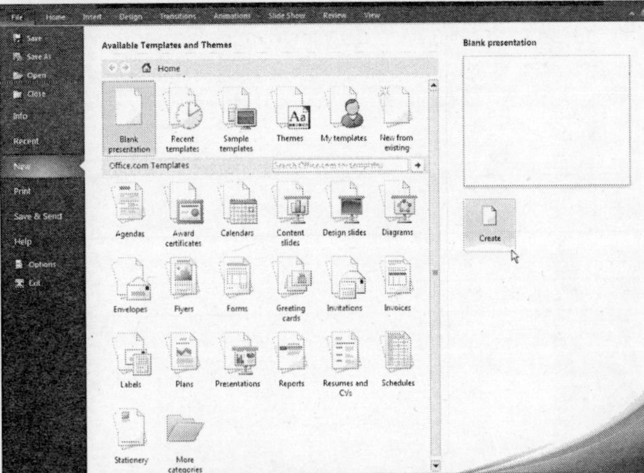

Figure 6.20 File Backstage view

➔ To create a presentation by using the blank template, do this:

1. Click the **File** tab. The Backstage view appears, displaying various options as shown in Figure 6.20.
2. Select the **New** option from the Backstage view.
3. The list of all available templates appears in the middle pane.
4. Under the **Available Templates and Themes** category, select the **Blank presentation** option.
5. Click the **Create** button.
6. The new presentation is created with the name Presentation2 as shown in Figure 6.21.

You can see that a blank presentation contains a single slide with text boxes (placeholders) to enter a title and a subtitle. You can also apply different styles and background to it.

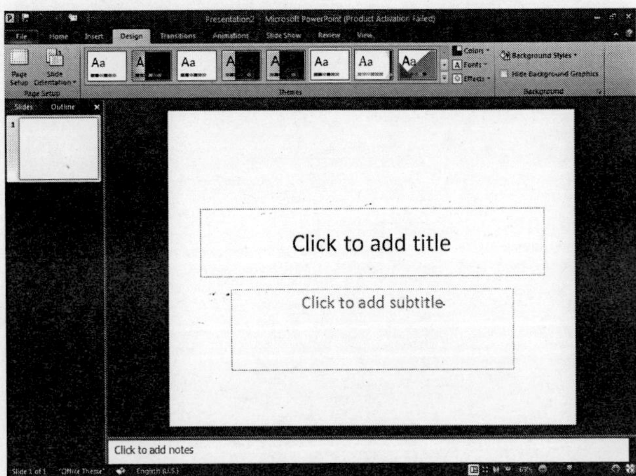

Figure 6.21 Blank presentation with the default name presentation2

Creating a New Template based on an Existing Presentation

You can create a template in almost the same way as you create a presentation. If you have a template that already has most of the features you want, you will save time by creating a new presentation based on that existing template.

1. Click the **File** tab on the ribbon. The Backstage view appears. A list of options appears as shown in 6.20.
2. Click the **New** option from the list.
3. Under **Available Template and Themes** click **New from existing** icon (See Figure 6.17).
4. The **New from Existing Presentation** dialog box appears as shown in Figure 6.22.

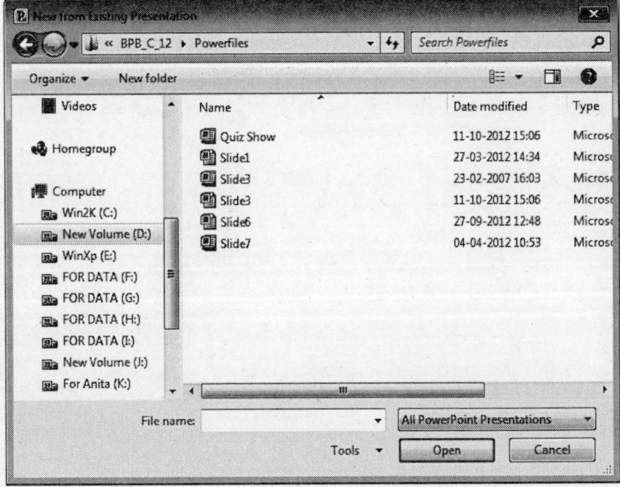

Figure 6.22 New from existing presentation

5. Select the template that is similar to the one that you want to create.

6. Then click **Create New**. Make the changes you want to apply, such as themes colors, fonts and other formats.
7. Click the **Save As** button to save the template.
8. The **Save As** dialog box appears. Give the new name to template file in the **File name:** drop-down list.
9. Select the PowerPoint template in the **Save as type:** drop-down list, and then click **Save** button (See Figure 6.16).

6.3.3 Entering and Editing Text

PowerPoint slide always contains text of some kind, even if it is just a title. Entering and editing text in PowerPoint is similar to entering and editing text in Word or Excel.

Entering Text to Slides

You can enter text in a presentation in two ways:

- Inserting a new slide with text placeholder.
- Inserting text in an existing slide.

Adding Text in a Placeholder

PowerPoint 2010 comes with predefined layouts you want to use, or you can add a blank slide and create a custom layout. Many of these layouts contain text placeholders for title, body and bulleted list.

➜ **To insert a new slide with text, do this:**

1. Click the **Home** tab. In the **Slides** group click New slide down pointing arrow. A list of layout slides appears as shown in Figure 6.23.

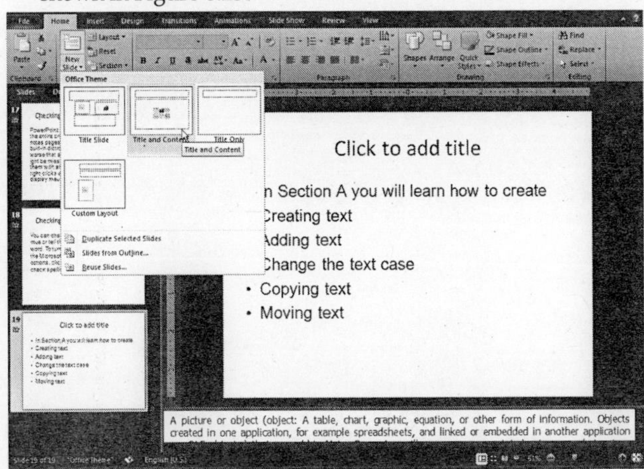

Figure 6.23 Selecting slide layout with title and contents

2. Click anywhere within a placeholder to select it. This border indicates that the current placeholder has been selected (See Figure 6.24).
3. The sample text disappears and an insertion point appears inside the placeholder, indicating that you can enter text.
4. In a title or subtitle placeholder, the insertion point may be centered.
5. In a bulleted-list placeholder, the sample text disappears and the bullet remains, with the insertion point positioned where the text will begin.
6. Type the text for the slide inside the selected placeholder and press Enter key.
7. In the case of bullets, press Enter key when you want to begin a new bulleted item. If the bulleted text is too long to fit on one line, PowerPoint automatically wraps the text to the next line and aligns the text.
8. When you finish entering text, deselect the object by clicking a blank area of the slide of the gray border around the slide.

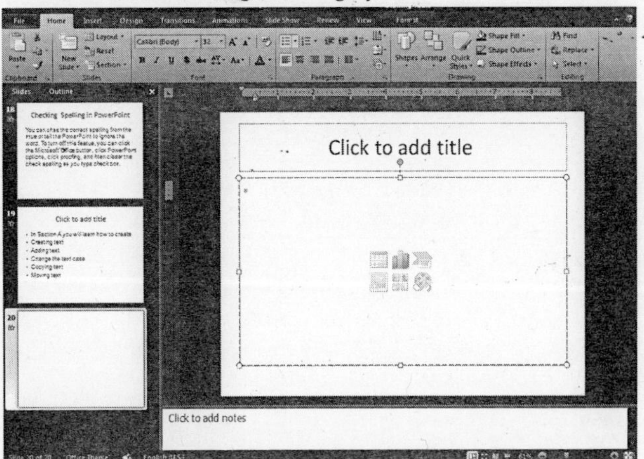

Figure 6.24 The Slide Layout with Placeholder

Editing Text on a Slide

You can make changes to the text in any text object simply by clicking the object. An insertion point appears, indicating that the text is ready for editing. Then you can start making changes to the text. Before you can change existing text, you have to select it by using the following techniques:

- Select an individual word by double-clicking it. The word and the space following it are selected.
- *Alternatively*, position the insertion point at the beginning of the text you want to select, hold down the Shift key, and either press an arrow key to select characters one at a time or click the end of the text you want to select.
- Select an entire slide title by clicking its slide icon on the Outline tab.
- Select all the text in a placeholder by clicking inside the placeholder and then clicking select and then **Select All** in the **Editing** group on the **Home** tab.

Copying Text

You can copy text that appears in one place to another place. Copying of text occurs with the assistance of the Windows Clipboard. The *Clipboard* is an area of your computer's memory that is used for holding data. As long as the data is on the Clipboard, you can place it anywhere in any Windows software application. The data stays on the Clipboard until you replace it with new data, or until you exit Windows.

➜ **To copy text using Ribbon command, do this:**

1. Select the text you want to copy.
2. In the **Home** tab, click copy icon on the **Clipboard** group or (press Ctrl+C keys together).
3. Move to the place in your presentation where you want to insert this text.

4. Click Paste down pointing arrow and choose Paste command on the **Clipboard** group (or press Ctrl+V) keys together.

Moving Text

The move operation is similar to the copy operation except that text is moved, i.e., it is deleted from the original location and copied to a new place.

➜ **To move the text using Ribbon command, do this:**

1. Click the text to put the text box in edit mode.
2. Select the text you want to move.

☞ *Using Cut and Paste is the way to move text around between slides. Just select and cut the text, move to the appropriate slide, and paste it where you want it.*

3. Right-click and choose Cut from the shortcut menu or click the Cut button on the **Home** tab (or press Ctrl+X keys together). Move to the new location, right-click, and choose Paste or click the **Paste** button on the **Home** tab or press Ctrl+V keys together.

Deleting Text

You can delete characters, words, or all the text in a text box. Using one of these methods:

- The Delete key erases the character to the right of the cursor.
- The Backspace key erases the character to the left of the cursor.

If you delete text accidentally, you can undo your action by clicking the Undo button on the Quick Access toolbar. You can also press Ctrl+Z keys together.

6.3.4 Inserting and Deleting Slides in a Presentation

➜ **To insert slide, do this:**

1. In the slide view, display the slide after which you want to insert the slide.
2. In the **Home** tab click **New Slide** drop-down arrow and then choose New slide with layout. The **New** slide is inserted.

Deleting Slides

➜ **To delete slide, do this:**

1. In the Slides pane select the slide you want to delete.
2. Press Delete key. The selected slide gets deleted.

6.4 PREPARATION OF SLIDES

6.4.1 Inserting Word Table or an Excel Worksheet

To add some tabulated data, you can do with many ways, such as inserting table from word file or can choose layout options of PowerPoint. You can insert data from Excel worksheet as well. You can also create a table in your presentation without using Word 2010.

➜ **To create a new slide with table, do this:**

1. Click the **Insert** tab. Click **New Slide** down pointing arrow in the **Slides** group. A list of slides appears.
2. Click the **Title and Content** Slide. A new slide appears as shown in Figure 6.25.

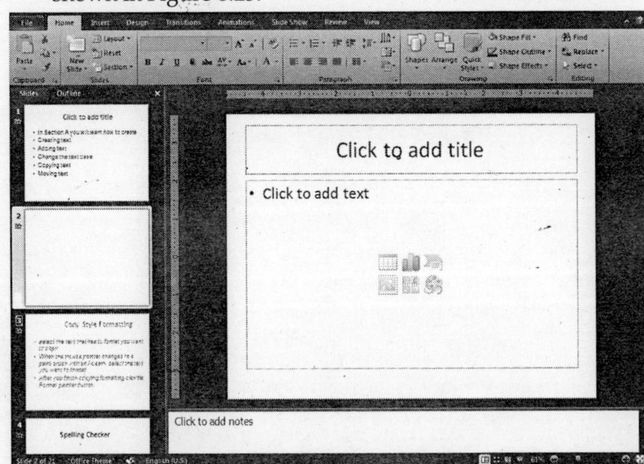

Figure 6.25 A new slide with table placeholder

3. Click the **insert table** placeholder. **Insert Table** dialog box appears as shown in Figure 6.26.
4. In the **Insert Table** dialog box, enter the number of *columns* and the number of *rows* you want to insert in the table. You can type the number of rows and the number of columns or click the up or down arrow on the right of the edit boxes to specify these numbers.
5. After you specify the number of rows and columns, click OK to create the table.
6. A table appears on the slide as shown in Figure 6.27.

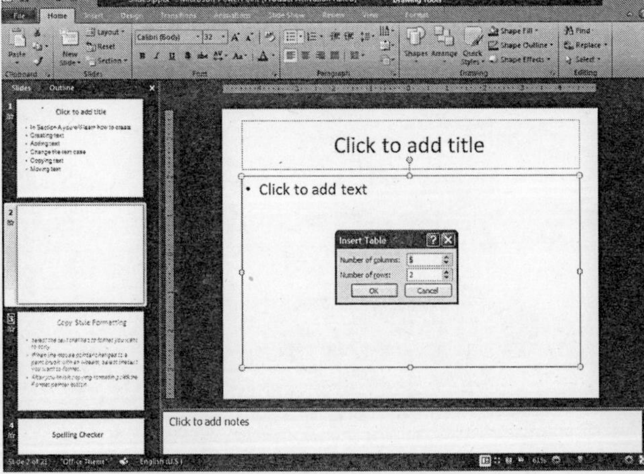

Figure 6.26 Insert Table dialog box

Entering Text in a Table

When you create a new table, an empty table appears within a gray frame on the slide as shown in Figure 6.27. When you insert a table, the insertion point flashes in the first cell in the upper left corner of the table. The text you type appears at the insertion point. After entering the text in the table and to exit the editing mode, click anywhere outside the table.

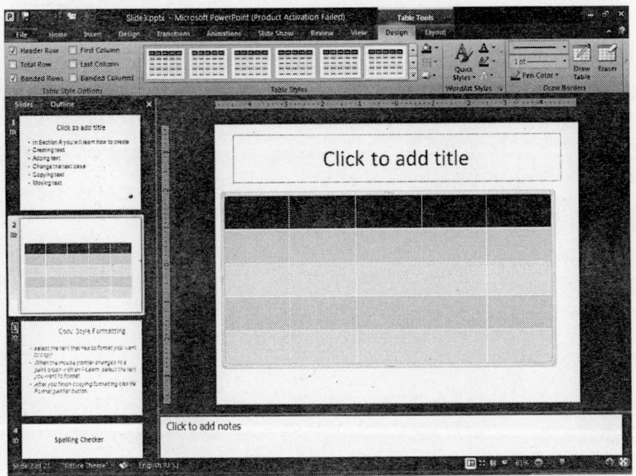

Figure 6.27 Slide with a Table

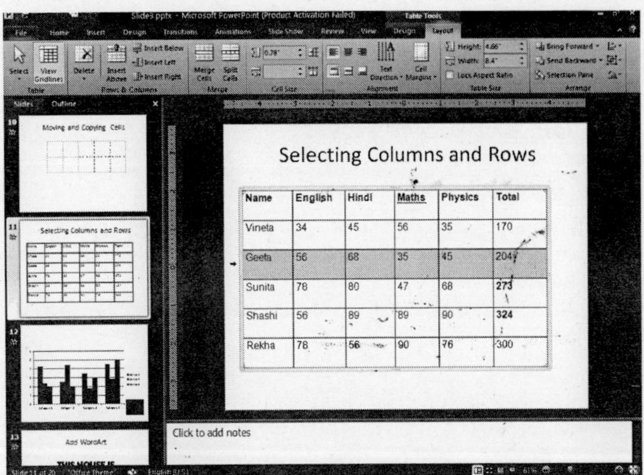

Figure 6.28 Selecting the entire row in a table

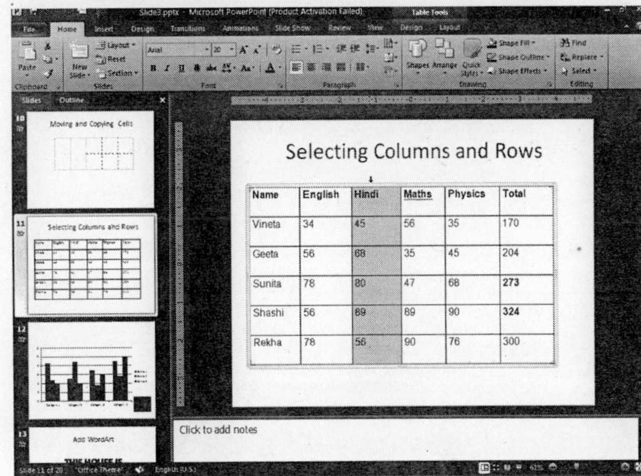

Figure 6.29 Selecting a Column

Editing a Table

Once you have created a table and entered text or numbers, you can modify its structure by *adding, deleting, moving* and *copying* cells, columns and rows. You can also change the width of columns, height of rows and merge or split cells to accommodate typed text in the cells.

Selecting Cells, Columns and Rows

➜ **To select cells, do this:**

1. For selecting a single cell, position the mouse pointer near the left inside edge of the cell. Once the pointer changes to a right arrow, click the cell.
2. To select adjacent cells in the same column, click anywhere in the first cell and drag the mouse pointer down the column.
3. To select adjacent cells in the same row, click anywhere in the first cell, and drag the mouse pointer across the row.
4. To select multiple cells click the first cell, press and hold down the Shift key, and click the other cell. Both the cells and any cell in between these two cells are selected.

➜ **To select a row of cells, do this:**

1. Position the mouse pointer near the left ledge of the table. Once the pointer changes to a right arrow, click the row as shown in Figure 6.28. *Alternatively*, in **Table Tools** contextual tab, click **Layout** tab. In **Table** group, click Select down pointing arrow and choose Select Row.

➜ **To select column or columns of cells, do this:**

1. Position the mouse pointer on the top border of the column or columns. The pointer changes to a down arrow. Click the left mouse button to select the entire column or columns (See Figure 6.29). *Alternatively*, in **Table Tools** contextual tab, click **Layout** tab. In **Table** group, click Select down pointing arrow and choose Select Column.

Adding Columns and Rows

➜ **To insert a column, do this:**

1. Click anywhere in the column next to where you want the new column to appear.
2. In **Table Tools** contextual tab, click **Layout** tab. In **Rows & Columns** group choose **Insert Columns to the Left** or **Right**. A column is inserted to the left or right of the selected column. Or

   Right click the mouse, choose Insert, a sub menu appears, choose Insert Columns to the Left or Right.

➜ **To insert a row, do this:**

1. Click anywhere in the row next to where you want the new row to be appeared.
2. In **Table Tools** contextual tab, click **Layout** tab. In **Rows & Columns** group choose **Insert Rows to the Above** or **Below**. A row is inserted to the above or below of the selected row. Or

   Right click the mouse, choose Insert Rows Above or Insert Rows Below. A row is inserted above or below of the selected row.

Deleting Columns and Rows

➜ **To delete columns/rows, do this:**

1. Select the columns/rows you want to be deleted.

2. In **Table Tools** contextual tab, click **Layout** tab. In **Rows & Columns** group choose Delete Columns or Rows. Or right click the mouse, choose Delete Rows or Columns.

Copying and Moving Cells

Once you select the contents of a cell, you can *copy* or *move* these to another location using drag and drop. *Alternatively*, use the Cut, Copy and Paste commands from the **Home** tab or from the shortcut menu that appears when you select a cell and click the right mouse button.

➔ To move or copy cell contents using drag-and-drop, do this:

1. Select the text you want to move or copy.
2. From the **Home** tab of **Clipboard** group or from the shortcut menu, choose **Cut** (to move) or **Copy**.
3. Click in the table, to position the insertion point where you want to insert the cut or copied text.

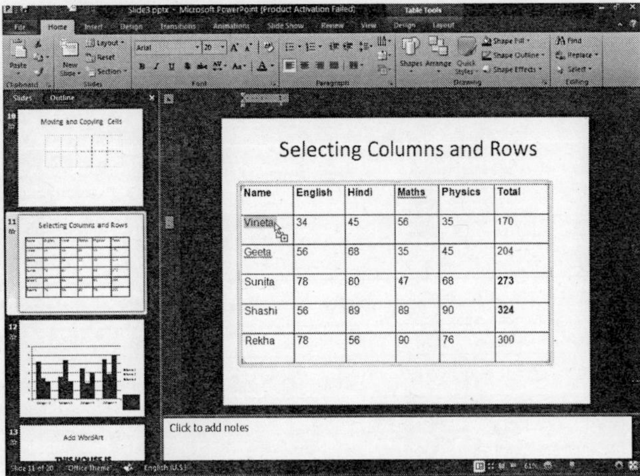

Figure 6.30 Copying a cell with contents

4. From the **Home** tab **Clipboard** group or from the Shortcut menu, choose **Paste**. Cut or copied selected text is moved or copied at the insertion point.
5. *To move the selected text* – Position the mouse pointer over the selected text, press and hold down the left mouse button and drag the text to the destination cell.
6. *To copy the selected text* – Position the mouse pointer over the selected text, press and hold the Ctrl key, press and hold down the left mouse button and drag the text to the destination cell.

   A *plus* sign appears next to the pointer to indicate that you are copying instead of moving (See Figure 6.30).

Changing Column Width and Rows Height

You can change the size of *rows* of a table by adjusting the height of the rows. Similarly, you can also change the size of the *columns* by adjusting the width of the columns.

Changing Column Width

➔ To change the width of a column in a table, do this:

1. Position the pointer anywhere on the column's right border

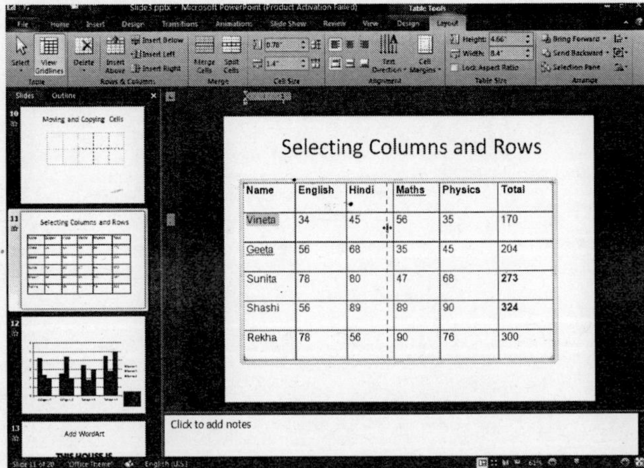

Figure 6.31 Changing column width

until the pointer changes to a double line and arrow (See Figure 6.31).

2. Drag the column border to the left or right to decrease or increase the column width. A dashed line indicates the target column width.
3. Release the mouse button. The column width is changed to the new size you specified by dragging.
4. In **Table Tools** contextual tab, click **Layout** tab. In the **Cell Size** group, click the **Table Column Width** up and down arrow, to set the width of the selected cells.

Changing Row Height

➔ To change the height of a row in a table, do this:

1. Position the pointer anywhere on the row's right border until the pointer changes to a double line and arrow.
2. Drag the row border up or down to decrease or increase the row height. A dashed line indicates the target row height (See Figure 6.32).

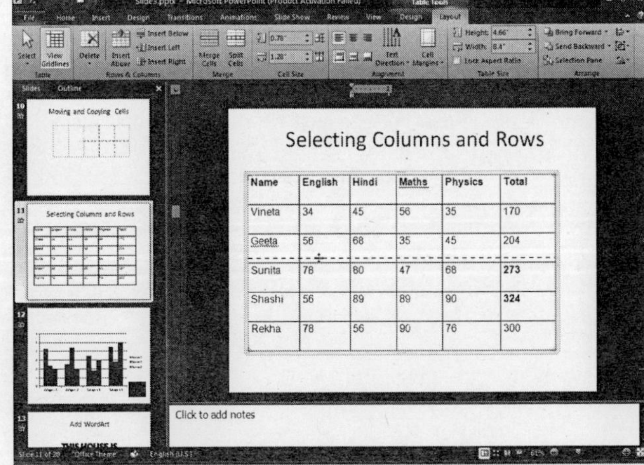

Figure 6.32 Changing row height

3. Release the mouse button. The row height is changed to the new size you specified by dragging.

4. In **Table Tools** contextual tab, click **Layout** tab. In the **Cell Size** group, click the **Row height up** and **down** arrow, to set the height of the selected cells.

Merging and Splitting Cells

To create one cell that spans two or more cells, you can merge adjacent cells. In Figure 6.33, merging cells allows you to enter a column heading in one large cell that occupies the same width as several smaller cells below.

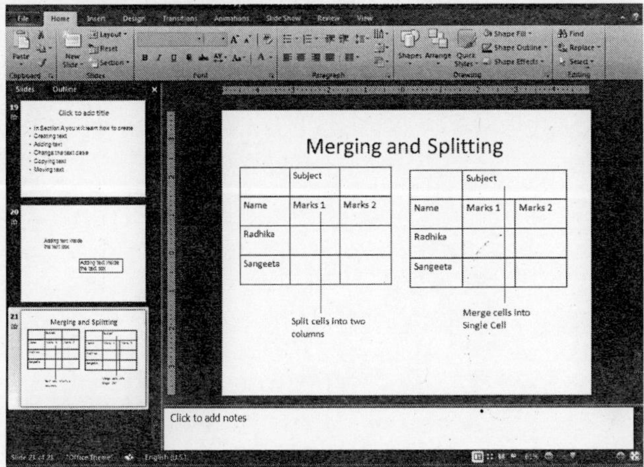

Figure 6.33 Merging in cell in first row and split it in two cells in row 2

➜ **To merge two or more cells, do this:**

1. Select the cells you want to merge.
2. Click the **Table Tools** contextual tab, click the **Layout** tab. Click **Merge** cells in the **Merge** group.
   Or right click the mouse and choose Merge Cells.

➜ **To split a cell, do this:**

1. Select the cell that you want to split. You can only split one cell at a time.
2. Click the **Table Tools** contextual tab, click the **Layout** tab. Click **Split** cells in the **Merge** group.
3. The cell is split into two cells of equal width, with any text appearing in the cell on the left. Or right click the mouse and choose Split Cells... .

☞ *After splitting a cell, you might want to adjust the cell width to make it look right in your current cell structure and layout.*

Adding Borders and Fills

PowerPoint establishes default borders around cells and the table itself, on the current presentation template. You can change borders separating cells, columns and rows or around the entire table.

Changing Table Borders

You may specify a variety of ways for border formatting in a table. You can choose:

1. The border format (*Top border, bottom border, Left border, Right border, All border*, etc.).
2. The border style (solid line, dashed line, dotted line, etc.).
3. The border width (1/4 point to 6 points).
4. The border color.

➜ **To select the table cells that you want to add or change the table border, do this:**

1. Select the entire table, or the cells, columns, or rows around which you want to specify the border.
2. Under **Table Tools**, on the **Design** tab, click **Border** down arrow in the **Table Styles** group. The actual name of this button changes depending on what was last selected. Borders option shows all the different border types (See Figure 6.34).

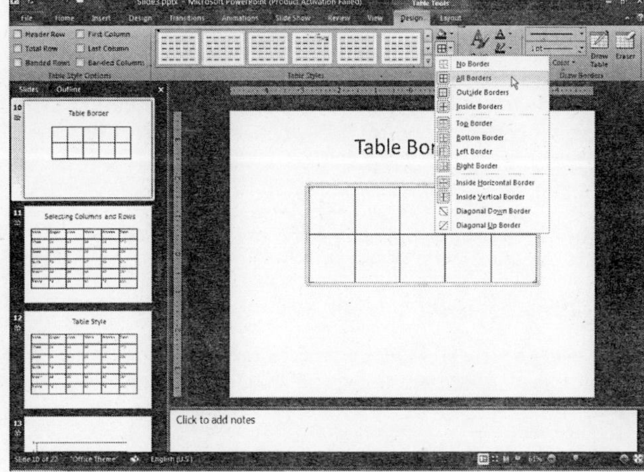

Figure 6.34 Borders palette

3. Click the border you want. The selected portion of the table changes to reflect the new border type.
4. If you want to change the border line style, click Draw borders down arrow, and choose Pen Style. Pen Style palette drop-down menu appears as shown in Figure 6.35.

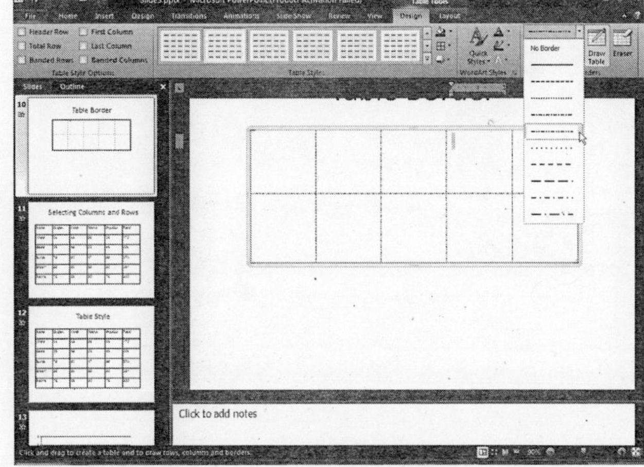

Figure 6.35 Borders Style drop-down list appears

5. Click the border style you want. The mouse pointer changes to pen style. Click the table row or column line. You can see the selected portion of your table changes to the new border style.

6. If you want to change the border width or border color, repeat Steps 2 to 4 with the border width and border color button. After making a change, click the Border button if necessary to redraw the table with the new formatting.

7. If you want to delete borders between table cells, click Eraser, or press and hold (Shift) key while the pointer is a pencil, and then click the borders that you want to delete.

Creating a Chart Slide

PowerPoint creates or modifies a chart using MS-Graph. MS-Graph is a graphing program shared by all components like *Word, Excel, PowerPoint*. So if you know how to create graphics in one of the components, you can use the same technique in other components also.

Charts that you create will be embedded in PowerPoint 2010, and the chart data is stored in an Excel 2010 worksheet that is incorporated in the PowerPoint file.

➜ **To create a chart slide, do this:**

1. Click the **New slide** in the **Slides** group. It displays, the slides after which you want to add the chart slide. Or click the **Insert** tab, on the **Illustrations** group, click the **Chart** icon.

2. The new slide appears. In the center of the slide contains *table, chart, Media clips, SmartArt*, etc., as shown in Figure 6.36.

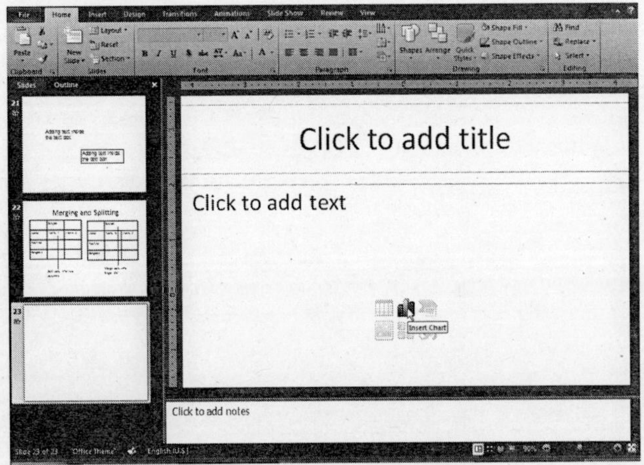

Figure 6.36 A new slide contains chart

3. Click the Insert Chart in the new slide. The Insert Chart dialog box appears as shown in Figure 6.37.

4. Select the chart type under **Templates**. For example, if you click the Column chart type, there are different types of columns in the column section. Select the desired chart type. Click OK.

5. A sample chart appears in the Excel worksheet and the data sheet window containing the sample data for the chart overlays as shown in Figure 6.38.

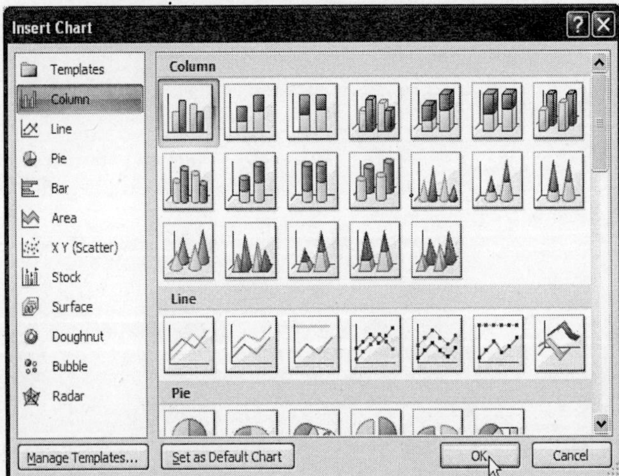

Figure 6.37 Insert Chart dialog box

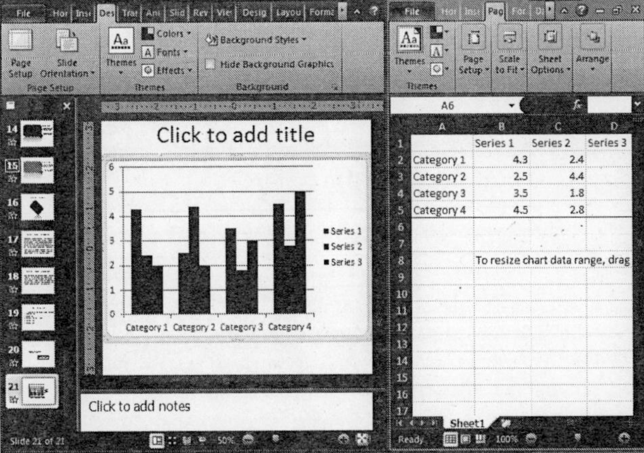

Figure 6.38 Sample Data graphically displayed

6. In Excel to replace the sample data, click a cell on the worksheet, and then type the data that you want. When you enter data in Excel you can see the PowerPoint the data as well chart also simultaneously appearing in the PowerPoint (See Figure 6.39).
7. In Excel, click the Office Button and then click **Save As**.
8. In the **Save As** dialog box in the **save in:** list, select the folder or drive that you want to save the worksheet.
9. In the **File name:** box, type a new name for the file.
10. Click **Save**.
11. In Excel, Click the Office button and then click Close.

Entering Data in the Datasheet

Entering data in the datasheet consists of two steps. These are:

- Entering the labels in the left most column and top most row.
- Entering the data to be graphed in the remaining cells.

➜ **To enter data in a datasheet, do this:**

1. Click the top cell in column A and enter the category labels across the top row. (The categories along the rows appear along the *X-axis* in the graph).

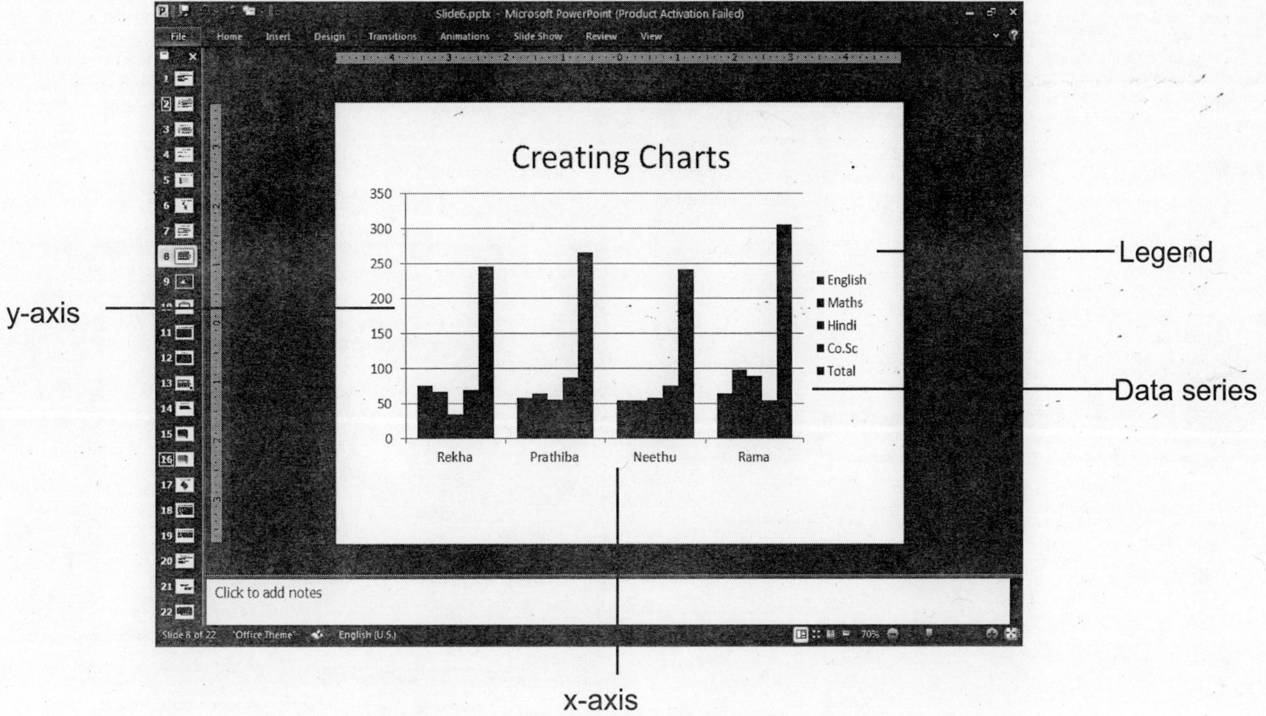

Figure 6.39 A Sample Chart appearing in PowerPoint

2. Enter the name of the data series along the column, starting from the first cell labeled. Each row represents the data series for each category.
3. Enter the values for each category in the cell (See Figure 6.40).

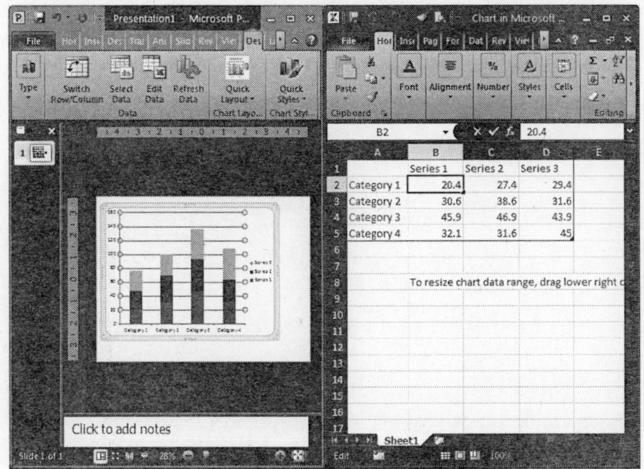

Figure 6.40 Entering Data in the cell B2 of the datasheet

Now type the numbers for each cell along the column and press Enter. For practice, enter the numbers given below.

20.4	27.4	29.4
30.6	38.6	31.6
45.9	46.9	43.9
32.1	31.6	45

6.4.2 Adding Clip Art Pictures

Clip Art gallery is a collection of graphic files in PowerPoint that you can insert in presentations. It has built a gallery of Clip Art images into the Clip Art gallery. But you also have your own collection of artwork available.

PowerPoint can help you select an appropriate piece of art for your slides by looking at keywords in your presentation and trying to find pictures to match.

Inserting a picture from the Clip Art Gallery

1. Select the slide that contain a Clip Art slide.
2. Click the Clip Art icon in the slide. A Clip Art task pane appears (See Figure 6.41).
3. Select the current entry in the Search for: box or click in the box if there is no entry, type animals, and then click Go. The task pane displays animals list.
4. Click the selected picture, once it appears at the center of the slide or select the picture, it appears a small arrow at the right of the side of the picture. Click the arrow and then Insert (See Figure 6.41).
5. When you are finished using the Clip Gallery, click the Close button on the Clip Gallery Title bar.

6.4.3 Inserting Other Objects

You may want to add a particular graphic to a presentation but not maintain it in the Clip Gallery. You can insert picture from another application.

➜ **To insert a picture from a file, do this:**

1. Click where you want to insert the picture.

Figure 6.41 Clip Art task pane

2. On the **Insert** tab, in the **Images** group, click **Picture**.
3. The **Insert Picture** dialog box appears as shown in Figure 6.42.
4. Search a file in the **Look in:** drop-down list.
5. Click **Insert** button to place the graphic on the current slide.

Figure 6.42 Insert Picture dialog box

6.4.4 Resizing and Scaling an Object

Resize an object

To resize or reshape an object, drag one of the object's handles in the direction you want. If you want to maintain the proportions of the object, hold down Shift key while drag a corner handle. If you want the object to grow out from its current center, hold down Ctrl while you drag a corner handle.

➔ **To resize an object, do this:**

1. Select the object you want to resize.
2. Drag a size handle until the object gets desired shape and size as you want (See Figure 6.43). Or

Scaling an object

Rather than drag objects into position, you can set object placements and sizing on the size and position tabs of the Format Picture.

➔ **To scale an object, do this:**

1. Select the object you want to scale.
2. Click the **Picture Tools** contextual **Format** tab in the **Size** group.

Figure 6.43 Object has to be resized

3. Enter the percentage you want change in the **Height:** and **Width:** boxes. *Alternatively*, click the **Size and Position** dialog box launcher dialog box.
4. The **Format Picture** dialog box appears as shown in Figure 6.44.
5. Click the Size tab, under the Scale, enter the percentage you want change in the **Height:** and **Width:** box.

☞ *To maintain the ratio between the object's height and width whenever to resize it, select the Lock aspect ratio check box on the size tab.*

6.5 PROVIDING AESTHETICS

PowerPoint is designed to give your slide presentations a consistent look. There are four ways that PowerPoint helps you control the look of your slides – with design templates, masters, color schemes, and layouts of slides.

6.5.1 Enhancing Text Presentation

Enhancing the text presentation makes your presentation in a more presentable manner by formatting features, such as bold, italic, underline, alignment of text, font size, font style, colors, etc.

Aligning Text in a Slide

Alignment is the way text is placed between the margins of a page or a text box on a slide. The alignment choices are summarized in Table 6.1.

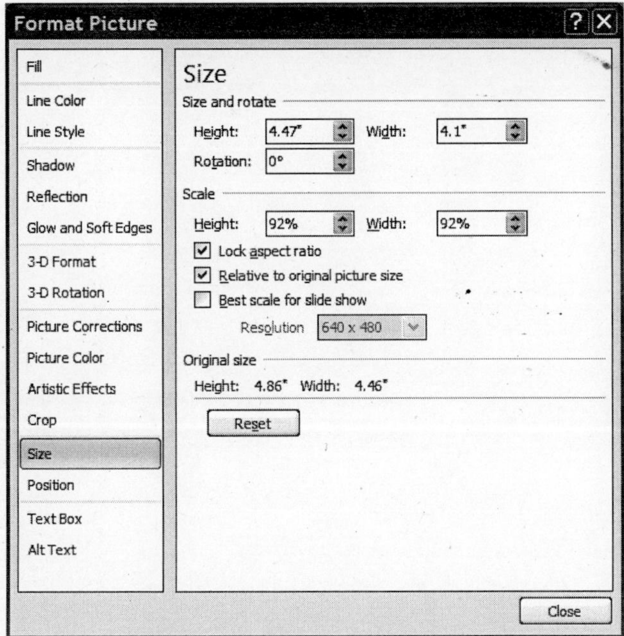

Figure 6.44 Format Picture dialog box

Table 6.1 Aligning Text in a Slide

Alignment	Effect
Left Align	The left margin of each line is at the same place on the left, while the right edge of each line ends wherever appropriate (called a *ragged right edge*).
Right Align	The right margin of each line is at the same place on the right. The left edge of each line falls in a different place, depending on the contents of the line (called a *ragged left edge*).
Center	Each line is centered. The left and right edges of each line will differ, depending upon the number and size of characters in the line.
Justified	Each line starts at the left margin and ends at the right margin. There are no ragged edges.

➜ To align the text, do this:

1. Select the text, then click the Left, Center, or Right alignment button on the Formatting toolbar. *Alternatively*, click the **Paragraph Launcher** dialog box and select the desired option in the alignment section.

Changing Fonts

Fonts are also called *typefaces* in computer programs. There are groups of characters that share the same style or look.

Fonts are divided into two groups.

- On the basis of the way, characters are spaced – *monospaced* or *proportionately* spaced (See Figure 6.45). In *monospaced* font, all the characters have the same width. In *proportionately* spaced font the widths are different, i.e., w has more width than i.
- On the basis of the finishing strokes. That is Serif and Sans Serif. In Sans Serif the finishing strokes are not there (See Figure 6.45). In Serif fonts the finishing strokes are there.

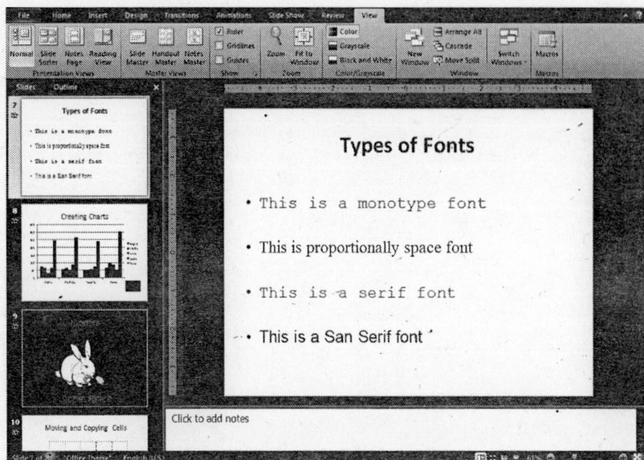

Figure 6.45 Display of various kind of fonts

While choosing fonts for your presentation, keep in mind the following points:

- Using too many fonts on the same slide looks unprofessional. It is advisable to use one font for the headline and another for the rest of the text or a third font for bulleted items. But do not use too many fonts.
- Fancy fonts, do not work well on slides, especially for headlines.
- Sans Serif fonts tend to have a more authoritative and bold look.
- Proportional fonts work extremely well in body text.

➜ To change the font of any text in a slide, do this:

1. Select the text you want to change.
2. Click the **Home** tab and choose **Font** group. Or select the text, a mini toolbar appears. Select the font themes appears choose the desired font you want to apply. Or

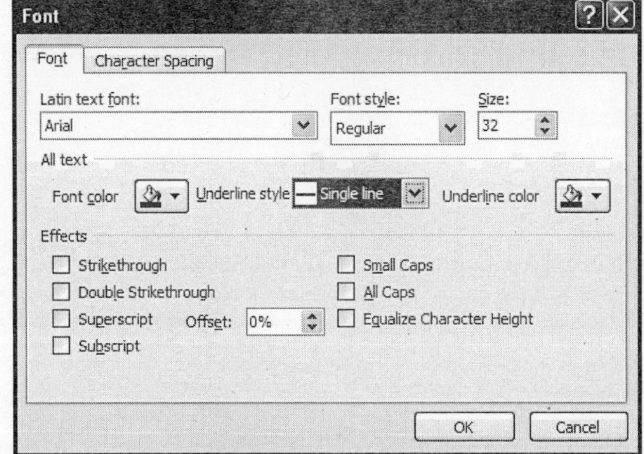

Figure 6.46 Font dialog box

3. Click the right mouse button and choose Font... from shortcut menu. The Font dialog box appears as in Figure 6.46. Click

the Font drop-down list and select the required font. *Alternatively*, click the down arrow to the right of the Font box on the Ribbon command. A drop-down list of available fonts appears.

☞ *Right type and size of font creates good impression on your audience.*

4. Click the font you want to use. The selected text changes to the selected font.

Changing the Text Size

Font size is measured in *points*, which is a height measurement, each point is 1/72 of an inch.

➜ **To change the size of text, do this:**

1. Select the text you want to change.
2. Click the **Home** tab and choose **Font** group. Or select the text. A mini toolbar appears. Choose the desired font size you want to apply. Or click the right mouse button and choose Font... . In the Font dialog box that appears, click the size drop-down list and choose the desired size or type the size. *Alternatively*, click the arrow to the right of the Font Size box on the Ribbon command to see the list of available sizes.
3. Select the new size. Or
4. Click the Increase and decrease font size on the Ribbon command.

Adding Special Effects to Text

One of the easiest ways to make text stands out is to add special formatting effects to *characters*, *sentences*, or *paragraphs*. PowerPoint makes these tasks very easy.

➜ **To add special effect, do this:**

1. Select text to which you want to apply special effect.
2. In the Font dialog box, the options Font style: box has the following:
   - Regular—The text appears in regular way.
   - Bold—Text appears bold or highlighted.
   - Italic—Text appears italic.
   - Bold Italic—Text appears bold and italic.

   The All text has this option:
   - Font color— Specifies the color of the selected text. In the box, select the color. You can see the color under the bucket.
   - Underline style— Specifies whether selected text is in underlined. Click None to remove underlining.
   - Underline color— Specifies the color of the underlined text. This option remains unavailable until you apply an underline style.

   The Effect Areas has following options:
   - Strikethrough—Draws a line through selected text.
   - Superscript—Text appears raised like x^2y.
   - Subscript—Text appears lowered like H_20.
   - Small caps—Selected text appears reduce size. It does not affect on numbers, punctuation, non-alphabetic characters.
   - All caps—It converts lowercase to capitals.
   - Equalize Character Height—It reformats text effects to apply an even character height to text.

The font style and special effects of above explanation as shown in Figure 6.47.

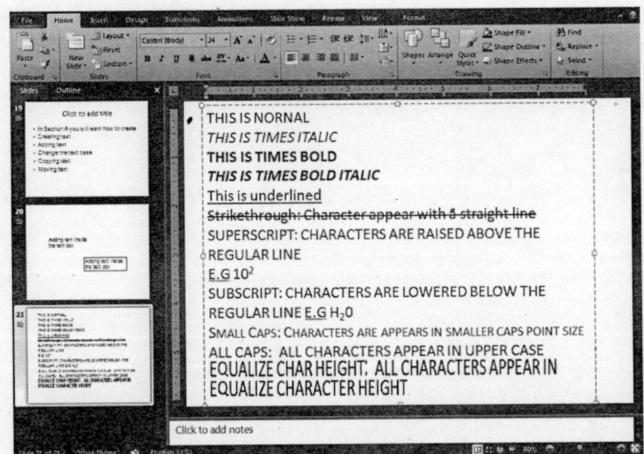

Figure 6.47 The font style effect

Changing Text Color

➜ **To change the text color, do this:**

1. Select the text you want to change.
2. In the **Home** tab, click the **Font** group. Click the font color by pointing arrow. The font colors theme palette appears.
3. Move the mouse pointer over the color, you can see the effect changes in the text. Choose the desired color you want to apply to the text.

Applying Character Formatting using the Keyboard

Most of the character formatting can also be applied using the keyboard shortcut as discussed in the following sections.

➜ **To format using shortcut keys, do this:**

1. Select the text you want to format and use the shortcut key combinations for the desired formatting effects.

Format	Shortcut
Bold	Ctrl+B
Italic	Ctrl+I
Underline	Ctrl+U
Superscript	Ctrl+Shift++
Subscript	Ctrl+=
Copy formatting	Ctrl+Shift+C
Paste formatting	Ctrl+Shift+V
Remove formatting	Ctrl+Spacebar
Change case of letters	Shift+F3
Change the font	Ctrl+Shift+F
Change the font size	Ctrl+Shift+P
Increase the font size	Ctrl+Shift+>
Decrease the font size	Ctrl+Shift+<

Bullets and Numbering

PowerPoint 2010 provides the ability to create bulleted, numbered lists. A bulleted list is a list with a graphic character, very small picture or bullet at the beginning of each paragraph in the list. You might also consider using SmartArt for many bulleted or numbered lists. The style of each list type can be changed and different bullets can be used.

➔ **To create a bulleted list, do this:**

1. Select the text you want to add bullet.
2. Click the down arrow of the bullets command icon, in the Paragraph group.

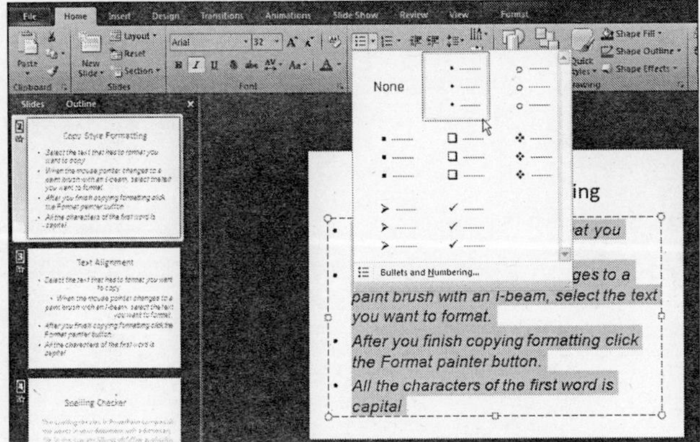

Figure 6.48 Selecting Bullets in the paragraph group

3. A drop-down list shows with the pre-defined bullet list.
4. Select the desired bullet type from the drop-down list. For example, we have selected the circled bulleted list (See Figure 6.48).
5. The selected bullet type is applied to the text as shown in Figure 6.49.

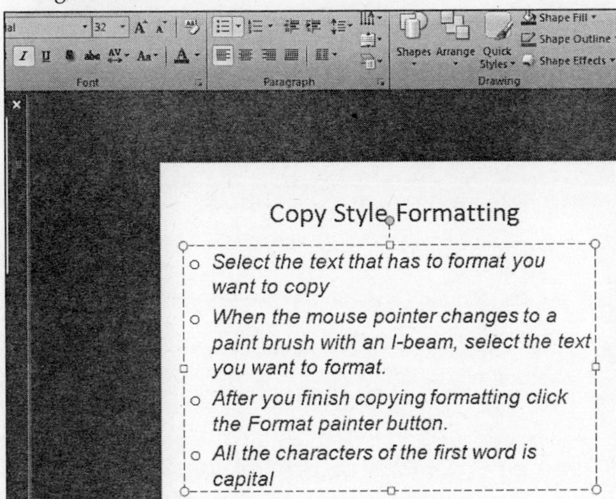

Figure 6.49 Bullet applied in selected paragraph

Adding Symbols

PowerPoint provides a full range of special symbol characters like the copyright or trademarks, registration symbol, etc.

➔ **To add symbol, do this:**

1. Click the **Insert** tab. In the **Symbols** group, click Symbol icon. The **Symbol** dialog box appears as shown in Figure 6.50.

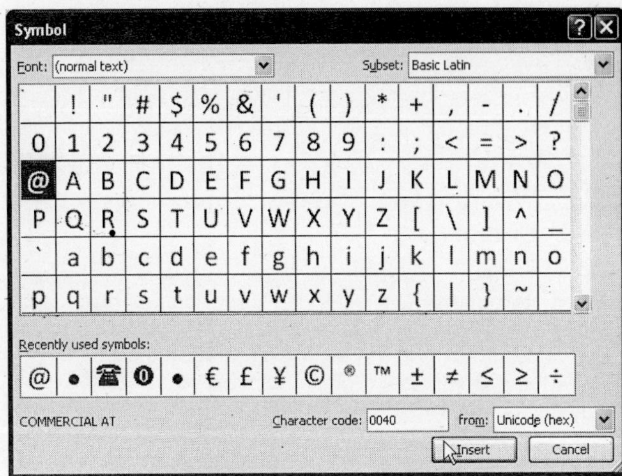

Figure 6.50 Symbol dialog Box

2. By default, the **Font:** box is set to Symbol. Click the down arrow to see the choices for fonts, each of which provides a different set of symbols.
3. Select the font with the symbols you want to use. Select the symbols to insert by clicking it once. Or click the Insert button to insert the symbol.
4. In the **Subset:** name box, specify a subset of special characters for the selected font, if available. A font subset can include an extended list of language characters, such as Greek or Russian (Cryillic), or a category of characters, such as Currency Symbols.
5. In Symbol list represents the full list of symbols that can be inserted from the selected Font and Subset.
6. In **Recently used symbols:** box, lists the most frequently used symbols that have been inserted.
7. **Description:** Provides a meaningful description of the selected symbol. For example, if the ® symbol is selected, the description will appear as Registered sign.
8. **Character code:** list box displays a unique code representing a symbol.
9. **From:** drop-down list, specifies the character set on which the character code is based on. ASCII (American Standard Code of Information Interchange) is a character-encoding standard based on the English alphabet. Unicode is a character-encoding standard that enables almost all of the written languages in the world to be represented by using a single character set.
10. Click Close to leave the Symbol dialog box and return to your slide.

Removing Bullets and Numbering

➔ **To remove bullets and numbering, do this:**

1. Select the text or placeholders you want to remove bullets and number form.
2. In the **Paragraph** group of **Home** tab, choose the bulleted down pointing arrow, a bullet palette list appears, choose None. Or

You can press Backspace to remove bullet or numbering from an item in a list. PowerPoint automatically adjusts the number sequence of a numbered list.

3. If you want to reorganize the elements of the list after removing bullets and numbering, use the promote and demote bullet on the Quick Access toolbar.

6.5.2 Working with Themes Color and Line Style

In earlier version color and line styles, contains a color scheme that provides the various parts of a presentation with a coordinated set of eight default colors. The most distinctive design element of the presentation is the background, so the first color in color scheme is background color. Other seven colors effectively complement the background colour and are applied to text, charts, and other objects that appear against the background.

A layout determines where text, graphics, charts and other elements appear on an individual slide. A theme determines the look of an entire presentations' colors, fonts, and overall format. A layout is to a slide what a theme is to an entire presentation. Both specify the way a slide or overall presentation looks.

In Latest version of PowerPoint 2010, Themes refer a set of unified design element that provides a look for your document by using *colors*, *fonts* and *graphics*. You can use predefined themes that come with PowerPoint, or you can define your own.

➜ To select a New slide and apply themes effect, do this:

1. Click the **Home** tab, in the **slides** group. Click the **New Slide** down pointing arrow. PowerPoint opens a layout list from which you can select (See Figure 6.51).
2. When you click to select a layout, PowerPoint inserts a new slide at that location in your presentation with that layout.
3. Click the **Design** tab, in the **Themes** group. In the Themes group click the **More** button at the lower right corner. A list of themes appears as shown in Figure 6.52.
4. Select a desired style you want to apply your presentation.
5. If you want to modify the theme, select from the *Font*, *Colors*, and *Effect* buttons to the right of the Themes group.
6. After you have modified a theme to your liking, click down arrow next to the Ribbon's themes and select Save Current Theme.

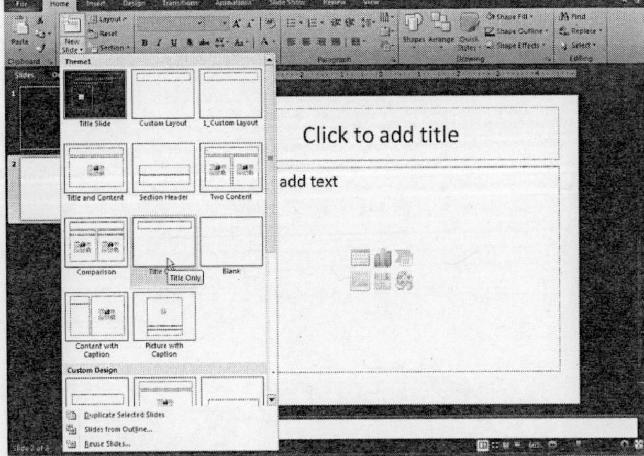

Figure 6.51 Selecting a New Slide from Home tab

Figure 6.52 Selecting a Themes from Design tab

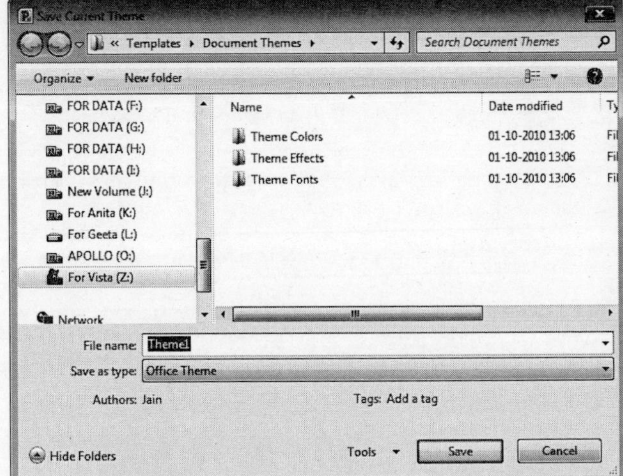

Figure 6.53 Save Current Theme dialog box

7. The **Save Current Theme** dialog box appears as shown in Figure 6.53.
8. In the **Save in:** drop-down list contains a default folder (Document Themes).
9. Give the name in the **File name:** in the drop-down list.
10. Click the **Save** button.
11. After giving a name to the theme, PowerPoint makes that theme available in the Themes list.

Change the Color, Style and Weight of a Line

You can change the look of a line shape by changing its color, line style, or weight.

- Add a Quick Style to a line
- Change the color of a line
- Make a line dashed
- Change the weight of a line

Add a Quick Style to a line

Quick Styles for lines include theme colors from the document theme, shadow, line styles and three-dimensional perspectives.

1. Select the line that you want to change.
   If you want to change multiple lines, select first line, and then press and hold Ctrl key while you select other lines.
2. Under **Drawing Tools** on the **Format** tab, in the **Shape Styles** group, click the Quick style that you want.
3. To see more Quick Styles, click the **More** button (See Figure 6.54).

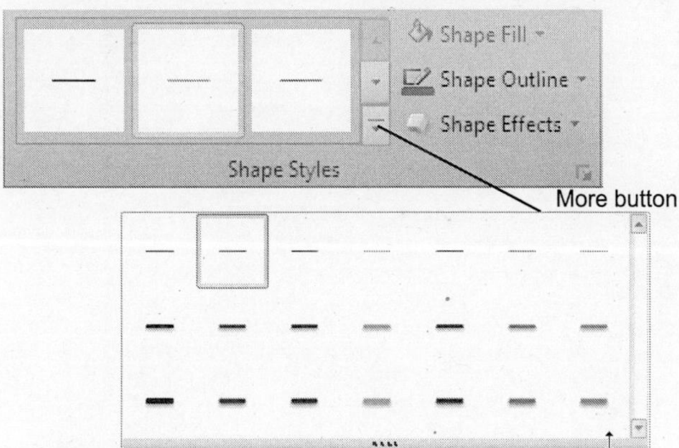

Figure 6.54 Select the line style from the More button

Change the Color of a Line

1. Select the line that you want to change.
2. Under the **Drawing Tools**, on the **Format** tab, in the **Shape Styles** group, click the arrow next to **Shape Outline**, and then click the color that you want (See Figure 6.55).
3. To change to a color that is not in the theme colors, click **More Outline Colors**, and then either click the color that you want on the **Standard tab**, or mix your own color on the **Custom tab**. Custom colors and colors on the Standard tab are not updated if you later change the document theme.

Figure 6.55 Select the color of a line from the Shape Outline drop-down list

Make a Line Dashed

You can change *thickness, style* and *color*. To format a line first select it by clicking it. For selecting multiple lines press and hold the Shift key while you click the lines. The selected lines appear dimmed and dashed.

1. Select the line that you want to change.
2. Under **Drawing Tools**, on the **Format** tab, in the **Shape Styles** group, click the arrow next to **Shape Outline**.
3. Point to **Dashes**, and then click the line style that you want (See Figure 6.56).
4. To create a custom style, click **More Lines**, and then choose the options that you want.

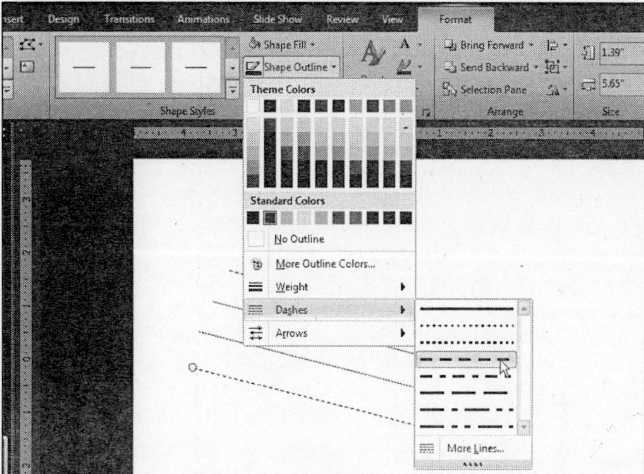

Figure 6.56 Select the line Dashes from the Shape Outline drop-down list

Change the weight of a line

1. Select the line that you want to change.
   If you want to change multiple lines, select the first line, and then press and hold Ctrl while you select the other lines.
2. Under **Drawing Tools**, on the **Format** tab, in the **Shape Styles** group, click the arrow next to **Shape Outline**.

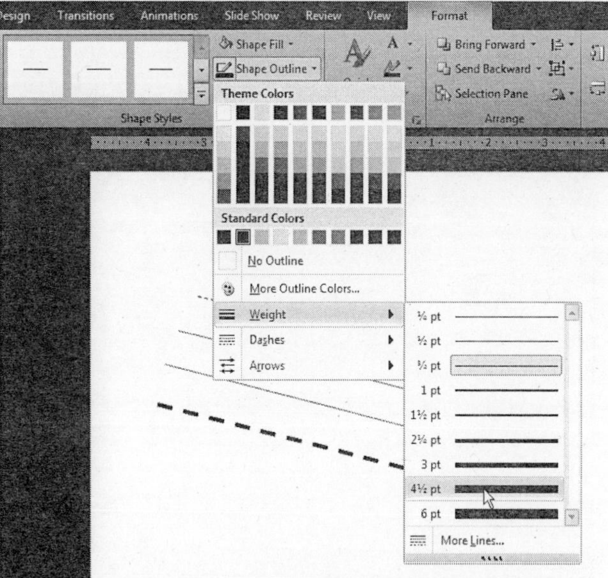

Figure 6.57 Select the line weight from the Shape Outline drop-down list

3. Point to **Weight**, and then click the line weight that you want (See Figure 6.57).
4. To create a custom style, click **More Lines**, and then choose the options that you want.

6.5.3 Adding Movie or (Video) and Sound

You insert a music, sound, or video clip on a slide where you want it to play during a slide show. You can choose either to have the sound or video start automatically when you move to the slide, or to have the sound or video start only when you click its icon during a slide show.

One of the exciting new features in PowerPoint 2010 is that you now have the ability to edit and style the video clips you add to your slides. You can insert video files from your computer, download them from the Web, or insert video clips from Microsoft Office Clip Art. This enables you to add life to your slides and share compelling stories in a way that is sure to hold your audience's attention.

PowerPoint supports videos in various formats, such as Audio Video Interchange (.avi), Motion Pictures Group (.mpg) and Movie (.mov).

➜ To insert a video from a Clip Art video, do this:

1. Insert the new slide or display the slide that will contain **Media Clip Art**.
2. Click the **Insert** tab.
3. Click **Video** button under the **Media** Group. A drop-down list appears as shown in Figure 6.58.

Figure 6.58 Selecting Video from file from the Insert tab

4. Select the Video from File option from the list.
5. The **Insert Video** dialog box appears as shown in Figure 6.59.

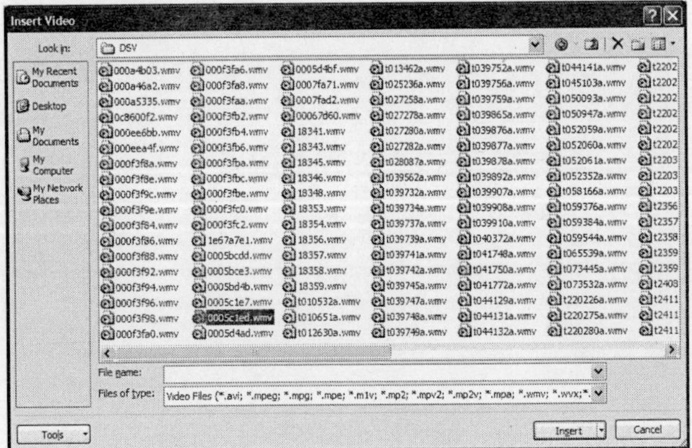

Figure 6.59 Insert video dialog box

6. Browse the location where the video is saved on your computer.
7. Select the desired video file. Then click **Insert** button.
8. The desired video is inserted in the slide as shown in Figure 6.60.

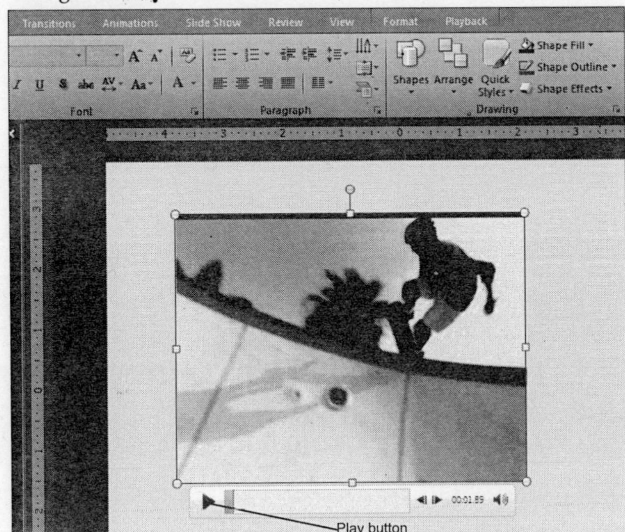

Figure 6.60 The video file is inserted in the presentation

9. Drag the sizing handles of the image to set the size of your video, and then drag it to the location you want.
10. Play the video by clicking the Play button.

Adding Sound file

In PowerPoint 2010, you can easily add sound effects, voiceovers and music to individual slides. You can add a soundtrack and narration to the presentation as well. Sound effects, such as music and voice recordings, can add another level of professionalism to slide presentations. Music is an effective way to introduce or end a presentation and it gives your audience something to listen to as they enter and leave the presentation room. You could play a movie theme song as background music for several slides, or play a voice recording that contains advertising slogans to insert on a single slide, for example.

There are many sound file formats. Two common types are wave files (with the .wav filename extension) and Musical Instrument Digital Interface (MIDI) files (with the .mid, .midi, or .rmi filename extension).

➜ To insert a sound, into the slide, do this:

1. Select the slide in which you want to insert the desired sound.
2. Click the **Insert** tab.
3. Click the **Audio** button under the **Media** group as shown in Figure 6.61.
4. A drop-down list appears.
5. Select the **Audio from file** option from the drop-down list as shown in Figure 6.61.
6. The **Insert Audio** dialog box appears as shown in Figure 6.62.
7. Browse the location where the sound clip is saved on your computer. For example, we have selected the Sample Music folder as shown in Figure 6.62.
8. Select the desired sound clip and then click OK button.
9. The audio file is inserted in the slide as shown in Figure 6.63.

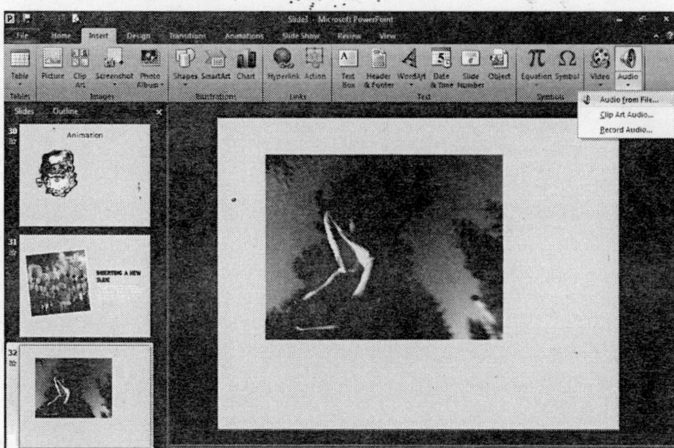

Figure 6.61 Slecting Audio from file from the Insert tab

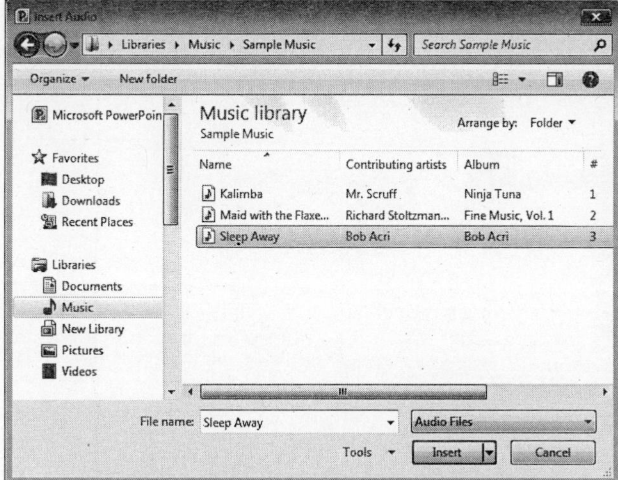

Figure 6.62 Insert Audio dialog box

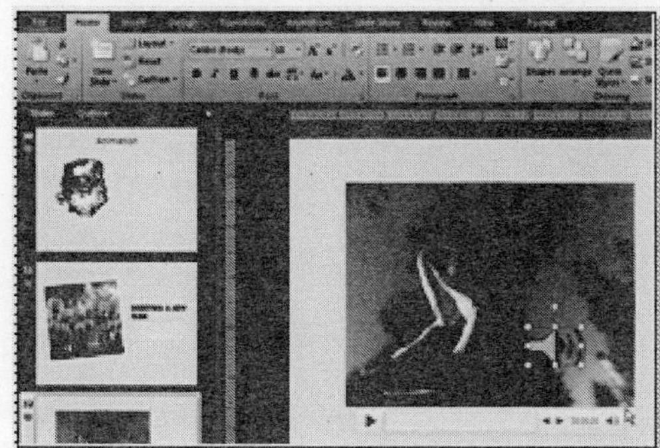

Figure 6.63 The audio file is inserted in the presentation

6.5.4 Adding Headers and Footers

You can add *headers, footers* and *page numbers* to each of the slide or the Note Pages.

➜ **To insert header and footer to the slide, do this:**

1. In the **Insert** tab, click **Header & Footer** in the **Text** group. Or in the **Print** Backstage view, click **Edit Header & Footer** link option.
2. The **Header and Footer** dialog box appears. Now click the **Notes and Handouts** tab property sheet as shown in Figure 6.64.

The Notes tab property sheet of Header and Footer dialog box offers the following options.

Date and time – If you select this option, the date and time appears in the upper-right corner of the page.

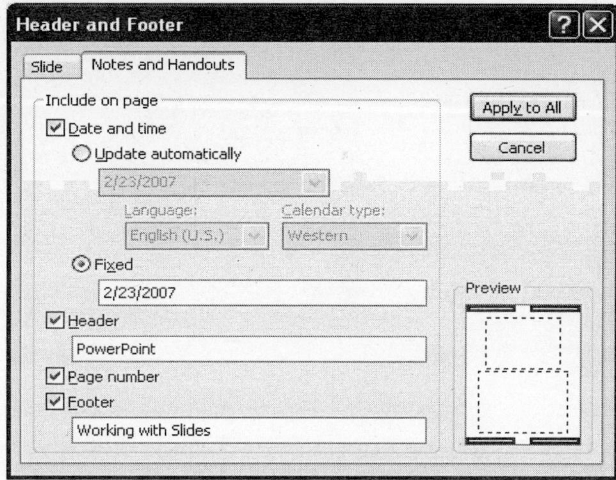

Figure 6.64 Header and Footer dialog box with Notes and Handouts Tab

- Update automatically – Select this option to print the actual date and time when printouts are made. Use the list box to select the format you would like the date and time to appear in.
- Fixed – Choose this option if you want to specify the specific date to be printed in text box.

Header – The header appears on the top left corner of the page. Enter the text for the header in the box below the option.

Page Number – The page numbers are shown as numerals only and appear in the lower-right corner of the page. Numbering is automatic increased once this option is on.

Footer – The footer appears in the lower-left corner of the page. Enter the text for the footer in the box below the option.

3. Click Apply to All to use the selected settings.

6.6 PRESENTATION OF SLIDES

6.6.1 Viewing a Presentation

PowerPoint offers five ways (*views*) to look at your presentation. Each view enables you to work on a different aspect of the presentation. The changes made in one view are also reflected in all other views.

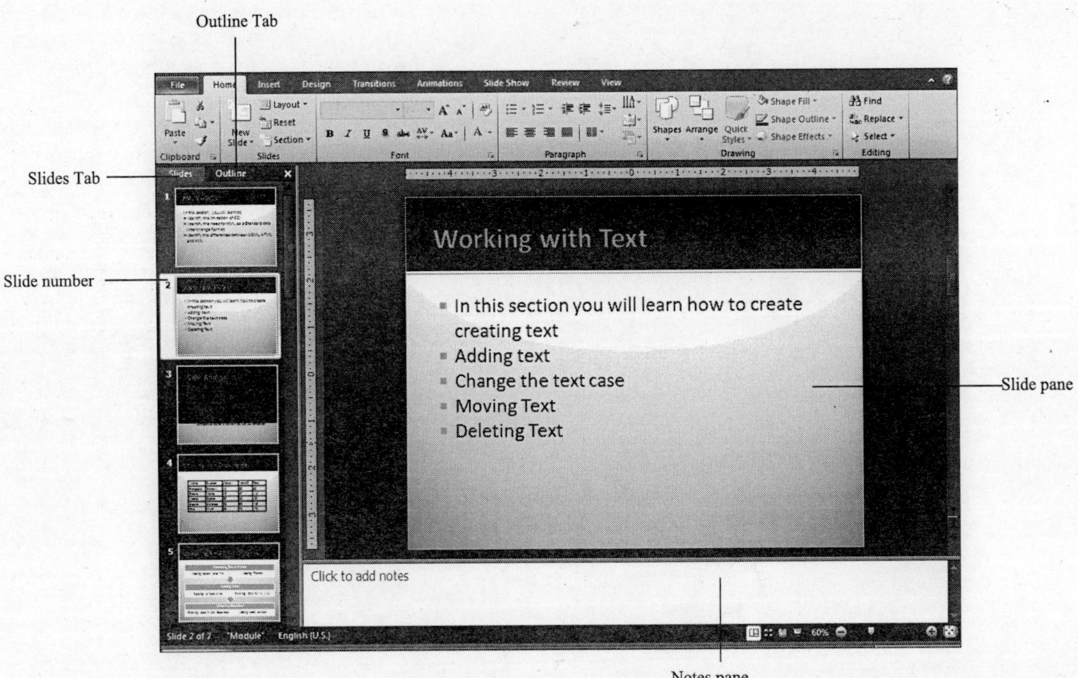

Figure 6.65 Normal View

To understand the function of views, consider that you are looking at a house. Now assume you are standing in front of a house, you see one view. Now you move to one of the sides and you see a different view of the same house. PowerPoint views also allow you to see a presentation in various ways.

The buttons located at the lower left corner of the PowerPoint window just above the Status bar as shown in Figure 6.65 help you to switch to different views.

In the following section, you will conceptually learn about the view.

Normal View

Normal view is the main editing view, where you write and design your presentation. The view has four working areas:

- Outline tab
- Slides tab
- Slide pane
- Notes pane

These panes let you work on all aspects of your presentation in one place. You can adjust the size of different panes by dragging the pane borders.

- **Outline tab:** Use the Outline tab to organize and develop the contents of your presentation. You can type all of the text of your presentation and rearrange bullet points, paragraphs and slides. The Outline tab shows your slide text in outline form.
- **Slides tab:** This is a great place to view the slides in your presentation as thumbnail-sized images while you edit. The thumbnails make it easy for you to navigate through your presentation and to see the effect of any design changes. You can also easily rearrange, add or delete slides.
- **Slide pane***:* In the slide pane, you can see how your text looks on each slide. You can add SmartArt graphics, movies and sounds, create hyperlink and add animations to individual slides.
- **Notes pane:** The Notes pane lets you add speaker notes or information you want to share with the audience. If you want to have graphic in your notes, you must add the notes in Notes page view.

  These pane are also shown when you save a presentation as a Web page. The only difference is that the outline pane displays a table of contents so that you can navigate through the complete presentation.

Slide Sorter View

The slide sorter view is a view of your slides in thumbnail form (See Figure 6.66). Working in this view is like laying out the pages of your presentation or report on the table so that you can see them all at once. In this view, you can see the design consistency and the flow of your presentation. If need be, you can easily reorder the slides, copy or delete the slides.

Notes Page View

This view helps you to prepare the speaker notes used while making the presentation to your audience. Notes pages view produces a smaller version of the slide on the top part of a page and leaves the lower part free for notes or keypoints (See Figure 6.67).

Slide Show View

This view of PowerPoint shows the progress of the presentation form slide to slide just like a real slide show. In this view, all

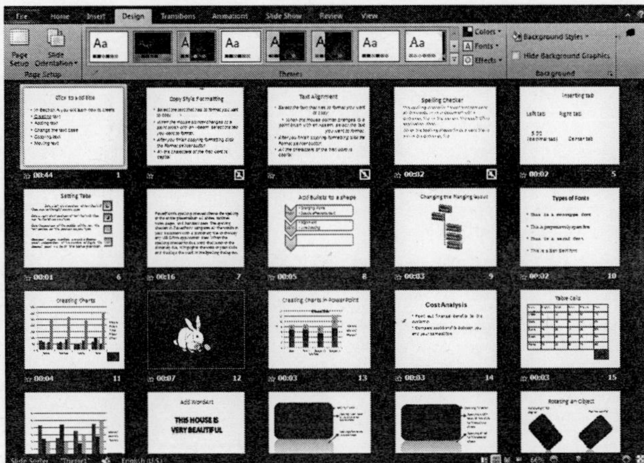

Figure 6.66 PowerPoint's Slide Sorter View

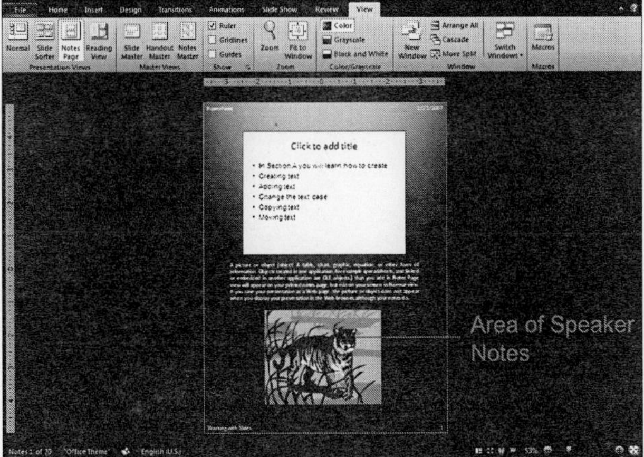

Figure 6.67 PowerPoint's Notes Pages View

menus, toolbars, rulers, status bar, scrollbars, and the Windows *taskbar* are removed from the screen (See Figure 6.68).

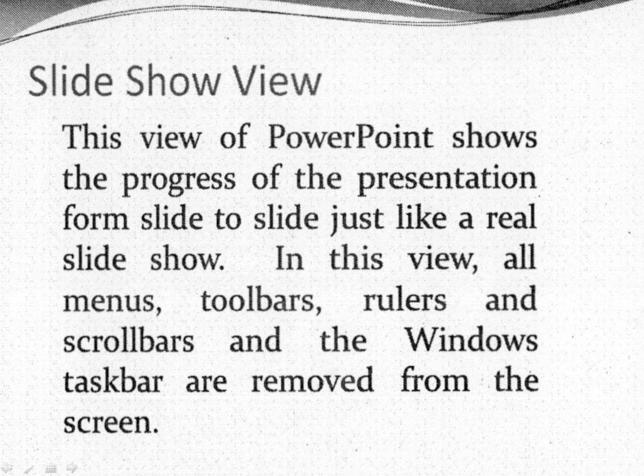

Figure 6.68 Slide Show View

6.6.2 Choosing a Set Up for Presentation

With the options in the Set up dialog box, you can choose the type of show to run and how the show should proceed.

Starting the Slide Show

When you view a slide show, you have following options:

1. Click **Slide Show** tab in the **Start Slide Show group**, choose Slide Show from beginning or press Shift+F5 keys together.
2. In the Slide show, you go to next slide, press N or click the Backspace key to go to the previous slide.

➜ **To set a slide show option, do this:**

1. Click **Slide Show** tab in the **Set Up** group, choose Set Up Show icon. The Set Up Show dialog box appears as shown in Figure 6.69.

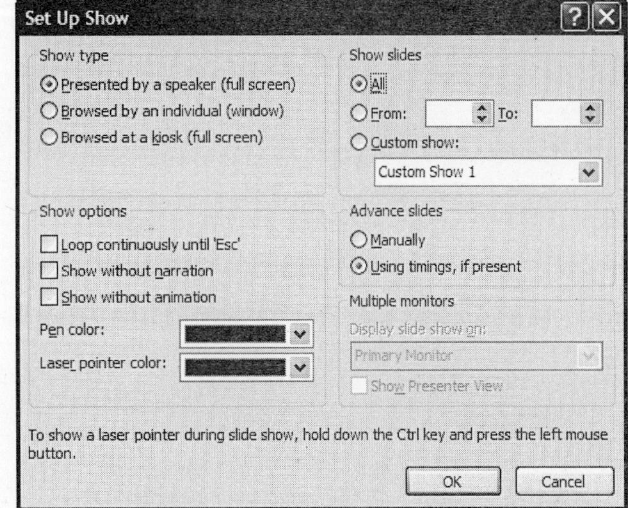

Figure 6.69 The Set Up Show dialog box

2. To Show all slides in your presentation, Click All in the Show slides section.
3. To show a specific group of slides from your presentation, enter a starting and ending slide in From: and To: edit boxes.
4. To start a custom slide presentation that derives from another presentation, click Custom Show: drop-down list and then click the presentation that you want to view as a custom show.

Giving Special Show

PowerPoint offers three special slide show types. These are available on the Set Up Show dialog box (See Figure 6.69).

1. *Click Presented by a Speaker (full screen)*: Is the traditional, full-screen slide show.
2. *Click Browsed by an Individual (window)*: Runs the slide show in a standard window.
3. *Click Browsed at a Kiosk (full screen)*: It displays a full screen as a self running show which restarts after 5 minutes.

6.6.3 Printing Slides and Handouts

Handout lets you include two, three, or six small images of the slides in your presentation. You can select the format when you print them.

Handouts can be created in the following two ways:

- Print the Handouts using the standard PowerPoint format, i.e., two, three or six slide on a page format.
- The Handout format can be customized to your requirement using the handout master.

If you make Handouts, PowerPoint shrinks the slides you have created and fits them on a page, according to the option you choose in the print Backstage view. To use standard Handout formats, you only have to select the number of slides you want to print on a page when you take the printouts for Handouts.

The header, footers, page numbers and the date on each handout will be printed if you have selected any of these items on your Notes Pages. The same is automatically applied to your Handouts.

In case you want to have different headers, footers, page numbers or dates on your Handouts as compared to the Notes Pages then you are required to change these in the Headers and Footer dialog box.

The golden rule in presentations is "Say more than you show and handout more than you say". Therefore the material that you hand out (either before or after your presentation) should be more than just pictures of your slides.

Printing Handouts

You can print your entire presentation – slides, outline, notes and audience handouts. You can also print specific slides, handouts, notes pages, or outline pages.

➜ To print handouts, do this:

1. Open the presentation you want to print.
2. Click the **File** tab, the Backstage view appears.
3. To click one or multiple slides per page in handout format, under **Handouts**, click the number of slides you want per page, and whether you want them to be appeared in order vertically or horizontally (See Figure 6.70).
4. After applying the desired option, click OK.

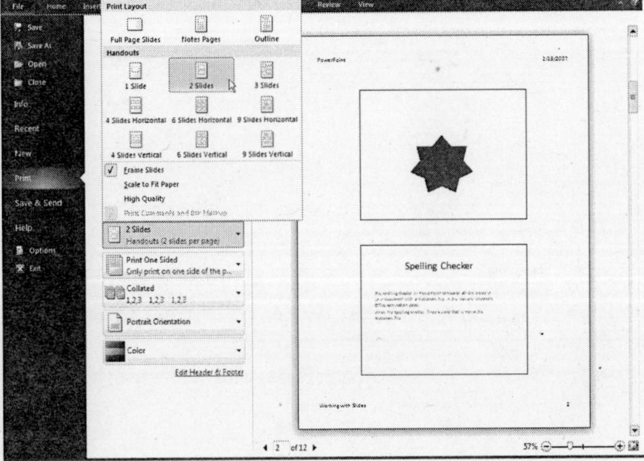

Figure 6.70 Selecting slides per page in handout format

Printing Slides

In PowerPoint 2010, you can either print all the slides or the current slide of a presentation.

➜ To print a slides, do this:

1. Open the presentation that you want to print.
2. Click the **File** tab on the Ribbon, click **Print** tab. The **Print** Backstage view appears as shown in Figure 6.71.
3. The name of the currently selected printer is shown at the under **Printer** drop-down arrow. To print the presentation on a different printer, select the desired printer from the **Printer** drop-down list.
4. Specify the number of copies you want to print, for each slide in the **Copies:** spinner box.

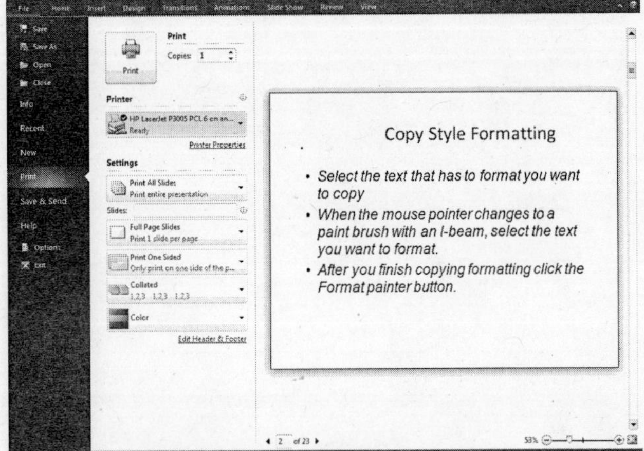

Figure 6.71 Print Backstage view

5. The **Setting** drop-down list has the option which allows you to select the pages you want to print.

Option	Description
Print All Slides	Choose Print All Slides option to print the entire presentation at one time.
Current slide	Choose the Current slide option to print the slide shown on the monitor.
Custom Range	Choose to print the selected slides, and enter the corresponding slide numbers in the **Slides:** edit box, e.g., to print slide 3 and 6 through 8, enter 3,6-8 in the Slides edit box.
Custom Show	Prints a certain custom show which has been set up. Each custom shows appears on the list.
Print Hidden Slides	If slides are hidden (do not display during a slide show), they can be printed by checking the *Print Hidden Slides* check box.

6. **Collate:** Specify if you want to arrange while printing multiple copies. When you choose collate option, each set is printed completely from first page to the last page. Then the next set is printed.
7. Click the Color button, and select the color setting for the printouts:
   - **Color**–This is default. When you use this settings with a black-and-white printer, it results in slides with grayscale or black backgrounds.
   - **Grayscale**–To print in grayscale, select the grayscale check box.

- **Pure black & white option**–Converts all colors in the presentation to either black or white. Prefer this option if you need to print on a printer that cannot print gray shades.

6.7 SLIDE SHOW

6.7.1 Running a Slide Show

When you develop a slide show in Slide Sorter view, you can get a preview of transition effects for all slides. But to see the transitions full-screen and to see animated or bulleted text slides, you must select the presentation as a slide show.

Assigning Slide Transitions

Slides transitions are the animation-like effects that occur in the slide show view, when you move from one slide to the next. You can control the speed of each slide transition effect, and you can also add sound.

➜ **To assign the transitions, do this:**

1. Select the slide(s) you want to add a transition effect.
2. Click the **Transitions** tab. In the **Transition to This slide** group, click down arrow and then select the effect that will be applied during the slide show. For example here we select *Flash* under **subtle** (See Figure 6.72).

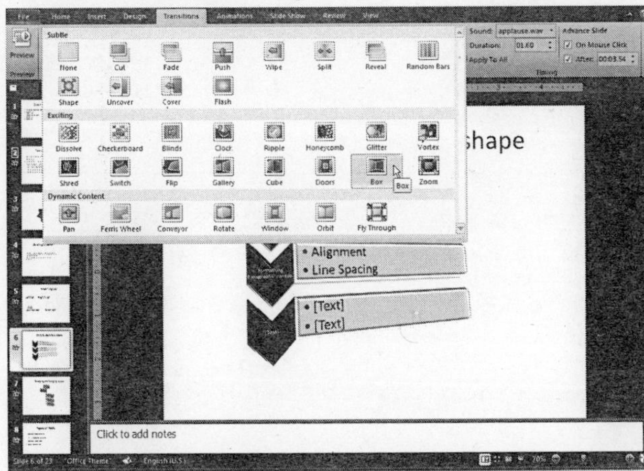

Figure 6.72 Selecting Transition effect to Slide

3. If you Apply to all slides, click **Apply To All** in the **Timings** group.
4. Select the Sound option to give sound transitions to your slide show from the **Sound:** drop-down list in the **Timings** group.
5. The Advance section has two options for transition:
   - On mouse click check box – If you want the transition to take place on clicking the mouse.
   - Automatically after – In this case, the transition takes place automatically after the time you specify in the *seconds* box.
6. After apply all options, you can see the effect in the Slide show. Click the **Slide Show** tab, in the **Start Slide Show** group, click **From Beginning** icon. Click the Next button, i.e., → to go to the next slide.
7. Click Preview command to preview the current transitions effect in the **Preview** group

Controlling the Slide Show with a Mouse

During a slide Show, you can use the pop-up menu button. A pop-up menu appears as shown in Figure 6.73. As mentioned earlier, the button appears in the lower left corner of the current slide as soon as you move the mouse pointer. You can then click the button to display slide show pop-up menu.

The Next and Previous commands on the pop-up menu let you move forward or backward through the slides in your slide show.

To move to a specific slide, click Go to Slide and then choose slide from the menu (See Figure 6.73).

To stop a slide show at any time during a presentation, simply choose End Show from the pop-up menu.

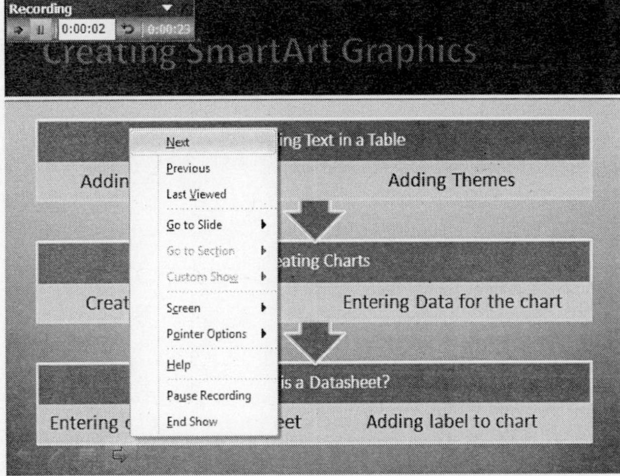

Figure 6.73 Pop-up menu during Slide show

Controlling the Slide Show with a Keyboard

In addition to the slide show pop-up menu, you can use the keys listed in Table 6.2 to control various aspects of the show.

Table 6.2 Slide Show keyboard controls

Press This	To Perform This Action
Spacebar, →, ↓, PgDn, N	Advance to next slide.
Backspace, ←, ↑, PgUp, or P	Return to previous slide
Slide number + Enter	Go to slide number
B or period	Blacks/Unblacks the screen
W or comma	Whites/Unwhite the screen
Ctrl+A	Show mouse pointer as arrow
Ctrl+P	Show mouse pointer as pen
S or + (numeric keypad)	Stop/Restart automatic show
H	Go to next slide if hidden.
T	Rehearse – use new time
O	Rehearse – use original time
Esc, Ctrl+break or (-)	End Show

6.7.2 Transitions and Slide Timings

If you do not want to move through a slide show manually, there are two ways you can set the length of time a slide appears on the screen. One way is to set a time manually for each slide, and then run the slide show and view the timings you set. The other way is to use rehearsal feature, where you can record timings automatically as you rehearse. You can also ajdust the timings you have already set and then rehearse the new ones.

Setting Slide Show Timings Manually

1. On the **Slide Show** tab, in the **Set Up** group, click **Rehearse Timings** to start the show in rehearsal mode.
2. It starts a full-screen slide show in which you can rehearse your presentation.
3. The Rehearsal dialog box appears in the slide show as shown in Figure 6.74. It starts slide timings in the first slide.

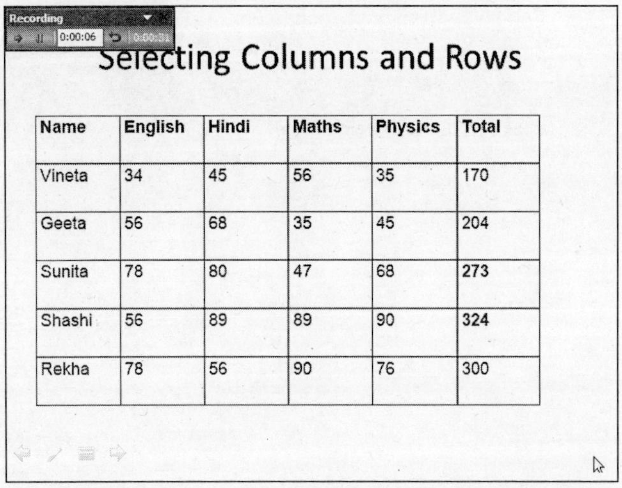

Recording 0:00:06 0:00:31

Selecting Columns and Rows

Name	English	Hindi	Maths	Physics	Total
Vineta	34	45	56	35	170
Geeta	56	68	35	45	204
Sunita	78	80	47	68	273
Shashi	56	89	89	90	324
Rekha	78	56	90	76	300

Figure 6.74 Rehearsal Timings dialog box appears in the slide show

4. Click Next button in the Rehearsal dialog box, and fix the time in the second slide.
5. When you reach the end of the slide show, the PowerPoint dialog appears. It asks *The Total time for the slide show was 0:00:42. Do you want to keep the new slide timings to use when you view the slid show?* Yes or No. Click Yes to accept the timings or No to try again.
6. The amount of time you spend on each slide is recorded and you can save those timings to run the show automatically in the future.

REVIEW QUESTIONS WITH ANSWERS

1. Multiple Choice

1.1 Which of the following views in not one of PowerPoint views?
a. Slide Sorter view b. Slide view
c. Slide Show view d. Sorter view

1.2 The Save As dialog box can be used:
a. For saving the file for the first time
b. To save file by some alternative name
c. To save file in a format other then Word
d. All of the above

1.3 In which tab is used to insert the video from file in PowerPoint 2010
a. Insert tab of Media group
b. Insert tab of Symbols group
c. Home tab of Editing group
d. Insert tab of Images group

1.4 An electronic page in a presentation in called:
a. Slide b. W-slide
c. E-page d. Page

1.5 Which of the following shortcuts is used to insert a New Slide?
a. Ctrl+M b. Ctrl+N
c. Ctrl+O d. None of the above

1.6 Which extension is given to PowerPoint document by default?
a. .EXT b. .COM
c. .PPT d. None

1.7 Which of the following menus has the Background?
a. Format b. View
c. Insert d. Slide Show

1.8 Which of the following is true in relation to Clip Art?
a. PowerPoint displays available pictures in the Clip Art Gallery
b. You can use a toolbar button or a placeholder to insert Clip Art
c. You can re-color Clip Art.
d. All of the above

1.9 In which view Notes pane appears:
a. Normal view c. Both a and b
b. Outline view d. None of the above

1.10 In Handout master, footer area appears at
a. Top of the page c. Center of the page
b. Bottom of the page d. None of the above

1.11 You can show the shortcut menu during the slide show by
a. Clicking the shortcut button on the ribbon
b. Right clicking the current slide
c. Clicking an icon on the current slide
d. Both a and b

1.12 Which of the following allows you to select more than one slide in a presentation?
a. Alt + click each slide c. Shift + click each slide
b. Shift + drag each slide d. Ctrl + click each slide

1.13 The PowerPoint view that displays only text (title and bullets) is:
a. Slide show c. Notes page view
b. Slide sorter view d. Outline view

1.14 To add a header or footer to your handout, you can use:
a. Title master c. Handout master
b. Slide master d. All of the above

1.15 What is the easy way to apply varied animations to test on slides?
a. Apply effects in the custom animation text pane
b. Apply an animation scheme
c. Customize bullets with animated ClipArt
d. All of above

1.16 How can you create a uniform appearance by adding a background image to all slides?
a. Design tab of background group
b. Insert tab of Illustrations group
c. Design tab of Themes group
d. None of the above

1.17 Which of the following is the default page setup orientation of slide in PowerPoint?
a. Vertical c. Portrait
b. Landscape d. None of above

1.18 What is defined by the handout master?
- a. Slide formatting
- b. Layout of audience handout notes
- c. Handout content formatting for Word export
- d. All of the above

1.19 Which command brings you to the first slide in your presentation?
- a. Next slide button
- b. Pg Up
- c. Ctrl + Home
- d. Ctrl + End

2. State whether the following statements are True or False

2.1 You can view a presentation using one out of ten views provided by PowerPoint.

2.2 The Slide Sorter View button automatically sorts the slides alphabetically.

2.3 Outline view, Slide view, and Slide Show are just different ways of viewing the same set of slides.

2.4 Closing a presentation and exiting PowerPoint are the same thing.

2.5 You can shut down PowerPoint 2010 by using the Close button.

2.6 The first time you save a presentation you must name it.

2.7 A text box can be placed anywhere on the slide.

2.8 Bullets and numbering appear in the Standard toolbar.

2.9 A table can be inserted in PowerPoint slide only if the MS Word is also installed.

2.10 Animation effects appear in the Design tab.

2.11 Both .wav and .mid files are the two kind of sound effects files that can be added to the presentation.

2.12 To edit a chart, you can click the chart object.

2.13 Rotate is the term used when a ClipArt image changes the direction of faces.

2.14 Inserting a new slide is used when you want to add a slide to an existing presentation.

2.15 Slide sorter view is the best view to use when setting transition effect for all slides in a presentation.

3. Match the following

3.1	Another name for the cursor is the	a.	selected text or graphics are removed
3.2	In a document when the "cut" command is used	b.	Sorter view
3.3	To re-arrange slides in	c.	Insertion point
3.4	The main area for adding slide content in PowerPoint window	d.	A title side for a new presentation appears
3.5	To start Powerpoint first	e.	Cannot be placed on a single slide
3.6	Two different color schemes	f.	The slide pane, in the middle of the window
3.7	Creating a new slide you choose a	g.	Allows you to set the time of animations
3.8	The use of Notes in Slides	h.	Format Slide
3.9	The use of Rehearse Timings	i.	Layout
3.10	Not the one of view options provided by PowerPoint to look and modify presentation	j.	To make design to your slides
3.11	Design tab	k.	This is just Note about the slide
3.12	Home tab	l.	To place text anywhere on your slide
3.13	Text box	m.	Transition Settings
3.14	Insert Clip Art	n.	It displays Clipboard, Slides, Font, Paragraph etc.
3.15	To add special effects to modify the appearance of the slides and the timing between each slide	o.	Double click a Clip Art placeholder
		p.	End a slide show

4. Fill in the blanks

a. Transitions	b. Notes Page	c. Update the presentation
d. Slide sorter view	e. Ctrl + Home	f. View tab
g. Insert	h. Ctrl + K	i. Shadow Effects
j. Slide master	k. Design	l. F5
m. Template	o. Landscape	p. Backspace

4.1 To place an organization chart on a slide, you must ________.

4.2 Special effects used to introduce slides in a presentation are called ________.

4.3 ________ view in PowerPoint can be used to enter speaker comments.

4.4 The best way to insert a new slide in a presentation is to use the ________.

4.5 Preset, Shadow, Reflection and Glow are ________

4.6 ________ command brings you to the first slide in your presentation.

4.7 Slide sorter of PowerPoint is available on ________ on the Presentation Views group.

4.8 To place something in the same position on every slide of presentation automatically, insert into ________.

4.9 ________ to insert a hyperlink in a slide.

4.10 ________ tab in the Text group to create a text box on a slide.

4.11 ________ tab is used to apply a design themes in PowerPoint.

4.12 ________ Function key on the keyboard can be used to view slide show.

4.13 ________ is the default page setup orientation for slides in PowerPoint.

4.14 A file which contains readymade styles that can be used for a presentation is called ________.

4.15 ________ key deletes text before, or the left of the insertion point.

Answers

1.	1.1	a	1.2	d	1.3	a	1.4	a	1.5	a	1.6	c
	1.7	a	1.8	d	1.9	c	1.10	b	1.11	b	1.12	c
	1.13	d	1.14	c	1.15	b	1.16	a	1.17	b	1.18	b
	1.19	c										
2.	2.1	F	2.2	T	2.3	T	2.4	T	2.5	T	2.6	T

2.7 T 2.8 F 2.9 T 2.10 F 2.11 T 2.12 F
2.13 T 2.14 T 2.15 T

3. 3.1 c 3.2 a 3.3 b 3.4 f 3.5 d 3.6 e
3.7 i 3.8 k 3.9 g 3.10 h 3.11 j 3.12 n
3.13 l 3.14 o 3.15 m

4. 4.1 c 4.2 a 4.3 b 4.4 d 4.5 i 4.6 e
4.7 f 4.8 j 4.9 h 4.10 g 4.11 k 4.12 l
4.13 o 4.14 m 4.15 p

Short Questions with Answers

1. What is animation?
2. Where is a transition icon displayed?
3. Why is a transition icon used for?
4. What is sound?
5. Describe the Photo Album feature.
6. Advantages and disadvantages to using Presentation software.
7. Define Custom show. How would you create a custom show.
8. What is the function of MS PowerPoint?
9. What is the difference between MS PowerPoint and MS Word?
10. What are the uses and features of MS PowerPoint?

Answers to Short Questions

1. An animation is a visual effect in which objects appear to be moved.
   a. Select the slide or text in which you want to animate.
   b. Click Animations tab in the Animation group.
   c. Click the more button to choose the desired animation to apply to objects in the slides.
2. A transition icon is displayed next to each slide in the Slides tab or below each slide in Slide Sorter view.
3. The transition icon is used to preview animations.
4. Sound is an audio file that can be added to a slide and played during a slide show.
5. The Photo Album feature is used to create a slide show of pictures.
6. Advantages

   Attract and hold audience attention.
   Presents information in many formats (auditary, graphic, text)
   Content is easy to edit.
   Presentation can be shown on any computer.
   Multiple sources of data, including Excel and Word files, can be incorporated.
   Create speaker notes.

   Disadvantages

   Computers and software are expensive.
   Technology can be unreliable.
   The "look" of a presentation may overcome the message.
   Too much time and effort may be spent on the "look" of the presentation.
7. To create a custom show, do this:
   - Select the Slide Show tab and locate the Start Slide Show group.
   - Click the Custom Slide Show command.
   - Select Custom Shows... . The Custom Shows dialog box appears.
   - Click New. The Define Custom show dialog box will appear.
   - Locate the Slide show name: box and type in a name for your custom show.
   - Select the slides in the Slides in presentation: box that you would like to include in your custom show, then click Add>> to add them to the Slides in custom show: box. You can also use the up and down arrows to reorder the addes slides.
   - Click OK.
   - Select Close to exit or Show to view your custom show.
8. PowerPoint is used to create slide shows, on screen projector, for printing or Web-based displays. PowerPoint is frequently used to create educational presentations at seminars.
9. PowerPoint was made to prepare and demonstrate presentations, and Word was made to write document, books, resumes and so on.

   Both MS Word and MS PowerPoint have similar features and can sometimes be replaced by each other, but it is necessary to remember that they are completely different adopted for different purposes.
10. PowerPoint is a very powerful program used to create and manipulate slideshows. It is commonly used in advertizing because of its wide range of visual effects. It is not difficult to create PowerPoint presentation with text and graphics. When you start to get better, the more powerful features are very useful. These include slide master, which allows you to modify aspects of every slide including copy/paste, custom animation schemes, slide transitions,

DESCRIPTIVE TYPE QUESTIONS

1. Open PowerPoint and Label the parts of the window.

a.	File Tab	d.	Slides Tab	g.	Zoom Slider
b.	Quick Access Toolbar	e.	Notes Pane	h.	Slide Pane
c.	Ribbon	f.	Views	i.	Window controls

2. What should be the features of a good presentation packages? What role do the presentation packages play in the field of Education?
3. What are the functions used in Slide Show tab of Ribbon command?
4. What is theme and layout in PowerPoint 2010? How do you apply theme effect in your presentation?
5. Explain the utility of Bullets and Numbering. Write down the steps to use bullets.
6. What are shapes and how do you make use of them?
7. Explain the steps involved to animate text and graphic objects in PowerPoint presentation?
8. Give difference between Handout master and Slide master.
9. What do you understand by a slide show? Explain with an example.
10. How would you copy a slide from one presentation to another? Give all the steps.
11. In PowerPoint, explain using a custom animation effect. How do you make text appear on a slide letter-by-letter?
12. Explain how animation is inserted in MS PowerPoint.
13. What are action buttons? Explain their utilities?

CHAPTER 7

HTML and Publishing Tools

7.1 INTRODUCTION

Every HTML (HyperText Markup Language) document should contain certain standard HTML tags. A tag is a coded HTML command that indicates how a part of Web page should be displayed. Each document consists of head and body tags. A tag is a coded HTML command that indicates how a Web page should be displayed. The head contains the title and the body contains the actual text that is made up of paragraphs, lists and other elements. Web browsers expect specific information because they are programmed according to HTML specifications.

A sample HTML document is shown in Figure 7.1.

Figure 7.2 shows the output when this document is read using the Internet Explorer.

```
<html>
  <head>
  <TITLE> A Simple HTML Example</TITLE>
  </head>
  <body>
  <H1>HTML is very EASY to Learn </H1>
  <P>Welcome to the world of HTML.</P>
  <P>This is the first paragraph. However
       short it is still a paragraph!
  </P>
  <p>And this is the second paragraph. </p>
  </body>
  </html>
```

Figure 7.1 A sample HTML document

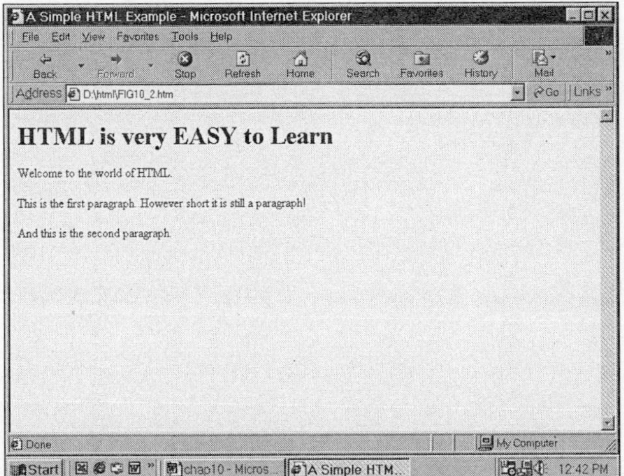

Figure 7.2 Result of code given in Figure 7.1

> ☞ *Every HTML document contains certain standard HTML tags. Each document consists of head and body tags.*

The required elements are the <html>, <head>, <title>, and <body> tags (and their corresponding terminating end tags). It is better to include end tags because you are not aware about the type of Internet browser that a Web surfer may be using.

7.1.1 HTML Page Structure

An HTML page consists of the following tags.

<HTML> : This tag specifies the document as an HTML document.

<HEAD> : This tag contains information about the document, including its title, scripts used, style definitions and document descriptions.

<TITLE> : This tag contains the document title. The title specified inside <Title> tag appears on the browser's title bar. You should be very careful while choosing the title because a title is also used to identify a Web page for search engines.

<BODY>: This forms the largest part of the HTML document. The <Body> tag encloses all the tags, attributes and information to be displayed in the Web page. The information written within the body tag is displayed in the browser window.

Above tags are explained in detail in the following sections:

7.1.2 Different HTML Tags

HTML Element <Html>

The HTML element tells the Web browser that the file contains HTML-coded information. The file extension **.html** indicates that this is an HTML document. An HTML document must contain this extension for it to be read by a Web browser.

HEAD Element <Head>

The Head element identifies the first part of the HTML-coded document containing the title. The title is shown as part of the browser's window.

Information placed in the Head is essential to the inner working of the document and has nothing to do with the content of the document. With the exception of information contained within the **<TITLE>... </TITLE>** tags, all information placed within the **<HEAD>...</HEAD>** tags is not displayed in the browser. The HTML tags used to indicate the start and end of the head section are as follows:

```
<HEAD>
   <TITLE> </TITLE>
</HEAD>
```

TITLE Element <Title>

The Title element contains the document's title and identifies its contents in a global context. The title is displayed somewhere in the browser window (usually at the top), but not within the text area. You should choose title head somewhat descriptive, unique and relatively short.

For example, you might include a shortened title of a book along with the Chapter contents:
Windows 2000 Guide: Installation. This tells the software name, the platform, and the chapter contents, which is more useful than simply calling the document *Installation*. Generally, you should keep the title limited to 64 characters or less.

ADDRESS Element <ADDRESS>

Just as the title can be placed in the title bar of the browser window, certain information is commonly placed at the foot of the Web page. For example, *Copyright* information, contact details of the company, etc.

The HTML tags used for this purpose are as follows:

<ADDRESS>...</ADDRESS>

The **<ADDRESS>** tag should be placed immediately after the last line of the textual material of the Web page. However, it could also be placed anywhere in the body of the document. The text typed within these **<ADDRESS>** tags appears in *Italics*.

BODY <BODY>

The second and largest part of your HTML document is the body, which contains the contents of the document (displayed within the text area of your browser window). The tags explained below are used within the body of your HTML document.

The tags used to indicate the start and the end of the main body of textual information are as follows:

```
<BODY>
=======
</BODY>
```

The default characteristics of a page, such as background color, text color, font size and font width, etc., can be specified as attributes of the **<BODY>** tag. The attributes for the **<BODY>** tag are given in Table 7.1.

Table 7.1 Different Attributes of <BODY> Tag

Attribute	Description
BGCOLOR	This command is used to changes the default background color as per the specified color.
BACKGROUN D	This command specifies the name of the GIF file (image) that will be used as the background of the document. The GIF tiles up across the page to give a background.
TEXT	This command changes the body text colour from its default value to the colour specified with this attribute.

Example 1

A sample HTML document containing **<BODY>** attributes is shown in Figure 7.3. This HTML document contains various elements described so far.

When you see this HTML document using any of the popular browsers, such as Internet Explorer or NetScape Navigator, you will find that the text is displayed in red color. If you do not use a color monitor, then the text will not be distinguishable from the rest of the screen display. Note the attribute Text = Red in the **<BODY>** tag in Figure 7.3.

```
<html>
<head>
<TITLE> A Simple HTML Example</TITLE>
</head>
<body TEXT = RED>
<H1>HTML is very EASY to Learn </H1>
<P>Welcome to the world of HTML.</P>
<P>This is the first paragraph. However
      short it is still a paragraph!
</P>
<p>And this is the second paragraph. </p>
</body>
</html>
```

Figure 7.3 Code for displaying text in red color

```
<html>
<head>
<TITLE> A Simple HTML Example</TITLE>
</head>
<body BGCOLOR = YELLOW>
<H1>HTML is very EASY to Learn </H1>
<P>Welcome to the world of HTML.</P>
<P>This is the first paragraph. However
      short it is still a paragraph!
</P>
<p>And this is the second paragraph. </p>
</body>
</html>
```

Figure 7.4 Code for yellow background

The program in Figure 7.4 gives the background as yellow. This is possible by giving the body attribute BGCOLOR as YELLOW.

Example 2

The program in Figure 7.5 gives the background as yellow but text displayed in red. This is possible by giving the body attribute BGCOLOR = YELLOW and TEXT = RED.

7.1.3 HTML Text

The most basic element of any HTML page is ASCII (American Standard Code for Information Interchange) text. HTML pages, while they include the .htm or .html file extensions, are simply ASCII text files. Any program that generates ASCII text files will work fine as an HTML editor.

☞ *An HTML document is simply a text file that contains the information you want to publish. It also contains embedded instructions, called elements, that indicate how a Web browser should present the document.*

```
<html>
<head>
<TITLE> A Simple HTML Example</TITLE>
</head>
<body BGCOLOR = YELLOW TEXT = RED>
<H1>HTML is very EASY to Learn </H1>
<P>Welcome to the world of HTML.</P>
<P>This is the first paragraph. However
        short it is still a paragraph!
</P>
<p>And this is the second paragraph. </p>
</body>
</html>
```

Figure 7.5 HTML code for yellow background and red text

7.1.4 What is an Element?

An *element* is a fundamental component of the structure of an HTML text document. Some examples of elements are heads, tables, paragraphs and lists.

☞ *You use HTML tags to mark the elements of a file for your browser to interpret and display them. Elements can contain plain text, other elements, or both.*

7.1.5 Types of HTML Elements

HTML elements can be categorized as

- Container elements
- Empty elements

Container Elements

This type of HTML elements require pair tags, i.e., a starting as well as an ending tag, for example <title> .... </title> <B>....</B>, etc. The end tag or *off* tag </Tag> is just like the start tag or ON tag <Tag>, except that it has a slash (/) in it. In HTML, elements that include both an *ON* and an *OFF* tag are called *container* elements. These tags affect everything that comes between their starting and ending tag.

Empty Elements

This type of HTML elements require just a starting tag and not an ending tag, for example <BR>, <HR>, etc.
 breaks a line and <HR> inserts a horizontal rule. Some elements have only an *ON* tag, but they do not have a corresponding end or *OFF* tag. These elements are called empty elements. Empty elements just carry out their specific job and do not act on blocks of text.

7.2 HEADING ELEMENT

HTML has six levels of section headings numbered 1 through 6, with 1 being the most prominent section. Text with heading tags is displayed in larger and/or bolder fonts than the normal body text by a Web browser. The first heading in each document should be tagged as **<H1>.**

The syntax of the heading element is as follows:

<Hn>*Text of heading* **</Hn>**

where **n** is a number between 1 and 6 specifying the level of the heading.

☞ *Do not skip levels of headings in your document. For example, if you start with a level-one heading (<H1>), then do not use a level-three (<H3>) heading next to it.*

7.3 BLOCK-ORIENTED ELEMENTS

The carriage returns in HTML documents are not important. Therefore, you should not worry about how long your lines of text are. Any number of lines can be written in your source file. Multiple spaces are joined into a single space by the Web browser.

☞ *In the text, a blank line always separates paragraphs. But in HTML, the tag* **<P>** *provides a blank line.*

In the HTML documents as shown in Figure 7.1, the first paragraph is coded as:

```
<P>Welcome to the world of HTML.
</P>
<P>This is the first paragraph.
However short it is still
a paragraph!</P>
```

In the source file, there are line breaks between sentences. A Web browser ignores the line breaks and starts a new paragraph only when it encounters another **<P>** tag.

☞ *You must indicate paragraphs with <P> elements. A browser ignores any indentations or blank lines in the source text. Without <P> elements, the document becomes one large paragraph.*

To preserve readability in HTML files, put headings on separate lines. Use a blank line or two where it helps you to identify the start of a new section and separate paragraphs with blank lines (in addition to the **<P>** tags). These extra spaces are needed to help you when you edit files. Note that the browser ignores the extra spaces because it has its own set of rules on spacing that do not depend on the spaces you put in your source file.

☞ *The </P> closing tag is optional. This is because browsers understand that when they encounter a </P> tag, it implies that there is an end to the previous paragraph. Note the sign / before P.*

Using the <P> and </P> as a paragraph container means that you can centre a paragraph by including the **ALIGN** = *alignment* attribute in source file.

Example 3

A sample HTML coding of an document containing the center alignment is shown in Figure 7.6. Here, the line "Welcome to the world of HTML" would be shown in the centre of the page when browsed.

Figure 7.7 shows how the document shown in Figure 7.6 appears using Internet Explorer.

7.3.1 Line Breaks

When text needs to start from a new line and not continue on the same line without skipping a blank line, you can insert Line Break **
** tag.

```
<html>
<head>
<TITLE> A Simple HTML Example</TITLE>
</head>
<body BGCOLOR = YELLOW TEXT = RED>
<H1>HTML is very EASY to Learn </H1>
<P ALIGN=CENTER>Welcome to the world of
             HTML.</P>
<P>This is the first paragraph. However
        short it is still a paragraph!
</P>
<p>And this is the second paragraph. </p>
</body>
</html>
```

Figure 7.6 Code using ALIGN attribute

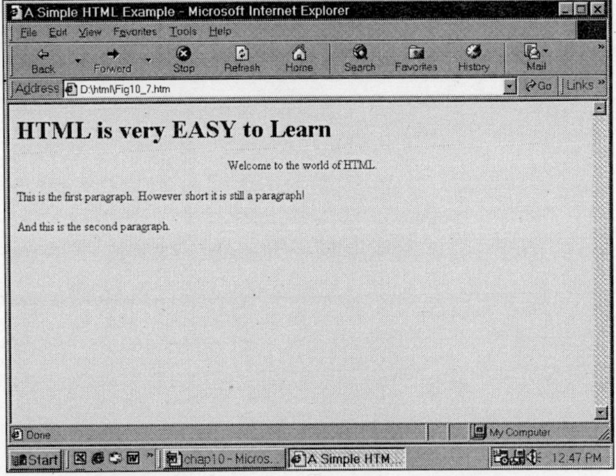

Figure 7.7 Result of code given in Figure 7.6

☞ *Every tag must close with '/'. For example, <P> is the paragraph tag which should end with </P>.*

Example 4

Figure 7.8 shows the line break tag **
** before the sentence "However short it is". When the document is browsed, this line will appear separate from the sentence "This is the first paragraph".

```
<html>
<head>
<TITLE> A Simple HTML Example</TITLE>
</head>
<body BGCOLOR = YELLOW TEXT = RED>
<H1>HTML is very EASY to Learn </H1>
<P ALIGN=CENTER>Welcome to the world
         of HTML.</P>
<P>This is the first paragraph. <BR>
```

(Contd...)

```
   However short it is still a paragraph!
</P>
  <p>And this is the second paragraph. </p>
  </body>
  </html>
```

Figure 7.8 Code for line break using <BR> tag.

7.3.2 Drawing Lines <HR>

The tag <HR> draws lines and horizontal rules. Table 7.2 gives the attributes of the <HR> tag.

Table 7.2 Different Attributes for the <HR> Tag

Attribute	Description
ALIGN	Aligns the line on the screen. ALIGN = LEFT (aligns the line to the left of the screen). ALIGN = RIGHT (aligns the line to the right of the screen). ALIGN = CENTER (aligns the line to the centre of the screen).
SIZE	It changes the size of the line.
WIDTH	It sets the width of the rule.

Example 5

The document in Figure 7.9 shows the line drawn under the last paragraph.

The appearance of the document when browsed through Internet Explorer is shown in Figure 7.10.

```
  <html>
  <head>
  <TITLE> A Simple HTML Example</TITLE>
  </head>
  <body BGCOLOR = YELLOW TEXT = RED>
  <H1>HTML is very EASY to Learn </H1>
  <P ALIGN=CENTER>Welcome to the world of
HTML.</P>
  <P>This is the first paragraph. <BR> How-
ever short it is still a paragraph !</P>
  <P ALIGN = CENTER> And this is the second
paragraph.
  <HR ALIGN = CENTER WIDTH = 100 SIZE = 10>
</P>
  </body>
  </html>
```

Figure 7.9 Code for a line drawn on the second paragraph

7.3.3 Text Styles

Tags for the text styles add the distinction to certain characters of the text.

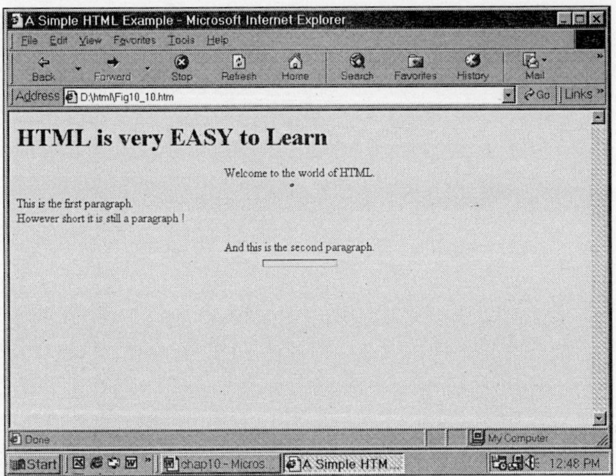

Figure 7.10 Result of code given in Figure 7.9

Boldface

The tags **<B>** and **</B>** will display text in **BOLD** face style.

> ☞ *Use proper character size to enable a reader to read text without much exertion.*

Italics

The tags **<I>** and **</I>** will display text in *ITALICS* face style.

Underline

The tags **<U>** and **</U>** will display text as UNDERLINED.

Example 6

The document in Figure 7.11 shows the text style tags as applied to the HTML document. The browsed output is shown in Figure 7.12.

```
  <html>
  <head>
  <TITLE> A Simple HTML Example</TITLE>
  </head>
  <body BGCOLOR = YELLOW TEXT = RED>
  <H1>HTML is very EASY to Learn </H1>
  <P ALIGN=CENTER><B>Welcome to the world of
HTML.</B></P>
  <P><I>This is the first paragraph.</I>
<BR>
  <U>However short it is still a paragraph
!</U></P>
  <P ALIGN = CENTER> And this is the second
paragraph.
  <HR ALIGN = CENTER WIDTH = 100 SIZE = 10>
</P>
  </body>
  </html>
```

Figure 7.11 HTML code using text style tags

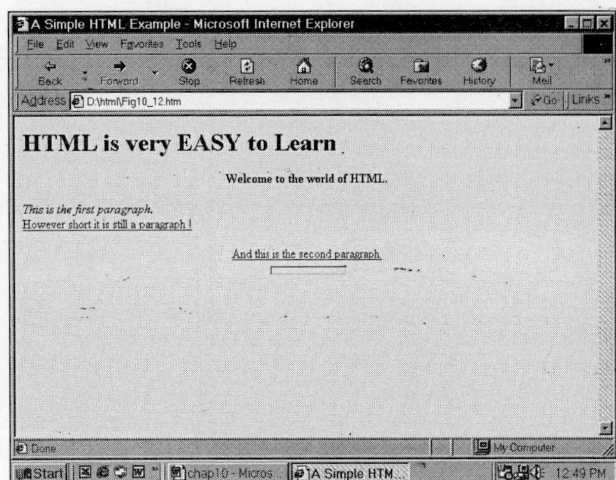

Figure 7.12 Result of code given in Figure 7.11

7.3.4 Font Size and Colour <FONT>

All text specified within the tags **<FONT>** and **</FONT>** will appear in the font, size and color as specified by the attributes of the tag **<FONT>**. Table 7.3 gives the attributes of the tag **<FONT>**.

Table 7.3 Different Attributes for the <FONT> Tag

Attribute	Description
FONT FACE	Sets the font to the specified font name.
SIZE	Sets the size of the text. It takes values between 1 and 7. The default value is 3. The size can also be a set relative to the default size. For example, SIZE = +X, where X is any integer value and will add up to the default size.
COLOR	It sets the color of the text. Color may be given as English color name or the hexadecimal value.

Example 7

Figure 7.13 shows the document containing a new type of font and its size for the last paragraph as well as the color for this paragraph only. Figure 7.14 shows the browser output.

7.4 LISTS

Using HTML, you can arrange items in lists in several ways. The two most commonly used methods are as follows:

a. Bulleted
b. Numbered

> ☞ *Text style changes the appearance of text in italics, bold, underlines or bold italics, etc., for clarity.*

7.4.1 Bulleted Lists <UL>

This is an unordered list. In this, each item (paragraph) is prefaced with a bullet. An unordered list is used for a list of items in which the ordering is not specific. The tags used for this are **<UL>** and **</UL>**. A browser adds a bullet for each item and indents it.

```
<html>
<head>
<TITLE> A Simple HTML Example</TITLE>
</head>
<body BGCOLOR = YELLOW>
<H1>HTML is very EASY to Learn </H1>
<P ALIGN=CENTER><B>Welcome to the world of
HTML.</B></P>
<P><I>This is the first paragraph.</I> <BR>
<U>However short it is still a paragraph !</U></P>
<P ALIGN = CENTER><FONT FACE = "Brush Script MT"
Size = 7 COLOR = RED> And this is the second
paragraph.</FONT> </P>
<P><HR ALIGN = CENTER WIDTH = 100 SIZE = 10> </P>
</body>
</html>
```

Figure 7.13 Code using text style tags

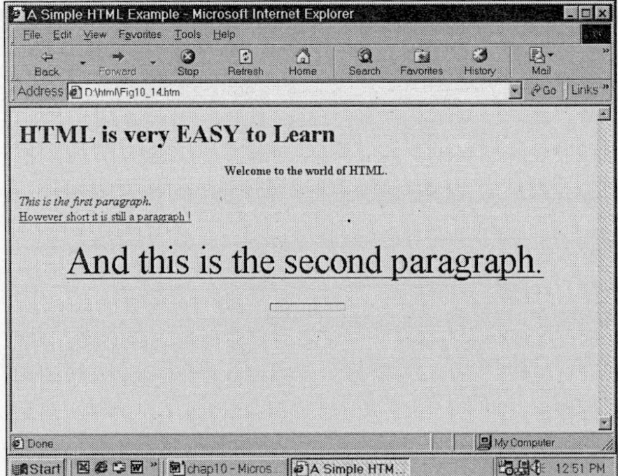

Figure 7.14 Result of code given in Figure 7.13

Example 8

Figure 7.15 shows an example of the unordered list. Figure 7.16 displays the document in Figure 7.15 when displayed in a Web browser.

```
<html>
<head>
<TITLE> A Simple HTML Example</TITLE>
</head>
<body BGCOLOR = YELLOW>
<H3>CHAPTER I</H3>
<P><UL>
<LI>Section 1
<LI>Section 2
<LI>Section 3
</UL></P>
</body>
</html>
```

Figure 7.15 Code for an unordered list

You can also put one list within another list (i.e., nesting of lists) simply by beginning the new list with the appropriate list tag. This allows you to create outlines.

☞ *Putting text in different paragraphs improves readability of the document.*

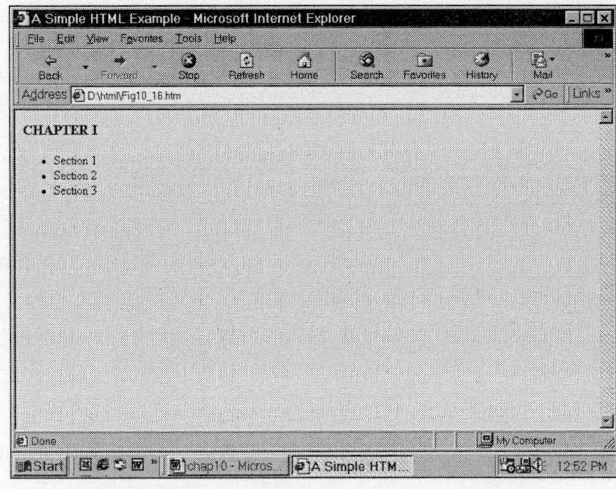

Figure 7.16 Result of code given in Figure 7.15

☞ *Listing the topics helps in improved presentation.*

```
<html>
<head>
<TITLE> A Simple HTML Example</TITLE>
</head>
<body BGCOLOR = YELLOW>
<H3>CHAPTER I</H3>
<P><UL>
<LI>Section 1
<LI>Section 2
<LI>Part A
<LI>Part B
<LI>Part C
</UL>
<UL>
<LI>Section 3
</UL></P>
</body>
</html>
```

Figure 7.17 Code for generating an unordered nested list

Example 9

The document in Figure 7.17 displays the nested list with Part A, Part B and Part C under Section 2. Figure 7.18 displays the browsed output.

7.4.2 Numbered List <OL>

Numbered list is a list with numbers arranged in an either ascending or descending order. It is an ordered list which defines a list in which order is taken into account. The tags used for this are **`<OL>`** **`</OL>`**. The browser applies the appropriate number to each line when it opens the page.

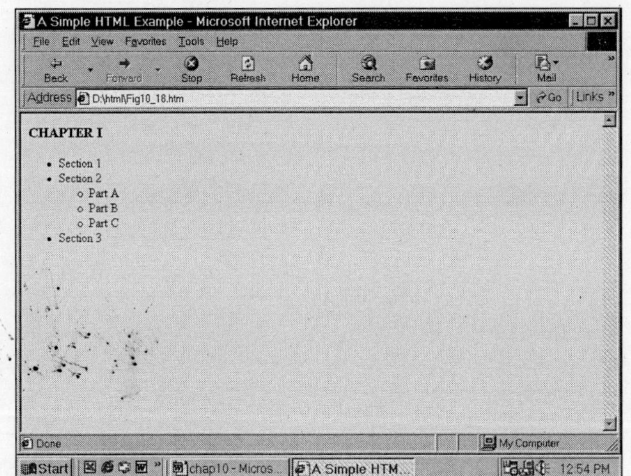

Figure 7.18 Result of code given in Figure 7.17

Ordered lists have additional attributes that you can use to specify the first number of the list as well as to create hierarchical information.

The <OL> element also has a start attribute that takes a numeric value to begin the list numbering. The number must be a positive integer. The start = "value" indicates the starting number for the list and type attribute defines the type of numbering sequence used for each listed item. For example, if you want to start ordering from the letter G, you would type <OL Type = 'A' START = "7">. This is because G is the 7th letter.

☞ *List within another list is called a nested list.*

Example 10

Figure 7.19 shows the HTML document with ordered list and Figure 7.20 shows the browsed output by Internet Explorer.

7.5 INLINE ELEMENTS

Inline elements are those HTML elements that can be used to add the description of the line in a document. Some of these elements are Image, Quote, Subscript and Superscript. Some of these are explained below.

```
<html>
<head>
<TITLE> A Simple HTML Example</TITLE>
</head>
<body BGCOLOR = YELLOW>
<H1 ALIGN=LEFT>Sample Lists</H1>
<OL>
<LI>Lions
<LI>Tigers
<LI>Bears
<LI>Oh, My!
</OL>
<OL TYPE=A>
<LI>Outlines use sequential lists with letters.
<LI>So do some (unpopular) numbering schemes for documentation.
</OL>
<UL TYPE=SQUARE>
<LI>Use bullets for non-sequential items.
<LI>Use numbers for sequential items.
</UL>
<UL >
<LI TYPE=CIRCLE> Use bullets for non-sequential items.
<LI TYPE=SQUARE> Use different bullets for visual interest.
</UL> <OL START=51>
<LI>This is the fifty-first item.
<LI>This is the fifty second.
<LI TYPE=i VALUE=7>This item was renumbered to be the seventh,
using lowercase roman numerals, just because we can.
</OL>
</body>
</html>
```

Figure 7.19 Coding for generating an ordered list

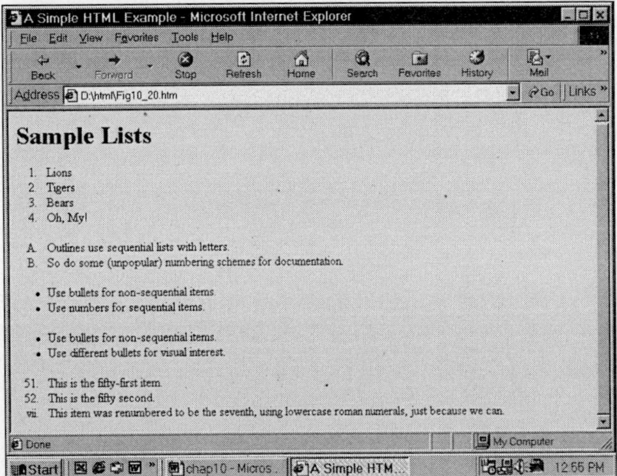

Figure 7.20 Result of code given in Figure 7.19

7.5.1 Quote Element <Q>....</Q>

A new HTML 4.0 element for citing inline quotes is the *quote* element. The quote uses **<Q>** and **</Q>** tags. It is similar to the blockquote element. The main difference is that the quote element is not block-level. It does not start a new paragraph but is used within a paragraph to mark a quotation.

Example 11

Figure 7.21 shows a sample example of Quote element.

```
<html>
<head>
<TITLE> A Simple Inline Element Exam-
ple</TITLE>
</head>
<body>
<H1>A new HTML 4.0 element for citing
inline quotes</H1>
<P>Churchil said, <Q> "We have chosen
shame and will get,"
</Q> but he was not talking about
1066.</P>
</body>
</html>
```

Figure 7.21 Code using inline element "Quote"

7.5.2 Subscript Element _{...}

The subscript element coded by **_{** and **}** tags will put the enclosed text in subscript (a bit lower than regular text). This element is useful for mathematical formulas. For example, the following line of HTML code contains the chemical formula for water (See Figure 7.23):

We all need H₂O.

7.5.3 The Superscript Element ^{...}

The superscript elements **^{....}** will render

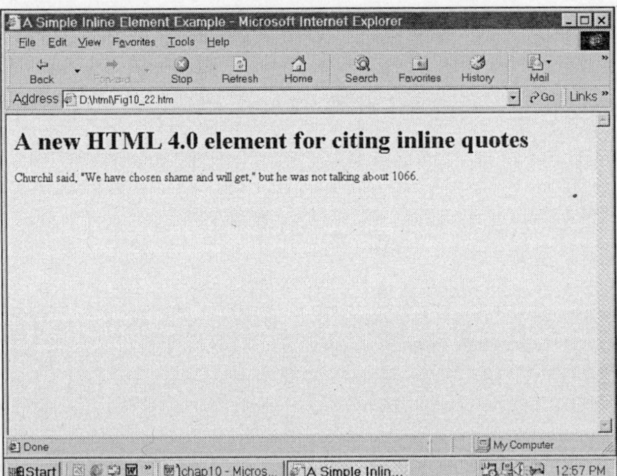

Figure 7.22 Result of code given in Figure 7.21

```
<html>
<head>
<TITLE> A Simple Inline Element
      Example</TITLE>
</head>
<body>
<H1>HTML Sub and Sup elements</H1>
<P>We all need H <SUB>2</SUB>O.</P>
<P>E = MC<SUP>2</SUP></P>
<P>Eat a Burger<SUP>TM</SUP> Today!</P>
</body>
</html>
```

Figure 7.23 HTML code using SUB and SUP elements

the enclosed text in superscript (a bit higher than regular text). This element is also useful for mathematical formulas. For example, the following is the HTML code for Einstein's famous equation (See
Figure 7.24).

> *Subscript and superscript are necessary for writing mathematical/chemical formulas.*

```
E = MC<SUP>2</SUP>
```

Another good use of the <SUP> tag is to put the trademark symbol in the document.

```
Eat a Burger<SUP>TM</SUP> Today!
```

7.5.4 Other Inline Elements

There are a few other inline elements that are new to HTML 4.0. These are as follows:

Object Element <OBJECT>...</OBJECT>

The Object element is also used to insert images, movies and multimedia files in your document.

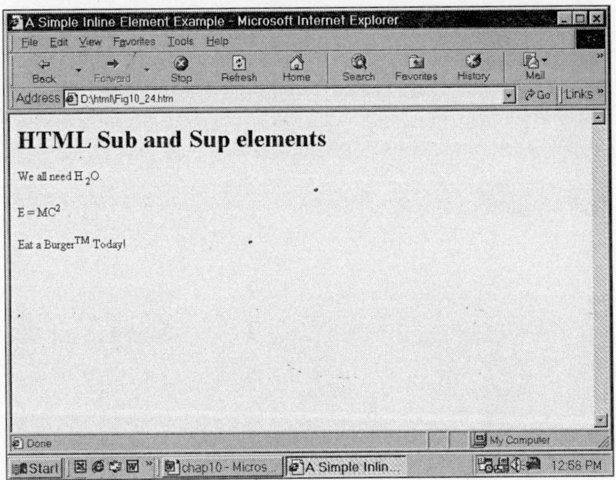

Figure 7.24 Result of code given in Figure 7.23

☞ *By putting text under quotes, you can draw attention of the reader.*

Bidirectional Override Element <BDO>...</BDO>

This element controls the direction in which the text is displayed for foreign languages (left-to-right or right-to-left) text.

Script Element <SCRIPT>...</SCRIPT>

This element can be used as a text-level element in HTML 4.0.

Span Element <SPAN>...</SPAN>

Span element is a text-level element and is commonly used with style sheets.

7.6 VISUAL MARKUP

The font element **<FONT>...</FONT>** is used to format the size, typeface and color of the enclosed text. This element changes body text for visual markup of the contents.

```
<html>
<head>
<TITLE> A Simple Visual Markup
     Example</TITLE>
</head>
<body>
<H1>HTML element BIG and SMALL</H1>
<P><BIG>The Big and Tall Company</BIG></P>
<P><FONT SIZE = "+2">The very Big and Tall
Company</FONT></P>
<P><SMALL>The Small and Short
          Company</SMALL></P>
</body>
</html>
```

Figure 7.25 HTML document with visual markup

The **<FONT>** tag can be used with three different attributes, namely, SIZE, FACE and COLOR.

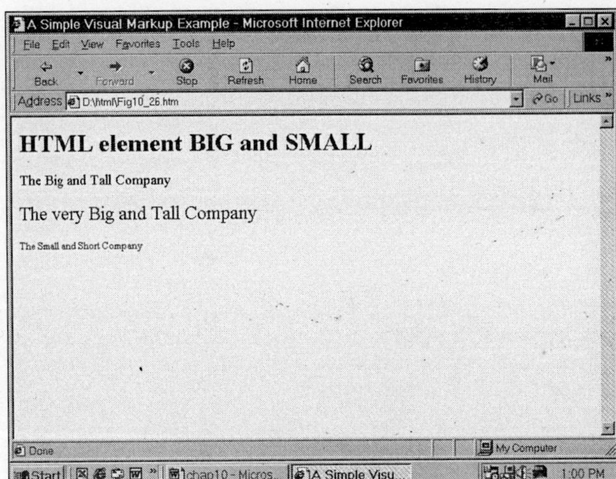

Figure 7.26 Result of code given in Figure 7.25

The SIZE attribute can be specified in absolute or relative values ranging from 1 (smallest) to 7 (largest). Using a relative font size (putting a plus or a minus sign before the number) will change the font size relative to the BASEFONT tag or the default font size. For example:

```
<FONT SIZE = "+4">
```

makes the font size four times bigger than the current size.

7.6.1 Big Element <BIG>...</BIG>

The big element **<BIG>...</BIG>** renders the enclosed text in a larger font (unless the document's font size is already as large as possible). The **<BIG>** tag has the same effect as: **<FONT SIZE = "+1">**.

More than one big element can be nested to render a larger text than is achieved with just one big element. The following examples explain this:

```
<BIG>The Big and Tall Company</BIG>
<FONT SIZE = "+2">The very Big and Tall
  Company</FONT>
```

7.6.2 Small Element <SMALL>...</SMALL>

The small element **<SMALL>...</SMALL>** renders the enclosed text in a smaller font. If your text is already at size 1 (the smallest size possible), still, the tag is ignored. The **<SMALL>** tag has the same effect as **<FONT SIZE = "-1">**. The following example explains this:

```
<SMALL>The Small and Short Company</SMALL>
```

Like the big element, more than one small element can be nested in order to render a smaller text size than is designated with just one small element.

☞ *Larger font size draws your attention but it consumes a larger area of the screen. However, takes much time to print on the printer.*

7.6.3 Teletype Element <TT>...</TT>

The Teletype elements **<TT>...</TT>** will render the enclosed text in Teletype font. This means that the text will be monospaced to look like a typewriter font.

7.6.4 FACE Attribute

The FACE attribute specifies a typeface that you would like to use for the text enclosed by the font element. You can use a single typeface (such as Arial or Courier), or you can give a list of typefaces separated by commas.

To specify font characteristics, follow these steps. You can set some or all of the following characteristics:

a. Identify the text to format with the <FONT> tag.

b. Select a specific font using the FACE = attribute.

c. Change the font size using the SIZE = attribute. You can set the size of text on a relative scale from 1 to 7 with the default size being 3.

   You may set the size absolutely with the number from 1 to 7 or relatively, with + or - to change the size. Take a look at the following example:

```
<P><BIG>The Big and Tall Company</BIG></P>
<P><BIG><FONT FACE = "Times New Roman,
Times" SIZE = "+2">The very Big and
Tall Company</FONT></BIG></P>
```

d. Add a COLOR = attribute to set color, using a color name or a #RRGGBB value. For example, the following HTML statement produces a different color along with the text:

```
<P><BIG>The Big and Tall Company</BIG></P>
<P><BIG><FONT FACE = "Times New Roman,
Times" SIZE = "+2" COLOR = "#FF0000">The
very Big and Tall Company
</FONT></BIG></P>
```

Figure 7.27 shows a sample HTML document with Face and Color attributes. The corresponding output when browsed with a browser is shown in Figure 7.28.

```
<html>
<head>
<TITLE> A Simple Visual Markup Exam-
ple</TITLE>
</head>
<body>
<H1>HTML element with FONT FACE</H1>
<P><BIG>The Big and Tall Company</BIG></P>
<P><BIG><FONT FACE = "Times New Roman,
Times" SIZE="+2"
COLOR = "#FF0000">The very Big and Tall
Company
</FONT></BIG></P>
</body>
</html>
```

Figure 7.27 HTML code using FACE and Color attributes

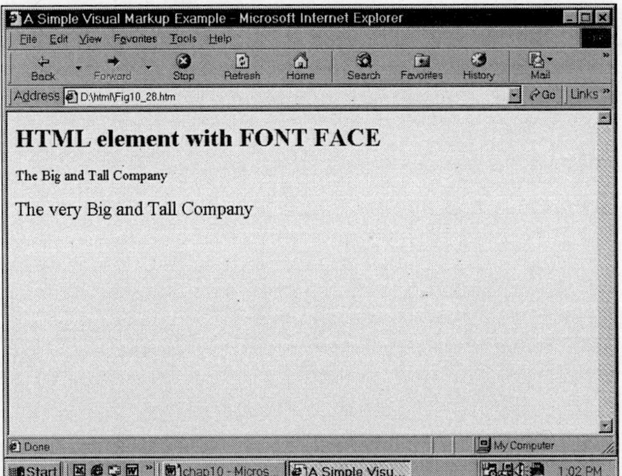

Figure 7.28 Result of code given in Figure 7.27

7.7 HTML LINKS

If one part of a document is required at another part of the same document, or if it needs to be referred to by another document, then a link can be created to call the required part. A browser highlights the identified text or image with color/underline to indicate that is a hypertext link or link.

☞ *Links (also called* ***anchors****) mark text or images as elements that point to other HTML documents, images, applets, multimedia effects or specific places within an HTML document.*

There are two types of links. These are:

a. Links to an external document.
b. Link (jumps) to a specific place within the same document or internal linking.

☞ *Background color can change the appearance of your message to a reader. Therefore, select the right color at all times.*

7.7.1 Link to an External Document

Links are created in a Web page by using the **<A> </A>** tags. Anything written between the **<A>...</A>** tags becomes a hyperlink/hotspot.

By clicking on the hyperlink, navigation to a different Web page or image takes place. However, a document to be navigated needs to be specified. By using the HREF (Hypertext Reference) attribute in the **<A>** tag, the next new navigable Web page or document can be specified.

A Web browser can distinguish hyperlinks from normal text using different color appearance of the link. In some cases, the hyperlink text or image can be shown as underlined. There is another alternate to show the link. When the mouse cursor is placed over it, the standard arrow-shaped mouse cursor changes to a shape of hand.

Links are made up of three parts. These are:

1. An anchor tag, **<A>**.
2. An attribute, HREF = " ", which is located within the opening anchor tag, like **<A HREF = " "> </A>**.

3. An address (called a URL or Uniform Resource Locator, which tells the browser about the file to link to. URLs identify file locations (addresses) on the Web or on your local hard drive. These addresses can be HTML documents or elements referenced by documents, such as *images, applets, scripts* and other *files*. The URL is always enclosed in quotes, for example, "address.html" (See Figure 7.29).

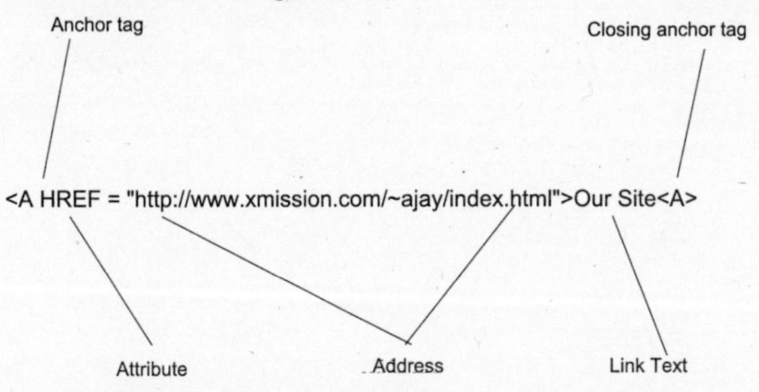

Figure 7.29 Link of an HTML document

The "link text" part of this example actually appears in the document. Text links usually appear as blue and underlined text, but this depends on your visitor's computer and browser settings. Image links generally appear in a border.

☞ *All links include an anchor tag, an attribute, and a URL. The specific address you use, however, depends on where the documents you link to are located.*

7.7.2 Link (jumps) to a Specific Place within the Same Document

Sometimes, a jump is required to a different location in the same document. Since the jump has to be targeted to a specific location, it is important to first identify a location with a name and then jump to that location using the name. Here, the file name will be the name of the file where you are linking the text, which means the same file where the link is located. An example is as follows:

```
<A HREF="#location_name">    </A>
```

☞ *The absence of the filename.htm before the # symbol indicates that a jump is required within the same document.*

Suppose you want to create a hypertext version of any chapter. To make it easy to navigate, you have to include a table of content at the top of the page that includes links to all the section headings. The first task is to add anchor tags to each heading. Here is the general format for an anchor:

```
<A NAME="Name">Anchor text goes here</A>
```

As you can see, an anchor tag looks like a regular hypertext link tag with the difference that the HREF part is replaced by NAME = "Name". Name is the name you want to give to the anchor. For example, the first section of the chapter is "DIGITAL SUBSCRIBER LINE". If you want to give a different name to this section like Section1, you may use the following anchor:

```
<A NAME="DSL">DIGITAL SUBSCRIBER LINE</A>
```

After setting the table of contents, you can create a link to this section by using a regular **<A>** tag (with the HREF thing) that points to the section's name. And, just so a Web browser does not confuse the anchor name with the name of another document, you have to use the anchor name with a hash sign (#). Here is how it looks:

```
<A HREF="#DSL">DIGITAL SUBSCRIBER LINE</A>
```

Coding for jumps to a specific place within the same document is given in Figure 7.30.

In Figure 7.31, when we click on **Local Area Network** link, it will jump to that point within the same document where the details of Local Area Network (LAN) is written (See Figure 7.32).

The output of the coding is given in Figure 7.31.

```
<H3>CHAPTER CONTENT</H3>
<H4><A HREF="#DSL" >DIGITAL SUBSCRIBER LINE</A></H4>
<H4><A HREF="#WWW" >WORLD WIDE WEB</A></H4>
<H4><A HREF="#INET" >INTERNET</A></H4>
<H4><A HREF="#LAN" >LOCAL AREA NETWORK</A></H4>
<H4><A HREF="#WAN" >WIDE AREA NETWORK</A></H4>
<H4><A HREF="#HLINK">HYPERLINK</A></H4>
<H4><A NAME="DSL">DIGITAL SUBSCRIBER LINE</A></H4>
<p> Here we have to write the details of digital subscriber line </p>
<H4><A NAME="#WWW" >WORLD WIDE WEB</A></H4>
<P> Here we have to write the details of world wide Web </P>
<H4><A NAME="#INET" >INTERNET</A></H4>
<P> Here we have to write the details of Internet </P>
<H4><A NAME="#LAN" >LOCAL AREA NETWORK</A></H4>
<P> Here we have to write the details of local area network </P>
<H4><A NAME="#WAN" >WIDE AREA NETWORK</A></H4>
<P> Here we have to write the details of wide area network.</P>
<H4><A NAME="#HLINK">HYPERLINK</A></H4>
<P> ere we have to write the details of hyperlink.</P>
```

Figure 7.30 Coding for linking from one place to another within the same document

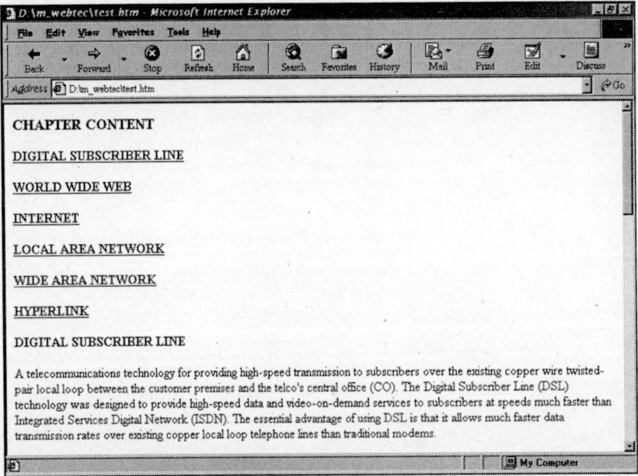

Figure 7.31 Output of code given in Figure 7.30

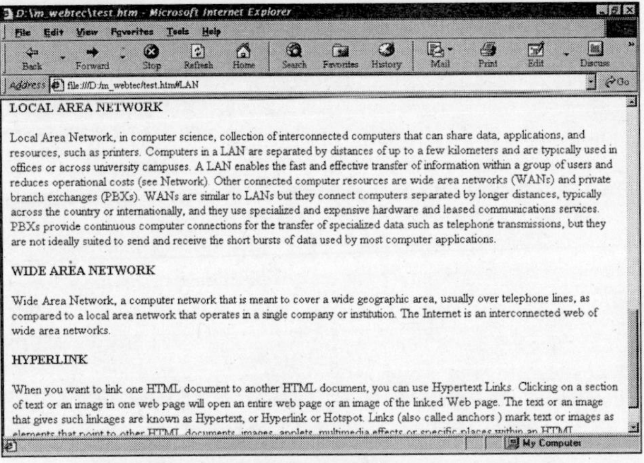

Figure 7.32 Jumping within the same document

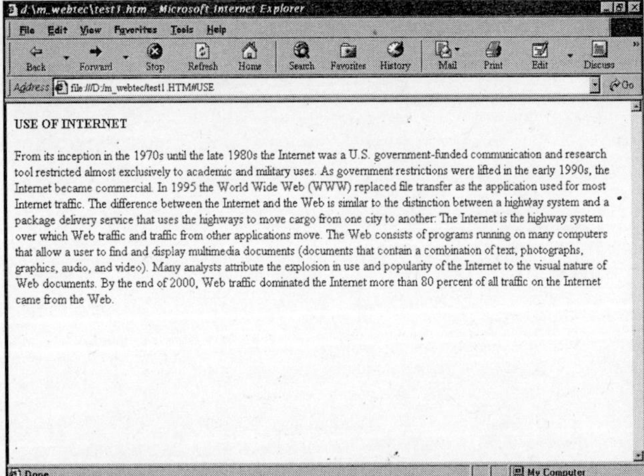

Figure 7.33 Linking of one file to another file

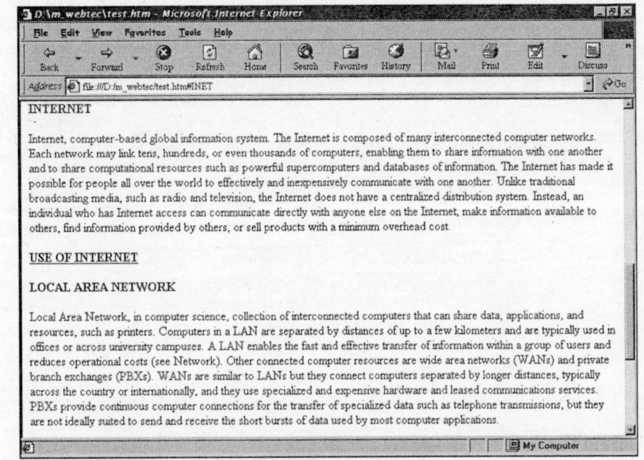

Figure 7.34 Displayed another file by linking

7.7.3 Link to Places in other HTML Documents

If you want to create a link from a file to another html file to a specific place, you have to perform the following task. Suppose, you want to create a link of test.html [the USE OF INTERNET section (which is written in the section INTERNET section) to its details] to test1.html, then you have to simply write the under-mentioned command in the test.html in section INTERNET.

```
<H4><A HREF="d:\m_Webtec\
    test1.htm#USE">USE OF INTERNET</A></H4>
```

And write the following command in test1.html above the details of USE OF INTERNET.

```
<H4><A NAME="USE">USE OF INTERNET</A></H4>
```

In Figure 7.33, when we click on the USE OF INTERNET section, it will jump to the test1.html and display the details of USE OF INTERNET (See Figure 7.34).

7.8 CREATING TABLES

Creating a table in HTML is fairly straightforward. We have to only provide the data. It is the task of the client-side Web browser to determine how to represent these data items to the user. One important thing is that the tables in HTML are organized in rows, which go horizontally from left to right.

To make tables, we need to start with a **<TABLE>** tag. Of course, we end our tables with the **</TABLE>** tag. If we want the table to have a border, we can use a **BORDER** attribute to specify the width of the border in pixels. A border size of 0 (or leaving the **BORDER** attribute out entirely) will make the border invisible, which is often handy when we are using a table as a page layout tool.

There are a number of optional attributes we can specify in the **<TABLE>** tag, but these are discussed after the creation of as simple table.

After the **<TABLE>**, the next thing we need is the **<TR>** tag. **<TR>** creates a table row, which contains one or more cells of information. To create these individual cells, we use the **<TD>** tag. **<TD>** stands for table data. We place the table information within the **<TD>** and **</TD>** tags. Within the table element, we use **<TH>** for table headers and the **CAPTION** element for the table's caption.

☞ *We can create as many cells as we want, but each row in a table should have the same number of columns as the other rows.*

Figure 7.35 gives a simple example. The output of the above program is shown in Figure 7.36.

```
<HTML>
<TABLE>
<CAPTION>The World Raffle Results.</CAPTION>
<TR><TH>Game</TH>
<TH>Red Wings</TH>
<TH>Black Hawks</TH></TR>
<TR><TD>1</TD><TD>3</TD><TD>2</TD></TR>
<TR><TD>2</TD><TD>4</TD><TD>1</TD></TR>
<TR><TD>3</TD><TD>0</TD><TD>8</TD></TR>
<TR><TD>4</TD><TD>8</TD><TD>7</TD></TR>
<TR><TD>5</TD><TD>2</TD><TD>1</TD></TR>
</TABLE>
</HTML>
```

Figure 7.35 HTML code to create a table

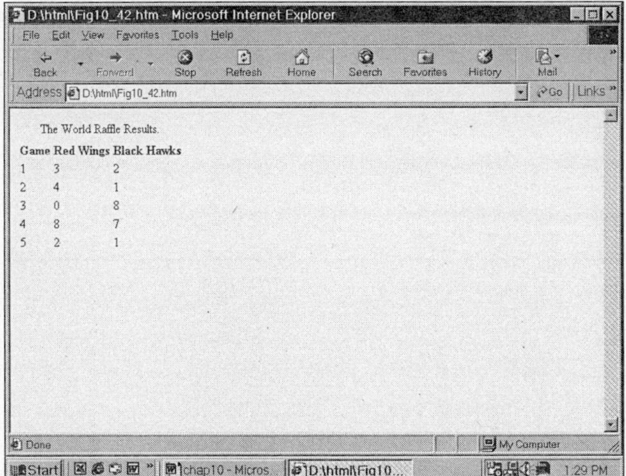

Figure 7.36 Output of the program given in Figure 7.35

7.9 TABLE ATTRIBUTES

7.9.1 Align

The horizontal alignment of the table on-screen (not the contents of the table) with possible values are as follows:
bleedleft: It is used to align the left window border.
bleedright: It is used to align the right window border.
center: It is used to center the text within margins.
justify: Table should fill space between text margins.
left: At the left text margin.
right: At the right text margin.
Border: Causes browser to render a border around the table. If missing, the table has no grid around it or its data. You can set the thickness of the border by giving this attribute an integer value. For example: Border="3" gives the table a three-pixel border.
Cellpadding: You can set this to the number of pixels you want to place between the cells of the table.
Cellspacing: You can set this to the number of pixels you want to place around the data in the cells.
Width: Specifies how wide the table will be; if given as NN%, the width is NN% of the width of the display; otherwise, the width is in pixels. It is not advisable to give the width in pixels, because you may not know how wide your users' browsers will be.

Figure 7.37 gives a sample example containing different table attributes.

The output of the program is shown in Figure 7.38.

7.9.2 Caption Element

It is used to label a figure or table. Its attribute is Align, which is used to position the caption relative to the figure or table. Values include top, bottom, left, and right.

7.9.3 TH Element

The TH element identifies a table header cell, and TD identifies a table data cell. Browsers usually treat these two elements differently in terms of how they are rendered. In general, a TH element's contents are placed in boldface and centered by default. A TD's elements contents usually are aligned to the left.

7.9.4 TD and TH Attributes

Align: Horizontal alignment of the paragraphs in a table row; values include left, center, right, justify, and decimal (text aligned on decimal points).
Colspan: Specifies the number of columns the cell spans.
No wrap: Prevents the browser from wrapping the contents of the cell.
Rowspan: Specifies the number of rows the cell spans.
Valign: Vertical alignment of material in a cell. Values include top, middle, and bottom.

The TR identifies a container for a row of table cells. Its attributes are the same as for TH and TD.

Working with tables is fairly easy and usually leads to pleasing results when you fine-tune your elements.

The following are some simple tips while working with tables:

a. Remember that table data can consist of lists, images, forms and other elements. The TD is a true container that can hold other HTML elements even more tables.
b. The TH element is typically rendered as bold text.
c. The TD element is typically rendered as regular-weight text.
d. Always use TRs as "holders" for THs and TDs. Think of building your table row-by-row. Each time you start a new row, you also should consider using a BR or P element to break the row, so that browsers that do not render tables will be able to show the contents of your table with each row's data on a separate line.

☞ *The browser sets the number of columns in a table to be the greatest number of columns in all the rows. Blank cells are used to fill extra columns in the rows.*

```
<HTML>
<TABLE Border="2" Cellpadding="3" Cellspacing="3">
<CAPTION>The EXTREME CUP RESULTS</CAPTION>
<TR><TH>Game</TH><TH>Red Wings</TH><TH>Black Hawks</TH></TR>
<TR><TD Align="center">1</TD Align="center">
<TD Align="center">3</TD Align="center">
<TD Align="center">2</TD Align="center"></TR>
<TR><TD Align="center">2</TD Align="center">
<TD Align="center">4</TD Align="center">
<TD Align="center">1</TD Align="center"></TR>
<TR><TD Align="center">3</TD Align="center">
<TD Align="center">0</TD Align="center">
<TD Align="center">8</TD Align="center"></TR>
<TR><TD Align="center">4</TD Align="center">
<TD Align="center">8</TD Align="center">
<TD Align="center">7</TD Align="center"></TR>
<TR><TD Align="center">5</TD Align="center">
<TD Align="center">2</TD Align="center">
<TD Align="center">1</TD Align="center"></TR>
</TABLE>
</HTML>
```

Figure 7.37 HTML code to keep data centered in a table

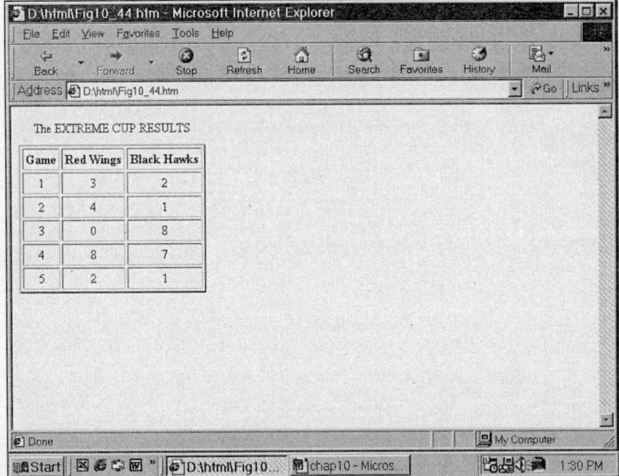

Figure 7.38 Output of the program given in Figure 7.37

7.10 FRAMES

One of the most significant developments that Netscape and Internet Explorer have contributed the introduction of frames. In olden days, we could see only one page at a time. Frames overcome this limitation. With the help of frames, we can divide the reader's browser window into multiple panes of information that can be viewed and changed independently. We can also display different HTML documents in each of the window. We can also control the display of one frame from another.

☞ *A **frame** is a rectangular region within the browser window that displays a Web page, alongside other pages in other frames. Or, it is basically a way of arranging and presenting several Web pages at a time.*

The main advantage of using frames becomes apparent when a user clicks on one of the links of any frame, the other frames on the same Web page do not change at all, but a new page is loaded and displayed in the same frame.

There are three ways to specify the dimensions of the frame. These are as follows:

a. As a *percentage* of the area allotted to the parent frame set.
b. As a '*relative size*'.
c. As an *absolute* (specific) number of screen pixels (e.g., 250).

The first two types are further elaborated in the successive paragraphs.

7.10.1 Percentage Dimension to Parent Frameset

We can specify the size of the ROWS or COLS as percentages of the total size of the browser window. For example, for three rows, the first and the last being smaller than the center row, we can give the following statement:

```
<FRAMESET rows = "20%, 60%, 20%">
```

Take another example, to clear the concept. For three rows, the first and the last being fixed height, with the remaining space assigned to the middle row, we will give the following statement:

```
<FRAMESET rows = "100, *, 100">
```

7.10.2 Relative Dimension to Parent Frameset

A *relative dimensions* is specified with an asterisk, e.g., '1*', '2*', '3*' ('1*' can also be written simply as '*'). For example:

```
<FRAMESET rows = "30%, 400, *, 2*">
  <FRAME ... >
  <FRAME ... >
  <FRAME ... >
  <FRAME ... >
</FRAMESET>
```

Suppose the browser window is currently 1000 pixels high. The first frame gets 30% of the total height, that is, 300 pixels; the second frame gets 400 pixels, since an absolute dimension was specified. This leaves 300 pixels to be divided between the other two frames. The fourth frame's height is specified as '2*', so it is twice as high as the third frame, whose height is only '*' (1*). Therefore, the third frame is 100 pixels high and the fourth is 200 pixels high.

A single '*' character is a "relative-sized" frame and is interpreted as a request to give the frame all remaining space. If multiple relative-sized frames are specified, the remaining space is divided evenly among them. If there is a value in front of the '*', the frame gets that much more relative space. "2*, *" would give 2/3 of the space to the first frame and 1/3 to the second.

☞ *Use **relative** and **percentage** sizes whenever possible. If you use an absolute size for one of your frames, be sure to use relative sizes for the others.*

7.11 <FRAMESET> TAG

To create a frame definition document, we use the **<FRAMESET>** tag. When we use **<FRAMESET>** tag in an HTML document, it is replacement for the **<BODY>** tag, as shown below:

```
<HTML>
<HEAD>
</HEAD>
<FRAMESET rows = "33%, 33%, 33%">
  <FRAMESET cols = "50%, 50%">
      <FRAME name = "frame1">
      <FRAME name = "frame2">
  </FRAMESET>
  <FRAME name = "frame3">
  <FRAME name = "frame4">
</FRAMESET>
<BODY>
..contents to display in non-frame-capable
user agent..
</BODY>
</HTML>
```

If we include a **<FRAMESET>** tag in an HTML document, we cannot include a **<BODY>** tag. Basically, the two tags are mutually exclusive. In addition, no other formatting tags, hyperlinks, or document text should be included in a frame definition document, except in one special case – the **<NOFRAME>** tag. **<FRAMESET>** tags contain only the definitions for the frames in this document.

☞ *A* frameset *is the set of frames defined by the <FRAMESET> tags in the frame definition document.*

7.11.1 Creating Two or More Columns (<FRAMESET COLS>)

When we define a **<FRAMESET>** tag, we must include one of the two attributes as part of the tag definition. The first of these attributes is the **COLS** attribute. The syntax of the **COLS** attribute is as follows:

```
<FRAMESET COLS = "column width, column width, ...">
```

The **COLS** attribute informs the browser to split the screen into a number of vertical frames whose widths are defined by column width values separated by commas. We define the width of each frame in three different ways:

a. Pixels,
b. Percentage of the total width of the <FRAMESET>,
c. An asterisk (*).

When we use *, the browser uses as much space as possible for the specified frame. The following **<FRAMESET>** tag creates a screen with three vertical frames. The first frame is 100 pixels wide, the second is 50 percent of the width of the screen, and the third uses all the remaining space.

```
<FRAMESET COLS = "100, 50%, *">
```

The **COLS** attribute defines the number of vertical frames or columns in a frameset.

☞ *To define a frameset with three equal-width columns, use COLS="*, *, *".*

7.11.2 Creating Two or More Rows (<FRAMESET ROWS>)

The ROWS attribute works in a similar way as the COLS attribute, except that it splits the screen into horizontal frames rather than vertical ones. For example, to split the screen into two equal-height frames, we write either of the following:

```
<FRAMESET ROWS = "50%, 50%">  or

<FRAMESET ROWS = "*, *">
```

The ROWS attribute defines the number of horizontal frames or rows in a frameset.

7.12 <FRAME> TAG

Within the **<FRAMESET>** and **</FRAMESET>** tags, we should have a **<FRAME>** tag indicating which HTML document to display in each frame. If we have fewer **<FRAME>** tags than the number of frames defined in the **<FRAMESET>** tag, any remaining frames will be left blank. We do not need to specify a closing **</FRAME>** tag.

7.12.1 <FRAME SRC> Attribute

The **<FRAME SRC>** attribute in each **<FRAME>** tag specifies the address of the document to be displayed in the frame. When omitted, the frame is displayed as a blank space. The syntax of the SRC attribute is shown below:

```
<FRAME SRC="document URL">
```

For each frame defined in the **<FRAMESET>** tag, we must include a corresponding **<FRAME>** tag, as shown in Figure 7.39.

```
<HTML>
<FRAMESET rows = "40%, 60%">
<FRAME src =
        "http://www.rediffmail.com/">
<FRAMESET cols = "50%, 50%">
<FRAME src = "http://www.google.com/">
<FRAME src =
        "http://www.epfindia.com/">
</FRAMESET>
</FRAMESET>
</HTML>
```

Figure 7.39 Code of <FRAME> tag to define the contents of each frame

Figure 7.40 Output of the program given in Figure 7.39

The coding shown in Figure 7.39 causes three frames to be displayed. The first (outer) **FRAMESET** element divides the browser window into two horizontal regions. The upper region contains a single frame displaying the document http://www.rediffmail.com/, and the lower region displays the frames defined in the second (inner) **FRAMESET** element. This **FRAMESET** divides the lower part of the window into two vertical frames, displaying the documents http://www.google.com/ and http://www.epfindia.com/ (See Figure 7.40).

7.12.2 <FRAME NAME> Attribute

The NAME attribute is used to assign a name to a frame so that it can be targeted by links in other documents. The NAME attribute is optional. By default, all windows are unnamed. Names must begin with an alphabetic character.

```
<FRAME SRC="main.htm" NAME="main">
```

This displays the main.htm page in that frame when the page loads, and names the frame "main." (The frame name need not match the name of its contents. It is given so in this example).

7.12.3 <FRAME MARGINHEIGHT> Attribute

To adjust the margin that appears above and below a document within a frame, set the **MARGINHEIGHT** to a number indicated by *pixels*. The general form of **MARGINHEIGHT** attribute is as follows:

```
MARGINHEIGHT="VALUE"
```

7.12.4 <FRAME MARGINWIDTH> Attribute

The **MARGINWIDTH** attribute enables you to adjust the margin on the left and right side of a frame to the number indicated by pixels. Margins cannot be less than one. This ensures that frame objects will not touch frame edges, and cannot be specified in a way that leaves no space for the document contents. **MARGINWIDTH** attribute is optional. The general form of **MARGINWIDTH** attribute is as follows:

```
MARGINWIDTH="VALUE"
```

7.12.5 <FRAME SCROLLING> Attribute

The **<FRAME SCROLLING>** attribute allows you to control scrollbar as and when the scrollbars appear in the frame. Normally, scrollbars are added only if there is not enough room to display all the contents in a frame. The general form of **SCROLLING** attribute is given below:

```
SCROLLING="YES|NO|AUTO"
```

The **SCROLLING** attribute is optional. The default value is "auto". Different parts of the SCROLLING attribute are as follows:

a. **AUTO (default):** By default, if the contents of a frame take up more space than the area available, the browser automatically adds scrollbars to either the side or the bottom of the frame so that the user can scroll through the document.
b. **NO:** Setting the value of **SCROLLING** to NO disables the use of scrollbars for the current frame. If we set **SCROLLING = "NO"** but there is more text in the document than can fit inside the frame, we will not be able to scroll the additional text into the frame view.
c. **YES:** If we set SCROLLING to YES, the scrollbars are included in the frame regardless of whether they are required or not.

7.12.6 <NORESIZE> Attribute

By default, users can move the position of borders around each frame on the current screen by grabbing the border and moving it with their mouse. To lock the borders of a frame and prevent them from being moved, we use the **NORESIZE** attribute. The **NORESIZE** attribute does not require a value. It can simply be used as a flag to indicate that the frame is not resizable by the user. The **NORESIZE** attribute is optional. However, all frames are resizable by default.

7.12.7 <NOFRAMES> Tag

If we load a frame definition document into a Web browser that does not support frames, we get only a blank page. To get around this problem, the **<NOFRAMES>** tag enables us to include body text as part of the document. **Frame-capable** browsers ignore all tags and data contained in a NOFRAME element.

In the code shown in Figure 7.41, the **<NOFRAMES>** element is used to include in a document a table of contents, which is otherwise displayed in a separate frame. The output is shown in Figure 7.42.

```
<BODY>
<H1>The Different Fish Species</H1>
<NOFRAMES> <!-- TOC for no frames display -->
  <UL>
   <LI><a href=#sec1>The fresh and sea water
      species</a>
   <LI><a href=#sec2>A subjective comparison</a>
  </UL>
</NOFRAMES>
<H1><a name=sec1>The fresh and sea water
species</a></H1>
Fishes can be classified into several categories starting by the type of water in which they
live.
...
<H1><a name=sec2>A subjective comparison</a></H1>
This section is clearly not objective. I much prefer sea water fishes which are generally
speaking more colorful and therefore more beautiful.
...
</BODY>
```

Figure 7.41 Use of <NOFRAME> tag

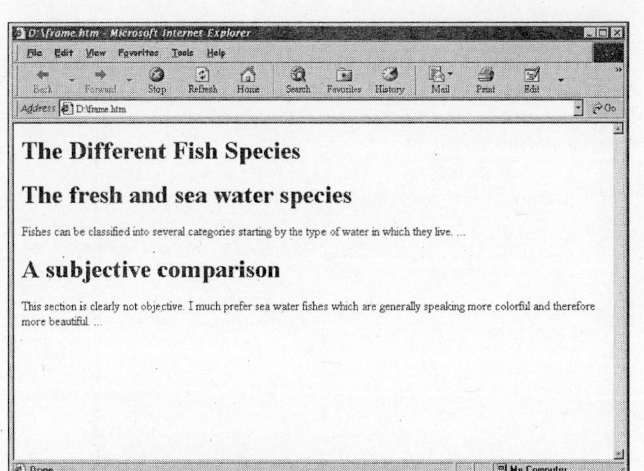

Figure 7.42 Output of the program given in Figure 7.41

☞ *Using both frames' content and tags inside <NOFRAME>, we can create pages that work well with browsers.*

7.13 IMAGES

HTML allows placing of static and animated images in a Web page. It accepts picture file formats *.gif* and *.jpg*. Using tools, such as GIF (Graphical Interchange Format) Constructor or Adobe PhotoShop, images can be created to suit the requirements of a Web page and saved in these formats.

An image can be inserted into a Web page using the tag **<IMG> </IMG>**. This tag takes the name of the image file (filename.gif) as an attribute. In addition, HTML also allows control of the height, width, border, etc., of every image placed on the Web page. The attributes associated with **<IMG>** tag are given in Table 7.4.

Table 7.4 Attributes associated with <IMG> Tag

Attribute	Function
ALIGN	Controls alignment of the text that appears after the image.
ALIGN = TOP	Shows the text after the image to be written at the top, next to the image.
ALIGN = MIDDLE	Shows the text after the image to be written at the middle, next to the image.
ALIGN = BOTTOM	Shows the text after the image to be written at the bottom, next to the image.
Controls for alignment of the image with respect to the VDU (Visual Display Unit) screen	
ALIGN = LEFT	Indicates the image is aligned to the left with respect to the screen. Similarly, for example, ALIGN = CENTER indicates the image is aligned to the centre with respect to the screen. Also, ALIGN = RIGHT indicates the image is aligned to the right with respect to the screen.
BORDER	Specifies the size of the border to place around the image.
WIDTH	Specifies the width of the image in pixels.
HEIGHT	Specifies the height of the image in pixels.
HSPACE	Indicates the amount of space to the left and right of the image.
VSPACE	Indicates the amount of space to the top and bottom of the image.
ALT	Indicates the text to be displayed in case the browser unable to display the image specified in the SRC attribute.

To add an image to the basic document, shown in Figure 7.43, note the following:

```
<html>
<head>
<TITLE>ASR Outfitters</TITLE>
</HEAD>
<BODY BACKGROUND="" BGCOLOR="#ffffff" TEXT="#000000"
LINK="#0000ff" VLINK="#800080" ALINK="#ff0000">
<CENTER><IMG SRC="c:\asrlogo.gif"><BR></CENTER>
We provide mountaineering equipment nationwide via postal order. <P>
<HR WIDTH=70% SIZE=8 NOSHADE>
Please select any one from the following links for more information :<P>
<UL>
<LI><A HREF="camping.htm">Camping News</A>
<LI><A HREF="catalog.htm">Catalog</A>
<LI><A HREF="clubs.htm">Clubs</A>
<LI><A HREF="contact.htm">Contact Us</A>
<LI><A HREF="weather.htm">Check Weather</A>
</UL>
<HR WIDTH=70% SIZE=8 NOSHADE>
</body>
</html>
```

Figure 7.43 HTML code with linking to GIF file

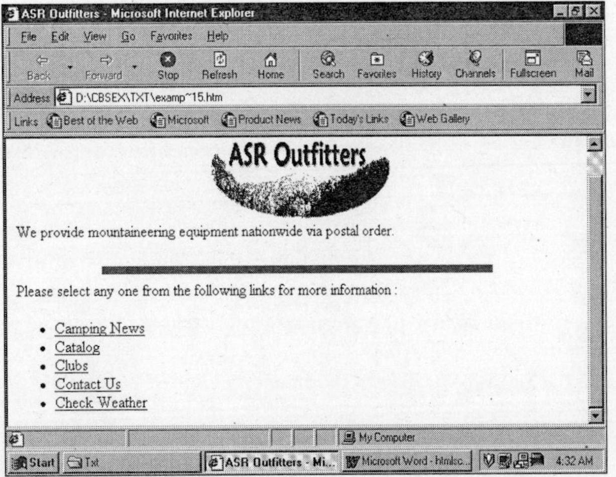

Figure 7.44 Result of code given in Figure 7.43

a. Insert an <IMG> tag where you want the image to be appeared.
b. Add an SRC="   " attribute pointing to the image file name. In this example, the file name is asrlogo.gif.
c. The first level heading was centered to consider adding a <CENTER> tag around the logo to center it.

☞ *The <IMG> tag supports ALIGN= attributes with values of TOP, MIDDLE, BOTTOM, LEFT and RIGHT, but does not support horizontal centering. To use horizontal centering, use the <CENTER> tag.*

The output of this program, as browsed by the Internet Explorer, is shown in Figure 7.44.

Alternative text indicated by the attribute ALT = describes an image that you have inserted. You include alternative text for the following reasons:

a. Some of your visitors may be using text-only browsers.
b. A visitor may have turned off images for faster loading of files on the Internet.
c. Sometimes, some browsers do not display images correctly.
d. Sometimes, images do not display when the links do not work properly.
e. Sometimes, browsers display alternative text while images load.

To add alternative text to your images, simply add the ALT = attribute to the <IMG> tag:

```
<IMG SRC = "c:\asrlogo.gif" ALT =
"ASR Outfitters Logo">
```

This will cause the alternative text to be displayed when the image cannot be shown due to the reasons mentioned above.

7.13.1 Specifying the Height and Width

Images can be loaded faster by specifying the height and width of an image. As the browser loads the page, it notes the height and width attributes and leaves that much space for the image. Next, it lays out the remaining text and then goes back and fills in the image. If you do not include these attributes, the browser has to load enough of the image to get the dimensions before it can lay out the rest of the text, thereby slowing the display of text.

To specify image height and width, add the HEIGHT= and WIDTH= attributes in the <IMG> tag as shown below:

```
<IMG SRC = "c:\asrlogo.gif" ALT =
"ASR Outfitters Logo" HEIGHT="192"
WIDTH="604">
```

7.13.2 Controlling the Border

You can control the border around an image with the BORDER=attribute. In most browsers, by default, the border is visible only on images that are used as links. To turn the border off for all images, add the BORDER="0" attribute to the <IMG> tag as shown here:

```
<IMG SRC = "c:\asrlogo.gif" ALT =
"ASR Outfitters Logo" HEIGHT="192"
WIDTH="604" BORDER="0">
```

Likewise, you can increase the border width around an image by increasing the value in the BORDER=attribute as in the following example:

```
<IMG SRC = "c:\asrlogo.gif" ALT =
"ASR Outfitters Logo" HEIGHT="192"
WIDTH="604" BORDER="7">
```

The resulting output is shown in Figure 7.45.

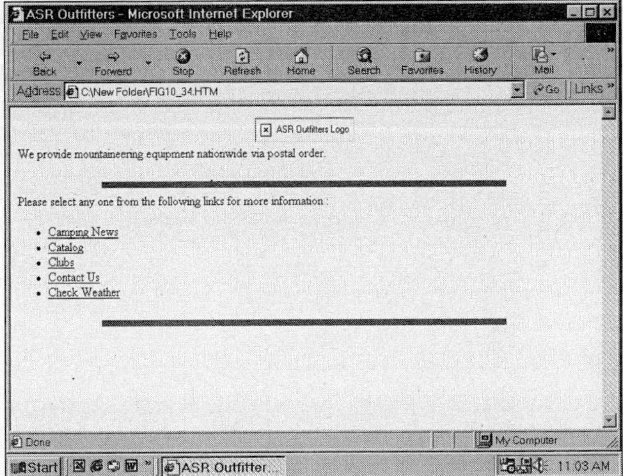

Figure 7.45 Linking alternate text to a GIF file

7.13.3 Creating Image Links

To add an image as a link, start by adding an image tag. The following steps need to be followed to add an image as a link in the HTML file program.

a. Add an image tag and an SRC=attribute to the document as shown below:

```
<IMG SRC="camping.gif">
```

Note that camping.gif is the file which will be used for linking.

b. Include an alternative text using the ALT=attribute as shown below:

```
<IMG SRC = "camping.gif" ALT = "Camping
News">
```

c. Add the remaining attributes you want to include, such as the HEIGHT= and WIDTH = and BORDER = attributes as follows:

```
<IMG SRC="camping.gif" WIDTH="300"
HEIGHT="80" BORDER="0" ALT="Camping News">
```

d. Add the link anchor tag, <A> before and after the image as shown below:

```
<A><IMG SRC="camping.gif" WIDTH="300"
HEIGHT="80"
 BORDER="0" ALT ="Camping News"></A>
```

e. Add the HREF=attribute to the opening anchor tag to specify the image file name as shown below:

```
<A HREF="camping.html"><IMG SRC="cam-
ping.gif" WIDTH="300" HEIGHT="80"
BORDER="0" ALT ="Camping News"></A>
```

Now you will get an image that acts as a link to the camping.html file as shown in Figure 7.46.

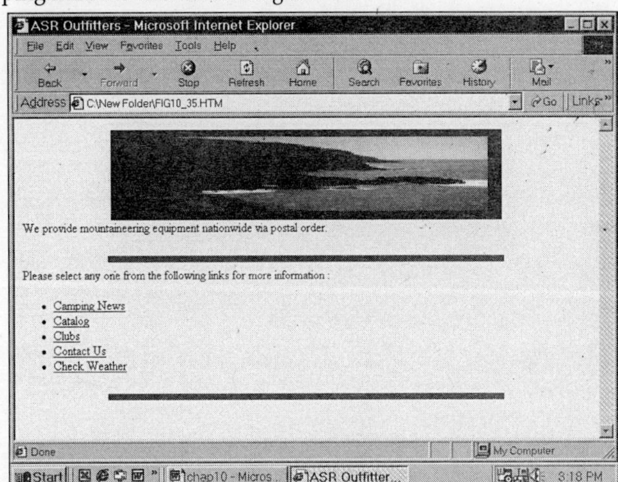

Figure 7.46 Controlling the border around the logo

7.13.4 Creating Image Maps

An image map, also called a clickable image, is a single image that contains multiple links. Clicking on a portion of an image map takes you to the link connected with that part of the visual presentation. For example, a physician might present an image map of the human body to a patient, with instructions for the patient to click where it hurts.

There are two types of image maps:

a. Server side
b. Client side

The feature distinguishing the two types of images is where the processing takes place. The processing can occur either on the server (hence the server side image map) or on the visitor's computer (hence the client-side image map).

The client-side image maps are more user-friendly than server-side image maps. When a visitor moves the cursor over an image-map link within a document, the status bar generally displays the URL of the link. Client-side image maps are better for you, because you can use and test them before you put the image map on the server. In contrast, server-side maps do not work until they have been installed on the server, making testing much more difficult.

7.14 PUBLISHING TOOLS

There are a number of Web publishing tools developed by various corporations. Some of the more popular ones are:

- Netscape Navigator Gold
- Macromedia's Backstage Desktop Studio
- Adobe's PageMill and SiteMill
- Other Web Publishing Tools, such as HotDog, HoTMetal and WebEdit.

7.14.1 Netscape Navigator Gold

As Visual Editor: Netscape Gold offers a visual editing environment that closely approximates that of a Web page and at the same time adopts many of the concepts used by word processors and document publishing tools.

☞ *Netscape Gold provides a Web publishing environment that looks and feels like a Web page.*

Netscape Gold generates true HTML code, but during the editing phase, this code is hidden from the user by the graphical interface. When creating complex Web pages, you will need to understand the principles behind the HTML language and its various constructs.

Using Templates and the Page Wizard, Netscape has reduced the amount of work you need to do when designing a Web page.

Menus for Editing Web Pages

The two important menus for editing Web pages are as follows:
- Insert menu
- Properties menu

Insert Menu: It contains a list of the different types of elements that you can add to a Web page. When you select any of the entries on this menu, Netscape Gold will automatically add the element to your Web page and you do not even need to know the HTML codes for it.

Properties menu: It enables you to control the appearance and actions of the various elements that you can place on a Web page. It is similar to the way that you can alter the appearance of text in a word processor. Most of the functions on the Properties menu are controlled by the type of text or element that is currently selected in the editing window.

☞ *Navigator Gold includes a number of paragraph formatting tools and pre-defined paragraph styles that you can assign to blocks of text and objects on your Web pages. The Paragraph Format toolbar lets you easily assign paragraph formatting to the text you have currently selected.*

7.14.2 Macromedia's Backstage Desktop Studio

Backstage Desktop Studio consists of a suite of tools to assemble and manage an end-to-end Website. The advantage of Macromedia is its excellence in multimedia Web authoring. By combining that experience in imaginary with the simplicity of a point-and-click, drag-and-drop, WYSIWYG (What You See Is What You Get) strategy for the implementation tools, Macromedia has one of the best tools for designing Web pages.

Macromedia's Backstage Desktop Studio is one of the new generation of tools that combine dynamic Web page authoring facilities with Website management features.

☞ *The word dynamic here means adding multimedia and database connectivity into pages whose information needs to change as often as the person viewing it changes.*

Advantages

The main advantages of the dynamic Websites are as follows:
- They involve the viewer. They enable viewers to correspond with Web page creators.
- They provide gateways to specific information.
- They help them to solve problems. They do it in interesting and creative ways.

Tools for Website Designing

Macromedia uses the following tools to design a Website:
- **Backstage Designer:** This provides a WYSIWYG authoring environment on the low end as a client. This helps in creating a Website fast.
- **BackStage Enterprise Studio:** This is a high-end Website creation and management software on the server side. It helps in creating professional looking sites for optimum multimedia pages. It also helps in client/server Web applications.

7.14.3 Adobe PageMill and SiteMill

PageMill and SiteMill from Adobe feature a WYSIWYG interface, which makes operating them easy. At the same time, it incorporates typical Macintosh ease of use.

SiteMill

SiteMill is the perfect choice for both managing and editing Web pages on the server. It catalogues a Website, checks each link, and displays all errors. Currently, both programs support HTML as well as Netscape plug-ins. A plug-in declares that of handles certain content types, such as audio/Motion Picture Experts Group Audio Layer 3 or MP3.

☞ *Because both PageMill and SiteMill share the same feature sets, techniques and tools learned on one program can be used on the other. Each of these tools offers an easy system for creating Web pages or managing a Website.*

Using PageMill

PageMill is an excellent choice for creating Web pages. It allows even a novice to create a Web page complete with forms, graphics and formatting. PageMill can be operated in two separate modes: Browse and Edit. The Browse mode is the default mode when you are opening a saved page. It shows a view of the page as though it were being served over the Internet to your browser. The Edit mode is for creating and editing your page. You can toggle between the two modes by simply clicking the Browse/Edit icon at the screen's upper right corner.

PageMill lets you easily create Web pages that have forms, backgrounds, internal links, external links, images, image maps, and detailed text formatting. You can accomplish all of this without any knowledge of HTML. PageMill supports normal cut-and-paste operation. If the dragged or copied text is (Rich Text Format) or RTF-formatted, the attributes and styles are preserved; otherwise, you have to reformat the text.

☞ *Rich Text Format (RTF) is a formatting option common in many word processors. Saving a file in RTF allows for cross-platform and cross-application compatibility without losing formatting.*

PageMill allows simple drag-and-drop inputting of images into any page. PageMill also contains a graphics editor that makes it easy to modify and enhance the image.

You can include an image by clicking the Insert Image button on the button bar. Once the image is included on the page, you can change its characteristics with the Image Editor, invoked by simply double-clicking on the image. You can also easily create image maps in the editor window by drawing rectangles, ovals, polygons, or other shapes inside the image, then linking that shape to either a URL (Uniform Resource Locator) or an anchor located in another part of the current page.

PageMill for Linking Pages

A link is a section of text or image that, when clicked, sends the browser to another location. PageMill enables you to do both types of linking, namely, the same page or pages on the same server (internal links) and another page on a different server (external links). External links send the browser to another server. This type of link is difficult to manage because you have no control over the name or content of pages on other servers.

PageMill for Creating Forms

PageMill makes it easy to create different types of forms. Forms are very versatile, because they let the owner of a Website know who is interested in the site or products and topics presented on the site's Web pages. Forms are an easy way to gather information from visitors to your Web page or to share information with them. Another use is for commerce, to sell merchandize at your Website. The visitor uses a form to send in the necessary information to complete a transaction. This information is then sent to the Web server, processed by a CGI (Common Gateway Interface), and stored for retrieval during normal business hours.

☞ *Although forms are versatile and helpful to a Website owner, it involves some effort to get them operating correctly.*

7.16.4 Other Web Publishing Tools

There is a wide variety of Web publishing tools. Many of these tools offer value for low price. These are described in the following subsections:

GoLive

Adobe GoLive boasts drag-and-drop authoring features that will have you building your own site in no time. Although Adobe was one of the first big software developers to release a drag and drop Web authoring package in the shape of PageMill, it did not offer a real contender until the release of GoLive. GoLive incorporates cutting-edge features.

HotDog and HotDog Pro

HotDog supports HTML, Netscape extensions to HTML, and Internet Explorer extensions to HTML. When you have multiple documents open in the editor, you can switch between them quickly using tabs at the bottom of the editor window. HotDog has a friendly interface.

HotDog lets you preview your pages without having to save the page. Other features include an advanced correction system that automatically replaces text and file paths when you publish your pages.

HotDog is designed for beginners and experts alike. You will know this immediately when you start HotDog. In addition to being able to insert many common tags into a page directly from the toolbar, HotDog has a dialog box for adding tags.

Creating forms with HotDog is easy just click the Forms icon on the toolbar and HotDog displays a form builder. The form builder provides a friendly interface for selecting the type of element you want to add to a form.

HotDog has other friendly tools for managing links, building tables and creating frames.

☞ *HotDog Pro separates itself from the standard edition with multi-level undo operation and the ability to handle files of unlimited size. It also has a spell-checker.*

With HotDog Pro, not only you can customize the toolbar, but also you can select the icons and labels for toolbar buttons. Another nice feature of HotDog Pro is the ability to define your own tags or tag sets that can be accessed via the menus.

HoTMetaL and HoTMetaL Pro

HoTMetaL is an editor from SoftQuad Incorporated (www.sq.com). There are two editions of HoTMetaL. HoTMetaL is available free! What is even better is that SoftQuad has made a serious commitment to continue to develop and improve this freeware editor.

HotMetaL Pro supports features that put it in the same league as Microsoft FrontPage and Macromedia Backstage. Still, SoftQuad has the market experience to back its offerings with solid support and continual upgrades. Versions of this editor are available for Windows, Macintosh, Power Macintosh, and UNIX.

☞ *HoTMetaL is a unique editor because it enters elements using a WYSIWYG approach. It has a unique interface that integrates a WYSIWYG approach with tag markers used by content generators.*

HoTMetaL Pro is an advanced authoring system that supports the most current HTML specification and extensions. It supports HTML, Java, ActiveX, objects, scripts and even Shockwave. HoTMetaL Pro follows an integrated WYSIWYG and tag marker approach.

Features of HoTMetal Pro

A feature you will want to check out is the multiple browser preview with which you can preview your page in any browser at the touch of a button. This feature is great if you want to test your page in several browsers. Other features include automatic conversion of other document formats to HTML. All you have to do is open any MS Word, WordPerfect, or AmiPro document in HoTMetaL Pro, and it is instantly converted to HTML. The best feature of HoTMetaL Pro is the template system. HoTMetaL Pro's templates are as advanced as they come. You will find hundreds of templates with which you can instantly create pages, ready-made tables, frames, Java applets, scripts, and Shockwave animation.

Another feature of HoTMetaL Pro is the Frames Editor, which is one of the most advanced Frames editors you will find anywhere. Creating a frame-enhanced page is done completely with an easy-to-use graphical interface. As you define frames, you can also define the document sources for the frames by dragging and dropping Web pages into your frames.

HoTMetaL Pro comes with a built-in graphics editor called *MetalWorks*. Whenever you want to manipulate an image, all you need to do is right-click the image to display a pop-up menu with which you can define image attributes, create transparent images, and build image maps. HoTMetaL Pro supports both server-side and client-side image maps.

Building an image map from an existing image is handled through a dialog box called *MetalWorks Map*. Using this dialog box, you can create very precise image maps by enlarging or shrinking the image to suit your needs. Before you can define hot spots on the map, you must select a shape for the hot spot. Hot spots can be circular, rectangular, or polygonal in shape.

WebEdit and WebEdit Pro

Both editions of WebEdit include a toolbar, shortcut keys, and a spell-checker, where the editions differ is in the automation routines for creating advanced HTML elements, such as forms and frames. The Professional edition has many wizards to guide you through the creation process but the Basic edition has only a few. Both editions of WebEdit fully support HTML, Netscape extensions to HTML, and Internet Explorer extensions to HTML.

Using WebEdit, you can open multiple documents open at a time. Although WebEdit does not use a Window or Document menu with which you may be familiar to access open documents, it does provide access to the documents using quick tabs.

Dreamweaver

In the space of two short years, Macromedia Dreamweaver has become the standard Web authoring tool for creative designers. Now in its latest version, the package is still in a position to take advantage of future developments on the Web. In the industry, e-business and e-commerce have become buzzwords and Dreamweaver acknowledges this with Roundtrip Coded data import. The program can be customized for specific projects so that team members and clients alike can use the same package in the development cycle. Dreamweaver also prepares us for Web development with a core built around XML (eXtensible Markup Language), CSS (Cascading Style Sheet), the extendible scripting language expected to go mainstream as browser support comes online. Dreamweaver lets you keep one eye on the future without forgetting what is important now.

REVIEW QUESTIONS WITH ANSWERS

1. Multiple Choice

1.1 The ___________ attribute indicates that there are two rows and they will display in 30% and 70% of the screen, respectively.

a. cols="30%, 70%" b. rows="30,70"
c. rows="30%, 70%" d. row="30%, 70%"

1.2 A frame definition file ___________.

a. Contains the layout of the frames on the Web page
b. Specifies the Web pages contents of the frames on the Web page
c. Includes the HTML for all of the Web pages to be contained in the frames on the Web page
d. Both b and c

1.3 On all Web pages that use image maps for navigation, you should also include:

a. Links referring visitors to the home page
b. A list of elements in the image maps
c. Captions for the images in the image maps
d. Text links to the URLs reflected in the image maps

1.4 What is the usage of Alt value in <img> tag?

a. Alternative text for an image b. Alternative source of an image
c. Caption of an image d. All of the above

1.5 Is it possible to insert a table within another table?

a. Yes, but there must be exactly 2 rows and 2 columns in first table
b. Yes, table can be inserted into cell of another table
c. Yes, but there must be no border in second table
d. No, it is not possible

1.6 Which tag is used to list the items with bullets?

a. <bullet>...</bullet> b. <list>...</list>
c. <ul>...</ul> d. <ol>...</ol>

1.7 Choose the correct HTML tag to left align the content of a cell:

a. <tdleft> b. <td leftalign>
c. <td valign="left"> d. <td align="left">

1.8 Which of the following is correct HTML for inserting an image?

a. <image source="www.pictures.com/ganesh.jpg"alt="This is me"/>
b. <img src="www.pictures.com/ganesh.jpg"alt="This is me" />
c. <img source="www.pictures.com/ganesh.jpg"alt="This is me" />
d. <img alt="This is me">www.pictures.com/ganesh.jpg</img>

1.9 Which of the following tags are related to Table in HTML?

a. <table><row><column> b. <table><tr><td>
c. <table><head><body> d. None of the above

1.10 Which of the following HTML Tag will insert a line break?

a. <p /> b. <lb />
c.
 d. <break />

1.11 How to set a picture as a background Web page?

a. <body background="peacock.gif">
b. <body backgroundimage="peacock.gif">
c. <background="peacock.gif">
d. <background image="peacock.gif">

1.12 Which HTML tag would be used to display power in expression $(A+B)^2$?

a. <SUP> b. <SUB>
c. <B> d. <P>

1.13 Choose the correct HTML tag to make the text bold?

a. <B> b. <BOLD>
c. <STRONG> d. Both a and c

1.14 Which of the following is an attribute of <Table> tag?

a. Src b. Link
c. Cellpadding d. Bold

1.15 What is the correct syntax in HTML for creating a link on a Web page?

a. <LINK SRC = "proj.html">

b. <Body Link = "proj.html">
c. <A SRC = "proj.html">
d. <A HREF = "proj.html">

1.16 Which is true to change the text color to red?
a. <BODY BGCOLOR=RED>
b. <BODY TEXT=RED>
c. <BODY COLOR=RED>
d. None of the above

1.17 <TD>...</TD> tag is used for __________.
a. Table heading b. Table Records
c. Table row d. None of the above

1.18 Using <P> tag will:
a. Start a new paragraph b. Break the line
c. End the current paragraph d. None of the above

1.19 <SCRIPT>...<SCRIPT> tag can be placed within _______.
a. Header b. Body
c. Both a and b d. None of the above

1.20 Common Gateway Interface (CGI) is a standard method used to generate _________ content on Web pages and Web application.
a. Static b. Text
c. Dynamic d. Integer

2. State whether the following statements are True or False

2.1 HTML does not allow a Web page to include an image.
2.2 Tables can be nested (table inside of another table)
2.3 The content of a single file of hypertext is called a Web page.
2.4 HTML files are text files only.
2.5 <HR> tag draws lines and horizontal rulers.
2.6 The <BODY> tag is assumed by the browser after the HEAD section, if you have omitted it in the HTML page.
2.7 Elements allowed within the <HTML> tag are the <HEAD> and <TITLE> elements.
2.8 The <ADDRESS> tag is similar to italics or emphasis.
2.9 Tags are used to define the structure of an HTML document.
2.10 The first way to break text into paragraph is to use <P>.
2.11 There are up to six levels of header tags in HTML.
2.12 In HTML, the tag <H1> is used to indicate that http is being used.
2.13 HTML does not allow a Web page to include an image.
2.14 You can participate in virtual world and join in "virtual chat" sessions on the Internet.
2.15 Some of the extensions of sound files are .Doc and .EXE.
2.16 The use of Web Font in HTML to enable to use fonts over the Web without installation.
2.17 The use of Forms in HTML to collect user's input.
2.18 <marquee>...</marquee> in HTML tab will use to scroll a text or image in a Web page.
2.19 Charles Babbage invented World Wide Web (WWW).
2.20 To define target in new page in HTML <a href = "http://www.interview.com/" target = "_blank">Click Here-</a>.
2.21 In HTML, Uniform Resource Identifer (URI) is used to customize the image in the Web page.
2.22 You can combine structures e.g, linear and hierarchical.
2.23 You do not have to connect to the Internet to verify changes to a Web page on your computer.
2.24 Because each computer differs in terms of what fonts it can display, each individual browser determines how text is to be displayed.
2.25 The two main file formats for images on the Web are GIF and TIF.
2.26 You cannot designate an inline image as a hypertext link.

3. Match the following

3.1	HTML tag for the largest heading	a.	Cell padding
3.2	<a> and </a> used for	b.	Adding links to your page
3.3	vlink means	c.	Visited link
3.4	Increase the distance between cell and content	d.	HTML element
3.5	<TITLE>...</TITLE>	e.	<H1>
3.6	 	f.	<HR>
3.7	Horizontal ruler	g.	<HTML>
3.8	Optional element	h.	Return a line break in Web browser
3.9	<UL>	i.	Label figure or table
3.10	CAPTION element	j.	Unordered list
3.11	RMF	k.	colspan=n can be added to tag
3.12	<td>	l.	<th>...</th>
3.13	A Web publishing tool developed by Microsoft	m.	Front Page
3.14	Authoring tools	n.	Rich Music Format
3.15	The HTML tags that creates a table header is	o.	Web publishing
3.16	Any Web document must begin and end with	p.	Web authoring
3.17	NetBeans and Eclipse are	q.	<HTML> and </HTML>

4. Fill in the blanks

a. <a>	b. LIST	c. Tags
d. 	e. <UL>	f. Relative, absolute
g. NORESIZE	h. Auto	i. Document
j. Internet Protocol	k. Tags, attribute	l. head, body
m. <TITLE>	n. Frames	o. SRC
p. ROWS, COLS	q. Interfacing	r. Dynamic HTML pages
s. PHP	t. Head	u. bgcolor
v. Streaming audio	w. <noframes>	

4.1 HTML tag for creating a line break is __________.
4.2 The most commonly used Head feature in HTML is the _______ tag.
4.3 The ________ tag is used for bulleted, unordered list.
4.4 The full form of IP is __________.
4.5 _____ tags are responsible for affecting the spacing and layout of the text.
4.6 The two major elements of HTML are ________ and ________.
4.7 HTML commands surrounded by < and > are called ________.

4.8 ________ tag is used to show a Web browser what text in your document constitutes a paragraph.

4.9 The first HTML tags are the __________ tags.

4.10 An HTML document has two parts: a _______ and a ________ .

4.11 ________ divide the reader's Window in multiple panes that can be viewed independently and changed independently.

4.12 The values of rows or columns can be _________ and ________ .

4.13 ________ and ________ take comma-separated list of values.

4.14 ________ attribute does not require a value.

4.15 The default value of SCROLLING attribute is ________ .

4.16 ________ specifies the address of the document to be displayed in the frame.

4.17 With ___________, we do not have to wait for playing sound until a file is completely downloaded.

4.18 __________ is the most widely used e-mail form script.

4.19 The page title is inside the ____________ tag.

4.20 ________ refers to the way the GIF file is saved by the graphics software.

4.21 The _________ attribute changes a frame's border color.

4.22 PHP is a scripting language to create ______________ .

4.23 You can use cols and rows in the _________ tag to set the number of columns and rows of the display area.

Answers

1.	1.1	c	1.2	b	1.3	c	1.4	a	1.5	b	1.6	c
	1.7	d	1.8	b	1.9	c	1.10	c	1.11	a	1.12	a
	1.13	d	1.14	c	1.15	d	1.16	b	1.17	b	1.18	a
	1.19	c	1.20	c								
2.	2.1	F	2.2	T	2.3	T	2.4	T	2.5	T	2.6	T
	2.7	T	2.8	T	2.9	T	2.10	T	2.11	T	2.12	F
	2.13	F	2.14	T	2.15	F	2.16	T	2.17	T	2.18	T
	2.19	F	2.20	T	2.21	F	2.22	F	2.23	T	2.24	T
	2.25	T	2.26	F								
3.	3.1	e	3.2	b	3.3	c	3.4	a	3.5	d	3.6	h
	3.7	f	3.8	g	3.9	j	3.10	i	3.11	n	3.12	k
	3.13	m	3.14	o	3.15	l	3.16	q	3.17	p		
4.	4.1	d	4.2	m	4.3	e	4.4	j	4.5	b	4.6	k
	4.7	c	4.8	a	4.9	i	4.10	l	4.11	n	4.12	f
	4.13	p	4.14	g	4.15	h	4.16	o	4.17	v	4.18	s
	4.19	t	4.20	q	4.21	u	4.22	r	4.23	w		

Short Questions with Answers

1. What is HTML?
2. How do I make a picture as a background on my Web pages?
3. How do I make it so that someone can mail me by just clicking on text with subject?
4. Who is making the Web standards?
5. Write HTML code background color in HTML.
6. Give the definition of HTML tag?
7. What are tags?
8. Do all HTML tags come in pair?
9. How do you insert a comment in html?
10. What bullet types are available?
11. How to center text in HTML?
12. How do I create a bullet and number list in HTML?
13. How would you add the height and width to the img src tag?
14. How would create an HTML back button?
15. How would create an image with a text description in HTML?

Answers to Short Questions

1. HTML is short for HyperText Markup Language, and is the language of the World Wide Web. It is the standard text formatting language used for creating and displaying pages on the Web. HTML documents are made up of two things: the content and the tags that formats it for proper display on pages.
2. Point the body background to the name of your image you wish to use as the background as shown below. The body line should be the first line after </head> tab.

   <body background="picture.gif">

   You can also have the background image fixed, so it does not move when using the scroll bar in the browser. To add the BGPROPERTIES tag as shown below. <body background="picture.gif" bgproperties="fixed">
3. Use the mailto command in your A HREF link tag as shown below.

   <A HREF="mailto:bpbonline.com">Click here to mail BPB Publications</A>
4. The World Wide Web Consortium (W3C Consortium).
5. <body style="background-color:yellow">
6. A HTML tag is nothing but a element which tells browser to execute it, when it gets loads.
7. Content is placed in between HTML tags in order to properly format it. It makes use of the less than symbol (<) and the greater than symbol (<). A slash symbol is also used as a closing tag. For example, </strong>Example</strong>.
8. No, there is single HTML tag that does not need a closing tab. Examples are the <img> tag and <br> tag.
9. Comments in html begins with "<!-" and ends with "->". For example, <!-- A Sample Comment -->.
10. With ordered lists, you can select to use a number of different list types including alphabetical and Roman numerals. The type attribute for unordered lists can be set to disc, square, or circle.
11. To center text in HTML, you can use the <center>...</center> tags or use a style sheet property.

    Using the <center>...</center> tags

    One way to center text is to enclose it within <center>...</center> tags, as in the following example.

    <center>This text needs to be centered!</center>
12. To create a bulleted list use the <ul><li></li></ul> tags and shown in the example below. To help remember these tags, "ul" is short for "unordered list" and "li" is short for "list item". Let us see the following example:

    <ul>
<li>Example 1</li>
<li>Example 2</li>
<li>Example 3</li>
</ul>
13. Adding the height and width attributes to your IMG SCR HTML tag allows the browser to know how much space to leave for an image. Without these values, the browser gives an image no space until the image is loaded, which means anything surroundings the image is adjusted after the image has loaded.
14. Adding the code below will direct a visitor back to the page they used to open your page. For example, this is a great feature to add to any error page to help get the visitor back to a working page.

```
<FORM><INPUT Type="button" VALUE="Back"
onClick="history.go(-1);return true;"></FORM>
```

In the above code the -1 tells the browser to go back one page.

15. Adding title to the IMG SRC tag displays a message for the image as shown in the below code.

```
<img src="http://www.bpbonline.com/logo.gif" alt="List of
Compute Science Books" title="Visit BPB Publications">
```

The above example displays "Visit BPB Publications" over the image in all browsers. In the above example, we also used the alt tag to describe the image.

DESCRIPTIVE TYPE QUESTIONS

1. Write an HTML program segments to print unordered, ordered lists.
2. What are the Web publishing tools? Discuss any two of them.
3. Write short notes on any two of the following Web publishing tools:
   a. Netscape Navigator Gold
   b. Adobe PageMill and SiteMill
   c. Macromedia's Backstage Desktop Studio
4. Write HTML commands to achieve the following:
   i) Put a Level two heading 'I am at top'.
   ii) Put 'I am BOLD' in bold face.
   iii) Render 'I am BIG' in a larger font.
   iv) Render 'I am SMALL' in a smaller font.
   v) Provide a link to http://www.microsoft.com.
5. How to create a link that goes to top of a Web page?
6. Write an HTML script to create the following Web page:

   LIST 1
      1. Breakfast
      2. Lunch
      3. Dinner

   LIST 2
      1. Cars
      2. Trucks
      3. Buses
7. Write HTML code for creating the following layout using frames. The underlined word(s)/phrases are hyperlinks and they should always open on clicking.

LOGO	**Address of DOEACC**
<u>Services</u> <u>Centers</u> <u>Imp. Phones</u>	Dispwin
<u>Contact Us</u> <u>Exam</u> <u>Result</u> <u>News</u> <u>Old Question Papers</u> <u>Project Guidelines</u> This site is maintained by DOEACC Society © Copyright 2002-2004	

8. Give an HTML script to achieve the following:
   a. Put the following in bold typeface "I am a boy"
   b. Put the following in italics typeface "I am a girl"
9. Give HTML code fragments to achieve the following text layout:

   This is a paragraph left aligned

   This is a paragraph center aligned

   This is a paragraph Right aligned
10. Write the HTML code for creating the following layout:

   THE EURO CUP RESULTS

GAME	BRAZIL	GERMANY
1	3	2
2	4	1
3	0	8
4	8	7
5	2	1

11. Differentiate between the following:
    a. Subscript and Quote elements
    b. The Big element and the Small element
12. What do you understand by the term "Inline Elements"? How does it differ from subscript element? Give an example of each of the two types of elements.
13. Write HTML tags for the following with examples:
    a. Making text italics
    b. Underlining the text
    c. Leave the text as it is
14. Write HTML script to create the following Web page:

List 1	**List 2**
1. Part 1	• Part 1
2. Part 2	• Part 2
3. Part 3	• Part 3

CHAPTER 8

Intellectual Property Right and Copyright Issue

8.1 INTRODUCTION

The Intellectual Property Rights (IPR) Act corresponds to the exclusive rights granted to creators of original works. IPR represents original works could stem from many sources and authors. IPR deals with trademark, patent and design rights. It deals exclusively with copyright issues, a specific branch of IPR that is relevant to all authors engaged in educational content.

Intellectual property rights are like any other property right. They allow creators, or owners, of patents, trademarks or copyrighted works to benefit from their own work or investment in a creation. These rights are outlined in Article 27 of the Universal Declaration of Human Rights, which provides for the right to benefit from the protection of moral and material interests resulting from authorship of scientific, literary or artistic productions. The importance of intellectual property was first recognized in the Paris Convention for the Protection of Industrial Property (1883) and the Berne Convention for the Protection of Literary and Artistic Works (1886). Both treaties are administered by the World Intellectual Property Organization (WIPO).

The Convention Establishing the World Intellectual Property Organization (1967) gives the following list of subject matter protected by intellectual property rights:

- Literary, artistic and scientific works;
- Performances of performing artists, phonograms, and broadcasts;
- Inventions in all fields of human endeavor;
- Scientific discoveries;
- Industrial designs;
- Trademarks, service marks, and commercial names and designations;
- Protection against unfair competition; and
- All other rights resulting from intellectual activity in the industrial, scientific, literary or artistic fields.

8.1.1 Types of IPR

The term "Intellectual Property" denotes the specific legal right. These are

- Copyrights (e.g. book)
- Patents (e.g. new drug)
- Trademark (e.g. symbol)
- Trade secrets (e.g. new method)

These are discussed in the following sections:

8.1.2 The Two Branches of Intellectual Property: Industrial Property and Copyright

Intellectual property is usually divided into two branches, namely industrial property, which broadly speaking protects inventions, and copyright, which protects literary and artistic works.

Industrial Property

Industrial property takes a range of forms. These include patents to protect inventions, and industrial designs, which are aesthetic creations determining the appearance of industrial products. Industrial property also covers trademarks, service marks, layout-designs of integrated circuits, commercial names and designations, as well as geographical indications, and protection against unfair competition.

Industrial property shall be apply not only to industry and commerce but also agricultural and extractive industries and to all manufactured or natural products, for example, wines, grain, tobacco leaf, fruit, cattle, minerals, mineral waters, beer, flowers, and flour. Industrial property takes a range of forms. These include patents to protect inventions; and industrial designs, which are aesthetic creations determining the appearance of industrial products.

Industrial property also covers trademarks, service marks, layout-designs of integrated circuits, commercial names and designations, as well as geographical indications, and protection against unfair competition. In some of these, the aspect of intellectual creation, although existent, is less clearly defined.

Copyright

Copyright may subsist in creative and artistic works (e.g. books, movies, music, paintings, photographs, and software) and give a copyright holder the exclusive right to control production or adaptation of such works for a certain period of time.

The expression copyright refers to the main act which, in respect of literary and artistic creations, may be made only by the author or with his authorization. That act is the making of copies of the work. The expression author's rights refers to the creator of the artistic work. It thus underlines the fact, recognized in most laws, that the author has certain specific rights in his creation which only he can exercise (such as the right to prevent a distorted reproduction). Other rights (such as the right to make copies) can be exercised by other persons, for example, a publisher who has obtained a license from the author.

Copyright covers literary works (such as novels, poems and plays), films, music, artistic works (e.g., drawings, paintings, photographs and sculptures) and architectural design. Rights related to copyright include those of performing artists in their performances, producers of phonograms in their recordings, and broadcasters in their radio and television programs.

While other types of intellectual property also exist, it is helpful for present purposes to explore the distinction between industrial property and copyright in terms of the basic difference between inventions and literary and artistic works.

Inventions may be defined in a non-legal sense as new solutions to technical problems. These new solutions are ideas, and are protected as such; protection of inventions under patent law does not require that the invention be represented in a physical embodiment. The protection accorded to inventors is, protection against any use of the invention without the authorization of the owner. Even a person who later makes the same invention independently, without copying or even being aware of the first inventor's work, must obtain authorization before he/she can exploit it.

Unlike protection of inventions, copyright law protects only the form of expression of ideas, not the ideas themselves. The creativity protected by copyright law is creativity in the choice and arrangement of words, musical notes, colors and shapes. So copyright law protects the owner of property rights against those who copy or otherwise take and use the form in which the original work was expressed by the author.

From this basic difference between inventions and literary and artistic works, it follows that the legal protection provided to each also differs. Since protection for inventions gives a monopoly right to exploit an idea, such protection is short in duration- usually about 20 years. The fact that the invention is protected must also be made known to the public. There must be an official notification that a specific, fully described invention is the property of a specific owner for a fixed number of years; in other words, the protected invention must be disclosed publicly in an official register.

8.1.3 Intellectual Property Rights in India

There is a well-established statutory, administrative and judicial framework to safeguard intellectual property rights in India, whether they relate to patents, trademarks, copyright or industrial designs, etc.

Well-known international trademarks have been protected in India even when they were not registered in India. The Indian Trademarks Law has been extended through court decisions to service marks in addition to trade marks for goods.

8.1.4 Features of IPR

- IPR are property rights over information, knowledge and ideas.
- IPR are exclusive, trade able and temporary.
- IPR differ in the information being protected (copyright, patent, trade secrets, trademarks).
- IPR protect information that has public good characteristics (non-excludability and non-rivalry consumption).

Why Promote and Protect Intellectual Property?

There are several convincing reasons. First, the progress and well-being of humanity on its capacity to create and discover new works in the areas of technology and culture. Second, the legal protection of new creations encourages the commitment of additional resources for further innovation. Third, the promotion and protection of intellectual property raise economic growth, creates new jobs and industries, and enhances the quality and enjoyment of life.

An efficient and equitable intellectual property system can help all countries to realize intellectual property's potential as a catalyst for economic development and social and cultural well-being. The intellectual property system helps strike a balance between the interests of innovators and the public interest, providing an environment in which creativity and invention can flourish, for the benefit of all.

What are the benefits of protecting copyright and related rights?

Copyright and related rights protection is an essential component in human creativity. Giving authors, artists and creators incentives in the form of recognition and fair economic reward increases their activity and output and can also enhance the results. By ensuring the existence and enforceability of rights, individuals and companies can more easily invest in the creation, development and global dissemination of their works.

This helps to increase access to and enhance the enjoyment of culture, knowledge and entertainment and also stimulates economic and social development.

How have copyright and related rights kept up with advances in technology?

The field of copyright and related rights has expanded enormously during the last several decades with the spectacular progress of technological development that has, in turn, yielded new ways of disseminating creations by such forms of communication as satellite broadcasting, compact disks and DVDs (Digital Versatile. Widespread dissemination of works via the Internet raises difficult questions concerning copyright and related rights in this global medium. WIPO is fully involved in the ongoing international debate to shape new standards for copyright protection in cyberspace. In that regard, the Organization administers the WIPO Copyright Treaty (WCT) and the WIPO Performances and Phonograms Treaty (WPPT), known as the "Internet Treaties". These treaties clarify international norms aimed at preventing unauthorized access to and use of creative works on the Internet.

How are copyright and related rights regulated?

Copyright and related rights protection is obtained automatically without the need for registration or other formalities. However, many countries provide for a national system of optional registration and deposit of works. These systems facilitate, for example, questions involving disputes over ownership or creation, financial transactions, sales, assignments and transfer of rights.

Many authors and performers do not have the ability or means to pursue the legal and administrative enforcement of their copyright and related rights, especially given the increasingly global use of literary, music and performance rights. As a result, the establishment and enhancement of Collective Management Organizations (CMOs), or "societies", is a growing and necessary trend in many countries. These societies can provide their members with efficient administrative support and legal expertise in, for example, collecting, managing and disbursing royalties gained from the national and international use of a work or performance. Certain rights of producers of sound recordings and broadcasting organizations are sometimes managed collectively as well.

8.1.5 Works Protected by Copyright

For the purposes of copyright protection, the term "literary and artistic works" is understood to include every original work of authorship, irrespective of its literary or artistic merit. The ideas in the work do not need to be original, but the form of expression must be an original creation of the author. The Berne Convention for the Protection of Literary and Artistic Works states: "The expression 'literary and artistic works' shall include every production in the literary, scientific and artistic domain, whatever may be the mode or form of its expression". The Convention goes on to list the following examples of such works:

- Books, pamphlets and other writings;
- Lectures, addresses, sermons;
- Dramatic or dramatico-musical works;
- Choreographic works and entertainments in dumb show;
- Musical compositions with or without words;
- Cinematographic works to which are assimilated works expressed by a process analogous to cinematography;
- Works of drawing, painting, architecture, sculpture, engraving and lithography;
- Photographic works, to which are assimilated works expressed by a process analogous to photography;
- Works of applied art; illustrations, maps, plans, sketches and three-dimensional works relative to geography, topography, architecture or science;
- Translations, adaptations, arrangements of music and other alterations of a literary or artistic work, which are to be protected as original works without prejudice to the copyright in the original work.
- Collections of literary or artistic works, such as encyclopaedias and anthologies which, by reason of the selection and arrangement of their contents, constitute intellectual creations, are to be protected as such, without prejudice to the copyright in each of the works forming part of such collections.

Computer programs are a good example of a type of work which is not included in the list in the Berne Convention, but which is undoubtedly included in the notion of a production in the literary, scientific and artistic domain. Computer programs are protected under the copyright laws of a number of countries, as well as under the WIPO Copyright Treaty (1996). A computer program is a set of instructions, which controls the operations of a computer in order to enable it to perform a specific task, such as the storage and retrieval of information. The program is produced by one or more human authors, but in its final "mode or form of expression," it can be understood directly only by a machine (the computer), not by humans. Multimedia productions are another example of a type of work not listed in the Berne Convention, but which clearly comes within the notion of creations in the literary, scientific and artistic domain.

8.1.6 Rights Protected

The most important feature of any kind of property is that the owner may use it exclusively, i.e., as he/she wishes, and nobody else can lawfully use it without his/her authorization. This mean that he can use it further of the legally recognized rights and interests of other members of society. Similarly the owner of copyright in a protected work may use the work as he wishes, and may prevent others from using it without his authorization. The rights granted under national laws to the owner of copyright in a protected work are normally exclusive rights to authorize a third party to use the work, subject to the legally recognized rights and interests of others.

There are two types of rights under copyright. Economic rights allow the rights owner to derive financial reward from the use of his/her works by others. Moral rights allow the author to take certain actions to preserve the personal link between himself-/herself and the work.

Most copyright laws state that the author or rights owner has the right to authorize or prevent certain acts in relation to a work. The rights of owner of a work can prohibit or authorize:

- Its reproduction in various forms, such as printed publications or sound recordings;
- The distribution of copies;
- Its public performance;
- Its broadcasting or other communication to the public;
- Its translation into other languages;
- Its adaptation, such as a novel into a screenplay.

These rights are explained in more detail in the following paragraphs.

Reproduction, Distribution and Related Rights

The right of the copyright owner to prevent others from making copies of his works without his authorization is the most basic right protected by copyright legislation. The right to control the act of reproduction of books by a publisher, or the manufacture by a record producer of compact disks containing recorded performances of musical works. It is the legal basis for many forms of exploitation of protected works.

Other rights are recognized in national laws in order to ensure that this basic right of reproduction is respected. Many laws include a right specifically to authorize distribution of copies of works. Obviously, the right of reproduction would be of little economic value if the owner of copyright could not authorize the distribution of the copies made with his/her consent. The right of distribution usually terminates upon first sale or transfer of ownership of a particular copy. This means, for example, that when the copyright owner of a book sells or otherwise transfers ownership of a copy of the book, the owner of that copy may give the book away or even resell it without the copyright owner's permission.

Another right which is achieving increasingly wide recognition, and is included in the WIPO Copyright Treaty, is the right to authorize copies of certain categories of works, such as musical works in sound recordings, audiovisual works, and computer programs. This became necessary in order to prevent abuse of the copyright owner's right of reproduction.

Finally, some copyright laws include a right to control importation of copies as a means to prevent erosion of the principle of territoriality of copyright; that is, the legitimate economic interests of the copyright owner would be endangered if he/she could not exercise the rights of reproduction and distribution on a territorial basis.

Certain forms of reproduction of a work are exceptions to the general rule, because they do not require the authorization of the rights owner. These exceptions are known as limitations on rights. An area of current debate relates to the scope of one particular limitation traditionally present in copyright laws, which allows individuals to make single copies of works for private, personal and non-commercial purposes. The continued justification for such a limitation on the right of reproduction is being questioned now that digital technology has made it possible to produce high-quality, unauthorized copies of works, which are virtually indistinguishable from the source - and thus a perfect substitute for the purchase of authorized copies.

Rights of public performance, broadcasting and communication to the public, and making available to the public

A public performance is considered under many national laws to include any performance of a work at a place where the public is or can be present; or at a place not open to the public, but number of persons outside the normal circle of a family and its close acquaintances is present. The right of public performance entitles the author or other copyright owner to authorize live performances of a work, such as a play in a theater, or an orchestra performance of a symphony in a concert hall. Public performance also includes performance by means of recordings. Thus a musical work is considered publicly performed when a sound recording of that work, or phonogram, is played over amplification equipment, for example in a discotheque, airplane, or shopping mall.

The right of broadcasting covers the transmission for public reception of sounds, or of images and sounds, by wireless means, whether by radio, television, or satellite. When a work is communicated to the public, a signal is distributed by wire or wireless means, which can be received only by persons who possess the equipment necessary to decode the signal. Cable transmission is an example of communication to the public.

Under the Berne Convention, authors have the exclusive right to authorize public performance, broadcasting and communication of their works to the public. Under some national laws, the exclusive right of the author or other rights owner to authorize broadcasting is replaced, in certain circumstances, by a right to equitable remuneration, although this sort of limitation on the broadcasting right is less and less common.

In recent years, the rights of broadcasting, public performance and communication to the public have been the subject of much discussion. New questions have arisen as a result of technological developments, in particular digital technology, which has introduced interactive communications. The user selects which works he wishes to have delivered to his computer. The WIPO Copyright Treaty (WCT) clarifies that it should be covered by an exclusive right, which the Treaty describes as the authors' right to authorize works available to the public in such a way that members of the public can access these works from a place and at a time individually. Most national laws implement this right as a part of the right of communication to the public, although some do so as part of the right of distribution.

Translation and Adaptation Rights

The acts of translating or adapting a work protected by copyright also require authorization from the rights owner. Translation means the expression of a work in a language other than that of the original version. Adaptation is generally understood as the modification of a work to create another work, for example adapting a novel to make a film; or the modification of a work for different conditions of exploitation, e.g., by adapting a textbook originally written for university students to make it suitable for a lower level.

Translations and adaptations are themselves works protected by copyright. So in order to publish a translation or adaptation, authorization must be obtained both from the owner of the copyright in the original work and from the owner of copyright in the translation or adaptation.

The scope of the right of adaptation has been the subject of significant discussion in recent years because of the greatly increased possibilities for adapting and transforming works which are embodied in digital format. With digital technology, manipulation of text, sound and images by the user is quick and easy. Discussions have focused on the appropriate balance between the rights of the author to control the integrity of the work by authorizing modifications, and the rights of users to make changes which seem to be part of a normal use of works in digital format.

8.1.7 Moral Rights

In relation to IPR, Moral Rights can be defined as the set of privileges granted to authors in order to allow them the right to have the quality and authorship of their work. Moral rights cannot be assigned, however it is possible for the author of a work to waive their moral rights. An infringement of an author's moral rights can be taken to court and where appropriate, damages can be awarded to the author.

The Berne Convention requires Member countries to grant to authors:

(i) The right to claim authorship of the work (sometimes called the right of paternity); and

(ii) The right to object to any distortion or modification of the work, which would be prejudicial to the author's honor or reputation (sometimes called the right of integrity).

These rights are generally known as the moral rights of authors. The Convention requires them to be independent of the author's economic rights, and to remain with the author even after he has transferred his economic rights. It is worth noting that moral rights are only accorded to individual authors. Thus even when, for example, a film producer or a publisher owns the economic rights in a work, it is only the individual creator who has moral interests at stake.

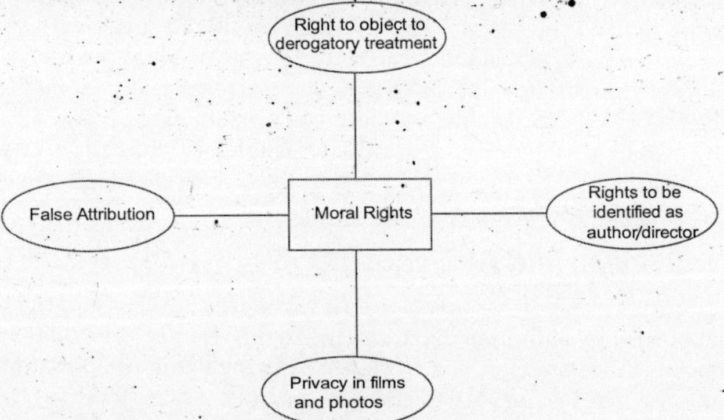

Figure 8.1 Moral Rights of Authors

There are four main rights are illustrated in Figure 8.1.

(i) Right to object to derogatory treatment
(ii) Right to be identified as the author
(iii) Rights to object to false attribution
(iv) Right to privacy in films and photographs

8.1.8 Limitations on Rights

The first limitation is the exclusion from copyright protection of certain categories of works. In some countries, works are excluded from protection if they are not fixed in tangible form. For example, a work of choreography would only be protected in dance notation or recorded on videotape. In certain countries, the texts of laws, court and administrative decisions are excluded from copyright protection.

The second category of limitations concerns particular acts of exploitation, normally requiring the authorization of the rights. Owner, which may, under circumstances specified in the law, be carried out without authorization. There are two basic types of limitations in this category: (a) Free use, which carries no obligation to compensate the rights owner for the use of his/her work without authorization; and (b) Non-voluntary licenses, which do require that compensation be paid to the rights owner for non-authorized exploitation.

Examples of free use include:

- Quoting from a protected work, provided that the source of the quotation and the name of the author is mentioned, and that the extent of the quotation is compatible with fair practice;
- Use of works by way of illustration for teaching purposes; and
- Use of works for the purpose of news reporting.

In respect of free use for reproduction, the Berne Convention contains a general rule, rather than an explicit limitation. Article 9(2) states that Member States may provide for free reproduction in special cases where the acts do not conflict with normal exploitation of the work and do not unreasonably prejudice the legitimate interests of the author. As noted above, many laws allow for individuals to reproduce a work exclusively for their personal, private and non-commercial use. However, the ease and quality of individual copying made possible by recent technology to narrow the scope of such provisions, including through systems which allow certain copying, but incorporate a mechanism for payment to rights owners for the prejudice to their economic interests resulting from the copying.

Non-voluntary licenses allow use of works in certain circumstances without the authorization of the owner of rights, but require that compensation be paid in respect of the use. Such licenses are called non-voluntary because they are allowed in the law, and do not result from the exercise of the exclusive right of the copyright owner to authorize particular acts. Non-voluntary licenses were usually created in circumstances where a new technology for the dissemination of works to the public had emerged, and where the national legislator feared that rights owners would prevent the development of the new technology by refusing to authorize use of works. This was true of two non-voluntary licenses recognized in the Berne Convention, which allow the mechanical reproduction of musical works and broadcasting. The justification for non-voluntary licenses is, however, increasingly called into question, since effective alternatives now exist for making works available to the public based on authorizations given by the rights owners, including in the form of collective administration of rights.

Fair use and Fair dealing

Copyright does not prohibit all copying or replication. In the United States, the fair use doctrine, modified by the Copyright Act of 1976. Section 107, permits some copying and distribution without permission of the copyright holder or payment to same. The statute does not clearly define fair use, but instead gives four non-exclusive factors to consider in a fair use analysis. These factors are:

1. The purpose and character of one's use.
2. The nature of the copyrighted work.
3. What amount and proportion of the whole work was taken.
4. The effect of the use upon the potential market for or value of the copyrighted work.

Duration of Copyright

Copyright does not continue indefinitely. The law provides for a period of time during which the rights of the copyright owner exist. The period or duration of copyright begins from the moment when the work has been created, or, under some national laws, when it has been expressed in a tangible form. It continues, in general, until some time after the death of the author. The purpose of this provision in the law is to enable the author's successors to benefit economically from exploitation of the work after the author's death.

In countries party to the Berne Convention, the duration of copyright provided for by national law is as a general rule. The life of the author not less than 50 years after his death. The Berne Convention also establishes periods of protection for works, such as anonymous, posthumous and cinematographic works, where it is not possible to base duration on the life of an individual author. There is a trend in a number of countries toward lengthening the duration of copyright. The European Union, the United States of America and several others have extended the term of copyright to 70!years after the death of the author.

Ownership, Exercise and Transfer of Copyright

The owner of copyright in a work is generally, the person who created the work, i.e., the author of the work. But this is not always the case. The Berne Convention contains rules for determining initial ownership of rights in cinematographic works. Certain national laws also provide that, when a work is created by an author who is employed for the purpose of creating that work, then the employer, not the author, is the owner of the copyright in the work. However, moral rights always belong to the individual author of the work, whoever the owner of economic rights may be.

The laws of many countries provide that the initial rights owner in a work may transfer all economic rights to a third party. (Moral rights, being personal to the author, can never be transferred). Authors may sell the rights to their works to individuals or companies able to the works, in return for payment. These payments are often made dependent on the actual use of the work, and are then referred to as royalties. Transfers of copyright may take one of two forms: assignments and licenses.

Under an assignment, the rights owner transfers the right to authorize or prohibit certain acts covered by one, several, or all rights under copyright. An assignment is a transfer of a property right. So if all rights are assigned, the person to whom the rights were assigned becomes the new owner of copyright.

In some countries, an assignment of copyright is not legally possible, and only licensing is allowed. Licensing means that the owner of the copyright retains ownership but authorizes a third party to carry out certain acts covered by his economic rights, generally for a specific period of time and for a specific purpose. For example, the author of a novel may grant a license to a publisher to make and distribute copies of his work. At the same time, he may grant a license to a film producer to make a film based on the novel. Licenses may be exclusive, where the copyright owner agrees not to authorize any other party to carry out the licensed acts; or non-exclusive, which means that the copyright owner may authorize others to carry out the same acts. A license, unlike an assignment, does not generally convey the right to authorize others to carry out acts covered by economic rights.

Licensing may also take the form of collective administration of rights. Under collective administration, authors and other rights owners grant exclusive licenses to a single entity, which acts on their behalf to grant authorizations, to collect and distribute remuneration. To prevent and detect infringement of rights, and to seek remedies for infringement. An advantage for authors in collective administration lies in the fact that, with multiple possibilities for unauthorized use of works resulting from new technologies. A single body can ensure that mass uses take place on the basis of authorizations which are easily obtainable from a central source.

A rights owner may also abandon the exercise of the rights, wholly or partially. The owner may protected material on the Internet and leave it free for anybody to use, or may restrict the abandonment to non-commercial use. Some very impressive cooperation projects have been organized on a model where contributors abandon certain rights as described in the licensing terms adopted for the project, such as the General Public License (GPL). They thereby leave their contributions free for others to use and to adapt, but with the condition that the subsequent users also adhere to the terms of the license. Such projects, including the open source movement, which specializes in creating computer programs, also build their business models on the existence of copyright protection, because otherwise they could not impose an obligation on subsequent users.

Enforcement of Rights

The Berne Convention contains very few provisions concerning enforcement of rights, but the evolution of new national and international enforcement standards has been dramatic in recent years due to two principal factors. The first concerns advances in the technological means for creation and use (both authorized and unauthorized) of protected material. Digital technology in particular makes it easy to transmit and make perfect copies of any information existing in digital form, including copyright-protected works. The second factor is the increasing economic importance in the realm of international trade of the movement of goods and services protected by intellectual property rights. Simply, trade in products embodying intellectual property rights is now a growing, worldwide business. This is acknowledged in the WIPO Copyright Treaty (WCT), which requires Contracting Parties to ensure that enforcement procedures are available under their law so as to permit effective action against any infringement of rights covered by the Treaty, including remedies to prevent infringements.

The Agreement on Trade-Related Aspects of Intellectual Property Rights (TRIPS), which contains more detailed provisions on the enforcement of rights, is wide evidence between intellectual property and trade. The following paragraphs identify and summarize some of the enforcement provisions found in recent national legislation. They may be divided into the following categories: conservatory or provisional measures; civil remedies; criminal sanctions; measures to be taken at the border; and measures, remedies and sanctions against abuses in respect of technical devices.

Conservatory or provisional measures have two purposes: first, to prevent infringements from occurring, in particular to prevent the entry of infringing goods into the channels of commerce, including entry of imported goods after clearance by customs; and second, to preserve relevant evidence in regard to an alleged infringement. Thus, judicial authorities may have the authority to order that provisional measures be enacted without advance notice to the alleged infringer. In this way, the alleged infringer is prevented from relocating the goods to avoid detection. The most common provisional measure is a search of the premises of the alleged infringer and seizure of suspected infringing goods, the equipment used to manufacture them, and all relevant documents and other records of the alleged infringing business activities.

Civil remedies compensate the rights owner for economic injury suffered because of the infringement, usually in the form of pecuniary damages, and create an effective deterrent to further infringement. This is often in the form of a judicial order to destroy the infringing goods and the materials which have been predominantly used for producing them. If there is a danger that infringing acts may be continued, the court may also issue injunctions against such acts, failure to comply with which would subject the infringer to payment of a fine.

Criminal sanctions are intended to punish those who willfully commit acts of piracy on a commercial scale and, as in the case of civil remedies, to deter further infringement. The purpose of punishment is served by substantial fines, and by prison sentences consistent with the level of penalties applied for crimes of corresponding seriousness, particularly for repeat offenses. The purpose of deterrence is served by orders for the seizure and destruction of infringing goods, and of the materials and equipment used predominantly to commit the offense.

Measures to be taken at the border are different from the enforcement measures described so far, in that they involve action by the customs authorities rather than by the judicial authorities. Border measures allow the rights owner to request that customs authorities suspend the release into circulation of goods that are suspected of infringing copyright. This is intended to give the rights owner a reasonable time to commence judicial proceedings against the suspected infringer, without the risk that the alleged infringing goods will disappear into circulation after customs clearance. The rights owner must (a) Satisfy the customs authorities that there is prima facie evidence of infringement, (b) Provide a detailed description of the goods so that they can be recognized and (c) Provide a security to indemnify the importer, the owner of the goods, and the customs authorities in case the goods turn out to be non-infringing.

The final category of enforcement provisions, which has achieved greater importance since the advent of digital technology, includes measures, remedies and sanctions against abuses in respect of technical means. In certain cases, the only practical means of preventing copying is through so-called copy-protection or copy-management systems. These use technical devices, which either entirely prevent copying, or make the quality of the copies so poor as to be unusable. Technical means are also used to prevent the reception of encrypted commercial television programs except with use of decoders. However, it is technically possible to manufacture devices to circumvent such copy-protection and encryption systems. The enforcement provisions are intended to prevent the manufacture, importation and distribution of such devices. Provisions to this effect are included in the WCT. So too are provisions to prevent the unauthorized removal or alteration of electronic rights management information, and the dissemination of copies of works from which such information has been removed. Such information may identify the author or rights owner, or contain information about the terms and conditions of use of the work. Removing it may result in the distortion of computerized rights management or fee-distribution systems.

8.1.9 Other Types of Intellectual Property Rights

Within the scope of digitization projects or the creation of online material, although copyright stands as the most relevant, other types of Intellectual Property Rights also need to be identified and measures implemented in order to make sure that the rights of third parties are not infringed and, where appropriate to maximize their full exploitation.

8.2 WHAT IS A TRADEMARK?

A trademark is a distinctive sign that identifies certain goods or services produced or provided by an individual or a company. Its origin dates back to ancient times when craftsmen reproduced their signatures, or "marks", on their artistic works or products of a functional or practical nature. Over the years, these marks have evolved into today's system of trademark registration and protection. The system helps consumers to identify and purchase a product or service based on whether its specific characteristics and quality – as indicated by its unique trademark – meet their needs.

8.2.1 What do Trademarks do?

Trademark protection ensures that the owners of marks have the exclusive right to use them to identify goods or services, or to authorize others to use them in return for payment. The period of protection varies, but a trademark can be renewed indefinitely upon payment of the corresponding fees. Trademark protection is legally enforced by courts that, in most systems, have the authority to stop trademark infringement.

In a larger sense, trademarks promote initiative and enterprise worldwide by rewarding their owners with recognition and financial profit. Trademark protection also hinders the efforts of unfair competitors, such as counterfeiters, to use similar distinctive signs to market inferior or different products or services. The system enables people with skill and enterprise to produce and market goods and services in the fairest possible conditions, thereby facilitating international trade.

8.2.2 What Kinds of Trademarks can be Registered?

Trademarks may be one or a combination of words, letters and numerals. They may consist of drawings, symbols or three dimensional signs, such as the shape and packaging of goods.

In some countries, non-traditional marks may be registered for distinguishing features, such as holograms, motion, color and non-visible signs (sound, smell or taste).

In addition to identifying the commercial source of goods or services, several other trademark categories also exist. Collective marks are owned by an association whose members use them to indicate products with a certain level of quality and who agree to adhere to specific requirements set by the association. Such associations might represent, for example, accountants, engineers or architects. Certification marks are given for compliance with defined standards but are not confined to any membership.

They may be granted to anyone who can certify that their products meet certain established standards. Some examples of recognized certification are the internationally accepted "ISO (International Organization for Standardization) 9000" quality standards and Ecolabels for products with reduced environmental impact.

8.2.3 How is a Trademark Registered?

First, an application for registration of a trademark must be filed with the appropriate national or regional trademark office. The application must contain a clear reproduction of the sign filed for registration, including any colors, forms or three-dimensional features. It must also contain a list of the goods or services to which the sign would apply. The sign must fulfill certain conditions in order to be protected as a trademark or other type of mark. It must be distinctive, so that consumers can distinguish it from trademarks identifying other products, as well as identify a particular product with it. It must neither mislead nor deceive customers nor violate public order or morality.

Finally, the rights applied for cannot be the same as, or similar to, rights already granted to another trademark owner. This may be determined through search and examination by national offices, or by the opposition of third parties who claim to have similar or identical rights.

8.3 WHAT IS A PATENT?

A patent is an exclusive right granted for an invention. A product or process that provides a new way of doing something, or that offers a new technical solution to a problem.

A patent provides patent owners with protection for their inventions. Protection is granted for a limited period, generally 20 years.

8.3.1 Why are Patents Necessary?

Patents provide incentives to individuals by recognizing their creativity and offering the possibility of material reward for their marketable inventions. These incentives encourage innovation, which, in turn, enhances the quality of human life.

8.3.2 What Kind of Protection do Patents Offer?

Patent protection means an invention cannot be commercially made, used, distributed or sold without the patent owner's consent. Patent rights are usually enforced in courts that, in most systems, hold the authority to stop patent infringement. Conversely, a court can also declare a patent invalid upon a successful challenge by a third party.

8.3.3 What Rights do Patent Owners Have?

A patent owner has the right to decide who may – or may not – use the patented invention for the period during which it is protected. Patent owners may give permission to, or license, other parties to use their inventions on mutually agreed terms. Owners may also sell their invention rights to someone else, who then becomes the new owner of the patent. Once a patent expires, protection ends and the invention enters the public domain. This is also known as becoming off patent, meaning the owner no longer holds exclusive rights to the invention, and it becomes available for commercial exploitation by others.

What role do patents play in everyday life?

Patented inventions have pervaded every aspect of human life, from electric lighting (patents held by Edison and Swan) and sewing machines (patents held by Howe and Singer), to Magnetic Resonance Imaging (MRI) (patents held by Damadian) and the iPhone (patents held by Apple).

In return for patent protection, all patent owners are obliged to publicly disclose information on their inventions in order to enrich the total body of technical knowledge in the world. This ever increasing body of public knowledge promotes further creativity and innovation. Patents therefore provide not only protection for their owners but also valuable information and inspiration for future generations of researchers and inventors.

How is a patent granted?

The first step in securing a patent is to file a patent application. The application generally contains the title of the invention, as well as an indication of its technical field. It must include the background and a description of the invention, in clear language and enough detail that an individual with an average understanding of the field could use or reproduce the invention. Such descriptions are usually accompanied by visual materials – drawings, plans or diagrams – that describe the invention in greater detail. The application also contains various 'claims', that is, information to help determine the extent of protection to be granted by the patent.

8.4 TRADE SECRETS

Trade secrets consist of confidential data, information or compilations used in research, business, commerce or industry. Universities and R&D (Research and Development) institutions, government agencies, business entities and individuals may own and use trade secrets. The information may include confidential scientific and technical data and business, commercial or financial information not publicly known that is useful to an enterprise and confers competitive advantage on one having a right to use it. The secrecy of the information must be maintained to conserve its trade secret status.

Trade secret information may be disclosed or shared under the terms of a confidentiality agreement. Confidential information may be created in sponsored research projects. In that case the sponsor will generally require the university or R&D institution and the creator to preserve the secrecy of the information. Trade secrets in the form of know-how may be vital to the working of patented inventions and other innovations. Trade secret information may have considerable value by itself or in conjunction with other forms of intellectual property.

A familiar example of a trade secret is the formula for Coca-Cola. If the formula had been patented, it would no longer be a secret, as patent law requires public disclosure of the invention. Anyone who independently and legitimately discovers the secret of the Coca-Cola formula can use that discovery, and the Coca-Cola Company would have no legal means of stopping them.

8.5 E-RESOURCE LICENSING

Systematic or programmatic downloading, retention, and printing are prohibited. For example, you cannot download entire issue of a journal or print out several copies of the same article. The following points of e-resource licensing are discussed below:

- Electronic distribution of content is generally restricted.
- Multiple copies of digital documents and their circulation is prohibited.
- Copyright laws protect published material in any format so that it cannot be copied except in accordance with fair use.

- Viewing, downloading, copying, printing and saving a copy of search results and individual articles.
- Using e-resources for scholarly, educational or scientific research, teaching, private study and clinical purposes.
- Sending a copy of an article to another authorized user (i.e., current faculty, students or staff).
- Posting the URL (Uniform Resource Locator) to the publisher's version of the article on a class Website (publisher links will allow)
- Use of robots or intelligent agents to do systematic, bulk or automatic downloading is not permitted.
- Use of robots or intelligent agents to do systematic, bulk or automatic downloading is not permitted.
- Systematic downloading or printing of entire journal issues or large portions of other e-resources is not permitted.
- Using e-resources for commercial gain is not permitted (i.e. reselling, redistributing or republishing).

8.6 THE ROLE OF WIPO

The World Intellectual Property Organization (WIPO) is an international organization dedicated to promoting creativity and innovation by ensuring that the rights of creators and owners of intellectual property are protected worldwide, and that inventors and authors are thus recognized and rewarded for their ingenuity. As a specialized agency of the United Nations, WIPO exists as a forum for its Member States to create and harmonize rules and practices to protect intellectual property rights. Most industrialized nations have protection systems that are centuries old. Many new and developing countries, however, are now building up their patent, trademark and copyright laws and systems. With the rapid globalization of trade during the last decade, WIPO plays a key role in helping these new systems to evolve through treaty negotiation, legal and technical assistance, and training in various forms, including in the area of enforcement of intellectual property rights.

The field of copyright and related rights has expanded dramatically as technological developments have brought new ways of disseminating creations worldwide through such forms of communication as satellite broadcasting, compact disks, DVDs and the Internet. WIPO is closely involved in the on-going international debate to shape new standards for copyright protection in cyberspace.

WIPO also provides an Arbitration and Mediation Center, which offers services for the resolution of international commercial disputes between private parties involving intellectual property. The subject matter of these proceedings includes both contractual disputes (such as patent and software licenses, trademark coexistence agreements, and research and development agreements) and noncontractual disputes (such as patent infringement). The Center is also now recognized as the leading dispute resolution service provider for disputes arising out of the abusive registration and use of Internet domain names.

8.7 EXCEPTIONS TO COPYRIGHT PROTECTION

Exceptions to protection break the monopoly of the right-holders by providing limited rights to use works without their consent. Steward says that the limitations on copyright are necessary to keep the balance between two conflicting public interests: the public interest in rewarding creators and the public interest in the widest dissemination of their works. Commenting on the scope of such exceptions, Fabiani argues that limitations on the author's exclusive rights may be imposed in order to facilitate the work's contribution to the intellectual and cultural enrichment of the community. However, the limitations must not be, such as to dampen the will to create and disseminate new works.

The exceptions specifically permitted by the Berne Convention include free use of otherwise protected works in public speeches, lectures and legal proceedings; use of short excerpts by way of quotation or illustration for teaching (in such cases the use must be compatible with fair practice and justified by the purpose); use justified in connection with the reporting of current events; use solely for the purposes of private study and research; and, finally, the convention contains a catch-all provision, allowing reproduction in certain special cases provided that such reproduction does not constitute exploitation of the work and does not unreasonably prejudice the legitimate interests of the author.

The three-step test, as set out by the Berne Convention, is made up of the following conditions:

1. Specific exceptions of limited scope for informational and educational purposes,
2. Limitations on the right of reproduction and
3. Non-voluntary licensing systems.

8.7.1 Exceptions for Informational and Educational Purposes

Rights of Quotation

The right to make quotations from a published work allows the inclusion of one or more passages from someone else's work in one's own to illustrate a theme or defend some proposition or to describe or criticise the work quoted.

There are three limits to check this licence to quote:

1. The work from which the extract is taken must have been lawfully made available to the public.
2. The quotation must be "compatible with fair practice", implying an objective appreciation of what is normally considered acceptable and is a matter for the courts to decide.
3. The quotation must only be to the extent justified by the purpose, which again is a matter for the courts.

Use for Teaching Purposes

This right permits the utilization of works by way of illustration in publications, broadcasts or sound or audiovisual recordings for teaching, subject to the same conditions that govern quotations. The work's source and author's name have to be mentioned.

Exceptions for the Benefit of the Media

The broadcasting or the communication to the public by wire of arts published in newspapers or periodicals on current economic, political or religious topics, and of broadcast works of the same character may also be permitted by national legislation, an exception of particular value to the news media. The source must always be clearly indicated to protect moral rights and an author has the right to expressly reserve his consent to such use.

Reporting Current Events.

Reporting current events allows the reproduction of works to make them available to the public, when they are circumstantial seen or heard in the background in the course of an event.

8.7.2 Limitations on the Right of Reproduction

The Three-Step Test of the Berne Convention:

Art.9 of the Berne Convention grants the Right of Reproduction. Art. 9(1) grants authors of literary and artistic works (including those of an audio or visual nature) the exclusive right of authorizing the reproduction of these works, in any manner or form. According to 9(2) the contracting parties may legally permit the reproduction of such works in certain special cases, provided that such reproduction does not conflict with a normal exploitation of the work and does not unreasonably prejudice the legitimate interests of the author.

In cases where there would be serious loss of profit for the copyright owner, the law should provide him with some compensation such as, for example, a system of compulsory licensing with equitable remuneration. Art. 10 WCT 1996 has extended the scope of Art. 9(2) of the Berne Convention to make it applicable to all authors' rights and not merely reproduction rights. This is also part of the WPPT or WIPO Performances and Phonograms (Art. 16) and the TRIPs (Trade-Related Aspects of Intellectual Property Rights) Agreement (Art. 13). The Information Directive recognizes the three-step test in it's own Art. 5(5) which regulates limitations and exceptions to the reproduction right as well as to the rights of communication to the public of works and making available to the public matter subject to related rights. It is an exhaustive list of permissible but not mandatory exceptions and the member states are free to choose for themselves what to allow.

8.7.3 Non-Voluntary Licensing Systems

This limitation in the form of statutory or compulsory licences allows the use of a work without the author's authorization under certain conditions, such as the payment of equitable remuneration. The compulsory licence for broadcasting and cable distribution was introduced in the Berne Convention in the interest of the public but it is restricted. Such licences only apply in countries which have provided for them, they may not prejudice the authors' moral rights and fair remuneration must be paid.

8.8 GUIDELINES FOR CLEARANCE

Clearance is the process of determining and negotiating any permissions that are needed to include use of someone else's intellectual property in your creative project. These process includes:

- Determining the owner(s) of the intellectual property.
- Contacting the owners and negotiating an agreement.
- Administering written contracts.
- Handling other issues related to the use and licensing of intellectual property.

8.8.1 Why do I Need Clearance?

If you use someone else's intellectual property without their permission, you can face some very serious consequences. The operative term here is property. If you use someone else's property without asking, then you are stealing. !The Copyright Act provides substantial penalties for copyright infringement ranging from $10,000 for accidental infringement to $250,000 for willful infringement. The copyright holder can also file an injunction against you, which can keep you from distributing or selling your work with their material in it. Examples of what can happen when clearance is not handled correctly can be found here.

8.8.2 What is Fair Use?

Another noteworthy exception to the exclusive rights previously described is referred to as the fair use doctrine. Fair use provides an absolute exception to the exclusive rights of the copyright owner when another uses the owner's work in specific ways. In cases where the fair use exception applies, permission from the copyright owner to use the work is unnecessary.

Generally, use of a copyrighted work for criticism, comment, news reporting, teaching (including multiple copies for classroom use), scholarship , or research qualifies as fair use. While no bright line rules exist for determining whether a particular use is fair, courts rely on a four factor test. The factors are:

- The purpose and character of the use, including whether the use is commercial or for non-profit educational purposes;
- The nature of the copyrighted work itself, in which courts typically evaluate whether the work is factual, scientific, or artistic in nature;
- The quantitative amount and substantiality, interpreted as the qualitative amount, of the work that is copied; and
- The effect of the use upon the potential market for or value of the work.

Generally speaking, uses for non-commercial purposes that will not diminish the copyright owner's ability to make money from the work are considered fair use. As a result, permission from the copyright owner for those uses is unnecessary. However, if there is doubt about whether a use is fair, err on the side of caution and get permission or speak with an attorney.

8.9 ELEMENTS OF COPYRIGHT

The copyright include three elements:

1. The symbol (C), word Copyright or abbreviation copr;
2. The year of first publication; and
3. The name or abbreviation of the owner of copyright.

In the cases of derivative works it is recommended to indicate a range of years for a work (although this is not required by law). For instance, a copyright notice may be specified according to any of the following variants:

-Copyright (c) BPB Publications
-(c) 2007 BPB Publications
-Copyright 2007 BPB Publications
-Copr. 2007 BPB Publications

An exception to the above relates to the copyright notice of sound recordings. Sound recordings embodied on phonorecords are required to include a special notice consisting of the letter in a circle followed by the year of first publication and by the name of the copyright holder.

Under the Copyright Act of 1909 if an authorized copy of a work was published without notice, the work would be placed permanently on the public domain. This would result in the loss of copyright ownership. This requirement changed when the US passed the Berne Implementation Act of 1998 which became effective on March, 1989. For works published after this date, the omission of the copyright notice does not result in loss of copyright protection. Despite this change in the law it still strongly recommended to use the copyright notice. The notice serves to inform the public that the work is protected and identifies the owner of the work. Additionally, the proper use of a copyright notice makes it significantly more difficult for defendants to claim innocent infringement.

8.10 Collaboration in Intellectual Property

Over the past two decades there has been an explosion in the number of patent awards across a wide variety of technologies, and a dramatic increase in the volume of patent litigation between rivals. Overlapping Intellectual Property (IP) rights create "patent thickets" which make it expensive for manufacturers to commercialize innovative products and difficult for inventors to extend the frontiers of technology. Knowledge-sharing organizations, such as patent ponds, alliances and standard-setting organizations - where owners of IP share patent rights with each other and third parties - have been proposed as a way for firms to work around the problem of patent thickets. This article explores the merits of knowledge-sharing organizations, and outlines a number of policy considerations that may serve to eliminate some of the tensions that can arise from such IP-focused collaborations.

Evidence suggests that companies are recognizing the benefits of participating in IP collaborations. In 2001, for example, sales of devices based in whole or in part on pooled patents were estimated to be at least US$100 billion. While the Information and Communication Technologies (ICT) industry, broadly defined, has accounted for the majority of patent pools over the last 20 years, there are indications of more widespread interest in such arrangements. The biomedical research community, for example, has expressed a keen interest in the development of patent pools for biomarkers for cancer, HIV/AIDS or Human Immunodeficiency Virus/Acquired Immune Deficiency Syndrome and Severe Acute Respiratory Syndrome (SARS), as well as for biotechnologies applied to agriculture and animal cloning.

8.10.1 Advantages of Collaboration

Patent pools present compelling reasons for firms to cooperate insofar as they can offer attractive "complementaries". For example, it may be far more efficient for multiple firms - each working to their own strengths - to work together to produce a complex technology. This has been particularly true within the ICT industry, where many different firms develop complementary and interoperable technologies. Take, for example, the respective roles of Dell, Intel and Microsoft in the sphere of personal computing, or Apple and its iPhone application developers. Collaborating with developers of such technologies can help coordinate investment schedules and promote interoperability in new product releases.

More generally, acquiring the foundational knowledge needed to produce cutting-edge technologies is a costly affair. Taking advantage of the experience of others can be much cheaper than gaining such experience first hand. Collaborating with another firm can be a way to leverage its experience without locking in to a commitment to build up the required knowledge internally. This is a particularly useful option when exploring new markets, geographies or technologies.

Investments in research and development (R&D) - the cost of labs, instrumentation, testing equipment and technical specialists - can be substantial. In some industries, such as those producing semiconductors or telecommunications equipment, the cost of a single R&D project can be beyond the reach of most companies. In more typical smaller-scale R&D operations, effective facilities not only require lab equipment but also ancillary services, such as administrative support, staff to maintain specialized equipment or hazardous materials and testing technicians. Collaborating with a player that has similar needs helps spread these costs. It also allows firms to share development risks and undertake projects that might otherwise be considered too risky.

8.10.2 Payments

Royalty is the payment of any kind, received as a fee for use of or entitled right to use any copyright on literary works, art or science works, including computer programs, other records on data carriers, video and audio tapes, cinematographic films or tapes for radio or television broadcasts; for any patent purchase, registered mark on goods and services or trademark, design, secret drawings, patterns, formulae, process, right for information concerning industrial, commercial or scientific expertise (know-how). Royalty shall not be the payment for obtaining property objects, defined in part 1 of this item, for possession and administration or ownership by the person or if the conditions of use of such property objects shall entitle the user to sell or alienate the property object by a different method or promulgate (disclose) secret drawings, patterns, formulae, processes, right for information concerning industrial, commercial or scientific expertise (know-how), except for the cases, when such promulgation (disclosure) shall be mandatory under the Laws of Ukraine. Royalty rates level in the current international trade fluctuates between 2 and 10% and amounts mainly to 3-5%. It shall depend upon economy branch, license layout, terms of agreement, volume of production, inner and export prices for the products, made under the license. Since royalty is usually paid by bank transfers, license agreements shall have bank guarantees for the part or total amount of payments with possible gradual reduction of a guaranteed amount.

Combined payment is a license payment which shall include royalty and lump-sum payment. If the parties have decided to carry out payments for use of intellectual property by means of combined payments, the agreement shall definitely include clear calculations, under which they shall be carried out. The parties shall also be entitled to specify royalty payment order (sale fee, fixed amount, non-cash payments, etc.)

REVIEW QUESTIONS WITH ANSWERS

1. Multiple Choice

1.1 Which of the following is not specifically protected by Intellectual property legislation?

a. Trade secrets b. Industrial designs
c. Patents d. Trademarks

1.2 Which of the following cannot be protected by copyright?
a. Literary works b. Folklore
c. Musical components d. Graphic works

1.3 What action would a person bring against someone who steals a trade secret?
a. Cyber law b. Copyright infringement
c. Patent law d. Trademark infringement

1.4 In Patent law, the invention must have which of the following characteristics?
a. The invention cannot have been in use by others.
b. The invention must have unique qualities.
c. The invention must be a concrete thing that can be constructed.
d. All of the above

1.5 Which of the following is false with regard to patent registration?
a. The first to apply has priority.
b. There is a 50-year monopoly over the invention.
c. The registration gives the patent holder exclusive rights to manufacture and sell the invention.
d. Patent law protects information about how to build-the invention.

1.6 What action would a person bring against someone who steals a trade secret?
a. Infringement action b. Violation of trademark law
c. Misappropriation d. None of the above

1.7 To be patented, an invention must be.
a. Non-abvious b. Useful
c. Novel d. All of the above

1.8 Trademarks are closely associated with:
a. Business image b. Patents
c. Reputation d. None of the above

1.9 It is possible for a new product to be protected using.
a. Copyright an patents b. Trade marks and copyright
c. Registered designs and patents d. All of the above

1.10 Which of the following principles is applicable to trademarks?
a. A trademark should not cause confusion with previous trademarks
b. A trademark should be distinctive
c. A trademark should be capable of distinguish goods or service
d. All of the above

2. State whether the following statements are True or False

2.1 Trademark registration can be renewed for an unlimited number of ten years.

2.2 .gov is a commerical use domain names will normally use the following suffix in their Website address.

2.3 Patents are valid for twenty years.

2.4 The Copyright Term Extension Act granted an individual copyright holder the right to own the copyright for the life of the author 95 years.

2.5 Sound recordings are considered tangible writings for copyright purposes.

2.6 The Berne Convention requires the copyright holder to put a copyright notice on the copyrighted material.

2.7 Material does not need to be copied word-for-word to have a copyright infringement claim.

2.8 The public-use doctrine permits certain limited unauthorized use of copyrighted materials.

2.9 Trademarks laws are designed, in part, to prevent consumers from being confused as to the origins of goods and services.

2.10 Agency theory is the same as stakeholder theory.

3. Match the following:

3.1	The commission of illegal acts through the use of the computer or against the computer system is called	a. TRIPS
3.2	A sets of initials refers to a major international agreement seeking to protect 'knowledge-based' aspects of international trade.	b. Copyright
3.3	Any sign capable of being represented graphically which is capable of distinguishing goods or services of one undertaking from those of another and which has legal effect.	c. Agent
3.4	Which of the following regimes offers the best prospects for intellectual-property protection for the film under these facts?	d. Computer crime
3.5	A party who agrees to act on behalf of another	e. Trademark
3.6	WIPO	f. Fair-use doctrine
3.7	Article 2 of the UCC (Uniform Commercial Code)	g. World Intellectual Property Organization
3.8	A doctrine that permits certain limited use of a copyright by someone other than the copyright holder without the permission of the copyright holder.	h. that governs the sale of goods
3.9	Unauthorized use of another's patent	i. Trade secret
3.10	A product formula, pattern, design, compilation of data, customer list, or other business secret	j. Patent infringement

4. Fill in the blanks

a. Certification	b. Trade secrets	c. Copyright infringement
d. Constitution	e. Infringement	f. Patent application
g. HTML	h. Trademark	i. Copyright
j. Tradename		

4.1 __________ set businesses apart from their competitors.

4.2 Express authority for patents is granted in the __________.

4.3 __________ occurs when a party copies a substantial and material part of a copyrighted work without permission.

4.4 Two computer languages used to exchange information are __________ and Java.

4.5 A(n) ________ containing a written description of the invention must be filed with the U.S. Patent and Trademark Office to request a patent.

4.6 Patent ________ is the unauthorized use of another person's patent.

4.7 Any work of an artistic, literary or scientific nature and the derivative work is covered by ________.

4.8 A ________ refers to the name or designation identifying and distinguishing an enterprise.

4.9 A ________ is a distinctive sign that identifies certain goods or services produced or provided by an individual or a company.

4.10 ________ marks are given for compliance with defined standards but are not confined to any membership.

Answers

1.	1.1	a	1.2	b	1.3	a	1.4	d	1.5	b	1.6	c
	1.7	d	1.8	c	1.9	d	1.10	d				
2.	2.1	T	2.2	F	2.3	T	2.4	F	2.5	T	2.6	F
	2.7	T	2.8	F	2.9	T	2.10	F				
3.	3.1	d	3.2	a	3.3	e	3.4	b	3.5	c	3.6	g
	3.7	h	3.8	f	3.9	j	3.10	i				
4.	4.1	b	4.2	e	4.3	c	4.4	g	4.5	f	4.6	e
	4.7	i	4.8	j	4.9	h	4.10	a				

Short Questions with Answers

1. What are "Intellectual Property Rights"?
2. What is the place of the TRIPS Agreement in the multilateral trading system?
3. What is WIPO?
4. What is covered by copyright?

Answers to Short Questions

1. Intellectual property rights can be defined as the rights given to people over the creations of their minds. They usually give the creator an exclusive right over the use of his/her creations for a certain period of time.
   Intellectual property rights are traditionally divided into two main categories:
   Copyright and rights related to copyright: i.e. rights granted to authors of literary and artistic works, and the rights of performers, producers of phonograms and broadcasting organizations. The main purpose of protection of copyright and related rights is to encourage and reward creative work.
   Industrial property: This includes (1) The protection of distinctive signs such as trademarks and geographical indications, and (2) Industrial property protected primarily to stimulate innovation, design and the creation of technology. In this category fall inventions (protected by patents), industrial designs and trade secrets.
2. One of the fundamental characteristics of the TRIPS Agreement is that it makes protection of intellectual property rights an integral part of the multilateral trading system, as exemplify in the WTO.
   The TRIPS Agreement is part of the single undertaking resulting from the Uruguay Round negotiations. That implies that the TRIPS Agreement applies to all WTO members.
3. The World Intellectual Property Organization (WIPO) was established by a convention of 14 July 1967, which entered into force in 1970. It has been a specialized agency of the United Nations since 1974, and administers a number of international unions or treaties in the area of intellectual property, such as Paris and Berne Convention.
4. Almost anything created by the exercise of the imagination is protected by copyright. The work must be in a tangible form (e.g. a book, a computer program, an image) – copyright does not protect the idea, but the manifestation of the idea.

DESCRIPTIVE TYPE QUESTIONS

1. What is a patent?
2. What are copyright exceptions?
3. What can be patented?
4. What inventions cannot be patented?
5. Discuss the features of Intellectual Property Rights
6. What are the types of intellectual property?
7. What is an industrial design?
8. What is a trademark?
9. What are well-known marks?
10. What is duration of trademark?

CHAPTER 9

Handheld Devices (Mobiles and Tabs)

9.1 INTRODUCTION

A mobile phone is also known as a cellular phone, cell phone, a hand phone, or even simply a phone. It is a phone that can make and receive telephone calls over a radio link while moving around a wide area. It connects to a cellular network provided by a mobile phone operator, allowing access to the public telephone network. In addition to telephony, modern mobile phones also support a wide variety of other services such, as text messaging, MMS (Multimedia Message Service), e-mail, Internet access, short-range wireless communications (infrared, Bluetooth), business applications, gaming, and photography. Mobile phones that offer these and more general computing capabilities are referred to as smartphones (See Figures 9.1 (a) and (b)).

(a) (b)

Figure 9.1 (a) Mobile phone

The first handheld cell phone was demonstrated by John F. Mitchell and Dr. Martin Cooper of Motorola in 1973. Using a handset weighing around 4.4 pounds (2kg). In 1983, the DynaTAC 8000x was the first to be commercially available. From 1990 to 2011, worldwide mobile phone subscriptions grew from 12.4 million to over 6 billion of the global population. These first generation ("1G") systems could support far more simultaneous calls, but still used analog technology. In 1991, the second generation (2G) digital cellular technology was launched in Finland by Radiolinja on the GSM (Global System for Mobile) standard.

A mobile operating system, also called a mobile OS. It is an operating system that is specifically designed to run on mobile devices, such as mobile phones, smartphones, PDAs (Personal Digital Assistant), tablet computers and other handheld devices. The mobile operating system is the software platform on top of which other programs, called application programs, can run on mobile devices.

The operating system is the functions and features available on your device, such as thumbwheel, keyboards, WAP, synchronization with applications, e-mail, text messaging and more. The mobile OS will also determine which third-party applications (mobile apps) can be used on your device.

9.1.1 Types of Mobile Operating Systems

In this section, you will learn about the mobile operating system before you purchase a device to ensure compatibility and support for the mobile applications you want to use.

9.1.2 Popular Mobile Operating Systems

Android OS

The Android mobile operating system is Google's open and free software that includes an operating system, middleware and also key applications for use on mobile devices, including smartphones. Updates for the open source Android mobile operating system have been developed under "dessert-inspired" codenames with each new version arriving in alphabetical order with new enhancements and improvements.

Bada

Bada is a Samsung mobile OS that was first launched in 2010. The Samsung Wave was the first smartphone to use this mobile OS. Bada provides mobile features, such as multipoint-touch, 3D graphics and of course, application downloads and installation.

BlackBerry OS

The BlackBerry OS is a proprietary mobile operating system developed by Research In Motion for use on the company's popular BlackBerry handheld devices. The BlackBerry platform is popular with corporate users as it offers synchronization with Microsoft Exchange, Lotus Domino, Novell GroupWise e-mail and other business software, when used with the BlackBerry Enterprise Server.

iPhone OS/iOS (Apple)

Apple's iPhone OS was originally developed for use on its iPhone devices. Now, the mobile operating system is referred to as iOS and is supported on a number of Apple devices including the iPhone, iPad, iPad 2 and iPod Touch. The iOS mobile operating system is available only on Apple's own manufactured devices as the company does not license the OS for third-party hardware. Apple iOS is derived from Apple's Mac OS X operating system.

MeeGo OS (Nokia and Intel)

A joint open source mobile operating system which is the result of merging two products based on open source technologies: Maemo (Nokia) and Moblin (Intel). !MeeGo is a mobile OS designed to work on a number of devices including smartphones, notebooks, tablets, in-vehicle information systems and various devices using Intel Atom and ARMv7 architectures.

Palm OS (Garnet OS)

The Palm OS is a mobile operating system (PDA operating system) that was originally released in 1996 on the Pilot 1000 handheld. The Palm OS have added support for expansion ports, new processors, external memory cards, improved security and support for ARM (Acorn RISC or Reduced Instruction Set Computer Machines) processors and smartphones. Palm OS 5 was extended to provide support for a broad range of screen resolutions, wireless connections and enhanced multimedia capabilities and is called Garnet OS.

Symbian OS (Nokia)

Symbian is a mobile operating system offers a high-level of integration with communication and Personal Information Management (PIM) functionality. Symbian OS combines middleware with wireless communications through an integrated mailbox and the integration of Java and PIM functionality. Nokia has made the Symbian platform available under an alternative, open and direct model, to work with some OEMs (Original Equipent Manufacturers) and the small community of platform development collaborators. Nokia does not maintain Symbian as an open source development project.

webOS (Palm/HP)

WebOS is a mobile operating system that runs on the Linux kernel. WebOS was initially developed by Palm as the successor to its Palm OS mobile operating system. It is a proprietary Mobile OS which was eventually acquired by HP (Hewlett-Packard) and now referred to as webOS (lower-case w) in HP literature. HP uses webOS in a number of devices including several smartphones and HP TouchPads. HP has pushed its webOS into the enterprise mobile market by focusing on improving security features and management with the release of webOS 3.x. HP has also announced plans for a version of webOS to run within the Microsoft Windows operating system and to be installed on all HP desktop and notebook computers in 2012.

Windows Mobile (Windows Phone 7)

Windows Mobile is Microsoft's mobile operating system used in smartphones and mobile devices with or without touch screens. The Mobile OS is based on the Windows CE 5.2 kernel. In 2010 Microsoft announced a new smartphone platform called Windows Phone 7.

9.1.3 Types of Phones

CDMA (Code Division Multiple Access)–A network that digitizes communication using a specific frequency like GSM. But are not compatible. Before traveling internationally, be sure to find out which is used to make sure your phone will work when you reach at your destination.

GSM (Global System for Mobile Communications)– A digital cellular network which behaves much like CDMA, but are not compatible. GSM is commonly used in Europe.

3G phones–"Third-generation" devices. Third generation technology makes it possible for cell phones to accommodate broadband wireless data in addition to traditional cell phone functionality (e.g. e-mail download and Internet access). There are other Internet technologies that perform similarly but are not called "3G" specifically.

9.2 MOBILE PHONE FEATURES

All mobile phones have a number of features in common, but manufacturers also try to differentiate their own products by implementing additional functions to make them more attractive to consumers. This has led to great innovation in mobile phone development over the past 20 years.

The common components found on all phones are:

- A battery, providing the power source for the phone functions.
- An input mechanism to allow the user to interact with the phone. The most common input mechanism is a keypad, but touch screens are also found in some high-end smartphones.
- Basic mobile phone services to allow users to make calls and send text messages.
- All GSM phones use a SIM (Subscriber Identity/Identification Module) card to allow an account to be swapped among devices. Some CDMA devices also have a similar card called a R-UIM (Removable User Identity Module).
- Individual GSM, WCDMA (wideband Code Division Multiple Access), iDEN (Integrated Digital Enhanced Network) and some satellite phone devices are uniquely identified by an International Mobile Equipment Identity (IMEI) number.

All mobile phones are designed to work on cellular networks and contain a standard set of services that allow phones of different types and in different countries to communicate with each other. However, they can also support other features added by various manufacturers over the years.

Accessories

Manufacturers offer a number of accessories that can make phones even more convenient to use, such as hands-free options (headsets, ear buds, bluetooth hands free devices), extra batteries, and portable charging adapters.

Battery Type

NiMH (Nickel-Metal Hydride) and Li-ion (Lithium-Ion) are the two primary types of mobile phone batteries. Li-ion is longer-lasting and lighter, but more expensive. Many mobile phone manufacturers use lithium–polymer batteries as opposed to the older lithiumion, the main advantages being even lower weight and the possibility to make the battery a shape other than strict cuboid. Phones use more battery life during calls than when they are turned on but not in use.

Bluetooth

This wireless communications technology links compatible mobile phones, personal computers, PDAs, hands free devices, and other devices across short ranges. To ensure compatability with current devices, look for bluetooth version 2.0.

Caller ID

A feature that displays the name and/or number of the calling party on the phone's display when an incoming call is received. Virtually all digital phones have this capability. While typically only the number is received, most phones will display the name, if the number matches an entry in the phone's built-in phone book.

Digital Camera

Allows you to take digital photos and transmit the images wirelessly. There is often an additional cost to transmit images. Currently, the image quality is lower than what you might find in a digital camera.

Display

Mobile phones have a display device, some of which are also touch screens. The screen size varies greatly by model and is usually specified either as width and height in pixels or the diagonal measured in inches.

Some mobiles have more than one display, for example the Kyocera Echo, an Android smartphone with a dual 3.5!inch screen. The screens can also be combined into a single 4.7!inch tablet style computer.

GPS

Some select phones offer GPS, or global positioning and navigation functionality. This feature can be especially useful to those who often travel.

International Support

Travelers may want to investigate a world phone, compatible with the respective frequencies (GSM or CDMA or (Code Division Multiple Access)) most commonly used in Europe, Asia, and North America. Users wanting international access will want to make sure to research which networks are used in areas they will be traveling, as GSM and CDMA are not compatible.

Multimedia

You can download digital ringtones to personalize your phone. Other devices allow you to download and play MP3s (Moving Picture Experts Group Layer-3), and stream video. If you will be using multimedia functionality, you may want to consider purchasing extra storage space, an external memory card which can be inserted under the phone battery.

SIM card

GSM mobile phones require a small microchip called a Subscriber Identity Module or SIM card, to function. The SIM card is approximately the size of a small postage stamp and is usually placed underneath the battery in the rear of the unit. The SIM securely stores the service-subscriber key (IMSI) used to identify a subscriber on mobile telephony devices (such as mobile phones and computers). The SIM card allows users to change phones by simply removing the SIM card from one mobile phone and inserting it into another mobile phone or broadband telephony device.

A SIM card contains its unique serial number, internationally unique number of the mobile user (IMSI), security authentication and ciphering information, temporary information related to the local network, a list of the services the user has access to and two passwords (PIN (Personal Identification Number) for usual use and PUK (Personal Unlocking Key) for unlocking).

SIM cards are available in three standard sizes. The first is the size of a credit card (85.60 mm x 53.98 mm x 0.76 mm, defined by ISO/IEC (International Standardization for Organiztion/International Electrotechnical Commission) 7810 as ID-1). The newer, most popular miniature version has the same thickness but a length of 25 mm and a width of 15 mm (ISO/IEC 7810 ID-000), and has one of its corners truncated (chamfered) to prevent misinsertion. The newest incarnation known as the 3FF or micro-SIM has dimensions of 15 mm x 12 mm. Most cards of the two smaller sizes are supplied as a full-sized card with the smaller card held in place by a few plastic links; it can easily be broken off to be used in a device that uses the smaller SIM.

Smartphone (Palm or Pocket PC)

Devices, with computing, Internet, and networking features, are often referred to as smartphones. They combine cell phone and Personal Digital Assistant (PDA) functions, eliminating the need to carry two separate devices, but are larger and more expensive than standard mobile phones.

Speakerphone

Commuters and drivers who want to keep their hands free can buy phones with built-in speakerphone capability.

Text Messaging

Text messaging allows short text messages to be received and displayed on the phone.

Video Recording

In much the same way many phones can take digital photos, many phones also have video recording capabilities.

Voice Dialing

This feature lets users speak a name to dial a number instead of entering a number manually or choosing it from the phone book. Most phones with this feature limit the number of voice dial entries to a small number.

Voice Mail

A feature that supports audio messages from callers. Users can leave spoken messages for one another and listen to the messages by executing the appropriate command. This is often a standard feature that comes with a mobile phone service.

Weight

Mobile phone manufactures consistently streamline their products; however, some phones are heavier and more awkward than others. Smartphones, combining PDA and phone features, are slightly heavier than the average mobile phone. And smaller is not always better; for instance, most users would not want to surf the Web on a postage-stamp sized display.

9.2.1 Five types of Mobile Devices

Today, powerful mobile devices are more powerful than ever, and are becoming increasingly important for software developers and websites. There are several common types of mobile devices.

Personal Digital Assistant (PDA)

A PDA is a small handheld computer with a touch-screen interface. A small pen-like device called a stylus is generally used to interact with the screen. Some of the activities that a typical PDA can perform include browsing the Web, working with office documents and spreadsheets, reading e-mail and playing games. In the late 2000s, most PDA models without mobile phone capabilities were phased out in favor of "smartphones," mobile phones with PDA features.

Mobile Phone

A mobile phone is a telephone that uses cellular radio networks to send and receive communication rather than physical phone lines. In addition to being used for telephone communications, most mobile phones have the ability to send and receive short text messages called Short Message Service (SMS) messages. Many modern phones have touch screen interfaces and can run software like a PDA.

Global Positioning Satellite (GPS) Receiver

GPS uses a network of satellites orbiting around the Earth for navigation and location finding. A GPS receiver has a small internal antenna and searches automatically for signals from GPS satellites when the user turns it on. Once a GPS receiver has signal from at least three satellites, it uses triangulation to determine your location. Many GPS receivers have screens and mapping software that you can use to find directions while driving. Others connect to laptop computers and PDAs via USB (Universal Serial Bus) or Bluetooth.

Portable Game Console

A portable game console is a mobile device designed primarily for playing games. Portable game consoles use cartridges, memory cards, optical disks and downloaded files for game storage, and have buttons, directional pads, thumb sticks or touch screens for control. Although games are the primary use for portable game consoles, many have other functions, such as Web browsing and viewing movies.

Media Player

A media player is a mobile device that is primarily used for playing music and videos. Increasingly, manufacturers have added functionality to media players to make them more like PDAs. Some media players might include cameras or have the ability to run applications and games.

9.3 SMARTPHONES

A smartphone is basically a mobile phone with numerous additional features that extend its functionality. A smartphone provides all of the functions of a standard cell phone. In addition, a smartphone supports e-mail and Web browsing capabilities as well as word processing, office productivity and collaboration applications. Smartphones typically come equipped with a full-featured QWERTY keyboard as well as touch-screen and voice-activated controls to enable easy data input. Most smartphones can also incorporate relatively high-resolution cameras, video recording capabilities and robust audio playback functions (See Figure 9.2).

Figure 9.2 Smartphone

The first smartphone was released by IBM (International Business Machines) in 1992 and was called the Simon. It was the first mobile phone to feature support for capabilities, such as e-mail, calendaring and word processing. However, it was not until Ericsson released its R380 model in 2000 that the term smartphone was first used to describe a mobile phone with extended capabilities. Since then, the term is broadly applied to a range of mobile communication devices including PDAs, such as the BlackBerry and the Palm.

Smartphones have their own operating systems and are capable of hosting mobile versions of applications that typically run on standard desktop and notebook computers. The most popular smartphone operating systems include Symbian, the BlackBerry OS, iPhone and Windows Mobile. In addition to these established vendors, Google recently entered the smartphone market with the release of its Google Android mobile platform.

From a functionality standpoint, high-end smartphones allow users to perform most of same tasks that they would be able to perform on a full-featured (Personal Computer) PC. Smartphones can typically be synced with Windows or Macintosh computers. This allows data from the computer to be easily transferred to the smartphone or vice versa. This capability is extremely useful for backing-up data from a smartphone or for downloading data, such as e-mail contact lists and phone books from a desktop or laptop computer.

Almost all major manufacturers of mobile devices today offer smartphone technologies. However, subscribers typically need to purchase a specific mobile plan in order to be able to take advantage of smartphone functionality. Mobile phone providers usually offer e-mail, Web browsing and other smartphone functions as separately priced options on top of whatever basic voice plans they may be offering. The subscription rates charged by service providers for a mobile plan for smartphones can vary substantially, so it pays to shop around if you want to find cheap mobile plans.

Multiple connectivity possibilities. A smartphone does not does not use solely GSM to connect to the world, but also brings you the Internet through 3G, Wi-Fi (Wireless Fidelity) and even WiMax connections. A smartphone also easily connects into a LAN (Local Area Network). Data transfer to and from computers and other devices, either simply through USB cables or Bluetooth adapters. VoIP (Voice over Internt Protocol) makes smartphones smarter, in the sense that it makes users save a lot of money on calls, and even make free calls world wide. It also adds many interesting features in calls that would not be possible with simply cellular communication, like call recording, voice mail, etc. Read more on using VoIP on mobile phones to save money.

9.3.1 Smartphone Operating Systems

The most important software in any smartphone is its operating system. An operating system manages the hardware and software resources of smartphones. An operating system designed with a user interface for the small touchscreens found in smartphones. The four major smartphone operating systems are iOS (iPhone/iPod touch/iPad), Android, BlackBerry and Windows Phone. Although more Symbian smartphones had been sold worldwide than any other, in 2011, Nokia switched from its native Symbian OS to the Windows Phone platform. Introduced in 2013, BlackBerry users were eager to try the completely revamped BlackBerry 10 phones.

9.3.2 Smartphone Hardware and Software

As long as we are talking details, let us have a quick look at smartphone hardware.

Some smartphones run on processors. Along with processors, smartphones also have computer chips that provide functionality. Phones with cameras have high-resolution image sensors, just like digital cameras. Other chips support complex functions such as browsing the Internet, sharing multimedia files or playing music without placing too great a demand on the phone's battery. Some manufacturers develop chips that integrate multiple functions to help reduce the overall cost.

You can visualize software for smartphones as a software stack. The stack consists of the following layers:

- Kernel–management systems for processes and drivers for hardware.
- Middleware–software libraries that enable smartphone applications (such as security, Web browsing and messaging).
- Application Execution Environment (AEE)–application programming interfaces, which allow developers to create their own programs.
- User interface framework–the graphics and layouts seen on the screen.
- Application suite –the basic applications users access regularly, such as menu screens, calendars and message inboxes.

9.3.3 Features of Smartphone

One of the biggest features of smartphones is their ability to make use of small computer programs called apps. These applications can perform a wide variety of functions for the user. Some of the features that can be found in smartphones, in addition to standard mobile phone services, include:

Web Browser

Smartphones are basically hand-held computers and, like any computer, they feature Web browsers. These browsers load and navigate Websites the way a typical computer browser would, although smartphones are sometimes directed to a company's mobile home page, which usually offers pared down features for faster downloading times. Most smartphones have a built-in browser, which is proprietary to the maker of the phone. However, recently major browsers have begun to develop versions of their software which will run on smartphone operating systems. This allows the user to choose what Internet browser they are most comfortable with.

Applications

Perhaps one of the most well-publicized features of a smartphone is its ability to use third-party applications, sometimes called apps. These applications include games, productivity tools, music services, e-readers, weather trackers and news aggregators, among others. Smartphones feature an applications store where users can browse, download and review both free and priced apps.

E-mail

Smartphones have helped to bridge the gap between personal digital assistants and regular mobile phones and therefore must provide features targeted to the business professional. Email capability is a must-have feature for all smartphones, allowing users to stay on top of their messages.

Larger Screen

Smartphones typically offer users a much larger screen than most other varieties of cell phones to deal with the Web browser, apps and e-mail. This large screen not only enhances the phone aesthetically but also provides a more comfortable reading, viewing and gaming.

Full Keyboard or Touchscreen

Regular cell phones usually have a numeric keypad that also can be used to type out letters, but most smartphones feature a full QWERTY keypad, a touchscreen or sometimes both. Because smartphone users are often heavy e-mail and Web users, a full keypad is a convenient feature, as well as a huge time-saver.

Internet Connectivity

The most basic feature of a smartphone is instant wireless connectivity to the Internet through the carrier's service. Most smartphones offer network-based Internet capabilities while many advanced models also offer Wi-Fi connections as well. This

Internet connection allows a user to check and send e-mails and surf Websites all on the wireless device. The various phones offer different Internet platforms based on the provider.

Global Positioning System (GPS)

Many smartphones offer the same GPS system that a person can get with a car unit. The phone works as a tracking device, allowing satellites to locate the user. Using either built-in maps on the phone or maps updated through an external server, the service then provides a mapping service and gives either voice or text-based directions.

Touch Screens

While many phones offer basic and slide out keyboards, more smartphones offer touch screens to both free up space and provide a larger display screen in its place. The downfalls to touch screens on telephones are smudging of the screen and inaccuracy of the sensors. While touch screens used to be simply about convenience, more phones use the technique to make it easier to surf through Websites, drag-and-drop items on the home screen and operate complex audio and video controls.

Synchronization

Many smartphones allow users to operate utilities like word documents and mail programs. One function of the smartphone is to allow the user to synchronize phone to computer. Most users can hook a smartphone into a PC with a USB connection to allow the user to update everything. Other phones are capable of wireless transfers using Bluetooth and other synchronization methods.

USB Connectivity

This is one of the mandatory feature which should form part of any smartphone. USB is a standard these days to connect to any other electronic device like a laptop or a digital camera. Smartphones generally do not have the USB of the same size as a laptop but they do carry a Micro USB and a converter cable to connect to laptop USB port.

Also, when you connect your smartphone and your laptop with this micro USB to USB connector, the phone's battery starts charging itself too. So, that is another great feature supported in many smartphones today.

RAM Memory

This is an important part of any smartphone. If you do not have sufficient RAM (Random Access Memory), you will not be able to run multiple applications. It should at least be 512 MB as per current standards.

Third party apps

No platform is so complete that it can entirely do without the enhancements of third party software.

9.4 TABLETS

The mobile technoloy is growing at a rapid pace and new gadgets, which are better and efficient than previous ones, are coming regularly in the market. A tablet computer, or simply tablet, is a mobile computer with display, circuitry and battery in a single unit. Tablets are equipped with sensors, including cameras, microphone, accelerometer and touch screen, with finger or stylus gestures replacing computer mouse and keyboard. Tablets may include physical buttons, e.g., to control basic features, such as speaker volume and power and ports for network communications and to charge the battery. An on-screen, pop-up virtual keyboard is usually used for typing. Tablets are typically larger than smartphones or personal digital assistants at 7 inches (18 cm) or larger, measured diagonally (See Figure 9.3).

Figure 9.3 Tablets

One of these gadgets is the tablet computer which is very popular these days. Tablets perform all the basic functions of mobile phones like sending and receiving calls, SMS, MMS and making video calls. They also give laptop like experience while surfing Web, creating and reading documents, watching videos or connecting through social networking because of their large screens.

9.4.1 How Tablets became Popular?

The tablets gained popularity after the launch of Apple's iPad tablet in 2010. Microsoft and Intel also launched tablets named 'Microsoft Tablet PC' and 'Intel Web Tablet' respectively in early 2000's. The Microsoft Tablet PC used the modified version of Windows XP and Intel's Web Tablet used Wind Rivers' operating system. It was the head of Apple, Steve Jobs who innovated the tablets and packed them with mobile operating system iOS, a longer battery life, Internet connectivity, stylish and sleek design, less weight and access to social networking and hundreds of smartphone applications. Steve Jobs presented the tablet in a cool and elegant way with very good features and performance. This is also the formula of the success of Apple's products. He launched the tablet under the name of iPad in 2010. Since then tablet's popularity is increasing day-by-day.

9.4.2 General Hardware Configuration of Tablets

Tablets are personal digital assistants with a capacitive or resistive touch screen and/or keyboard. The input to the tablet is given mainly through the touch screen. Keyboard are connected through USB port or wireless keyboard can also be used, some tablets have keyboard integrated to them similar to laptops.

Similarly a mouse can also be connected. Some tablets also have a stylus pen for better input through touch screen. The hardware of the tablet consists of a processor, RAM, internal memory, Graphics card, Keyboard, battery, capacitive touch screen, microphone and primary and secondary camera.

A typical tablet in India can have following hardware configuration: 1 GHz dual core processor, 1GB RAM (DDR2 (Double Data Rate 2 or DDR3), ARM Mali-400 GPU (Graphics Processing Unit) (graphics card), 3 MP Primary camera with 1.3 MP Secondary camera (optional), 8 or 16 GB internal memory and a 3500 mAh battery. The internal memory can be expanded with a memory card of 16 GB/32 GB. Their are also some tablets which allow the users to connect external hard drives and thus providing memory space with the computers. The hardware configuration of tablets will get better in the coming time and their performance will match with that of laptops and desktop computers in future.

9.4.3 Software Compatible with Tablets

The early tablets which came before the iPad had a modified desktop operating system or a primitive operating system. After the iPad, tablets became longer battery life. Almost all tablets in the markets have a mobile operating system which is user friendly and easy to use.

The mobile operating system enables the users to easily surf the Internet, use e-mails, read PDF documents and have hundreds of smartphone applications and games. It also let users get access to social networking websites such as Facebook, Google+ and Twitter almost anywhere and anytime. The most popular mobile operating system at this time is Google's Android operating system based on the Linux operating system. The Apple's iOS operating system is also widely used due to the large sales of ipad tablets and iphones. Many tablets also use Microsoft' Windows 7 operating system and Windows 8 will be used in the future Windows-based tablets. The future versions of Windows will be tablet compatible and can be used in tablets as well as computers. Apart from these three, their are few Linux/GNU operating system based tablets. Some companies like Research In Motion (BlackBerry OS) have also launched their own operating system for their tablets.

9.4.4 Features of the Tablets

Many companies are offering tablets with different cost and features to suit everybody's needs. The main criteria for buying a tablet is its performance and features, and design if you want your tablet trendy and good looking. Performance of the tablet means how well the hardware and software of the tablet works. If the tablet boots slowly and the applications are launced slowly then the performance of the tablet's processor is poor. Features refer to the quantity of hardware and software the tablet is offering. For example, a tablet having a 1.6 GHz dual core processor and both primary and secondary camera is certainly better than the one having a single core 932 MHz processor with no camera. The former is said to be better in terms of processor and camera features than the latter. When buying a tablet, one must first decide what features he/she wants from the tablet and what performance he/she expects from them. After that it's easy to choose from the wide array of tablets in the market.

- **High Quality Web Anytime and Anywhere:** The Web access speed is faster for its technical specifications and can be accessed from anywhere.
- **Connect via GPRS or Wi-Fi:** Can connect to the web either via GPRS or Wi-Fi like your smartphone but the bandwith and speed differs positively.
- **GPRS (General Packet Radio Service):** Embedded modem eliminates the need for external dongles and allow Internet access everywhere. Unlike the laptop or any other earlier portable devices, you need not to carry your USB modem to connect to the Internet as it is embedded with modem (in-built modem)
- **Wi-Fi:** Allows fast Youtube videos at hotspots. Do not have to get irritated or wait for video buffering and breaking video streaming or slow loading of video even through Wi-Fi.
- Fast Web access even on GPRS networks, across the country using DataWind's patented acceleration technology. No state barriers or network service provider barriers anymore to rely on connectivity speed.
- Web, E-mail, Facebook, Twitter and much more. Lots of Social Networking applications and easy to access options for widely used Web applications.
- High Quality Video Streaming and HD (High Defintion) Quality Video Playback. Having better and advanced video quality high-definition videos can be watched in its original pixels.
- Games, Full Office suite, Educational software and Over 150,000 apps. Like a computer, easy to view and edit documentation applications and educational oriented applications are available.
- Expandable memory up to 32 GB. It comes with 2 GB Flash memory.
- Use any other ordinary pen drive. Just like a PC the ports provided here supports any normal pen drive.
- It is a phone to make and receive voice calls. The uniqueness is that it is a phone having all other above features and advantages.

Internet Connectivity in Tablets

Tablets are just like laptops and desktop computers because it can also connect to Internet. Some tablet models have LAN ports to enable wired connectivity to the Internet. All tablets can connect to the Internet via wireless LAN and Wi-Fi. It is handler to use compared to Laptop, especially in Internet surfing because of its touchscreen interface.

All tablets have 2G Internet support and many new tablets also have 3G support. Their are few new tablets which also have 4G Internet support. These tablets will come to India when 4G is established in our country. Many tablets also have Wi-Fi and bluetooth support and almost all tablets have USB ports to connect USB or Bluetooth dongle to them for Internet connectivity. Many tablets also have HDMI (High Defintion Multimedia Interface) port to connect the tablet with HD TV (High Definition Television). Some tablets even connect with Xbox or Playstation to let the users enjoy games on their tablet screen.

Portability

Tablets are not as portable as smartphones because of its large size. Due to their lighter weight and thinner size compared to laptops, you can easily transport tablets with ease.

Large Screen compared to Smartphone

Smartphones also have powerful processors, larger memory, and greater graphics engine compared to older mobile phones. They can also play high definition videos considering the specifications of the smartphone. The disadvantage is the small screen size of smartphones compared to laptops or desktop monitors. Tablets are optimized also for high definition video playback. They have more advanced graphics capabilities than smartphones. In addition, tablets have larger crystal clear LED (Light Emitting Diodes) screen.

Storage Capacity

Tablets have larger memory and storage space compared to smartphones, so you can store more application and software in it. You can store more files and documents, presentations, videos, music, etc. You will have your personal files wherever you go and you can easily access them using your tablet.

Call and Messaging Functions

Tablets are also optimized for calls and messaging functionalities. Most tablets can be slotted with a SIM card so you can use a regular phone service from a network service provider in your area. Since tablets can also connect to the Web easily, it is also possible to use VoIP services like Internet call and teleconferencing. A VoIP service provider like RingCentral offers these features.

9.5 INTRODUCTION TO ANDROID OS FOR HANDHELD DEVICES

Android is an operating system based on the Linux kernel with a user interface based on direct manipulation, designed primarily for touch screen mobile devices, such as smartphones and tablet computers, using touch inputs. Despite being primarily designed for touch screen input, it also has been used in televisions, games consoles, digital cameras, and other electronics.

Mobile phone industry is not only developing in its hardware sector but the mobile phone software sector is where the development is being concentrated these days and the most phenomenal progress is in the mobile phone operating systems development. The companies are spending millions of dollars to get the best operating software for the mobile phones and it is a continuous process which also includes constant debugging and improvement in the operating system so that it never loses its worth.

Here are the top five popular mobile phone operating systems in the world:

9.5.1 Android OS

Two most common ones are Windows and Android. Android and iOS may be the top operating systems for tablets.

Android is most used OS for tablet computers. It can be found on various tablets, especially on slates. Operating system was initially developed by Android Inc. Company was sold to Google in 2005. Android operating system is based on a modified version of the Linux kernel. Java programming language is used for Android programs. A large base of developers is writing applications for this operating system. Due to its popularity and number of developers, a lot of new functionalities are added to Android devices. Primarily it was developed as mobile phone operating system. But lately it is widely used also in tablet PC computers.

9.5.2 Windows OS

Microsoft is not only ruling the PC world but also has invaded the mobile phone operating systems and has made a mark for itself and is one of the most popularly used mobile phone operating devices from among the many in the market today.

Majority of convertible notebooks and notebooks are equipped with latest Microsoft Windows 7 operating system. OS editions range from Starter to Professional. A fork of Windows 8 (Windows 8 RT), specially designed for ARM CPU (Central Processing Unit) has been released in 2012. Windows 8 for ARM processors features a similar user interface as Windows 8 for PC. Main difference is instant quicker boot of device.

Proprietary OS

Some manufactures integrate their proprietary operating systems into the products. Two of the most popular, Apple's iPad, BlackBerry PlayBook and HP TouchPad come with own OS installed.

9.5.3 Apple iOS

This is the operating system found in the iPad and iPad 2 and is also used in the iPhone and iPod Touch. The operating system beginning with iPhone in 2007 and was called iPhone OS. A different name became essential after the iPad was released and Apple announced the change in June 2010. iOS devices need to be synchronized with PC or Mac to download music and videos. iOS' identity is through its grid-like layout which has been in place of iPhone. By default, the bar at the bottom of the iPad's screen includes the icon for your browser, mail, photos and music, though you can replace these with any icon you like.

The latest iOS version is 4. It introduced folders to the OS so you can group icons and you can move icons between different home screens should you have enough apps downloaded. You're also able to completely configure your iPad through iTunes including the position of the apps and the apps you currently have installed on your iPad. Operating system updates are also available through iTunes.

All of the new Android tablets are running version 3.0 of the software. This 'Honeycomb' has been designed with tablets, rather than modified from a phone OS. Tablets, such as the Motorola Xoom and Samsung Galaxy Tab 10.1 use Honeycomb. Some tablets released with older versions of Android. The HTC (High-Tech Computer) Flyer tablet to run Android 2.4.

Android's big difference to iOS is that it does not connected to a PC or Mac for updates. Everything, is controlled online via Wi-Fi using Google. Google Account is associated with your device. The advantage is that, if you lose your tablet, everything is backed up. The disadvantage is that Google has all the information from your contact details to your latest e-mails. All your information safeguarded by Google's Privacy Policy.

9.5.4 webOS

There are two other tablet operating systems. The first is inside the BlackBerry PlayBook, called the BlackBerry Tablet OS. The second is HP's tablet OS, called webOS.

webOS started in 2009 Palm Pre smartphone and, HP bought Palm in 2010 and it would be using webOS devices. The HP TouchPad is the first tablet form - webOS 3.0. webOS uses touch in a similar way to the iPad, but application windows run in separate called cards. This means you can flick between different app screens - perhaps a Web pages and an open e-mail - all of which are displayed on 'cards'.

You move between these on the screen by flicking from left to right or from right to left on the screen to cycle through the open cards, while you can close anything by flicking the card off the screen. There are not huge numbers of apps at the moment, but HP says they will only grow in number (See Figure 9.4).

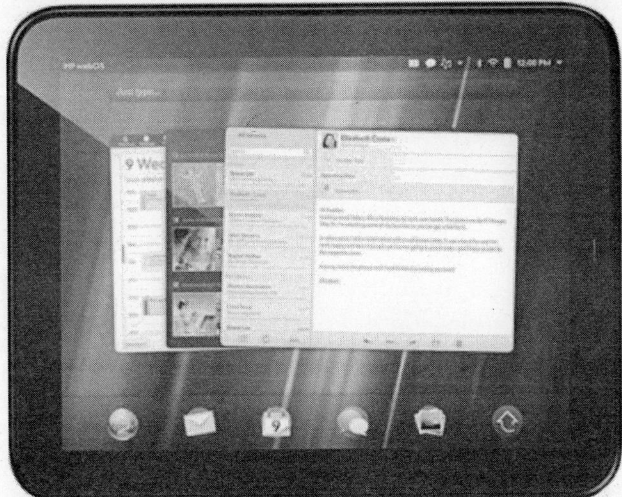

Figure 9.4 webOS

Apps can be started from a Launcher which displays all your apps, while there's also a Quick Launch bar for popular apps at the bottom of the screen.

When changing the orientation of the tablet it does not respond instantly. There is a pause with Android 3.0 Honeycomb, but the TouchPad takes a lot longer.

9.5.5 BlackBerry Tablet OS

The new BlackBerry Playbook by RIM (Research in Motion), and BlackBerry Tablet OS is integrates with the hardware like tablet. The Playbook's bezel packs hidden secrets. Swiping your finger from the edge of the device, across the bezel and onto the screen will bring up all manner of options and features, depending on which side you choose to swipe from and which app you are using.

For instance, in the web browser, a swipe from the top down pulls down the tab menu where you can either switch to another tab or open a new one. There is also great multitasking with the Playbook - far better than in iOS, for example. There's no doubt that, while it's probably a more business-orientated tablet to fit in with Blackberry's core audience, the Playbook is a pretty handy entertainment machine to boot with HD video support (See Figure 9.5).

Tablet Forms

Tablet computers are available in variety of forms. To make comparison charts easier to read, we divided all tablet PCs into two main categories:

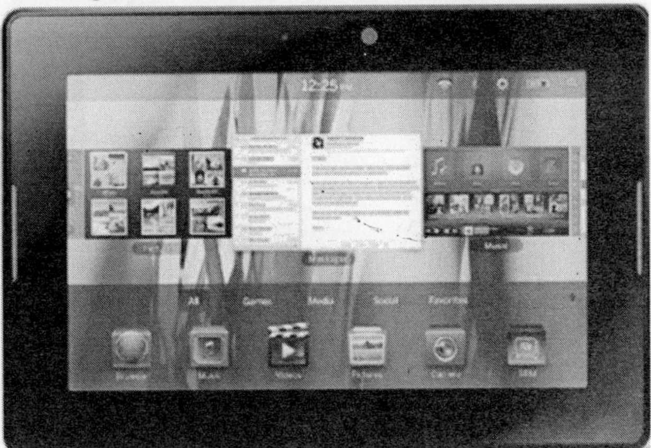

Figure 9.5 BlackBerry

Slates–Slate tablet pc's got their name from writing slates, since they reassemble their form and a manner how to use them. The main difference from other forms of tablet computers is that they don't have a dedicated keyboard. Instead a touch screen keyboard or stylus is used to interact with computer. Lately this is a prevailing form of tablet PC computers. As a matter of fact, nowadays a term "slate tablet PC", is simply shortened to tablet (See Figure 9.6).

Figure 9.6 Slate Form Tablets

Hybrids–Tablets are new technology hence new forms are emerging. Latest trend are hybrid tablets. In short these are tablets with keyboard. Keyboard can be integrated into tablet or detachable, hence hybrid tablets can be further divided into:

Detachables–Tablet and keyboard are two separate parts and can be usually bought separated. Together they form a laptop like portable computer. Optional detachable keyboard serves as input device, docking station and can also provide additional battery for tablet (See Figure 9.7).

Figure 9.7 Detachable Form

Convertibles–Keyboard is integrated into tablet and can not be detached. Keyboard or display can slide, flip, rotate or twist in order to convert from laptop into tablet (See Figure 9.8).

Figure 9.8 Convertibles Form

Other forms–Beside these two prevailing forms others less typical can be found.

Rugged tablets are one of these. They were used for data acquisition on terrain. Rugged tablets have touch screen and usually come with stylus and integrated buttons for navigation and other dedicated tasks.

Convertible laptops are another reincarnation of tablets. They are considered to be predecessors of current tablets. Convertible laptops can be notebooks or notebooks with touch screen capability and a special construction which permits to fold them around a swivel.

Booklets are another special form of tablets. These are dual screen tablets that can be folded like a book.

Tablet PC Screen

Touch screen technology has brought about a revolution in the new-age and broadcast media industries and is now widely adopted by Television, computer, mobile phones and camera manufacturers. Tablet computers are among the most visible manifestations of this technology and are seen as a possible replacement for regular desktops and laptops in the foreseeable future.

Majority of the tablets are available in 2 sizes: 7 inch and 10 inch. Some tablet manufacturers make also 8 inch and 9 inch tablets. Few models can be found with large than 10 inch display sizes, in majority these are Windows based tablet computers.

Display Resolution

Screen resolutions vary according to the manufacturer and the price range in which the tablet is sold. From the QXGA (Quad eXtended Graphics Array) resolution on the New IPad to the WVGA (Wide Video Graphics Array) or resolution that is found in the most basic models, there is a wide choice available for the consumer depending on his or her personal needs.

Typically, the screen resolution can be categorized as follows:
QXGA: 2048 x 1536
WXGA (Wide eXtended Graphics Array) : 1366 x 768 or 1280 x 800
XGA (eXtended Graphics Array): 1024 x 768
WSVGA (Wide Super Video Graphics Adapter) : 1024 x 600
WVGA: 800 x 600

Tablets of smaller sizes such as the 7 inch can do well with a lower resolution screen. Higher screen resolution becomes relevant as the tablet size increases.

Screen coating, Brightness and Protection

Since tablets are highly portable devices, they are widely used indoors and outdoors. While screen brightness is not really an issue when used indoors, these tablets can become highly reflective in outdoor daylight conditions and therefore needs the screen brightness to offset the ambient brightness. Most manufacturers have overcome the problem by using a coating that prevents glare while also protecting the glass from scratches and dirt. If your tablet display is protected using a toughened glass, such as Gorilla Glass, the chances of screen cracking due to the tablet accidentally falling on the ground is minimized.

Screen Viewing Angles

While this may not be a major concern if you are using the tablet as a handheld device, screen dimming and colour change can be an irritant if you are placing the tablet on a stand or keeping it on a table for people around you to see. This problem is normally found in LCD (Liquid Crystal Displays) displays made using TN (Twisted Nematic) technology. Colours like red, blue or green become darker and the screen becomes dimmer as you move away from the centre of the screen. Make sure that you get to test this out on a demo piece at the retailer before you choose your tablet. Most modern tablets do not use the TN technology in their LCD display.

Screen Technology

There are 2 prominent TFT (Thin Film Transistor) LCD Screen technologies available today. Plane to Line Switching or PLS is a relatively new LCD technology and was developed by Samsung in Korea and has lower manufacturing costs as compared to other LCD technologies. In-Plane Switching or IPS technology was developed in Japan in response to the viewing angle problems caused by LCDs-based on twisted nematic display technology. IPS LCD screens have almost no viewing angle color changes.

Battery Capacity

Battery capacity is nothing but the amount of charge it can store something like the fuel capacity in your car. It is usually measured in Ah or Ampere Hours. However, in the case of tablets, most manufacturers rate in mAh or milli ampere hour. For example, the Samsung Galaxy Tab 10.1 battery is rated 7000 mAh. The battery is likely to last a lot longer with higher mAh. In addition to mAh ratings, most manufacturers also provide additional battery consumption information, such as video play, audio play back and standby time.

Power Consumption

Continuing with the same analogy of car and its fuel capacity, your car is likely to give a better mileage if you drive it on lower revs, accelerate and brake gradually. Similarly, your tablet computer's power consumption is directly dependent on how power hungry the various components in your tablet are.

Battery life benchmark tests

Most battery life tests will involve running videos continuously at bright screen settings or running graphics heavy game till the battery dies. Depending on the reviewer, there will be different methods of doing the tests. Since there are different test results including some that are regularly updated, it is best to go online and find out the latest results.

Battery Care - How to improve battery life?

Calibrating your tablet battery is one of the most important steps to ensuring longer battery life. Check your tablet manufacturer's documentation to see if there are any recommended methods of calibration. Battery calibration and maintenance techniques will vary depending on whether the battery is made of lead acid, lithium-ion or nickel base. One of the most popular and effective ways of calibrating your battery is to charge and discharge the battery completely the first few times and then ensuring that you discharge the battery completely at least once every three months. Once the tablet is completely charged, do not leave the charging cable connected to the tablet. As far as possible, keep the tablet in its ideal operating temperature range as it will help keep the battery performing at optimum levels.

Symbian 60

Nokia's phones are one of the most selling phones in the world and it has one of the most used mobile operating systems. It is not only Nokia that uses symbian OS but almost every mobile phone manufacturer has models which have Symbian OS. Out of the many Symbian OS produced, it is the most sought after. It has ruled the market for a long time and still is one of the most sought after by people looking for simple OS.

Mobile phone operating systems provide a lot to choose from and it is the user and his or her needs that define which mobile phone operating system they want to use and it is not that a single OS is ever going to satisfy the needs of all the users and so the variety in the market of business and technology is a much needed one.

9.5.6 Versions of Android

Each version of Android since 1.5 has been developed with a specific codename. The following names are used for the currently existing Android releases.

- Note that versions 1.0 and 1.1 were not publicly named. However, Android 1.1 was internally referred to as "Petit-Four".
- Android 1.5 released in April 2009. Code name of is Cupcake. The Features are Bluetooth A2DP (Advanced Audio Distribution Profile) and AVRCP (Audio/Video Remote Control Profile) support. Uplading videos to YouTube and pictures to Picasa.
- Android 1.6 releasaed in sept 2009. Code name of is Donut. The features are WVGA Screen revolution support. Google free turn-by-turn support.
- Andropid 2.0/1 released in Oct 2009 and its code name is Eclair. The features are (HyperText Markup Language) or HTML5 file support. Microsoft exchage server Bluetooth 2.1.
- Android 2.2 released in May 2010 and its code name is Froyo. The features are USB tethering and Wi-Fi hotsport functionality. Adobe flash 10.1 support.
- Android 2.3 Gingerbird Dec 2010 Multi touch software keyboard. Support for Extra Large screen size and resolution.
- Android 3.0 Honeycomb May 2011. Optimized tablet support with a new user interface. 3D desktop. Video chat and Gtalk support.

9.5.7 Features Available in Android

Application framework–It enables reuse and replacement of components.

Integrated Browser–It is based on the open source Web kit engine.

Optimized Graphics–It is powered by a custom 2D graphics library; 3D graphics based on the OpenGL ES 1.0 specification. Other features include **SQLite, Media support, GSM Technology, Bluetooth, EDGE (Enhanced Data rates for GSM or Global System for Mobile Evolution), 3G, Wi-Fi, Camera, GPS (Global Positioning System), Compass, etc.**

Messaging–SMS and MMS are available forms of messaging, including threaded text messaging and Android Cloud To Device Messaging (C2DM) and now enhanced version of C2DM, Android Google Cloud Messaging (GCM) is also a part of Android Push Messaging service.

Web browser–The Web browser available in Android is based on the open source Blink (previously WebKit) layout engine, coupled withChrome's V8 JavaScript engine. The browser scores 100/100 on the Acid3 test on Android 4.0.

Voice-based features–Google search through voice has been available. Voice actions for calling, texting, navigation, etc., are supported on Android 2.2. As of Android 4.1, Google has expanded Voice Actions with the ability to talk back and read answers from Google's Knowledge Graph when queried with specific commands.

Multi-Touch–Android support for multi-touch which was initially made available in handsets, such as the HTC Hero. The feature was originally disabled at the kernel level (possibly to avoid infringing Apple's patents on touch screen technology at the time).

Multitasking–Multitasking of applications, with unique handling of memory allocation, is available.

Screen capture–Android supports capturing a screenshot by pressing the power and volume-down buttons. Prior to Android 4.0, the only methods of capturing a screenshot were through manufacturer and third-party customizations or otherwise by using a PC connection (DDMS (Dalvik Debug Monitor Server) developer's tool). These alternative methods are still available with the latest Android.

Video calling–Android does not support native video calling, but some handsets have a customized version of the operating system that supports it, either via the UMTS (Universal Mobile Telephone System) network or over IP. Video calling through Google Talk is available in Android 2.3.4. Gingerbread allows Nexus S to place Internet calls with a SIP account. This allows for enhanced VoIP dialing to other SIP accounts and even phone numbers. Skype 2.1 offers video calling in Android 2.3, including front camera support. Users with the Google+ Android app can video chat with other Google+ users through hangouts.

9.6 CONCEPTS OF APPLICATIONS

Android is a powerful operating system supporting a large number of applications in Smartphones. These applications make comfortable and advanced for the users. Hardwares that support Android is mainly based on ARM architecture platform. Some of the current features and specifications of android are:

Android comes with an Android market which is an online software store. It was developed by Google. It allows Android users to select, and download applications developed by third party developers and use them. There are around 2.0 lack+ games, application and widgets available on the market for users.

Android applications are written in Java programming language. Android is available as open source for developers to develop applications. There are around 200000 applications developed for android with over 3 billion+ downloads. Android relies on Linux version 2.6 for core system services, such as security, memory management, process management, network stack, and driver model. For software development, Android provides Android SDK (Software Development Kit).

These are the basics of Android applications:

- Android applications are composed of one or more application components (activities, services, content providers, and broadcast receivers)
- Each component performs a different role in the overall application behavior, and each one can be activated individually (even by other applications)
- The manifest file must declare all components in the application and should also declare all application requirements, such as the minimum version of Android required and any hardware configurations required.
- Non-code application resources (images, strings, layout files, etc.) should include alternatives for different device configurations (such as different strings for different languages)

In order to understand the Android application architecture you need some basic knowledge regarding Android applications key concepts. Understanding these elements will allow you to control:

- application components
- application lifecycle
- application resources

These are described all these key concepts in order to highlight their role, utility and importance. The main characteristics of an Android application are:

- It is a Java application executed by a Dalvik Virtual Machine (VM); the Dalvik VM runs .dex files, obtained from Java .class files. It is optimized for mobile devices.
- It is distributed in an Android Package, which is a .apk file.
- It is executed by the Android Operating System (a multi-user Linux) in a sandbox. Each application has a unique user ID and its resources can be accessed only by that user. Each application runs in its own Linux process and its own Virtual Machine instance; despite this, two different applications can be assigned same user ID in order to share their resources.
- Critical operations (access to Internet, read or write contacts, monitor SMS, access GPS module) can be restricted or can require user permission, using the application manifest file.
- An Android application is represented by one or more activities (an activity can be associated with a user screen or window) and Linux process; an activity life cycle is not related to the application process life cycle; the activity can run even if its process does not exists any more (this is different than C, C++ or classic Java applications where an application has a process);
- An application can start a component (activity) from another application; the component is executed by its parent application process;
- An Android application does NOT have a single entry point, like the `main()` method in Java, C or C++ applications;
- SQLite

9.6.1 Components of Android Applications

The most important components of the Android application are:

Activity

- Represents a user interface screen, window or form.
- An Android application can have one or more activities; an agenda application can have an activity to manage contacts, an activity to manage meetings and one to edit an agenda entry.
- Each Activity has its own life cycle independent from the application process life cycle.
- Each Activity has its own state and it is possible to save it and restore it.
- Activities can be started by different applications (if it is allowed).
- Has a complex life cycle because applications can have multiple activities and only one is in the foreground; using the Activity Manager, the Android System manages a stack of activities which are in different states (starting, running, paused, stopped, destroyed).
- In the Android SDK is implemented using a subclass of Activity class which extends the Context class.

Intent

- Represents an entity used to describe an operation to be executed. It is a message transmitted to another component in order to announce an operation.
- Somehow similar to the event-handler concept from .NET or Java.
- An asynchronous message used to activate activities, services and broadcast receivers.
- Implemented by the Intent class.

Service

- A task that runs in the background without the user direct interaction.
- Implemented by a subclass of Service.

Content provider

- A custom API (Application Programming Interface) used to manage application private data.
- An data management alternative to the file system, the SQLite database or any other persistent storage location.
- Implemented as a subclass of `ContentProvider`.
- A solution to share and control (with permissions) data transfer between applications (i.e., Android system provides a content provider for the user's contact information).

Broadcast receiver

- A component that responds to system-wide broadcast announcements.
- Somehow similar to the global (or system event) handler concept.
- Implemented as a subclass of `BroadcastReceiver`.

Activity Life Cycle

The Android application Activity is one of the most important components (with services and broadcast receivers) of Android applications because it is related to the user interface. An activity is used to manage a user screen and is equivalent to the window or form desktop applications.

Understanding and knowing how to control the Activity allows you to:

- Use the Activity lifecycle to create, view, use and stop activities.
- Save user data before the Activity is stopped and restore it when it is brought back to the foreground.
- Create applications with multiple views or activities.

The Activity life cycle describes the state in which an Activity can be at one moment:

- ***Running***–The Activity has been created (`onCreate()`) and started (`onStart()`) and it is displayed on the device screen. If the Activity was used before and the application has saved its state (`onSaveInstanceState()`), it is resumed from that point (`onRestoreInstanceState()` and `onResume()`); in this state the user interacts with the Activity through the device input interface (keyboard, touchscreen, display).
- ***Paused***–The Activity looses the foreground position (`onPause()`) because another Activity is executed, like a dialog box or alert; also, if the device enters sleep mode, the Activity is paused; the activity may resume its execution (`onResume()`) and placed back to the foreground.
- ***Stopped***–The Activity is not more in use and because it is stopped (`onStop()`) is not visible; in order to be reactivated (the Activity already exists), the Activity must be restarted (`onRestart()` and (`onStart()`) and resumed (`onResume()`).
- ***Destroyed***–The Activity is destroyed (`onDestroy()`) and its memory is released because it will not be needed or the systems needs more memory; because memory management is an important issue for the Linux OS of the mobile device, the process that hosts the paused, stopped or destroyed Activity can be killed to release memory for new activities; only processes that hosts running activities are protected.

The previous image the Activity has multiple states with clear transitions between them only one Activity can be in the foreground. The other system manages the states and the transitions, not the programmer (not directly, because when you start a new Activity you implicitly change the state of the current one)

- `onCreate(Bundle)` –called when the Activity is created. Using the method argument you can restore the Activity state that has been saved from a previous session; once the Activity has been created is going to be started (`onStart()`);
- `onStart()` – called when the Activity is going to be displayed; from this point the Activity can come to the foreground (`onResume()`) or stay hidden (`onStop()`).
- `onRestoreInstanceState(Bundle)`– called when the Activity is initialized with data from a previous saved state; by default, the system restores the state of the user interface.
- `onResume()` – called when the Activity is visible and the user can interact with it; from this state, the Activity can go in the background becoming paused (`onPause()`).
- `onRestart()` – called when the Activity is going back to the foreground from a stopped state; after that, the Activity is started (`onStart()`) once again.
- `onPause()` – called when the system is bringing into the foreground another Activity; the current Activity is set into the background and later it may be stopped (`onStop()`) or resumed and displayed (`onResume()`); this is a good moment to save application data to a persistent storage (files, database).
- `onSaveInstanceState(Bundle)` – called to save the Activity state; by default, the system saves the state of the user interface.
- `onStop()` – called when the Activity is not longer used and not visible as another Activity is interacting with the user; from this point, the Activity can be restarted (`onRestart()`) or destroyed (`onDestroy()`);
- `onDestroy()` – called when the Activity is deleted and its memory released; this can happen if the system requires more memory or if the programmer terminates it by calling the Activity `finish()` method.

Because the state transitions are regulated by different calls to onXXX() methods. The Activity life cycle can be described by their possible calling sequence.

9.6.2 Android Application Resources

Applications use text strings, bitmaps, video and audio files to enhance the user experience. All these represent resources. Despite they are controlled from the source code as they are external resources and the recommendation is to externalize.

- Internalization is done by providing different languages and format user interface.
- Application portability is applicable on different devices.

Resources are stored in the res directory inside the Android project. In order to manage different types of resources, the project res directory contains specific subfolders:

Directory	**Resource**
res/animator/	XML (eXtensible Markup Language) files that define property animations.
res/anim/	XML files for tween animations.
res/color/	XML files that define colors and color state list resource.
res/drawable/	Bitmap files (.png, .jpg, .gif) or XML files that define drawable resource subtypes.
res/layout/	XML files that define a user interface layout.
res/menu/	XML files that define application menus.
res/raw/	arbitrary files in their raw format (binary or text files)
res/values/	XML files that contain simple values, such as strings, integers, and colors. It is recommended to use filename conventions for particular types of resources: arrays.xml (typed arrays), colors.xml (color values), dimens.xml (dimension values), strings.xml (string values), styles.xml (styles).
res/xml/	XML files that can be read by calling `Resources.getXML()`

All the resources from the res subdirectories are packed by the compiler. In order to facilitate the access and control of resources from the application code, the compiler generates a class, called `R`, that contains static identifiers used to reference each resource.

9.6.3 Some Popular Applications

There are more newest android applications which have been developing and publishing in the Android Market. But not every applications are usable and reliable for users. Some of them, are sometimes does not work properly as we need. To find a best application, we have to categorize the application according to our needs.

During this year, Android provides more than 200,000 android applications with 26 categories. But some categories are related to each other, such as Business, and Productivity. Both are from different category, but provide a related application. As you have seen in the Android Market that those categories are look similar to each other. So we are going to make it more simple and easier for you to see and choose one of the android Applications you may be needed. We give our recommended apps for each category.

WhatsApp Messenger

WhatsApp Messenger is a cross-platform instant messaging service for smart phones and selected feature phones that uses the Internet for communication.

This app is the most downloaded revolutionary communication app which says good bye to SMS. Now, you do not need to depend on SMS service to send messages to your friends and family. This app is famous for all Mobile operating systems. You can use 3G and Wi-Fi service to send messages to your friends. You can send and receive messages and share pictures, audio and notes (See Figure 9.9).

Figure 9.9 WhatsApp application

WhatsApp Inc. was founded in 2009 by US citizens Brian Acton and Jan Koum, both former employees of Yahoo!. The company is currently in the process of takeover after Facebook Inc. announced its acquisition of WhatsApp Inc. on February 19, 2014.

KakaoTalk

This is the some what similar to app WhatsApp Messenger and this is the number one Android app in communication category. The service is very stable when using KakaoTalk users. You can use a group chat with your friends. You can add and chat with unlimited number of friends in a group chat. You can play your voice note in any Android phone. You can add your friends with there id's or phone numbers. They added some new emoticons which can be used in both iPhone and Android OS (See Figure 9.10).

Figure 9.10 KakaoTalk application

Twitter

Twitter is an online socila networking and microblogging service that enable users to send and read short 140-character text messages called "tweets". You can do anything which you want from your twitter account like sharing links and media, sending direct messages to your friends and retweet, tweet, reply and receive messages and updates from them instantly. You can observe four tabs in this app which are timeline, @mentions, messages and lists tab. The app also suggest you to add people in your contacts who have a twitter account already. The interface is fast and attractive. You can shorten the links and notify the settings too (See Figure 9.11).

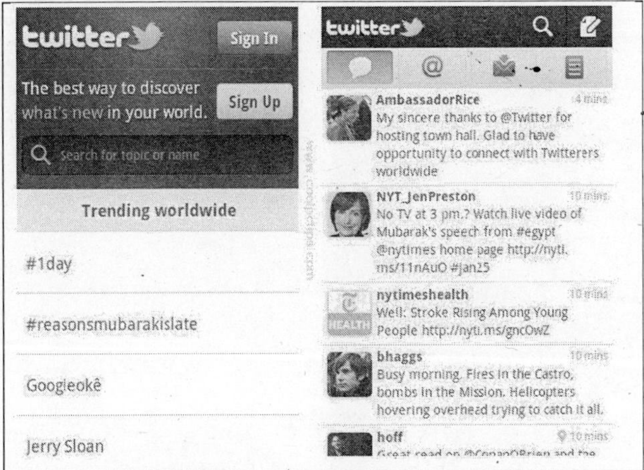

Figure 9.11 Twitter application

Facebook for Android

Now-a-days any person who does not have a Facebook account. People are so addicted to share the things with there friends. This app will allow you to stay connected with your friends and share info. You can share status from anywhere you want, you can chat with them, send messages, check your news feed, looking at your friend wall, upcoming events, user info and you can also upload pictures, watch videos and share links. You will never get a feeling that you are away from Facebook with this app. The app has some technical problems like its takes too much of time to load and improper login errors which have been fixed recently (See Figure 9.12).

Figure 9.12 Facebook application

Pandora Internet Radio

Pandora radio Web services are very famous in the past years and it has been a great success so far. Now Pandora radio has hit the android with similar expectations as its previous versions. This free app is a personalized radio service which streams music on your phone. Pandora radio can make a complete station of music according to your selected artist, songs or classical composers. The best way is to make your own account and create a station to keep your music preferences. You can even login to your station which you were listening lastly when you logged out. Its very easy to use this app.

Figure 9.13 Pandora application

Google Maps

Google Maps app is the most wonderful app which provides complete mapping for mobile phones. You will see at the information provided by various locations and places in your phone when you use this app. This app is a open source and anyone can add stuff to the app under Google's staff monitoring. The Google maps database has complete access to all the places for mapping and navigation. Some of the main features of the Google Maps are Navigation, 3D Maps, Places with hotspots, Compass mode, Offline reliability, Directions, Places page, Latitude, My location, Traffic, Street view, layers and etc., (See Figure 9.14).

Figure 9.14 Google Maps

Lookout Mobile Security

This is a award winning security app which protects your phone. This app is frequently app in the Android. It also protects your phone from newly found DroidDream Light malware effectively. The security widget will scan block and remove malware. You can schedule your scans and the database is very consistent which regularly updates automatically. You can make your phone ring, even if it is in a silent mode, and also you can locate via GPS from any browser if your phone is lost. You can also backup the data and restore them. You can access all your backed up data from PC. The best use of this app is its lightweight, Phone locator and backup options.

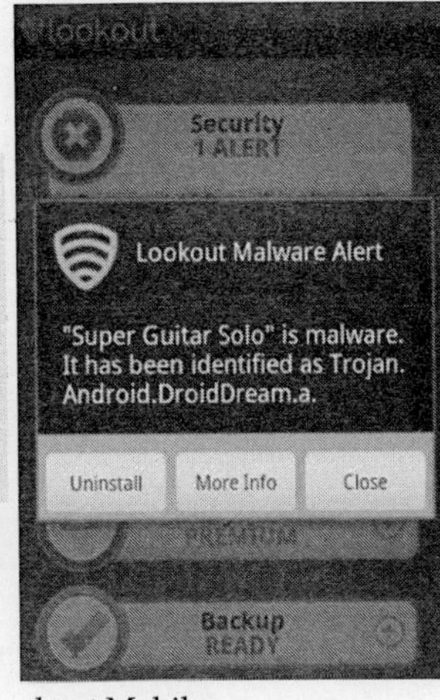

Figure 9.15 Lookout Mobile

The Weather Channel

This free app is considered to be most downloaded app in the category of weather widgets. You can exactly know what will be weather in the upcoming week too. The animated RADAR and easy to access options made the app more professional. You can also check the severe weather alert indicator which is really a good option in bad conditions (See Figure 9.16).

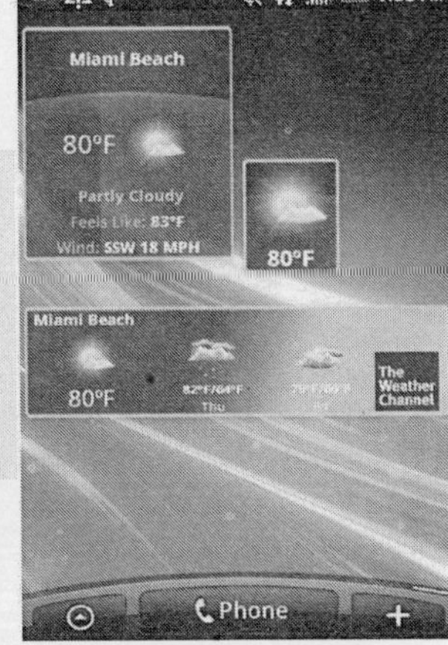

Figure 9.16 Weather Channel

TweetCaster for Twitter

This advanced twitter app uses a wide range of classic and new features of twitter. You can zip tweeters or twitter friends without unfollowing them. You can select a custom color for your tweets. You can post directly to Facebook and also you can manage two accounts at a time. You can also retweet with or without comments, and also create lists. This is really an excellent free app which gives complete access to twitter. The app is really easy to use and navigate. The few options of this app is integrated with tweets, Notifications, Offline tweet caching, photo attachment, tweet filtering and etc. (See Figure 9.17).

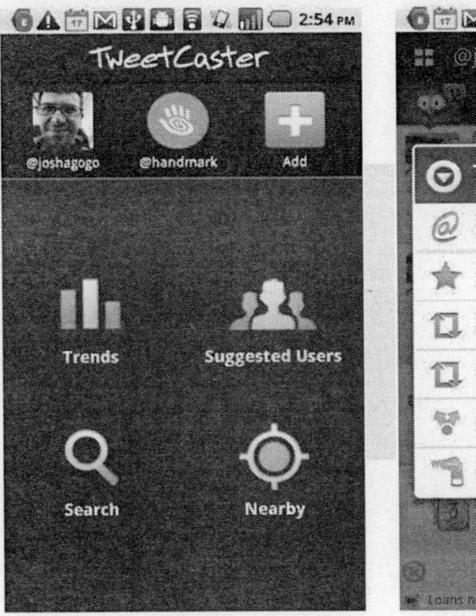

Figure 9.17 TweetCaster for Twitter

Antivirus Free

If you want to keep your phone protected then you must have this app. Very useful and powerful indeed. The app will scan all your apps, settings, files and real time viruses and malwares. It will also check those apps which will install later in your smart phone. You can backup and restore all of your data and also if you have lost your phone, you can track it via Google maps, the ultimate GPS. To assure security and privacy there is awesome option with which you can lock, wipe your data from the device immediately. It will also work as a task killer and end processes up.and also you can increase your battery backup. The 5 in 1 antivirus free has been so far the best antivirus app in Android (See Figure 9.18).

Opera Mini Browser

This app is considered to be the most downloaded app in the browsers category. Opera Mini compresses the pages with opera servers and make the page to download even more better and faster. It reduces the quality of images in page, we do not need to worry much about it. The Opera Mini shows 9 mini grids which we have visited recently. The browser bar can easily access bookmarks, favorates, downloads and settings from the (O) icon in the browser bar. You can also configure the font size, image quality, show/hide browser bar, status bar and etc. The browser will be really fast and it consumes less battery and less data (See Figure 9.19).

Dropbox

People always worry about there data and how to store it. Your data is stored on a Web storage where you can share and access anytime. The cloud computing technology which is used by dropbox. Data exactly is stored in the form of Web storage devices. You can backup all our data from this app to the cloud

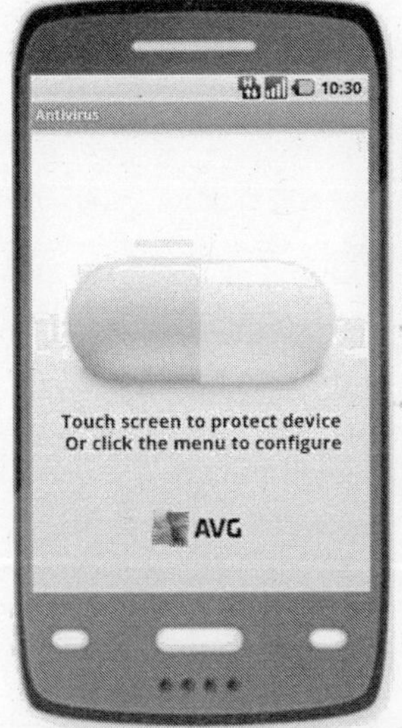

Figure 9.18 Antivirus free

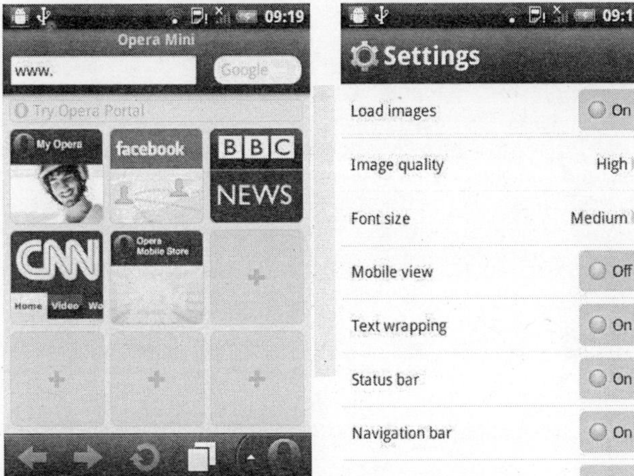

Figure 9.19 Opera Mini Browser

Figure 9.20 Dropbox

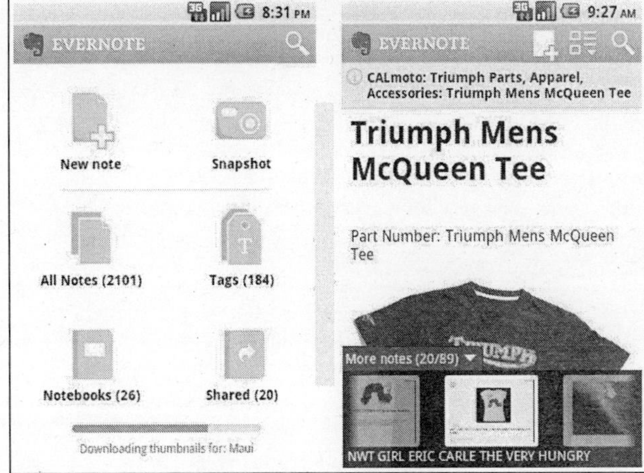

Figure 9.21 EVERNOTE

server of dropbox. You can save almost everything like contacts, photos, SMS, APPS and create a dropbox account where you will be given a free 2 GB disk space and an additional 250 MB for each friend you refer. Once if you have uploaded the data to dropbox, you can access it anytime and anywhere you want. Just login and access (See Figure 9.20).

EVERNOTE

Evernote is an award winning app which is really easy to use and very important to day-to-day life. Whenever we want to note something suddenly, we will do strange things like writing on hands or sending the message to yourself and etc. Instead of doing all such weird things, you can use a simple app which notes down all those brief texts, verses and the freaking ideas which we get suddenly. This incredibly useful app is very easy to use and simple to understand. This best app is very useful when you make a to-do lists while shopping or noting down a recipe and etc. (See Figure 9.21).

Paradise Island

This is really fun-oriented free excitement game for the people who love sea, sun and beaches. You can build your own sunny island of your wish. The game allows you to run your own business and attract rich tourists. In this game you can create your own empire. You can build Casino, Hotel, Entertainment center, Restaurant and Disco to entertain tourists. You can create your own resort and manage it accordingly. The rich graphics are very beautiful but be careful since it is an extremely addictive game.

Angry Bird Rio

This is a very popular game loved by millions of users world wide. In this game you can destroy the greedy pigs fortresses. Angry Bird Rio is an extension of its original game Angry bird. In this story mode, the other angry birds are caged and are shipped to Rio. They get very angry with this and want to take revenge on the pigs. You can find two friends Blu and Jewel fighting for there friends to set them free. The excellent game play will give a real film experience to the user. There are a total of 60 levels with hidden fruits and exciting gifts. You will love the game when you find the smugglers and take them out.

Paper Toss

Paper Toss game has been developed for the iOS (iPad, iPhone, iPod Touch) operating system. This game was developed by Backflip Studios. It comes with two versions: free ad-supported and paid ad-free. This Android game is generally set in an office. The player starts with flicking a piece of paper into a bin. In this setup, there is a fan running in the space, and as a result the wind track and speed are displayed on the platform. The wind track and speed are used to be accounted for when flicking the piece of paper. Players are scored on the number of times they pitch the paper into the bin before omitted.

Bubble Blast 2

Bubble blast is a game where there is a start but no end. you can play the games for ages. This game is a puzzle game in which we have to blast bubbles to trigger in a chain reaction to eliminate them. The game offers two modes. One is arcade and another is puzzle mode.

World War

This is a massive Multiplayer online game which is played by millions of people everyday. In this game we run with a good story mode of 2012 nuclear war which will create history and 5 countries will merge to become a massive force with superpowers in this war. You can battle with other players live. You can found millions of people playing the game online. Around 2.8 millions of player will be active every time when you login.

Jewels

Jewels is very simple game, but quite polished and fun match 3 puzzle game. The game is very addictive. You can complete with players all over the world. Global, cross-platform leader boards. The graphics are really neat and clean, the game is very smooth. The game has four different modes, Normal, Timed, Quick and Infinite and also the game is available for iphone.

Mouse Trap

This simple puzzle game is very addictive and very interesting. All you have to do is to find the way out of a mouse which is trapped. You can do it by sliding the blocks out of the mouse way and unblock each of the maze. You can unlock bonuses and gain coins as the game progresses. With the gain coins you can unlock various level packs and hidden features in the game bonus store.

Astro File Manager

This is the best application in Android which allows us to download any file which we want from any browser. We can Extract Zip Files, Create and Browse files. You can backup all your files to SD Card, Send file attachments Images, Text and also its the best way to manage the files on your phone without the need of a computer. You can also use the common commands like Cut, Copy, Paste, Delete and Move. The best part is that you can search your files whenever you want. You can backup your Android apps to your SD card and uninstall the app and again reinstall it when required.

AK Notepad

Ak Notepad will allow you to write whatever you want and allow us to send that notes via SMS or e-mails whenever you want. The app allows us to save remainders and also it allows us to keep the remainders in the Home page for easy access and you can sort the notes accordingly with custom titles with LED notifications.

Swype

Swype is a faster and a easier way of typing text on any mobile screens. You can use your phone stylus motion or a finger to type text. You can be able to type 40 wpm text with the help of swype. Works perfectly on phones, gaming consoles, kiosks, T.V, Virtual screens and tablets. The main advantages of swype are its Easy, Fast, Finger Tip Operation, Auto-Spacing, Input Slider, 50+ symbols, Auto Correction, 65000+ words English dictionary and many more.

Tweet Deck

Tweet Deck is an Android application which allows All Social Networking like Facebook, Twitter, Google Buzz and etc. You can Retweet and track your comments, likes and tweets in a ME Column. It has a Foursquare fluent where you can check your location and venue in maps. You can customize the sound, and light for each columns and also vibration. You can instantly sign in all your accounts with a single Tweet Deck App. You can also Speed dial your contacts and also you can control your messaging services.

VPlayer Alpha

This Android App will allow us to play different media formats in our phone. It supports Flv, RMVB, Divx/Xvid, AVI, WMV, MP4. The application will allow you to play almost all videos formats.

Task Manager

The Task manager is the best Android App which allows us to manage tasks, phone information, devices, SD card and etc. You can terminate the apps which are not working or not needed. You can uninstall bulk apps at a single time. And assign shortcuts to your useful tools.

K9 Mail

K-9 Mail is an open source and independent mail application for the Android operating system. The features of K-9 Mail include working with Internet Message Access Protocol or IMAP, Post Office Protocol or POP3, and Exchange 2003 and 2007 along with Web Distributed Authoring and Versioning (WebDAV) accounts. One of the unique features of K-9 Mail is that this application can be encrypted with Android Privacy Guard (APG) support which allows users to encrypt, decrypt, sign, and verify signatures for text, e-mails, and files.

REVIEW QUESTIONS WITH ANSWERS

1. Multiple Choice

1.1 The main components of Android are:
a. Activity b. Intent
c. Service d. All of the above

1.2 What is the driving force behind an Android application and that ultimately gets converted into a Dalvik executable?
a. Java Source code b. R-file
c. The emulator d. The SDK

1.3 Which of the following files specifies the layout of your screen?
a. Manifest file b. Layout file
c. Strings XML d. None of the above

1.4 The XML file that contains all the text that your application uses.
a. Stack.xml b. text.xml
c. strings.xml d. String.java

1.5 Which of the following is not a state in the life cycle of a service?
a. Starting b. Running
c. Destroyed d. Paused

1.6 What do the letters GSM currently mean?
a. Global Special Mobile
b. Greater System's Mobile
c. Global Systems for Mobile Communications
d. None of the above

1.7 The major operating systems of smartphone are:
a. iOS b. Android
c. BlackBerry d. All of the above

1.8 What was the first phone released than ran the Android OS?
a. Google gPhone b. T-Mobile G1
c. Motorola Droid d. None of the above

1.9 Android is based on Linux for the following reason:
a. Security b. Portability
c. Networking d. All of the above

1.10 Skype runs on a number of platforms including
a. Windows XP b. OS X
c. Linux d. All of the above

2. State whether the following statements are True or False

2.1 Google licensed some proprietary apps.
2.2 Muffin is one of the nickname of a version of Android.
2.3 Dalvik is a part of Android's native libraries.
2.4 A device with Android installed is needed to develop apps for Android.
2.5 Skype was released in August 2003 and it was created by Janus Friis.
2.6 The most important feature of a tablet computer is the touch screen.
2.7 Android does not make any assumptions about a device's screen size, resolution and chipset.
2.8 WhatsApp Messenger is a cross-platform instant messaging service for smart phones.
2.9 In 2006, Google purchased Android.
2.10 Android is built upon the Java Micro Edition (J2ME) version of Java.
2.11 Android is an open source operating system.
2.12 Tablets are typically larger than smart phone.

3. Match the following:

3.1	All mobile phones are designed to work on	a. Cell
3.2	Android is licensed under which open source licensing license	b. International Mobile Equipment Identity
3.3	SIM	c. Subscriber Identity Module
3.4	Cell phone networks are divided into specific areas called	d. Cellular networks
3.5	Unique number of the mobile user	e. Bluetooth
3.6	Sending and receiving pictures and videos through MMS	f. Apache/MIT
3.7	A consortium of various firms to develop open standrds fro mobile devices	g. Skype
3.8	It is a Voice over IP service and instant messaging client	h. Linux operating system
3.9	It is used as the base of the Android stack.	i. Open Handset Alliance
3.10	.apk extension	j. Dalvik
		k. Application package

4. Fill in the blanks

a. Capacitive	b. Slates, Hybrids	c. SIM Card
d. Multimedia Messaging Services	e. Android	f. Dropbox
g. Analog FM	h. Peer-to-peer, client/server	i. Martin copper
j. Data	k. Gingerbread	

4.1 ________ and ________ are available in a variety form of Tablets.
4.2 MMS stands for ____________.
4.3 __________ which stores information such as phone book, contacts that can be tranferred from one cell phone to another.
4.4 __________ touch screens tend to be less accurate, but more responsive than resistive devices.
4.5 Skype is a hybrid _________ and _________ system.
4.6 ___________ is the inventor of cell phone.
4.7 __________ is most used OS for tablet computers.
4.8 __________ is a file hosting service that allows users to create a special folder on each of their computers.
4.9 First generation of cellular systems, such as AMPS (Advance Mobile Phone Service) use _________.
4.10 A collection of facts in raw forms that become information after processing is called _________.

Answers

1.	1.1	d	1.2	a	1.3	b	1.4	c	1.5	d	1.6	c
	1.7	d	1.8	b	1.9	d	1.10	d				
2.	2.1	T	2.2	F	2.3	F	2.4	F	2.5	T	2.6	T
	2.7	T	2.8	T	2.9	F	2.10	F	2.11	T	2.12	T

3. 3.1 d 3.2 f 3.3 c 3.4 a 3.5 b 3.6 e
3.7 i 3.8 g 3.9 h 3.10 k
4. 4.1 b 4.2 d 4.3 c 4.4 a 4.5 h 4.6 i
4.7 e 4.8 f 4.9 g 4.10 j 4.11 k

Short Questions with Answers

1. What is Android?
2. What is MT SMS Message?
3. How to find your mobile model number?
4. What are the use of mobile phone?

Answers to Short Questions

1. Android is a stack of software for mobile devices which has Operating System, middleware and some key applications. The application executes within its own process and its own instance of Dalvik Virtual Machine. Many Virtual Machine run efficiently by a DVM device. DVM executes Java Language's byte code which later transforms into .dex format files.
2. In general terms, if you send any SMS message and if you get SMS response for that message, then the sending message is called Message Originate (MO) and the response SMS message you receive is Message Terminate (MT).
3. Detach the battery. You can find the Model Number on the label. Or you can also find the model number in the settings menu on your phone.
4. Mobile phones are used for a variety of purposes, including keeping in touch with family members, conducting business, and having access to a telephone in the event of an emergency. Some people carry more than one cell phone for different purposes, such as for business and personal use. Multiple SIM cards can also be used for local calls, long-distance call, international calls or roaming.

DESCRIPTIVE TYPE QUESTIONS

1. What are the advantages of Android?
2. Write the names of different Android version.
3. What is Smartphone? State three features of Smartphone.
4. What are the different type of mobile operating systems?
5. Name five types of mobile devices.
6. Explain PDA.
7. Name any five features of smartphone.
8. Describe Android application architecture.
9. Why to use Android?
10. What are the features of Android?
11. What do you mean by Tablets?

CHAPTER 10

Basic Networking and Internet

10.1 OVERVIEW OF THE INTERNET

Internet is an interconnection between several computers of different types belonging to various networks across the world. It is a network of networks. Millions of people use the Internet to search and share information and ideas, etc. It has grown into an important infrastructure supporting a widespread, multi-disciplinary community. This community now consists of students, scientists and researchers, large corporations, non-profit organizations, government agencies, and individual consumers.

The Internet is an immensely complex combination of thousands of technologies and dozens of services used by millions of people around the world each day. Figure 10.1 shows a Web of computers which is laid around the globe. The Internet links thousands of computer networks. Every network and every computer in these networks exchange information according to certain rules called protocols. These different computers and networks are united with the common thread of two protocols, i.e., Internet Protocol (IP) and Transmission Control Protocol (TCP).

☞ *The Internet is a computer-based worldwide information network. It is the network of computers connected with one another all over the world.*

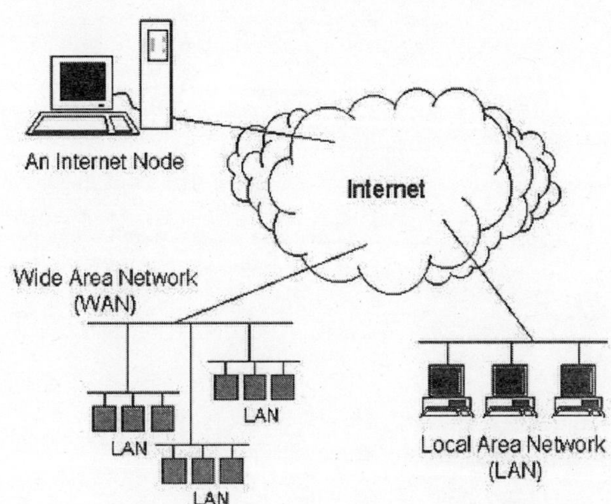

Figure 10.1 Internet: network of networks

10.1.1 What are Characteristics of Internet?

Internet has the following characteristics:

- *A Complex Network*–with the simplified definition as a "network of networks" that comprises of over 150 million computers.
- *Disorganized*–the Internet can be cumbersome and confusing, even for experienced users.
- *A Decentralized System*–millions of individual networks and over 140 million individual computers connected throughout the world.
- *Composed of Billions of Files*–files pertaining to thousands of subjects, disciplines, and professions are available in a numerous of file formats.
- *Widely Used*–more than 147 million people use the Internet, over 40 million of whom use it daily.
- *International in Scope*–this global network is accessed by people in approximately 140 countries; people in over 155 countries use e-mail services.
- *Dynamic*–changing every minute of every day. On an average, a new network is connected to the Internet every 30 minutes.
- *Expanding Exponentially*–the Internet is growing at a rate of 12% per month; it doubles in size every 18 months.

10.1.2 Advantages of Internet

The Internet provides opportunities and can be used for a variety of things. Some of the things that you can do via the Internet are:

(a) **E-mail:** E-mail is an online correspondence system. With e-mail you can send and receive instant electronic messages, which works like writing letters. Your messages are delivered instantly to people anywhere in the world.

(b) **Access Information:** The Internet is a virtual treasure trove of information. Any kind of information on any topic under the sun is available on the Internet. The 'search engines' on the Internet can help you to find data on any subject that you need.

(c) **Shopping:** Along with getting information on the Internet, you can also shop online. There are many online stores and sites that can be used to look for products as well as buy them using your credit card. You do not need to leave your house and can do all your shopping from the convenience of your home.

(d) **Online Chat:** There are many 'chat rooms' on the Web that can be accessed to meet new people, make new friends, as well as to stay in touch with old friends.

(e) **Downloading Software:** This is one of the most happening and fun things to do via the Internet. You can download innumerable, games, music, videos, movies, and a host of other entertainment software from the Internet.

10.1.3 Disadvantages of Internet

There are certain dangers related to use of the Internet. These are as follows:

(a) **Theft of Personal Information:** If you use the Internet, you may be facing grave danger as your personal information, such as name, address, credit card number, etc., can be accessed by other culprits to make your problems worse.
(b) **Spamming:** Spamming refers to sending unwanted e-mails in bulk, which provide no purpose and needlessly obstruct the entire system.
(c) **Virus Threat:** Virus is nothing but a program which disrupts the normal functioning of your computer systems. Computers attached to the Internet are more prone to virus attacks and they can end up into crashing your whole hard disk, causing you considerable headache.
(d) **Pornography:** This is perhaps the biggest threat related to your children's healthy mental life. A very serious issue concerning the Internet. There are thousands of pornographic sites on the Internet that can be easily found and can be a detrimental factor to letting children use the Internet.

10.2 ANATOMY OF INTERNET

Anatomy refers to the study of structure. While studying the structure of the Internet, it can be broadly said that the Internet is a network of computer networks. It brings together computers through the communication media and protocols. It also enables the computers to communicate with one another.

A study of the Internet outlines the following major components of the structure:

- Internet Services
- Elements of the Internet
- Uniform Resource Locators (URLs)
- Internet Protocol

All these are explained in detail in the following sections.

10.2.1 Internet Services

The Internet is a combination of many networks and a large number of databases and other services. The major services offered on the Internet are given in Table 10.1.

Most of the services can be accessed through a Web browser, such as Netscape Navigator or Microsoft Internet Explorer. Web browsers also provide e-mail as well as access to mailing lists (See Figure 10.2).

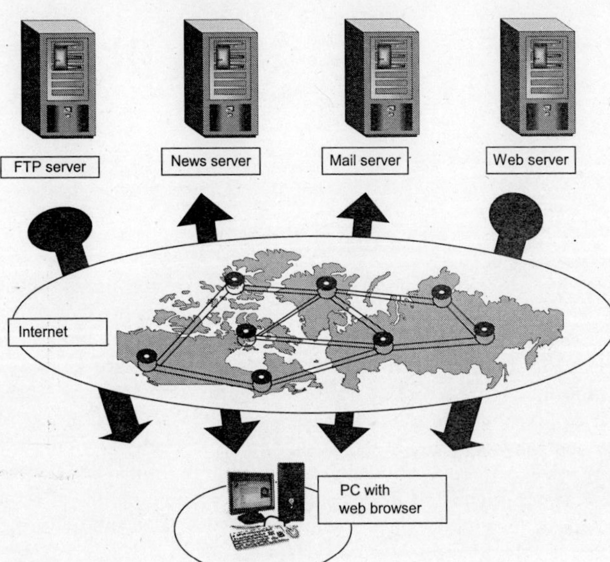

Figure 10.2 Internet services accessible with a Web browser, using Internet Explorer

10.2.2 Elements of the Internet

A simplified hierarchical model of the Internet includes client PCs (Personal Computers), server computers and networks (composed of both clients and servers).

Clients, Servers and Networks

Clients PCs–These are the computers that request information from servers. Client computers typically maintain intermittent (part-time) connections. If your personal computer has access to the Internet, it is categorized as a client computer.

☞ *A Web client is the requesting program associated with the user. The Web browser is a client that requests HTML files from the Web server.*

Server Computers–A server is a computer that holds the files for one or more Websites. These are relatively powerful computers with a persistent (full-time) Internet connection and can provide data to multiple client computers simultaneously.

Table 10.1 Major Internet Services

Internet Service	Started In	Description
E-mail (Electronic mail)	1970	E-mail is the most common service of the Internet.
Mailing Lists	1981	Mailing lists are a group-based messaging service. Once subscribed, you can receive mailing list messages via a standard e-mail account. There are currently over 90,000 Internet mailing lists.
FTP (File Transfer Protocol)	1973	An Internet service designed for transferring files among computers. Files are available for downloading on the Internet using FTP.
Newsgroups (Usenet)	1979	Usenet is a public messaging and "bulletin board" system. It comprises more than 34,000 individual forums, and each one pertains to a specific topic.
World Wide Web (Web, WWW, W3)	1992	This service features user-friendly publishing and multimedia documents and files. Web pages are created using HTML (HyperText Markup Language), JavaScript and Java.

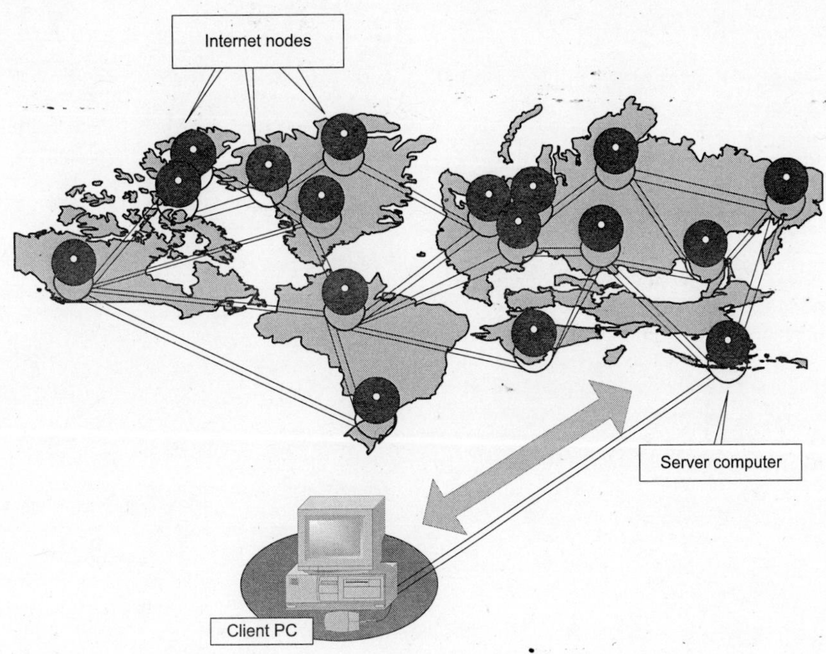

Figure 10.3 Major elements of the Internet: clients, servers and nodes

Networks–These are composed of one or more server computers and multiple client PCs.

Nodes–"Node" is a generic term used to describe a client, server, or network (composed of clients and servers). Figure 10.3 illustrates major elements of the Internet, which are clients, servers and nodes.

10.2.3 Uniform Resource Locators

Uniform Resource Locators, or URLs, are the unique addresses of Internet resources. A URL is divided into four parts as shown in Figure 10.4.

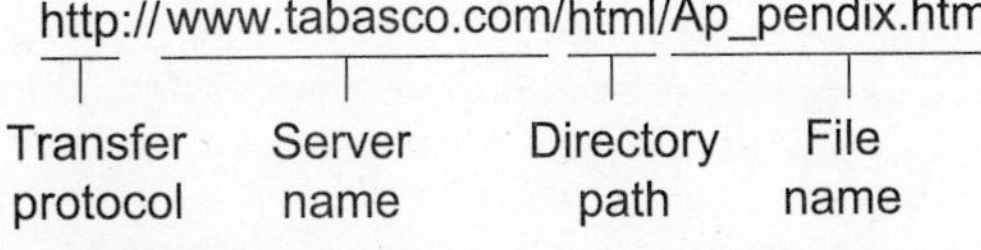

Figure 10.4 Syntax used in specifying URL

- Transfer protocol
- Server name
- Directory path
- File name

☞ *Be careful while typing a URL into a Web browser; a single wrong character in the address will give an error message or download the wrong Web page.*

10.2.4 Internet Protocol (IP)

IP (Internet Protocol) is a method by which data is sent from one computer to another over the network. Each computer that is connected to the Internet has at least one IP address which uniquely identifies this computer from other computers. All other types of protocols, which are used to send data on the Internet.

10.3 BASIC INTERNET TERMINOLOGIES

A simplified hierarchical model of the Internet includes the following basic terminologies:

10.3.1 Modem

A *modem* (short form for modulator–demodulator) is a computer peripheral that allows you to connect and communicate with other computers via telephone lines. When digital data are to be sent over telephone lines, the digital signals must be converted to analog form. The technique by which a digital signal is converted to its analog form is known as *modulation*. The reverse process, i.e., the conversion of analog signal to its digital form at the destination device is called *demodulation*. The process of modulation and demodulation, i.e., the conversion of digital data to analog form and vice versa is carried out by the *modem*.

10.3.2 Internet Protocol

A *protocol* is a set of rules for exchanging information on the Internet. Internet Protocol (IP) is responsible for the addressing and sending of data from one computer to another.

Internet Information Server (IIS)

IIS is a group of Internet servers (HTTP or HyperText Transfer Protocl) server and FTP server) including the additional capabilities of Windows NT and Windows 2000.

Transmission Control Protocol (TCP)

It uses a set of rules to exchange messages with other Internet points at the information packet level.

Internet Service Provider (ISP)

ISP (Internet Service Provider) is a company that provides access to the Internet. An ISP is one gateway to the Internet. In most cases, you connect to an ISP by using a PC modem to dial into your ISP's modem over a standard telephone line. Your modem connects to a single modem among a bank of modems at your ISP. This is called a dial-up connection. Users within corporations and large organizations typically connect to an ISP via a high-speed link (typically over fiber-optic cabling but not phone lines) called a *direct connection*.

Requirements to Make Your Computer a Part of the Internet

1. Internet connection
2. Modem
3. Telephone line
4. Program which controls the communication of data over the hardware component.

10.3.3 Internet Connection by ISP

Internet Service Provider (ISP) allows you to connect your computer to the Internet.

Internet connections are provided by Internet Service Providers who install a main server and through the server they give connections to users. Server is a computer with high storage capacity and memory. It is, in turn, connected to other servers installed at different places in the world through satellites. Connections issued through the server are allotted private place on the servers in order to store the e-mails for the connected user. Some of the ISP's are:

1. Tata VSNL (Videsh Sanchar Nigam Limited)
2. MTNL (Mahanagar Telephone Nigam Limited)
3. Reliance
4. Airtel

10.3.4 Internet Access Techniques

There are several ways to connect to the Internet. The more expensive services provide more features, more flexibility, and greater data transfer capacity. Different types of Internet Access techniques have been described below.

Telephone Line Options

If you are using the telephone system (old land-line) to get onto the internet your telecommunication connection follows either the normal phone system or an ISDN (Integrated Services Digital Network) or ADSL (Asymmetric Digital Subscriber Line), line until it reaches the telephone company's central office. The central office router calls to a long distance carrier's point of presence or POP (Post Office Protocol). The POP is the point at which a local call is handed off to a long distance company. The call is then routed to the central office nearest your ISP.

Dial-up connections through the telephone system

A dial-up connection is a temporary connection, setup between your computer and ISP server. A dial up connection is established using a modem, which uses the telephone line to dial-up the number of ISP server. The modem converts electronic signals to analog signals and vice versa.

☞ *In a dial-up connection to the Internet, you use a modem to connect your computer with the ISP's computers on your normal regular telephone line.*

Advantages

1. It is simple access to Internet.
2. It is less expensive as compared to leased line.
3. Dial up connection makes the Internet available to you as long as you remain connected.

Dedicated Connections

The most popular Internet access for companies and institutions is a dedicated phone line connecting your LAN (Local Area Network) to the Internet 24 hours a day. However, a dedicated Internet access requires substantial initial investment in equipment. The main continuing cost is a flat monthly fee for the use of the line. It varies with line capacity, and line capacity determines how many users can connect to Internet simultaneously.

In dedicated connection, the speed of direct line is very high. It is very fast but expensive.

☞ *Dedicated connections are also called leased lines. Leased lines are direct cables laid to connect your computer to an ISP's server.*

Leased lines

An inexpensive modem-based connection, which is set up only when it is needed, is the ideal solution for occasional user on the Internet. Running a Web server, handling a large volume of mail, connecting an entire network of users or, offering other information services require a permanent connection to the Internet and higher bandwidth than a normal modem can deliver.

The solution is a leased line connection to the Internet which is fast and permanent. Depending on your bandwidth requirements, ISP's can provide leased line ranging from 10 Mbps to 100 Mbps or more.

Advantages

1. The speed of direct line is very high.
2. Modem is not required for connection.
3. It is very fast but expensive.
4. A leased line is like a direct connection to Internet and is available 24 hours a day.

Broadband Connections

A high-speed Internet connection is termed as a Broadband connection. A channel may be broadband if it sends a signal without modulation on a carrier. The signal covers the whole range of frequency that medium can carry. It services at a high-speed Internet access of minimum 512 Kbps and upto a maximum of 100 Mbps.

A customer basically uses land line phone for providing this service. He/She can use his/her telephone for a normal telephone call even while he/she is browsing Internet. There is no separate telephone charges for the connection to the Internet. The access to the Internet will be around 8 times faster than a normal dial-up access. The advantage are:

(i) Cost (ii) Speed (iii) No setup time (iv) Always On

Dial-up uses regular phone lines to connect, whereas broadband uses a variety of other means. There are different types of Broadband service. These are as follows:

DSL Broadband Digital Subscriber Line (DSL) is a technology that delivers broadband over your phone line to be used in home or office. With DSL technology, large volumes of information are sent over a copper cable at rapid speed. DSL allows you to download Web pages, text, graphics, music and video in real-time.

Cable Broadband Cable is another broadband connection option, where the cable operator provides the Internet connection. It requires a special modem which is connected to the cable TV box. Majority of the cable companies provide packages which have telephone and TV channels as well as a broadband Internet connection.

Satellite Broadband Satellite is the ultimate option for people living in remote areas and who can not receive any other form of broadband Internet. It requires the installation of a special satellite dish. There are mainly two types of connections: one-way connections and two-way connections. In the one-way connection, you will be able to receive data, but for sending data, you will need a dial-up modem through a telephone line or IDSN line. In the two-way connection, data is both sent and received through the satellite dish, though it is more expensive. Satellite transmission may be affected by weather conditions. The cost of installing and running satellite broadband can be quite expensive compared with other types of broadband.

SLIP (Serial Line Internet Protocol)

This is the standard protocol developed for UNIX environments and that supports TCP/IP (Transmission Control Protocol/Internet protocol) networking over a serial transmission lines which is connected by a modem. It is an older serial line protocol that does not support automatic negotiation of network configurations. It has been replaced by PPP (Point-to-Point Protocol) because of the following reasons:

- SLIP supports only TCP/IP.
- SLIP requires the user to write script for automating logon process.
- It requires host's TCP/IP parameters configured manually.
- Windows 2000 cannot accept connection from SLIP clients.

PPP (Point-to-Point Protocol)

Point-to-Point Protocol provides router-to-router and host-to-network connection over synchronous and asynchronous circuits. It was designed to work with several network layer protocols such as IP, IPv6 (Internet Protocol version 6), IPX (Internetwork Packet eXchange) and AppleTalk. PPP frames can be transmitted over a serial transmission line, such as Old Telephone Services, ISDN (Integrated Services Digital Network). It includes LCP (Link Control Protocol and NCP (Network Control Protocol) for establishing, testing WAN (Wide Area Network) connections and performing modification in network communication using each network protocol. It is the supervisor of SLIP (Serial Line Internet Protocol), because:

- It supports IPX.
- Negotiates the TCP/IP parameters.
- Supports Password Authentication Protocol (PAP) and Challenge Handshake Authentication Protocol (CHAP) for sending your qualifications to the PPP server.

Wi-Fi (Wireless Fidelity) Connection

Wi-Fi is the acronym for Wireless Fidelity, essentially a set of standards for transmitting data over a wireless network. Wi-Fi allows you to connect to the Internet at broadband speed without cables, as long as you have the right equipment and, in most cases, a regular Internet service provider and a Wi-Fi account.

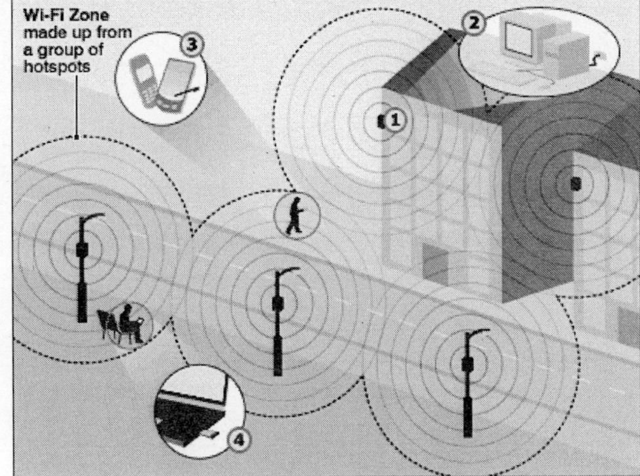

Figure 10.5 Wi-Fi connection

To understand the technology behind Wi-Fi, imagine using a walkie-talkie. Your voice is picked up by a microphone, encoded onto a radio frequency and transmitted with the antenna to another walkie-talkie, which decodes your voice. Wi-Fi works in broadly in the same way, but using a better radio that is capable of handling a lot more data per second (See Figure 10.5).

1. Wi-Fi uses antennas around which Wi-Fi "hotspots" are created. The hotspots are outlets equipped to receive the radio waves that power wireless networking.
2. The source Internet connection is provided by a PC or server to which the antennas are connected either wirelessly or via a cable.
3. Some mobile phones and Personal Digital Assistants (PDA) now have Wi-Fi chips installed. With mobile phones, this means conventional networks can be bypassed and inexpensive long-distance calls made over the Web (using Voice over Internet Protocol or, VoIP).
4. Many laptops and handheld computers now come with built-in Wi-Fi connectivity; it is also possible to add Wi-Fi to your computer with a special card that plugs into a port on your laptop.

WiMAX Connection

WiMAX is a new technology that promises to deliver high data rates in two separate frequency bands. The lower band is in the frequency range 2-11 GHz and the higher band is in the range 10-66 GHz. At the higher frequencies, line of sight is required as the frequencies tend to become directional at these frequencies. In the lower region, the signals will propagate without the requirement for line of sight. WiMAX is a point to multipoint technology that will allow for ad-hoc networks to be created.

WiMAX connection has the capacity to transfer large amount of information and it has large data transmitting capacity. These two definite qualities of WiMAX connection make it suitable for a number of purposes. It is used for providing connection between the points that allows Wi-Fi access. WiMAX connection is also a desirable option that enables convenient access of the broadband. WiMAX connection is a viable system which is also more affordable than broadband connections. (See Figure 10.6)

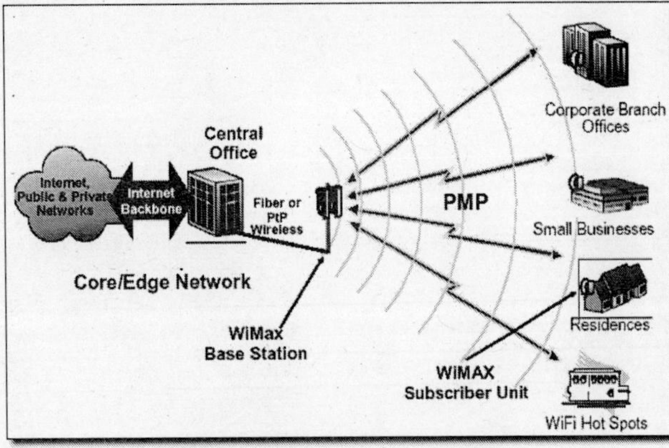

Figure 10.6 WiMAX connection

10.4 WHAT IS WORLD WIDE WEB?

The World Wide Web, or simply "the Web" is a global information system that is the fastest-growing area of the Internet. In other words, World Wide Web is a series of servers that are interconnected through hypertext. *Hypertext* is a method of presenting information in which certain text are highlighted, that, when selected, displays more information on that particular topic.

The Web, like all Internet services, is based on the interaction and transfer of data between special server computers (Web servers) and your PC (using Web browser software, such as Internet Explorer from Microsoft).

☞ *Different browsers may format and display the same file differently, depending on the capabilities of the hardware and the default layout options for the browser itself.*

10.4.1 Hypertext (Non-linear Information)

Conventional information systems like the text books present information on printed pages in a linear fashion. To read and comprehend a novel, you must begin at page 1 and read every successive page until you reach the end of the book.

Hypertext information systems, on the other hand, allow you to navigate through a flood of "information space" following any path of your choice. Hypertext, as implemented on the Web, allows Web pages to be created with links to any other page on the Web. This system allows you to choose from various links on a single Web page that typically leads to other Web pages at different Web sites geographically located anywhere in the world.

Hyperlinks

Hyperlinks, or *links* are Web navigation elements that allow you to move, or navigate, between Web pages. They also allow you to download audio, video, and other types of multimedia files. Web pages accessed via a link may reside at the same Website as the source link or at another site anywhere on the Web.

There are three types of hyperlinks.

- Text hyperlinks
- Image hyperlinks
- Image maps (containing multiple hyperlinks)

Functionally, all the three categories of hyperlinks are identical. Text hyperlinks are generally denoted in blue color and underlined, while image hyperlinks and maps are indicated by a blue colored border. In all the three cases, the mouse pointer will change from an arrow to a pointing hand when it passes over a hyperlink.

10.5 WEB BROWSERS AND WEB SERVER

The World Wide Web is based upon clients and severs. A WWW client is called a Web browser or simply a browser, and a WWW server is called a Web server.

10.5.1 Web Browser

A browser or Web browser is a program you use to view pages on Net and navigate the World Wide Web. Browsers are sometimes referred to as Web clients. A wide range of Web browsers are available for every type of systems you can imagine, including graphical user interface, and text-only for dial-up UNIX connections. Most browsers are freeware. All you have to do is to get a browser downloaded from the Internet. For example, Internet Explorer 8 comes free as part of Windows 7. The relationship between Web server and Web browser is shown in Figure 10.7.

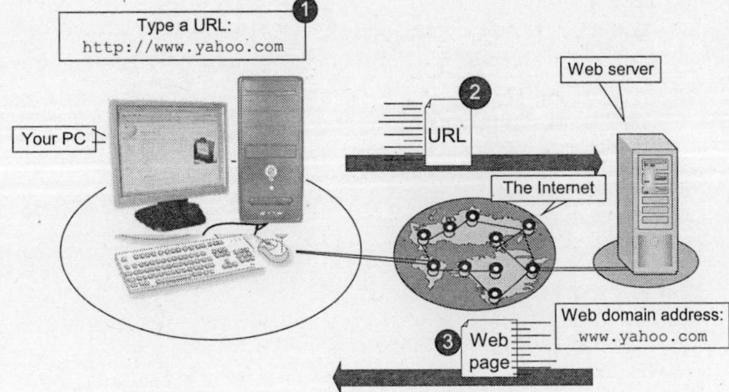

Figure 10.7 Relationship between a Web browser and a Web server

☞ *Web browser is a versatile, multi-function software package designed to access, download, and display multimedia hypertext documents called Web pages.*

Some popular Web browsers are briefly described in the following paragraphs:

Internet Explorer

This browser was made by Microsoft Corporation and bundled together into Windows operating system. The latest operating system, Windows 7 comes with Microsoft's latest Web browser named Internet Explorer 8. If you purchase a genuine copy of Windows 7 you will get Internet Explorer 8 for free otherwise it is free for downloading from Microsoft Website (**http://www.microsoft.com/ie/**).

☞ *Internet Explorer, usually is just called Explorer. Explorer runs on all versions of Windows OS and Macintosh, etc. If you love to browse the Internet without any hassle, use Internet Explorer available free.*

Mozilla Firefox

The latest official version of Mozilla Firefox is Firefox 3.6. Mozilla. Firefox has become popular because it is fast, full-featured Web browser and makes browsing very efficient. Firefox includes pop-up blocking, tab-browsing, integrated Google searching, simplified privacy controls. It lets you cover tracks more effectively. A streamlined browser window that shows you more of the page than any other browser and has a number of additional features that work with you to help you get the most out of your time online. This browser is also available free of cost.

☞ *Mozilla Firefox protects you from Internet threats while maintaining fast browsing, twice faster than Internet Explorer. If you prefer speed to come with style and additional functions, then use Mozilla Firefox.*

Google Chrome 6

Google built Google Chrome just for speed for any type of user to browse the Web. It has become popular due to its fast loading speed. Google Chrome designed with minimal-istic user interface. It is built with fast browsing engine. There is no task bar to display commands such as *File, Edit, Bookmarks* and *Help* as in Mozilla Firefox and Internet Explorer browsers.

☞ *If you prefer speed while browsing the Internet, use Google Chrome.*

10.5.2 Web Server

A Web server is the program that runs on a Website and is responsible for replying to Web browser requests for files. You need a Web server to publish documents on the Web. To avail the services of Web pages, Websites need "a host" a computer and server software that runs on the host. The host manages the communication protocols and related software required to create a Website on the Internet. The server software resides on the host and serves up the pages and otherwise acts on the requests sent from the client browser software.

☞ *In MHTML document, Web page archive format saved from a .HTML file and encoded with .MIME (Multipurpose Internet Mail Extensions) encoding and includes resources linked from the Web page, such as images, Flash animations, Java applets, audio files, etc; can be opened and viewed without being online.*

Types of Servers

There are different types of server software (database servers or network servers, etc.) that perform different types of services for different types of clients. Specifically, a Web server is an HTTP server and its function is to send information to the client software (typically a browser) using the HTTP. The client browser requests and the server return a Hypertext Makup Language HTML document. The server receives this request and sends back a response.

10.5.3 Website

A Website is a collection of Web pages associated with a particular person, business, government, school and organization. Websites are stored on a Web server, a special computer that makes Web pages available for people to browser.

Websites can consist of only a few Web pages or many humdreds of Web pages. For example Microsoft's Website currently offers over 250,000 Web pages.

Steps for connecting to Website are explained below.

1. Type the URL for a Website say **www.yahoo.com** into your Web browser.
2. Your browser attempts to make a connection to the Web server.
3. The Web server receives the request.
4. The Website Home page is downloaded from the Web server to your PC.
5. The Web page is displayed by your Web browser and the connection between the server and your browser is closed.

☞ *Website is a collection of information stored as Web pages which may be on one or more computers.A Web page is an electronic document written in computer language called HTML.*

10.5.4 Web Page

World Wide Web information is presented on Web pages, which you download to your computer using a Web browser, such as Internet Explorer. Each Web page can combine text with images, sound, music and video.

☞ *A Web page is an electronic document written in computer language called HTML. Each web page has a unique address, called a URL that identifies its location on the network.*

A Website has one or more related Web pages. Web pages on a site are linked together through a system of hyperlinks to jump between them by clicking on a link. On the Web, you navigate through pages of information according to your interests.

The first page of the Website is called the Home Page. The Home page provides an overview of what you will find at the Website. A site can have one page or many pages. If there is a lot of information, the home page may be the only page. But usually, you will find at least a few other pages.

10.5.5 Web Addresses

When entering a Web page address into your Web browser, you need to follow certain rules. For example, if you mail a letter via the postal service, you should write address comprising *city*, *state*, and *pin code* on your letter. Otherwise it will not be delivered. Similarly, the rules also apply when you attempt to access a Web page on the Internet.

Enter a Web Page Address

If you know the address of a specific Web page, you can type the address into the Web browser and the program will display the page. Internet Explorer's Address bar list the Web page addresses you have entered most recently. By pulling down the list you can see these recent addresses and select one to return to that site.

➔ **To type a Web page address, do this:**

1. Click in the address bar.
2. Type the address of the Web page. For example, we have typed http://www.gmail.com (See Figure 10.8).
3. Click the **Go** button or press **Enter**. The Web page appears (See Figure 10.9).

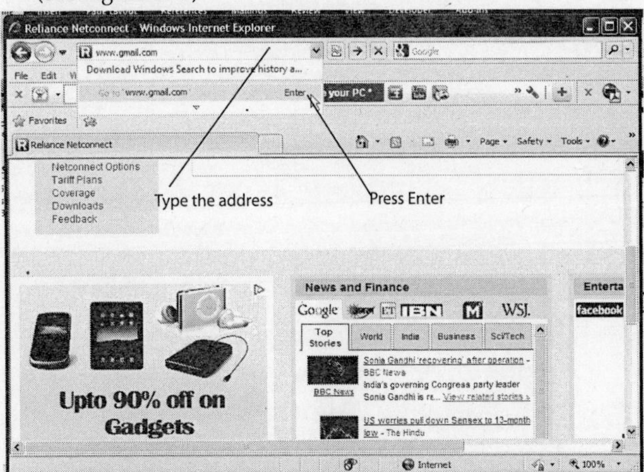

Figure 10.8 Type the address in the address bar

10.5.6 Domain Name Servers

DNS is known as Domain Name Server, System or Service. Its purpose is to translate domain names into IP addresses. Whenever we use a domain name, a service is used for translating domain names into IP addresses and is known as DNS. For example, the domain name www.computer-games.com might translate to 192.111.221.2. So what DNS did in above examples as it translated the Domain name "computer-games" into corresponding IP address.

If one DNS server does not know how to translate the particular domain name it asks another DNS server and this process continues until the correct IP address is returned. As in above example, if one domain server does not know how to translate www.computer-games.com then it will move to another DNS until the corresponding IP address 192.111.221.2 is returned. DNS scheme uses alphabets and it is easier to remember, but actually each domain name has an address and DNS scheme is used to convert this domain name into its corresponding address.

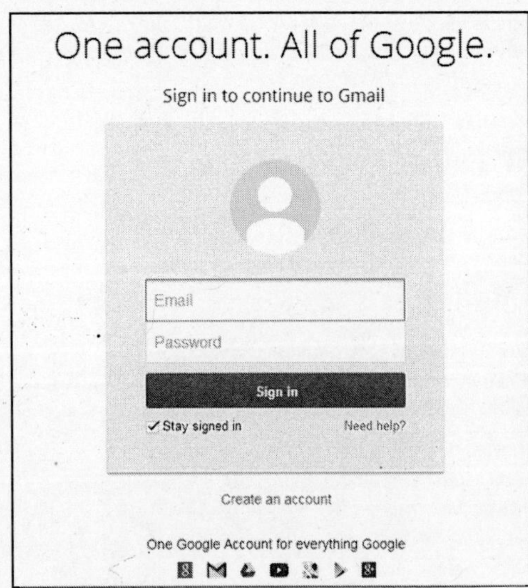

Figure 10.9 Gmail Web page appears

In the Internet, the domain name space (tree) is divided into three different sections:

(a) Generic domains
(b) Country domains
(c) Inverse domains

Generic Domains

The *generic domains* define registered hosts according to their generic behaviour. Each node in the tree defines a domain, which is an index to the domain name space database. The first level in the generic domain section allows seven possible three-character labels. These labels describe the organization types as listed in Table 10.2.

Table 10.2 Generic domain names

Label	Description
com	Commercial organization
edu	Educational institutions
gov	Government institutions
int	International organizations
mil	Military groups
net	Network support centers
org	Non-profit organizations

Recently a few more first-level labels have been proposed. These are listed in Table 10.3.

Table 10.3 Additional first labels proposed

Label	Description
art	Cultural organizations
firm	Business or firms
info	Information service providers
nom	Personal nomenclatures
rec	Recreation/entertainment organization
store	Business offering goods to purchase
web	Web-related organizations

Country Domains

The *country domain* section follows the same format as the generic domains but uses two-character country abbreviations (e.g., "us" for United States) in place of the three-character organizational abbreviations at the first level. Second-level labels can be organizational, or they can be more specific, national destinations. The United States, for example, uses state abbreviations as a subdivision of "us" (e.g., ca.us.).

Inverse Domain

The *inverse domain* is used to map an address to a name. This may happen, for example, when a server has received a request from a client to do a task. Whereas the server has a file that contains a list of authorized clients, the server lists only the IP address of the client (extracted from the received IP packet). To determine if the client is on the authorized list, it can send a query to the DNS server and ask for a mapping of address to name.

10.6 E-MAIL

E-mail is a method of sending messages, voice, video and graphics over digital communication link, such as the Internet, anywhere in the world at cost-effective rates. Technically, e-mail is a type of client/server application that provides a routed, stored message service between any two e-mail accounts. Because all modern computers can be connected to the Internet, users can send e-mail over the Internet to any location that has telephone or wireless digital service.

☞ *The backbone of an electronic mail system is communications network that connects remote terminals to a central system or a LAN that interconnects personal computers. Users can send mail to a single recipient or broadcast it to any number of selected users on the system.*

There are two broad procedures available for e-mail.

- Subscribe to e-mail service, such as Hotmail, Rediffmail, etc.
- Install your own e-mail server on the Internet.

The first option is not advisable for business setups due to the following reasons:

- E-mail belonging to your business may be carrying someone else's advertisement.
- Your name might be used by someone else. It means that your mail is not safe.

However, the following are some advantages of using this method:

- Administering your own e-mail setup is avoided.
- When the number of messages are small, an exclusive setup for e-mail is not cost-effective.
- Your e-mail address does not identify you. So it may not be easy for the sender to locate you thus saving you from receiving *junk* or useless mail called spams.

The advantages of setting up your own e-mail server are as follows:

- You can host your Web pages as well as run your mail server.
- The initial cost of setting up your own mail server may be high but as the volume of e-mail messages increases, the overheads may not go up. Therefore, the price you pay per message will come down.

The following steps are required for sending an e-mail:

1. Start an e-mail program on your PC.
2. Write the address of the e-mail recipient.
3. Compose a message.
4. Click on the Send button to send your message.

10.6.1 Advantages of E-mail

Speed: An e-mail is a quicker means of correspondence than ordinary postal system. A message can reach any part of the world in a fraction of a second.

Content: The message may consist of only a few lines of text or of several hundred lines. Unlike the postal service, the message is not charged by weight.

Cost: E-mail is an extremely cost-effective way to move information quickly. A three-page letter to U.S.A can cost Rupee 400 through courier, or about Rupee 100 through fax. The same letter can be sent by e-mail for the cost of one local call.

Ease of use: It is easy to send an e-mail than a letter through a normal postal system. In postal system, we have to write a letter, find an envelop, buy a stamp, and then find a mail box to drop it.

Receiving Messages: We need not be at our computer all the time to receive a message. The message is stored by our service provider. It will deliver the message to us when we ask for it.

Multiple Copies: We can send the same message to multiple users without retyping the message again and again.

10.6.2 Limitation of E-mail

Hardware Requirement: We have to be at a computer to read or print e-mail.

A Hasty Medium: Because e-mail is easy to use, it is also easy to send a message that you might later regret.

Hard to Convey Emotion: Without the extra clues of voice, posture and expression, it is easy to misunderstand what someone really means in a message.

E-mail is Not Private: As message is passed from one system to another, there are chances that someone might intercept or read your e-mail.

10.6.3 Features of E-mail

Reply to a Message: We can reply to a message sent by others. Our reply includes the original message, also known as quoting. Quoting helps the reader to know of the message being replying to.

Forward a Message: We can forward a message we have received to someone else, without retyping the message.

Store a Message: Important messages can be stored. This gives us the option to go through the message again later on.

Delete a Message: We can delete unwanted messages; otherwise the mail will pile up in our Inbox.

Print a Message: A message can be printed to make a hard copy.

10.6.4 Structure of E-Mail Message

An e-mail message is made up of binary data, usually in the ASCII text format. ASCII (American Standard Code for Information Interchange) is a standard that enables any computer, regardless of its system or hardware, to read the text. ASCII code describes the characters you see on your computer screen.

On the subject line, you may type in the subject of your message or a very brief summary. At the bottom of the message is a "signature" area that can contain personalized information about you. Some mail programs will automatically append this signature to the bottom of every message you send. Signatures areas are not required and are used at the discretion of the person who creates the e-mail message. Signature portion should not exceed five lines.

There are five sections of an e-mail message:

(a) E-mail address
(b) header
(c) body
(d) signature (optional)
(e) attachment(s) (optional)

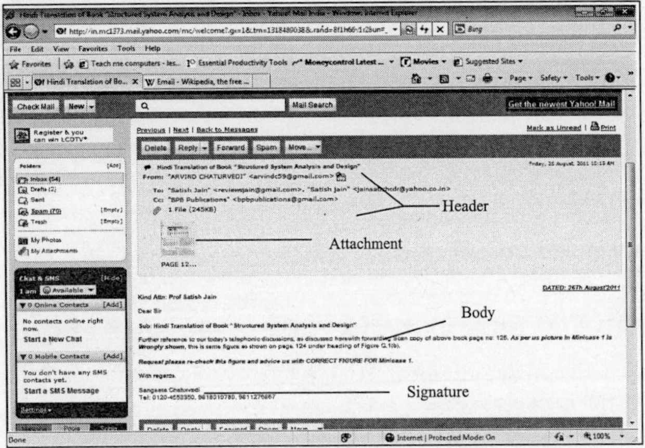

Figure 10.10 Major sections of an e-mail message

Figure 10.10 shows the major sections of an e-mail message. Note that signatures and attachments are optional.

E-Mail Address

An e-mail address is composed of two separate parts.

(a) The domain name of the mail server computer on which you have an e-mail account.
(b) Your personal identity or account name (user name) on that mail server.

For example, 100 people have e-mail accounts with the same ISP or organizations. All 100 users will share the same domain name (say **hotmail.com**), but each person will possess a unique user name, such as "rakesh" or "aparna." The user name and domain name are separated by an @ ("at") symbol. Together, they form a complete e-mail address.

The components of a typical e-mail address are shown in Figure 10.11. Users with multiple e-mail accounts – perhaps with different ISPs or organizations– will have a different e-mail address for each account.

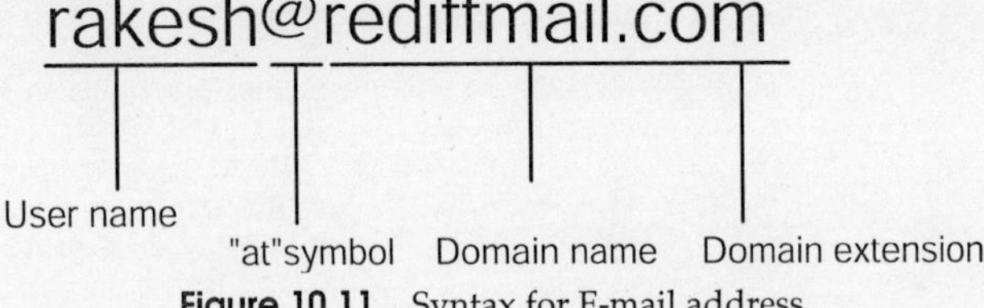

Figure 10.11 Syntax for E-mail address

☞ *Note that there are no spaces in the above address; e-mail software and server computers will not accept spaces in an address. Messages will not reach their destination if spaces are included.*

Header

The header of e-mail message is the upper-most section. It displays information regarding the status of the messages. A header records message information and provides it to the recipient(s) of the message. Headers are present in both outgoing (sent) and incoming (received) messages.

The header shows information, such as:

(a) Time and date of a message,
(b) Subject of a message (as typed by the sender),
(c) Whether carbon copies were sent to others
(d) Whether files are attached to the message, and
(e) The e-mail address of the sender.

Body

The body of e-mail message is the primary focus because it contains the actual message. Although there is no limit to the size (number of characters) of an e-mail message, but many Internet Service Providers do limit the size of an e-mail message.

Attachments

E-mail has become all the more attractive to businesses because it allows users to attach a file to any e-mail message. Any file format, such as *word processing documents*, *spreadsheets*, *images*, or *video* files–can be attached to an e-mail message. E-mail allows complex data as attachments but not in the body.

☞ *E-mail messages cannot contain viruses, but viruses can still be sent through attachments. Therefore, you should scan all e-mail attachments with a virus detection and eradication software program, such as McAfee VirusScan or Norton Anti Virus before opening, or forwarding attachments.*

Most e-mail applications alert you if an incoming message contains an attachment. Such e-mail applications show an icon within the body of the messages to represent an attached file. The icon indicates the type of file that is attached and allows the recipient to double-click the icon to automatically launch the attachment on their computer.

Signature

The signature for an e-mail message is the personal information which automatically appears at the bottom of the outgoing message. Use of a signature is optional. You can provide any signature information you wish.

Information in a signature block may include the following:

(a) Full name
(b) Job title/position
(c) Organization name and division
(d) Phone and fax numbers
(e) Physical (snailmail) address
(f) E-mail address
(g) Website address (URL)

☞ *By utilizing the signature feature of the e-mail software, you can avoid typing information for each outgoing message.*

Carbon Copy (CC)

This feature lets you send a copy, i.e., carbon copy of the mail to another recipient. In this case, the main recipient is informed about the other people who receive the same message.

Blind Carbon Copy (BCC)

In this option, the recipient of the first e-mail copy does not come to know the name of the other recipients, who receive the carbon copies of the same message.

10.7 CONCEPT OF MULTIMEDIA STREAMING

Multimedia is the integration of multiple forms of media. This includes text, graphics, audio, video, etc. For example, a presentation involving audio and video clips would be considered a "multimedia presentation." Educational software that involves animations, sound, and text is called "multimedia software." CDs (Compact Disks) and DVDs (Digital Video/Versatile Disk) are often considered to be "multimedia formats" since they can store a lot of data and most forms of multimedia require a lot of disk space.

Streaming is a method of delivery of sound and video files over the Web. The computer begins playing the file when sufficient data for playback has been downloaded and it continues to receive the rest of it, keeping ahead so playback does not pause or break up.

Audio/video streaming allows the user to listen or view video files on the Internet in real time, with no need to download an entire file before playback. It is entirely different from when user has to download files to listen to it. In streaming, both the client and server cooperate for uninterrupted motion. The client side stores a few seconds of audio/video in a buffer (files created by buffering are temporary, and are gone when playback is complete) before it starts sending it to the screen and speakers. Throughout the session, it continues to receive data ahead of time.

Purpose of Streaming Audio/Video Files:

(i) A file with streaming cannot be copied, downloaded, or edited. Therefore, illegal act of piracy or copyright infringement is not possible. Streaming will keep sources secured in the Website.

(ii) Audio/video media can be used in online advertising, live Webcasts, and e-learning training and solutions. Connecting media to the computer is easier with streaming.

(iii) It is also beneficial for people who work overseas and wanted to listen to their favorite local artists. Players like Windows Media Player work well with streaming.

(iv) Streaming is a cheapest way to create music albums, DVDs, or videos. The innovation of streaming eliminated the shipment process and promoted a faster way of transferring files.

(v) Streaming allows you to know who are listening to your music file or watching your videos. Viewers experience will also be improved because you get to know the statistics of your media playback.

10.8 WHAT IS COMPUTER NETWORKING?

A network is a group of computers connected in some fashion in order to share resources. A group of computers in a network would provide greater storage capacity and processing power than that by stand-alone independent machines. In addition to computers, a network also consists of peripheral devices with carriers and data communication devices used for the purpose of exchanging data and information.

☞ *By using computer networks, the cost of data transfer can be made economical because computers can send data at a very fast speed.*

Computers enable us to reduce both cost and time in transferring data or information when networked. In a network, computers of different make can be connected together and users can work together in a group. Software packages have been developed for group working in Database Management System (DBMS) as well as in graphical artworks. Also, data from different departments located at distant places can be transferred and stored on a central computer. This data can then be accessed by the computers located in different departments. Data at the central computer is updated and accessed by all users. This method would prevent any bottlenecks in the smooth functioning of the organization because all the users will get the latest information (for example, inventory) stored in the central computer.

10.8.1 Advantages of Networking

The following advantages of computer networking are:

1. **Resource Sharing:** The aim is to make all programs, data and peripherals available to authorized users on the network irrespective of the physical location of the resources.
2. **Reliability:** This is provided by having an alternative source of supply. For example, files can be replicated on two or three machines, so if one of them is unavailable (due to hardware failure), the other copies can be used. In addition, the presence of multiple CPU's (Central Processing Unit) means that if one goes down, the others may be able to take over its work. This is of utmost importance for military, banking, air traffic control, etc., which need to continue operating in case of hardware problems.
3. **Financial Benefits:** Small computers (PC) have better price-to-performance ratio compared to large ones. A mainframe computer may be ten times faster than a PC, but it may cost about a hundred times more. As a result most of the organizations prefer to maintain a computer network consisting of a set of personal computers rather than centralized large computer.
4. **Better Communication Medium:** In an organization with a number of branches at far off places, networking of computers facilitates cheap and easy mode of communication. It is possible to transfer any information to any other destination immediately. Whenever a user updates a file, it is visible to the other users logged onto the network.
5. **Access to Remote Database:** By getting access to the remote database, it is possible to get rid of unnecessary trouble and wastage of precious time especially in works, such as airplane and railway reservations, booking hotels, etc., from a

remote place in any part of the world, a man can book an air ticket from one city to another, accommodation in hotels and get instant confirmation also.

10.8.2 Types of Networks

Networking has been developed on all levels, from local to international, in diverse sectors of society. Examples are networks used by government organizations for rapid retrieval of information from databases at central locations, networks used by banks and retail merchants for the transfer of funds or credit verification or by corporate offices to get information of activities at its branch offices etc. There are many types of computer networks that are described as follows:

- **Local Area Network (LAN):** A system of networked computers and other hardware, like printers, that are in relatively close proximity to one another. LAN is a computer network that spans a relatively small area. Most LANs are confined to a single building or group of buildings. However, one LAN can be connected to other LANs over any distance via telephone lines and wireless circuits. LANs are capable of transmitting data at very fast rates, much faster than data that can be transmitted over a telephone line. But the distances are limited. There is also a limit on the number of computers that can be attached to a single LAN. There are several different protocols (Ethernet, Token Ring, etc.), each with its own advantages and disadvantages. The owners usually provide and maintain the transmission media for a LAN maximum data transfer rate of 100 Mbits/sec or more.
- **Wide Area Network (WAN):** The term Wide Area Network (WAN) usually refers to a network which covers a large geographical area. Numerous WANs have been constructed, including public packet networks, large corporate networks, military networks, banking networks, stock brokerage networks and airline reservation networks. Some WANs are very extensive, spanning the globe.
- **Metropolitan Area Network (MAN):** A Metropolitan Area Network (MAN) is a network that interconnects users with computer resources in a geographical area or region larger than that covered by even a large local area network but smaller than the area covered by a wide area network. It is data network designed for a town or city. MANs are usually characterized by very high-speed connections using fibre optical cable or other digital media. A MAN can support both data and voice, and might even be related to the local cable television network. Usually provides a "backbone" which connects several LANs, may be owned by one organization or may lease services to users. Several protocols exist namely, FDDI (Fiber Distributed Data Interface), DQDB (Distributed Queue Double Bus), each with its own topology. They may have a high data transfer rate, 100 Mbits/sec or more.
- **Value-Added Network (VAN):** It is communications channel leased from a telephone company to offer customers with modems access to network services through a local or toll-free number.
- **Backbone:** It is a high-speed network that connects various LAN segments. These LANs should be interconnected with a backbone – a network that has direct connections to all the LANs segments. When a LAN has a backbone, then each pair of LAN segments can communicate without passing through a third party LAN segment.
- **Campus Area Networks (CANs):** The computers are within a limited geographic area, such as a campus or military base.
- **Home Area Networks (HANs):** It is a network contained within a user's home that connects a person's digital devices.
- **Wireless/Mobile Networks (HANs):** In these networks, transmission media includes infra-red light, radio channels, microwave radio, cellular telephone systems and satellite relays. Here the transmission rates vary with the media, from under 1 Mbit/sec up to Gbit/sec range for satellite relays.

10.9 NETWORK TOPOLOGIES

Topology is the method in which networks are physically connected together. Topology determines the complexity of connecting computers and therefore decides the cost of network cable installation. Cable installation can often be a major cost factor for network system. Topology also determines the strategy for physically expanding the network, in future. Different topologies are described in the following sub-sections.

10.9.1 Bus Topology

In linear bus topology, all computers are connected by a single length of cable with a terminator at each end (See Figure 10.12).

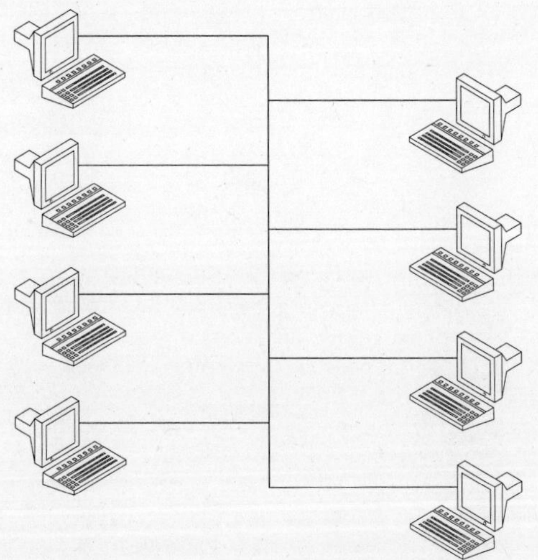

Figure 10.12 A linear bus topology

The bus topology is the simplest and most widely used local area network design. It is a passive topology which means only one computer at a time can send a message. Hence, the number of computers attached to a bus network can significantly affect the speed of the network. A computer must wait until the bus is free before it can transmit. Each node is connected to two others except the machines at either end of the cable, which are connected only to one other node.

☞ *Ethernet 10Base2 (also known as thinnet) is an inexpensive network based on the bus topology.*

The network operating system keeps track of a unique electronic address for each node, and manages the flow of data based on this addressing scheme. This topology has the advantage of not requiring that every computer be up and running in order for the network to function. But because a single cable is dedicated to all the information traffic, performance can be slow at times. This topology is often found in client/server systems, where one of the machines on the network is designated as a file server meaning that it is dedicated solely to the distribution of data files, and is not usually used for information processing.

Advantages of the Bus Topology

(a) The bus topology is simple, reliable, easy to use and understand in small sized local area networks.
(b) The bus requires the least amount of cable to connect the computers together and is therefore less expensive than other cabling arrangements.
(c) It is easy to extend a bus. Two cables can be joined into one longer cable with a connector, making a longer cable and allowing more computers to join the network.

Disadvantages of the Bus Topology

(a) Heavy network traffic can slow down a bus considerably. Because any computer can transmit at any time, and computers on most bus networks do not coordinate with each other to reserve time slots to transmit. A bus network with many computers can spend a lot of its bandwidth (capacity for transmitting information) with the computers interrupting each other instead of communicating. The problem only gets worse as more computers are added to the network.
(b) It is difficult to troubleshoot a bus. A cable break or malfunctioning computer anywhere between two computers can cause them not to be able to communicate with each other. Cable break or loose connector will also cause reflections and bring down the whole network, causing all network activity to stop.

10.9.2 Ring Topology

This layout is similar to the linear bus, except that the nodes are connected in a circle using cable segments (See Figure 10.13). In this layout, each node is physically connected to only two other nodes. Each node passes information along to the next, until it arrives at its intended destination. Since each computer retransmits what it receives, a ring is an active network and is not subject to the signal loss problems which a bus topology experiences. There is no termination because there is no end to the ring.

Performance on this type of topology is faster because each portion of the cabling system is handling only the data flow between two machines. This type of topology can be found in peer-to-peer networks, in which each machine manages both information processing and the distribution of data files.

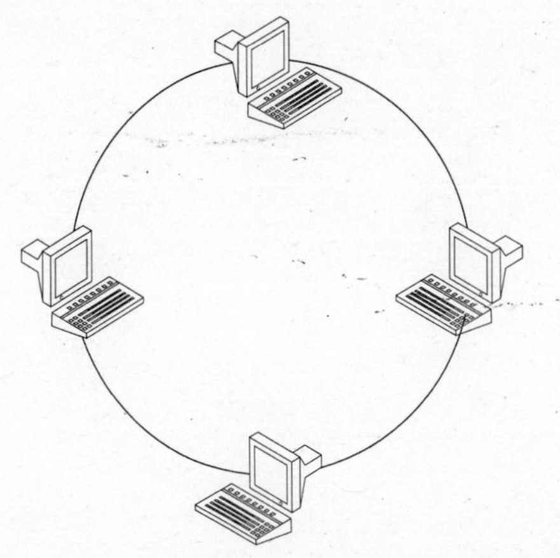

Figure 10.13 Computers connected in a ring or circular topology

☞ *Fiber Distributed Data Interface (FDDI) is a fast fiber-optic network-based on the ring topology.*

Advantages of Ring Topology

(a) Because every computer is given equal access to the token, no one computer can monopolize the network.
(b) The fair sharing of the network allows the network to degrade gracefully. It continues to function in a slower, manner rather than fail.

Disadvantages of Ring Topology

(a) Failure of one computer on the ring affects the whole network.
(b) It is difficult to troubleshoot a ring network.
(c) Adding or removing computers disrupts the network.

☞ *In Ring topology, computers are arranged in a circle. Data travels around the ring in one direction, with each device on the ring acting as a repeater. Ring networks typically use a token passing protocol.*

10.9.3 Star Topology

Each computer on a star network communicates with a central hub that re-sends the message either to all the computers (in a broadcast star network) or only to the destination computer (in a switched star network.) The hub in a broadcast star network can be active or passive (See Figure 10.14).

An active hub regenerates the electrical signal and sends it to all the computers connected to it. This type of hub is called a multiport repeater. Active hubs and switches require electrical power to run. A passive hub merely acts as a connector point and does not amplify or regenerate the signals. Passive hubs do not require electrical power to run.

☞ *Ethernet 10BaseT is a popular network based on the star topology.*

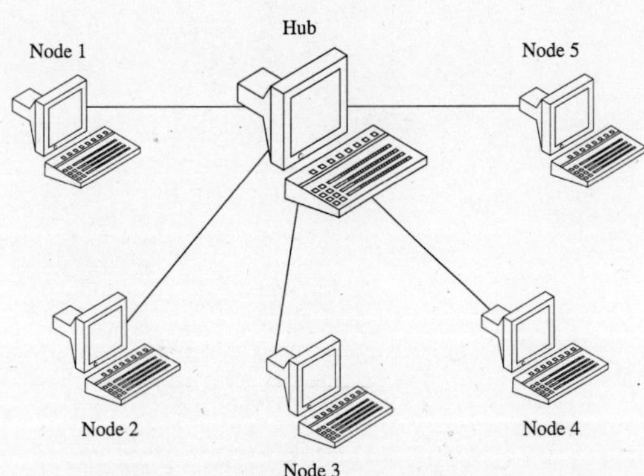

Figure 10.14 A Star topology

You can use several types of cable to implement a star network. Hybrid hub can accommodate several types of cable in the same star network. You can expand a star network by placing another star hub where a computer might otherwise go, allowing several more computers or hubs to be connected to that hub. This creates a hybrid star network.

Advantages of Star Topology

(a) It is much easier to modify or add new computers to a star network without disturbing the rest of the network. You simply run a new line from the computer to the central location and plug it into the hub. When the capacity of the central hub is exceeded, you can replace it with one that has a larger number of ports to plug lines into it.

(b) The center of a star network is a good place to diagnose network faults. Intelligent hubs (hubs with microprocessors that implement features in addition to repeating network signals) also provide for centralized monitoring and management of the network.

(c) Single computer failures do not necessarily bring down the whole star network. The hub can detect a network fault and isolate the offending computer or network cable and allow the rest of the network to continue its operation.

(d) You can use several cable types in the same network with a hub that can accommodate multiple cable types.

☞ *Out of all the topologies, the Star topology is the most flexible and the easiest to diagnose when there is a network fault.*

Disadvantages of Star Topology

(a) If the central hub fails, the whole network fails to operate.

(b) Many star networks require a device at the central point to rebroadcast or switch the network traffic.

(c) It costs more to cable a star network because all network cables must be pulled to one central point, requiring more cable length than other networking topologies.

10.9.4 Mesh Topology

It is a type fo network setup where each of the computers and network devices are interconnected with one another, allowing for most transmissions to be distributed, even if one of the connections go down. A mesh topology is most often used in large backbone networks in which failure of a single switch or router can result in a large portion of a network going down. This topology is expensive, because it has redundant connection to every computer. This type of topology is commonly used for wireless networks. Figure 10.15 is a visual example of a simple computer setup on a network using a mesh topology.

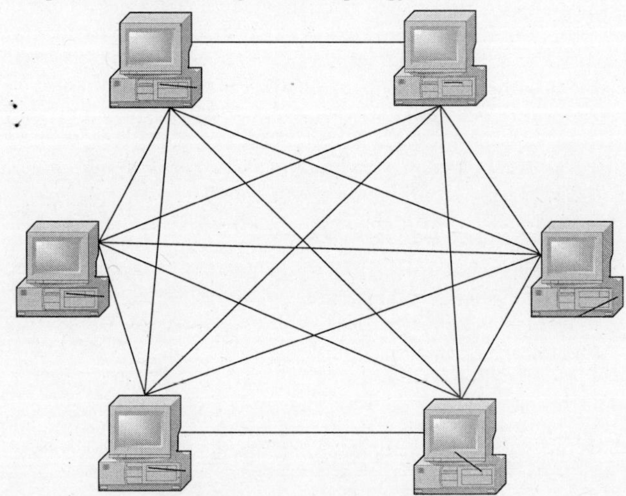

Figure 10.15 Mesh Topology

10.9.5 Tree Topology

Tree is a network topology containing zero or more nodes that are linked together in a hierarchical fashion. The topmost node is called the root. The root may have zero or more child nodes, connected by edges (links); the root is the parent node to its children. Each child node can in turn have zero or more children of its own. Nodes sharing the same parents are called siblings. Every node in a tree has exactly one parent node (except for the root, which has none), and all nodes in the tree are descendants of the root node. These relationships ensure that there is always one and only one path from one node to any other node in the tree (See Figure 10.16).

10.9.6 Graph Topology

In this method of connection, zero or more nodes are linked together in an arbitrary fashion. Any two nodes in a graph may (or may not) be connected by a link. Not all the nodes in a graph need to be connected, but if a path can be traced between any two nodes, the graph is a connected one.

10.10 ACCESS NETWORKS

An access network is a user network that connects subscribers to a particular service provider and, through the carrier network, to other networks, such as the Internet.

Some types of access networks:

(a) Ethernet is the most commonly installed wired LAN technology. Ethernet LAN typically uses coaxial cable or special grades of twisted pair wires.

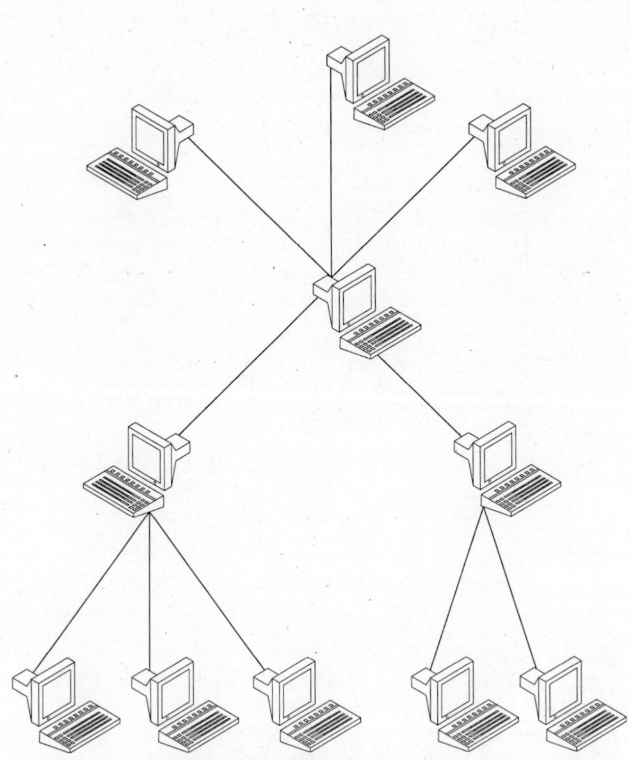

Figure 10.16 A tree topology

(b) Wireless LANs allow mobile users to connect through a wireless (radio) connection.

(c) Fibre optic networks, such as Fiber To The Home (FTTH) use optical fiber from a central point directly to individual buildings, such as residences, apartment buildings and businesses.

(d) ADSL (Asymmetric Digital Subscriber Line) is a technology for transmitting digital information at a high bandwidth on existing phone lines to homes and businesses.

Ethernet

Ethernet is the most widely-installed local area network technology. Specified in a standard, IEEE (Institute of Electronic and Electric Engineers) 802.3, Ethernet was originally developed by Xerox from an earlier specification called ALOHAnet (for the Palo Alto Research Center Aloha network) and then developed further by Xerox, DEC, and Intel. An Ethernet LAN typically uses coaxial cable or special grades of twisted pair wires. Ethernet is also used in wireless LANs. The most commonly installed Ethernet systems are called 10BASE-T and provide transmission speeds up to 10 Mbps. Devices are connected to the cable and compete for access using a Carrier Sense Multiple Access with Collision Detection (CSMA/CD) protocol.

Fast Ethernet or 100BASE-T provides transmission speeds up to 100 Megabits per second (Mbps) and is typically used for LAN backbone systems, supporting workstations with 10BASE-T cards. Gigabit Ethernet provides an even higher level of backbone support at 1000 Megabits per second (1 GB 1 Billion bits per second). 10 Gigabit Ethernet provides up to 10 Billion bits per second.

Ethernet was named by Robert Metcalfe, one of its developers, for the passive substance called "luminiferous (light-transmitting) ether" that was once thought to pervade the universe, carrying light throughout. Ethernet was so- named to describe the way that cabling, also a passive medium, could similarly carry data everywhere throughout the network.

Wireless LAN

A wireless LAN (or WLAN, for Wireless Local Area Network, sometimes referred to as LAWN, or Local Area Wireless Network) is one in which a mobile user can connect to a local area network through a wireless (radio) connection. The IEEE 802.11 group of standards specify the technologies for wireless LANs. 802.11 standards use the Ethernet protocol and CSMA/CA (Carrier Sense Multiple Access with Collision Avoidance) for path sharing and include an encryption method, the Wired Equivalent Privacy algorithm.

High-bandwidth allocation for wireless will make possible a relatively low-cost wiring of classrooms in the U.S. A similar frequency allocation has been made in Europe. Hospitals and businesses are also expected to install wireless LAN systems where existing LANs are not already in place.

Using technology from the Symbionics Networks, Ltd., a wireless LAN adapter can be made to fit on a Personal Computer Memory Card Industry Association (PCMCIA) card for a laptop or notebook computer.

Fiber Optic

Fiber optic (or "optical fiber") refers to the medium and the technology associated with the transmission of information as light impulses along a glass or plastic wire or fiber. Fiber optic wire carries much more information than conventional copper wire and is far less subject to electromagnetic interference. Most telephone company long-distance lines are now fiber optic.

Transmission on fiber optic wire requires repeating at distance intervals. The glass fiber requires more protection within an outer cable than copper. For these reasons and because the installation of any new wiring is labor-intensive, few communities yet have fiber optic wires or cables from the phone company's branch office to local customers (known as local loop).

ADSL

ADSL (Asymmetric Digital Subscriber Line) is a technology for transmitting digital information at a high bandwidth on existing phone lines to homes and businesses. Unlike regular dialup phone service, ADSL provides continously-available, "always on" connection. ADSL is asymmetric in that it uses most of the channel to transmit downstream to the user and only a small part to receive information from the user. ADSL simultaneously accommodates analog (voice) information on the same line. ADSL is generally offered at downstream data rates from 512 Kbps to about 6 Mbps. A form of ADSL, known as Universal ADSL or G.lite, has been approved as a standard by the ITU-TS.

Table 10.4 Different terms of Coaxial Cable Implementation

Terms	Implementation
10Base2	An implementation of the 802.3 Ethernet standard on thin Ethernet (RG-58) coaxial cable. It has a data transfer rate of 10 megabits per second and a maximum cable segment length of 185 metres.
10Base5	An implementation of the 802.3 Ethernet standard on thick Ethernet coaxial cable. It has a data transfer rate of 10 megabits per second and a maximum cable segment length of 500 metres over a bus topology.
10BaseF	Emerging 802.3 standards that define the use of an Ethernet over fiber-optic cable.
10BaseT	An implementation of the 802.3 Ethernet standard over Unshielded Twisted-Pair (UTP) wiring. It is similar to the wiring used with modern telephone systems using RJ-45 connectors. The standard is based on a star topology, with each node connected to a central wiring centre and a maximum cable segment length of 100 metres.
Thick Ethernet	Connecting coaxial cable used on an Ethernet network. The cable is 1 centimetre (0.4 inch) thick, and can be used to connect network nodes up to a distance of approximately 1006 metres.
Thin Ethernet	Connecting coaxial cable used on an Ethernet network. The cable is 5 millimetres (0.2 inch) thick, and can be used to connect network nodes up to a distance of approximately 165 metres. Normally used for office installations.

ADSL was specifically designed to exploit the one-way nature of most multimedia communication in which large amounts of information flow toward the user and only a small amount of interactive control information is returned. Several experiments with ADSL to real users began in 1996. In 1998, wide scale installations began in several parts of the U.S. In 2000 and beyond, ADSL and other forms of DSL are expected to become generally available in urban areas. With ADSL (and other forms of DSL), telephone companies are competing with cable companies and their cable modem services.

10.11 PHYSICAL MEDIA

There are several types of physical channels (communication media) through which data can be sent from one point to another in a LAN. Some of the most common data transmission media are briefly described in the following subsections:

10.11.1 Twisted-pair Wire

A twisted-pair of wires consists of two insulated copper wires, typically about 1 mm thickness (See Figure 10.17). The wires are twisted together in a helical shape. The purpose of twisting the wires is to reduce electrical interference from similar pairs that are close by.

Twisted-pair wires as shown in Figure 10.17 are commonly used in local telephone communication and for digital data transmission over short distances up to 1 km. When many twisted-pairs as shwon in Figure 10.18 run in parallel for a substantial distance, such as all the wires coming from a multistory apartment building to the telephone exchange, they are bundled together and placed in a protective sheath.

☞ *The pairs in these bundles would interfere with one another if they are not twisted.*

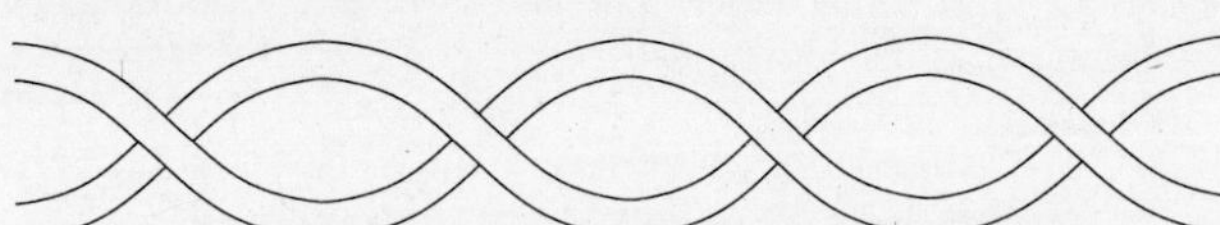

Figure 10.17 A twisted-pair of wires

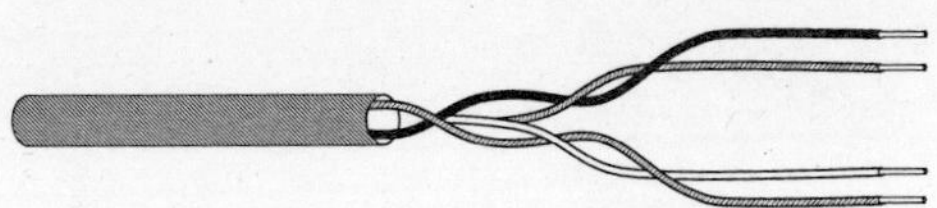

Figure 10.18 Unshielded twisted-pair cable

Wire pairs are normally used to connect terminals to the main computer up to short distances from the main computer. Data transmission speeds up to 9600 bits per second can be achieved if the distance is not more than 100 meters.

Advantages

(a) Being the oldest method of data transmission, trained manpower to repair and service this media of communications are easily available.
(b) In a telephone system, signals can travel several kilometres without amplification when twisted-pair wires are used.
(c) This media can be used for both analog and digital data transmission. The bandwidth depends on the thickness of the wire and the distance traveled, but several Mbps can be achieved for a few kilometres in many cases.
(d) It is the least expensive media of transmission for short distances.
(e) If portion of a twisted-pair cable is damaged, the entire network is not shut down as it may be the case with coaxial cable.

Disadvantages

(a) Easily picks up noise signals which results in higher error rates when the line length exceeds 100 metres.
(b) Being thin in size, it is likely to break easily.
(c) It can support 19,200 bps up to 50 feet on RS-232 port. On a 10BaseT, which supports 10 Mbps, twisted-pair wires can be used up to 100 metres.

☞ *Unshielded twisted-pair, is by far the more common of the two configurations.*

Shielded wire is used in an electrically noisy environment to limit the effects of noise absorption (See Figure 10.19). Twisted-pair wiring is more commonly used for LAN media. The twisted pair version of Ethernet is designated as 10BASE-T, in which 10 refers to the Ethernet rate of 10 Mbps.

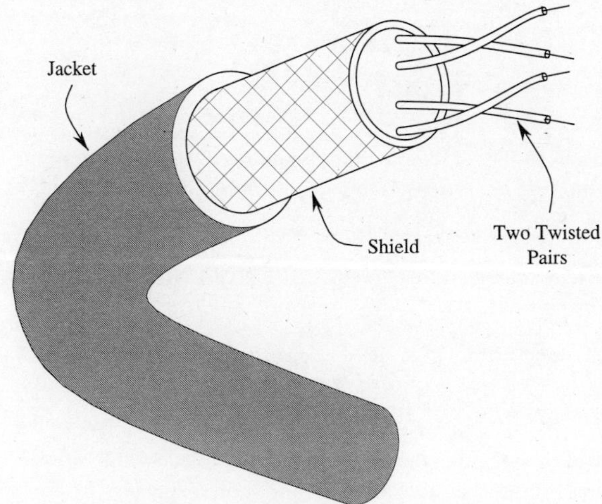

Figure 10.19 Shielded two pair cable

Twisted-pair cabling comes in several varieties. In computer networks, two of these are important. Category 3 twisted-pair's cable consists of two insulated wires gently twisted together. Four such pairs are typically grouped together in a plastic sheath for protection and to keep the eight wires together. Another more advanced category, 5 twisted-pairs were introduced. They are similar to category 3 pairs, but with more twist per centimeter and Teflon insulation, which results in less crosstalk and better quality signal over longer distances, making them more suitable for high-speed computer communication.

10.11.2 Coaxial Cabling

Coaxial cable consists of a stiff copper wire as the core, surrounded by an insulating material. The insulator is encased by a cylindrical conductor, often as a closely woven braided mesh. The outer conductor is covered in a protective plastic sheath. A cut-away view of a coaxial cable is shown in Figure 10.20. The signal is transmitted by the inner copper wire and it is electrically shielded by the outer metal sleeve. Table 10.4 gives a summary of different types of coaxial cable terms and their implementation.

Two kinds of coaxial cable are widely used. One kind, 50-ohm cable, is commonly used for digital transmission. The other kind, 75-ohm cables, is commonly used for analog transmission in cable TV transmission.

IEEE uses the 10Base5 designation for thick Ethernet coaxial cable and 10Base2 for the thin Ethernet coaxial cable. Coaxial cable can support data rates of up to several tens of Mbps at distances up to several thousand feet. Certain types of signaling enable high data rates over distances of several miles.

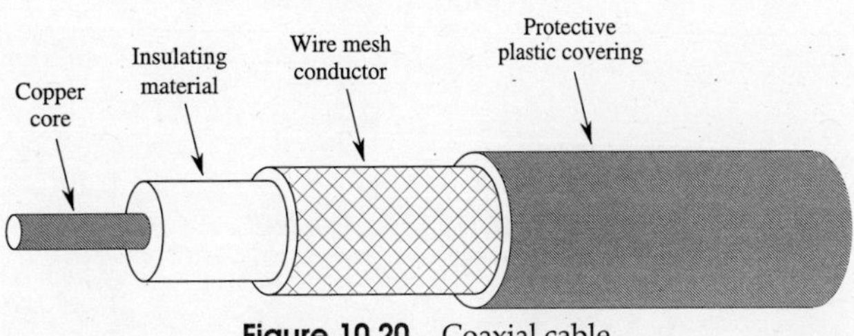

Figure 10.20 Coaxial cable

Baseband networks are the networks where the entire bandwidth of the cable is utilized for a single channel. Broadband is basically a frequency division multiplexed situation, where the coaxial cable's bandwidth is separated into subchannels of either equal or varying frequency ranges that can be treated as separate communication media.

Coaxial cable is difficult to connect to network devices and generally requires more planning than twisted-pair system. Many coaxial systems require the connectors on the main cable to be attached directly to the adapter on the PCs. This reduces flexibility in locating workstations and servers.

Installation

Coaxial cable is typically installed in two configurations: daisy-chain (from device to device–Ethernet) and star (ARCnet). The daisy-chain configuration is shown in Figure 10.21.

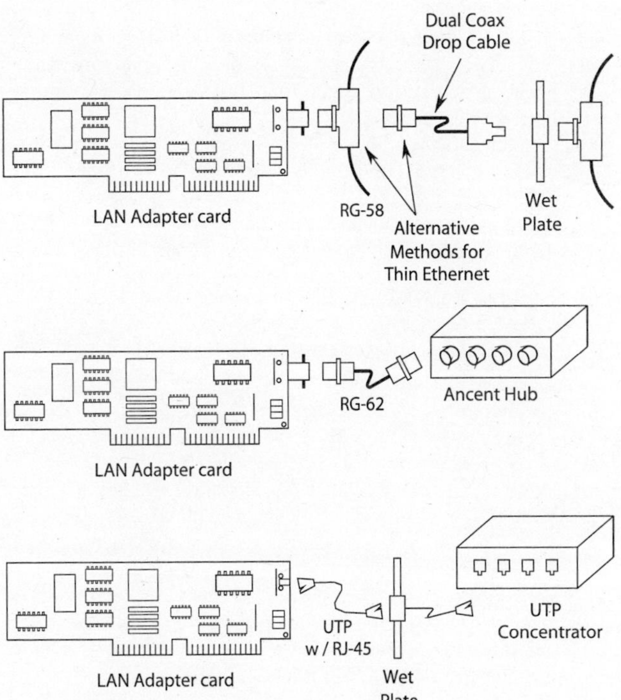

Figure 10.21 Coaxial cable wiring configuration

Table 10.5 Characteristics of different types of Cable Media (Bounded Media)

Factor	Unshielded Twisted-pair cable (UTP)	Shielded Twisted-pair cable (STP)	Coaxial Cable	Fiber optic
Cost	Lowest	Moderate	Moderate	Highest
Installation	Easy	Fairly easy	Fairly easy	Difficult
Bandwidth Capacity	1 to 155 Mbps (typically 10 Mbps)	1 to 155 Mbps (typically 100 Mbps)	typically 100 Mbps	2 Gbps (typically 100 Mbps)
Attenuation	High (Range of a few hundred metres)	High (Range of a few hundred metres)	Lower (range of a few kilometres)	Lowest (range of tens of kilometres)
Electromagnetic Interference (EMI)	Most vulnerable to EMI and eavesdropping	Less vulnerable than UTP but still vulnerable to EMI and eavesdropping	Less vulnerable than UTP but still vulnerable to EMI and eavesdropping	Not affected by EMI or eavesdropping

The Ethernet cabling is an example of *Thinnet,* which uses RG-58 type cable. Devices connect to the cable by means of T-connectors. Cables are used to provide connections between T-connectors. One characteristic of this type of cabling is that the ends of the cable must be terminated by a special connector, called a *terminator*. The terminator contains a resistor that is matched to the characteristics of the cable. The resistor prevents signals that reach the end of the cable from bouncing back and causing interference.

Advantages of Coaxial Cable

(a) It has better shielding against electromagnetic interference than twisted-pair cable. Thus, it can span longer distances at higher data bits per second (bps).

(b) It can be used for both analog and digital data transmissions. For analog data transmission, 75-ohm broadband coaxial cable is used and for digital data transmission, 50-ohm baseband cable is used.

(c) Coaxial cable has higher bandwidth and excellent safe guard against electrical noise (noise immunity). RG-58 cable (10Base2) is a thin coaxial cable (50-ohm) in widespread use for Local Area Network LAN connections. RG-11 (10Base5) cable is a coaxial cable that is much thicker and sturdier and can withstand more rugged surroundings and can be used with much longer segment lengths. RG-59, a 75-ohm coaxial cable and RG-62 (93-ohm) cable are used in ARCnet local area networks or the (International Business Machines) IBM 3270 applications.

(d) It is inexpensive as compared to twisted-pair wires and UTP cables but easy to handle.

(e) Coaxial cable has a bandwidth in the range of 300-400 MHz. It is capable of carrying over 50 standard 6 MHz color TV channels or thousands of channels of voice-grade and/or low-speed data over a single cable. CD-quality audio (1.4 Mbps), or a digital bit stream at 3 Mbps can be mixed on coaxial cable for transmitting video signal. Broadband cable is inferior to baseband cable for sending digital data but has the advantage that a huge amount of broadband cable is already available in the cable TV systems.

☞ *Cable TV systems may begin operating as Metropolitan Area Network's, and offer telephone and Internet services at low cost.*

Trade-off between Coaxial Cable and Twisted-pair Wiring

Following factors give the comparison between the coaxial cable and twisted-pair wiring as transmission media. A brief comparison is given in Table 10.5.

Cost In general, coaxial cable is more expensive by a factor of two or three, than twisted pair, and more expensive by a smaller factor than shielded twisted pair.

Data rate The difference between coaxial and twisted-pair is more apparent in the data rate that they support. For comparable distances to be spanned, twisted-pair will typically be suitable for data rates of at least an order of magnitude. If the data rate of choice is 1 Mbps, then either coaxial cable or twisted-pair will suffice at distances out to several hundred metres.

Security Cables that employ copper conductors can easily be breached by listening equipment. If the main consideration is security, then fiber cable is the only choice to avoid espionage. However, it is to be remembered that no system can ever be perfectly secure. Even fiber-optic lines can be tapped without detection.

Electromagnetic compatibility Coaxial cable emits less radiation which may cause less interference with the communication equipment as compared to twisted wires.

10.11.3 Optical Fiber

Optic fiber is the newest form of bounded media. This media is superior in data handling and security characteristics. The fiber-optic cable transmits light signals rather than electrical signals. It is by far more efficient than the other network transmission media. Each fiber has an inner core of glass or plastic that conducts light. There are two types of light sources for which fiber cables are available. These sources of light are:

(a) Light Emitting Diodes (LEDs)

(b) Light Amplification by Stimulated Emission Radiation (LASER)

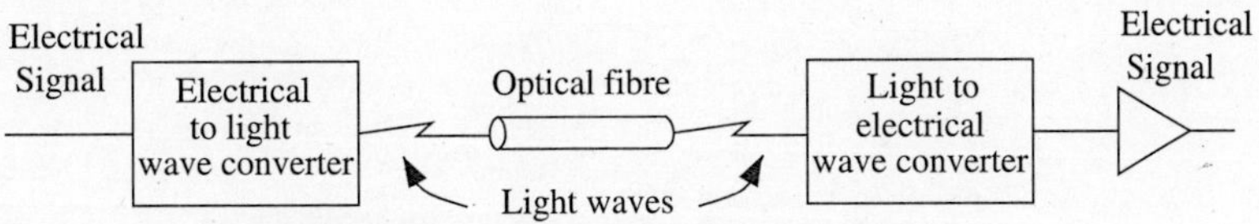

Figure 10.22 Transmission through optical fibers

Figure 10.22 shows the principle of operation of the fiber-optic system. The system basically consists of fiber-optic cables that are made of tiny threads of glass or plastics. In a single-mode fiber, the core is 8 to 10 microns (about the size of hair). In multi-mode fibers, the core is of about 50 microns in diameter.

Towards its source side is a converter that converts electrical signals into light waves. These light waves are transmitted over the fiber. Another converter placed near the sink converts the light waves back to electrical signals by photoelectric diodes. These electrical signals are amplified and sent to the receiver. Each fiber has an inner core of glass or plastic that conducts light. The inner core is surrounded by cladding. Cladding is a layer of glass that reflects the light back into the core. Each fiber is surrounded by a plastic sheath (See Figure 10.23).

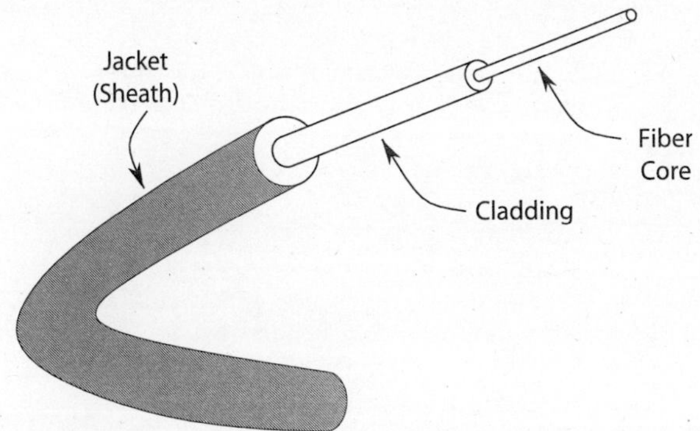

Figure 10.23 Fiber-optic cables with cladding and jacket (sheaths)

☞ *Optical fibers may be of the type of multi-mode or single-mode.*

Single-mode fibers allow a single light path and are typically used with *laser* signaling. Single-mode fiber can allow greater bandwidth than multi-mode but it is more expensive. Multi-mode fibers use multiple light paths. The physical characteristics of the multi-mode fiber make all parts of the signal (those from the various paths) arrive at the same time, appearing to the receiver as though they were just one pulse. Figure 10.24 shows the single-mode and multi-mode optical fibers and the transmission of light through them.

☞ *Optical fibers are differentiated by core/cladding size and the mode of operation.*

Following are the common types of fiber-optic cables:

(a) 8.3-micron core/12.5-micron cladding, single-mode,
(b) 62.5-micron core/125-micron cladding, multi-mode

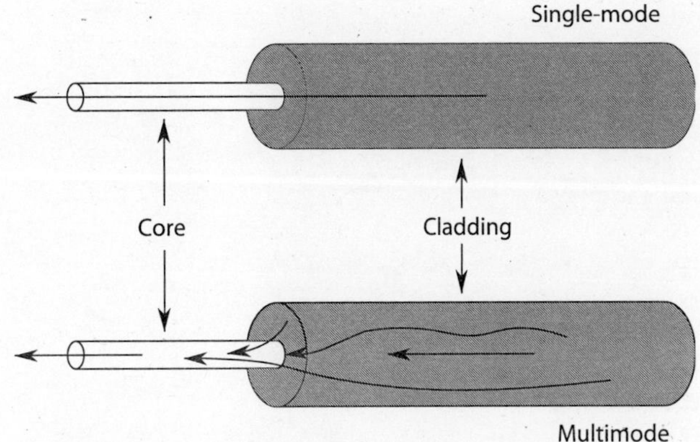

Figure 10.24 Single-mode and multi-mode optical fibers

(c) 50-micron core/125-micron cladding, multi-mode and 100-micron core/140-micron cladding, multi-mode

Micron is one millionth of a meter = 1/25,000 inch (approximately).

Characteristics of Fiber-optic Cable

Fiber-optic cable has the following characteristics:

Cost Fiber-optic cable is more expensive than copper cable, but fibre cable costs are falling. Associated equipment costs can be much higher than for copper cable, making fiber-optic networks much more expensive. Single mode fiber devices are more expensive and more difficult to install than multi-mode devices.

Installation Fiber-optic cable is more difficult to install than copper cable. Every fiber connection and splice must be carefully made to avoid obstruction of light path. Also the cables have a maximum bend radius, which makes cabling more difficult.

Bandwidth capacity Because it uses light, which has higher frequency than electrical signals, fiber-optic cabling provides data rates from 100 Mbps to 2 Gigabits per second (Gbps). The data rate depends on the fiber composition, the mode, and the wavelength (frequency) of transmitter light. A common multi-mode installation can support 100 Mbps over several kilometres.

Node Capacity In the case of Ethernet network, fiber-optic cables have the useful upper limit of around 75 nodes on a single collision domain.

Attenuation Fiber-optic cable has much lower attenuation than copper wires, mainly because the light is not radiated out in the way electricity is radiated from copper cables. It has a different problem, namely *chromatic dispersion*. Different wavelengths of light travel through glass differently, and the colors of a single pulse of light spread apart slightly as they travel down a cable. At a distance of several miles, 1 bit may shift into the next bit, causing data to be corrupted or lost. Single-mode fiber-optic cable conveys only one frequency of light down the cable, so it does not suffer from chromatic dispersion.

Electromagnetic interference Fiber-optic cable is not subjected to electrical interference. In addition, it does not leak signals, so it is immune to eavesdropping. Because it does not require a ground, fiber-optic cable is not affected by potential shifts in the electrical ground, nor does it produce sparks. This type of cable is ideal for high-voltage served areas or installations where eavesdropping could be a problem.

Mode of transmission Fiber-optic channels are *half-duplex*, which means that light signals can only move in one direction at a time. A full-duplex circuit would cause light wave interference without special electronics and hence it is generally not economically viable. Moreover, a bend radius that is too tight causes distortion and attenuation of the light signal due to changes in the electrical and physical characteristics of the inner core.

☞ *Fiber-optic cables are particularly appropriate for campus and multi-building backbones and for high security applications, such as financial transactions, military operations, and public safety.*

Uses of Optical Fiber Media

Fiber-optic media can support high bandwidth applications such as video conference, digital voice/image/graphics networking in LAN. Fiber-optic media are the basis for several high bandwidth networking standards, such as Fiber Distributed Data Interface (FDDI) and Synchronous Optical Network (SONET).

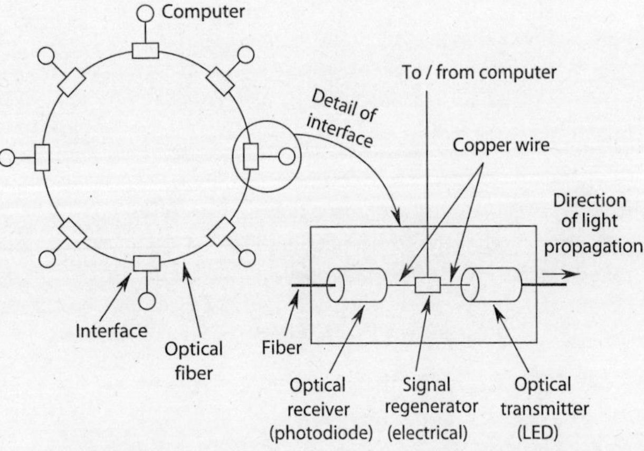

Figure 10.25 A fiber-optic ring with active repeaters

Fiber optics can be used for LANs as well as for long transmission (See Figure 10.25). The interface at each computer passes the light pulse stream through to the next link and also serves as a T junction to allow the computer to send and accept messages. The figure shows the active repeater. The incoming light is converted to an electrical signal regenerated to full strength if it has been weakened, and re-transmitted as light. The interface with the computer is an ordinary copper wire that comes into the signal regenerator.

Comparison of Fiber-Optics and Copper Wire

Advantages Fiber-optic cable has many advantages over copper wire as a transmission media. These are the following:

(a) It can handle much higher bandwidth than copper. Due to the low attenuation, repeaters are needed only about every 30 km on fiber lines, versus about every 5 km for copper.
(b) Fiber is not affected by power surges, electromagnetic interference, or power failures. Nor is it affected by corrosive chemicals in the air, making it ideal for factory environments where electrical interference is very high.
(c) Fiber cable is lighter than copper cable. One thousand twisted pairs copper cables of 1 km long weigh 8000 kg. But fibers have more capacity and weigh only 100 kg, which greatly reduces the need for expensive mechanical support systems that must be maintained.
(d) Fibers do not leak light and are quite difficult to tap. This gives them excellent security against potential wire-tappers.

Disadvantages Fibers have the following disadvantages over copper wires:

(a) Fiber is an unfamiliar technology requiring skills which may not be easily available.
(b) Since optical transmission is inherently unidirectional, two-way communication requires either two fiber cables or two frequency bands on one fiber.
(c) Fiber interfaces cost more than electrical interfaces.

10.12 CONCEPT OF OSI PROTOCOL LAYERS

The problem of getting a computer of one brand to accept data created by another manufacturer's machine has confronted users of these devices since their early days. At one time the only practical way to get around this barrier was to retype the data from the computer into the second. This is a very time consuming procedure and has the chances of lot of errors.

As the computers proliferated, interfaces or adapters were invented that translated one machine's code into a form that others could understand, allowing a variety of computers to be hooked together in networks. But these interfaces were expensive. Because a substantial number of them were needed to establish a large network. Moreover, each type of computer needed an interface of its own. Thus, there was little opportunity to spread the cost of developing the given interfaces by selling many copies of it.

☞ *Networking would be facilitated and the expense much reduced if computer manufacturers could agree on how to construct their products, so that each could communicate with the other.*

Towards this end, in 1977, the Geneva-based International Organization for Standardization set forth the *Open Systems Interconnection* (OSI) model. A master plan for computer-to-computer dialo, the OSI model divides the communications process into seven layers. The model sets standards that permit a wide variety in the design of computer hardware and software. The model demands only that communication tasks remain in their assigned layers and that the output of each layer precisely matches the format established for it.

10.12.1 Open System Interconnection (OSI) Model

The OSI model was developed to standardize the procedures for exchange of information between processing systems. The OSI is a communications reference model that has been defined by the International Standards Organization (ISO). It is a seven-layer communications protocol intended as a standard for the development of communications systems worldwide.

Most vendors and suppliers of computer communications equipment have agreed to support OSI in one form or another. However, adherence to this standard is vital in order to achieve smooth universal communications. This model conceptually organizes the process of communications between computers in terms of seven layers called protocol stacks. The seven layers of the OSI model provide a way for you to understand how communications across various protocols take place.

10.12.2 Protocol Stacks

A protocol stack is a group of rules or procedures called protocols arranged on top of each other as part of a communication process. Each layer of the OSI model has different protocols associated with it. When more than one protocol is needed to complete a communication process, the protocols are grouped together in a stack. A popular protocol stack is TCP/IP, which is widely used for UNIX and the Internet. Each layer in the protocol stack receives services from the layer below it and provides services to the layer above it. That means, layer N uses the services of the layer below it (layer N-1) and provides services to the layer above it (layer N+1). For two computers to communicate, the same protocol stacks must be running on each computer.

☞ *Each layer of the protocol stack on one computer communicates with its equivalent, or peer, on the other computer. The entities comprising the corresponding layers on different machines are called peers.*

The computers can have different operating systems and still be able to communicate if they are running the same protocol stacks. For example, a Windows 2000 machine running TCP/IP protocol stack can communicate with a IBM AS400 machine running TCP/IP (See Figure 10.26).

10.12.3 Layers and their Functions

When a message is sent from one machine to another, it travels down the layers on one machine and then up the layers on the other machine. This route is illustrated in Figure 10.27. As the message travels down the first stack, each layer it passes through (except the physical layer and application layer) adds a header. These headers contain pieces of control information that are read and processed by the corresponding layer on the receiving stack.

As the message travels up the stack of the other machine, each layer strips the header added by its peer layer.

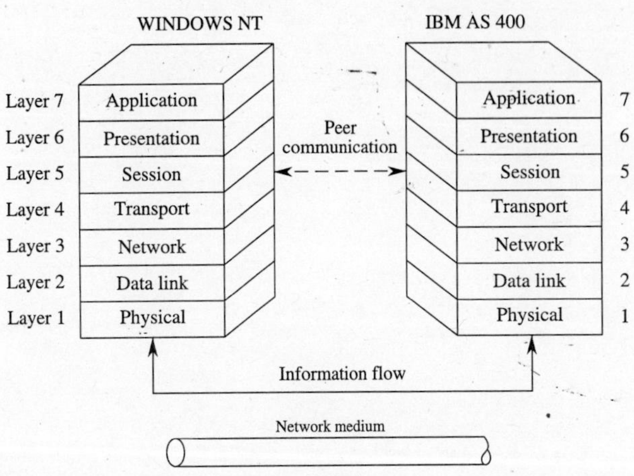

Figure 10.26 Peer-to-peer communication between two computers

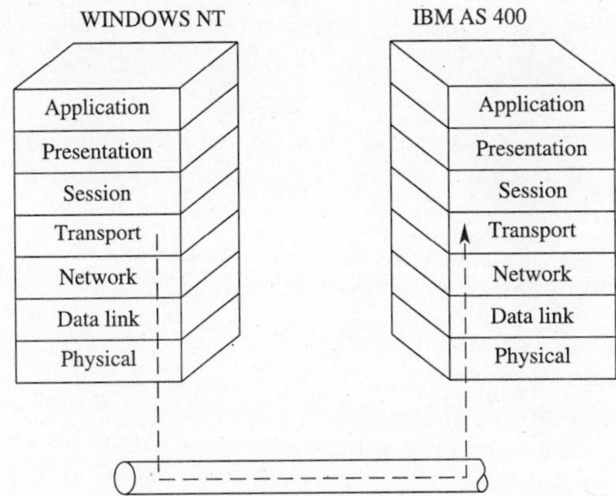

Figure 10.27 A message sent from one peer layer to another peer layer

For example, suppose we are using two networked applications based on the Windows 2000, a popular network operating system from Microsoft Corporation and IBM AS400 operating systems. At layer 7, the Windows NT application requests something from the IBM AS400 application. This request is sent to the Windows NT application's layer 6. The layer receives the request as a data packet, adds its own header, and passes the packet

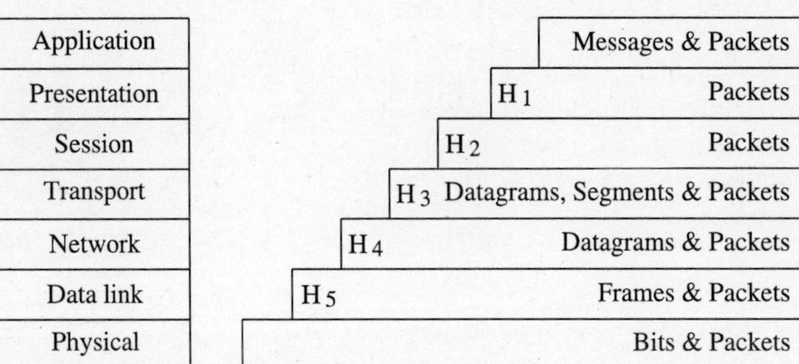

Figure 10.28 Common data package names

down to layer 5, where the process is repeated. As the request travels down the layers, headers are added until the request reaches the physical layer (which does not add a header).

Next, this requested packet travels across the network transmission media and begins its journey up the layers on the IBM AS400. The header that was put on at the data link layer of the Windows NT application is stripped at the data link layer of the IBM AS400 application. The IBM AS400 data link layer performs the tasks requested in the header and passes the requests to the next higher layer. This process is repeated until the IBM AS400 application's layer 7 receives the packet and interprets the request inside. At each layer, the data packages, called service data units, are made up of data and headers from the layers above. For this reason they are commonly referred to by different names when they are at different layers, as shown in Figure 10.28. The term packet is applicable to a service data unit at any layer.

☞ *The OSI model divides communication tasks into smaller pieces called subtasks. Protocol implementations are computer processes that relate to these subtasks. Specific protocols fulfill subtasks at specific layers of the OSI model. When these protocols are grouped together to complete a whole task, we get a protocol stack.*

Layers 1 and 2 are mandatory in order to transmit and receive messages in any communications system. Layers 3, 4 and 5 are provided by the controlling network software (network control programs and network operating systems) and have typically been treated as one layer by vendors. Layers 4, 5 and 6 are often combined into one or two layers in existing communications systems.

Control is passed from one layer to the next, starting at the application layer in one station, proceeding to the bottom layer, over the communications channel to the next station and back up the hierarchy.

☞ *In reality, no data is directly transferred from layer n on one machine to layer n on another machine. Instead, each layer transfers data and control information to the layer immediately below it, until the lowest layer is reached. Below layer 1 is the physical medium through which actual communication occurs.*

From top to bottom, the layers of the OSI model are shown in Figure 10.29. These layers are further described in the following section.

Layer 1 — Physical Layer

The physical layer defines the actual set of wires, plugs and electrical signals that connect the sending and receiving devices to the network. The RS-422 interface is a common standard in this layer. However, RS-232 interface is a common standard for PCs (See Figure 10.30).

☞ *A physical layer makes a physical circuit with electrical, optical or radio signals. Passive hubs, simple active hubs, terminators, couplers, cables, connectors, repeaters, multiplexers, transmitters, receivers, and trans-receivers are devices associated with the physical layer.*

Layer 2 — Data Link Layer

The data link layer is responsible for gaining access to the network and transmitting the physical block of data from one device to another. It includes the *error checking* necessary to ensure an accurate transmission. This layer uses the communications protocol that is most commonly referenced and often implies the specifications for Layer 1 as well.

Layer 3 — Network Layer

The network layer makes *routing decisions* and forwards packets for devices that are farther away than a single link. A link connects two network devices and is implemented by the data link layer. Two devices connected by a link communicate directly with each other and not through a third device. In larger networks there may be intermediate systems between any two end systems, and the network layer makes it possible for the transport layer and layers above it to send packets without being concerned about whether the end system is immediately adjacent or several hops away.

The network layer translates *logical network addresses* into physical machine addresses. This layer also determines the quality of service (namely, priority of the message) and the route a message will take if there are several ways a message can get to its destination.

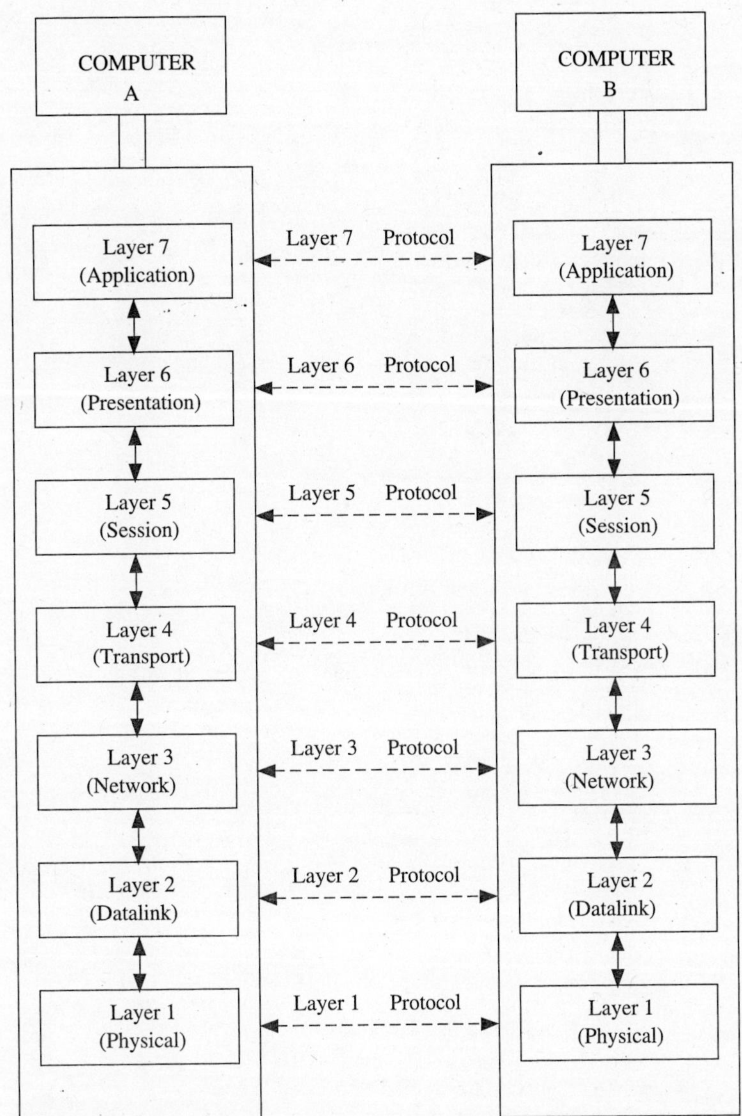

Figure 10.29 The International Standards Organization's (ISO) seven layers of control for open systems

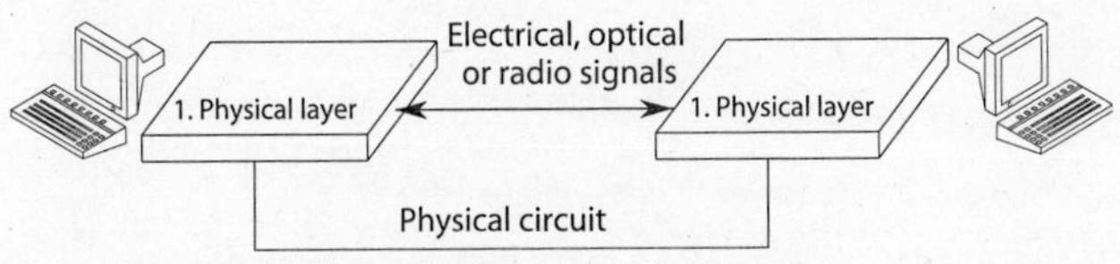

Figure 10.30 Physical Layer

The network layer may also break large packets into smaller chunks if the packet is larger than the largest data frame the data link layer will accept. The network reassembles the chunks into packets at the receiving end.

The network layer performs several important functions that enable data to arrive at its destination. The protocols at this layer may choose a specific route through an internetwork to avoid the excess traffic caused by sending data over networks and segments that do not need access to it.

☞ *Routers and gateways operate in the network layer.*

Layer 4 — Transport Layer

Layer 4 is known as transport layer. The transport layer breaks large messages from the session layer into packets to be sent to the destination computer and reassembles packets into messages to be presented to the session layer. The transport layer typically sends an acknowledgment to the originator for messages received.

Layer 5 — Session Layer

Layer 5 establishes and terminates the session, queues of the incoming messages and is responsible for recovering from an abnormally terminated session. This layer allows applications on separate computers to share a connection called a session. This layer provides services, such as name lookup and security to allow two programs to find each other and establish the communication link. The session layer also provides for data synchronization and check points so that in the event of a network failure, only the data sent after the point of failure need to be re-sent.

The session layer also controls the dialog between two processes determining whom they can transmit and from whom can they receive at what point during the communication.

☞ *The session layer provides for dialog between application programs.*

Layer 6 — Presentation Layer

The presentation layer translates data between the formats the network requires and the formats the computer expects. The presentation layer does protocol conversion, data translation, compression and encryption, character set conversion, and the interpretation of graphics commands. A network redirector is what makes the files on a file server visible to the client computer.

The network redirector also makes remote printers act as though they are attached to the local computer. The network redirector operates at presentation layer. Figure 10.31 shows how the presentation layer operates.

☞ *The presentation layer adapts information to the local environment.*

Layer 7 — Application Layer

The application layer is the topmost layer of the OSI model. It provides services that directly support user applications, such as database access, e-mail, and file transfers. It also allows applications to communicate with applications on other computers as though they were on the same computer. When a programmer writes an application program that uses network services, this is the layer the application program will access. Electronic mail and query languages are examples of this layer (See Figure 10.30).

☞ *The Application layer provides for the connection of application programs on separate machines.*

A summary of functions performed by different layers in the OSI model is given in Table 10.5.

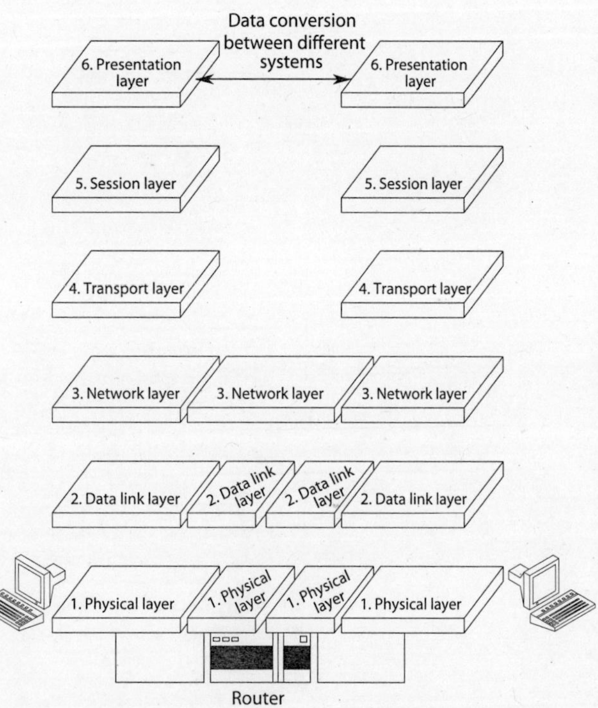

Figure 10.31 The Presentation Layer

Table 10.5 Function performed by different layers in the OSI model

Layer Number	Layer Name	Description
7	Application layer	Interfaces user applications with network functionality, controls how applications access the network, and generates error messages. Protocols at this level include HTTP, FTP (File Transfer Protocol), SMTP (Simple Mail Transfer Protocol), and NFS (Network File System).
6	Presentation layer	Translates data to be transmitted by applications into a format suitable for transport over the network. Redirector software, such as the Workstation service for Microsoft Windows 2000, is located at this level. Network shells are also defined at this layer.
5	Session layer	Defines how connections can be established, maintained, and terminated. Also performs name resolution functions.
4	Transport layer	Sequences packets so that they can be reassembled at the destination in the proper order. Generates acknowledgments and retransmits packets. Assembles packets after they are received.
3	Network layer	Defines logical host addresses, such as IP (Internet Protocol) addresses, creates packet headers, and

(Contd...)

Layer Number	Layer Name	Description
		routes packets across an internetwork using routers and Layer 3 switches. Strips the headers from the packets at the receiving end.
2	Data link layer	Specifies how data bits are grouped into frames, and specifies frame formats. Responsible for error correction, flow control, hardware addressing (such as MAC or Media Access Control addresses), and how devices, such as hubs, bridges, repeaters, and Layer 2 switches operate. The Project 802 specifications divide this layer into two sublayers, the Logical Link Control (LLC) layer and the MAC layer.
1	Physical layer	Defines network transmission media, signaling methods, bit synchronization, architecture (such as Ethernet or Token Ring), and cabling topologies. Defines how Network Interface Cards (NICs) interact with the media (cabling). You can think of each layer as being logically connected to the same layer on a different computer on the network. For example, the application layer on one machine communicates with the application layer on another machine. But this communication is logical only; physical communication occurs when packets of data are sent down from the application layer of the transmitting computer, encapsulated with header information by each lower layer, and then put on the wire at the physical layer of the transmitting computer. After traveling along the wire, the packets are picked up by the physical layer of the receiving computer, passed up the seven layers while each layer strips off its associated header information and then passes to the application layer of the receiving computer, where the receiving application can process the data.

10.12.4 Enhancements to the OSI Model

The bottom two OSI layers, the Physical layer and the Data Link layer, define how multiple computers can simultaneously use the network without interfering with each other.

The IEEE 802 project worked with the specifications in those two layers to create specifications which have defined the dominant LAN environments.

The 802 Standards Committee decided that more detail was needed at the Data Link layer. They divided the Data Link layer into two sublayers (See Figure 10.32):

(a) Logical Link Control (LLC)–error and flow control
(b) Media Access Control (MAC)–access control

Logical Link Control Sublayer

The LLC manages data link communication and defines the use of logical interface points, called Service Access Points (SAPs). Other computers can refer to and use SAPs to transfer information from the LLC sublayer to the upper OSI layer. These standards are defined by 802.2.

Media Access Control Sublayer

The Figure 10.33 indicates the Media Access Control sublayer. It is the lower of the two sublayers, providing shared access for the computer's network adapter cards to the Physical layer. The

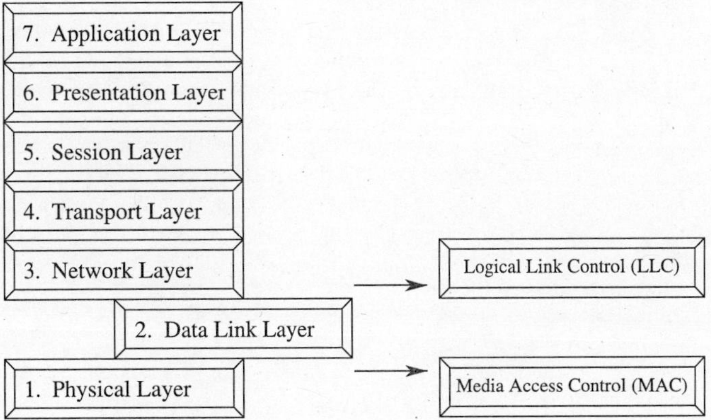

Figure 10.32 Sub-layers of Data link layer

Media Access Control layer communicates directly with the network adapter card and is responsible for delivering error-free data between two computers on the network. Categories 802.3, 802.4, 802.5 and 802.12 define standards for both this sublayer and OSI layer 1, the Physical Layer.

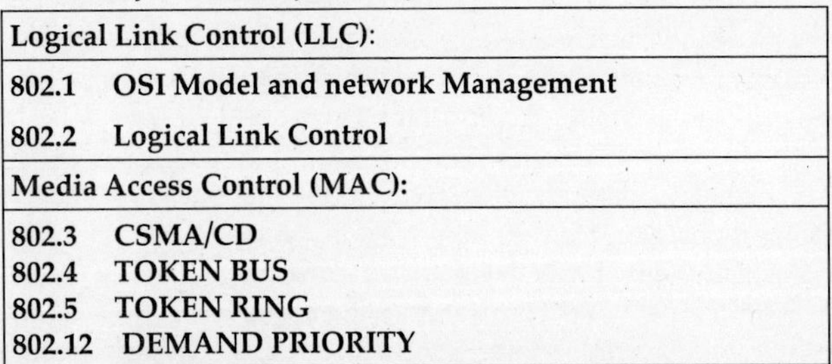

Logical Link Control (LLC):	
802.1	OSI Model and network Management
802.2	Logical Link Control
Media Access Control (MAC):	
802.3	CSMA/CD
802.4	TOKEN BUS
802.5	TOKEN RING
802.12	DEMAND PRIORITY

Figure 10.33 standards for LLC and MAC

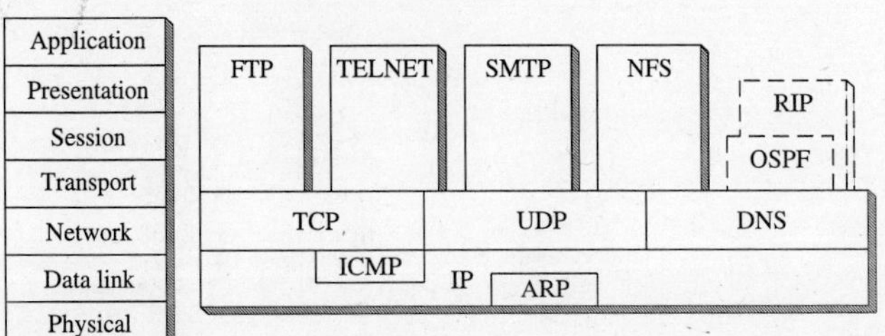

Figure 10.34 The relationship between the Internet Protocol suite and the OSI model

10.13 TCP/IP PROTOCOL

TCP/IP is an industry-standard protocol suite for wide area networks developed in the 1970s and 1980s by the U.S. Department of Defense (DoD). TCP/IP is a routable protocol that is suitable for connecting dissimilar systems (such as Microsoft Windows and UNIX) in heterogeneous networks. It is the protocol of the worldwide network known as the Internet. The Internet began as a project funded by the United States Department of Defence in the 1970s to interconnect educational institutions and government installations. At that time it was called ARPAnet (Advanced Research Projects Agency Network). Over time it has evolved into the huge, worldwide network known as the Internet. The protocols that make up the Internet protocol suite, the best known being TCP (Transmission Control Protocol) and IP (Internet Protocol), have become de-facto standards because of the success of the Internet. The entire protocol suite is referred to as TCP/IP.

☞ *The Internet Protocol suite is unique in that it is made up of non-proprietary protocols. This means that they do not belong to any one company and that the technology is available to anyone who wishes to use it. As a result, the Internet protocol suite is supported by the widest variety of vendors.*

The Internet suite was developed about ten years before the OSI model was defined and can therefore be only roughly mapped to it. The Internet protocol suite was defined according to its own model, known as the Internet or DoD model. Figure 10.34 illustrates the relationship between the Internet protocol suite and the OSI reference model.

The four DoD model layers are shown in Figure 10.35 and the OSI model layers they correspond to are as follows:

(a) The network access layer corresponds to the physical and data link layers of the OSI model.

(b) The Internet layer corresponds to the OSI network layer. Protocols at this layer are concerned with transporting packets through the internetwork. The main Internet layer protocol is IP.

(c) The host-to-host layer corresponds roughly to the OSI transport layer. Protocols at this layer communicate with peer processes in other hosts or networked devices. An example of a host-to-host protocol is TCP.

OSI Model | Internet (DOD) Model

OSI Model	Internet (DOD) Model
Application	Process/ Application
Presentation	
Session	
Transport	Host-to-Host
Network	Internet
Data link	Network
Physical	

Figure 10.35 The Internet (DoD) model mapped to the OSI model

(d) The Process/application layer corresponds to the OSI session, presentation and application layers. Protocols at this layer provide applications services on the network. Examples of protocols at this layer are Telnet (a Terminal Emulator) and FTP.

Figure 10.35 shows the Internet (DoD) model and various protocols mapped to the OSI model. The Internet protocols do not cover the lower two layers of the OSI model. This is because the designers of TCP/IP used existing physical and data link standards, such as Ethernet and Token Ring, to make TCP/IP hardware independent. As a result, the protocols of the Internet suite are widely used to connect heterogeneous systems.

As the Internet Protocol suite does not include lower-layer protocols, we shall discuss the individual protocols at the middle layers.

The OSI model's network and transport layers are concerned with transporting packets across the internetwork. TCP/IP and other Internet protocols use three types of addresses for network addressing. These are as follows:

(a) Hardware or physical addresses are used by the data link and physical layers. Physical addresses are usually hard coded into the network cards at each device.

(b) IP addresses provide logical node IDs. IP addresses are unique addresses assigned by an administrator according to certain guidelines. They are expressed in four-part dotted-decimal notation. For example, 123.144.131.12.
(c) Logical node names are easier to remember than an IP address. For example, BANIYA. COM.

Each layer of the TCP/IP protocol suite has its associated component protocols, the most important of which are as given below.

(a) **Application layer protocols:** Responsible for application-level access to TCP/IP networking services. These include Dynamic Host Configuration Protocol (DHCP), Domain Name System (DNS), HyperText Transfer Protocol (HTTP), File Transfer Protocol (FTP), Telnet, Simple Mail Transfer Protocol (SMTP), and Simple Network Management Protocol (SNMP). In the Microsoft implementation of TCP/IP, application layer protocols interact with transport layer protocols by using either Windows Sockets or NetBIOS over TCP/IP (NetBT).
(b) **Transport layer protocols:** Establish communication through connection-oriented sessions and connectionless broadcasts. Protocols at this layer include Transmission Control Protocol (TCP) and User Datagram Protocol (UDP).
(c) **Internet layer protocols:** Responsible for routing and encapsulation into IP packets. Protocols at this layer include Internet Protocol IP, Address Resolution Protocol (ARP), Internet Control Message Protocol (ICMP), and Internet Group Management Protocol (IGMP).
(d) **Network layer protocols:** It places frames on the network. The protocols include the various local area network architectures (such as Ethernet and Token Ring) and WAN telecommunication service technologies, such as Plain Old Telephone Service (POTS), Integrated Services Digital Network (ISDN) and Asynchronous Transfer Mode (ATM).

☞ *TCP/IP is a constantly evolving protocol suite whose development is steered by such bodies as the Internet Society (ISOC), the Internet Architecture Board (IAB), and the Internet Engineering Task Force (IETF). Internet Protocol version 6 (IPv6) is the latest revision of Internet Protocol. It was developed by the Internet Engineering Task Force (IETF) to deal with the long-anticipated problem of IPv4 (Internet Protocol version 4) address exhaustion.*

10.13.1 Internet Protocol (IPv4)

IP works at the network layer. The functions it handles and methods it uses are as follows:

(a) For addressing, IP uses the logical network address.
(b) For switching purposes, it uses the packet-switching method.
(c) For route selection, it uses the dynamic routing method.
(d) For connection services, IP provides error control.

IP is a connectionless, datagram protocol. IP packets are also called as IP datagrams. IP uses packet switching. It performs route selection by using dynamic routing tables that are referenced at each hop. The packets making up a message could be routed differently through the internetwork depending on the state of the network at each hop. For example, if a link were to go down or become congested, packets are to be sent through a different route.

Appended to each packet is an IP header. The header includes source and destination information. IP uses sequence numbering if it is necessary to fragment a packet into smaller parts and reassemble it at its destination or at an intermediate point. IP performs error checking on the header information by way of a checksum.

IP addresses are unique, 4 byte addresses that must be assigned to every addressable device or node on the internetwork (See Figure 10.36). In this Figure, you will notice that a big message is divided into smaller packets by the TCP. These are given a header and then enveloped by the IP to be sent to the addresses by various routes using the router. At the receiving end, each envelop is placed in order and the message is reassembled by the TCP and forwarded to the addressee.

☞ *A checksum is an error-checking method in which the data is submitted to an algorithm and the result is appended to the packet. When the packet arrives at its destination, the same calculation is performed on the data to see whether it matches the checksum value.*

Depending on the class of IP address, a certain number of bytes specifies the network portion and a certain number of bytes specifies the host or node portion. If a connection to the Internet is desired, a unique IP network address must be requested from a governing body called SRI (Systems Research Inc) Network Information Center. This ensures that the new network will have an address different from any other on the Internet. IP addresses are assigned according to three classes of networks that are as follows:

(a) **Class A addresses:** These are used for systems with a small number of networks and a large number of hosts. These addresses use the first byte to specify the network and the last three bytes to specify the host. The first byte of a Class A address can be in the range from 0-127 e.g., 80.23.102.3. The available IP addresses for this class have already been exhausted and not available for further distributions.
(b) **Class B addresses:** Provide for an equal number of networks and hosts by assigning the first two bytes to the network and the last two bytes to the host. The range of values for the first byte of a Class B address is 128-191. For example, 132.45.67.28. This class is most often assigned to universities and commercial organizations.
(c) **Class C addresses:** They use the first three bytes of the address to specify the network and the last byte to specify the host. Because there is only one byte available for host addresses, a Class C network will only support a small number of hosts (or nodes). The range of values for the first byte of a Class C address if it ranges between 192-223. For example, 194.123.45.7.

Datagram

Packets in the IP layer are called datagrams. Figure 10.37 shows the *IP datagram* format. A datagram is a variable-length packet (up to 65,536 bytes) consisting of two parts:

(a) Header
(b) Data

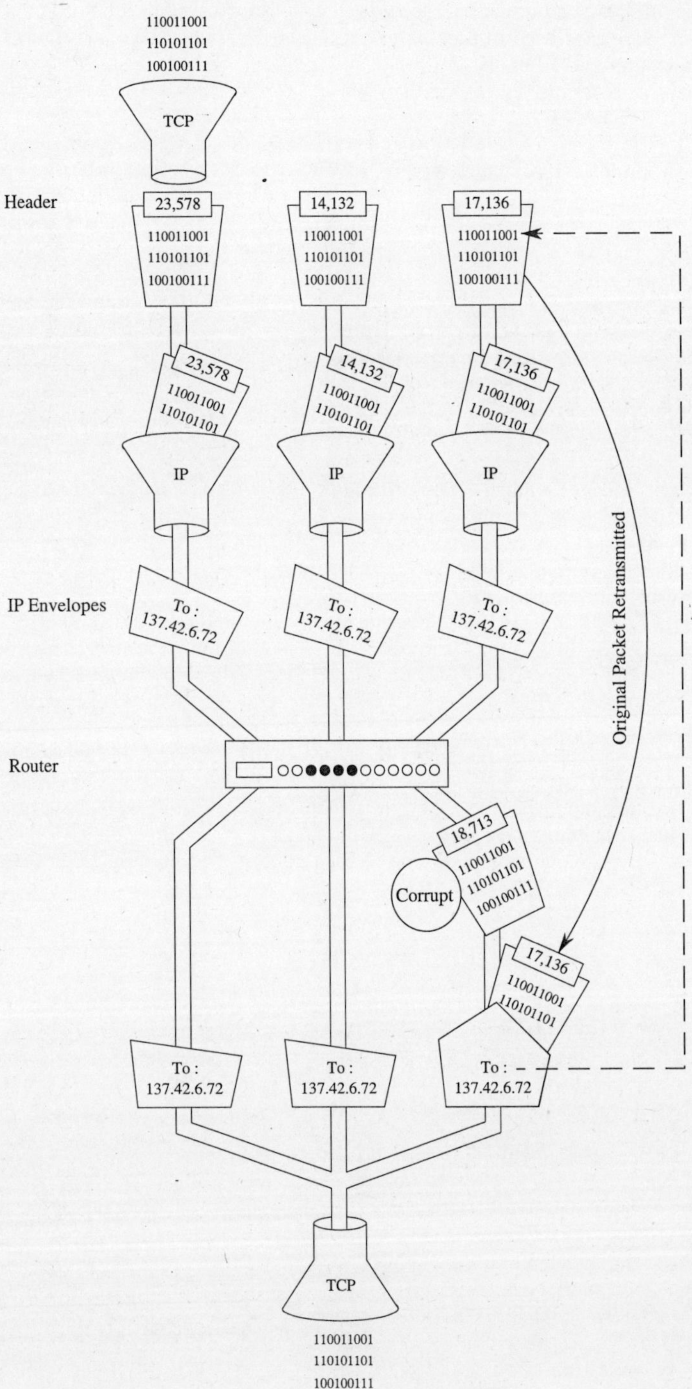

Figure 10.36 Working of TCP/IP Protocol

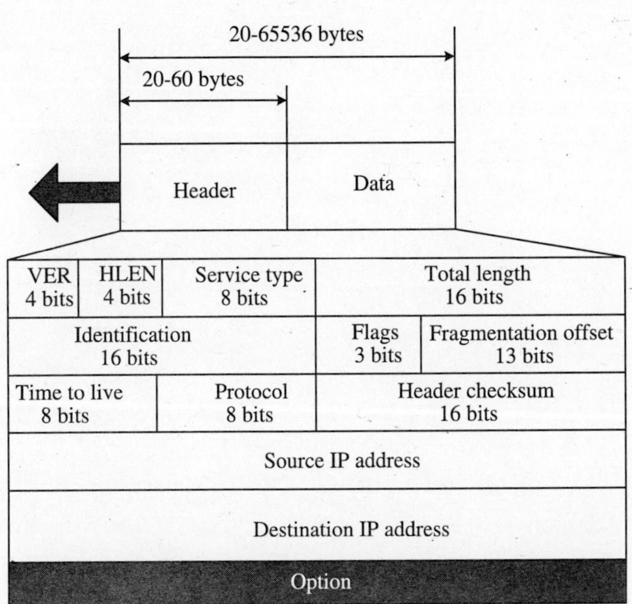

Figure 10.37 IP diagram format

Header The header can be from 20 to 60 bytes and contains information essential to routing and delivery. It is customary in TCP/IP to show the header in four byte sections.

A brief description of each field in the header is as follows:

(a) *Version:* The first field defines the version number of the IP. The current version is 4 (*IPv4*), with a binary value of 0100. The newer version 6 (IPv6) is under development.

(b) *Header Length (HLEN):* The HLEN field defines the length of the header in multiples of four bytes. The four bits can represent a number between 0 and 15, which, when multiplied by 4, gives a maximum of 60 bytes.

(c) *Service type:* The service type field defines how the datagram should be handled. It includes bits that define the priority of the datagram. It also contains bits that specify the type of service the sender desires, such as the level of throughput, reliability, and delay.

(d) *Total length:* The total length field defines the total length of the IP datagram. It is a two-byte field (16 bits) and can define up to 65,535 bytes.

(e) *Identification:* The identification field is used in *fragmentation*. A datagram, when passing through different networks, may be divided into fragments to match the network frame size. When this appears, each fragment is identified with a sequence number in this field.

(f) *Flags:* The bits in the flags field deal with fragmentation.

(g) *Fragmentation offset:* The fragmentation offset is a pointer that shows the offset of the data in the original datagram (if it is fragmented).

(h) *Time-to-live:* The time-to-live field defines the number of hops a datagram can travel before it is discarded. The source host, when it creates the datagram, sets this field to an initial value. Then, as the datagram travels through the Internet, router by router, each router reduces this value by 1. If this value becomes 0 before the datagram reaches its final destination, the datagram is discarded.

(i) *Protocol:* The protocol field defines which upper-layer protocol namely, TCP, UDP, ICMP (Internet Control Message Protocol), etc., are encapsulated in the datagram.

(j) *Header checksum:* This is a 16-bit field used to check the integrity of the header, not the rest of the packet.

(k) *Source address:* The source address field is a four-byte (32-bit) Internet address. It identifies the original source of the datagram.

(l) *Destination address:* The destination address field is a four-byte (32-bit) Internet address. It identifies the final destination of the datagram.

(m) *Options:* The options field gives more functionality to the IP datagram. It can carry fields that control routing, timing, management and alignment.

Addressing

In addition to the physical addresses contained on network interface cards that identify individual devices, the Internet requires an additional addressing convention. This address identifies the connection of a host to its network.

Each *Internet address* consists of four bytes (32 bits), defining three fields:

(a) Class type
(b) Netid
(c) Hostid

These parts are of varying lengths, depending on the class of the address (See Figure 10.38).

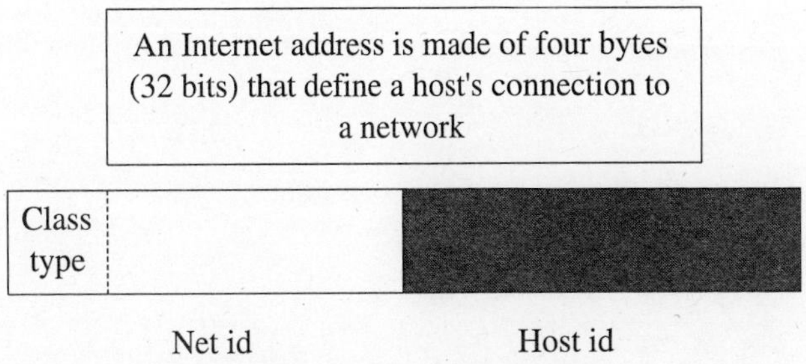

An Internet address is made of four bytes (32 bits) that define a host's connection to a network

Class type

Net id   Host id

Figure 10.38 Internet address

Classes There are five different field-length patterns in use, each defining a *class of address*. All such classes are designed to cover the needs of different types of organizations. For example, Class A addresses are numerically the lowest. They use only one byte to identify class type and netid, and leave three bytes available for hostid numbers. This division means that Class A networks can accommodate far more hosts than can Class B or Class C networks, which provides two- and one-byte hostid fields, respectively.

☞ *Currently both class A and class B are full. Addresses are available in class C only.*

Class D is reserved for *multicast addresses. Multicasting* allows copies of a datagram to be passed to a select group of hosts rather than to an individual host. Multicasting allows transmission to a selected subset. Class E addresses are reserved for future use. Figure 10.39 shows the structure of each *IP address class.*

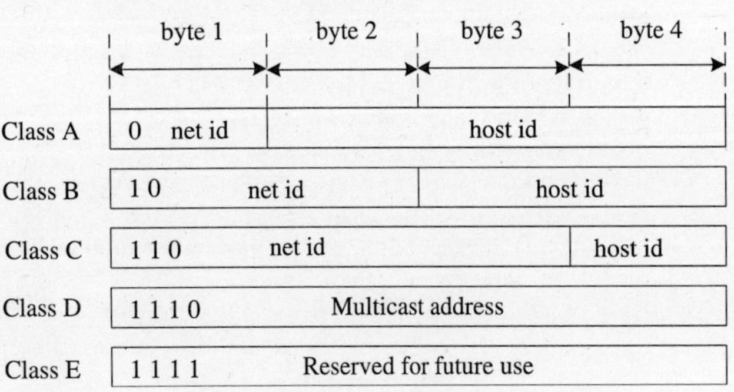

Figure 10.39 IP address classes

Example 1 What is the class of each of the following addresses?

(a) 11011101 10001111 11111100 11001111
(b) 10011101 10001111 11111100 11001111
(c) 01111011 10001111 11111100 11001111
(d) 11110101 10001111 11111100 11001111
(e) 11101011 10001111 11111100 11001111

Solution The first bits define the class:

(a) Class C
(b) Class B
(c) Class A
(d) Class E
(e) Class D

Dotted-Decimal Notation: Internet addresses are usually written in decimal form with decimal points separating the bytes–*dotted-decimal notation*. This is done to make the 32-bit form shorter and easier to read. Figure 10.40 shows the bit pattern and decimal format of a possible address.

Figure 10.40 IP addresses in decimal notation

Looking at the first byte of an address in decimal form, we can determine at a glance to which class a particular address belongs (See Figure 10.41).

Example 2 Write each of following in dotted-decimal notation:

(a) 11011101 10001111 11111101 00001111
(b) 10011101 10001111 11111100 11001111
(c) 11111110 10000001 01111110 00000001
(d) 11111101 10001010 00001111 00111111
(e) 01011101 00011111 00000001 11110101

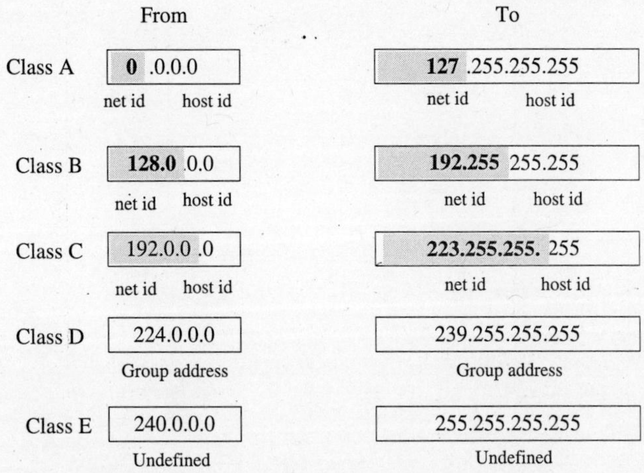

Figure 10.41 Class ranges of Internet addresses

Solution Each byte is converted to a decimal number between 0 and 255.

(a) 221.143.253.15
(b) 157.143.252.207
(c) 254.129.126.1
(d) 253.138.15.63
(e) 93.31.1.245

Example 3 Find the class of each address:

(a) 226.34.78.7
(b) 4.22.145.90
(c) 245.7.3.8
(d) 197.76.9.23
(e) 28.6.8.4

Solution The first byte defines the class

(a) Class D
(b) Class A
(c) Class E
(d) Class C
(e) Class B

Example 4 Find the network for each address:

(a) 227.34.78.7
(b) 4.23.145.90
(c) 198.76.9.23
(d) 129.6.8.4
(e) 246.7.3.8

Solution First find the class and then find the network address

(a) Class D, no network address
(b) Class A, network address: 4.0.0.0
(c) Class C, network address: 198.76.9.0
(d) Class B, network address: 129.6.0.0
(e) Class E, no network address

Example 5 Find the netid and hostid for each address:

(a) 227.34.78.7
(b) 4.23.145.90
(c) 198.76.9.23
(d) 129.6.8.4
(e) 246.7.3.8

Solution First find the class and then find the netid and hostid

(a) Class D, no hostid or netid
(b) Class A, netid: 4 hostid: 23.145.90
(c) Class C, netid: 198.76.9 hostid: 23
(d) Class B, netid: 129.6 hostid: 8.4
(e) Class E, no hostid or netid

10.13.2 Internet Protocol (IPv6)

The network layer protocol in the TCP/IP protocol suite is currently IPv4 (Internet Protocol version 4). IPv4 provides host-to-host communication between systems in the Internet. Although IPv4 is well-designed, it has some deficiencies that make it unsuitable for the fast-growing Internet. These deficiencies are as follows:

(a) IPv4 has two-level address structure (netid and hostid) categorized into five classes. The use of address space is insufficient. This method of addressing system has reduced the address space of IPv4. There may not be any addresses left to assign to any new system that wants to be connected to the Internet. The subnetting and supernetting strategies have solved some of the addressing problem while making routing more complicated.
(b) The Internet must accommodate real-time audio and video transmission. This type of transmission requires minimum delay. Reservation of resources are not provided in the IPv4 design.
(c) The Internet must accommodate encryption and authentication of data for some applications but no encryption or authentication is provided in the IPv4.

To overcome these deficiencies, IPv6 was proposed and is now a standard. In IPv6, the Internet Protocol was extensively modified to accommodate the unforeseen growth of the Internet.

IPv6 is the latest level of the Internet Protocol and is now included as part of the IP support in many products including the major computer operating systems. Formally, IPv6 is a set of specifications from the Internet Engineering Task Force (IETF). IPv6 was designed as an evolutionary set of improvement to the current IP version 4. Network hosts and intermediate nodes with either IPv4 or IPv6 can handle packets formatted for either level of the Internet Protocol. Users and service providers can update to IPv6 independently without having to coordinate with each other.

The most obvious improvement in IPv6 over the IPv4 is that IP addresses are lengthened from 32 bits to 128 bits. This extension will take care of future growth of the Internet. This will provide relief for what was perceived as an impending shortage of network addresses.

IPv6 describes rules fro three types of addressing. These are as under:

(a) *Unicast:* one host to one other host.
(b) *Anycast:* one host to the nearest of multiple hosts.
(c) *Multicast:* one host to multiple hosts.

Some of the advantages of the IPv6 are as following:

(a) Options are specified in an extension to the header that is examined only at the destination. Thus, network performance are speed up.
(b) The introduction of an "any cast" address provides the possible gateway hosts. With this idea, any one of them can manage the forwarding of the packet to others. Anycast messages can be used to update routing tables along the line.
(c) Packets can be identified as belonging to a particular "flow". Thus, packets that are part of a multimedia presentation, which needs to arrive in "real-time" can provide higher quality-of-service relative to other customers.
(d) The IPv6 header now includes extensions that allow a packet to specify a mechanism for authenticating its origin. This helps for ensuring data integrity, and privacy.

10.14 BASICS OF WIRELESS COMMUNICATIONS

In wireless communication, the frequency resources are limited and there are more number of users than the available resource (i.e., frequency band). Therefore, the communication channel should be assigned on demand. This increases the utilization factor of the channel. Further, channel capacity should be wisely and systematically allocated to each user. A common transmission medium like air space need to be shared among many mobile stations. This sharing of transmission medium, like air space is called Multiple Access.

☞ *Multiple Access is use of a communications system by more than one user simultaneously.*

Each user's transmitted signal should be kept uniquely distinguishable from other user's transmitted signals to allow private communications among them without interference. Users can be separated by arbitrarily defined "channels" established in frequency, time, or any other variable imaginable. The most commonly used multiple access techniques are Frequency Division Multiple Access (FDMA), Time Division Multiple Access (TDMA) and Code Division Multiple Access (CDMA).

10.14.1 Code Division Multiple Access (CDMA)

In CDMA, all users use the same frequency and may transmit simultaneously. The narrow band message signal is multiplied by a codeword. Each user has its own codeword (orthogonal to others). The receiver (intended destination) detects only the desired codeword. The rest of the signals appear as noise to it. In CDMA, the receiver must know the transmitter's codeword.

CDMA transmission can access a Base Station (BS) on demand and hence may occupy the channel's entire bandwidth for small intervals. This kind of transmission is more suited to military communication where mobile stations may communicate among themselves for brief time periods.

Hence, the CDMA technology optimizes the utilization of the frequency bandwidth, by equalizing Signal-to-Noise Ratio (SNR) among all the users. CDMA provides more equitably frequency band in sharing the system power resources among the users.

However, CDMA has three main disadvantages. These are:

(a) The capacity of a CDMA channel in the presence of noise and uncoordinated stations is typically lower than what TDM can achieve.

(b) With 128 chips/bit (a common value), although the bit rate may not be high, the chip rate will be, necessitating a fast, expensive transmitter. In CDMA, each bit is subdivided into *m* short intervals called chips.
(c) Few practicing engineers actually understand CDMA, which decrease their chances of using it, even if it is the best method for a particular application.

☞ *CDMA has been used by the military for decades and is now becoming more common in commercial applications as well.*

The signals are encoded in such a fashion that the information from an individual transmitter can be recovered only by the receiving station that has its own coded address and the transmitting station modulates its transmission with the address of the receiving station. CDMA transmission can access a transponder on demand and hence may occupy the transponder's entire bandwidth for small intervals. This kind of transmission is more suited to military communication where mobile stations may communicate among themselves for brief time periods.

10.14.2 GSM (Global System for Mobile Communications)

GSM stands for Global System for Mobile Communication. It is a digital cellular system developed by Group Special Mobile of Conference Europeenne des Postes et Telecommunications (CEPT) and its successor European Telecommunications Standard Institute (ETSI). It was adopted in 1982 and is a globally accepted standard for digital cellular communication. GSM is a revolutionary technology that combines both Time Division Multiple Access (TDMA) and FDMA.

An important goal of GSM development process was to offer compatibility of cellular services among European countries. It provides the specifications, that is the function and interface requirements, but does not address the hardware. This is done in order to allow buying hardware equipments from different vendors.

In the early 1980s, analog cellular telephone systems experienced rapid growth in Europe. Every country developed its own system, which was incompatible with everyone else's in hardware equipment and operation. This was an undesirable situation, because not only was the mobile equipment limited to operation within national boundaries, but there was also a very limited market for each type of equipment. Realising this, in 1982, the CEPT set up a committee known as *Groupe Special Mobile* (GSM), later known as *Global System for Mobile Communications*. Its purpose was to define a mobile system that could be introduced across Europe in the 1990s. The proposed system was expected to meet the following criteria:

(a) Good subjective speech quality.
(b) Low terminal and service cost.
(c) Support for international roaming.
(d) Ability to support handheld terminals.
(e) Support for range of new services and facilities.
(f) Spectral efficiency and
(e) ISDN compatibility.

Although standardized in Europe, GSM is not only a European standard now. Over 200 GSM networks (including DCS (Digital Cordless System) 1800 and PCS 1900) are operational in 110 countries around the world. In the beginning of 1994, there were 1.3 million subscribers worldwide which has grown to more than 55 million by October 1997. With North America making a delayed entry into the GSM field, with PCS1900, GSM systems exist throughout the world and GSM now stands for Global System for Mobile communications.

The GSM interfaces, protocols and protocol stacks are related to the Open System Interconnection (OSI) model. The GSM architecture provides independence between network elements such as the BS Controller (BSC), Mobile Switching Center (MSC), and the Home Location Register (HLR). This simplifies design, testing and implementation of the system. Thus, modification to one network element, in a system, can be made without any impact on the others.

GSM 900 has been adopted in many countries, namely as Europe, North Africa, Middle East, East Asia and Australia. In most cases, roaming agreements exist to make it possible for subscribers to travel to different parts of the world and at the same time continue to enjoy their telecommunication services with a single number and a single bill.

☞ *One adaptation of GSM at 1800 MHz, DCS 1800, is also spreading to East Asia and certain South American countries. PCS1900, a derivative of GSM for North America, is expected to cover a substantial part of United States.*

All these forms of GSM will enjoy a form of roaming, known as *Subscriber Identity Module.*(SIM) roaming. A subscriber of any of these GSM forms can access telecommunication services by using a SIM card in a handset suitable for the network in the visited system. Eventually, one phone could be used worldwide. This globalization is going to make GSM and its derivatives the leading competitors of cellular and Personal Communications Services (PCS).

10.14.3 General Packet Radio Service (GPRS)

General Packet Radio Service (GPRS) is a new service designed for digital cellular networks (GSM, DCS, PCS, etc.). It utilizes a packet radio principle and can be used for carrying end user packet data protocol (such as IP and X.25) information from/to a GPRS terminals to and from other GPRS terminals and/or external packet data networks. GPRS is standardised in ETSI (European Telecommunications Standards Institute).

GPRS (General Packet Radio Service) is an enhancement of the GSM. It extends the capabilities of GSM and provides connection to external packet data networks, through the GSM infrastructure, with brief access time to the network. GPRS supports higher data rates and longer messages. It helps sending point-to-point and point-to-multipoint messages. Some of the benefits of GPRS GSM are:

(a) No hardware changes to the BTS/BSC
(b) Easy to scale
(c) Support for voice/data and data only terminals
(d) High-throughput (up to 21.4 kbps)
(e) User-friendly billing

GPRS uses a packet-mode technique to transfer high-speed and low-speed data and signalling in an efficient manner over GSM radio networks. GPRS optimizes the use of network resources and radio resources. Strict separation between the radio subsystem and network subsystem is maintained, allowing the network subsystem to be reused with other radio access technologies. GPRS does not mandate changes to an installed MSC base.

Applications based on standard data protocols are supported and interworking is defined with IP networks and X.25 networks. Specific point-to-point and point-to-multipoint services are supported for applications, such as traffic telematics. GPRS allows SMS transfer over GPRS radio channels.

GPRS is designed to support everything from intermittent and bursty data transfers to occasional transmission of large volumes of data. Four different quality of service levels are supported. GPRS is designed for fast reservation to begin transmission of packets, typically 0.5 to 1 second. Charging will typically be based on the amount of data transferred.

☞ *The General Packet Radio Service (GPRS) is a new value added service that allows information to be sent and received across a mobile telephone network. It supplements today's Circuit wireless Switched Data and Short Message Service.*

10.14.4 3G and 4G (3rd Generation and 4th Generation)

Third generation (3G) of digital cellular/PCS systems are being explored presents to replace earlier second generation systems. The focus of 3G mobile systems is on economical networks and radio protocols to deliver seamless services across many networks (wireless and wireline).

In Europe, four related network platforms are currently the subject of intensive research. These are Universal Mobile Telecommunications System (UMTS), IMT-2000 (International Mobile Telecommunications beyond the year 2000), Mobile Broadband Systems (MBS) and Wireless Local Area Network (WLAN).

One of the driving forces of modern communication technology is the trend towards *Universal Personal Telecommunications* and *Universal Communications Access*.

Universal Personal Telecommunications concept refers to the ability of a person to identify himself or herself easily and use conveniently any communication system in an entire country, over a continent, or even globally, in terms of a single account.

The Universal Communications Access refers to the capability of using one's terminal in a wide variety of environments to connect to information services (e.g., to have a portable terminal that will work in the office, on the street, and on airplanes equally well). The GSM system does achieve these goals considerably.

In telecommunications, 4G is the fourth generation of cellular wireless standards. It is a successor to the 3G and 2G families of standards. In 2008, the ITU-R organization specified the IMT-Advanced (International Mobile Telecommunications Advanced) requirements for 4G standards, setting peak speed requirements for 4G service at 100 Mbit/s for high mobility communication (such as from trains and cars) and 1 Gbit/s for low mobility communication (such as pedestrians and stationary users).

A 4G system is expected to provide a comprehensive and secure all-IP based mobile broadband solution to laptop computer wireless modems, smart phones, and other mobile devices. Facilities such as ultra-broadband Internet access, IP telephony, gaming services, and streamed multimedia may be provided to users.

Pre-4G technologies such as mobile WiMAX and first-release 3G Long term evolution (LTE) have been on the market since 2006 and 2009 respectively. The current versions of these technologies did not fulfill the original ITU-R requirements of data rates approximately up to 1 Gbit/s for 4G systems. Marketing materials use 4G as a description for Mobile-WiMAX and LTE in their current forms.

10.15 INTRODUCTION TO WI-FI

Short for "wireless fidelity", Wi-Fi is one of the most popular wireless communication standards on the market. Wi-Fi is technically a trademarked brand name for the wireless standard owned by the Wi-Fi Alliance. Wi-Fi technology was almost solely used to wirelessly connect laptop computers to the Internet via local area networks (LANs).

Using the 2.4 GHz band, available globally for unlicensed low-power uses, two Bluetooth devices within 10 m of each other can share up to 720 Kbps of capacity. Bluetooth is intended to support an open-ended list of applications, including data (such as schedules and telephone numbers), audio, graphics, and even video. For example, audio devices can include headsets, cordless and standard phones, home stereos, and digital MP3 players.

The most familiar standards are 802.11b and 802.11g (Wireless B and G) which are used in the majority of commercial Wi-Fi devices. Both of these standards operate in the 2.4 GHz band.

REVIEW QUESTIONS WITH ANSWERS

1. Multiple Choice

1.1 Which of the following is a function of e-mail system?

a. Mosaic b. Netscape
c. Internet Explorer d. All the above

1.2 In OSI network architecture, the dialogue control and token management are responsibilities of?

a. Session Layer b. Network Layer
c. Transport Layer d. Data Link Layer

1.3 What is the main function of transport Layer?

a. Node to node delivery
b. Process to process message delivery
c. Synchronization
d. updating and maintenance of routing tables

1.4 To deliver a message to the correct application program running on a host, the address must be consulted?

a. port b. physical
c. IP d. None of the above

1.5 The technique by which a digital signals must be converted to analog form is known as:

a. Modulation b. Demodulation
c. Decryption d. Encryption

1.6 A technology that delivers broadband over your phone line to be used in home or office is known as:

a. Synchronous Circuit b. Wireless Fidelity
c. Asynchronous Circuit d. Digital Subscriber Line

1.7 Name the topology in which computers are arranged in a circle:
a. Star topology b. Bus topology
c. Ring topology d. Graph topology

1.8 The most commonly installed wired LAN technology is known as
a. PCMCIA b. Ethernet
c. ADSL d. Fiber optic

1.9 Shielded wire is used in an electrically noisy environment to limit the effects of:
a. Noise absorption b. Network devices
c. Insulating material d. Frequency ranges

1.10 A seven-layer communications protocol intended as a standard for the development of communications systems worldwide:
a. TCP/IP b. OSI
c. Peer-to-peer d. DoD

1.11 Which of the following layers is the topmost layer of the OSI model?
a. Presentation layer b. Data link layer
c. Application layer d. Session layer

1.12 Which of the followoing classes is reserved for multicast address?
a. Class A b. Class A
c. Class B d. Cladd D

1.13 Internet addresses are usually written in decimal form with decimal points separting the bytes:
a. Dotted-Decimal Notation
b. Binary Notation
c. Dotted-Address Notation
d. Point-to-point Notation

1.14 GPRS uses a packet-mode technique to transfer high-speed and low-speed data and signalling in an efficient manner over GSM:
a. X.25 networks b. Radio networks
c. Local area networks d. Wide area networks

2. State whether the following statements are True or False

2.1 A modem is a comptuer peripheral that allows you to connect and communicate with other computers via telephone lines.

2.2 Leases lines re direct Internet connection laid to connect your computer to an ISP server.

2.3 Wi-Fi (Wireless Fidelity) is a set of standard for transmitting data over a wireless network.

2.4 SLIP does not support TCP/IP.

2.5 WiMAX connection is a viable system which is also more affordable than broadband connections.

2.6 The signature for an e-mail message is the personal information which automatically appears at the bottom of the incoming message.

2.7 The bottom two OSI layers, the Physical layer and the Data link layer, define how multiple computers can simultaneously use the network without interfering with each other.

2.8 The Media Access Control (MAC) manages data link communication and defines the use of logical interface points, called Service Access Points (SAPs).

2.9 A checksum is an error-checking method in which the data is submitted to an algorithm and the result is appended to the packet.

2.10 In datagram, the HLEN field defines the length of footer in multiples of four bytes.

2.11 OSI Model has severn layers.

2.12 IPv4 has flow control mechanism.

3. Match the following:

3.1	Internet	a.	A variable-length packet
3.2	Study of structure	b.	Internet Protocol
3.3	A public messaging and Bulletin board system	c.	Presentation layer
3.4	Unique addresses of Internet Resources	d.	Half-duplex
3.5	Info first-level label	e.	Robert Metcalfe
3.6	Ethernet was named by	f.	Information service providers
3.7	Fiber-optic channels are	g.	URL
3.8	The network redirector operates at	h.	Usenet
3.9	IPv4	i.	Anatomy
3.10	Datagram	j.	Network of networks

4. Fill in the blanks

a. Ethernet 10Base2	b. Class A	c. Channel
d. Network layer	e. Access network	f. Home Page
g. LAN	h. Backbone	i. IEEE 802.11
j. Spamming	k. 32	

4.1 __________ refers to sending unwanted e-mails in bulk, which provide no purpose and needlessly obstruct the entire system.

4.2 The first page of the Website is called the __________.

4.3 __________ is a computer network that spans a relatively small area.

4.4 __________ is a high-speed network that connects various LAN segments.

4.5 __________ (also known as thinnet) is an inexpensive network based on the bus topology.

4.6 An __________ is a user network that connects subscribers to a particular service provider and, tthrough the carrier network to other network, such as the Internet.

4.7 The __________ group of standards specify the technologies for wireless LANs.

4.8 Baseband networks are the networks where the entire bandwidth of the cable is utilized for a single __________.

4.9 In OSI Model, the __________ makes routing decisions and forwards packets for devices that are farther away than a single link.

4.10 __________ addresses are used for systems with a small number of networks and a large number of hosts.

4.11 IPv4 network addressing requries ______ bit address.

Answers

1.	1.1	d	1.2	a	1.3	b	1.4	a	1.5	a	1.6	b
	1.7	c	1.8	d	1.9	a	1.10	b				
2.	2.1	T	2.2	F	2.3	T	2.4	F	2.5	T	2.6	F
	2.7	T	2.8	F	2.9	T	2.10	F	2.11	T	2.12	T
3.	3.1	j	3.2	i	3.3	h	3.4	g	3.5	f	3.6	e
	3.7	d	3.8	c	3.9	b	3.10	a				
4.	4.1	j	4.2	f	4.3	g	4.4	h	4.5	a	4.6	e
	4.7	i	4.8	c	4.9	d	4.10	b	k			

Short Questions with Answers

1. Name the major components of the Internet structure.
2. What do you mean by Internet Information Services?
3. Name the wireless network access pint which is used by devices to connect to a network resource.
4. Write the difference between OSI Model and TCP/IP Model.
5. Who coined the term datagram? Name the two components of datagram.

Answers to Short Questions

1. A study of the Internet outlines the following major components of the structure.
   (a) Internet services (b) Elements of the Internet
   (c) Uniform Resource Locators, and (d) Internet Protocol
2. Internet Information Services or IIS is an extensible Web server which supports HTTP (HyperText Transfer Protocol), HTTPS (HyperText Transfer Protocol Secure), FTP (File Transfer Protocol), FTPS (File Transfer Protocol Secure), SMTP (Simple Mail Transfer Protocol) and NNTP (Net Nes Transfer Protocol).
3. Many devices use Wi-Fi, for example, personal computers, video game consoles, Smartphones, tablet digital audio players. These can connect to a network resource, such as the Internet via a wireless network access pint (hotspot).
4.

OSI Model	TCP/IP Model
Theoretical model	Model around which the Internet is developed.
This model has seven four architectural layers.	This Model has four architectural layers.
Protocol-independent standard	Protocol-dependent standard

5. The term datagram was coined by Louis Pouzin. Each datagram has two components, a header and a data payload.

DESCRIPTIVE TYPE QUESTIONS

1. Discuss the advantages of the Internet.
2. Describe the different types of broadband service.
3. Illustrate the concept of multimedia streaming with the help of example.
4. Explain bus and star topology.
5. Why is fast Ethernet used? Explain.
6. Write the advantages and disadvantages of twisted-pair and coaxial cabling.
7. Make a list of comparision of fiber-optics and copper wire.
8. Explain all layers present in OSI Model.
9. Dicuss the working process of TCP/IP protocol.
10. What are the advantages of CDMA? Discuss.

CHAPTER 11

Information Technology and Society

11.1 SOCIAL NETWORKING

A social networking service is an online service, platform, or site that focuses on building and reflecting of social networks or social relations among people, who share interests and activities. A social network service essentially consists of a representation of each user (often a profile), his/her social links, and a variety of additional services. Most social network services are Web-based and provide means for users to Interact over the internet, such as e-mail and instant messaging, video calling, chat, file sharing, discussion groups, voice chats, e-mails, blogging and so on. Social networking sites allow users to share ideas, activities, events, and interests within their individual networks.

Social networking is all about communication. People with common interests are able to share information with each other via a huge variety of social networking sites. Sites created specifically to make sharing, communicating, and creating information as simple and efficient as possible.

11.2 TODAY'S SOCIAL NETWORKS

While traditionally, social networks were made up of people who might gather face-to-face, today's social networks are predominately online. Examples of today's social networks include social networking sites, such as LinkedIn, Facebook, MySpace and others. With increasing mobile phone popularity and enhanced cell phone technology, even Twitter might be considered a social network of sorts where you can let your network of friends know what you are doing or thinking at any given moment.

The top social network, MySpace, has over two-hundred and fifty million subscribers, with actors, authors, musicians and comedians counted among them. For example, Newegg.com, a computer hardware reseller, has a profile highlighting computer deals offered at their Website. Today's social networks are predominately free to join, which makes them extremely popular.

11.2.1 Use of Social Networks for Job Search

Social networks can be useful for those who are seeking legal work at home jobs. Most social networks include job search tools that you can use frequently. In the case of LinkedIn, access to some job postings is limited to members only.

11.2.2 Social Networks for Business Promotion

Social networks like **Facebook** and **MySpace** are being increasingly used for promoting every type of business from a small one-person business to mega corporations. From its birth, LinkedIn was geared more to fostering network connections within the business community and it is common for entrepreneurs and corporate managers alike to seek out partnership opportunities for their business.

11.2.3 Additional Features

Some social networks have additional features, such as the ability to create groups that share common interests or affiliations, upload or stream live videos, and hold discussions in forums. Geo-social networking co-opts Internet mapping services to organize user participation around geographic features and their attributes.

Lately, mobile social networking has become popular. In most mobile communities, mobile phone users can now create their own profiles, make friends, participate in chat rooms, create chat rooms, hold private conversations, share photos and videos, and share blogs by using their mobile phone. Some companies provide wireless services which allow their customers to build their own mobile community and brand it, but one of the most popular wireless services for social networking in North America and Nepal.

11.3 TWITTER

Twitter is a free social networking and micro-blogging service that has changed the way of many people to communicate. It is a message service that allows people to send and receive short messages (called tweets) within your Twitter community. Twitter community consists of:

1. ***People You Follow:*** You define your community by following other Twitter users. You see the tweets created by everyone you follow. Following someone means that you subscribe to their tweets.
2. ***People Who Follow You:*** Other people read your tweets and decide to follow you. Your followers see the tweets you send out.

Twitter was created by a software development team to solve their own communication challenges. They took features from other communication tools like e-mail, chat, and instant messaging and mashed them together to create Twitter.

11.3.1 How to find People on Twitter

There are several ways to find people to follow on Twitter. These are as under:

1. Name Search
2. E-mail Search
3. Keyword Search

11.3.2 Types of Tweets

There are three types of tweets:

1. ***General Tweets:*** A public tweet is sent to everyone who follows you.

2. ***@Replies:*** A public tweet is sent to a specific person on Twitter. You may send an @reply in response to a tweet sent out by a person or you can use @reply to send a message to anyone on Twitter.
3. ***Direct message:*** A private tweet is sent to a person who follows you. You cannot send a direct message to someone who does not follow you.

☞ *While creating account, use your real name if you want people to find you using the Twitter search feature.*

11.3.3 How to Tweet?

In order to tweet, you will have to go to the Home Page of twitter, and sign-in as shown in the Figure 11.1.

Figure 11.1 Sign in Screen Twitter dialog box

After sign-in, you will be able to type your 'tweet' - a 140 character message. (This limit was set to make the service compatible to text messages). While you type your tweet, the interface itself will show you how many characters are left as shown in Figure 11.2.

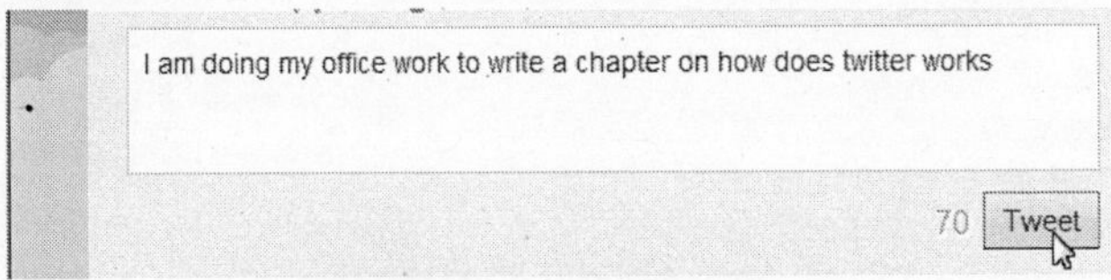

Figure 11.2 Message box

How to Send a Tweet on Twitter?

Twitter is an extremely interesting and versatile application that you can use to talk with friends, conduct business and even promote a blog or other type of Website. Each update you enter into Twitter is known as a "tweet." A tweet can be no longer than 140 characters, and you can send a general tweet to everyone, reply to a specific person or direct a tweet to only one person.

➜ **To send a tweet on twitter, do this:**

1. Log in to Twitter via the Twitter Home Page, or via a Twitter API application such as Twhirl. You can also update Twitter via Facebook and several other applications that use the Twitter API (Application Programming Interface)
2. Enter your message in the box with the label "What are you doing?" Keep in mind that your tweet can be no longer than 140 characters at the most. This limitation exists because Twitter uses the SMS (Short Message Service) network to send notifications via cell phone to those who desire it.
3. Click "Update" to send the Tweet to everyone on Twitter.
4. Type "d USERNAME" before your tweet to send a direct message to a particular user. Only that user will see the message.
5. Put "@USERNAME" at the beginning of your tweet to send a reply to a particular user. That user, your followers and that user's followers will all be able to see the tweet, but it will not appear on the public timeline.

Finding People on Twitter

How to find people by name

1. Type the person's name into the **search box** at the top of your Twitter Home Page.
2. Results for your search will show up under the **People tab** on the search page. Or
3. You can also search by typing the person's name into the search box on the **Connect page**.
4. The list of **People results for Sachin Tendulkar** appears as shown in Figure 11.3.

Figure 11.3 People Search Results

To send a direct message via the Web

1. Sign in to Twitter account.
2. Click on the envelope icon in the top right navigation bar.
3. You will see a pop up showing your direct message history. Click the **New message** button.
4. In the address box, type the name or username of the person you wish to send a message to.
5. Enter your message and click **Send message.**

☞ *Make sure that user follows you. You can only send a direct message to your followers even though you can receive messages from all users you follow.*

To delete a direct message via the web

1. Click on the **envelope** icon in the top right navigation bar.
2. You will see a pop up showing your direct message history. Click the conservation containing the message you would like to delete.

3. Locate the desired message and hover your mouse over it. A **trash icon** will appear as shown in Figure 11.4. Click it.
4. A message will show at the bottom of the DM inbox asking "Are you sure you want to delete this message?" Click **Delete message**.

Figure 11.4

Types of Tweets

Specific types of tweets will appear on others user's profiles. For instance, where your @reply will appear once you have sent it? The outline of General tweets are explained below.

General Tweets

Figure 11.5 General tweets

Definition: Any message with fewer than 140 characters posted to Twitter as shown in Figure 11.5.

Where it appears for the sender: On the Sender's profile page and Home timeline.

Where it appears for the recipient: In the Home timeline of anyone who is following the sender.

Places it will never appear: On anyone else's profile page, unless they retweeted the message.

@Replies:

Support @Support 30 Nov
@lukester Thanks for your feedback, I'll share it with the team!
View conversation Reply Retweet Favorite More

Figure 11.6 @Replies

Definition: A Tweet that begins with another user's username and is in reply to one of their Tweets.

Where it appears for the sender: On the Sender's profile page.

Where it appears for the recipient: In the recipient's Mentions and Interaction tabs. Like mentions, @replies will also appear in the recipient's Home timeline if they are following the sender. Anyone following the sender and the recipient of an @reply will see it in their Home timeline as shown in Figure 11.6.

Places it will never appear: On anyone's profile page, unless they wrote/sent the message.

Direct Messages:

Definition: A personal message sent directly to someone who follows you or sent directly to you from someone you follow.

Where it appears for the sender: In the sender's direct message folder. A direct message will disappear completely if either the sender or the recipient deletes it.

Where it appears for the recipient: In the recipient's direct messages. It will disappear if the sender deletes it.

Places it will never appear: In any public timeline or public search.

Using hashtags on Twitter

The # symbol, called a hashtag, is used to mark keywords or topics in a Tweet. It was created organically by Twitter users as a way to categorize messages.

Using hashtags to categorize Tweets by keyword

- People use the hashtag symbol # before a relevant keyword or phrase (no spaces) in their Tweet to categorize those Tweets and help them show more easily in Twitter Search.
- Clicking on a hashtagged word in any message shows you all other Tweets marked with that keyword.
- Hashtags can occur anywhere in the Tweet at the beginning, middle, or end.
- Hashtagged words that become very popular are often Trending Topics.

☞ *In the Tweet below, @eddie included the hashtag #FF. Users created this as shorthand for "Follow Friday," a weekly tradition where users recommend people that others should follow on Twitter. You will see this on Fridays (See Figure 11.7).*

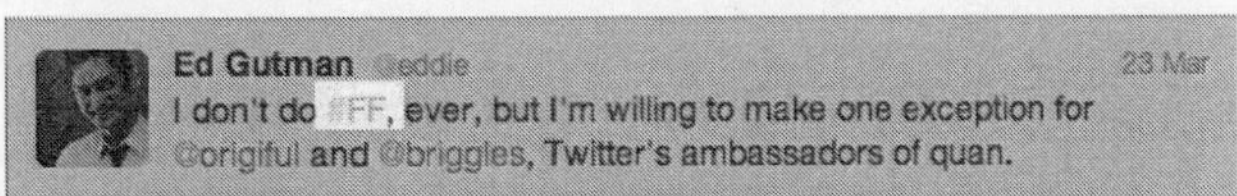

Figure 11.7 Using hashtag to categorize tweets

11.4 USING FACEBOOK

Facebook is a social networking Website intended to connect friends, family, and business associates. It is the largest networking site. People have been 'facebooking' each other for about 6 years now, making Facebook the most used social network all over the world.

11.4.1 How does Facebook Work?

Facebook uses a variety of services, tools, and programming languages to make up its core infrastructure.

The Front End of Facebook Website

At the front end, their servers run on a LAMP (Linux, Apache, MySQL, and PHP or (Personal Home Page) stack with Memcache.

Linux is a computer operating system. It is open source, very customizable, and good for security. Facebook runs the Linux operating system with Apache HTTP (Hypertext Preprocessor) Servers.

Apache is also free and is a a most popular open source Web server in use.

For the database, Facebook utilizes MySQL because of its speed and reliability.

Facebook uses PHP because it is a good Web programming language with extensive support from an active developer community. It is good for rapid iteration also. PHP is a dynamically typed/interpreted scripting language.

Memcache is a memory system that is used to speed up dynamic database-driven Websites (like Facebook) by caching data and objects in RAM to reduce reading time.

The Back End of Facebook Website

Facebook's back end services are written in a variety of different programming languages including C++, Java, Python, and Erlang. There is a large list of all Facebook open source development tools. Some of the essential tools are as under:

Thrift (protocol): Thrift is a lightweight remote procedure call framework for scalable cross-language services development. It is quick, saves development time, and provides a division of labor of work on high-performance servers and applications.

Scribe (log server): Scribe is a server for aggregating log data streamed in real-time from many other servers. It is a scalable framework useful for logging a wide array of data.

Cassandra (database): Cassandra is a database management system designed to handle large amount of data spread out across many servers. It powers Facebook Inbox Search feature and provides a structured key-value store with eventual consistency.

HipHop for PHP: HipHop for PHP is a source code transformer for PHP script code and was created to save server resources. It transforms PHP source code into optimized C++ programming language code.

11.4.2 Creating an Account

➔ To create Facebook account, do this:

1. Go to **www.facebook.com**.
2. Enter your name (first name and last initial), e-mail address, and a password in the text boxes provided for them (See Figure 11.8).
3. Then click on **Sign Up**.

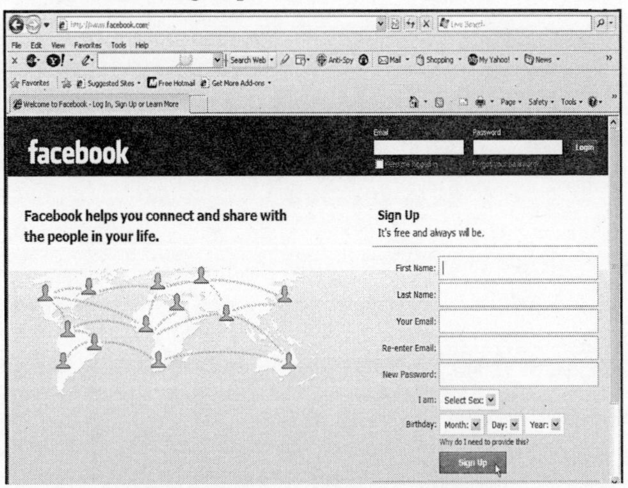

Figure 11.8 Facebook Sign in Window

4. After that a security code appears and you have to enter that code.
5. A confirmation link would be sent to your e-mail address. You need to click on that link and once you do that, you will be directed to the **'Getting Started'** page of Facebook. If anyone has been on the lookout for you, their names would appear, and you can opt to add them in your friends list.

Exploring the Facebook Toolbar and Tabs

The Toolbar at the top of your screen lets you navigate through Facebook.

Use Facebook button

Use the Facebook button to return to your Facebook Home Page. You can also use the Home button to return to your Home Page. Your Facebook page displays information about your Facebook friends. A series of tabs are displayed at the top of the screen that allow you to easily navigate through your Facebook page. There are five default tabs for your Facebook Home Page:

1. **News Feed:** This tab displays stories about your friends, such as when they add friends, post updates or write on a friend's wall. The amount of information displayed about a friend depends on their privacy settings. You can customize the amount of news that you receive about a particular friend in your News Feed.
2. **Status Updates:** This tab displays status updates posted by your friends. It does not include other stories about your friends, such as when they join a group or add a new friend.
3. **Photos:** This tab displays your friend's photo albums. The photo albums displayed in this tab depends on the privacy setting selected for the photo album.
4. **Posted Items:** This tab displays all posted by friends.
5. **Live Feed:** This tab displays all news stories about your friends, such as status updates, friends they have added and groups they have joined.

➔ To add application tabs to your Facebook page, do this:

1. Select the arrow at the far right of the tabs.
2. From the drop-down list, select the application feeds you want displayed on your tabs. The tabs are added to your Facebook Home Page.

Use Profile button

Use the Profile button view and edit your profile. Your profile is the place where you share information with your friends, such as photos, information and messages. You can use this to determine who sees your profile. You can set your profile to Public so that everyone on Facebook can see your profile.You can also restrict your profile to only friends that you have approved. There are also restrictions you can set that only affect specific information in your profile.

There are four default tabs for your Profile page. These are:

1. **Wall:** This tab displays messages that your friends leave for you. You can use Wall to write a message back to your friend.
2. **Info:** This tab displays your profile information. To edit information, click Edit Information.
3. **Photos:** This tab displays pictures that you posted.
4. **Videos:** This tab displays videos that you posted.

➔ To add additional tabs to your profile page, do this:

1. Select the plus sign button at the far right of the tabs.
2. From the drop-down list, select the applications you want displayed on your tabs. The tabs are added to your Profile page.

11.4.3 How to use your Facebook Inbox button?

Use this button to read messages from your friends and send messages to your friends. Messages are a way to communicate with friends individually without posting a public message on their wall.

1. From the Inbox menu, select Compose New Message.

2. Enter the name of the person you want to send a message to, the subject and the message. Click the Send button.
3. To read messages sent to you, select View Message Inbox from the Inbox menu.

11.4.4 Finding Friends on Facebook

Facebook has been programmed to ask you whether you want it to search your e-mail list. If you opt to go ahead and allow Facebook to search for people, it would search for those people who are on your e-mail list and check if they are on Facebook. If there is anyone on Facebook who is also there in your e-mail list, the Website would suggest you those names. You can opt to add them in the list of your friends list and you do not need to include anyone whom you do not want to include.

☞ *Avoid creating a profile with the name of your organization. Facebook requires accounts to represent real individuals. If you do not want to use your own name, try using a first name and last initial.*

Find and Add Friends

After you join Facebook, this screen is displayed. You can add friends now or you can access this screen later by clicking Find Friends in the right side of the screen.

How to Find Friends? One of the easiest ways to find Friends is to allow Facebook to access and import contacts from your email and various other social accounts. Facebook uses this information to connect you with Friends based on your contact list.

1. To find friends, locate and select Find Friends on the Toolbar. The Find Friends page will appear as shown in Figure 11.9.

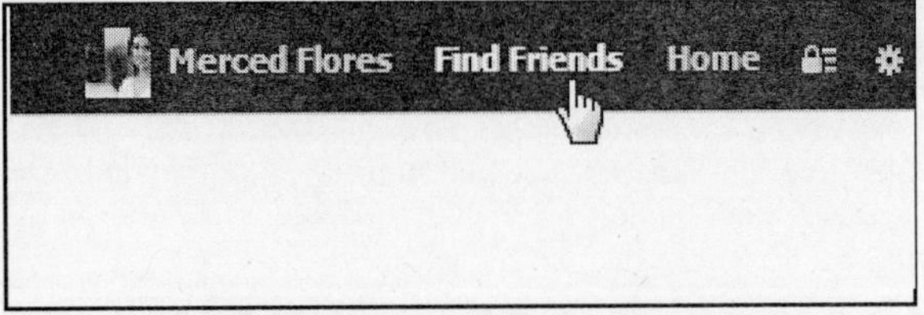

Figure 11.9 Selecting Find Friends

2. Click the buttons in the interactive below to learn about the different ways to find Friends on Facebook as shown in Figure 11.10.

To Send a Friend Request Once you find your Friends, you will need to send them a Friend Request to become their Facebook Friend.

1. Click **Add as Friend** as shown in Figure 11.11.
2. The **Friend Request** will be sent. Keep in mind that the person will have to confirm you as a Friend on Facebook before they will be added to your Friends list (See Figure 11.12).

Find Friends you Instant Message

To Find Friends who you instant message, click on the Find Friends You Instant Message link:

1. Select the button for America Online Instant Messenger or AIM or Windows Live Messenger. Enter your screen name and AIM password, then click on the Find Friends button.

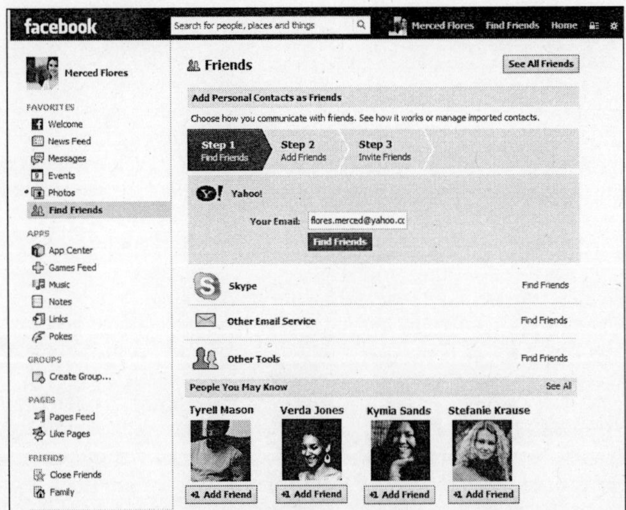

Figure 11.10

Figure 11.11 Sending a Friend request

Figure 11.12 Sent Friend request

☞ *Depending on your instant messaging provider, you may be directed to your IM provider's Website to enter your password directly on their site. Many e-mail providers require that you sign an agreement allowing Facebook to access your IM account.*

2. A list of people who you instant message with and are registered on Facebook is displayed. Click the check box next to each friend that you want to add.
3. To add all people that are displayed, click on the Select All Friends checkbox. If you do not want to add any of the friends displayed, click on the Skip button.
4. To add the friends you have selected, click on the Add as Friends button. An e-mail is sent to the friend for them to approve your request to be added as a friend.

How to Use the Different Facebook Applications?

Facebook is one of the most popular social media networking site where friend and known persons can keep in touch with each other. As a popular social media networking site, Facebook offers its users a wide array of applications that make their Facebook session even more exciting. You can enjoy a lot of online games through the Facebook application. Making birthday list, sending a friend a smile, poking a friend, sending virtual gifts and creating photo collages are some of the popular applications of Facebook. These small applications help you stay connected to your friends in a better way and helps them bond with you in a better way. You are sure to have a wonderful fun filled time with these Facebook applications. You can also enjoy Horoscope, creating events and groups through these applications on Facebook. Learn about the many Facebook applications like groups, events and horoscope in this free educational video clip.

11.4.5 Start Networking

If you know friends who are already on Facebook, you can add them by first searching as shown in the Figure 11.13, and then sending an invitation.

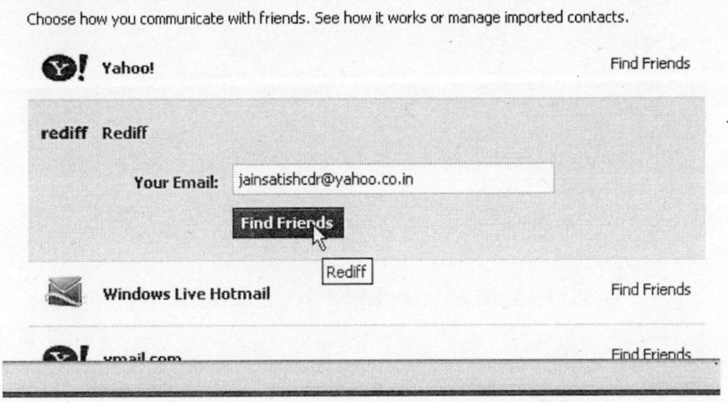

Figure 11.13 Searching Friends on the Facebook

☞ *You can create a group to stay in touch with your friends or like minded people.*

They need to accept your invitation and once accepted you can start networking with them by sending messages, pictures, videos, etc. Moreover, Facebook gives you the option to add or ignore a person from being your friend. Once these steps are done, it means you have successfully created a Facebook profile.

11.4.6 Keep Updating

Once you have created a profile, you can choose to keep it updated so that people know what you have been up to and whatever you have been thinking. You can add photos and share information which you want. You can also set preferences to as much or as little information you want to share with people who are not in your list of friends.

11.4.7 Groups on Facebook

Apart from staying in touch with your closest friends, there are many other reasons to learn how to create a group on Facebook. These reason are:

☞ *With Facebook, you can connect with your friends and acquaintances and it depends on you whom to choose or ignore. You can also play a few games, so go ahead and try it.*

1. Groups on Facebook of people share common interests. For example, if you are learning how to play the Guitar and are looking for help on one of the song, you can join a group made for Guitar players and ask the question and find your answers.
2. It brings together the people of one institution, whether it is a workplace or a college, and makes it easier for them to communicate with each other.
3. It can also be a platform for a celebrity to communicate with his/her fans and get important reviews from them about his/her work.

11.4.8 How to Create Group on Facebook?

In order to create a group on Facebook, firstly you have to go to the Home Page of Facebook.

1. Log-in to Facebook.

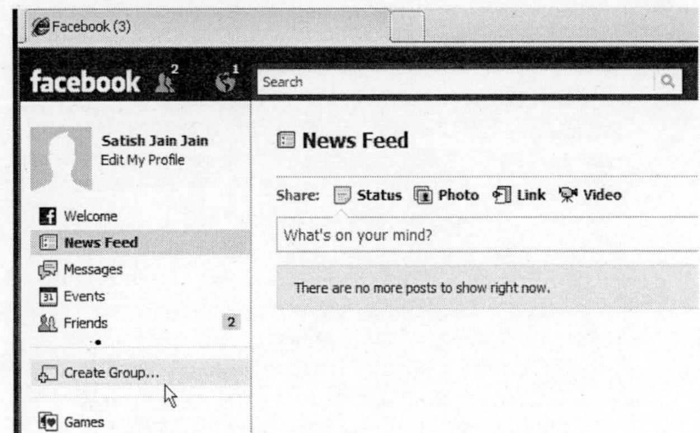

Figure 11.14 Create groups on Facebook

2. After log-in, on the left hand side of the same page, click on **Create a group**.
3. Search a person who is in your new group dialog box. Here you have to fill the basic information about your group and modify the settings as per your requirements whether you want to give access only to the members or to anyone on Facebook.
4. Then click on **Create Group** button.

Figure 11.15 Add a new group

11.5 WHAT IS LINKEDIN?

LinkedIn is a social network within the larger world of social media that is geared toward business. LinkedIn is very popular with those who are seeking work and trying to build their network of contacts so they can reach out to employers. LinkedIn is also popular as a way of marketing a business, because business owners can interact with those who are interested in their services by answering questions, participating in discussions and more.

11.5.1 How to use LinkedIn?

LikedIn is a popular Website for professionals to network, and college students also use it to meet someone in a company that they want to work for. It is advantageous to have a LinkedIn account, and here are some ways to make the most out of the online networking experience.

1. **Network with those you already know**–If you are new to LinkedIn, the best and easiest way to increase your connections is to add those you already know in person. LinkedIn allows you to import friends from your email accounts such as **Gmail, Yahoo, AOL (American Online), Windows Live**.
2. **Online Identity**–LinkedIn helps you build an online profile or recreate a professional identity. LinkedIn usually gets top ranking on Google, when someone plugs your name in the search engine, your professional profile comes up first. This is beneficial when you want to establish that you are professional identity because what they see on LinkedIn is a mini resume.
3. **Jobs**–Although LinkedIn is more popular as a networking tool that allows you to contact people and companies. There is also a jobs section on the page. You can apply for these jobs through the jobs page, but also utilize your knowledge of the contact person by being more assertive and contact them directly regarding the position.
4. **Find people**–LinkedIn is also useful when you want to look for someone in a particular company, or to find out what positions people hold in a particular organization. LinkedIn has a feature that helps you to "approach" someone and send them a message or e-mail.
5. **Recommendations**–LinkedIn has a built-in page for recommendations. You can receive recommendations from colleagues, and you can also give recommendations to those who work for you. These recommendations are helpful since you can showcase your achievements and gain credibility.

11.5.2 How to Create a LinkedIn Login?

You can use LinkeIn to find jobs, promote yourself or your business and much more. But first, you will need to create a LinkedIn login (account) in order to start using LinkedIn.

How to Create a LinkedIn Account?

In order to get started with LinkedIn, you will need to create an account. Once your accout is set up you can then start adding others to your network and building a powerful tool.

Start Creating Your LinkedIn Login

1. Open your Web browser and go to **LinkedIn.com**.
2. Complete the information in the **Join Linked** (right) area of the page.
   Type your First Name in the **First Name:** box.
   Type your Last Name in the **Last Name:** box.
   Type a valid email address where you receive e-mail in the **Email:** box.
   Type a Password for your account in the Password: box. The password needs to be at least six letters. It's a good idea to use both lowercase and capital letters along with at least one number or special character (*, !, etc.) to create a strong password. Don't leave any blank spaces.
   Click **Join Now** button as shown in Figure 11.16. This will move you to the next LinkedIn screen as shown in Figure 11.17.

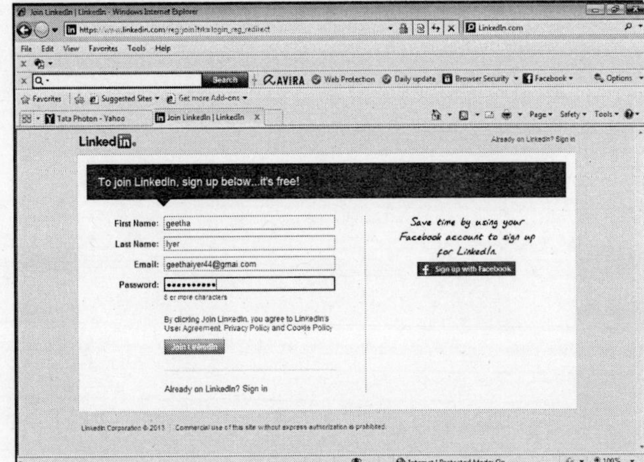

Figure 11.16

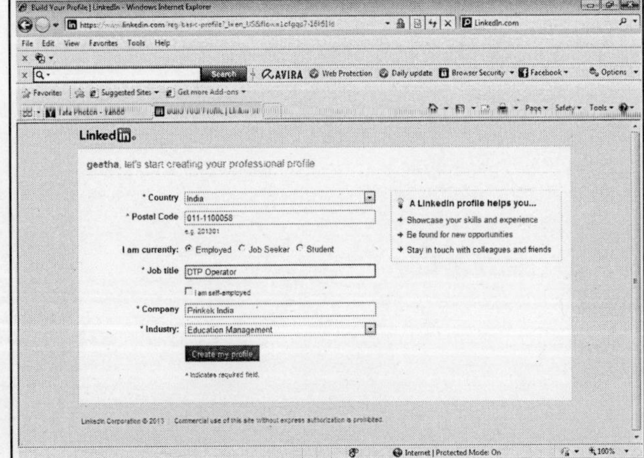

Figure 11.17

3. The next step in creating a LinkedIn login is to provider your employment status and location information.

4. Select one of the following options in the **I am currently:** drop-down list. These are: Employed with Company, A Business Owner, Working Independently or A student.
5. For example, if you selected **Employed** the remaining fields you will need to complete will be Company, Job Title, Country and Zip Code as shown in Figure 11.17.
6. **Create my profile** button.

Importing your E-mail Contacts (Optional)

In order to start building contacts, you have the option to import email addresses during the LinkedIn login setup process as shown in Figure 11.18. If you choose to take this optional step, LinkedIn will check to see if any of the e-mail addresses in you address book belong to existing LinkedIn members.

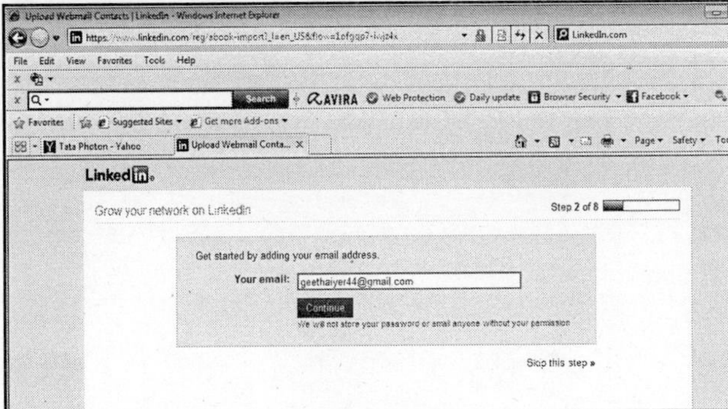

Figure 11.18

Keep in mind:

- If you do not want to use this feature, click the Skip this step link near the bottom of the screen.

Once you have eithe gone through the e-mail address or skipped over it, a confirmation screen displays to let you know that a confirmation e-mail has been sent to the e-mail account you just registered with LinkedIn. If LinkedIn recognized your e-mail provider, a button will be available that you can click to go directly to your (Webmail) e-mail provider, where you can log in and receive the confirmation message sent by LinkedIn (See Figure 11.19)

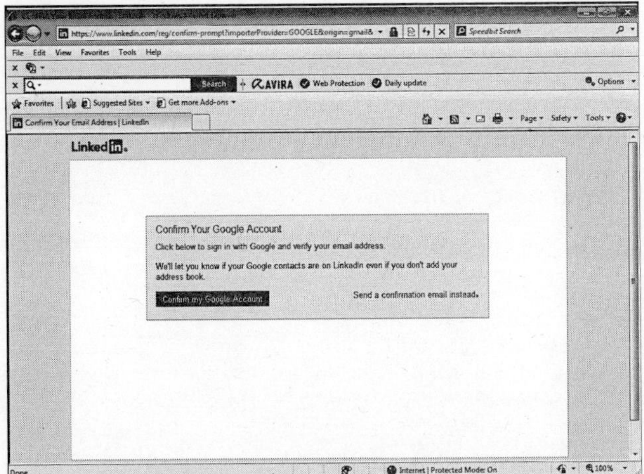

Figure 11.19

You may receive LikedIn's confirmation immediately or it could take several minutes. Once you receive the message, you need to do is:

1. Click the link in LinkedIn's confirmation message.
2. Log in to LinkedIn with the login you just created.
3. Start using LinkedIn!

What is a LinkedIn public profile?

Your public profile appears when people search for you using a public search engine like Google, Yahoo!, Bing, etc. You can edit your public profile from the Edit Profile page.

To hide your public profile do this:

1. Move your cursor over **Profile** at the top of your Home Page and select **Edit Profile** as shown in Figure 11.20.

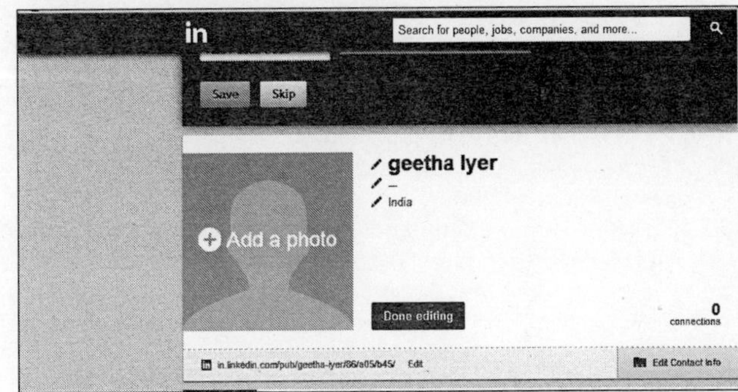

Figure 11.20

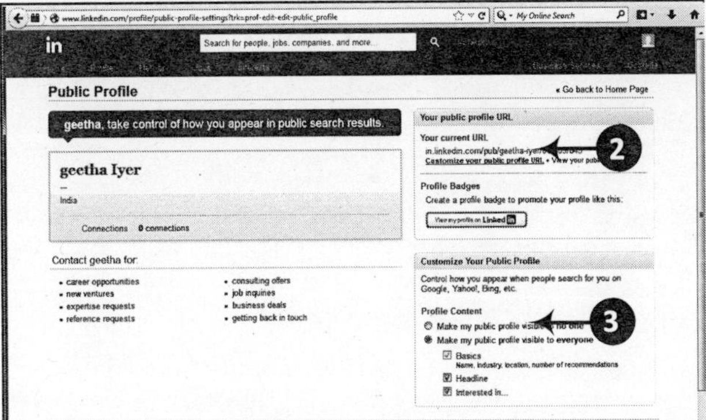

Figure 11.21

2. Click the **Edit** link next to your public profile URL in the top section of your profile. It will be an address like www.linkedin.com/in/yourname.
3. Click the button next to "Make my public profile visible to no one" on the right as shown in Figure 11.21. Your LinkedIn profile would not appear in search engines and would not be visible to non-LinkedIn members.

To show your public profile, do this:

1. Move your cursor over **Profile** at the top of your Home Page and select **Edit Profile**.
2. Click the **Edit** link next to your public profile URL in the top section of your profile. It will be an address like www.linkedin.com/in/yourname.
3. Click Next button to "Make My Public Profile Visible to Everyone". Your basic information displays by default.

4. Check or uncheck the boxes to select which additional sections you would like to display. The changes take effect immediately and you will be able to see them reflected on the page. Click View Your Public Profile to see the full page. You may need to reload that page to see the changes you have made.

11.6 E-GOVERNANCE

E-Governance is the application of modern information and Communication Technologies, such as Internet, local area networks, mobiles, etc., by Government to improve the effectiveness, efficiency, service delivery and to promote democracy.

It also use technology to enhance the access to and delivery of government services to benefit citizens, business partners and employees. Focus of these definitions range from those focusing on Information and Communication Technologies (ICTs) to those focusing on ICT-enables government and governance transformations. Some examples of such defintions include:

(a) The use of ICTs, and particularly the Internet, as a tool to achieve better government.

(b) The use of informaton and communciation technologies in all facts of the operations of a government organization.

(c) The continuous optimization of service delivery, constituency participation and governance by transforming internal and external relationships through technology, the Internet, etc.

E-governance is a form of public administration by using information and communication technologies to enhance the access and delivery of Government Services to benefit citizens, employees and management of urban local bodies, exchange of information, communication transactions, integration various stand-alone systems and services between Government and Citizens (G2C), Government and Business (G2B). It is as well as back office processes and interactions within the entire Government frame work. The aim is to strengthen the government's drive toward effective governance and increase in transparency to better manage social and economic resources for development.

11.6.1 Why E-Governance?

E-Governance can transform citizen service, provide access to information to empower citizens, enable their participation in government and enhance citizen economic and social opportunities, so that they can make better lives, for themselves and for the next generation.

Through the e-governance, the Government services will be made available to the citizens in a convenient, efficient and transparent manner.

☞ *Governments are specialized institutions that contribute to governance. Representative governments seek and receive citizen support, but they also need the active cooperation of their public servants. Governance is the outcome of politics, policies and programs.*

Government of India (GoI) has launched a National e-governance Plan (NeGP). NeGP intends to institute and enable mechanisms to improve the system of governance and thus provide better services to the citizens by effective use of ICT. In addition, e-governance in municipalities is one of the Mission Mode Projects under the NeGP, which is expected to result in improved service delivery by local governments for the citizens.

11.6.2 Difference between E-Government and E-Governance

While E-Government has traditionally been understood as being centered around the operations of government whereas, is also understood to extend the scope by including citizen engagement and participation in governance.

11.6.3 Activities of E-Government using E-Governance

E-governance models are built around objectives that include better use of information, quicker dissemination of information, transparency in government-people transactions, and creating services that cover as broad a spectrum of society as possible. The primary delivery models of e-governance to provide services to citizens, businesses and other arms of the government can be divided into:

(a) Government-to-Citizen or Government-to-Consumer (G2C)

(b) Government-to-Business (G2B)

(c) Government-to-Government (G2G)

(d) Government-to-Employees (G2E)

Within each of these interaction domains, four kinds of activities take place:

(a) Pushing information over the Internet, e.g., regulatory services, general holidays, public hearing schedules, issue briefs, notifications, etc.

(b) Two-way communications between the agency and the citizen, a business, or another government agency. In this model, users can engage in dialogue with agencies and post problems, comments, or requests to the agency.

(c) Conducting transactions, e.g., lodging tax returns, applying for services and grants.

(d) Governance, e.g., online polling, voting, and campaigning.

11.6.4 Risks and Benefits of E-Governence

Risks

There are many considerations and potential implications of implementing and designing e-government, including disintermediation of the government and its citizens, impacts on economic, social, and political factors, vulnerability to cyber attacks, and disturbances to the status quo in these areas.

Hyper-surveillance

Increased contact between government and its citizens goes both ways. Once e-government begins to develop and become more sophisticated, citizens will be forced to interact electronically with the government on a larger scale. This could potentially lead to a lack of privacy for civilians as their government obtains more and more information on them. In a worse case scenario, with so much information being passed electronically between government and civilians. When the government has easy access to countless information on its citizens, personal privacy is lost.

Cost

Although "a prodigious amount of money has been spent" on the development and implementation of e-government, some say it has yielded only a mediocre product. The outcomes and effects of trial Internet-based governments are often difficult to gauge or unsatisfactory.

Inaccessibility

An e-government site that provides web access and support often does not offer the potential to reach many users including those who live in remote areas, are homebound, have low literacy levels, exist on poverty line incomes, suffer from chronic illness, are single parents or older adults.

Benefits

It is convenient and cost-effective for businesses, and the public benefits by getting easy access to the most current information available without having to spend time, energy and money to get it.

E-government helps simplify processes and makes access to government information more easily accessible for public sector agencies and citizens. For example, the Indian Bureau of Motor Vehicles simplified the process of certifying driver records to be admitted in county court proceedings. The anticipated benefits of e-government include:

(a) Efficiency
(b) Improved services
(c) Better accessibility of public services
(d) Transparency and accountability

Democratization

One goal of e-government will be greater citizen participation. Through the Internet, people from all over the country can interact with politicians or public servants and make their voices heard. Blogging and interactive surveys will allow politicians or public servants to see the views of the people they represent on any given issue. Chat rooms can place citizens in real-time contact with elected officials, their offices or provide them with the means to replace them by interacting directly with public servants, allowing voters to have a direct impact and influence in their government. These technologies can create a more transparent government, allowing voters to immediately see how and why their representation in the capital is voting the way they are. This helps voters better decide who to vote for in the future or how to help the public servants become more productive. A government could theoretically move more towards a true democracy with the proper application of e-government. Government transparency will give insight to the public on how decisions are made and hold elected officials or public servants accountable for their actions. The public could become a direct and prominent influence in government legislature to some degree.

Environmental Bonuses

Proponents of e-government argue that online government services would lessen the need for hard copy forms. Due to recent pressures from environmentalist groups, media, and public, some governments and organizations have turned to the Internet to reduce this paper use.

Speed, Efficiency, and Convenience

E-government allows citizens to interact with computers to achieve objectives at any time and any location, and eliminates the necessity for physical travel to government agents sitting behind desks and windows. Improved accounting and record keeping can be noted through computerization, and information and forms can be easily accessed, equaling quicker processing time. On the administrative side, access to help find or retrieve files and linked information can now be stored in databases versus hardcopies stored in various locations. Individuals with disabilities or conditions no longer have to be mobile and to be active in government and can be in the comfort of their own homes.

Public Approval

Recent trials of e-government have been met with acceptance and eagerness from the public. Citizens participate in online discussions of political issues with increasing frequency, and young people, who traditionally display minimal interest in government affairs, are drawn to e-voting procedures.

☞ *E-governance has given citizens easy access to tangible benefits, be it through simple applications such as online form filling, bill sourcing and payments, or complex applications like distance education and tele-medicine.*

11.6.5 E-governance Websites and their Societal Impacts

We will describe about e-governance Websites. Although, there are hundreds e-governance projects running in India. But, here we shall discuss only some of them.

Central Excise Mission Mode Project

The Automation of Central Excise and Service Tax (ACES) *(URL: http://aces.excisegst.com)* is a Mission Mode Project under the National e-governance Plan being implemented by the Central Board of Excise and Customs (CBEC) in India (See Figure 11.22). It is targeted at the 20,000 users of the CBEC in 245 cities across India and seeks to automate the processes of CBEC along with providing e-services to the users both online and through facilitation centres.

In order to achieve its objective, areas that needed immediate attention were prioritized. It provides the following facilities to the taxpayers:

(a) Online Registration of Central Excise Assesses and online amendment.
(b) Online Registration of Service Tax Assesses and online amendment.
(c) Electronic filing of Central Excise Returns.
(d) Electronic filing of Service Tax Returns.
(e) Electronic filing of claims, permissions, intimations submitted by assesses in the course of business with the Department.
(f) Instant e-acknowledgement of documents with an Unique Document Identification (UDI) Number.

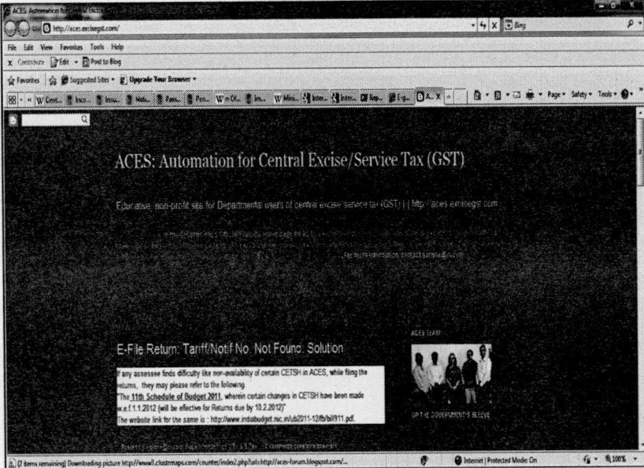

Figure 11.22 Home Page of ACES

Immigration, Visa and Foreigner's Registration & Tracking (IVFRT) Project

In order to Modernize and upgrade the Immigration services, "Immigration, Visa and Foreigners Registration & Tracking (IVFRT)" has been identified *(URL: http:www.immigrationindia.nic.in/)*. The core objective of this Project is to develop and implement a secure and integrated service delivery framework that facilitates legitimate travelers while strengthening security. The scope of the project includes 169 Missions, 77 ICPs (Immigration Check Posts), 5 FRROs (Foreigners Regional Registration Offices), and FROs (Foreigners Registration Offices) in the State/District Headquarters (See Figure 11.23).

Figure 11.23 Website of Bureau of Immigration, India

The implementation of this project provides the following services:

(a) It enables authentication of traveler's identity at the Missions, Immigration Check Posts (ICPs) and Foreigners Registration Offices (FROs) through use of intelligent document scanners and biometrics.

(b) It also updates foreigner's details at entry and exit points, improved tracking of foreigner's through sharing of information captured during visa issuance at Missions, during immigration check at ICPs, and during registration at FRRO/FROs.

Income Tax (IT) Department of India

The Income Tax Department of India is implementing a plan for setting up a comprehensive service that enables citizens to transact all businesses with the Department on an anywhere, anytime basis (See Figure 11.24).

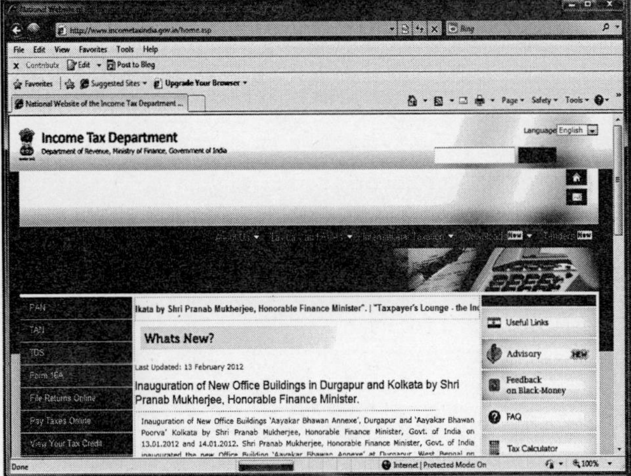

Figure 11.24 Web site of Income Tax of India

Some of the services provided by the Income Tax Department are as follows *(URL: incomtaxindia.gov.in)*:

(a) Distribution of Permanent Account Number (PAN)
(b) Tax accounting
(c) Taxpayer complaint redressal
(d) Taxpayer correspondence
(e) Tax compliance
(f) Online submission of returns
(g) Processing of tax return
(h) Processing of Tax-Deducted-at-source (TDS) return

Passport Seva Project

The Passport Seva Project was launched by the Ministry of External Affairs with the objective of delivering Passport Services to the citizens in a comfortable environment with wider accessibility and reliability (See Figure 11.25) *(URL:http://www.meaindia.nic.in)*. The project controls 77 Passport Seva Kendras (PSKs) across the country, a Data Centre and Disaster Recovery Centre, Call centre operating 18x7 in 17 languages, and a centralized nationwide computerized system for issuance of passports. The entire operation will function in a "less paper" environment with an attempt being made to deliver passports within 3 working days to categories not requiring police verification.

Pensioner's Portal

Pensioner's Portal *(URL: http://pensionersportal.gov.in)* project has been set up with the two components (See Figure 11.26). Non-interactive component provides updated information on pension issues and Interactive component monitors grievance redressal at three interlinked levels as follows:

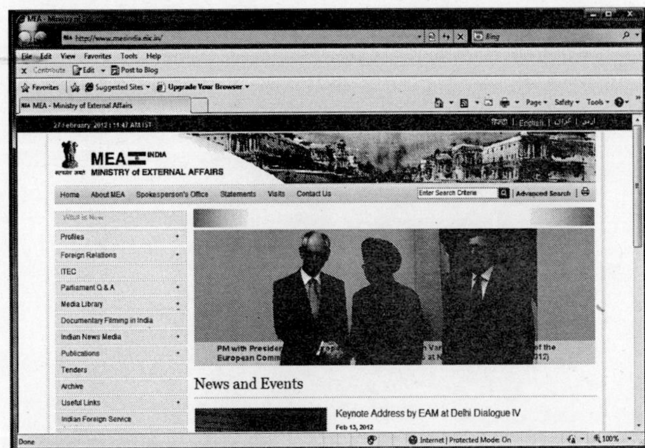

Figure 11.25 Website of Ministry of External Affairs (MEA)

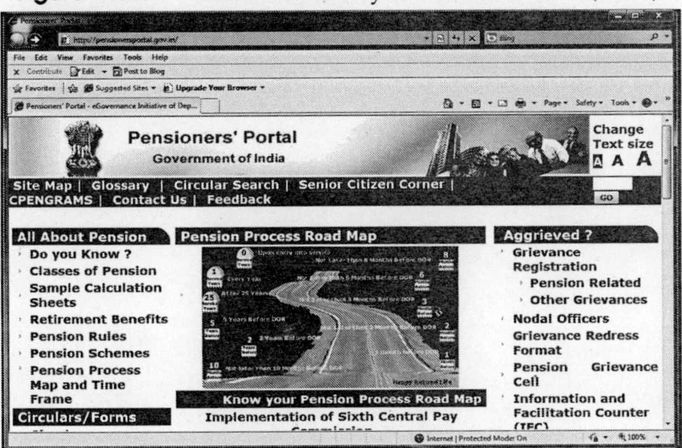

Figure 11.26 Website of Pensioners' portal

(a) Central-level in Department of Pensions & Pensioners' Welfare (nodal point)
(b) Central Ministries/ Department-level
(c) Pensioners' Associations-level (field level)

Pensioners registering their grievances on the portal and get unique access codes, which helps them to monitor the progress of their cases. The designated nodal officer at the level of Department of Pension & Pensioners' Welfare and at the level of Central Ministry/Department can also monitor the progress of such registered cases.

11.6.6 E-governance Challenges

With the use of e-governance, a citizen can avail multiple government services from a single point. With respect to managing its relationship with the citizen/customer, the government has the strategies in terms of various delivery channels that it can use for e-governance. These channels include Internet, digital TV, tablets, and mobile phones. As with every new enterprise, initiating and sustaining e-governance ventures has its own set of challenges.

All implementers and drivers of e-governance initiatives agree that the biggest challenge of deploying e-governance is not technology but change management. Change management is important not only in terms of cultural change but also in terms of changing operations and processes workflow that the automated environment will introduce.

The key challenges with e-governance are not technology or Internet issues but organizational issues like the following:

(a) Redefining rules and procedures
(b) Information transparency
(c) Legal issues
(d) Infrastructure, skill and awareness
(e) Access to right of information
(f) Interdepartmental collaboration
(g) Tendency to resist the change in work culture

Other obstacles are geographical distances, lack of trained human resources, and lack of ICT penetration in remote areas. For example, a good e-governance application will not benefit anybody in remote areas if there are no supporting infrastructures such as electricity, computers and connectivity.

The other set of challenges lie in extending the reach of e-governance services to 70% of Indian population that lives in villages. These include:

(a) Assessment of local needs and customizing e-governance solutions to meet those needs
(b) Connectivity
(c) Content (local content based on local language)
(d) Building Human Capacities
(e) E-commerce
(f) Sustainability

To overcome from these challenges, government organizations need administrative support. In order to obtain this, they need to first convince the bureaucracy of the benefits of e-governance. Legacy systems need to be incorporated into the e-governance infrastructure. Information needs to be prepared almost in real time to the government, business partners, and citizens.

A government department's work processes will have to be altered to accommodate CRM (Customer RElationship Management) and e-governance. This will require educating employees at all levels about the benefits of technology. The various benefits and advantages of e-enabling the system should be communicated clearly right at the beginning to ensure popular support which will lead to greater chances of success. In addition to this, explain to people that the introduction of IT will not take away existing jobs but will make them easier, and if less manpower is required for operations the staff can be re-deployed elsewhere with no threat to their career growth path.

E-governance Challenges in India

Following points list down some of the challenges which are specific to India:

(a) *Lack of Integrated Services:* Most of the e-governance Services offered by state or central governments are not integrated. Non-integration results in lack of communication between different departments. So the information that resides with one department has no or very little meaning to some other department of Government.
(b) *Lack of Key Persons:* e-governance projects lack key persons, not only from technological aspect, but from other aspects as well.

(c) *Population:* Apart from being an asset to the country, population is one of the biggest challenge in India. It offers some unique issues, an important one being Establishing Person Identities. There is no unique identity of a person in India. Apart from this, measuring the population, keeping the database of all Indian nationals are some other related challenges.

(d) *Different Languages:* A challenge due to the diversity of the country. It enforces need to do governance (upto certain level), in local languages. Ensuring e-governance in local language is a big task to achieve.

11.7 E-COMMERCE

Electronic commerce or e-commerce refers to a wide range of online business activities for products and services. It also pertains to any form of business transaction in which the parties interact electronically rather than by physical exchanges or direct physical contact.

E-commerce is usually associated with buying and selling over the Internet, or conducting any transaction involving the transfer of ownership or rights to use goods or services through a computer-mediated network. A more complete definition is: E-commerce is the use of electronic communications and digital information processing technology in business transactions to create, transform, and redefine relationships for value creation between or among organizations, and between organizations and individuals.

E-commerce allows consumers to electronically exchange goods and services with no barriers of time or distance. Electronic commerce has expanded rapidly over the past five years and is predicted to continue at this rate, or even accelerate. In the near future the boundaries between "conventional" and "electronic" commerce will become increasingly blurred as more and more businesses move sections of their operations onto the Internet.

Electronic commerce draws on such technologies as *electronic funds transfer, supply chain management, Internet marketing, online transaction processing, Electronic Data Interchange* (EDI), *inventory management systems,* and *automated data collection systems.* Modern electronic commerce typically uses the World Wide Web (WWW) at least at one point in the transaction's life-cycle, although it may encompass a wider range of technologies such as e-mail, mobile devices and telephones as well.

The Information Technology Act, 2000 governs the activities of e-commerce in India.

Some common applications related to electronic commerce are the following:

- Enterprise content management
- E-mail
- Automated online assistants
- Instant messaging
- Newsgroups
- Online shopping and order tracking
- Electronic tickets
- Teleconferencing

11.7.1 Different Types of E-Commerce

There are different types of e-commerce and we need to know what e-commerce is and how different it is from e-business. E-commerce is used for business transactions through the internet medium while e-business involves one or more organizations making and individuals making commercial transactions through a digital medium.

You can classify e-commerce into five main categories.

- *Business-to-Consumer (B2C):* Online transactions which are made between businesses and individual consumers. B2C is the indirect trade between the company and consumers. It provides direct selling through online. For example, if you want to sell goods and services to customer so that anybody can purchase any products directly from supplier's Website.

  Directly interact with the customers is the main difference with other business model. As B2B it manages directly relationship with consumers, B2C supply chains deal with business that are related to the customer.
- *Business-to-Business (B2B):* businesses make online transactions with other businesses. It consists of largest form of Ecommerce. This model defines that buyer and seller are two different entities. It is similar to manufacturer issuing goods to the retailer or wholesaler.
- *Business-to-Business-to-Consumer (B2B2C):* E-commerce model in which a business provides some product or service to a client business that maintains its own customers.
- *Consumer-to-Business (C2B):* E-commerce model in which individuals use the Internet to sell products or services to organizations or individuals and seek sellers to bid on products or services they need.
- *Consumer-to-Consumer (C2C):* E-commerce model in which consumers sell directly to other consumers. It helps the online dealing of goods or services among people. Though there is no major parties needed but the parties will not fulfill the transactions without the program which is supplied by the online market dealer, such as eBay.
- *Peer-to-Peer (P2P):* Technology that enables networked peer computers to share data and processing with each other directly. It can be used in C2C, B2B and B2C e-commerce.
- *Mobile commerce (M-commerce):* E-commerce transactions and activities conducted in a wireless environment.
- *Location-based commerce (L-commerce):* L-commerce refers to the localization of products and services through mobile commerce and framework aware computing technologies. This service works around various service areas, such as Location, Navigation, Tracking, Mapping and Timing.
- *Intrabusiness e-commerce:* E-commerce category that includes all internal organizational activities that involve the exchange of goods, services, or information among various units and individuals in an organization.

11.7.2 What is B3B E-commerce?

B2B e-commerce is simply defined as e-commerce between companies. This is the type of e-commerce that deals with relationships between among businesses. About 80% of e-commerce is of this type, and predict that B2B e-commerce will continue to grow faster than the B2C. The B2B market has two primary components: e-frastructure and e-markets. E-frastructure is the architecture of B2B, primarily consisting of the following:

- Logistics - transportation, warehousing and distribution (e.g., Procter and Gamble);

- Application service providers - deployment, hosting and management of packaged software from a central facility (e.g., Oracle and Linkshare);
- Outsourcing of functions in the process of e-commerce, such as Web-hosting, security and customer care solutions (e.g., outsourcing providers, such as eShare, NetSales);
- content management software for the facilitation of Website content management and delivery (e.g., Interwoven and ProcureNet); and
- Web-based commerce enablers (e.g., Commerce One, a browser-based, XML-enabled purchasing automation software).

E-markets are simply defined as Websites where buyers and sellers interact with each other and conduct transactions. The more common B2B examples and best practice models are IBM, Hewlett Packard (HP), Cisco and Dell. Cisco, for instance, receives over 90% of its product orders over the Internet.

B2B applications are in the areas of supplier management (especially purchase order processing), inventory management (i.e., managing order-ship-bill cycles), distribution management (especially in the transmission of shipping documents), channel management (i.e., information dissemination on changes in operational conditions), and payment management (e.g., Electronic payment systems or EPS).

11.7.3 What is B2C E-commerce?

Business-to-consumer e-commerce, or commerce between companies and consumers, involves customers gathering information; purchasing physical goods (i.e., tangibles such as books or consumer products) or information goods (or goods of electronic material or digitized content, such as software, or e-books); and, for information goods, receiving products over an electronic network.

It is the second largest and the earliest form of e-commerce. Its origins can be traced to online retailing (or e-retailing). Thus, the more common B2C business models are the online retailing companies, such as Amazon.com, Drugstore.com, Beyond.com, Barnes and Noble and ToysRus. Other B2C examples involving information goods are E-Trade.

11.7.4 What is B2G E-commerce?

Business-to-government e-commerce or B2G is generally defined as commerce between companies and the public sector. It refers to the use of the Internet for public procurement, licensing procedures, and other government-related operations. This kind of e-commerce has two features: first, the public sector assumes a pilot/leading role in establishing e-commerce; and second, it is assumed that the public sector has the greatest need for making its procurement system more effective.

11.7.5 What is C2C E-commerce?

Consumer-to-consumer e-commerce or C2C is simply commerce between private individuals or consumers. This type of e-commerce is characterized by the growth of electronic marketplaces and online auctions, particularly in industries where firms/businesses can bid for what they want from among multiple suppliers.

This type of e-commerce comes in at least three forms:

- Auctions facilitated at a portal, such as eBay, which allows online real-time bidding on items being sold in the Web;
- Peer-to-peer systems, such as the Napster model (a protocol for sharing files between users used by chat forums similar to IRÇ) and other file exchange and later money exchange models; and
- Classified ads at portal sites, such as Excite Classifieds and eWanted (an interactive, online marketplace where buyers and sellers can negotiate).

Advantages of C2C sites

Consumer-to-consumer ecommerce has many benefits. The business model of C2C is very interesting. The primary benefit which consumers get is reduction in cost as compared to buying space of their adds on other ecommerce sites which seem to be quite expensive. People interested in selling their items can post their respective items for free or with minimal charge depending on the C2C website. C2C websites form a perfect platform for buyers and sellers who wish to buy and sell products of similar interest. Another benefit is that business owners can easily afford the low cost of maintaining C2C websites and earn good profits instead of buying or hiring a shop which could cost a lot.

Disadvantages of C2C sites

There are a couple of disadvantages to these type of sites as well. Doing transaction on these type of Websites requires co-operation between the buyer and seller. It has been noted many times that these two do not co-operate with each other after a transaction has been made. They do not share the transaction information which may be via credit or debit card or internet banking. This can result in online fraud since the buyer and seller are not very well versed with each other. Companies which handle consumer to consumer e-commerce Websites seem to have becoming very cautious to prevent online crime.

What is M-commerce?

M-commerce (mobile commerce) is the buying and selling of goods and services through wireless technology, i.e., handheld devices such as cellular telephones and Personal Digital Assistants (PDAs).

As content delivery over wireless devices becomes faster, more secure, and scalable, some believe that m-commerce will surpass wireline e-commerce as the method of choice for digital commerce transactions. This may well be true for the Asia-Pacific where there are more mobile phone users than there are Internet users.

11.7.6 Importance of E-commerce

E-commerce proved its importance based on the fact where time is essence. In the commercial markets, time plays an important role to both the business and consumers. From the business perspective, with less time spent during each transaction, can be achieved on the same day. As for the consumer, they will save up more time during their transaction. Because of this, e-commerce steps in and replaced the traditional commerce method where a single transaction can cost both parties a lot of valuable time. For instance, a banking transaction can be completed through the Internet within a few minutes compared to the traditional banking method which may take up to hours. This fact obviously proves that e-commerce is beneficial to both business and consumer wise as payment and documentations can be completed with greater efficiency.

From the business view point, e-commerce is much more cost effective compared to traditional commerce method. This is due to the fact where through e-commerce, the cost for the middle person to sell their products can be saved and diverted to another aspect of their business.

To both the consumers and business, connectivity plays an important part as it is the key factor determining the whole business. From the business point of view, e-commerce provides better connectivity for its potential customer as their respective Website can be accessed virtually from anywhere through Internet. e-commerce proves to be more convenient as online trading has less compared to traditional commerce method.

11.7.7 Advantages and Disadvantages of E-Commerce

E-commerce provides many new ways for businesses and consumers to communicate and conduct business. There are a number of advantages and disadvantages of conducting business.

E-commerce Advantages

Some advantages that can be achieved from e-commerce include:

- **Being able to conduct business:** E-commerce systems can operate all day every day and every hour. Your physical storefront does not need to be open in order for customers and suppliers to be doing business with you electronically. This is the greatest way to conduct the business.
- **Access the global market place:** It is possible to do business with any business or person who is connected to the Internet. Simple local businesses are able to market and sell their offerings internationally using e-commerce.
- **No need to wait:** Electronic communications allow messages to traverse the world almost instantaneously. There is no need to wait weeks for a catalog to arrive by post: that communications delay is not a part of the Internet/e-commerce world.
- **High market space:** The market place in which Web-based businesses operate is the global market. It may not be evident to them, but many businesses are already facing international competition from Web-enabled businesses.
- **Opportunity to reduce costs:** This is the greatest way to purchase the product. The Internet makes it very easy to 'shop around' for products and services that may be cheaper or more effective than we might otherwise settle for. It is sometimes possible to, through some online research, identify original manufacturers for some goods-thereby by passing wholesalers and achieving a cheaper price.
- **Computer platform-independent:** Computers have the ability to communicate via the Internet independent of operating systems and hardware. Customers are not limited by existing hardware systems.
- **Efficient applications development environment:** In many respects, applications can be more efficiently developed and distributed because the can be built without regard to the customer's or the business partner's technology platform. Application updates do not have to be manually installed on computers. Rather, Internet-related technologies provide this capability inherently through automatic deployment of software.
- **Allowing customer self service and 'customer outsourcing:** People can interact with businesses at any hour of the day that it is convenient to them, and because these interactions are initiated by customers, the customers also provide a lot of the data for the transaction that may otherwise need to be entered by business staff. This means that some of the work and costs are effectively shifted to customers; this is referred to as "customer outsourcing".

E-commerce disadvantages

Some disadvantages and constraints of e-commerce include the following.

- **Time for delivery of physical products:** E-commerce is often used to buy goods that are not available locally from businesses all over the world, meaning that physical goods need to be delivered, which takes time and costs money. In some cases there are ways around this, for example, with electronic files of the music or books being accessed across the Internet, but then these are not physical goods.
- **Physical product and delivery uncertainty:** When you walk out of a shop with an item, it's yours. You have it; you know what it is, where it is and how it looks. In some respects e-commerce purchases are made on trust. This is because, firstly, not having had physical access to the product, a purchase is made on an expectation of what that product is and its condition. Secondly, because supplying businesses can be conducted across the world, it can be uncertain whether or not they are legitimate businesses and are not just going to take your money.
- **Perishable goods:** Transport can be used, goods bought and sold via the Internet tend to be durable and non-perishable: they need to survive from the supplier to the purchasing business or consumer. This shifts the bias for perishable and/or non-durable goods back towards traditional supply chain arrangements, or towards relatively more local e-commerce-based purchases, sales and distribution. In contrast, durable goods can be traded from almost anyone to almost anyone else, sparking competition for lower prices. In some cases this leads to disintermediation in which intermediary people and businesses are bypassed by consumers and by other businesses that are seeking to purchase more directly from manufacturers.
- **Limited sensory information:** The Internet is an effective conduct for visual and auditory information: seeing pictures, hearing sounds and reading text. However it does not allow full scope for our senses: we can see pictures of the flowers, but not smell their fragrance; we can see pictures of a hammer, but not feel its weight or balance. There are many ways in which the Internet does not convey the richness of experiences of the world. This lack of sensory information means that people are often much more comfortable buying

via the Internet generic goods - things that they have seen or experienced before and about which there is little ambiguity, rather than unique or complex things.

- **Returning goods:** Returning goods online can be an area of difficulty. The uncertainties surrounding the initial payment and delivery of goods can be worsened.
- **Privacy, security, payment, identity, contract:** Many issues arise - privacy of information, security of that information and payment details, whether or not payment details (e.g. credit card details) will be misused, identity theft, contract, and, whether we have one or not, what laws and legal jurisdiction apply.
- **Defined Services and the unexpected:** E-commerce is an effective means for managing the transaction of known and established services, that is, things that are everyday. It is not suitable for dealing with the new or unexpected.
- **Personal service:** Although some human interaction can be facilitated via the web. e-commerce cannot provide the richness of interaction provided by personal service. For most businesses, e-commerce methods provide the equivalent of an information-rich counter attendant rather than a salesperson. This also means that feedback about how people react to product and service using e-commerce approaches. Successful business use of e-commerce typically involves strategies for gaining and applying customer feedback. This helps businesses to understand, anticipate and meet changing online customer needs and preferences, which is critical because of the comparatively rapid rate of ongoing Internet-based change.
- **Size and number of transactions:** E-commerce is most often conducted using credit card facilities for payments, and as a result very small and very large transactions not to be conducted online. The size of transactions is also impacted by the economics of transporting physical goods.

11.8 E-LEARNING

The term *e-learning* (also known as electronic learning), refers to use of computers and communication technologies in the teaching to enhance its effectiveness or we can say, it is a method of education used for web-based distance education, wherein there is no face-to-face interaction (See Figure 11.27).

☞ *E-learning provides the potential to give the right of information to the right people at the right time and places using the right medium.*

E-learning is based on three fundamental criteria:

- It is networked, instant updating, storage and retrieval, distribution and sharing of information is therefore possible.
- It is delivered to the end-user via a computer using standard Internet technologies.
- It focuses on the broadest view of learning.

☞ *E-learning is very beneficial in adding value in organizational matters, like it is easier to access information and there is flexibility with respect to time and place. It is a facility that reduces the travel time and associated costs. It eliminates the expense and inconvenience of getting the teachers and students in the same premise.*

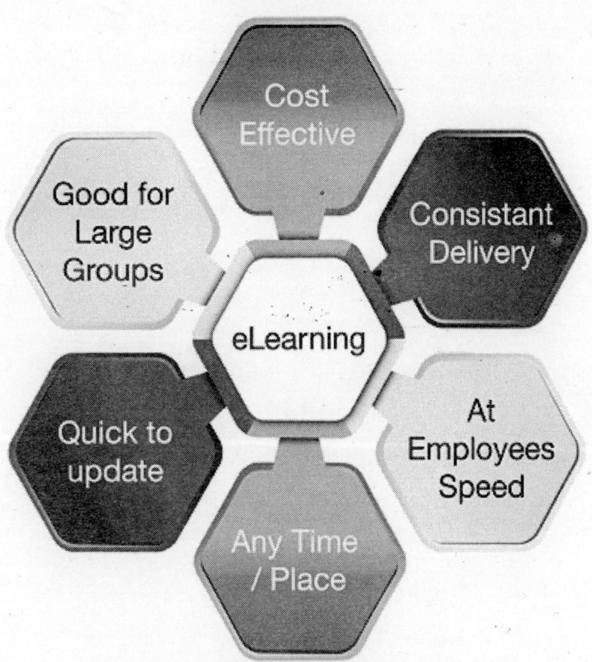

Figure 12.27 E-learning concept

In traditional way learning, the teacher and the students assemble at one prespecified place – the classroom, normally – at a specified time. If a student comes late or is at the wrong place, he/she would miss the instruction. Similarly, all students are expected to follow the same speed set by the teacher.

But, in e-learning, there is no need to gather at one single place. The teacher and the students can be at different geographical places, but the time synchronization is retained. Video lectures broadcast live is an example of instruction by this mode. In addition, there is no need for the teacher and students to be available at a common time. Contents available on the Website in the form of video, slides, notes, etc., so that the students can access and peruse them when they want to. Apart from this, different students can follow the course at their own individual pace–a fast learner can finish the course in shorter time than not so fast learner.

☞ *E-learning means anytime, any place, any pace learning (See Figure 11.27).*

11.8.1 Why E-learning?

The need for e-learning has as many different answers as the number of different perspectives on e-learning that people have. E-learning is seen as desirable from a number of perspectives. We outline some of these as given below:

(a) *Teacher shortage*–In many educational institutional, shortage of qualified teachers is the main problem. The quality of the available teachers is another major concern. Attractive opportunities given in the MNCs (Multinational Companies) and poor academic environment lead to teaching job as last preference. Therefore, in this context, it is necessary to expand the reach of the available teachers.

(b) *A3 (Any Time, Any Place, Any Pace) learning*–As mentioned earlier, for many, the need to come together at a fixed place at a fixed time is a major constraint. This is particularly true for those pursuing courses in part-time mode, the just-in-time learners, adult learners, etc. The freedom to connect to the course setup at any time of your choice, and from any place is a major incentive for e-learning. It also enables learners to take to studying when they feel is the best time for them to study.

(c) *Enhanced learning experience*–This is a very important, but often ignored and under-explored aspect. When exploited effectively, e-learning enables a high degree of personalization and a wide range of instructional methods. Powerful simulation environments, multimedia capability and high-end visualization support enables a learner to relate to the subject much more deeply and hence understand well. Online assessments provide a world of opportunities to further enhance the TLP (Teaching Learning Process). This ought to be the best reason for a teacher to adopt e-learning. The opportunity to incorporate the vast variety of contents and resources from the Web is also a significant benefit.

(d) *Content creation*–India, despite her IT-brains, is still a poor contributor of content in the Web. It means very few of our teachers are on-line. Adopting e-learning enables and encourages them to do this naturally.

(e) *Enhancing quality of teaching*–When one gets into practicing e-learning to any significant degree, one will be creating much of the course material electronically. These are a lot more reusable compared to written notes, used otherwise. These can also be shared with other teachers, can be improved over the years using user feedback, and hence results in better quality of material.

(f) *More systematic feedback and evaluation*–Bringing assessment and other activities under e-learning enables us to gather much more detailed feedback on various aspects of the course. These include quality of questions, quality of content, qualitative judgement on students' performance, etc. These can be used to enhance the quality of instruction at an institutional level.

11.8.2 Benefits of E-Learning

Effective e-learning comes from using Information and Communication Technologies (ICT) to broaden educational opportunity and help students develop the skills they and their countries. E-learning can deliver substantial benefits. These benefits are as under:

(a) *Flexibility, accessibility, convenience:* Users are now able to proceed through a program at their own pace. Users can access an e-learning course anytime, anywhere, and learn only as much as they need.

(b) *Cross-platform:* E-learning can be accessed by Web browsing software on any platform. A training program can be delivered to any machine over the Internet or Intranet without having to author a program for each platform.

(c) *Browser software and Internet are widely available:* Most computers have access to a browser, are connected to the organization's Intranet or the Internet.

(d) *Inexpensive worldwide distribution:* There is no need for a separate distribution mechanism.

(e) *Ease of updating information:* If changes need to be made in a program or courseware after the first implementation, these changes are made on the servers storing the program or courseware. Everyone worldwide can instantly access the updated information.

(f) *Travel costs and time savings:* There are no travel costs for bringing remote employees to a centralized workshop.

(g) *Efficiency:* Training efficiency is increasing significantly not only from a qualitative view but also from a quantitative view.

Now let us come to the advantages of e-learning to Students, teachers and institutions.

Benefits to Students (Learners)

Benefits of e-learning for the students are given as under:

- Students can log-in and get all course contents on the Web.
- Students can learn independently in anytime and place because e-learning is self-paced and the learning sessions are available all the time.
- Students can customize the course material as per their own needs. They have added control over their learning process and are able to better understand the subject.
- Students get single central location for all course materials.
- Students get a chance for enhanced exchange with other students and qualified teachers which are based on communication and information technologies.
- Students can deal with teachers who are highly qualified, but cannot be reached because of distance barriers. Now with e-learning coming in scene, such teachers can give their inputs and help students in their research.
- Students have an option to choose what they like. E-learning draws students to topics they like and enjoy.

Benefits to Teachers (Trainers)

Benefits of e-learning for the teachers are given as under:

- Method of teaching becomes more interactive.
- Teachers can prepare single document for all types of students, so that they do not need to do it again and again.
- Timing is also flexible for teachers. They can do this with continuation to their regular classes in schools.
- They can get more and more information on the Internet and they can embed it in their course material.
- Interaction with students become more appropriate. When students are sharing their problems with teachers, since it is not face-to-face they fear less and can ask their problems freely.

Benefits to School (Institution)

Benefits of e-learning for the schools (institutions) are given as under:

- Schools now provide more effective instructional leadership because they had better visibility into students' progress and work products.
- Enhanced connectivity also improved school capacity to communicate with parents, faculty, and district leaders, and enabled them to perform their responsibilities more efficiently.
- Alternative training mode from offsite personnel.
- Instructors are not held by geographic boundaries.

- More students can view a presentation at one time.
- Faster delivery of appropriate training to needed staff members.
- Higher rates of student completion than found in self-paced training.
- Flexibility to modify or change content and to make it accessible on demand.
- Reduction of internal training costs.
- Reduced time away from work for participants.
- Dramatically reduce travel costs.
- Flat fee pricing structures give institutions unlimited access to training for the year.

11.8.3 Advantages of e-Learning

- Class work can be scheduled around personal and professional work.
- Reduces travel cost and time to and from school.
- Learners may have the option to select learning material that meets their level of knowledge and interest.
- Learners can study wherever they have access to a computer and the Internet.
- Self-paced learning modules allow learners to work at their own pace.
- Different learning styles are addressed and facilitation of learning occurs through varied activities.
- Development of computer and the Internet skills that are transferable to other facets of learner's lives.
- Successfully completing online or computer-based courses builds self-knowledge and self-confidence and encourages students to take responsibility for their learning

11.8.4 Disadvantages of e-Learning

- Unmotivated learners or those with poor study habits may fall behind.
- Students may feel isolated or miss social interaction.
- Instructor may not always be available on demand.
- Slow or unreliable Internet connections can be frustrating.
- Managing learning software can involve a lower learning curve.
- Some courses, such as traditional hands-on courses can be difficult to simulate.

11.8.5 E-learning Websites and their Salient Features

Now-a-days e-learning is one of the best methods that is followed by numbers of educational institutions and corporate houses to train their students and employees respectively. This is not only a cost-effective method but also time saving and highly influencing in nature. In today's e-learning market, a number of Websites offers different courses to the learners. Here, we will discuss about some of the popular e-learning Websites.

Beginners.co.uk

This site provides both paid and free courses to the learners. All its courses are focused on newcomers from IT field. These courses include JavaScript, Flash, PHP (Personal Home Page or Hypertext), HTML (HyperText Markup Language), Java, .NET, SQL (Structured Query Language), C++, C#, VB (Visual Basic), ASP (Active Server Pages) and many more. This site also offers online tutorials for the above mentioned courses. The paid courses of this site include near bout 250 on-line training courses. Here, the learners have to pay annually for continuing their study. The course fee varies from course to course.

Ehow.com

Ehow.com site is completely dedicated to teach people how to do the real world activity in a hassle free manner (See Figure 11.28). This site offers solutions on staff-written, review and edits on different topics. Marriage, Finance/Business Computers, Relationships, Dating, Pets, Travel, Crafts, Fashion, Health, Hobbies, Education, Carrier are some examples of categories over which this site offers solutions to the learners.

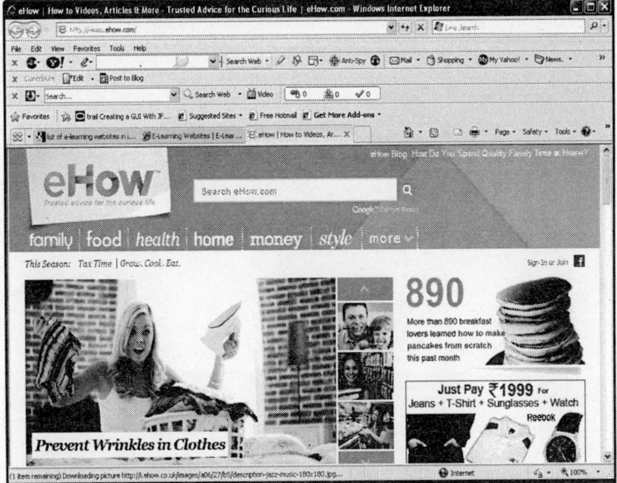

Figure 11.28 Home page of Ehow.com

Techtutorials.com

This is one of the best Website for free computer courses. Presently, this site contains around 1700 free computer tutorials and cover courses like computer hardware, networking, databases, Linux, UNIX, Programming and many more (See Figure 11.29). It

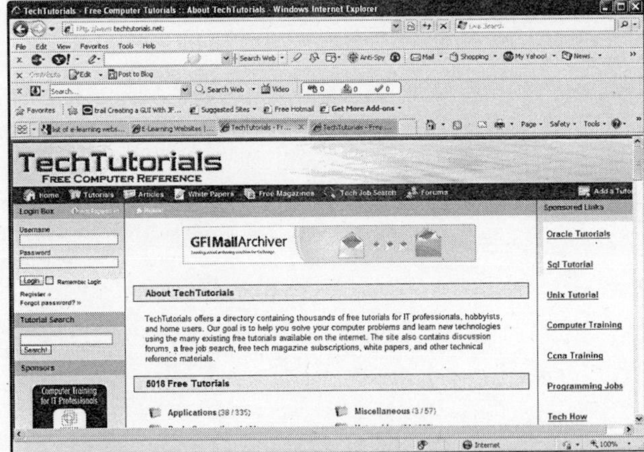

Figure 11.29 Home Page of Techtutorials.com

is a sister concern of **mcmcse.com** that helps the student for Microsoft's MCSE (Microsoft Certified Systems Engineer) examination.

Worldwidelearn.com

This Website offers a teaching of courses to the adults all over the world. All its courses are offered on-line. Its courses include more than 40 subjects, such as personality development, photography, copy writing, accounting, Linux training, e-commerce and many more. This site also offers MBA (Master in Business Administration) courses and other degree and collage courses.

Howstuffworks.com

This is a perfect site to answer the question "how anything works and why it works so" (See Figure 11.30). You can get answer of the questions that you really want. Topics that covered by this sits include, engines & automotive, science & technology, body & health, aviation & transport, electronics & telecom, computers & Internet and machines etc.

Figure 11.30 Home Page of Howstuffworks.com

Free-ed.net

It offers all free courses through Internet. Here, the user does not need to give payment for visiting any page or searching any information or downloading the information. This site has network with best tutorials, outlines, course notes, e-texts and courses. Here, the user can take part in different community activities, can study and can take courses free of cost. It offers courses on more than 120 different academic and vocational disciplines. The course catalog of this site is divided as IT or Information Technology course catalog and the General course catalog.

Beside theses sites there are a number of small and local sites offering e-learning courses for kids, students and professionals. Today, e-learning is not a mere system of getting certificate or adding some more qualification to the CV. E-learning offers education which can enable you to get a job in a reputed organization and also help you develop your practical skills in different fields.

11.8.6 E-learning Challenges

Some of the challenges that e-learning Education Management could be facing are as under:

- If learners were self-driven, sometimes their experience with poor e-learning courses in the past would have made them develop an aversion for this medium.
- For those Institutions who are offering a pure online e-learning course, awarding a recognized degree for students might become imperative. Most students and their prospective employers are happy only when a certifying endorsement is given.
- Many online institutions offering courses with spurious certificates, which may not have any value.
- The biggest challenge with learning practitioners is to create a culture of e-learning. If learners do not participate, then there is no improvement in their performance, if there is no improvement, there is no business impact for the organization, if there is no impact, there is no further commitment from leadership, with leadership not being clearly committed, learners have no incentives, and so the vicious cycle continues.
- Since the e-learning method is self-paced and self-learnt, the attention span of the student may not be enough for him/her to learn concepts effectively.
- Generally, the duration of the course also matters in this mode of lesson delivery.
- Measuring the level of success would be difficult.
- Last but not the least is the legal implications of e-learning. One should not forget that e-learning over Internet is across geographical borders. This makes it all the more, tougher for the enforcing authorities to have a global legal framework for the Internet offender.

11.9 IT-ETHICS

Information technology, or IT, has changed human interactions and business operations. People who work in IT must follow certain governing principles of conduct, known as ethics, because IT is at the core of virtually every aspect of society.

Every achievement in information technology is accompanied by at least one ethical problem. From Facebook to email updates, computer users are unaware of the fine balance between ethics and profit struck by providers. Software developers, businesses and individuals must think about the rights and wrongs of using information technology every day. The fundamental issues underlying the world of information technology are the end user's expectation of privacy and the provider's ethical duty to use applications or email responsibly.

The common thread in much of the history of IT ethics has been the protection and advancement of human values, such as privacy, security and protection of intellectual property. Some of the IT ethics are:

11.9.1 Privacy

There are four issues related to IT privacy. First is freedom from intrusion, which is the right to be left alone from telemarketers and spam. Second is control of personal information, which means securing the information provided to banks and online stores. Third is protection against unauthorized surveillance, such as software cookies that gather information from your computer. And the fourth issue is anonymity, which involves guaranteeing the confidentiality of people seeking help on sensitive topics either in person or online.

11.9.2 Encryption

Encryption protects sensitive information by altering plain text into code. It allows secure communications between individuals, businesses and government agencies. However, it also raises the issue of balancing privacy and confidentiality with public security interests.

11.9.3 Intellectual Property

Some people believe that information and software should be open and free. Others believe that, as in the case of pharmaceutical drugs, companies will not invest adequate resources in research and development if there are no enforceable intellectual property laws governing unauthorized duplication and reverse engineering.

11.9.4 Internet Ethics

The Internet Activities Board declared the Internet to be a "national facility" and that "irresponsible use of this critical resource poses an enormous threat to its continued availability to the technical community." It characterized as unethical and unacceptable several activities, including seeking unauthorized access and compromising user privacy.

11.9.5 Code of Ethics

Non-profit IT associations often establish codes of ethics for their members, which include a commitment to improving the understanding of technology and report system vulnerabilities. Businesses usually embed IT ethics guidelines in their corporate governance and computer usage policies.

11.9.6 Social Networking

The social networking craze may allow people around the world to speak with each other but it has also brought up several IT ethics issues. Facebook initiated a program called Beacon in 2007 to turn each user's personal information into an advertisement, allowing a greater amount of connectivity between the website's members. Facebook's developers failed to create an opt-in system that gave willing users the chance to participate of their own accord. Beacon came under fire for pulling information from Facebook profiles and breaking down privacy boundaries common in the real world. Another ethical issue for social networking Websites is the amount of security they should use when registering members. Several abductions in recent years have been connected to MySpace, bringing up concerns that social networking sites are not doing enough to protect young users.

REVIEW QUESTIONS WITH ANSWERS

1. Multiple Choice

1.1 Which of the following is a business-oriented social networking service?

a. MySpace b. LinkedIn
c. Facebook d. None of the above

1.2 What is Facebook?

a. A blog b. A content site
c. A social networking d. None of the above

1.3 Which phrase best describes what people do at social networking sites?

a. They interact with other people.
b. They browse articles and other content.
c. They code pages in HTML.
d. None of the above

1.4 ________ is the encompassing term that involves the use of electronic platforms - intranets, extranets and the Internet - to conduct a company's business.

a. E-commerce b. E-procurement
c. E-marketing d. E-business

1.5 Which of the following is not one of the benefits of e-commerce to sellers?

a. E-commerce can help to reduce costs
b. E-commerce offers greater flexibility in meeting customer needs
c. E-commerce increases the net cost per contact
d. E-commerce is a powerful tool for customer relationship building

1.6 The E-commerce domain that involves business activity initiated by the consumer and targeted to businesses is known as

a. Consumer to Consumer (C2C) b. Business to Business (B2B)
c. Consumer to Business (C2B) d. Business to Consumer (B2C)

1.7 A ________ is a B2B trading network that links a particular seller with its own trading partners.

a. Bitstream b. Private trading network
c. Web community d. Virtual network

1.8 By Electronic commerce mean:

a. Commerce of electronic goods
b. Commerce which depends on electronics
c. Commerce which is based on the use of internet
d. Commerce which is based on transactions using computers connected by telecommunication network

1.9 For carrying B2B e-commerce the following infrastructure is essential:

a. World Wide Web b. Corporate work
c. Electronic Data Interchange standards d. Secure Payment Service

a. a, b, c b. b, c, d
c. b, c, d d. a, b, c, d

1.10 For carrying out C2C e-cmmerce the following infrastructure is essential

a. World Wide Web b. Corporate work
c. Electronic Data Interchange standards d. Secure Payment Service

a. a and b b. b and d
c. a and c d. a and d

2. State whether the following statements are True or False

2.1 B2C commerce includes services, such as legal advice.
2.2 Disadvantages of e-commerce in India are Credit card payment security is not yet guaranteed.
2.3 Electronic Data Interchange is necessary in B2C e-commerce.
2.4 EDI requires data entry operators by receivers.
2.5 E-commerce refers to the physical transfer of goods on the Internet.
2.6 All process in e-commerce are expressed in terms of numeric values.
2.7 C2B is not an e-commerce activity.
2.8 E-cash is a type of electronic payment.
2.9 EDI over internet uses MIME to attach EDI forms to e-mail messages.
2.10 LinkedIn is mainly used for professional networking.

3. Match the following:

3.1	Facebook, a social networking site	a.	A video-sharing Website
3.2	LAMP	b.	Bernard Luskin
3.3	Windows Live Messenger	c.	E-commerce Model
3.4	E-Governance	d.	Live exchange of information
3.5	E-Commerce	e.	Words prefixed with a '#' sign
3.6	Hashtag in Tweeter	f.	Trading in products or services using computer networks, such as the Internet
3.7	Teleconferencing	g.	Application of ICT
3.8	Consumer-to-Consumer	h.	MSN Messenger from 1999 to 2006
3.9	A pioneer of e-learning	i.	Linux, Apache, MySQL, PHP
3.10	YouTube	j.	Founded in 2004

4. Fill in the blanks

a.	Scribe	b.	free-ed.net	c.	E-learning
d.	eHow	e.	Government-to-Government	f.	Twitter
g.	Home Page	h.	PHP	i.	Cisco
j.	Facebook Mobile				

4.1 __________ is an online social networking service that enables users to send and read short 140-character messages called Tweets.
4.2 Some companies provide wireless services that allow their customers to build their own mobile community and brand it; one of the most popular wireless services for social networking in North America and Nepal is _________.
4.3 A _________ also know index page is the initial or main Web page of a Website.
4.4 ________ is a server-side scripting language designed for Web development but also used as a general-purpose programming language.
4.5 __________ is a server for aggregating log data streamed in real-time from a large number of servers.
4.6 __________ is the online non-commercial interaction between Government organizations, departments, and authorities and other Government organizations, departments, and authorities.
4.7 __________ Systems, Inc. is an American multinational corporation which designs, manufactures, and sells networking equipment.
4.8 ________ is the use of electronic media, educational technology and ICT in education.
4.9 _________ is an online source of written articles and step-by-step instructions where articles and videos are created by freelancers and cover a wide variety of topics organized into a hierarchy of categories.
4.10 You can browse the virtual campus with ____________.

Answers

1.	1.1	b	1.2	c	1.3	a	1.4	d	1.5	c	1.6	c
	1.7	b	1.8	d	1.9	c	1.10	c				
2.	2.1	T	2.2	T	2.3	F	2.4	F	2.5	F	2.6	F
	2.7	T	2.8	T	2.9	T	2.10	T				
3.	3.1	j	3.2	i	3.3	h	3.4	g	3.5	f	3.6	e
	3.7	d	3.8	c	3.9	b	3.10	a				
4.	4.1	f	4.2	j	4.3	g	4.4	h	4.5	a	4.6	e
	4.7	i	4.8	c	4.9	d	4.10	b				

Short Questions with Answers

1. What is e-governance?
2. Is g-governance better than normal governance? Explain.
3. What are objectives of e-governance?
4. List the advantages of e-governance.
5. What is e-learning? Why is e-learning used?
6. How is e-learning useful to organization and students?
7. Why is e-learning preferred?
8. What advantage does e-learning offers as compared to normal learning? Explain.

Answers to Short Questions

1. E-governance is the use of modern information and communication technologies, such as Internet, local area network, mobiles, etc., by government to improve effectiveness of their services.
2. Yes because of the following reasons:
   (a) It provides better control at affordable cost and in fastest possible time.
   (b) It saves time.
   (c) It provides transparency.
   (d) It provides simplicity in work.
3. The objectives of e-governance are as under:
   (a) It improves Government processes.
   (b) It increases the efficiency and speed in a transparent manner.
   (c) It simplifies the administrative transactions.
   (d) It provides a facility for citizens to participate in decision making process.
4. Advantages of e-governance are as follows:
   (a) It improves the quality of information and information supply.
   (b) It reduces the process time.
   (c) It reduces the cost.
   (d) It improves the service level.
   (e) It increases efficiency

5. E-learning is a delivery of learning, training or education program by electronic means. E-learning is used to teach through technology.
6. E-learning for organization:
   (a) Reduced overall cost
   (b) Reduced learning time
   (c) Increased retention and application to job.
   E-learning for students:
   (a) It enables students to complete training conveniently at off-hours or form home.
   (b) It provides self pacing for slow and quick learners reduces stress and increased satisfaction.
   (c) Interactivity engage users, pushing them rather than pulling them through training, etc.
7. E-learning is preferred because of the following reasons:
   (a) It provides faster learning at reduced cost.
   (b) It increased accessed to learning.
   (c) It clears accountability for all participants in the learning process.
8. E-learning offers many things as compared to normal learning. These are as under:
   (a) Use of technology
   (b) Learning on demand
   (c) Participation of all

DESCRIPTIVE TYPE QUESTIONS

1. Give the social impact of e-governance.
2. What is the difference between e-business and e-commerce?
3. What are the importances of e-commerce?
4. Discuss the advantages and disadvantages of e-learning.
5. Define e-governance. How it is beneficial for common man?
6. How has society benefitted from e-governance? What are the limitations of e-governance?
7. What is meant by e-governance model? How e-government interacts Citizen, Business and Government.
8. Describe the advantages and disadvantages of e-commerce.
9. How has society benefitted for e-learning? Discuss its societal impacts?
10. What are the importances of e-commerce?
11. Discuss some of the e-learning Websites and their salient features.

GLOSSARY

Absolute cell address A cell address or range name in a formula that always refers to the same cell or range of cells. To make a cell address absolute, prefix the row and column with a dollar sign ($); for example, $AX$2.

Action buttons Pre-drawn button icons that can be placed on a PowerPoint slide and associated with an animation effect.

Active area The part of the current worksheet into which you have entered data or have formatted cells. The active area starts at cell A1 and ends at the lowest and rightmost filled or formatted cell.

ADSL Asymmetric Digital Subscriber Line, abbreviated as ADSL, is used for the transmission of digital information using high bandwidths on existing phone lines. ADSL technology is characterized by high download and low upload rates.

Alignment The placement of text along the left margin, right margin, or both margins.

Alphanumeric Pertaining to a character set that contains letters, digits, and usually other special characters, such as the comma, dollar sign, plus sign, etc.

ALU (Arithmetic Logic Unit) It is one of the components of the Central Processing Unit (CPU) of the computer which performs all mathematical and logical operations.

Anchored range A range of cells in which one corner is fixed. You can adjust the other corner with the pointer-movement keys. To anchor a range, press the period key (.).

Animate To add a special visual or sound effect to text or an object. For example – you can have your text bullet points fly in from the left, one word at a time, or hear the sound of applause when a picture is uncovered. You can animate any number of objects on a slide, and you can even animate elements of a chart.

Animation A set of images, pictures, or drawings displayed in sequence to imply movement. Computer animation files can be inserted in programs, such as PowerPoint and run by the speaker or viewer.

Applet A small application unable to run by itself. When you purchase PowerPoint or another application, it may come with additional applets. For example, PowerPoint comes with applets for manipulating fonts (WordArt), drawing graphs (Microsoft Graph), and creating graphics (Microsoft Draw).

Application program Software designed for a specific purpose, such as pay calculation, processing of examination results, stores accounting and inventory control, etc.

Applications Specific uses for a program. With Word, for example, you can create letters, mailing lists, proposals, resume, timetables, etc.

Architecture The overall design, construction, organization and interconnecting of the various components of a computer system. It refers particularly to the processor hardware and the size and ordering sequence of its bytes.

Archive Backup storage. Usually a secondary storage medium, such as magnetic tape or a mass storage device that operates on semi-direct access and sequential principles.

ARPANET The acronym stands for Advanced Research Projects Agency Network. ARPA of the United States Department of Defense developed ARPANET, which became the world's first packet switching network. Internet is the successor of ARPANET.

ASCII File It is a document file in the universally recognized text *format* called ASCII (American Standard Code for Information Interchange). An ASCII file contains characters, spaces, punctuation, carriage return, and sometimes tabs and an end-of-file marker, but it contains no formatting information, like bold or italic character.

Attribute Features of an object that you can mani-pulate using the PowerPoint tools and commands, including line, fill, shadow, embossing, colour, and shape. Both graphic and text objects have attributes.

AutoLayout object area The bordered areas, in addition to the title placeholder, that appear when your create a new slide. There are many kinds of object placeholders: placeholders for text, graphs, tables, organizational charts and clip art. Just click to add text in a placeholder, or double-click to add the specified object.

Automated Office A general term that refers to the merger of computers, office, electronic devices and telecommunications technology in an office environment.

AutoShape A menu on the PowerPoint Drawing toolbar that contains a variety of common shapes (also called AutoShapes) which can be drawn automatically by clicking and dragging the cursor across a slide.

Background colour The underlying colour of a PowerPoint slide. If you are painting on a white canvas, for example, your background colour is white. You can paint any other colour on top of it, but the underlying colour remains white; everywhere you do not add paint, the white shows. The background colour on a slide works the same way.

Backup Alternate facilities of programs, data files, hardware equipments, etc., that are used in case the original one is destroyed, lost, or fails to operate.

Backup File A duplicate of another file, which you create for safekeeping. A special kind of backup file, .bak, is automatically created by Word when you save the file you have been editing. You can not edit a .bak file.

Bar code A coding structure in which characters are represented by means of a series of parallel bars.

Base The total number of digits (symbols) available to represent numbers in a positional number system.

BIOS (Basic Input Output System) Bios is responsible for handling the details of input/output operations including the task of relating a program's logical records to a peripheral device physical records.

Bit Acronym for **bi**nary digi**t** which stands for one binary piece of information. This can be either 0 or 1.

BLOB Binary Large Object. Essentially, a long bit of string used for complex data.

Block A portion of text ranging in length from one word to several pages. During editing, you mark blocks in order to move, copy, or delete text.

Blogs Blogs are the expressions of the common masses about social or political issues or simply anything. Blogs can often be in the form of creative write-ups by writers in different parts of the world.

Broadband Internet Broadband connectivity to the Internet provides the users with a high-speed Internet access.

Buffer Either a device or a storage area where data are temporarily stored.

Bug An error in a computer program.

Byte A fixed number of adjacent bits that represent a particular character or symbol. Normally a byte consists of eight bits.

Cache Web browsers maintain a cache of recently visited web pages. Some of them use an external proxy web cache, which is a server program through which web requests pass. This enables the browsers to cache frequently visited pages. Even search engines make available already indexed web pages through their caches.

CAD (Computer Aided Design) Use of computers to automate design operations.

CAI (Computer Aided Instruction) A general term that refers to teaching with the help of a computer. Also called CAE (Computer Aided Education).

CAM (Computer Aided Manufacturing) Use of computers to automate manufacturing operations.

Cell The intersection of a column and a row in an Excel worksheet. The cell is the basic unit of a worksheet.

Cell address A cell's location in the grid of worksheet/column/row intersections. The cell address consists of the worksheet letter, a colon, and the column letter plus the row number.

Cell pointer The highlighted rectangle in the worksheet displays area that marks the current cell. You can move the cell pointer with arrow keys and a number of other keys on the keyboard.

Chain printer A printer in which the characters are embossed on a chain or a band. The chain is in the form of a loop which rotates at a high-speed and print heads are activated to print specified characters.

Character A single digit, letter, punctuation mark, space, or other symbol which the computer can read or write.

Character string Any group of contiguous characters (letters, numbers, punctuation marks, special symbols, etc.) enclosed in quotation marks and used in formulas and macros.

Chart A pictorial representation of data. A chart is also sometimes referred to as a graph.

Chip A thin wafer of silicon on which integrated electronic components are deposited.

Clip Art A collection of images you can use in your documents. Clip is often distributed on CD-ROM in large collections (thousands of Clip Art pieces) organized into categories. Various Clip Art formats are sold, and the most popular are Computer Graphics Metafile (CGM), Windows (WMF), Bitmap (BMP), and Graphics Interchange Format (GIF) format files. PowerPoint comes with a set a Clip Art contained in the Clip Gallery 3.0.

Color palette A display consisting of various colour blocks; you can select a colour fill to add to an object or slide from a color palette.

Column selector A horizontal bar at the top of a column that you click to select an entire column in the query design grid or the filter design grid.

COM (Computer Output Microfilm) An output device that records computer output on microfilm.

Command An instruction transmitted to your computer when you press specified keys.

Communication Bandwidth It refers to the data that can be transferred between two points in a given period of time. It is expressed in terms of bits per second. It is commonly known as the bit rate.

Compile To convert or translate a program written in a high-level language to an absolute or machine language form.

Computer An electronic equipment designed to automatically accept and store input data, manipulate them, and produce output results under the direction of a detailed step-by-step stored program or instructions.

Computer graphics The area of computer science which is concerned with the generation, manipulation and display of pictures with the aid of a computer.

Computer network A distributed data processing system in which multiple computers are linked together for the purpose of data communication and resource sharing.

Computer system The various components (input and output devices, storage, CPU) of a computer integrated together to perform the steps called for in the program being executed.

Container document The document on the receiving end of a linked object which comes from the source document. A PowerPoint presentation that includes linked objects is a container document.

Control commands Commands issued to the computer when you press a key (or keys) while holding down the Ctrl key.

Control handle A square that appears to indicate a vertex of a freeform shape or a polygon. You can edit freeform shapes and polygons by adding, deleting, and moving their control handles.

Control Key Ctrl A key, often represented by the caret symbol (^), used with other keys to command the computer to perform specific functions.

Control panel A tool in Windows operating system which allows you to install software and change different settings fo Windows, such as Date, Time, Keyboard, Mouse, Password, Display, Sound Settings, etc.

Control Unit Part of the central processor which directs the sequence of operations, interprets the coded instruction, and checks the execution of program instructions.

CPU (Central Processing Unit) Control unit and arithmetic logic unit of a computer system are jointly known as the CPU. All calculations and comparisons are made inside the CPU and the CPU is also responsible for activating and controlling the operations of the other units of a computer system.

Crop To trim vertical or horizontal edges of a picture by using the cropping tool on the Picture toolbar. After you crop a picture, you can always uncrop it. Photos are often cropped to focus attention on a particular portion of the photo.

CRT (Cathode Ray Tube) An electronic tube with a TV like screen upon which information may be displayed.

Cryptography A system of secret communications to improve the security of confidential computerized files.

Cursor Usually a small rectangle or line of light on the screen, marking your place in the text. Cursor shapes differ with different operating systems.

Custom Animation A feature in PowerPoint that allows you to set special effects and the sequence of slides in an on-screen presentation.

Custom Shows A feature in PowerPoint that allows you to save different subsets of slides in a presentation to create different versions of the show from the same set of slides.

Cyberspace This term coined by William Gibson, is used to refer to the computer networks connected to each other and the content they host. It is often used to refer to the Internet.

Cylinder In a disk pack, a set of corresponding tracks in all the surfaces is called a cylinder. All tracks of a cylinder are accessible by a single movement of the access mechanism.

Daisy wheel printer A letter-quality printer that uses a printing head with the appearance of daisy and/or a wheel. Each petal of the daisy wheel has a character embossed on it.

DASD Acronym for Direct-Access Storage Device. It is the online secondary storage which is always available to a processor.

Data A collection of facts in raw form that become information after proper organization or processing.

Data file A group of related pieces of information called records, stored together on a disk. A record belongs to a mailing list, for example, might contain all the information about a single addressee. One field within that record might contain name, street address, city, etc.

Data label Values or words that appear next to above, or below the data points on a graph.

Data range The range of cells containing the data records to be sorted or graphed.

Database server A system that receives requests from client applications over a network and responds by returning requested data (the answer set). Each database server is made up of a computer, an operating system, and database server software.

Database system A combination of software and hardware for performing some task or group of tasks that involve in handling a large amount of information.

Date number Excel's internal method of keeping track of dates. Excel starts its calendar at January 1, 1900. It assigns the number 1 to that date, 2 to January 2, 1900, and so on.

Debugging Process of finding and correcting program errors (bugs).

Default An automatic setting that the computer uses unless you specify another setting.

Design Visual elements of a slide. When changing presentation templates in PowerPoint, the Apply Design command is used. A template contains various design elements for slides, such as graphic objects and a colour scheme.

Design template A template whose format and colour scheme you apply to a presentation. A large selection of professionally designed templates come with PowerPoint, and you can also use any presentation as a template.

Dial-up It is the means to connect to the Internet using the copper phone lines and a modem. Dial-up connections are capable of sending information from the client's end at very slow speeds of about 56kbps.

Dial-up Internet In this type of access to the Internet, the user's computer is attached to a modem connected to a telephone line. Dial-up Internet access involves a modem that dials into an Internet service provider to establish a connection.

Digitizer An input device used to convert graphic and pictorial data into binary, numeric inputs for a digital computer.

Direct access Pertaining to storage devices where the access time is effectively independent of the location of the data.

Disk A flat, circular plate coated with a magnetic material on which data can be stored by magnetization of portions of the flat surface.

Docked toolbar A toolbar that is attached to one edge of the program window. You can dock a toolbar below the program title bar or to the left, right, or bottom edge of the program window. When you drag a toolbar to the edge of the program window, the toolbar outline snaps into place along the length of program window edge.

Domain Name System DNS, as it is called, refers to the hierarchical naming system used for computers, resources and services on the Internet. It translates the computer hostnames to IP addresses. By way of the implementation of DNS, the domain name 'www.buzzle.com' translates to its IP address, say, 208.70.178.150. With the help of DNS, domain names can be assigned to Internet users.

Downtime The period during which a computer is malfunctioning or not operating correctly due to machine failures.

Drag-and-drop To perform a move operation by selecting and dragging icon from one location to another location and then releasing the mouse button.

Drum printer A line printer that uses a solid, rotating, cylindrical drum on which the characters to be printed are embossed.

Dumb terminal A terminal that has no local processing capability.

DVD DVDs have much more storage capacity as compared to CDs. These are of three types: DVD-ROM, DVD-R and DVD-RW.

Edit To change a cell entry. You modify a cell entry by pressing the Edit (F2) key, which displays the current entry in the second line of the control panel so that you can make changes to it. Press Enter to complete an edited entry.

Electronic mail A general term to describe the transmission of messages by the use of computing systems and telecommunications facilities.

Electronic slide show A pre-defined list of slides displayed sequentially on-screen or using a LCD projector.

Electronic spreadsheet An application package usually available with microcomputers that displays the equivalent of a worksheet made up of rows and columns. It may be used for computation or display of information in a tabular form.

Electrothermal printer A high-speed printer that uses heated elements to create characters as matrices of small dots on heat-sensitive paper.

E-mail It is a store-and-forward method of writing, sending and receiving written messages. Electronic mail is an Internet e-mail system that uses network-based protocols to exchange messages between network subsystems.

E-mail Address It identifies the network location to which an email can be delivered. An email address is a combination of the user name of the mail user and the host name of the mailing system. It is of the form, 'username@domain-name'. An email alias is a forwarding email address. It simply forwards emails to specific email addresses.

E-mail Client It is also known as a mail user agent (MUA). An email client is a front-end computer program or an agent that acts as a client for the email server.

E-mail Scams With the increase in the use of email systems, its security needs also rose. Fraudulent users started tampering with the email systems to breach security.

E-mail Virus It is a computer code that is transmitted through an email in the form of an attachment. The email attachment causes the destruction of some of the files on the receiver computer's hard disk and is programmatically emailed to the contacts in the address book of the receiver.

Emulator A program that permits one computer to execute the machine-language instructions.

End user Any individual who uses the information generated by a computer based system.

EPROM (Erasable Programmable Read Only Memory) A semi-conductor memory which allows the eraser of the information stored in it by exposure to ultraviolet light. Later, new information can be stored in it.

Error message A statement that appears on your screen when your computer is unable to continue processing. The message tells you what the problem is and how to solve it.

Expand A function in Outline view of PowerPoint that allows you to open up all the lines of an outline to display all the detail points.

Extended ASCII Extended ASCII provides added capability by allowing for 128 additional haracters, such as accented letters, graphics characters, and special symbols.

Extended memory Main memory beyond 1 Mb in PC systems based on the Intel microprocessors. Extended memory is not typically available to MS-DOS programs. But Windows 9X makes use of this memory for better performance of the packages.

Extranet It is a private network that uses Internet technology to share a part of the business information and operations with suppliers and customers. It can be a part of a company's intranet that provides access to the users outside the company.

Facebook It is a place where people can express their views and discuss things in an open way, as they can and do in may other places.

Facsimile (FAX) Transmission of pictures, texts, maps, graphs, etc., over transmission lines, phone lines, and other carriers between geographically separated points. An image is scanned at a transmitting point and duplicated at a receiving point.

File A collection of related records.

File Management System (FMS) A software package that allows users to define data items, place these items into specified records, combine these records into designated files, and then manipulate and retrieve stored data in various ways to achieve user's goals.

Fills color PowerPoint uses to fill objects with colours that contrast with both the background colour as well as the lines and text colour to make round out your colour scheme. You can change a fill colour any time which you want.

Firmware A sequence of instruction (software) that is substituted for hardware and stored in Read Only Memory (ROM). Another example of Firmware is PROM, i.e., programmable read only memory.

First-in, First-out (FIFO) A technique for processing jobs on a first-come, first-served basis.

Flash Memory It is electrically erasable and programmable permanent type memory. Its entire contents can be erased in one operation. Flash memory modules upto 4 GB capacity are available. The modules are available as flash cards and flash drives. Flash drives can replace hard disk drives in some applications. They are static and faster and hence costlier.

Floating-point numbers Signed numbers held in a fraction-exponent format. For example, 3216 would be represented as 0.3216×10^4 in floating-point notation.

Font The typeface, type size, and type attributes of text or numbers.

Font size The size of a font is actually the height of a character, which is measured in points. A 72-point font has characters that are roughly one inch high.

Footer Text or graphics that appears at the bottom of page.

Format The way you arrange text on your screen, using commands for setting margins, centering text, etc.

Formula A mathematical expression that performs calculations on values in the worksheet. Formulas can contain numbers and arithmetic operators, as well as cell addresses, range names, and functions.

Frame Using a drawn object, such as a square as a border around another object on a slide.

Free rotate A PowerPoint function that allows you to turn an object in any direction, for example 360 degrees.

Front-end processor A CPU designed specifically to handle the communications between processing task. Its main purpose is to off-load communications processing task from the host computer, so that the host computer can be dedicated for applications and data processing jobs.

General purpose computer A computer capable of performing a variety of business and scientific applications.

General software package A software package, such as payroll and word processing, developed for users.

Googling The Google search engine, being the most popularly used one, has made the word, 'google' synonymous to the concept of search engines. Searching the Internet by using the Google search engine is known as googling.

Gradient A subtle shading from lighter to darker in a background of one or two colours giving the effect of a light source form the selected direction.

Graph A visual way to present data. A graph can often illustrate trends and projections more clearly and effectively than worksheet numbers.

Graph file A file in which you store a graph for use. The graph file can then be printed or edited by other software programs.

Graphic Graphic images come in all shapes and sizes. Typical graphics include Clip Art images, drawings, photographs, scanned images, signature files, etc.

Graphic display terminal A visual display terminal which has a screen to display a graph or drawing as well as alphanumeric information.

Graphic format The protocol used to save a graphic file, such as GIF or EPS.

Group A multiple selection that you treat as a single object by using the Group command on the Draw menu. Nested groups are multiple groups of objects, in a drawing, for example, Clip Art often is built with nested groups.

Hacking Hacking is the activity of programmatically gaining access to a computer application that is otherwise inaccessible. The act of gaining an unauthorized access to a computer is known as hacking. Hacking of passwords that leads to breach of email privacy is a threat to communication over the Internet. Internet crime refers to all the criminal activities that are carried over the Internet.

Handouts Printed output of PowerPoint presentation containing miniature versions of two, three or six slides. Audience handouts are intended to be distributed to presentation viewers to help them follow a presentation.

Hard copy Printed or filmed output from a computer device in human readable form.

Hardware The physical components of a computer system, such as electronic, magnetic, and mechanical devices.

Header Text or graphics that appears at the top of every page.

Hidden object Slide or element on slide that does not temporarily appear on-screen and is not included in printed output of a PowerPoint presentation.

Hidden slide A slide that does not automatically display during a slide show. You decide which slide or slides you want to be "hidden" and whether you want them to appear during your show. That way you can tailor a show to fit several different audiences.

High-level language A programming language whose structure is application oriented and is independent of the structure of the computer.

High-Low-Close-Open (HLCO) graph A graph that plots up to four data points as a series of vertical lines. HLCO graphs are typically used to track the performance of a stock equity over time. They plot the high, low, closing, and opening prices of the stock. They are also called stock market graphs.

Highlight Emphasize, a character, word, or block of text by making it either brighter or dimmer than the surrounding text.

Home Page The term home page is used to refer to the page that is the default page of any website. It is the main page of a complex website.

Host computer Main control computer in a network of distributed processors and terminals.

HTTP Hypertext Transfer Protocol, abbreviated as HTTP, is a communications protocol used for the transfer of information over the Internet. A client makes an HTTP request using a web browser to which an HTTP response is sent from the server.

Hyperlink A reference in a document to another section of the document or to another document is termed as a hyperlink. Hyperlinks are used to redirect the user from one section of a page content to another.

I/O (Input/Output) Pertaining to the techniques, media, and devices used for man-machine interaction.

IMAP Internet Message Access Protocol, as it is called, is another Internet standard protocol used for retrieval of emails.

Indexed file A file that includes an index directory to facilitate random access.

Indexed sequential access method A method whereby records are organized in a sequential order and can be referenced directly through an index based on some key or characteristic.

Information Result of data manipulation or processing which can be used to help people in making decisions.

Information hiding The principle which states that the state and implementation of an object or module should be private to that object or module and only accessible via its public interface (same as encapsulation).

Information Technology (IT) IT encompasses any combination of equipment (hardware) that facilitates the acquisition, creation, modification, retrieval, storage and transmission of information using electronic media. Thus, IT includes both computing and communications technology. Various aspects of IT are hardware, software, connectivity, telecommunications, science and human-computer interface.

Input Data entered into a data processing system.

Input/Output Input refers to any information coming into the computer. Output refers to processed information going out of a computer.

Input device A device used to enter information into a computer or other data processing devices; for example keyboard.

Insertion point A linking vertical line that appears on-screen at a location where you can enter data. The insertion point is sometimes called a cursor. Characters that you type appear to the left of the insertion point.

Intelligent terminal A terminal having local processing capability. It has a built-in CPU and can perform specific functions, such as editing data, controlling other terminals, etc.

Interactive A PowerPoint or other multimedia presentation is interactive when the viewer is able to make selections as to how the presentation runs or what is displayed, in effect interacting with the presentation itself.

Internet assistant A programmed series of steps a PowerPoint user can invoke to create a folder of presentation files to be moved to an Internet server.

Internet Chat It is a real-time Internet chat or synchronous conferencing that is used for group communication as well as one-to-one communication over the Internet. Jarkko Oikarinen, a Ph.D. from the University of Oulu is the developer of the first Internet chat network. He developed the client and server programs for Internet Relay Chat in August 1988.

Internet Protocol Suite It is a set of communication protocols, which are used for the Internet. Transmission Control Protocol (TCP) and Internet Protocol (IP) were the two pioneering protocols to be introduced in the Internet protocol standard. The Internet protocol suite is composed of a set of layers wherein; each layer provides a service to the upper layers in the set. The upper layers deal with abstract data while the lower layer protocols translate data into physically transmittable forms.

Internet Search Engine It is an information retrieval system that is designed to help find information over the Internet. Search engines use algorithms to scan the huge information base of the Internet and sort it making it retrievable for the web users.

Internet security It is one of the major concerns today. As the Internet acts as a communication platform that can be accessed by millions of users around the world, it becomes necessary that proper measures be implemented. Issues like Internet safety that deal with the content that is made accessible over the Internet are equally important. Internet privacy relates to safeguarding the privacy of the web users and the sensitive information on the web from hackers and stalkers.

Internet Service Provider A company, which provides users with an access to the Internet, is known as an Internet service provider or Internet access provider. ISP, as it is called, offers email accounts and other services like remote storage of files for its customers.

Intranet It is a relatively smaller private network that uses the Internet protocols and connectivity. It is an extension of the Internet and is privately used by organizations.

IP Address It is a way of numerically identifying an entity on a computer network. The original addressing system known as IPv4, used 32 bit addresses. With the growth of the Internet, IPv6 came to be used wherein the addresses are composed of 128 bits. You might want to know how to find your IP address.

ISAM (Index Sequential Access Method) Relating to a file design technique whereby records organized in a sequential order can be accessed directly through an index (directory) based on some key or characteristic. Permits both sequential and random access of records.

Justification The alignment of text within given margins. The left margin is justified as you enter your text. Word Wrap justifies the right margin by adding small spaces between words.

K (Kilo) Used to represent $2^{10} = 1024$ in computers only.

Key-to-disk A device used to enter data onto a disk device.

Key-to-tape A device used to enter data onto a magnetic tape.

Kiosk A booth or display area where an on-screen computer presentation may be set up for use by those visiting the area. An example of a kiosk would be an information counter in a shopping small or booth at a trade show.

Label Any cell that begins with a letter or a label-prefix character is a label.

Label prefix Indicates that a cell entry is a label, as opposed to a value. Label prefixes include the apostrophe (') for left-aligned labels, the quotation mark (") for right-aligned labels, the caret (^) for centered labels, the back slash (\) for repeating labels, and the vertical bar (|) for printer setup strings and non-printing rows.

LAN (Local Area Network) A digital communication system capable of interconnecting a large number of computers, terminals and other peripheral devices within a limited geographical area, typically within 1 km.

Landscape orientation A printer mode that causes text and graphs to be printed sideways on the page, across the long dimension.

Layering In PowerPoint, the process of placing objects one on top of another on your slide to give the appearance of a stack of objects. Objects can be brought forward to appear to be placed at the top of the stack, or sent back to any of the layers behind the first object.

Layout In PowerPoint, layouts (also called Auto Layouts) are applied to each slide in a presentation displaying various of placeholders used for entering slide content. Placeholders include title, bulleted lists, Clip Art, charts, organization charts, and multimedia clips.

Legend Legends explain the patterns, symbols, and colours used to identify the A through F data ranges on a graph. The legends and patterns, symbols, and colours appear beneath the graph.

Light pen A pen shaped device that is used as an input device to computers by writing or sketching on the screen of a cathode ray tube.

Line graph A graph that represents worksheet values as a continuous line, a sequence of symbols, or both. Line graphs are generally used to show one or more values changing over time. The x-axis defines a specific period of time; the y-axis is a numbered scale.

Linux Linux is an operating system kernal that behaves and performs similar to the famous UNIX operating system from AT & T Bells Labs. It has all the features of a modern operating system: true multitasking, threads, virtual memory, shared libraries, demand loading, shared, copy-on-write executables, proper memory management, loadable device driver modules, video frame buffering, and TCP/IP networking.

LISP (LISt Processing) A high-level programming language suitable for handling logical operations and non-numeric applications. It is used in the areas of pattern recognition, artificial intelligence and simulation of games.

Local storage Storage areas, called registers, used by the CPU to interpret instructions and perform arithmetic and logical operations.

Logical operator Used in formulas to test for equality, inequality, and other conditions. The relational operators are : <, < =, >, > =, =, < >. The logical operators are #NOT#, #OR#, and #AND#. A logical formula evaluates either TRUE (1) or FALSE (0).

Long label A label that is longer than the column width of the cell.

Looping macro A set of macro instructions that executes repeatedly. The macro commands {BRANCH} and {FOR} can create a loop in a macro.

Low-level languages Programming languages that normally translate from one source instruction to one object instruction. These languages are machine dependent.

MAC Address Media Access Control address (MAC) is the physical hexadecimal address assigned to each device on a network.

Machine language A low-level language that is directly understandable by the computer system. Each model of a computer has a unique machine language.

Macro A set of instructions for automating Excel's task. Macros include key strokes, macro commands, values, and labels. They can duplicate simple keyboard operations but can also be self-contained applications. Any Excel's task you can perform can be automated with a macro.

Macro command A special Excel's command that has meaning only within a macro. A macro command tells Excel to perform a built-in programming function. Each macro command consists of a keyword and its arguments (if any), enclosed in braces.

Macro library A file that contains Excel macros. When a macro library is in memory, you can run the macros in the library from any active file.

Magnetic-Ink Character Recognition (MICR) An input device that can read cards and paper documents printed with a special magnetic ink.

Magnetic bubble memory An electronic secondary storage device constituted of solid-state electronic chips. It uses the properties of certain materials, under applied magnetic fields, to represent binary 1s and 0s.

Magnetic storage Storage devices, such as disks, drums, tapes, cores, etc., that utilize the magnetic properties of materials to store data.

Magnetic tape A secondary storage device that uses a long plastic strip coated with a magnetic material as a recording medium.

Mail Server It can also be called Mail Transfer Agent (MTA) and is responsible for receiving incoming email from local users and forwarding outgoing mails for delivery. A mail server application forms the heart of a messaging system that performs all the functions to keep the mails moving over the network.

Master A special slide or page on which you define formatting for all slides or pages in PowerPoint presentation. Each presentation has a master for each key component – slides, title slides, speaker's notes, and audience handouts. If you have pictures, text, or special formatting you want to appear on every slide, title slide, notes page, or audience handout, add it to the corresponding master.

Master title The formatted placeholder for slide titles on the Slide Master. It is here that you set the font, color, size, and alignment of slide titles as well as the title's attributes, the shape of the title text box, and its placement on the slide.

Memory A device or medium that can accept data, hold them, and deliver them on demand at a later time.

Menu A screen display that list options or commands from which you can choose.

Menu pointer A pointer which is used to select a menu item and display its description. To select a menu command, use the pointer-movement keys to move the pointer and then press Enter key, or type the first letter of the command.

Merge A feature that enables you to combine information, such as names and addresses, with a document, such as a letter. The result of a typical merge is personalized letters and envelopes.

Metting Minder A PowerPoint feature used to coordinate the running presentation conference and take meeting minutes.

Mixed cell address A cell address in which part of the address is relative as well as absolute. A dollar sign ($) precedes the part of the address that is absolute. When a mixed cell address is used in a formula and the formula is copied, the relative part of the address adjusts to the new location while the absolute part stays at the same place.

Modem It is a device that modulates analog carrier signals to encode digital information and demodulates carrier signals to decode information. A cable modem provides access to data signals sent over the cable television infrastructure. Modems are commonly used for facilitating Internet access.

Netiquette This term is short for net etiquette and refers to the principles of courtesy and consideration for the people using the Internet. It refers to certain basic principles to adhere to while using the Internet. The general ethical principles to be followed in relation to using mailing systems of the Internet are termed as email etiquette.

Network interface card A chip-based circuit board used to connect the PC to a network or server. The card is activated by loading software on the PC.

Nibble 4 bits, half a byte.

Node An end point of a branch in a network, or a common junction of two or more network branches.

Non-impact printer A non-impact printer is a printer that prints without banging a ribbon onto paper, such as a thermal, inkjet and laser printer.

Non-volatile storage A storage medium that retains its contents even in the absence of power.

Notes Master A PowerPoint feature that controls the components and formatting features of all notes pages.

Nudge To move a drawing object on a slide by a very small, preset increment.

Object A single component of your drawing. You can draw objects with the text and drawing tools using Drawing and AutoShape toolbars. Objects can be rectangles, squares, circles, ovals, rectangles with rounded corners, diamonds, trapezoids, stars, freeforms, arcs, graphs, etc.

Octal number system A number system with a base of 8. The octal digits range from 0 to 7. It is commonly used as a shortcut notation for groups of three binary digits.

Offline A device which is not directly connected to the CPU.

Online A device or system directly connected to the CPU.

Operating system An integrated set of programs used to manage various resources and overall operations of a computer system.

Optical bar-code reader An input device that can interpret combinations of marks (bars) representing data.

Optical Character Reader (OCR) An input device which can read characters directly from an ordinary piece of paper by using a scanning mechanism. These characters are written in special type fonts.

Optical Mark Reader (OMR) An input device that can interpret pencil marks on paper media.

OR search You can conduct an OR search on a database when you want to find records that can match at least one criterion in the given criteria range.

Organization chart A chart object that can be placed in a PowerPoint presentation representing the hierarchical structure of an organization, such as a Corporation.

Orientation For printer paper, indicates whether the document is to be printed normally (for example, in Portrait mode) or sideways (in Landscape mode).

OSI Model The Open System Interconnection Model is used to describe a layered communication and network protocol design of a network. It is composed of seven layers, each of which performs certain functions and provides the layers above it with some services.

Outline Titles and main text from your slides. Pictures and other visuals do not appear in an outline. Other text that you have added using the Text tool and embedded text and graphics will not show up either, since they are not part of the main text.

Output Finished result of processing by a system.

Output range The range into which Excel copies extracted records.

Output unit The unit of a computer system that supplies information and results of computation to the outside world.

Overlapping objects Elements on a slide which appear to be stacked so that one is "behind" the other.

Page Break A place in text where one page ends and another begins. You can direct Word to place a page break between two blocks of text so that they will print on separate pages.

Palette A collection of tools. For example, in PowerPoint, there is a color palette that displays the colours available to use in creating a graphic.

Parity bit An extra bit added to a string of bits that enables the computer to detect internal errors in the transmission of binary data.

Password A code by which a user gains access to a computer system. It is used for security purposes.

PC Card PC cards offer large data storage and I/O capability, networking, modem and other functions with lower power consumption and fast data access speed in a compact size measuring the length and width of a credit card.

Peripherals devices Since the input and the output devices are on the periphery (edge) of the main processing unit, they are sometimes referred to as peripheral devices.

Personal computer A small and inexpensive computer (usually a microcomputer) used by individuals for applications, such as entertainment, home management, and hobbies.

Phishing It is a fraudulent activity of acquiring the sensitive information by the use of a fake identity during electronic communication. It is implemented by means of emails and instant messages wherein a user is lured to enter his/her details, which are actually captured by a fraudulent website.

Picosecond One trillionth of a second or 10^{-6} second.

Pie chart A graph in the form of a circle divided into slices, where each slice stands for a value in the range. Pie charts show what proportion of the total each graphed value represents; if one value is twice as large as another, it gets a slice that is twice as large.

Pixel A picture element. It is used to represent one point in a raster scan display device.

Placeholder On a PowerPoint slide, an area that can accept text, graphics or objects (such as charts).

Plotter An output device that converts computer output into a graphic, hardcopy form.

Point-of-sale device An I/O device capable of immediately updating sales and inventory records at a central CPU and producing a printed sales transaction receipt.

Pointing Moving the cell pointer or highlight to a cell; menu choice; file, graph, or range name; or help screen choice.

POP3 Short for Post Office Protocol, POP3 is an application layer Internet standard protocol. It is used to retrieve mails from a remote server.

Portrait mode A printer orientation in which the printer prints across the short dimension of the page, from top to bottom.

PowerPoint Animation Player An add-on program that works with a Web browser to play animated PowerPoint presentations on the Internet.

PowerPoint object Any shape you draw in PowerPoint or any graphic or picture you change from its original format to the PowerPoint format – for example, an AutoShape you draw or Clip Art you ungroup.

PowerPoint Viewer An application that comes with PowerPoint that's designed to support in preparing electronic slide shows.

PPP Point-to-Point protocol (PPP) is a data link protocol that facilitates the establishment of a direct connection between two nodes on a network.

Presentation A group of related slides you can create using PowerPoint.

Primary key When you sort a database, you select a primary key to make index and sort the database.

Primary memory A section of the CPU that holds program instructions, input data, intermediate results, and the output information produced during processing. Also known as primary storage, internal storage and main memory.

Printer An output device used to produce hard copy of computer output that is readable by human beings.

Processor A unit of a computer system that interprets instructions and executes them.

Program A set of sequenced instructions used to direct and control the operations of the computer in order to solve a problem or to perform a particular task.

Programming language A language used to express algorithms in computer understandable form.

PROM Similar to read only memory with the exception that these chips can be re-programmed by using special external equipments.

Promote To indent a line of text less than the previous line, indicating a greater level of importance.

Protect You protect a worksheet, file, or range to avoid accidentally erasing or changing cell contents and settings accidentally.

Proxy Server Client machines on a network connect to the proxy server, which forwards the client requests to other servers and returns responses to the clients.

Publisher The source document that creates an object you place in a PowerPoint presentation. Whenever a publisher is changed, the object in your presentation will be updated.

Query To query a database is literally to ask questions to it. When you query a database, you search for specific database records by establishing selection criteria.

Random Access Memory (RAM) Semiconductor-based memory that can be read and written by the microprocessor or other hardware devices. The storage locations can be accessed in any order. The term RAM is generally understood to refer to volatile memory, which can be written as well as read.

Range A cell or a group of contiguous cells in the worksheet file.

Range name The name you give to a single cell or to a range of cells.

Real-time systems Pertains to online computer processing systems which receive and process data quickly enough to produce output to control, direct, or affect the outcome of an ongoing activity or process.

Record In a database, a record is contained in a single row and a field in a column.

Record A collection of related items.

Record length A measure of the size of a record usually specified in units, such as characters.

Relative cell address A cell address in a formula that changes when you copy the formula to a different part of the worksheet file.

ROM (Read Only Memory) Special memory chips containing instructions which can be read only, therefore preventing accidental destruction of the instructions. ROM is used to store firmware.

Router A router connects two or more logical subnets and performs the functions of routing and forwarding information.

Satellite Internet Internet services that make use of the satellite communication media are termed as satellite Internet services. They are used in locations that are mobile thus making terrestrial Internet connectivity, an impossibility.

Scroll Move the screen view (or "window") up, down, to the right or to the left. You can scroll one line, one column, or one whole screen at a time.

Secondary key You select a secondary key when you need to specify the sort order of records whose primary keys are the same.

Secondary storage Devices like hard disk to store data permanently.

Security A process to protect data from unauthorized user, and also save data and information from tampering, or destruction.

Seek time In a disk system, the time required for a read/write head to move to the track where the record to be read or written is stored. Maximum seek time equals the time taken for the head to move from the outermost track to the innermost track.

Segment The fragments of a physical record that are arranged in a hierarchical fashion.

Segmentation A method of providing virtual memory. A multidimensional linear address space implementation differentiates it from paging.

Select To define a section of text so that you can take action on it, such as copying, moving or formatting.

Semantic-Level Model A data model concerned with the interpretation and meaning of stored data.

Sequential File Organization A file organization technique in which records are organized in order of the value of selected field.

Serial access A storage device or medium where the access time is dependent upon the location of the data. Magnetic tape is a typical serial access medium.

Serial adder An adder in which the bits of the operands are added one after another.

Server An object which performs operations according to the client's requests but may not act upon other objects. It may only send messages to other objects as a result of a request from them unless it is also a client of other servers.

Session It is an exchange of information between a computer and its user. It is established for a certain period of time after which it ends.

Shape The form of an object. A rectangle is a shape, and so is a circle, a triangle, and a trapezoid. Shape is also an attribute – you can change an object's shape without redrawing the object.

Shortcut key The keystroke combination that can be used to quickly execute commands (rather than opening a menu and choosing a command).

Sizing handle A square handle that appears at each corner and along the sides of the rectangle that surrounds a selected object. You can drag a handle to resize an object.

Slide The term for the working desktop area in Slide view of PowerPoint, as well as for each page of output of a PowerPoint presentation.

Slide icon A small icon that appears next to each slide title in Outline view. PowerPoint adds icon to show you where each slide begins. A slide icon will tell you if there are any graphics on the slide as well.

Slide master Slide that holds the formatted placeholders for the titles, main text, and any background items you want to appear on all slides in a presentation. If you make a change to the slide master, the change affects all slides in your presentation based on the master.

Slide show A term used for a PowerPoint presentation.

Slide Sorter A view in PowerPoint that shows miniatures of all slides in a presentation.

Slide transition A special effect used to introduce a slide during an electronic slide show.

SMTP Short for Simple Mail Transfer Protocol, SMTP is the standard for the transmission of electronic mails. The electronic mail server software uses SMTP to send and receive mail messages. ESMTP, that is known as extended or enhanced SMTP refers to the protocol extensions made to SMTP and is widely used today.

Social Networking Social networking is about building online communities of like-minded people. Serving as an excellent platform for sharing of information, social networking is a rage today.

Soft copy Computer output which is displayed on the screen.

Software A set of computer programs, procedures, and associated documentation related to the effective operation of a computer system.

Sort The process of arranging data into a desired sequence.

Sort key Specifies a field on which sorting process is done.

Source document A document on which data that are to be recorded in machine-readable code originates, that is, the original hand-written or typewritten document or a time card.

Spamming The act of sending unsolicited bulk messages over an email system is known as spamming. It is an undesirable use of the electronic messaging systems.

Special character A graphic character that is neither a letter, a digit, nor a space character; for example, the dollar sign, comma, period, etc.

Speech recognition The ability to input data directly into a computer system by speaking to it.

Speech synthesis Computer output in the form of spoken word. No cassette tapes are involved, rather a small LSI microchip is used which has the capability of reproducing the human voice via a small loudspeaker amplifier. Presently multimedia is using this concept.

Spooling A technique that has been successfully used on a number of computer systems to reduce the speed mismatch between slow speed I/O devices and fast CPU.

Spreadsheet A structure used for numeric or financial calculations. Spreadsheets contain columns and rows that intersect to form a pattern of boxes, called cells, each of which can hold a value.

SQL SQL is the abbreviated form of structured query language. A relational data-access language created by IBM. Most database server engines use SQL, as a standard way of accessing data from client applications.

Stack A memory in which the information stored last is on top and is retrieved first. Also known as LIFO (Last-In-First-Out) storage.

Stacked bar graph A bar graph in which related bars are placed on top of each other (stacked) rather than placed side by side. The height of the stack of bars usually represents a total.

Stacking Placing objects on top of one another.

Structure The framework of a worksheet, as opposed to the data the worksheet manipulates. Worksheet structure includes titles, labels, and formatting specifications that control the worksheet's appearance.

Submenu A list of additional commands available when you select a main menu command. Many menu commands bring up a submenu. Some submenu commands, in turn, bring up additional submenus.

Syntax The set of rules of a programming language that define the pattern or structure of the word order and punctuation of an instruction. It is analogous to the rules of grammar in languages like English.

Syntax errors Errors in computer programs that typically involve incorrect punctuation, incorrect word sequence, undefined terms, or misuse of terms. These errors are automatically detected and pointed out by language processors.

Template A blueprint that Microsoft applications, such as Word and PowerPoint use to create documents and slides respectively. The template includes the formatting options, colour, and graphics necessary to create a particular look.

Terminal An input/output device which allows a user to communicate directly with a computer system.

Text tool A tool on the Drawing toolbar, used to add text anywhere on a slide.

Textured background A background design that emulates a texture, such as wood or marble.

Thermal printer A printing device that utilizes paper that is sensitive to heat.

Throughput The total amount of useful processing carried out by a computer system within a given time period. It is a measure of efficiency of a computer system.

Timing The amount of time a slide stays on the screen during a slide show.

Title Titles always remain in view as you scroll through the worksheet.

Title master The slide that holds the formatted placeholders for a title and subtitle for your presentation. If you make a change to the title master, the change affects all slides in your presentation that are based on the title master.

Title placeholder The title box that appears when you create a new slide. Click in the title placeholder and type to make your slide title.

Transaction file A file in which the current data are stored for subsequent processing usually in combination with a master file.

Ungrouping Act of disassociating objects which have been grouped together to function as a single object.

UNIX A popular operating system for 32 and 16-bit mini and micro computers that was designed by Bell Telephone Laboratories, USA.

URL It specifies the location of a resource on the Internet. It consists of the basic address and path.

Usenet Usenet can be considered as a worldwide bulletin board. Usenet newsgroups serve as a repository of messages posted from users around the world.

Utilities Programs to perform some frequently required processes in the operation of a computer system-e.g., sorting, merging, transferring data files from one device to another.

Validation The process of making sure that the forms and documents from a particular transaction are correct.

Video Display Unit (VDU) An I/O device that consists of a television-like screen for displaying outputs and a keyboard for entering inputs.

Virtual memory The technique of using disk space to make programs believe that the system contains more RAM than is actually available. This can be implemented by using pure segmentation, pure paging, or a combination of both. Same as virtual storage.

Virtual Private Network It is a private network that allows the exchange of information between computers over a shared or a public network.

VLSI (Very Large Scale Integration) An electronic circuit with about 10,000 transistors fabricated in a single silicon chip.

Voiceband data A communication system that handles moderate volumes of data, typically from 300 to 9600 bauds. Phone lines that we use to talk to other people is an example.

Volatile storage A storage medium that loses its contents in the event of power failure or when the power is switched off.

W3C It is the acronym used for the World Wide Web Consortium, which develops standards for the web community.

Web Browser A web browser is a software application that facilitates user interaction with the text, audio, video and other information that is located on the web.

Web camera A simple Web camera consists of a digital camera attached to the computer through USB or parallel port.

Web Cookie Also known as an HTTP cookie, it is piece of text that is exchanged between the web client and the web server. It is sent by the web server to the web client and returned unchanged by the client each time it accesses the server. You might want to know how do websites use cookies?

Web Crawler Popularly known as a spider, a web crawler is a program that browses the World Wide Web in an automated manner. Search engines use the crawling technologies to index pages on the web.

Web Page Web pages are resources of information. They are generally created in the HTML format and provide the web users with navigational abilities through hyperlinks to other web pages on the web.

Web Server A web server is a computer program that accepts HTTP requests from web clients and provides them with HTTP responses.

Website A website is a set of web pages consisting of text, audio and video. Web servers host websites.

What-if scenario A calculation that uses variables in formulas to determine potential outcomes of different hypothetical situations.

Wide Area Network (WAN) A digital communication system which interconnects different sites, computer installations and user terminals, and may also enable LANs to communicate with each other. This type of network may be developed to operate nationwide or worldwide and the transmission medium used are normally public systems such as telephone lines, microwave and satellite links.

Wireless Networking It refers to computer networking that is carried out over the wireless media.

Word processing The use of computers to create, view, edit, format, store, retrieve, and print text materials for human communication.

WordArt A feature which allows you to create text enhancement effects.

Workbook An Excel file that contains one or more worksheets.

Worksheet A grid of 256 columns by 8192 rows.

Workstation A desktop computer in a local area network for services provided by the network. It usually has its own processing capability.

WWW It is a collection of interlinked documents that are accessible over the Internet. It consists of millions of web pages that contain text, images, voice and videos. Sir Tim Berners-Lee, a British scientist working at CERN, created the World Wide Web. It also called the Web, and W3 an interlinked collection of hypertext documents (Web pages) residing on Web servers and other documents, menus, and databases, available via URLs.

XY graph A graph that displays cell values as points. XY graphs use both a scaled x-axis and a scaled y-axis, so each point on the graph has an X value and a Y value. XY graphs are used to show how two different types of data are correlated. They are also known as scatter charts.

MAT.O1.R0 : Introduction to Information Technology Question Paper Sept 2014

Total Time : 3 Hours

Total Marks 100
(Part One - 40 Part Two - 60)

PART – ONE

1. Multiple Choice

1.1 What is the BCD equivalent of decimal 45 is
a. 00101101 b. 01000101
c. 11010011 d. None of the above

1.2 IPV4 network addressing requires _________ bit address.
a. 32 b. 64
c. 128 d. None of the above

1.3 Which one of the following is system software?
a. MS Word b. MS Excel
c. Compiler d. None of the above

1.4 One petabyte memory means how many bytes?
a. 2^{30} b. 2^{40}
c. 2^{50} d. None of the above

1.5 USB stands for
a. Universal Serial Bridge b. Universal Serial Bits
c. Unique Serial Bus d. None of the above

1.6 Android applications are written in ________ language.
a. JAVA b. PROLOG
c. LISP d. None of the above

1.7 The various units that used to measure computer memory is ________.
a. bits b. bytes
c. Both a & b d. None of the above

1.8 RAM stands for
a. Read-write Access Memory
b. Read Access Memory
c. Random Access Memory
d. None of the above

1.9 What is the process of recognizing a pre-specified type of mark made by pencil?
a. ATM b. OMR
c. MICR d. None of the above

1.10 The register which contains the instructions that are to execute is known as
a. Index registers b. Instruction register
c. Memory address register d. None of the above

2. State whether the following statements are TRUE or FALSE.

2.1 IPV4 has flow control mechanism.
2.2 Storage capacity of CD is greater than DVD.
2.3 OSI model has seven layers.
2.4 ALU is called brain of the computer system.
2.5 IPV6 has larger address space than IPV4.
2.6 Android is an open source operating system.
2.7 Semi-conductor memory is used as secondary storage.
2.8 Tablets are typically larger than smart-phones.
2.9 The base of octal number system is 7.
2.10 CU is part of CPU.

3. MATCH words and phrases in Column X with the nearest in meaning in Column Y.

	X		Y
3.1	Android	A	Non-volatile
3.2	IPV4	B	Wireless technology
3.3	CPU	C	Java-based
3.4	ROM	D	32-bit address
3.5	BIOS	E	Translator
3.6	MS-Excel	F	Secondary storage
3.7	Wi-Fi	G	5 layers
3.8	TCP/IP	H	Application software
3.9	DVD	I	System software
3.10	Compiler	J	Brain of computer

4. FILL IN THE BLANKS in the following questions by choosing the most appropriate word or phrase from the following list.

a	MS-Excel	b	DVD	c	Linker
d	Taskbar	e	154	f	Android
g	Network	h	MS-Word	i	Loader
j	Menu bar	k	145	l	256
m	RAM	n	128	o	Transport
p	Assembler				

4.1 Most commonly used protocol in _________ layer in Internet Protocol.
4.2 Auto Fill handle is available in __________.
4.3 Each worksheet is made of ____________ columns.
4.4 Example of primary memory is ____________.
4.5 __________ is a program that combines object modules to form an executable program.
4.6 IPV6 has ________ bit address.

4.7 __________ is a program which translates assembly languge to an object file.

4.8 Gingerbread is the name of __________ OS version.

4.9 The octal equivalent of 01100101 is __________.

4.10 Start button of Windows 7 is located on __________.

PART – TWO

(Answer any four questions. Each question carries 15 marks)

5. (a) Briefly describe the function of different components of digital computer with a suitable block diagram.

(b) Convert from one number system to another

(i) Convert $(10110110)_2$ to octal

(ii) Convert $(36.25)_{10}$ to binary

(iii) Convert $(2AD)_{16}$ to decimal

(iv) Convert $(493)_{10}$ to octal

(c) What is BCD? What are the advantages of BCD? [6+6+3 =15]

6. (a) Explain the memory hierarchy pyramid, also explain the relation of cost, speed and capacity.

(b) Explain three types of ROM.

(c) Can a ROM be also a RAM? Justify your answer. [5+6+4=15]

7. (a) What is OS? Write the different functions of OS.

(b) Write the difference between Compiler and assembler.

(c) What is BIOS? Where is it located? What is the purpose of BIOS?

[6+4=5=15]

8. (a) What is Android? Write the names of different Android version.

(b) State three features of Smartphone.

(c) Explain bus and start topology. [8+3+4=15]

9. (a) What is e-governance? Write the benefits of e-governance.

(b) What are the challenges of e-governance?

(c) Explain four types of E-commerce model. [5+4+6=15]

10. (a) State the difference between Linux and Windows.

(b) Explain relative cell addressing and absolute cell addressing in MS-Excel.

(c) Define the following tags of HTML with examples.

(i) BR (ii) IMG

[3+8+4=15]

Specimen Answersheet for Writing Answers to Objective Questions

PAPER CODE [ ] DATE [ ]

1. Multiple choice

(shade the box corresponding to your answer)

	a	b	c	d
1.1.				
1.2.				
1.3.				
1.4.				
1.5.				
1.6.				
1.7.				
1.8.				
1.9.				
1.10.				

2. Selecting TRUE or FALSE statements

(shade the box corresponding to your answer)

	True	False
2.1.		
2.2.		
2.3.		
2.4.		
2.5.		
2.6.		
2.7.		
2.8.		
2.9.		
2.10.		

3. Matching words/phrases in two columns

(write the alphabet corresponding to your answer in the box)

3.1.	
3.2.	
3.3.	
3.4.	
3.5.	
3.6.	
3.7.	
3.8.	
3.9.	
3.10.	

4. Fill in the blanks

(write the alphabet corresponding to your answer)

4.1.	
4.2.	
4.3.	
4.4.	
4.5.	
4.6.	
4.7.	
4.8.	
4.9.	
4.10.	

BOOKS *by Prof. Satish Jain*

'O' Level made simple Books (According to NIELIT (DOEACC) Syllabus effective from July, 2010 Examination)

- **IT Tools and Business Systems** *(covering M1-R4, A1-R4 and B1.1-R4 papers)*
- **Internet Technology and Web Design** *(covering M2-R4, A2-R4 and B1.2-R4 papers)* ***(Also available in Hindi)***
- **Programming and Problem Solving through 'C' language** *(covering M3-R4, A3-R4 and B1.3-R4 papers)* ***(Also available in Hindi)***
- **Application of .Net Technology** *(covering M4.1-R4 paper)*
- **Introduction to Multimedia** *(covering M4.2-R4 paper)*
- **Introduction to ICT Resources** *(covering M4.3-R4 paper)*

'A' Level made simple Books (According to NIELIT (DOEACC) Syllabus effective from July, 2010 Examination)

- **Computer System Architecture** *(covering A4-R4 and B1.4-R4 papers)*
- **Structured System Analysis & Design** *(covering A5-R4 and B1.5-R4 papers)* ***(Also available in Hindi)***
- **Data Structure Through C++** *(covering A6-R4 and B2.1-R4 papers)* ***(Also available in Hindi)***
- **Introduction to Database Management Systems** *(covering A7-R4 and B2.2-R4 papers)*
- **Basics of OS, Unix and Shell Programming** *(covering A8-R4 and B2.3-R4 papers)*
- **Data Communication and Network Technologies** *(covering A9-R4 and B2.4-R4 papers)*
- **Introduction to Object Oriented Programming through Java** *(covering A10.1-R4 and B2.5.1-R4 papers)*
- **Software Testing and Quality Management** *(covering A10.2-R4 and B2.5.2-R4 papers)*

'O' & 'A' Level BPB's Golden Solutions for NIELIT (DOEACC) Examination Question Papers

- 'O' Level–**IT Tools and Business Systems** *(Also covering A1-R4 and B1.1-R4 papers)*
- 'O' Level–**Internet Technology & Web Design** *(Also covering A2-R4 and B1.2-R4 Papers)*
- 'O' Level–**Programming & Problem Solving through 'C' language** *(Also covering A3-R4 and B1.3-R4 Papers)*
- 'O' Level–**ICT Resources** *(covering M4.3-R4 paper)*
- 'O' Level–**Introduction to Multimedia** *(covering M4.2-R4 paper)*
- 'A' Level –**Data Communication and Network Technologies** *(Also covering A9-R4 and B2.4-R4 papers)*

For B.E., MCA, M.Sc.(IT), B.Sc.(IT), BCA, PGDCA, and other IT Related Examinations for leading Indian Universities and Engineering Colleges

- **Introduction to Database Management**
- **Systems Analysis, Design and Management Information System**
- ***Computer Networks***
- **Principles of Electronics–Analog and Digital**
- **Computer Organization and Architecture**
- **Data Structures** *Made Simple*
- **Advanced Computer Networking**
- **Wireless Communications and Networking**
- **Software Testing and Quality Management**
- ***Guide to*** **Digital Electronics and Devices** *(Ques. & Ans.)*
- ***Guide to*** **Computer Networks and Data Communications** *(Ques. & Ans.)*
- ***Guide to*** **Systems Analysis, Design and MIS** *(Ques. & Ans.)*
- ***Guide to*** **Data Structures** *(Ques. & Ans.)*
- ***Guide to*** **Database Management Systems** *(Ques. & Ans.)*
- ***Guide to*** **Advanced Computer Networking** *(Ques. & Ans.)*
- ***Guide to*** **Computer Organization and Architecture** *(Ques. & Ans.)*
- ***Guide to*** **BPO and IT JOBS** *(Ques. & Ans.)*

For MBA, PGDBM and other Business Related Examinations for leading Indian Universities and Management Colleges

- **Computers in Business Management** *Principles and Practice*
- ***Guide to*** **Computers in Business Management** *(Ques. & Ans.)*
- **Information Technology Concepts** *(2nd Revisied and Updated Edition)*
- **BPB's Computer Course** *made simple (2nd Revisied and Updated Edition) (Windows 7/XP with MS Office 2007)*
- **BPB's Computer Course** *(Windows 7 with MS Office 2010)*
- **BPB's MS Office 2010 and Windows 7 Course**

'O' Level CHM (Computer Hardware Maintenance) Made Simple (According to DOEACC Syllabus)

- **Electronics Components and PC Hardware** *(covering CHM–O1 paper)*
- **Computer Peripherals and Networking** *(covering CHM–O3 paper)*
- **System Software, Dignostics and Debugging Tools** *(covering CHM–O4 paper)*

Training Guides for Application Packages

- **Windows 8** ***Training Guide***
- **Dreamweaver CS5** ***Training Guide***
- **Flash Professional CS5** ***Training Guide***
- **Illustrator CS5** ***Training Guide***

For Class IX, X (According to C.B.S.E Syllabus)

- *Introductory* **Information Technology** *Vol I*
- *Introductory* **Information Technology** *Vol II*

For Class XI & XII (According to C.B.S.E Syllabus)

- **Informatics Practices** *Vol I (Code 065)*
- **Informatics Practices** *Vol II (Code 065)*
- **Computer Science with C++** *Vol I (Code 083)*
- **Computer Science with C++** *Vol II (Code 083)*
- **Computer Science with Python** *Vol I (Code 083)*
- **Multimedia & Web Technology** *Vol I (Code 067)*
- **Multimedia & Web Technology** *Vol II (Code 067)*

Made Simple Books for Application Packages

- **Word 2007** and **2010** *(made simple)*
- **Excel 2007** and **2010** *(made simple)*
- **PowerPoint 2007** and **2010** *(made simple)*